Dictionary of Literary Biography

1 *The American Renaissance in New England,* edited by Joel Myerson (1978)

2 *American Novelists Since World War II,* edited by Jeffrey Helterman and Richard Layman (1978)

3 *Antebellum Writers in New York and the South,* edited by Joel Myerson (1979)

4 *American Writers in Paris, 1920-1939,* edited by Karen Lane Rood (1980)

5 *American Poets Since World War II,* 2 parts, edited by Donald J. Greiner (1980)

6 *American Novelists Since World War II, Second Series,* edited by James E. Kibler Jr. (1980)

7 *Twentieth-Century American Dramatists,* 2 parts, edited by John MacNicholas (1981)

8 *Twentieth-Century American Science-Fiction Writers,* 2 parts, edited by David Cowart and Thomas L. Wymer (1981)

9 *American Novelists, 1910-1945,* 3 parts, edited by James J. Martine (1981)

10 *Modern British Dramatists, 1900-1945,* 2 parts, edited by Stanley Weintraub (1982)

11 *American Humorists, 1800-1950,* 2 parts, edited by Stanley Trachtenberg (1982)

12 *American Realists and Naturalists,* edited by Donald Pizer and Earl N. Harbert (1982)

13 *British Dramatists Since World War II,* 2 parts, edited by Stanley Weintraub (1982)

14 *British Novelists Since 1960,* 2 parts, edited by Jay L. Halio (1983)

15 *British Novelists, 1930-1959,* 2 parts, edited by Bernard Oldsey (1983)

16 *The Beats: Literary Bohemians in Postwar America,* 2 parts, edited by Ann Charters (1983)

17 *Twentieth-Century American Historians,* edited by Clyde N. Wilson (1983)

18 *Victorian Novelists After 1885,* edited by Ira B. Nadel and William E. Fredeman (1983)

19 *British Poets, 1880-1914,* edited by Donald E. Stanford (1983)

20 *British Poets, 1914-1945,* edited by Donald E. Stanford (1983)

21 *Victorian Novelists Before 1885,* edited by Ira B. Nadel and William E. Fredeman (1983)

22 *American Writers for Children, 1900-1960,* edited by John Cech (1983)

23 *American Newspaper Journalists, 1873-1900,* edited by Perry J. Ashley (1983)

24 *American Colonial Writers, 1606-1734,* edited by Emory Elliott (1984)

25 *American Newspaper Journalists, 1901-1925,* edited by Perry J. Ashley (1984)

26 *American Screenwriters,* edited by Robert E. Morsberger, Stephen O. Lesser, and Randall Clark (1984)

27 *Poets of Great Britain and Ireland, 1945-1960,* edited by Vincent B. Sherry Jr. (1984)

28 *Twentieth-Century American-Jewish Fiction Writers,* edited by Daniel Walden (1984)

29 *American Newspaper Journalists, 1926-1950,* edited by Perry J. Ashley (1984)

30 *American Historians, 1607-1865,* edited by Clyde N. Wilson (1984)

31 *American Colonial Writers, 1735-1781,* edited by Emory Elliott (1984)

32 *Victorian Poets Before 1850,* edited by William E. Fredeman and Ira B. Nadel (1984)

33 *Afro-American Fiction Writers After 1955,* edited by Thadious M. Davis and Trudier Harris (1984)

34 *British Novelists, 1890-1929: Traditionalists,* edited by Thomas F. Staley (1985)

35 *Victorian Poets After 1850,* edited by William E. Fredeman and Ira B. Nadel (1985)

36 *British Novelists, 1890-1929: Modernists,* edited by Thomas F. Staley (1985)

37 *American Writers of the Early Republic,* edited by Emory Elliott (1985)

38 *Afro-American Writers After 1955: Dramatists and Prose Writers,* edited by Thadious M. Davis and Trudier Harris (1985)

39 *British Novelists, 1660-1800,* 2 parts, edited by Martin C. Battestin (1985)

40 *Poets of Great Britain and Ireland Since 1960,* 2 parts, edited by Vincent B. Sherry Jr. (1985)

41 *Afro-American Poets Since 1955,* edited by Trudier Harris and Thadious M. Davis (1985)

42 *American Writers for Children Before 1900,* edited by Glenn E. Estes (1985)

43 *American Newspaper Journalists, 1690-1872,* edited by Perry J. Ashley (1986)

44 *American Screenwriters, Second Series,* edited by Randall Clark, Robert E. Morsberger, and Stephen O. Lesser (1986)

45 *American Poets, 1880-1945, First Series,* edited by Peter Quartermain (1986)

46 *American Literary Publishing Houses, 1900-1980: Trade and Paperback,* edited by Peter Dzwonkoski (1986)

47 *American Historians, 1866-1912,* edited by Clyde N. Wilson (1986)

48 *American Poets, 1880-1945, Second Series,* edited by Peter Quartermain (1986)

49 *American Literary Publishing Houses, 1638-1899,* 2 parts, edited by Peter Dzwonkoski (1986)

50 *Afro-American Writers Before the Harlem Renaissance,* edited by Trudier Harris (1986)

51 *Afro-American Writers from the Harlem Renaissance to 1940,* edited by Trudier Harris (1987)

52 *American Writers for Children Since 1960: Fiction,* edited by Glenn E. Estes (1986)

53 *Canadian Writers Since 1960, First Series,* edited by W. H. New (1986)

54 *American Poets, 1880-1945, Third Series,* 2 parts, edited by Peter Quartermain (1987)

55 *Victorian Prose Writers Before 1867,* edited by William B. Thesing (1987)

56 *German Fiction Writers, 1914-1945,* edited by James Hardin (1987)

57 *Victorian Prose Writers After 1867,* edited by William B. Thesing (1987)

58 *Jacobean and Caroline Dramatists,* edited by Fredson Bowers (1987)

59 *American Literary Critics and Scholars, 1800-1850,* edited by John W. Rathbun and Monica M. Grecu (1987)

60 *Canadian Writers Since 1960, Second Series,* edited by W. H. New (1987)

61 *American Writers for Children Since 1960: Poets, Illustrators, and Nonfiction Authors,* edited by Glenn E. Estes (1987)

62 *Elizabethan Dramatists,* edited by Fredson Bowers (1987)

63 *Modern American Critics, 1920-1955,* edited by Gregory S. Jay (1988)

64 *American Literary Critics and Scholars, 1850-1880,* edited by John W. Rathbun and Monica M. Grecu (1988)

65 *French Novelists, 1900-1930,* edited by Catharine Savage Brosman (1988)

66 *German Fiction Writers, 1885-1913,* 2 parts, edited by James Hardin (1988)

67 *Modern American Critics Since 1955,* edited by Gregory S. Jay (1988)

68 *Canadian Writers, 1920-1959, First Series,* edited by W. H. New (1988)

69 *Contemporary German Fiction Writers, First Series,* edited by Wolfgang D. Elfe and James Hardin (1988)

70 *British Mystery Writers, 1860-1919,* edited by Bernard Benstock and Thomas F. Staley (1988)

71 *American Literary Critics and Scholars, 1880-1900,* edited by John W. Rathbun and Monica M. Grecu (1988)

72 *French Novelists, 1930-1960,* edited by Catharine Savage Brosman (1988)

73 *American Magazine Journalists, 1741-1850,* edited by Sam G. Riley (1988)

74 *American Short-Story Writers Before 1880,* edited by Bobby Ellen Kimbel, with the assistance of William E. Grant (1988)

75 *Contemporary German Fiction Writers, Second Series,* edited by Wolfgang D. Elfe and James Hardin (1988)

76 *Afro-American Writers, 1940-1955,* edited by Trudier Harris (1988)

77 *British Mystery Writers, 1920-1939,* edited by Bernard Benstock and Thomas F. Staley (1988)

Documentary Series

Yearbooks

1980 edited by Karen L. Rood, Jean W. Ross, and Richard Ziegfeld (1981)

1981 edited by Karen L. Rood, Jean W. Ross, and Richard Ziegfeld (1982)

1982 edited by Richard Ziegfeld; associate editors: Jean W. Ross and Lynne C. Zeigler (1983)

1983 edited by Mary Bruccoli and Jean W. Ross; associate editor: Richard Ziegfeld (1984)

1984 edited by Jean W. Ross (1985)

1985 edited by Jean W. Ross (1986)

1986 edited by J. M. Brook (1987)

1987 edited by J. M. Brook (1988)

1988 edited by J. M. Brook (1989)

1989 edited by J. M. Brook (1990)

1990 edited by James W. Hipp (1991)

1991 edited by James W. Hipp (1992)

1992 edited by James W. Hipp (1993)

1993 edited by James W. Hipp, contributing editor George Garrett (1994)

1994 edited by James W. Hipp, contributing editor George Garrett (1995)

1995 edited by James W. Hipp, contributing editor George Garrett (1996)

1996 edited by Samuel W. Bruce and L. Kay Webster, contributing editor George Garrett (1997)

1997 edited by Matthew J. Bruccoli and George Garrett, with the assistance of L. Kay Webster (1998)

1998 edited by Matthew J. Bruccoli, contributing editor George Garrett, with the assistance of Denis Thomas (1999)

Concise Series

Concise Dictionary of American Literary Biography, 6 volumes (1988-1989): *The New Consciousness, 1941-1968; Colonization to the American Renaissance, 1640-1865; Realism, Naturalism, and Local Color, 1865-1917; The Twenties, 1917-1929; The Age of Maturity, 1929-1941; Broadening Views, 1968-1988.*

Concise Dictionary of British Literary Biography, 8 volumes (1991-1992): *Writers of the Middle Ages and Renaissance Before 1660; Writers of the Restoration and Eighteenth Century, 1660-1789; Writers of the Romantic Period, 1789-1832; Victorian Writers, 1832-1890; Late-Victorian and Edwardian Writers, 1890-1914; Modern Writers, 1914-1945; Writers After World War II, 1945-1960; Contemporary Writers, 1960 to Present.*

British Novelists
Since 1960
Third Series

British Novelists
Since 1960
Third Series

Edited by
Merritt Moseley
University of North Carolina at Asheville

A Bruccoli Clark Layman Book
The Gale Group
Detroit, Washington, D.C., London

Printed in the United States of America

The paper used in this publication meets the minimum requirements
of American National Standard for Information Sciences–Permanence
Paper for Printed Library Materials, ANSI Z39.48-1984. ∞™

Library of Congress Cataloging-in-Publication Data

British novelists since 1960. Third series / edited by Merritt Moseley.
    p. cm.–(Dictionary of literary biography: v. 207)
"A Bruccoli Clark Layman book."
Includes bibliographical references and index.
ISBN 0-7876-3101-9 (alk. paper)
1. English fiction–20th century–Bio-bibliography–Dictionaries. 2. Novelists, English–20th century–Biography–Dictionaries. 3. English fiction–20th century–Dictionaries. I. Moseley, Merritt, 1949– . II. Series.
PR881.B733 1999
823'.91409'03–dc21   99–14525
[B]   CIP

10 9 8 7 6 5 4 3 2 1

To Madeline

Contents

Plan of the Series

... Almost the most prodigious asset of a country, and perhaps its most precious possession, is its native literary product—when that product is fine and noble and enduring.

Mark Twain*

The advisory board, the editors, and the publisher of the *Dictionary of Literary Biography* are joined in endorsing Mark Twain's declaration. The literature of a nation provides an inexhaustible resource of permanent worth. We intend to make literature and its creators better understood and more accessible to students and the reading public, while satisfying the standards of teachers and scholars.

To meet these requirements, *literary biography* has been construed in terms of the author's achievement. The most important thing about a writer is his writing. Accordingly, the entries in *DLB* are career biographies, tracing the development of the author's canon and the evolution of his reputation.

The purpose of *DLB* is not only to provide reliable information in a convenient format but also to place the figures in the larger perspective of literary history and to offer appraisals of their accomplishments by qualified scholars.

The publication plan for *DLB* resulted from two years of preparation. The project was proposed to Bruccoli Clark by Frederick C. Ruffner, president of the Gale Research Company, in November 1975. After specimen entries were prepared and typeset, an advisory board was formed to refine the entry format and develop the series rationale. In meetings held during 1976, the publisher, series editors, and advisory board approved the scheme for a comprehensive biographical dictionary of persons who contributed to North American literature. Editorial work on the first volume began in January 1977, and it was published in 1978. In order to make *DLB* more than a reference tool and to compile volumes that individually have claim to status as literary history, it was decided to organize volumes by

*From an unpublished section of Mark Twain's autobiography, copyright by the Mark Twain Company

topic, period, or genre. Each of these freestanding volumes provides a biographical-bibliographical guide and overview for a particular area of literature. We are convinced that this organization—as opposed to a single alphabet method—constitutes a valuable innovation in the presentation of reference material. The volume plan necessarily requires many decisions for the placement and treatment of authors who might properly be included in two or three volumes. In some instances a major figure will be included in separate volumes, but with different entries emphasizing the aspect of his career appropriate to each volume. Ernest Hemingway, for example, is represented in *American Writers in Paris, 1920–1939* by an entry focusing on his expatriate apprenticeship; he is also in *American Novelists, 1910–1945* with an entry surveying his entire career, as well as in *American Short-Story Writers, 1910–1945, Second Series* with an entry concentrating on his short stories. Each volume includes a cumulative index of the subject authors and articles. Comprehensive indexes to the entire series are planned.

Since 1981 the series has been further augmented by the *DLB Yearbooks*, which update published entries and add new entries to keep the *DLB* current with contemporary activity. There have also been *DLB Documentary Series* volumes which provide biographical and critical source materials for figures whose work is judged to have particular interest for students. One of these companion volumes is entirely devoted to Tennessee Williams.

We define literature as the *intellectual commerce of a nation:* not merely as belles lettres but as that ample and complex process by which ideas are generated, shaped, and transmitted. *DLB* entries are not limited to "creative writers" but extend to other figures who in their time and in their way influenced the mind of a people. Thus the series encompasses historians, journalists, publishers, book collectors, and screenwriters. By this means readers of *DLB* may be aided to perceive literature not as cult scripture in the keeping of intellectual high priests but firmly positioned at the center of a nation's life.

DLB includes the major writers appropriate to each volume and those standing in the ranks behind them. Scholarly and critical counsel has been sought in deciding which minor figures to include and how full their entries should be. Wherever possible, useful references are made to figures who do not warrant separate entries.

Each *DLB* volume has an expert volume editor responsible for planning the volume, selecting the figures for inclusion, and assigning the entries. Volume editors are also responsible for preparing, where appropriate, appendices surveying the major periodicals and literary and intellectual movements for their volumes, as well as lists of further readings. Work on the series as a whole is coordinated at the Bruccoli Clark Layman editorial center in Columbia, South Carolina, where the editorial staff is responsible for accuracy and utility of the published volumes.

One feature that distinguishes *DLB* is the illustration policy—its concern with the iconography of literature. Just as an author is influenced by his surroundings, so is the reader's understanding of the author enhanced by a knowledge of his environment. Therefore *DLB* volumes include not only drawings, paintings, and photographs of authors, often depicting them at various stages in their careers, but also illustrations of their families and places where they lived. Title pages are regularly reproduced in facsimile along with dust jackets for modern authors. The dust jackets are a special feature of *DLB* because they often document better than anything else the way in which an author's work was perceived in its own time. Specimens of the writers' manuscripts and letters are included when feasible.

Samuel Johnson rightly decreed that "The chief glory of every people arises from its authors." The purpose of the *Dictionary of Literary Biography* is to compile literary history in the surest way available to us—by accurate and comprehensive treatment of the lives and work of those who contributed to it.

The *DLB* Advisory Board

Introduction

In October 1996, as chair of the panel of judges that presented the Booker Prize to Graham Swift for his novel *Last Orders,* Carmen Callil took advantage of the occasion to mount a provocative defense of contemporary English novelists, along with an analysis of what she considered widespread critical negativism, or "cultural cringe" about the state of fiction. Her remarks are balanced and repay consideration here.

> Forty years ago, when I first came to England, there were still one or two literary personages who took it for granted that the English novel was the centre of the universe.
>
> However, it's many years now since that has been true. The English novelist now writes on the far edges of the great centres of English literature which reside in Ireland, America, Canada and India, and the Pacific countries.
>
> But English fiction has benefited hugely from the richness of Commonwealth and American writing and has been in good shape for some time now. . . . Despite this, every year, for as long as I can remember, there's been a ritual moan about the dire state of the English novel.

Callil goes on to declare that 1996 had been a vintage year for English novels; at the same time it was a vintage year for critical dismissal of English novels. Why this tendency on the part of English critics to knock, or apologize for, English books? Callil suggests three reasons:

> First, I'm not too sure how many English novelists these critics have actually read. . . . Second, obsessive denigration of English fiction is the dying chirrup of some sort of imperial misery. English novelists are no longer the greatest in the world, therefore they must be the worst. This is also tied up with an unhealthy obsession with American fiction, a sort of pistol-packing approach very much associated with the straitjacket of fashionable taste dictated by the old *Granta* in the 1980s. Third, there is a kind of political correctness about most of our literary assessment. Abroad yes, here no. Guarded praise is the most one is permitted.

Swift's *Last Orders* was welcomed as a Booker winner by many observers; written by an Englishman, set in England, dealing with ordinary English life, it marked a change (they seemed to feel) from the foreign and exotic (for example, Ben Okri's *The Famished Road,* 1991), the Celtic and inferentially anti-English (such as Roddy Doyle's *Paddy Clarke Ha Ha Ha,* 1993, and James Kelman's *How Late It Was, How Late,* 1994), and the backward-looking historical (Barry Unsworth's *Sacred Hunger,* 1992, and Pat Barker's *The Ghost Road,* 1995): the kinds of books which, in recent years, have replaced the novel written about what happens in England. As William Leith argued in *The Independent on Sunday* (2 May 1993), "Not writing about contemporary England seems to be a growth industry."

Callil is an Australian, and perhaps it required a foreigner to speak plainly about the strengths of English fiction to a readership and critical establishment that she accused of a "tiresome and destructive" attitude of denigration. Her statement is a good starting point for some observations about the state of contemporary English fiction writing, including the culture of publishing and book selling that supports it.

Callil is best known in the United Kingdom as a feminist publisher. In 1973 she and Ursula Own, along with other advisers and helpers who reportedly met around a kitchen table, founded Virago, the first all-women publishing house. Callil was the charismatic figure, the "godmother" of feminist publishing; without her, a commentator in the *Electronic Telegraph* (2 November 1996) asserted, "many women writers would have remained unknown, and the British publishing world would still be a bastion of stuffy, self-serving old boys." Virago was always more of a reprint house than a home for new writers—it published many Americans, such as Edith Wharton and Willa Cather, older (and then out of print) Englishwomen such as Elizabeth Taylor, and women authors—George Eliot, for example—who had by no means been shut out of the market. Among the new writers to British readers by Virago and Callil were Maya Angelou, Pat Barker, Shena Mackay, Michèle Roberts, and Angela Carter. Carter edited two books of fairy tales for Virago that were influential among younger writers. In 1982 Callil left Virago and went to work for mainline literary publishers Chatto and Windus. She left Chatto in 1994.

Her high profile, and the visibility and apparent success of Virago (which is now owned by Little, Brown), are part of a larger phenomenon in which women readers, writers, and critics, are more determined to see justice done to women writers. The most striking development in this area may be the creation of the Orange Prize, the only women-only fiction award. Kate Mosse explains its genesis this way:

> The Orange Prize was the brainchild of a group of senior women in the publishing industry—editors, journalists, booksellers, managing directors, authors, librarians, agents, teachers—who got together over several bottles of wine in the winter of 1992 to work out why it was that disproportionately few novels by women were making it to the shortlists of the established literary awards. Then, as now, rumour and research suggests women not only write more novels than men, but they also read more novels and borrow more fiction from libraries than men. Bearing this in mind, the figures for who won what looked decidedly lop-sided.
>
> The catalyst for the meeting was the shortlist for the 1991 Booker Prize for Fiction. Not a single woman in sight. There had been two all-male shortlists before, which had not been without their critics. It happens. But 1991 was a year where writers of the stature of Angela Carter, Margaret Atwood and Michèle Roberts had novels eligible. We tried to imagine the accusations of archaic feminist bias that would've been levelled at an all-woman list.

Not without controversy, including the unwillingness of some women novelists to permit their books to be considered, the Orange Prize has nevertheless achieved remarkable publicity considering that it has only been given three times. It may bring a mixed message for English writers; determinedly open to any author who writes in English, it has been dominated by North Americans, with most of the shortlisted titles and two of the three winners from the United States or Canada. The first Orange Prize was awarded in 1996, ironically as Carmen Callil was chairing the Booker Prize judging panel, which awarded the prize to Swift.

In the late 1970s another emigrant, an American named Bill Buford, purchased the title of *Granta,* which had a long history as a literary magazine headquartered in Cambridge, and used it as the vehicle for his ambitious project to revivify British fiction—which he thought "critically and aesthetically negligible"—by introducing British writers to the best American writing, which he considered "some of the most challenging, diversified, and adventurous writing today." This editorial policy is the "sort of pistol-packing approach very much associated with the straitjacket of fashionable taste dictated by the old *Granta* in the 1980s" mentioned by Carmen Callil. Whether the Americans he

published or the movement he named for them ("dirty realism") had anything to do with the revival of British writing or not, Buford contributed to the careers of many younger fiction writers by printing their work in *Granta.* For instance, he ran an excerpt from the unknown Salman Rushdie's *Midnight's Children* (1981) in his third issue. *Granta* did help to form fashionable taste.

In 1983 the magazine helped to publicize a list, "The Best of Young British Novelists." The list included twenty writers, all under forty years old, chosen in an unspecified way by the British Book Marketing Council, an arm of the publishing industry. In 1993 a panel selected by *Granta,* made up of Salman Rushdie, A. S. Byatt, John Mitchinson (head of Waterstone's bookshops) and Buford, selected another list of the twenty best young British novelists. In each case *Granta* published some selection of their work. Without doubt the lists achieved the purpose of foregrounding some strong and impressive writers and demonstrating that British fiction was not (or at least no longer—four years had now passed) critically and aesthetically negligible.

Best of Young British Novelists 1983

Martin Amis
Pat Barker
Julian Barnes
Ursula Bentley
William Boyd
Buchi Emecheta
Maggie Gee
Kazuo Ishiguro
Alan Judd
Adam Mars-Jones
Ian McEwan
Shiva Naipaul
Philip Norman
Christopher Priest
Salman Rushdie
Lisa St. Aubin de Teran
Clive Sinclair
Graham Swift
Rose Tremain
A. N. Wilson

Best of Young British Novelists 1993

Iain Banks
Louis de Bernières
Anne Billson
Tibor Fischer
Esther Freud
Alan Hollinghurst
Kazuo Ishiguro

A. L. Kennedy

Philip Kerr

Hanif Kureishi

Adam Lively

Adam Mars-Jones

Candia McWilliam

Lawrence Norfolk

Ben Okri

Caryl Phillips

Will Self

Nicholas Shakespeare

Helen Simpson

Jeanette Winterson

The lists prompt several reflections. The sense of the cosmopolitanism of the "British novelist" derives its force from the significant presence of African, Asian, and East Indian authors on the list. In the second list openly gay and lesbian authors are more highly visible. In each case six of the twenty novelists were women. William Leith points to some of these versions of difference when he declares that

> Our youngest novelists, growing up in a dying literary landscape, possibly believing that British society is unimportant, are both writing about England and not writing about England—many of them are describing an England unrecognisable to the English; a place of introspection, or private culture. Of course, a writer's early works have almost always been fictionalised versions of his or her immediate experience, so the contemporary-Britain strike rate is higher here–Adam Mars-Jones, Jeanette Winterson, Alan Hollinghurst and Hanif Kureishi have all recently written novels about contemporary Britain. That is to say, they've all written fascinating accounts of what it is like to be outsiders in contemporary Britain; Mars-Jones, Hollinghurst and Winterson are all gay, and Kureishi writes from an Anglo-Asian background.

Another, less satisfying reflection is that the need on the part of *Granta* to be at the leading edge of fashion forestalled much sober reflection. Adam Mars-Jones was listed twice among the twenty best British novelists, even though he had as of 1993 published no novel. Esther Freud, Will Self, and Lawrence Norfolk published their first novels in 1992. Helen Simpson had published only short fiction.

All these discussions, and almost all the prizes given for fiction in the United Kingdom (with the notable exceptions of the W. H. Smith Thumping Good Read and the now-discontinued *Sunday Express* Fiction Award) are devoted to what may be called "serious literary fiction." In this category, which generally excludes genre fiction such as thrillers, mysteries, and

costume romance, the big names are such as A. S. Byatt and Martin Amis.

The reading public has always been divided in two, however; the novels and novelists that receive the most critical attention and those which sell the most copies—in other words, please the most people—occupy two classes which almost never overlap. As a *Private Eye* reviewer, writing on Francis Wheen's *Lord Gnome's Literary Companion* (1994), declared:

> One of the ironies of the book trade in this country is that most of the attention is paid to the books that nobody buys. The young novelist commended by the Sunday newspapers as "a writer to watch out for," the biographer neatly anatomizing some Bloomsbury hanger-on: both may receive plenty of review coverage, both add lustre to a publisher's list, but nobody much will actually pay money for their work.
>
> The great British book-buying public reserves its book tokens for the great stodgy monsters which will pay a publisher's Garrick Club bill long after the slim first novels are nestling in the remainder bin.

These comments are an exaggeration, of course, and a recent list of best-sellers from the *Sunday Times* (24 January 1999) showed Booker Prize winners and critical favorites Arundhati Roy and Ian McEwan, along with "literary" novelists Sebastian Faulks and Louis de Bernières, side by side with thrillers, detective novels, and science-fiction titles.

Perhaps a surer sign of the public taste—since buying books, especially hardbacks, is a practice that varies widely by region and class—is library circulation. The Public Lending Right Scheme, which remunerates authors or their estates based on the number of times their books are loaned by libraries, publishes a record of the most-borrowed authors. The list for the year from July 1996 to June 1997 contains no name in the top twenty that has ever appeared on a Booker shortlist. The top five names are Catherine Cookson, Danielle Steele, Dick Francis, Ruth Rendell, and Agatha Christie, and twelve of the twenty are women. A reading public divided between highbrows and middlebrows is as much a feature of British life today as it was for Q. D. Leavis in *Fiction and the Reading Public* (1932).

Perhaps such a dichotomy does not matter so long as publishers are willing to continue publishing both serious literary fiction and popular books. One school of thought holds that domination of the book trade by a few enormous best-sellers is the inevitable outcome of domination of the bookselling industry by a few enormous chains. The defender of the good mid-list title is thus the independent bookshop. Tom Stoppard declared in 1997 that independent bookshops and publishers were the mark of a healthy literary culture and that their loss would mean fewer books published. "When a potential author fails to exist, there is a thought which fails to come into existence," Stoppard argued.

He was testifying in favor of the Net Book Agreement, a curious arrangement, dating from 1900, under which publishers and booksellers agreed not to sell books below the cover price dictated by the publisher. This price-fixing agreement began to collapse in 1995, when, under pressure from supermarkets, W. H. Smith and Waterstone's, two major book-retail chains, and Random House and HarperCollins, two of the most important publishers, withdrew from the agreement and began discounting titles. The Restrictive Practices Court was then asked to declare the agreement unlawful. Stoppard was arguing for its retention, as was Auberon Waugh, who said that abolishing it was "gratuitous philistinism." Nevertheless, the court ruled in 1997 that the agreement was anticompetitive and struck it down. It is too early to tell if the projected bonanza of discounted books or the loss of independent booksellers has resulted.

Clearly both the British publishing and bookselling industries have been conglomerated, as in the United States. HarperCollins, part of the News International Corporation owned by Rupert Murdoch—which also owns the *Sun,* the *News of the World,* the *Times* (London), and the *Sunday Times* newspapers and BSkyB television—is a giant concern, having absorbed many formerly independent publishing imprints, and the object of considerable misgiving.

W. H. Smith occupies a somewhat analogous position in the book-retailing trade. From its beginnings in the nineteenth century as a chain of railway-station bookstalls, it has become a large company of high street bookshops; but it also has a middle- or even down-market niche. W. H. Smith is popularly considered the bookstore to choose if one is actually shopping for a pen, a postcard, a compact disc, or a poster, but not necessarily for a wide range of books. In 1982 Waterstone and Co. Ltd. was established as a more-specialized quality bookseller, and its stores rapidly spread through the United Kingdom. Alongside it were similar competitors, particularly Hatchards, Dillons, and Blackwells (branching out from its headquarters in Oxford, one of the biggest and most comprehensive bookshops in Europe). All these companies operate large stores with knowledgeable staffs and display many more titles than the average independent shop.

Waterstone's was so successful that it was acquired by W. H. Smith in 1993; the newly augmented W. H. Smith group turned over £2 billion in sales at its six hundred outlets by 1994.

A new development in the United Kingdom is online book-buying. One of the first companies in this area was the Internet Book Shop, which was joined by Blackwell's Online. W. H. Smith has acquired the Internet Book Shop as well, and the British market has also been penetrated by the American firm Amazon.com. Just as large bookstore chains may well represent a threat to the local independents because of their mass purchases, their inventory control, and even their ability to secure favorable prices from publishers—thus, in Tom Stoppard's fears, "creaming off the custom for books with large print runs" and jeopardizing retailers without their market muscle—so the online marketers, which have no high-street rents to pay, no salespeople, and less warehousing, may threaten the success of Waterstone's and Dillons. A recent sampling of the Internet Book Shop inventory showed that for one randomly chosen author, Nicholas Shakespeare, seven different books were offered, comprising five titles, and all were discounted between 7.5 and 20 percent. Shakespeare's not-yet-published biography of Bruce Chatwin could already be ordered at a 20 percent discount. The discounting practices of Internet booksellers is a more serious matter than the aftermath of the collapse of the Net Book Agreement, when, according to one report, the average Waterstone's branch was offering only 12 discounted titles out of 100,000.

Stoppard, speaking as an author as well as a consumer, says "If you cannot spread the word you wish to write, there is no point in writing it, and in the end there is no point in thinking it either." Callil, speaking from the publisher's perspective, insists, "God knows, we need fewer and better books." Hardly anyone would disagree with Callil; the concern is about a system that delivers fewer and worse books. Given the changes since 1980 (including publishing on the Internet—one Internet title was considered by the Booker judging panel in 1998), it is impossible to predict how the dramatic developments in the system for choosing, publishing, distributing, and selling books will affect the British novelist in the twenty-first century.

—*Merritt Moseley*

Acknowledgments

This book was produced by Bruccoli Clark Layman, Inc. Karen L. Rood is senior editor for the *Dictionary of Literary Biography* series. Charles Brower was the in-house editor.

Production manager is Philip B. Dematteis.

Administrative support was provided by Ann M. Cheschi, Tenesha S. Lee, and Angi Pleasant.

Accountant is Neil Senol.

Copyediting supervisor is Phyllis A. Avant. The copyediting staff includes Ronald D. Aiken II, Brenda Carol Blanton, Worthy Evans, Thom Harman, Melissa D. Hinton, William Tobias Mathes, Raegan E. Quinn, and Audra Rouse. Freelance copyeditors are Brenda Cabra, Rebecca Mayo, Nicole M. Nichols, and Jennie Williamson.

Layout and graphics staff includes Janet E. Hill and John F. Henson.

Office manager is Kathy Lawler Merlette.

Photography editors are Margo Dowling, Charles Mims, Scott Nemzek, Alison Smith, and Paul Talbot. Digital photographic copy work was performed by Joseph M. Bruccoli.

SGML supervisor is Cory McNair. The SGML staff includes Tim Bedford, Linda Drake, Frank Graham, Alex Snead, and Joann Whittaker.

Systems manager is Marie L. Parker.

Database manager is Javed Nurani. Kimberly Kelly performed data entry.

Typesetting supervisor is Kathleen M. Flanagan. The typesetting staff includes Karla Corley Brown, Mark J. McEwan, Patricia Flanagan Salisbury, and Kathy F. Wooldridge. Freelance typesetters include Deidre Murphy and Delores Plastow.

Walter W. Ross and Steven Gross did library research. They were assisted by the following librarians at the Thomas Cooper Library of the University of South Carolina: Linda Holderfield and the interlibrary-loan staff; reference-department head Virginia Weathers; reference librarians Marilee Birchfield, Stefanie Buck, Stefanie DuBose, Rebecca Feind, Karen Joseph, Donna Lehman, Charlene Loope, Anthony McKissick, Jean Rhyne, and Kwamine Simpson; circulation-department head Caroline Taylor; and acquisitions-searching supervisor David Haggard.

British Novelists
Since 1960
Third Series

Dictionary of Literary Biography

J. G. Ballard
(15 November 1930 –)

John Fletcher
University of East Anglia

and

James Whitlark
Texas Tech University

SELECTED BOOKS: *Billennium* (New York: Berkley, 1962);

The Wind from Nowhere (New York: Berkley, 1962; Harmondsworth, U.K.: Penguin, 1967);

The Voices of Time and Other Stories (New York: Berkley, 1962; revised edition, London: Orion, 1974);

The Drowned World (New York: Berkley, 1962; London: Gollancz, 1963);

The Four-Dimensional Nightmare (London: Gollancz, 1963);

Passport to Eternity (New York: Berkley, 1963);

The Burning World (New York: Berkley, 1964); expanded as *The Drought* (London: Cape, 1965);

The Terminal Beach (London: Gollancz, 1964); revised as *Terminal Beach* (New York: Berkley, 1964);

The Crystal World (New York: Farrar, Straus & Giroux, 1966; London: Cape, 1966);

The Impossible Man and Other Stories (New York: Berkley, 1966);

By Day Fantastic Birds Flew Through the Petrified Forest. . . (Brighton: Esographics for Firebird Visions, 1967);

The Day of Forever (London: Panther, 1967; revised, 1971);

The Disaster Area (London: Cape, 1967);

The Overloaded Man (London: Panther, 1967);

The Atrocity Exhibition (London: Cape, 1970); republished as *Love and Napalm: Export U.S.A.* (New York: Grove, 1972); revised, with annotations by Ballard, as *The Atrocity Exhibition* (San Francisco: Re/Search, 1990);

J. G. Ballard at the time of the U.S. publication of Cocaine Nights
(photograph © 1998 by John Foley)

Chronopolis and Other Stories (New York: Putnam, 1971);

Vermilion Sands (New York: Berkley, 1971; London: Cape, 1973);

Crash (London: Cape, 1973; New York: Farrar, Straus & Giroux, 1973);

Concrete Island (London: Cape, 1974; New York: Farrar, Straus & Giroux, 1974);

High-Rise (London: Cape, 1975; New York: Holt, Rinehart & Winston, 1977);

Low-Flying Aircraft and Other Stories (London: Cape, 1976);

The Unlimited Dream Company (London: Cape, 1979; New York: Holt, Rinehart & Winston, 1979);

The Venus Hunters (London: Granada, 1980);

Hello America (London: Cape, 1981; New York: Carroll & Graf, 1988);

Myths of the Near Future (London: Cape, 1982);

Empire of the Sun (London: Gollancz, 1984; New York: Simon & Schuster, 1984);

The Day of Creation (London: Gollancz, 1987; New York: Farrar, Straus & Giroux, 1987);

Running Wild (London: Hutchinson, 1988; New York: Farrar, Straus & Giroux, 1988);

Memories of the Space Age (Sauk City, Wis.: Arkham House, 1988);

War Fever (London: Collins, 1990; New York: Farrar, Straus & Giroux, 1991);

The Kindness of Women (London: HarperCollins, 1991; New York: Farrar, Straus & Giroux, 1991);

Rushing to Paradise (London: Flamingo, 1994; New York: Picador, 1995);

A User's Guide to the Millennium: Essays and Reviews (London: HarperCollins, 1996; New York: Picador, 1996);

Cocaine Nights (London: Flamingo, 1996; Washington, D.C.: Counterpoint, 1998).

Collections: *The Best of J. G. Ballard* (London: Futura, 1977);

The Best Short Stories of J. G. Ballard (New York: Holt, Rinehart & Winston, 1978).

J. G. Ballard is one of the most significant of those British novelists who have established themselves since 1960. Although he established his literary reputation as a science-fiction writer, he has come to believe that the present, rather than the future, is the period of greatest moral urgency for the writer, and that science fiction is central to the literary mainstream, to the extent that it concerns itself not with outer but "inner space." In a 1975 interview, he commented:

> I began writing in the mid-Fifties. Enormous changes were going on in England at that time, largely brought about by science and technology—the beginnings of television, package holidays, mass merchandising, the first supermarkets. . . . The only form of fiction which was trying to make head or tail of what was going on in our world was science-fiction. . . . I wanted a science-fiction of the present day. . . . I am not interested in imaginary alien planets.

Ballard's fiction has at times included many of the conventions of science fiction, but his writing is distinct from those genre examples that suggest a space western, with ray guns instead of six shooters. Perhaps partly because of this distinctiveness, Ballard has never had much success in the American science-fiction market, where his early books were published in paperback by Berkley; his reputation in Great Britain has grown over his career so that he has become something of a literary institution, published by such discriminating fiction houses as Jonathan Cape. His books have been well received in France, where his particular blend of erotic fantasy and surrealistic imagery seems less unfamiliar than it has in the English-speaking world.

His American recognition, however, has begun to change since the publication of his best-selling autobiographical novel, *Empire of the Sun* (1984), a work that helped to account for many of Ballard's familiar idiosyncrasies by showing their source in his childhood. James Graham Ballard was born on 15 November 1930 in Shanghai, China, into the privileged world of the British colonial class. His father ran a British textile plant there. Living in a home with nine servants and a chauffeur-driven Packard, young Ballard enjoyed the collage of eastern and western cultures of the city, which he later considered an introduction to his favorite artistic style—surrealism.

The fortunes of the Ballard family were almost completely reversed during World War II, when from 1942 to 1945 Ballard, his parents, and younger sister, Margaret, were interned in a Japanese prison camp. According to various interviews, autobiographical articles, and above all his novels *Empire of the Sun* and *The Kindness of Women* (1991), young Ballard partly enjoyed the experience despite the privations. From 1946 to 1949 he attended the Leys School, Cambridge, then studied medicine at King's College, Cambridge University. For a time Ballard considered becoming a psychiatrist, and although he abandoned his studies in the field after two years, his fiction generally reflects his ongoing interest in that discipline. While he was at Cambridge, a short story of his was the joint winner of a university competition, leading to his first publication in a student periodical. After leaving King's College, Ballard next studied English at London University. In 1954 his longtime interest in flight led him to join the Royal Air Force, and he was sent to Canada for training.

Ballard was in the air force for little more than a year, but while in Canada he was first exposed to science fiction by the racks of American paperbacks in the airbase cafeteria. Back in England, he married Helen Mary Matthews in 1955. After a lean period of literary apprenticeship, Ballard published his first commercial story, "Prima Belladonna," in the December 1956 issue

Ballard with his children at their Shepperton home, 1965

of *Science Fantasy*. With his first child, James Christopher, to support, Ballard was compelled to supplement his income by editing technical journals. While working on the trade magazine *Chemistry and Industry* he read the scientific material that informed much of his fiction. During this period his daughters, Fay and Beatrice, were born as well, in 1957 and 1959, respectively. Feeling trapped in a routine of editorial work and commuting, Ballard wrote his first novel, *The Wind from Nowhere* (1962), in a desperate burst of energy during a two-week vacation. Although it followed quickly on the former, *The Drowned World* (1962) won more commercial and critical success. These novels, along with his next two, *The Burning World* (1964) and *The Crystal World* (1966), and approximately eighty short stories composed during the early years of his career, have just enough futuristic trappings to be nominally considered science fiction.

Being more literary than the norm of that genre, the first three novels were compared by Frederick Bowers to T. S. Eliot's poetry. There is, however, a striking difference. For Eliot, paradisiacal garden and waste land are antitheses; for Ballard, they are identical–an exten-sion of his paradoxically joyous and harrowing experience in the Japanese camp. Even in the most conventional of his books, *The Wind from Nowhere,* the planet-devastating dust storms are described as a "cosmic carousel," suggesting that the destruction can be likened to an amusing children's ride. As Ballard revealed in his 1963 essay "Time, Memory and Inner Space," the setting for *The Drowned World,* in which rising temperatures and melting glaciers make a swamp of the future London, was based on "the drowned paddy fields and irrigation canals . . . of Shanghai." What remains above the rising waters has to come to resemble an "insane Eden," reminding the protagonist of the "drowned world of my uterine childhood." Rather than follow the rest of his party to the last remaining human outposts near the poles, he follows "the lagoons southward through the increasing rain and heat, attacked by alligators and giant bats," becoming "a second Adam searching for the forgotten paradises of the reborn Sun." When an editor asked him to send the character north toward survival for a happier ending, Ballard countered that the character's apparent suicide was a form of "psychic fulfillment." Similarly, *The Drought* concerns willed self-destruction, this time in a desert—also paradoxically described as Edenic—where a new barbarism allows its characters to indulge varieties of self-absorption.

The Crystal World, which was composed in several stages following the sudden death of Ballard's wife, takes his favorite theme of withdrawal into one's own psyche further than its predecessors. In this novel the catastrophe is an apocalyptic plague of crystal that encrusts human flesh; yet, at the African *leproserie* where much of the novel is set, the lepers joyously accept the form of immortality the crystallization provides. Because Ballard's theme is so often the passing of civilization, Darko Suvin identified it with the loss of the British Empire. When Pringle asked Ballard about this, he quipped that his works chronicled "the fall of the *American* empire."

The Crystal World could be said to mark an important transition point in Ballard's literary development. Although the novel involves a science-fiction convention, a fantastic plague of mysterious origin, the social structure of the novel is that of the present (unlike his first three novels, where governments of the near future have had time to react to the emergencies). In Ballard's later works, the apocalyptic problems often are entirely psychological extrapolations from current conditions. This change in focus accorded with his association with the science-fiction writers collectively known as the British New Wave, whose works de-emphasize the "hard" sciences of physics and chemistry in favor of "soft" ones such as psychology and anthropology. One of the distinctive traits of New Wave authors is the degree of literary sophistication they brought to the genre: Ballard's acknowledged literary antecedents are not the popular practitioners of science fiction but are instead a diverse group of writers only tangentially related to the genre, if at all—William S. Burroughs, Jean Genet, Louis-Ferdinand Celine, and Graham Greene.

The growth of the New Wave was contemporary with the considerable social strife of the 1960s. Sympathetic with the student rebellions and anti-Vietnam protests of the time, the authors of the New Wave satirized the fruits of technological advances as a dangerous product of the military-industrial complex and championed formal experimentation as a way of breaking free from old shibboleths. A favorite target of their vitriol was the American space program; Ballard's attitude toward space travel is expressed most succinctly in his epigraph to his short-story collection *Memories of the Space Age* (1988): "By leaving his planet and setting off into outer space man had committed an evolutionary crime. . . ." Instead, reflecting his preference for exploring altered states of consciousness, Ballard at one point

issued through *Ambit* magazine the offer of a £40 prize "for the best fiction or poetry written under the influence of drugs."

Ballard's reputation as a novelist of the New Wave depends largely on four works: *The Atrocity Exhibition* (1970), *Crash* (1973), *Concrete Island* (1974), and *High-Rise* (1975). *The Atrocity Exhibition* collected pieces that had previously appeared as short stories in periodicals but were here brought together as an experimental novel. Each chapter of the novel relates the apparent schizophrenic perceptions of a protagonist whose name changes from chapter to chapter in response to the "increasing fragmentation of his external environment—a backdrop of splintered mass-cultural icons," as Andrea Juno and V. Vale characterize it in their introduction to the 1990 annotated edition to the work. According to Ballard in a marginal comment added to the 1990 edition, the protagonist's "core identity is Traven, a name taken consciously from B. Traven, a writer I've always admired for his extreme reclusiveness—so completely at odds with the logic of our own age, when even the concept of privacy is constructed from publicly circulating material." Traven may be a doctor or a patient—or both—at an unnamed psychiatric institution, at which the patients are exhibiting their artistic creations, the "atrocity exhibition" of the work's title: "A disquieting feature of this annual exhibition—to which the patients themselves were not invited—was the marked preoccupation of the paintings with the theme of world cataclysm, as if these long-incarcerated patients had sensed some seismic upheaval within the minds of their doctors and nurses." Traven projects himself as a series of other personae, including the projected first casualty of World War III and, in the section "You and Me and the Continuum," a Christ figure who descends to Earth in an atomic bomber. Throughout the work, the imagery is deliberately controversial. Even before the book's publication, when the section "Plan for the Assassination of Jacqueline Kennedy" appeared in *Ambit,* Winston Churchill's son Randolph denounced it and proposed that the magazine be deprived of its Arts Council grant. When another chapter about Ronald Reagan became involved in a pornography trial, Ballard told the court that he intended it to be pornographic as a way of shocking readers out of their complacency. Upon seeing the first American printing, Nelson Doubleday commanded his press to pulp its whole press run.

Despite such difficulties, Ballard continued to court notoriety, expanding one of the most disturbing sections of the book into the novel *Crash.* He further explored the themes that inform *Crash* in an exhibition entitled "Crashed Cars" at the New Arts Laboratory Gallery in London in April 1969, an episode that is

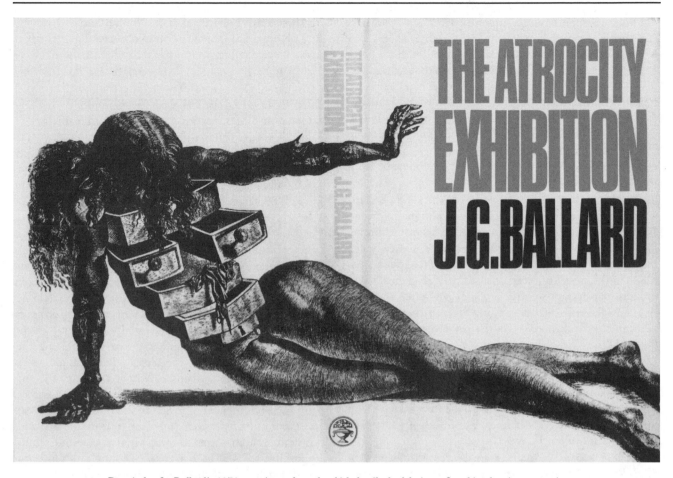

Dust jacket for Ballard's 1970 experimental novel, which details the delusions of a schizophrenic protagonist

rccountcd in *The Kindness of Women.* When he submitted the novel for publication, one publisher's reader offered the opinion that the author must be insane. No doubt such a conclusion was encouraged by Ballard's decision to give the obsessive narrator his own name in the novel; as he observed in a 1976 interview with James Goddard, it was "the honest thing to do." In *The Kindness of Women* Ballard seems to suggest that the origin of *Crash* lies in the self-destructive driving of a friend and fellow internee from the Japanese camp at Lunghua, a man whose post-traumatic stress causes him to pursue annihilation with an almost sexual fervor. In *Crash* the character Ballard, following a near-fatal collision, finds his imagination dominated by the conceptual possibilities of automobile accidents. Encouraged by Vaughan, a former talk-show host whose career ended as the result of a disfiguring accident, Ballard visualizes "absurd deaths of the wounded, maimed and distraught. I think of the crashes of psychopaths, implausible accidents carried out with venom and self-disgust, vicious multiple collisions contrived in stolen cars on evening freeways among tired office-workers." The

novel has had a cult following since its publication, and when a film adaptation was released in 1996, its subject matter was still sufficiently controversial for the movie to be banned in Britain (thereby increasing the readership of the book). His reputation among scholars was strengthened when postmodern theorist Jean Baudrillard included an essay on it in his *Simulacra and Simulation* (1994), in which he refers to *Crash* as "the first great novel of the universe of simulation." Along with *The Atrocity Exhibition, Crash* represents Ballard's turning away from tales about ecological disasters or mutations to an unsentimental scrutiny of the dehumanized eroticism and brutality that he feels are inseparable from the new technologies.

Similar in theme but shorter is *Concrete Island,* in most ways a more straightforward account of a character's pathology that lacks the lyricism of *Crash.* In the opening scene of the novel Robert Maitland is seriously injured in a hit-and-run accident after his car has a flat tire on one of the highways surrounding London. Knocked down the slope of a huge concrete embankment, Maitland is unable to gain the attention of passing motorists and is consequently stranded Robinson Crusoe–like on the grotesque concrete island. Later Maitland learns that he shares the island with a tramp, Proctor, and Jane, a prostitute; he finds that he can survive on garbage dumped regularly over the perimeter fence by truckers serving the restaurant trade. Maitland establishes an ambiguous relationship with his fellow inhabitants, but eventually Proctor is killed and Jane leaves. Still incapacitated from his injuries, Maitland is clearly going to make no serious attempt to escape from the island.

Although *Concrete Island* represents for Ballard something of a return to more conventional plotting, Ballard leaves ambiguous the motivations of his characters and the relationships between events, somewhat in the manner of the novels of Alain Robbe-Grillet. Incidents in the novel proceed as a series of detached, vivid images that juxtapose arrestingly the nightmarish qualities of Maitland's situation along with the new pleasure he seems to find therein. As the reviewer for *TLS: The Times Literary Supplement* noted, "The skill with which Mr. Ballard manages, in the most uncontrived way, to have Maitland compulsively regress to self-discovery is itself considerable; that in doing so he reveals undertones of savagery and desolation beneath a metaphor of apparent neutrality is a tribute to him as our foremost iconographer of landscape."

The urban landscape also figures prominently in *High-Rise,* in which the setting is a habitat for the upper middle class that is repeatedly·referred to as a prison. As David Pringle observes, "the high-rise building is not so much a machine for living as a brutal playground full of essentially solitary children." Drawn into tribal feuds between floors, the inhabitants of the building cease to return to work or bring in new provisions. They regress through childhood, barbarism, and animality, become nocturnal, eat each other's pets and, finally, one another. Occupying the penthouse, the social summit of the high rise, is its architect, Royal, who resembles a "fallen angel." In a typically Ballardian display of hubris, he is attempting to "colonize the sky" and create a "new Jerusalem" that would be a "paradigm of all future high-rise blocks."

High-Rise "makes the point that the high-rise building is not so much a machine for living as a brutal playground full of essentially solitary children," as Pringle observes. The people who live in Ballard's elegant forty-story tower block are "living in a future that had already taken place." In his review of *High-Rise,* John Sutherland in the *TLS* referred to a comment made by Ballard's friend and fellow New Wave writer, Brian Aldiss, that Ballard had not resolved the problem of "writing a novel without having the characters pursue any purposeful course of action." Typical of the critical response to Ballard's fiction, Sutherland's review is decidedly mixed; he went on to observe that "As usual, Mr. Ballard contrives to unsettle and tease the reader."

Ballard's fiction is frequently set in locations familiar to the author. The setting for his 1979 novel, *The Unlimited Dream Company,* for example, is the London suburb of Shepperton, not far from Heathrow Airport, a residential area famous for its film studios. The choice of setting contributes to Ballard's intended ironic effect, making the events of the novel more disturbing by contrasting them with the familiarity of urban London. The visionary Blake, an aircraft cleaner at London Airport, steals a light aircraft that catches fire and crashes into the Thames at Shepperton. He drowns in the crash but somehow survives and proceeds to haunt the burghers of Shepperton with his dreams so that the whole community becomes an "unlimited dream company." He carries on his chest bruises that he assumes were caused by whatever lifesaving action was necessary after he was rescued. Eventually he encounters his own corpse, however, and the two struggle together desperately for life. "I realised then," Blake says, "whose mouth and hands I had tried to find since my arrival in this small town. The bruises were the scars of my own body clinging to me in terror as I tore myself free from that dying self and escaped from the drowned aircraft." He manages to calm his alter ego and reunify himself, and then he is free to celebrate in an airborne wedding feast with his bride, Dr. Miriam, with whom he has been in love since he crashed in Shepperton near her clinic. The two of them part, but Blake is confident, in the closing paragraph of the novel, that he and she will eventually be reunited for eternity:

> This time we would merge with the trees and the flowers, with the dust and the stones, with the whole of the mineral world, happily dissolving ourselves in the sea of light that formed the universe, itself reborn from the souls of the living who have happily returned themselves to its heart. Already I saw us rising into the air, fathers, mothers and their children, our ascending flights swaying across the surface of the earth, benign tornadoes hanging from the canopy of the universe, celebrating the last marriage of the animate and inanimate, of the living and the dead.

As is often the case in Ballard's fiction, the protagonist's internal journey involves imagery of aeronautics. His promise to teach the inhabitants to fly sometimes precedes his absorbing them into his body, an emblematic act in that it is really internal. Despite the pervasiveness of flight, throughout much of the book Blake feels imprisoned in Shepperton. His only recourse is to plunge further within the place. "I *had* escaped from Shepperton, by submerging myself in their bodies. . . ."

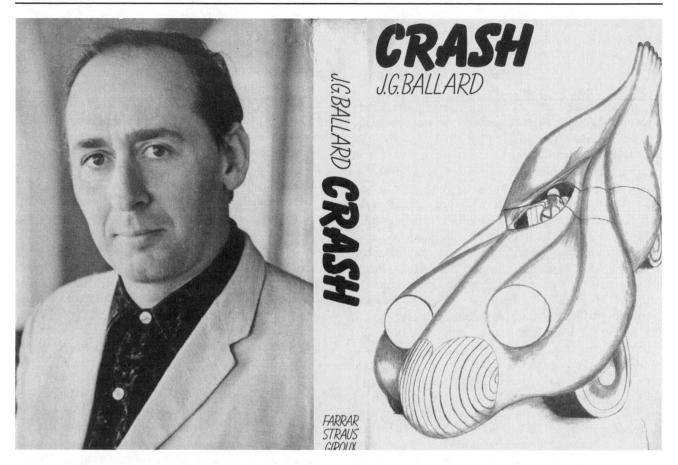

Dust jacket for the first U.S. edition of Ballard's 1973 novel, in which a protagonist named Ballard becomes obsessed with automobile collisions

The result seems solipsistic, particularly because of the narrator's repeated comparisons of himself to a god.

In a review for *Foundation* John Clute connects *The Unlimited Dream Company* to such fantasies of posthumous existence as William Golding's *Pincher Martin* (1956) and Ambrose Bierce's "An Occurrence at Owl Creek Bridge" (1956). Peter Brigg, however, insists on the novel's independence from these because it abounds in paradoxical characters that embody Ballard's oscillation between the actual Shepperton he knows well and his sexual fantasies. There is, for instance, a woman doctor with whom he flies magically, yet she is drawn back toward her science. Similarly, a stunt man, representative of film illusion, shoots Blake in defense of reality. In his *99 Novels* (1984) Anthony Burgess chose the book as one of the best English novels since 1939.

Somewhat less distinguished is *Hello America* (1981), although Galen Strawson has praised its "wealth of images." A burlesque of science-fiction writers' penchant for predicting grim futures, it took seven years to find an American publisher after its British debut. In the novel President Jerry Brown lacks the resolve to administer the country and withdraws to a Japanese monastery after pointless fiddling. "In his Millennial Address to Congress in the year 2000, President Brown recited a poignant Zen tantra and then made the momentous announcement that henceforth the operation of private gasoline driven vehicles would be illegal." (Ballard's use of the phrase "Zen tantra," which confuses the Mahayana and Vajrayana varieties of Buddhism, is representative of a certain superficial interest in the religion that recurs in his fiction.) *Hello America* is marred by equally questionable assertions about American culture. In several short stories Americans lose faith in their way of life and abandon large parts of their country for no adequate reason. Likewise, in *Hello America* the depletion of fossil fuels causes the United States to be almost deserted by the population's immigration to Europe and Asia, which also lack fuels, thus rendering migration pointless. Also implausible is Ballard's choice to have his villain flaunt his iconoclasm by naming himself after Charles Manson. According to Ballard's protagonist, the core of American democracy was for its citizens to explore their most bizarre fantasies. Ballard's portrayal of America is intentionally sensationalized, and such stereotypical depictions could help to account for relatively poor sales of his books in the United States.

Ballard's next novel, *Empire of the Sun,* however, overcame such popular indifference: in addition to being nominated for Britain's most prestigious literary award, the Booker Prize, it earned his best sales in the United States and was adapted for film by Steven Spielberg from a screenplay by Tom Stoppard. Rather than treating the fall of the American empire, the novel celebrates Americana. Its protagonist, Jim, is fascinated with everything American, and G.I.s are depicted as the heroes who liberated the camps. The novel's graphic horrors come from Ballard's childhood observations, as he notes in his foreword: "For the most part this novel is an eyewitness account of events I observed during the Japanese occupation of Shanghai and within the camp of Lunghua." Yet, the work is distinct from autobiography. Whereas Ballard accompanied the rest of his family to Lunghua, Jim is separated from his, starves for an extended period on the dangerous streets of Shanghai, and is unprotected in the camp. As in children's adventure tales, Jim is heroic, but he is a typically Ballardian protagonist in his willingness to accept his incarceration. On the streets, despite feeling that surrender is un-British, he tries desperately to be captured. He finally achieves that goal by being arrested for breaking into his own house, and his journey to the prison camp is "the first time he felt able to enjoy the war," which the British were losing. Consorting with his Japanese captors, Jim realizes that he feels closer to them than to the British. He jokes about joining the Japanese air force and gradually becomes more defeatist. When he hears news of Allied victories later in the war, he wishes "that the Americans would go back to Hawaii. . . . Then Lunghua Camp would once again be the happy place that he had known in 1943." He does, though, like the bombing: "He welcomed the air raids, the noise of the Mustangs as they swept over the camp, the smell of oil and cordite, the deaths of the pilots and even the likelihood of his own death. Despite everything, he knew he was worth nothing." During a forced march from his camp to the city of Nantao, Jim witnesses in the distance the first nuclear bomb blast, which he experiences as a moment of ecstasy. Jim shares the moment with a ragged Japanese soldier: "Jim smiled at the Japanese, wishing that he could tell him that the light was a premonition of his death, the sight of his small soul joining the larger soul of the dying world." In its ambiguity the passage links Jim with the Japanese, united in an imagined global annihilation. In the chaos that accompanies the end of the war, Jim is eventually left on his own again for months. He finds the body of a young Japanese pilot near the remnants of

the prison camp; while the Japanese military ignores one of its last kamikazes, Jim identifies with him: "Unlike the war in China, everyone in Europe clearly knew which side he was on, a problem that Jim had never really solved." Jim realizes his old world has died, and he wanders in a life-in-death state until being reunited with his parents. In *Empire of the Sun,* this death and rebirth motif has the conventional meaning of Jim's going from childhood to adulthood, with an unusually strong sense of the difficulty of the passage. The novel closes with Jim and his mother on a ship to England: "Below the bows of the *Arrawa* a child's coffin moved onto the night stream . . . only to be swept back by the incoming tide among the quays and mud flats, driven once again to the shores of this terrible city."

Ballard's next novel, *Running Wild* (1988), is written in the form of the forensic diaries of psychologist Richard Greville as he investigates the circumstances behind the massacre of the thirty-two adults of the Pangbourne community by their thirteen children. *Running Wild* depicts upper-class families living in the sort of cramped conditions usually associated with the poor, although the affluent parents spy electronically on their offspring. Denied by bourgeois decorum of an appropriate safety valve for the pressures of such intimate living, the children decide that they can no longer tolerate their comfortable prison. Using the videotape of the Pangbourne community's surveillance system, Greville reconstructs the children's brutal response to the "sensory depravation" of parental protection. Later they assassinate a former prime minister, and the young terrorists are still on the loose at the end of the novel.

Although a sequel to *Empire of the Sun, The Kindness of Women* (1991) does not begin where the other ends; instead, it repeats the protagonist's childhood internment, thus establishing the centrality of the camp experience in his life. The first section of the novel, "A Season for Assassins," starts with Jamie, a seven-year-old, whose chief worry is that "the war would be over before I noticed that it had begun." (The idea occurs also in Ballard's short story "The Secret History of World War 3," about a conflict so brief that only the narrator notices it.) The long and terrible Japanese occupation of Shanghai, however, is imminent. On "Bloody Saturday," as the invasion came to be known, Jamie is reading Daniel Defoe's *Robinson Crusoe* (1719), a work often mentioned in Ballard's writings because of its themes of isolation and of the individual's potential to build his own world. Jamie's parents are going out, but they tell him to stay home reading about the cannibals; he wants to go to the local British garrison's tattoo or to a performance by the Hell Drivers, a group of daredevils. (Obviously, this early scene is meant to allude to Ballard's later obsessions—the cannibalism to

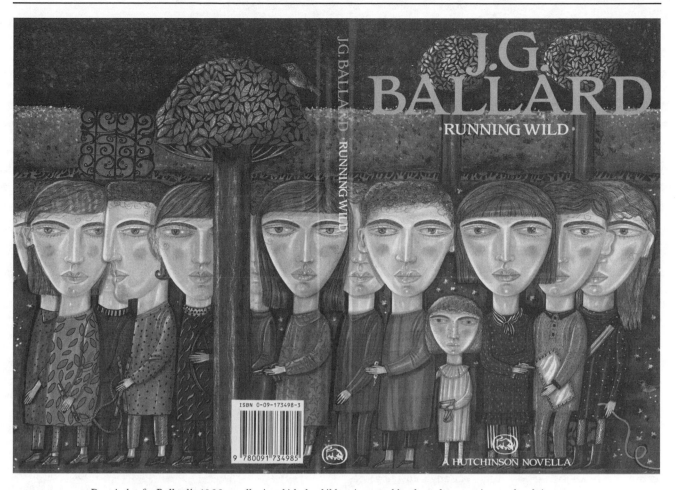

Dust jacket for Ballard's 1988 novella, in which the children in a wealthy planned community murder their parents

which his characters are so often reduced, their penchant for violent display, and the pathological fascination with automobile accidents that overflows *Crash*.) Later that day, Jamie is among 1,007 people wounded by a bomb that lands in a nearby amusement park and kills 1,012 others: "As everyone constantly repeated, proud that Shanghai had again excelled itself, this was the largest number killed by a single bomb in the history of aerial warfare." Jamie is separated from his parents—though without the extended adventures Jim experiences in *Empire of the Sun*. As in that novel, in *The Kindness of Women* Japanese airpower figures in Jamie's fantasies: "I watched the exhaust of the Japanese fighters, warming myself with the thought of their powerful engines." Whereas his friend David tries to flee the prison, Jamie's plan is to break into the food shed. "Far from wanting to escape from the camp, I had been trying to burrow ever more deeply into its heart." When the Japanese guards leave temporarily, the other prisoners rejoice, but Jamie feels "secretly relieved" at their return. After finally leaving, he speaks to Japanese soldiers who are slowly suffocating a Chinese youth with wire—Ballard as a child actually witnessed the horrible event. Despite realizing the danger of that situation, Jamie later recalls, "I keep thinking I should have stayed."

After the war, Jamie tries medical school, where he becomes obsessed with the cadaver he is assigned in anatomy class: "Exposing herself to young men with knives in their hands, she set a kind of order on my memories of the dead Chinese and Japanese I had seen during the war." He joins the air force, where he prepares to be a pilot of nuclear payloads and has dreams of starting World War III. He spends his spare time amid prostitutes in the company of his childhood friend David, who is also reliving his childhood traumas. "Sex, for David, was as close as he could get to that terrifying evening in the guardhouse" after being caught in his escape attempt. For Jamie, sex is a way "of re-creating the pearly light I had seen over the rice fields of Lunghua beside the railway station." Not quite as dominated by the past as David, Jamie manages to marry, have children, and pursue a writing career, although his wife dies suddenly. He becomes involved in the burgeoning counterculture of the time and tries LSD, ostensibly as part of a television documentary on the drug. During a traumatic hallucinatory trip he sees the "same light" that "lay over Lunghua on the day the war ended." Voicing one of Ballard's obsessions, he decides that humanity feels trapped in time, and that "war was the means by which nations escaped from time." Still thinking about the death of the Chinese youth, he believes that the Japanese tortured him to "release the mainspring of war" and thereby dissolve time.

David finds his escape from time and his Lunghua trauma in car crashes: he is the model for Vaughan in *Crash*. Jamie becomes drawn into his neurosis and mounts an art exhibition of crashed cars, which ends, as did Ballard's actual exhibition, in debauchery. David, however, enters an asylum, likened to a prison, and suggests that it may soon be Jamie's turn to join him. The book ends with the filming of Jamie's novel about his Shanghai experiences.

The title of Ballard's next novel, *Rushing to Paradise* (1994), parodies W. B. Yeats's "Running to Paradise," a poem of fin de siécle desire to leave for fairy land. In Ballard's novel Dr. Barbara Rafferty, a bisexual euthanasiast, starts a crusade, ostensibly to save the albatrosses being slaughtered on the island of Saint-Esprit but actually to seize it as her own concentration camp and killing field. The endangered albatross alludes to one of Ballard's favorite poems, Samuel Taylor Coleridge's *The Rime of the Ancient Mariner*, where its death means loss of soul and self-destruction. Seducing her victims, often through their own self-destructive impulses, Dr. Barbara tricks conservationists into bringing her endangered animals, which she eats, and becoming her slaves. She delivers them from their own self-consciousness and sense of responsibility, as a member of her expedition, David Carline, realizes: "All the self criticism and dissatisfaction of the years before his meeting with Dr. Barbara had been banished by his decision to follow her to the end." His lack of self-respect comes from "a world that had given him everything at his birth and then, piece by piece, taken it all back from him"—like Ballard in the Japanese camp. The protagonist, a teenager named Neil Dempsey, who has previously had little but swimming on his mind, joins Dr. Barbara, seemingly to stop nuclear testing on the island but actually because of his "childish infatuation with nuclear death," another trait he shares with the protagonist of *The Kindness of Women*. Neil finds Dr. Barbara more seductive the more homicidal she becomes. Although he is rescued from her attempts on his life, he still wants to return to the island and to "be embraced again by Dr. Barbara's cruel and generous heart."

Perhaps indicative of Ballard's increased popularity, in 1996 he published *A User's Guide to the Millennium*, collecting book reviews and other short essays, some of which date back to the early days of the British New Wave. These pieces celebrate the artists who have influenced him, including Franz Kafka, Salvador Dali, William Burroughs, the Marquis de Sade, and Andy Warhol, as well as others who have portrayed the attractiveness of destruction. About the director Stanley Kubrick, for example, he writes: "By enlisting us on the side of our darkest fears, Kubrick exposes all the sinister glamour and unconscious logic of technological death." In "The Coming of the Unconscious," he writes admiringly of the Dada art movement, which was "out to perpetrate any enormity that would attract attention to its mission—the total destruction of so-called 'civilized' values." In "The Innocent as Paranoid" he credits Dali for diagnosing through his paintings the twentieth-century's "death of affect," the "demise of feeling and emotion" that has paved the way for all our most real and tender pleasures—in the excitements of pain and mutilation . . . what our children have to fear are not the cars on the freeways of tomorrow but our own pleasure in calculating the most elegant parameters of their deaths." In "Project for a Glossary of the Twentieth Century" he defines his favorite genre, science fiction, as "the body's dream of becoming a machine," in other words, without emotion and, in a sense, dead. In a review of two encyclopedias of comic books, he takes an opportunity to comment on American reading tastes: "It is . . . depressing to reflect that American comics are read by virtually the entire US population well into adult life, and have probably been the dominant force in shaping the American imagination, a sobering thought for any British novelist hoping to sell his introverted crochet-work to an American audience."

If Ballard's short articles may be passed over quickly, his short stories deserve more attention. Like most science-fiction authors of his generation, when magazine fiction still flourished, he began by pursuing the shorter form, and he has published twelve collections since, as well as two "best of" collections. In this medium he has won the high regard of Burgess, among others. As David Pringle points out in *Earth Is the Alien Planet* (1979), Ballard is not a writer to be judged by his novels alone: "He is very much at home in shorter lengths, and his talents are often displayed to the full within the compass of, say, 10,000 words. Ballard tends to compression; at one extreme this leads to the remarkable density of the *Atrocity Exhibition* pieces (few of which are more than three or four thousand words long)." As Pringle notes, both *The Drowned World* and *The Crystal World* began as magazine novellas, and Ballard has commented in his notes to *The Best of J. G. Bal-*

lard (1977) that some of his early stories, such as "The Sound Sweep" and "The Voices of Time" were over-compressed novels, while some of his recent novels are really extended short stories. Of the stories in *Low-Flying Aircraft* (1976), Michael Irwin has said: "He taps our memories of disused railway-stations or airstrips, dumped cars, derelict cinemas or factories. The world he creates seems credible because it has already begun to exist." Five of the stories in the volume are "works of real imaginative force, dreamlike, vivid, unpredictable in their effect." A common feature of the stories are the memorable landscapes, of which Ballard is an undisputed master in contemporary fiction. Of an earlier collection of stories, *Vermilion Sands* (1971), a reviewer said that the stylistic effects of his landscapes were comparable to those of the painter Dali insofar as they showed "a mixture of appalling clarity and the exotic."

Ballard's most recent story collection is *War Fever* (1990). Its title narrative has Beirut as a new kind of concentration camp, a city where orphans are sent by the United Nations and manipulated into killing each other. Dr. Edwards, one of the manipulators, is "curiously addicted to the violence and death, as if tending the wounded and dying satisfied some defeatist strain in his character." In trying to explain the experiment, he reports that, aside from Beirut, the whole world is at peace. Consequently, the U.N. needs to generate the civil war in Lebanon to study violence like a disease. The story acquires its power not from this dubious notion but from its psychological study of defeatism and claustrophobic aggression within the politically quarantined city. Most tales in the volume are variations on this theme of precarious enclosure. In "The Enormous Space," traumatized by a divorce and business reverses, a man stays at home, consuming neighbors' pets and other visitors. A mutagen in "Dream Cargoes" transforms an isolated island into an Eden whose metamorphosed inhabitants feel they are outside time, but the rest of the world sees them as a threat. "The Largest Theme Park in the World" unites Europe; most of its citizens then confine themselves from 1995 to 1997 to the Riviera, bodybuilding and learning martial arts, until they become barbarians and begin the invasion of their previous homes. An American counterpart to that story is "Memories of the Space Age": having lost faith in NASA, those few Floridians who do not flee the state slip into violence and psychotic timelessness. Four of the stories are experimental in form: "The Object of the Attack," like *Running Wild*, is a case from the "forensic diaries" of Richard Greville;

"Answers to a Questionnaire" reveal a former convict who believes he has killed the "Son of God"; "Notes Towards a Mental Breakdown," in which each word in an unreliable sentence of narrative is annotated by a mental patient; and "The Index," which relates another life of madness and confinement, is told by way of the index of a book. Through their ellipses, these experimental narratives bring the readers into the confusion of their subjects.

War Fever shows Ballard practicing an originality that puts him in the company of Kafka and Jorge Luis Borges. His work has changed much since his first sallies into science fiction. What has remained constant, as critic David Punter rightly remarks, is Ballard's "almost manic fertility of idea and form" along with a hallucinatory portrayal of "the claustrophobia of excessive information and the corresponding breakdown of selective retrieval systems." From nearly every point of view, his achievements as a writer are solid, and the advances of his most recent fiction have more than justified his dramatic rise in literary stature.

Bibliography:

David Pringle, *J. G. Ballard: A Primary and Secondary Bibliography* (Boston: G. K. Hall, 1984).

References:

Jean Baudrillard, *"Crash,"* in his *Simulocra and Simulation,* translated by Sheila Faria Glaser (Ann Arbor: University of Michigan Press, 1994), pp. 111–119;

Peter Brigg, *J. G. Ballard,* Starmont Readers' Guide 26 (Mercer Island, Wash.: Starmont House, 1985);

James Goddard and David Pringle, *J. G. Ballard: The First Twenty Years* (Hayes, U.K.: Bran's Head, 1976);

Colin Greenland, *The Entropy Exhibition: Michael Moorcock and the British "New Wave" in Science Fiction* (London & Boston: Routledge & Kegan Paul, 1983);

Roger Luckhurst, *The Angle between Two Walls: The Fiction of J. G. Ballard* (New York: St. Martin's Press, 1997);

David Pringle, *Earth Is the Alien Planet: J. G. Ballard's Four-Dimensional Nightmare* (San Bernardino, Cal.: Borgo Press, 1979);

Gregory Stephenson, *Out of the Night and Into the Dream: A Thematic Study of the Fiction of J. G. Ballard* (New York: Greenwood Press, 1991);

V. Vale and Andrea Juno, eds., *Re/Search,* special Ballard issue, 8/9 (1984).

Stan Barstow

(28 June 1928 –   )

Elizabeth Allen
Regent's College, London

See also the Barstow entry in *DLB 14: British Novelists Since 1960, First Series* and *DLB 139: British Short-Fiction Writers, 1945–1980*.

BOOKS: *A Kind of Loving* (London: Joseph, 1960; Garden City, N.Y.: Doubleday, 1961);

The Desperadoes and Other Stories (London: Joseph, 1961); revised as *The Human Element and Other Stories,* edited by Marilyn Davies (London: Longman, 1969);

Ask Me Tomorrow (London: Joseph, 1962);

Joby (London: Joseph, 1964);

The Watchers on the Shore (London: Joseph, 1966; Garden City, N.Y.: Doubleday, 1967);

Ask Me Tomorrow (play), by Barstow and Alfred Bradley (London & New York: S. French, 1966);

A Raging Calm (London: Joseph, 1968); republished as *The Hidden Part* (New York: Coward-McCann, 1969);

A Kind of Loving (play), by Barstow and Bradley (London: Blackie, 1970);

A Season with Eros (London: Joseph, 1971);

Stringer's Last Stand, by Barstow and Bradley (London & New York: S. French, 1972);

Twenty Pieces of Silver, and Waiting, edited by Ronald Barnes (Cambridge: Cambridge University Press, 1975);

The Right True End (London: Joseph, 1976);

A Casual Acquaintance and Other Stories, edited by Davies (London: Longman, 1976);

Joby: A Television Play, edited by Davies (London: Blackie, 1977);

A Brother's Tale (London: Joseph, 1980);

The Human Element and Albert's Part: Two Television Plays (London: Blackie, 1984);

The Glad Eye and Other Stories (London: Joseph, 1984);

Just You Wait and See (London: Joseph, 1986);

B-Movie (London: Joseph, 1987);

Give Us This Day (London: Joseph, 1989);

Next of Kin (London & New York: Joseph, 1991).

Collection: *A Kind of Loving: The Vic Brown Trilogy* (London: Joseph, 1981).

Stan Barstow

PLAY PRODUCTIONS: *Ask Me Tomorrow,* by Barstow and Alfred Bradley, Sheffield, Yorkshire, 1964;

A Kind of Loving, by Barstow and Bradley, Sheffield, Yorkshire, 1965;

An Enemy of the People, adapted from the play by Henrik Ibsen, Harrogate, Yorkshire, 1969;

Listen for the Trains, Love, music by Alec Glasgow, Sheffield, Yorkshire, 1970;

Stringer's Last Stand, by Barstow and Bradley, York, 1971.

TELEVISION: *The Human Element,* script by Barstow, 1964;

The Pity of it All, script by Barstow, 1965;

The Desperadoes, script by Barstow, 1965;

A World Inside, documentary by Barstow and John Gibson, 1966;

Mind You, I Live Here, documentary by Barstow and Gibson, 1971;

A Raging Calm, script by Barstow, 1974;

South Riding, script by Barstow, adapted from the novel by Winifred Holtby, 1974;

We Could Always Fit a Sidecar, script by Barstow, 1974;

Joby, script by Barstow, 1975;

The Cost of Loving, script by Barstow, 1977;

Travellers, script by Barstow, 1978;

A Kind of Loving, script by Barstow, 1982.

OTHER: *Through the Green Woods: An Anthology of Contemporary Writing about Youth and Childhood,* edited, with an introduction, by Barstow (Leeds: E. J. Arnold, 1968);

"We Could Always Fit a Sidecar," in *Out of the Air: Five Plays for Radio,* edited by Alfred Bradley (London: Longman, 1978);

Henrik Ibsen, *An Enemy of the People,* adapted by Barstow (London: Calder, 1978).

Stan Barstow is a major figure in an important postwar movement in English fiction, one that for the first time put working-class novelists, most of them from the north of England, in a visible and celebrated position. Like John Braine, David Storey, Keith Waterhouse (all of them, like Barstow, from Yorkshire), and Alan Sillitoe from Nottingham, Barstow wrote about the daily reality of contemporary life among classes and characters not previously at the center of British literature. He and the others attracted considerable critical attention in the late 1950s and the 1960s; sometimes the criticism went no further than pigeonholing them in the "provincial angry young man school" of writers, a kind of lumping together that the writers came to resent. As D. J. Taylor observes, "By the mid-1960s . . . class had once again become a definite concern of the English novel." This time working-class writers such as Barstow—rather than upper-middle-class figures such as Anthony Powell and Evelyn Waugh—dictated the concern.

Like others in this group, Barstow diversified into other media, most notably television and stage plays. Keith Waterhouse adapted Barstow's first novel for the screen; later Barstow adapted Winifred Holtby's *South Riding* (1936). Unlike others among his northern contemporaries, who moved to London and the southeast of England, Barstow still lives in the north, and his most recent novels continue to draw on the same industrial towns and communities for his materials.

His later novels differ somewhat from his early work in being more retrospective, particularly his account, in the related texts *Just You Wait and See* (1986), *Give Us This Day* (1989), and *Next of Kin* (1991), of Yorkshire life during World War II. Though set within his own living memory, Barstow's novels of the 1980s and 1990s have turned slightly away from contemporary life to the middle decades of the twentieth century, which he portrays as the matrix of the kinds of lives he explored early in his career.

Born on 28 June 1928 in the village of Horbury in Yorkshire, Stan Barstow was the only child of Wilfred Barstow, a coal miner, and his wife, Elsie; his upbringing was not one to encourage literary pretensions. He has said: "My circumstances and background didn't seem a very helpful breeding ground. . . . There were no writers in the family. (There were, in fact, few real readers)." After passing the necessary examination, he attended high school in the nearby town of Ossett but was not academically ambitious, and in 1944 he left school to work in the drawing office of an engineering firm in the same town. Only then did he feel the urge to write: "It was the total frustration of my working life which led me to write: I had no alternative outlet."

The experiences of Wilf Cotton in *Ask Me Tomorrow* (1962) may serve to illuminate the youthful Barstow's situation. Among Wilf's peers at school—even the more intelligent—there is little ambition and imagination about life's possibilities. "The highest most of them looked was a teaching position at a local school, with short hours and long holidays. For the rest there was the vague idea of some job without physical labour." Wilf takes on one of these nonmanual positions, working as a wages clerk at the colliery where his father and brother are miners. "For Wilf . . . the restlessness was not long in making itself felt. . . . What nagged more and more was a dissatisfaction with his life as a whole, which grew out of a dawning awareness of a world and values outside the village and the knowledge that the opportunity given him . . . he had largely wasted." As in the case of his author, Wilf's dissatisfaction and restlessness find a creative outlet in writing, although Wilf is less conscious than Barstow of the problems facing an aspiring writer in that place and time. Barstow says of his own experience: "The important thing, the thing that can't be over-emphasised, is the extreme isolation of myself and other regional and working class writers in the mid-fifties. We had the temerity to think we could write but no teachers and no models." Such was the case before regional and working-class settings gained the vogue that they later achieved through the success of Barstow himself—together with Braine, Sillitoe, Storey, and Waterhouse—

The Pity of it All   STAN BARSTOW   3.

Now she was telling Nancy that she'd had a reply from a guest house in Bournemouth, whose address a new friend had given her, and they could have accommodation for the last two weeks in August. Nancy's mother thought the south coast would be a pleasant change, but if Nancy wanted to go elsewhere with a friend it would be no trouble for her and Nancy's father to take little June with them. But no, there was nowhere else that Nancy wanted to go.

Afterwards, Nancy found she could remember that moment in vivid clarity, though its components were all familiar ones she had seen and heard many times before. There was the attitude of her mother's body as she held the vacuum cleaner while she wound the flex on to the hooks; the sudden rush of water in the automatic washer as it performed its last rinse; the sunlight on the step outside the scullery door. The voices of the children were no longer close

"Just have a look out for June, will you," she said as she opened the washer and passed clothes over into the drying compartment. "They've gone quiet."

And then a minute or so must have passed, but it seemed like no time at all before Nancy's mother was calling from the end of the passage: "June! June, where are you? Ey, you two, bring June back here. Don't you know how busy that road is? No, keep hold of her! Don't let her —!" And Nancy was out and running across the flagstones and into the street, as though she knew before she heard that awful screech of tyres and saw the car slewed round and the little legs in the blue-and-white Marks & Spencer socks, washed just once, and the stupid, stupid little girls who had led her into it, standing, petrified, soundless, and she herself making no sound — not yet — while her mother set up an endless chanting moaning chant beside her: "Oh, oh, oh, oh, oh———"

Page from the manuscript for Barstow's 1965 television play The Pity of it All *(Collection of Stan Barstow)*

as a novelist and through the popularity of television plays and series with these backgrounds.

While Barstow began to try his hand as a writer, he continued to earn his living at the engineering firm. In 1951 he married Constance Mary Kershaw, and they later had two children, Neil (born in 1954) and Gillian (born in 1957). Barstow, lacking any clear sense of possibilities, began writing what he imagined to be commercial stories, inspired by his belief that "many of the stories that I read in magazines weren't very good and that with a bit of application I ought to be able to do as well." The stories that he wrote were not successful in any sense: "I found that writing insincerely rarely works and realised that what I ought to be writing about was the kind of working-class life that I knew from my own experience." An important influence at this time was the work of H. E. Bates, in particular his short stories, which offered a positive model. Yet, although Barstow was clearer about the need to write from his own working-class experience, "It quickly became apparent to me that very few people wanted to know about this kind of life. I sold only four short stories in the first nine years of my writing life." The conviction that he had found his authentic voice paid off, however. As Gordon Taylor in *A Brother's Tale* (1980) tells the painter Ted, "If you find your own real way of looking at things, you'll also find the audience that takes pleasure in the way you paint." Other working-class regional novelists were beginning to find an audience at this same time, and in 1960, with *A Kind of Loving,* Barstow found his.

Critics were eager to praise Barstow's skill: according to the *Punch* reviewer, "It is not often that a first novel gives me the feeling that its author is a natural writer who must have been born with some of the tricks of the trade." Critics also lauded the application of this skill to a world newly discovered by contemporary literature. The reviewer in the *Sunday Times* (London) said, "Like D. H. Lawrence, Mr Barstow is a miner's son, but Lawrence's genius swept him inevitably and rapidly out of this world: Mr Barstow has no need to waste his talent, his intellectual energy, on escaping from a world rich, lively with possible change, and scarcely scratched yet by its born writers."

Set, as are most of Barstow's novels, in Cressley, an unattractive industrial town in West Yorkshire, *A Kind of Loving* is the story of Vic Brown and his relationship with Ingrid Rothwell as they move through romantic tender infatuation, growing physical obsession, and attendant emotional numbness to a marriage forced by pregnancy. Because of their relative poverty, they live after their marriage with Ingrid's parents. Mrs. Rothwell's dislike of Vic, her snobbery, and intellectual poverty increase the strains on the couple's fragile re-

lationship. Vic, goaded beyond patience, leaves; encouraged by the strictures of Chris, his admired elder sister, however, he resolves on a further attempt to "make a go of it." The ending offers not joy but the peace of resignation. Vic envies the relationship of his sister, Chris, and her husband and is determined to do the best he can. "And, who knows, one day it might happen like Chris said: we might find a kind of loving to carry us through. I hope so, because it's for a long, long time." Refusing either sentimental reconciliations or dramatic partings, the novel offers instead a low-key, painful honesty. Barstow later tampered with this effective resolution, however, by continuing the story of Vic and Ingrid in two further novels.

A Kind of Loving demonstrates the strengths of a novel written from intimate knowledge of a particular society. It is full of small details that are part of the novel's fabric, not grafted on as local color: Vic's pleasure in cleaning shoes, the smell of ironing filling the house, the difficulty of getting out of bed on a winter morning in a house without central heating. Barstow also demonstrates an exact ear for dialogue in the bantering between Vic and his workmates, the strained conversations between Vic and Ingrid, and the continuous criticism of Vic's mother, which is born more of custom than conviction.

While the use of such a milieu for central characters was relatively untried in 1960, it was not social novelty alone that gave the novel its critical and popular success. A further strength is its convincing representation of Vic's changing feelings toward Ingrid, of Vic as young man far from ideal but capable of suffering and of enlarging his understanding. The portrait of Mrs. Rothwell verges on caricature, but Vic and Ingrid maintain the reader's sympathy and understanding.

A Kind of Loving was a Book Society choice and was adapted for the screen in 1962. The novel's success allowed Barstow in 1961 to leave the engineering company, where he was by that time a sales executive, to become a full-time writer. In the same year, *The Desperadoes and Other Stories* (several of which had been read on BBC radio) was published to further favorable reviews. "The dialogue positively leaps out from the page," said Anthony Burgess. The reviewer for the *Guardian* wrote that the stories "have that very rare compassion and pity that distinguishes the really good writer from the merely able. Some of these stories are right up in the same class as D. H. Lawrence"—a comparison that has inevitably been raised thoughout Barstow's career. The social setting, like that of *A Kind of Loving,* is a world of narrow morality and close family ties. Barstow understands the crucial ways in which material conditions affect responses: in "One Wednesday Afternoon," for example, when Jack Lister hears that his wife has been

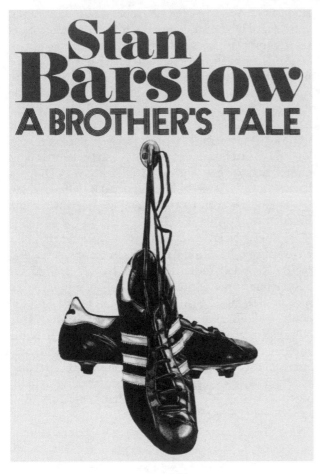

Dust jacket for Barstow's 1980 novel, about a schoolteacher whose life is disrupted by his football-star brother

seriously injured in an industrial accident, he travels to the hospital by bus—taking a taxi is not possible.

In 1969 a selection of stories from *The Desperadoes* was edited for use in schools and published under the title *The Human Element*. Barstow contributed a special essay to the edition, in which he observes that the short-story writer "must . . . leave the reader with a sense of completeness at the end. . . . This instinctive feeling for saying not too much or too little, but just enough, that is the mark of the real short story writer." Some of these stories fail to achieve that balance: in several the moral is drawn too explicitly, leaving little to inference or imagination. Overall, however, the collection provides a nice blend of humor, compassion, and the bizarre, with the title story giving an interesting account of a young man's motives for social aggression: "You've got to have a bit of fun. . . . You spend all day working to fill somebody else's pockets with brass, and everybody allus on to you. . . . Sometimes you feel you can't rest until you've smashed summat."

When some critics and readers complained that the absence of any overt disapproval of these desperadoes implied the author's endorsement of their attitudes and behavior, Barstow replied: "I think that the answer of most writers to such a charge would be that it is not their job to judge their characters, only to tell about them and leave the rest to the reader." This response seems oddly disingenuous from an author whose characters usually make a conscious choice to endorse or reject the specific moral frameworks within which they find themselves.

Such a character is Wilf Cotton, the coal miner's son and aspiring writer in *Ask Me Tomorrow,* whose dissatisfaction with the conditions of his life and work echoes Barstow's own. Wilf leaves home to concentrate on writing his first novel. Eschewing the romantic discomfort of starvation in a garret, he takes a mentally undemanding job by day and finds comfort in the bed of his landlady, Marguerite Fisher, at night. Wilf's struggles as a writer and his conviction of his vocation are the central concerns of the novel, and his discussions with Marguerite suggest Barstow's own views. When Wilf distinguishes between "the caterers," who "work to satisfy a ready made market," and the "creators," who "work to make their own market," one remembers Barstow's account of his early efforts to write commercially and his rejection of the caterer's approach. Marguerite supports Wilf's decision to write from the perspective of the provincial working class: "What you're trying to do is to put down on paper a kind of life that hasn't had its fair due in fiction."

Wilf, too, expresses belief in the kind of novel that he is writing, and the reader can infer from Wilf's assertions Barstow's sense of what is important in fiction. Of his just-finished novel Wilf says: "It was good because it was real and true . . . his was an authentic world, his people harsh and dour without the comic idiosyncrasies designed to appeal to the illusions of people who never travelled north of the Trent." In none of Barstow's other novels is there such detailed discussion of the process of writing, of "the need to express the throb and quiver of life on the page." Wilf reappears briefly in *The Watchers on the Shore* (1966), however, in which he comments on the regional novel from the vantage point of several years later: "People won't take north country working class stuff for its novelty value any more. It's got to be good in its own right."

As the reviewer in *The Times Literary Supplement (TLS)* noted, the creation of Wilf shows Barstow's developing ability to handle an evolving character. There is, however, a weakness in the novel's moral structure in that Barstow offers no wider perspective on the ideas and attitudes advanced by Wilf. In his attitudes to and relationships with women he has much in common with Vic Brown of the later novels and Gordon Taylor of *A Brother's Tale*. Each is ready to love a young woman who, while she may not be a virgin, gives an impression of sexual moderation. At the same time each evinces distrust of and contempt for women perceived as sexually voracious: June in *Ask Me Tomorrow*, Miriam in *The Right True End* (1976), Eunice in *A Brother's Tale*. Both Wilf and Gordon are able to accept sexual release with older, large-breasted, nurturing women seen as sexually unthreatening. Wilf at least recognizes the ambivalence of men who require that women enjoy sex while distrusting that enjoyment: "You looked for uninhibited sexuality and suspected it when you found it of being more licence." Yet, Wilf, in protecting his brother, acts with an instinctive, hard morality. Marguerite claims that most Englishwomen regard sex as "something not quite nice," a threat to the stability of marriage and the family unit. This belief in a tension between sexuality and married love perhaps underlies the hostility of the male characters toward those women who they suspect may prefer sensuality to stability, thus threatening traditional roles and society's security.

Ask Me Tomorrow did not make the public impact of *A Kind of Loving* but won some approving critical notice. While thinking little of Barstow's ability to construct plot, the *TLS* reviewer stated: "Mr. Barstow can do most of the essential things. He can write a vivid scene and give it tension . . . a book full of promise and life."

The novel that followed, *Joby* (1964), differs in style and subject matter from all Barstow's other works. The detail in the experiences of the eleven-year-old boy in the months before World War II is again vivid and evocative of a period, with its account of the "two-penny rushes," cheap cinema matinees where the children crowd in for the Flash Gordon serial and throw pellets during the advertisements; the holiday clubs where one saves through the year—"They would be splashing the lot on one glorious week away from washing and cleaning and cooking"; and the hospital where children cannot be admitted as visitors. Again Barstow offers authentic dialogue in the pointless, repetitious bickering of the adults and the status-conscious conversations of the children. The story is told from Joby's viewpoint although not limited to his vocabulary: in one funny but touching incident he is embarrassed by the nature of the operation for which his mother is in the hospital. He understands that it concerns her breast but knows only the word *tit*, whose vulgarity certainly cannot be applied to his mother.

Reviews of *Joby* were polite rather than enthusiastic: "An honest, agreeable book" said the *TLS*, "All the same it is something of a disappointment. It is careful

and sympathetic but a little thin." Frederick Bowers in *Contemporary Novelists* points out the thematic link between this novel and *A Kind of Loving*, finding in both "the presentation of a workaday human love not only as the best one can hope for but also as an essential condition of life." In the late 1970s *Joby* was being widely read as a set text in British schools.

In Barstow's next novel, *The Watchers on the Shore*, however, Vic Brown from *A Kind of Loving* has found himself unable to settle for workaday human love: "The thought that comes to me time and time again is: is this all?" His wife, Ingrid, is portrayed in this novel as an intellectual constraint on Vic: "Common in the mind, in the way she never searches for anything herself but just sits back and lets it all wash over her." One finds here, as elsewhere in Barstow, echoes of Lawrence in women who, to protect the stability of their homes, emasculate their menfolk sexually and intellectually. Vic leaves Cressley for a job near London, while Ingrid remains with her now widowed and sick mother. While there is no formal break, Vic determines to explore possibilities outside the society he knows. By the end of this second novel in the trilogy, in his love for the actress Donna he has found justification for his hope that relationships between men and women can offer more than he has found with Ingrid. The discovery makes it inevitable that he leave her, although not for a happy ending, as Donna—pregnant by another man, he believes—has abandoned him. The novel ends with Vic's recognition of the pathos of a situation that leaves Ingrid "small and scared and lonely in that flat and me, small and scared and lonely here."

Ten years later, in *The Right True End*, Barstow chose to continue and complete the story of Vic, Ingrid, and Donna. This final novel in the trilogy opens with the acrimonious divorce and then jumps ten years to find Vic an established business executive, Ingrid remarried, and Donna about to make a comeback both in Vic's life and her acting career. Barstow seems generally uncertain as to how to tie the trilogy's three sections together. The use of flashbacks to conversations in *A Kind of Loving* is not a successful device, and neither of the sequels has the solidity and emotional conviction of that first novel. Sympathy for Vic's yearning for a true relationship and his refusal to comply with family pressures is undercut by his easy acceptance of the business world in which he moves, with its dirty jokes and macho ethics working against any honest man-woman relationships. He offers an interesting portrait of a mid-1970s man who can accept new social mores in certain areas—young women with none of Ingrid's guilt and a new competence with contraception—but who does not question the status quo in the northern family, whose ethics require his sister Christine to give up emigration

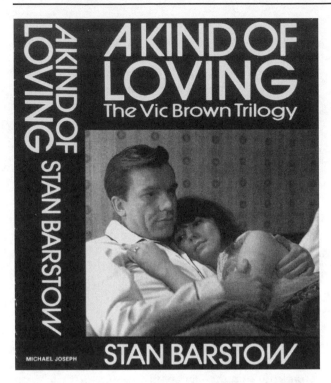

Dust jacket for the 1981 collected edition of Barstow's Vic Brown novels: A Kind of Loving *(1960),* The Watchers on the Shore *(1966), and* The Right True End *(1976)*

plans to care for her parents: "It's women's work and Chris will have to cope, as she expects to, as I suppose it was written into her future that she would one day." His orthodox liberal views on education and the apartheid system do not extend to any analysis of family roles and values. While this characterization could be read as a representation of complex and inconsistent attitudes in a quickly shifting moral world, there is no sense that the author invites any response to Vic other than the sympathy invoked by his genuine and generous love for Donna.

The ending of Vic's story was judged weak by several reviewers. In the *Sunday Times* David Pryce-Jones commented: "Sentimentality and realism go here hand in hand." Sue Limb wrote: "Isn't Romantic Reconciliation with a lost love who happens to be an actress rather a sentimental and unlikely cop-out for tough old Vic Brown?" While the accusations of sentimentality ignore the soft center of the tough talking that characterizes Vic throughout the trilogy, they have good foundation.

In *The Watchers on the Shore* and *The Right True End* political comment is fleeting, merely background detail or a single index allowing for the accurate placement of a character. The novel that appeared between these two offers a more complex analysis, an account of a society where political convictions are presented as the bedrock

of character. The book is a serious and sustained effort to marry beliefs and behavior. *A Raging Calm* (1968) is in the strong tradition of George Eliot's *Middlemarch* (1871–1872) and Elizabeth Gaskell's *North and South* (1855), regionally based novels with a wide cast of characters engaging both private and public concerns.

A Raging Calm has two main stories, both love relationships, but they are strongly linked and complemented by other relationships—between parent and child, friend and friend, political colleagues and opponents. The long affair between Alderman Simpkins and Norma Moffat is a positive fulfillment of the "kind of loving" that Vic had sought with Ingrid, while the relationship between schoolteacher Philip Hart and Andrea Warner, Simpkins's secretary, offers that sense of an absolute love that is the grail of Vic's quest. There is a strong sense of balances sought and sometimes achieved, with both love and other responsibilities acknowledged, and no easy answers are offered.

As in the earlier novels, the setting is a northern industrial town. Barstow has said that he considers himself to be "non-metropolitan oriented," and this setting, like the northern scenes in the Vic Brown trilogy, has an interest and conviction that is absent in the London-based *The Right True End*. Philip and Andrea may watch trendy French films, and Norma's son, Nick, may find himself the object of desire of both a man and a woman, but this is still a world where homes do not have telephones and where one does not linger in cold winter bedrooms. Political beliefs, represented by the socialism of Nick and Philip and the cautious, kind pragmatism of Tom Simpkins, are integrated into the fabric of their lives and discussions, with the occasional piece of overt analysis, such as Nick's irritation at his mother's outmoded (as he sees it) deference to authority, in character and essentially interesting.

Critical reaction was positive. The quality of feeling was praised by the *Tribune* reviewer: "This is the core of (Barstow's) power as a writer: he cares about people. It needs more than narrative skills to manage this; it takes imaginative warmth and a rare balance of sensibilities." The *Guardian* critic observed that "deeply felt and skilfully told, the novel will certainly enhance Mr. Barstow's already high reputation."

A Season with Eros (1971) was a second collection of short stories, some of which had been read on British Broadcasting Corporation radio while others had been published in periodicals as diverse as *Penthouse* and the *Guardian*. Two of the stories, "Love and Music" and "A Bit of a Commotion," tend to the overly neat, insistently ironic conclusion, but while these stories demonstrate the same mixture of black humor and compassion as the earlier collection, overall they call for a greater variety of response.

In the title story Ruffo marries the sensuous Maureen and enjoys a brief season of sexual ecstasy until Maureen's mother convinces her of the excesses of her sexy underwear and unbridled behavior, and the realities of pregnancy and properly rationed sex are asserted. The story is both funny and thought-provoking; while seeing the horror of the prudery that denies the demands of Eros, one is made to see too the selfishness and unreality of Ruffo's demands. Quite simply, his desires and those of Maureen are shown to be irreconcilable: "he had thought he was moulding her, but now in a flash of intuition he perceived his fate as a function of the phases of *her* life."

Several of the stories speak for the value of affection over reason and respectability–although there is a tendency to make women the cleaners of hearth and language, the disapprovers and life-deniers, another echo of Lawrence. One story, "Holroyd's Last Stand," in which the wife and daughters of an elderly miner who is having a final mild fling trick him into bringing his other woman to Sunday tea, is an oddity in the casual cruelty of its humor. The women may be realistic, but their defense of home and morality is shown to lack all conscience and affection: the mother "spends a very interesting time discussing with her daughters new ways of making his life miserable." A different kind of story is "Estuary"; here Barstow parallels the great tides of an estuary to the sexual needs of a woman. It is not a strikingly new metaphor but functions effectively as a way of focusing the reader's response and represents a new technique for Barstow.

The collection contains two longer stories, "Madge" and "The Assailants." The former offers a strong story line but an overly contrived moral, while the latter provides some of the complexities and difficult resolutions offered by the novels. The final story, "This Day, Then Tomorrow," has a special interest in that Ruth, whose first novel is accepted for publication, is in many ways an amalgam of Wilf and Marguerite in *Ask Me Tomorrow;* her belief in the value of her creation and her sense of concerned responsibility toward it are those of Wilf, while her emotional history is in part that of Marguerite.

Much of Barstow's work during the 1970s was for television, radio, and the theater. Two of his plays, written with Alfred Bradley, were published: an adaptation of *Ask Me Tomorrow* (1966) and *Stringer's Last Stand* (1972). His most successful work of this period, however, was probably that done for television, in particular his popular adaptation of Winifred Holtby's Yorkshire novel *South Riding* and the serialization of his own *A Raging Calm,* both in 1974. That same year the Writers' Guild of Great Britain awarded him the prize for the best British dramatization, and in 1975 he won the Royal Television Society Writer's Award.

A Brother's Tale appeared in 1980. The brothers of the title are Gordon and Bonny Taylor: Gordon is a schoolteacher with some small success as a writer, Bonny an inspired football star who has cracked under the pressure of expectation and fame. Bonny takes refuge with his brother and sister-in-law, Eileen, but the nature of his presence is such that it attracts disaster, both in ways directly attributable to him and in others that he cannot control. Not only does his presence destroy his brother's marriage and cause the usually equable Gordon to abuse colleagues and become involved in barroom brawls, but it also precipitates such events as dead birds falling down chimneys and a neighbor killing the husband who has been systematically battering her. The sense of violence and disaster lurking not far beneath the surface of ordinary lives has been present in several of Barstow's earlier novels, but here it is made manifest. What social analysis of the characters there is tends to the simplistic: "She was a potential battered wife who found a battering husband." The novel's strength lies rather in its depiction of recurring violence, which because of its unfathomability raises wider questions about the existence of cruelty and evil. There is an interesting discussion between Gordon and a fellow teacher about the dangers of creative writing for the unpracticed, about the necessity of properly and safely making patterns of one's experience in order to control it and give it significance. The novel raises problems that cannot be tackled by the expedients of decency and quiet affection alone; they are more intractable, on a wider than the human scale, than those raised by the earlier novels. That scale is suggested by the clearly religious discourse employed by Barstow in the questions that end the novel: "What was to become of us, the three of us? How were we to be saved?"

This hint of asking questions that might require a different kind of answer has not been borne out by Barstow's subsequent work, which has been dominated by the publication of a second Yorkshire trilogy and a consistent movement away from representations of contemporary life and manners. While the Vic Brown trilogy was set in contemporary Yorkshire and London, the Ella Palmer novels take place immediately before, during, and just after World War II. The novel that separates the first two parts of the trilogy, *B-Movie* (1987), is set in the 1950s and dramatizes the influence of postwar austerity and a reaction against its constraints.

Just You Wait and See works within the familiar setting of a Yorkshire industrial town in which the citizens know and understand each other and the moral framework by which they evaluate personal and public events. Here the sense of right and wrong is much clearer than in *A Brother's Tale:* evil is the war, not mysterious surges from the unknown; salvation is surviving the bombing of the towns by German planes or years in a Japanese prisoner-of-war camp and finding love that is kind and sustainable.

The heroine of *Just You Wait and See,* and of the trilogy as a whole, is Ella Palmer, daughter of a large family, the principal occupation of whose menfolk is working in the coal mines. Ella is a heroine, not merely the protagonist: although initially young and confused by the need to make choices between two men whose different attractions she finds it hard to evaluate, she develops into a strong woman, able to make decisions based on sound principles and to act on them despite family and community pressures. She is initially attracted to the subtle middle-class charms of Howard Strickland, an insurance agent, but is repulsed by his penchant for dishonesty and marries Walter, a butcher at the cooperative shop whose worth she appreciates.

The novel is concerned not only with Ella's emotional and marital progress, however, but also with the life of her wider family. Her sister and brothers and their own failures and small triumphs are an important thread in all three novels of the trilogy. Perhaps the most interesting character is Winnie, Ella's sister-in-law, a feckless housewife and poor manager derided by the prudent women of the family and physically abused by her husband, Thomas. In an extended monologue Winnie tells Ella of her meeting with Thomas and their courtship, a story made more touching for its reliance on the teller's plain and concrete vocabulary. She recounts faithfully the unromantic dialogue in which they registered their interest in each other, and by the end few readers could dissent from her sad conclusion: "God help us! we weren't married ten minutes. We had our fifth anniversary only last month. And now it's all over. But what I've told you's a love story. It is, isn't it. Ella?" This chapter follows an account, also deliberately low-key and unheroic, of a pit disaster in which Thomas has been killed. Such passages benefit greatly from Barstow's insistence on sincerity and authenticity.

Just You Wait and See is also the story of a community waiting, mainly in dread, for the threatened war and its reverberations. This sense of doom is usually specific and rendered in dialogue. There is one occasion that seems to look back to the more abstract sense of evil raised in *A Brother's Tale,* when Ella contemplates the future: "It was a curious moment during which she felt she had peered into an abyss and she remembered it all her life." This perception is an isolated instance, however, not properly realized in the text.

The period setting allows comparisons to be drawn between what is accepted in the late 1930s and the 1980s: "She could not know that she would live to see an age when girls would go out with whom they pleased, would live with men out of wedlock and, even in some cases, share a bed with them under their parents' roof." This kind of underlining, arguably better left to the reader, occurs only occasionally. Reviewers commented on "the incidental pleasures of observation and memory" that the novel demonstrated.

Barstow next temporarily abandoned Ella for a different kind of novel. *B-Movie* is set in the 1950s, with the prologue making much of this aspect of the setting and the different aspirations and experiences of those living in this immediate postwar period: "In those days people still went on holiday by train and bus. . . . Spain was where the onions came from." This heavy emphasis on the past as another country where matters are ordered differently allows for a commentary on the penal sanctions then prevailing, the fact that capital punishment was still in force, a period detail that has particular force as the plot unfolds. "They still hanged people in those days. . . . They hanged Ruth Ellis who shot her lover dead outside a pub in Hampstead. They hanged Derek Bentley who never shot anybody, but happened to be caught in a robbery with a lad who did. . . ." The shadow of the gallows throws a particular frisson over the deceptively ordinary events of the novel's early pages.

B-Movie marks a departure for Barstow in that plot and suspense form central interests. The plot concerns two cousins who have been brought up together in Cressley and are "mates" and virtual brothers, despite differences in temperament. Frank is a professional musician of serious disposition, ready to commit himself emotionally, and Arny, who works in London in a business dealing with gambling machines, is always looking out for the main chance, whether in business or sex. They leave for a weekend of bright lights and good times in Blackpool, but the consequences of a botched and brutal robbery pursue them. Frank, while watching Arny making his sexual moves and talking up life in London, is forced to accept that his cousin is guilty of a murderous attack on a pawnbroker and is persuaded to play a crucial role in his cousin's capture.

The main plot of the short novel develops simply and effectively. Frank's crisis of loyalty is purposely underplayed: although not relishing his role as decoy, he has no doubts as to his moral obligation. Less effective is a flashback section about Frank's former lover, Doris, a singer with a band with which Frank played; while presumably intended to develop Frank's character, the passage distracts from the story's main thrust. As always in Barstow's fiction, the small details of the milieu are crucial in constructing a sense of place and time: the "skimpy carpet with an indeterminate pattern" of the bed-and-breakfast where the cousins stay, the predictable constituents of the salad they are offered for their evening meal ("A few leaves of lettuce, a tomato, a hard-boiled egg, a slice or two of cucumber, a few rings of raw onion, maybe a radish . . . and a couple of slices of boiled ham"), and the regimental organization of the dancing at the crowded Tower Ballroom, where the men go hoping to pick up willing women. The waiting hangman casts a shadow over the novel's other period details, however, and explains Arny's despair and decision to make a quick end in the midst of the lights and noise of the tawdry seaside.

The tone of *B-Movie* is tougher than that of any of Barstow's other novels. The dialogue between the men is more crudely and explicitly sexual than elsewhere in his work. The language often has a punchy liveliness: Arny, scoffing at the claim that the dead pawnbroker was a "kindly" man, comments, "He'd nip a currant in two." The novel is less successful in those sections in which gentler human feelings are involved, such as Arny's father on the disappointments of fatherhood, which ring sentimental and portentous. The *Listener* reviewer praised the novel as demonstrating Barstow's gifts as a "natural storyteller," but the venture into new territory has not been repeated. Barstow's next novel was a return to the familiar with a sequel to *Just You Wait and See.*

Give Us This Day has the same cast of characters, with Ella again at the center of a family that grows as her siblings produce children and grandchildren. The war is now raging, with Walter fighting in the RAF in the Far East and believed lost in battle. Even for those remaining in Yorkshire, however, the war has direct as well as indirect impact, with bombs falling on Sheffield and wiping out the sympathetic cousins whom Ella and her mother have just visited. Barstow characteristically avoids sentimentalizing the war experience through stereotypical portrayals of plucky Brits smiling through. The air-raid warden who admonishes Ella and Walter, home on leave, is shown to be a petty tyrant, and the woman running a station buffet is a "cantankerous old cow." While Sheffield burns, Ella's older sister, Ada, a lady's maid much influenced by the fascist leanings of her rich employers, talks of appeasement and reconciliation with Hitler.

This last instance points to an emphasis in *Give Us This Day* not apparent in *Just You Wait and See*—an explicit concern with national political issues. Ella dreams of the house she hopes to possess after the war: "fitted kitchen with a floor standing gas-cooker and plenty of cupboards. In one of those cupboards would be an electric vacuum cleaner." She links this dream with political aspirations, however: "It needed no great flight of imagination. There were houses like that not far away. All it needed was for the war to sort out other

Dust jacket for Barstow's 1987 novel, about two cousins in the 1950s

things besides beating Germany. To bring about a state of affairs where everybody had work and could save for the better things so far always denied her kind." This dawning recognition of new possibilities for living accurately reflects the new political consciousness that resulted in the success of the Labour party in the 1945 national elections.

The reviews of *Give Us This Day* enthused about those aspects of Barstow's work that were agreed to represent his strong points. The *Times* reviewer praised his "sympathy for characters" and "distinctive generosity of spirit," while the *Mail* reviewer commented on the novel's "honesty, guts, compassion" and noted its author's "brilliantly accurate ear for dialogue."

The war continues in the third volume of the trilogy, *Next of Kin,* and the political debates become ever more central to the immediate concerns of Ella and her family, friends, and colleagues. Some of these debates, such as those over a miner's strike, are complicated and divisive. Ella's nephew George defends the miners' rights against an ignorant elderly man but nevertheless thinks that "they *shouldn't* be out. This war's being fought to defeat Fascism and nowt else matters besides that." Since mining and its attendant labor disputes have played such an important role in British politics, Barstow cannot resist another proleptic leap: George's "destiny would acquaint him with heady triumph in 1974 and close his working life again in bitter defeat in 1985."

The issue of women's roles in society is also raised consistently in the novel's debates, never in an abstract way but always as pertaining directly to the lives and livelihoods of the characters. In one scene, for instance, a union organizer at the factory where Ella works is challenged by the most feisty woman on equal pay. This is a world where women teachers have to give up their jobs on marriage: "Jobs have to go to t'men first, love. And there's never enough to go round." With respect to sex roles, however, there is a sense that these rules are not immutable, as when the factory woman promises: "There'll have to be some changes when this lot's over."

The coming end of the war is seen as the herald of change. Howard Strickland reappears and clears his name with Ella if not with the law. He becomes her lover, and the two discuss the likelihood and need for change. To Ella's dispirited comment that "We're all in this war together, but I expect they'll still have the upper hand when it's over," Howard responds, "There's a feeling among service-men, you know, that things mustn't go back to what they were." His comment is endorsed near the end of the novel when electioneering gets underway in 1945: "The forces vote would be the key—it wouldn't be registered for the old gang." A cabinet minister preaches on the need for social reforms outlined in the Beveridge Report, the "blueprint" for the National Health Service.

Next of Kin gives a strong sense of a community waiting for change, which they feel will at last offer them some material wealth and thus new comforts and respect. Some changes, however, are viewed more ambivalently by Ella and perhaps by Barstow. Ella comments on the furnished flat rented by her lover Howard and its implications: the apartment "smacked of the foreign life of cities, with people coming and going, all strangers. The web of the family and familiar streets—a life at ground level—was a reassurance as well as an entanglement. . . . The life represented by this flat was a step nearer the outer darkness."

It is perhaps significant that Barstow has retreated from an engagement with this view of life in his later works by setting them in a past that offers, in the phrase of the critic Raymond Williams, "knowable communities" and clearer sets of values. The communities that Barstow has realized so vividly have undergone shattering changes in the last twenty years, with the closure of the coal mines and the decline of heavy industry bringing a crisis of identity and shifts in traditional family roles. It remains to be seen if Barstow will bring his particular talent for compassion and observation to this new social setting. He is a writer who has always eschewed the lure of the trendy and novelty for its own sake, asserting that "As writers we should just do the best we can."

Nina Bawden

(19 January 1925 –   )

Gerda Seaman
California State University, Chico

See also the Bawden entries in *DLB 14: British Novelists Since 1960* and *DLB 161: British Children's Writers Since 1960, First Series.*

BOOKS: *Who Calls the Tune* (London: Collins, 1953); republished as *Eyes of Green* (New York: Morrow, 1953);

The Odd Flamingo (London: Collins, 1954);

Change Here for Babylon (London: Collins, 1955);

The Solitary Child (London: Collins, 1956);

Devil by the Sea (London: Collins, 1957; Philadelphia: Lippincott, 1959);

Just Like a Lady (London: Longmans, 1960); republished as *Glass Slippers Always Pinch* (Philadelphia: Lippincott, 1960);

In Honour Bound (London: Longmans, 1961);

The Secret Passage (London: Gollancz, 1963); republished as *The House of Secrets* (Philadelphia: Lippincott, 1964);

Tortoise by Candlelight (London: Longmans, 1963; New York: Harper & Row, 1963);

On the Run (London: Gollancz, 1964); republished as *Three on the Run* (Philadelphia: Lippincott, 1965);

Under the Skin (London: Longmans, 1964; New York: Harper & Row, 1964);

A Little Love, A Little Learning (London: Longmans, 1966; New York: Harper & Row, 1966);

The White Horse Gang (London: Gollancz, 1966; Philadelphia: Lippincott, 1966);

The Witch's Daughter (London: Gollancz, 1966; Philadelphia: Lippincott, 1966);

A Handful of Thieves (London: Gollancz, 1967; Philadelphia: Lippincott, 1967);

A Woman of My Age (London: Longmans, 1967; New York: Harper & Row, 1967);

The Grain of Truth (London: Longmans, 1968; New York: Harper & Row, 1968);

The Runaway Summer (London: Gollancz, 1969; Philadelphia: Lippincott, 1969);

The Birds on the Trees (London: Longmans, 1970; New York: Harper & Row, 1970);

Nina Bawden

Squib (London: Gollancz, 1971; Philadelphia: Lippincott, 1971);

Anna Apparent (London: Longmans, 1972; New York: Harper & Row, 1972);

Carrie's War (London: Gollancz, 1973; Philadelphia: Lippincott, 1973);

George Beneath a Paper Moon (London: Allen Lane, 1974; New York: Harper & Row, 1974);

The Peppermint Pig (London: Gollancz, 1975; Philadelphia: Lippincott, 1975);

Afternoon of a Good Woman (London: Macmillan, 1976; New York: Harper & Row, 1976);

Rebel on a Rock (London: Gollancz, 1978; Philadelphia: Lippincott, 1978);

Familiar Passions (London: Macmillan, 1979; New York: Morrow, 1979);

The Robbers (London: Gollancz, 1979; New York: Lothrop, Lee & Shepard, 1979);

Walking Naked (London: Macmillan, 1981; New York: St. Martin's Press, 1981);

William Tell (London: Cape, 1981; New York: Lothrop, Lee & Shephard, 1981);

Kept in the Dark (London: Gollancz, 1982; New York: Lothrop, Lee & Shepard, 1982);

The Ice House (London: Macmillan, 1983; New York: St. Martin's Press, 1983);

St. Francis of Assisi (London: Cape, 1983; New York: Lothrop, Lee & Shepard, 1983);

The Finding (London: Gollancz, 1985; New York: Lothrop, Lee & Shepard, 1985);

Princess Alice (London: Deutsch, 1985);

Circles of Deceit (London: Macmillan, 1987; New York: St. Martin's Press, 1988);

Keeping Henry (London: Gollancz, 1988); republished as *Henry* (New York: Lothrop, Lee & Shepard, 1988);

The Outside Child (London: Gollancz, 1989; New York: Lothrop, Lee & Shepard, 1989);

Family Money (London: Gollancz, 1991; New York: St. Martin's Press, 1991);

Humbug (London: Gollancz, 1992; New York: Clarion, 1992);

The Real Plato Jones (London: Gollancz, 1993; New York: Clarion, 1994);

In My Own Time: Almost an Autobiography (London: Virago, 1994; New York: Clarion, 1995);

A Nice Change (London: Virago, 1997).

During a long writing career, Nina Bawden has produced a large and significant body of novels for adults, children, and juveniles. Unlike some writers who "move up" from young people's fiction to more mainstream books for adults, she has continued to work in both fields. The awards she has received, including the *Yorkshire Post* Novel of the Year Award and a Booker Prize nomination, as well as many prizes for her children's books, testify to her achievement. She began her career as a writer of two elegantly plotted murder stories and then worked her way through several other novel genres, including the Gothic romance, the Bildungsroman, and the horror story. In 1960 her first effort at social satire, *Just Like a Lady,* was published, and, since her early formal explorations, she has mostly used her adult novels for the psychological dis-

section of modern British middle-class existence. Bawden is perhaps best known for her incisive satirical enquiry into the family relationships of the educated middle class. With an urbane irony and often surprising violence, she exposes the uneasy alliances that keep chaos at bay and provides a circumstantial account of the domesticated brutality at the heart of modern life.

Nina Mabey was born in London on 19 January 1925, the daughter of Charles and Ellalaine Ursula Mabey. She remained there until the outbreak of World War II, when her family was evacuated. They spent the war years in a South Wales mining village and on a farm in Shropshire. She lived with various mining families during the school year and learned during her summers on the farm to drive a tractor and care for farm animals. She even organized a group of Italian prisoners of war, conscripted as farm laborers. Her experience as an evacuee, which is reflected in her books *Carrie's War* (1973) and *Keeping Henry* (1988), may help account for her belief that children "are a kind of subject race, always at the mercy of the adults who mostly run their lives for them." Following graduation from grammar school, Mabey was awarded a scholarship to Somerville College, Oxford, where she studied politics, philosophy, and economics. She graduated in 1946, took an M.A. in 1951, and in 1960, following the publication of six novels, she attended the Salzburg Seminar in American Studies.

On her graduation, Nina Mabey married H. W. Bawden. She had two sons from this marriage. She married her present husband, Austen Kark, former managing director of the external services for the BBC, in 1954. They have a daughter.

In her autobiography Bawden relates that she began writing at an early age: "I wrote plays for my toy theater and an epic poem in blank verse." This writing seems to have functioned as a stay against the confusions of experience, and as almost palpable protection. In her 1981 novel, *Walking Naked,* the main character (a novelist) explains this notion: writers, she says, "are compulsive rearrangers, obsessional shapers of patterns," but only "to make the truth clearer." In the same novel the protagonist also speaks of the rewards of writing: "I can always make myself brave with words, drawing them on like a comforting garment against the cold weather." Bawden admits that her own "love of pattern" has sometimes led to flaws in her novels, although it has also been a source of strength. Her work reveals a writer of great integrity whose search for truth in style and content has not invariably been successful, but whose insights and technical skills have developed with each successive novel.

Bawden's initial ambition was to write like Graham Greene, and her early novels are thrillers with an edge of menace. *Who Calls the Tune* (1953) is a carefully plotted thriller praised by the *New Statesman* as having the cunning of Agatha Christie. Her next novel, *The Odd Flamingo* (1954), presents a respected and brilliant headmaster who is accused of seduction and murder. The search for the killer is conducted by a lawyer friend of the headmaster's—a sort of Doctor Watson character—with the appropriate name of Will Hunt. Hunt's slavish admiration for his arrogant friend makes him a rather confused investigator, but he is not an uninteresting one. The setting of the novel, however, is unconvincing. The writer does not seem at home with the scenes of the London underworld to which she introduces her characters. Bawden has described her interest in the crime story as providing her with a frame for her comments on "the bizarre complexity of motive behind simple actions." The genre, she says, also allows her to explore "the difference between what people say and what they actually mean."

Change Here for Babylon (1955) is a story in which the protagonists are enmeshed in the defects of their own characters. It opens with the execution of Geoffrey Hunter, then relates the events that led to it. Hunter is displeased that his wife, Emily, is having an affair with the novel's self-absorbed "hero," Tom Harrington. Hunter is a manipulative upper-class scoundrel who assumes that the world owes him status and privilege, and he is willing to kill for them. He is outwitted by Harrington, whose grubby adultery fades into relative insignificance beside Hunter's more robust crimes.

Bawden's next novel, *The Solitary Child* (1956), is a mostly conventional Gothic romance. Harriet, the heroine, marries James Random, who has been tried and acquitted of murdering his first wife. Even her best friends warn her against the marriage, but Harriet not only moves back to the ancestral farmhouse, she also ignorantly cherishes Maggie, her husband's psychopathic daughter, who is the real cause of the evils in the neighborhood. The heroine's lack of self-esteem is well drawn, but on the whole both characters and plot seem unconvincing.

With *Devil by the Sea* (1957) Bawden began a new phase. In its opening lines she demonstrates the elegant satiric touch for which she has become famous: "The first time the children saw the Devil, he was sitting next to them in the second row of chairs in the bandstand. He was biting his nails." The devil turns out to be a dim-witted and crazed derelict who murders an objectionable child called Poppet and is recognized as the murderer by Hillary, the ten-year-old heroine of the novel. Hillary's equivocal relationship with her father and mother prevents her from explaining her predicament, and thus she is unable to find protection among the adults who should shelter her. Although her father

Bawden in 1936

comes to understand her, he dies before he can help, and it is another child, Hillary's friend Wally, who alerts the police and thus saves her life.

Hillary's plight is one of Bawden's recurring concerns: the vulnerability of the child in a world where "other people are not to be relied upon . . . promises can be broken; loyalty abandoned." Bawden puts it only slightly differently in *Walking Naked:* "We all know (or believe secretly) that when we were children we were happy and trusting and hopeful and good, and that we would still be all these pleasant things if sometime, somewhere, somehow, we had not been betrayed." Children, for Bawden, often seem to live in a prelapsarian moral world. Their betrayal into maturity has consequences that are the basis for the explorations of her adult characters.

In 1960, with *Just Like a Lady,* Bawden began writing what she has called her "social comedies with modern themes and settings." Her gift is strongly satiric, but she does not take up the classical satiric stance that decries modern moral failure while referring the reader to some accepted standard. She is an ironist

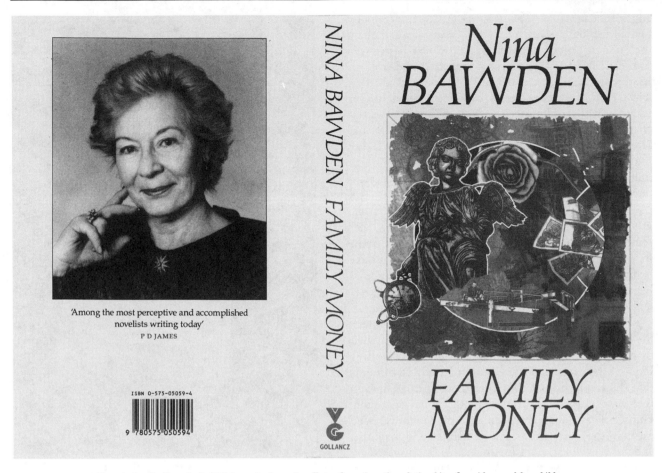

Dust jacket for Bawden's 1991 novel, about the effects of greed on the relationship of a widow and her children

who shows effects of the absence of standards of morality from much of the adult world. She offers no elaborated standard for contrast other than the notion that one is, or should be, his brother's keeper.

Though leaning decidedly toward satire, Bawden's novels often have strong, almost classical, comic elements. They are particularly noticeable in two witty reversals of the classic comic recognition scene. In *George Beneath a Paper Moon* (1974) the protagonist learns that his passion for a young woman is not incestuous when he recognizes that she is not, as he had believed, his daughter, and Mary Mudd of *Familiar Passions* (1979) finds an inherited taste for dissembling and her own "healthy vein of coarseness" when she discovers that her adoptive father is in fact her real father.

Just Like a Lady presents the story of a romantically inclined young lady named Lucy, an orphan brought up by relatives in near squalor. She expects much from life but finds instead a pompous husband and a tepid lover. *In Honour Bound* (1961) is the story of an upper-class hero whose antique virtues do not mesh with the England to which he returns after World War II. Johnny Prothero is courageous and charming, but untrained intellectually and emotionally to earn his living. His wife, Mary, whose origins are lower middle class, admires him but also sees that for him the world can only remain "a decent place as long as one is buttressed with money." The war had lengthened the "period of his illusion so that by the time it ended the facts of life were distorted beyond his power of correction." Johnny's assumptions about honor are jolted, but he has nothing with which to replace them. His business partner betrays him; his wife is unfaithful to him; and his final act, a dramatic suicide, is a useless anachronistic gesture toward the heroic ideal.

Tortoise by Candlelight (1963) offers a child's perspective once more. Emmie, the fourteen-year-old heroine, is committed to her responsibility to the members of her family: "the things that drain the spirit out of people, illness and pain and hope deferred, had not touched her yet." Emmie's commitment is also her shield, however. She draws her family around her like a cloak, protecting her younger brother from the consequences of his pilfering and pointing out to her older sister that her sensuality may prove to be at odds with her ambition to be a nurse. Emmie must fight time and adult weaknesses, both physical and moral.

The characters of this novel are beautifully drawn. Certain incidents stand out: Alice, the older sister, strapping up her breasts with adhesive tape for want of a decent bra; and Emmie, humiliated by her encounter with a neighbor's jealous wife, diving frantically into the gravel pit. Emmie wins out in the end in a gratuitously violent plot resolution, but along the way there are insights into the ambiguous tensions that affect the sensitive adolescent. Bawden's work has regularly dealt with the powerlessness of children, although they often succeed in overcoming that powerlessness.

In 1962, following what she refers to as "the failure" of a novel for adults, Bawden's husband suggested she write a book for children. Since then eighteen of her children's novels have been published, many to literary acclaim and all to popular success. As Mary Stoltz said of *The Runaway Summer* (1969): "she should be as much valued by children as she is by her adult audience." When asked about the relationship between her novels for children and those for adults, Bawden pointed to *Squib* (1971), which deals with one child's concern for another—a frequent theme in her work. Following the tale of Squib, Bawden said she was puzzled as to how such a child would turn out when he grew up. She wished to explore the character further. She did so in *Anna Apparent* (1972), in which the battered boy of the earlier novel is metamorphosed into a girl protagonist.

The *London Observer* described *Under the Skin* (1964) as a book that deals "perceptively with the problems of an intelligent young couple who befriend a charming Negro student and discover that neither 'prejudice' nor 'enlightenment' are as straightforward as they had thought, and that goodwill is not enough." John Grant has visited Africa and met Jay Nbola. When Nbola comes to study at the London School of Economics, Grant and his wife invite him to stay in their home, but small family hatreds are enlarged by the Grants' anxiety to appear liberal and decent, and the suffering inflicted on their guest drives him out of their home. Bawden offers no easy answers in this novel, which ends with the Grants about to embark on an African visit; the reader is left with the uneasy suspicion that the Grants may learn their real lesson in Africa.

Like *Tortoise by Candlelight, A Little Love, A Little Learning* (1966) is the story of a young girl growing into adulthood. The story is told by Katey, who looks back on the twelfth year of her life. Katey lives with her mother, her stepfather, and her two sisters in a small parochial English town. There she and her sister

Joanna learn that actions have consequences that reach far beyond original intentions. Katey discovers that "the strength of personal virtues" will not always serve to protect good men such as her stepfather, that to put one's trust in them is "an old-fashioned and innocent delusion that people wiser in the world had discarded." Yet, it is Katey's repetition of the kind words her stepfather says about her real father that saves the family from emotional disaster, and so, in a sense, virtue does triumph. The strength of this novel lies in the exploration of the children's need to test their parents' affection.

Bawden's protagonists are usually female, but she does not regard feminism as a crucial theme. When asked about her attitude to women's issues generally, she mentioned what she called her "women's lib novel," *A Woman of My Age* (1967). Few would agree that this book is a feminist novel, although it is about the difficulties and inequities of marriage. The novel is, however, a fine study of an ignorant, idealistic girl, Elizabeth, who marries because she is pregnant and stays married because she has no real alternatives. Her husband, Richard, is ashamed of his social origins but revels vindictively in the notion of hierarchy when he categorizes people as having first- or second-class minds. Elizabeth can feel nothing for this man, perhaps because she is obsessed by what she ought to feel, as defined by conventional middle-class expectations. A chorus rings in Elizabeth's head: "*Elizabeth is such a nice person, she puts herself out for the most boring people.*" When she gives up her work for the Labour Party, which gives her at least a limited sense of power, she does so because she wants to feel that she is doing the "right thing." She knows that her husband's new kindness and solicitude are sentiments one might devote to a caged bird. The marriage is dissected during a crucial few days of a North African holiday. Bawden employs a brilliant juxtaposition of scenes. The present is linked and opposed to the past in order to illuminate the characters in action. The ending is foreshadowed in an early incident in the novel: Elizabeth, watching several men recapture a horse, muses, "It was as if he hadn't really wanted freedom, only to assert his right to be free if he chose." She stays with Richard.

Bawden's next novel, *The Grain of Truth* (1968), is not entirely successful, but it is her first real experiment with a variety of narrative points of view. The novel is somewhat schematic in its deliberate alternation of perspectives. It opens and closes with Emma's fearful and manipulative cry for help: "Someone listen to me." Emma, like Hilary of *Devil by the Sea* and like many children described in psychiatric literature, fears she has killed someone. This fear has complex psychological functions. It is first a source and justification for self-hatred: Emma thinks of herself as being so wicked that

Bawden at her second home, in Nauplion, Greece

she is not worth loving, but with a part of her mind she is also aware that it was not "anything I had done but what I knew I was capable of doing." This conception of a potential for evil, or even for impure motives, is a source of masochistic self-doubt for many of Bawden's heroines. The same fear also functions to control and manipulate Henry, Emma's husband. Her best friend, Holly, points out that Emma, like her mother, believes "unhappiness gives you a moral advantage." When Emma insists on going to the police with a confession of guilt for her father-in-law's death, Holly lies to save her, insisting that Emma's disclosure is the figment of a distressed mind.

It is Emma's husband who uncovers the truth that feeds Emma's fear. Readers may be persuaded that they understand Emma and even that she will learn to come to terms with her problems, but they likely remain unconvinced that a husband like Henry is capable of psychological insight. Like many of Bawden's male characters, he is portrayed as basically self-deceiving. Such men in her fiction vary from the kindly to the brutally inept. Rarely do they seem capable of insight into their own predicaments, much less into the psychological intricacies of their wives. Bawden has suggested that perhaps her own experience of a frequently absent marine engineer father might have contributed to the portraits of these frequently passive male characters. She reserves her sharpest ironies, however, for her women characters—for domineering mothers such as Emma's or for their insecure, approval-seeking daughters.

The Birds on the Trees (1970) is the story of Toby, a sensitive and charming dropout. He has a psychotic episode while on drugs and later gets a girl pregnant. Bawden treats this apparently banal 1960s material with the delicacy of a gifted miniaturist. No element of the story is out of place, and the interweaving of perspectives is perfectly controlled. One of her admirers has linked it to the works of Guy de Maupassant, but the writing is far less sardonic. It is her most compassionate work. Although the work is intimately linked with Bawden's own experience with a schizophrenic son who drowned, there is no element of self-pity.

Annie May, the protagonist of *Anna Apparent,* is rescued from brutal foster care by an egotistical and vain woman for whom the child represents an opportunity to play a new role. Crystal Golightly has recently been abandoned by her husband, and her outrage and sense of failure are alleviated by the chance to exercise benevolent dictatorial powers: "She was marvellous with the child; no less so because that was how she saw her behavior. To act in a way that would be seen to be admirable had become the main spring of her life." Annie survives this upbringing to become "Crystal's good girl," going so far as to marry Crystal's real son, Giles, a man whose emotional parasitism is only slightly more perverse and sophisticated than his mother's. Annie becomes Anna, the model wife and mother. Only her nightmares suggest that she wants "to smash something." Although Anna is in some senses a special case, she is Bawden's first clear portrayal of a woman who discovers that she needs to define herself. Her sense of herself in which "the others" are real and she is "only the stage on which they moved" leads her to a monstrous explosion of rage and the death of an innocent stranger.

George, the travel-agent hero of *George Beneath a Paper Moon,* is from a different, more comic world. Somehow reality only comes secondhand to George. He interprets his life through the anecdotes of his friends and acquaintances and occasionally even through parables. It is therefore not surprising that he grows rich on the creation of fantasy for others, although he thinks of it with "missionary innocence" as the fulfillment of their need for "romance and excitement, beauty and truth." It takes Turkish intrigue and an earthquake before George can appreciate that life is not a fairy tale, but by a glorious irony he does get his own fairy-tale ending after discovering that the girl he wants is not his daughter, as he had thought.

In 1968 Bawden was appointed a justice of the peace in Surrey, a role in which she served for eight years. The experience provided the basis for her novel *Afternoon of a Good Woman* (1976) and its heroine, Penelope, also a justice of the peace. She has decided to leave her husband for a lover who needs her more, and as she sits in judgment on the bench she also assesses her own past and present. Part of what she discovers is her own unconscious affinity for weakness, and with this insight she comes to acknowledge that she might prefer to respond to strength. She finally decides to leave both men. The skillful interweaving of the life and situation of the accused with that of the accuser creates a tapestry in which life and law expose each other.

Familiar Passions, Bawden's next work, starts from an almost directly opposed plot premise: this time it is the heroine's husband who has decided to leave. On their thirteenth wedding anniversary he takes her to an expensive dinner and then breaks the news. Bridie Starr, whose very name is her husband's creation, goes back to being Mary Mudd. An adoptive child, she sets out to discover who she is by finding her real mother and father. Bridie's genealogy proves less important than her discovery that she must learn to define herself. She finds her natural mother, who is willing to give her information about her birth and ancestors but unwilling to provide emotional support. With a splendid lack of sentimentality she tells Bridie: "I think this has been the most interesting conversation we are ever likely to have." Bridie is thus forced to learn for herself that her nature includes an aptitude and a taste for intrigue and deception and that being "good" as defined for her by others—including her angelic adoptive mother—is not a necessary corollary of being a woman. As Bawden puts it, "having to be good twists people; you're so afraid you won't be loved."

Walking Naked received mixed reviews. It so irritated Auberon Waugh that he headed his piece: "If only nasty Laura had kept her clothes on. . . ." Bawden attributes this lack of sympathy in part to Laura's unforgivable act—she sends the two children of her first marriage to her ex-husband and his new wife, assuming that they will prefer living there—but far more radical incidents and assumptions appear in the novel. *Walking Naked* is at least partly about a woman who makes a choice between a deeply affectionate, apparently erotic, friendship with a woman and marriage to her second husband.

The two protagonists of *The Ice House* (1983), one an abused child, the other an overindulged one, are childhood friends whose adult paths cross in a comic mélange of betrayal and loyalty. Ruth, the good girl of the plot, has suffered brutal abuse at the hands of her father and grows up seeking always to placate the adults around her. She finds herself suddenly confronted with an adulterous husband whose self-pity in the face of his self-indulgence she is expected to condone. Though she does not know it at first, it is her best friend, Daisy, who is her rival. When the latter's hus-

band, forced into early retirement, kills himself, both women must come to terms with their marriages and themselves. Daisy, spoiled and sexually predatory, has almost always taken what she wants. Ruth, careful and creative, whose marriage had been her retreat, now seems to have only her skills and success as designer and maker of elegant clothes.

In a final section of the novel, against the backdrop of Egypt and London, the women confront themselves and each other honestly, with both direct hostility and deep affection. Bawden allows the reader a degree of satiric distance that makes it possible to respond with amused indulgence. Once more the men tend to be the weaker sex, while the women move actively toward a new adaptive selfhood.

Circles of Deceit, shortlisted for the 1987 Booker Prize, is the story of a painter who specializes as a copyist. Its cover illustration is Peter Brueghel's *The Fall of Icarus,* and the painting serves as a kind of wry, intertextual commentary on the themes of the novel. The painter, talented, honest, and perceptive in his work, cannot summon the same gifts to his personal life. While he wants to see himself as kindly, thoughtful, and tolerant, his actions, often when he thinks of himself as most gentle and understanding, are self-destructive and destructive to others. In consequence, he falsifies both his private and his public lives and colludes with those who would deceive him. Bawden has always had a painterly eye, and this gift is beautifully demonstrated here, as she shows the painter using the characters in his private life to illuminate his artistic insights. The somewhat solipsistic play of this novel makes it the most postmodern of Bawden's writings.

In *Family Money* (1991) Bawden once more probes the conflicting and often contradictory motives that govern the design and the development of family relationships. Fanny Pye, recently widowed, owns a fine house in one of the newly gentrified parts of London. The novel is set in the era of Thatcherism, with its property boom and attendant economic scrambling. Even Fanny's children, despite their basic decency, are not immune. When Fanny is injured while witnessing a street brawl, the issue of her future comes into sharp focus both for her and her children. Her amnesia and her trauma following the injury make her afraid for her own safety and vulnerable to the often violent emotions that beset her. Her children wonder whether she is mentally competent, their concern tainted by their desire for the safe cushioning of at least some of her money. Fanny, often willful and sometimes even spiteful, is determined to lead her own life and survives to face her fears and make her own choices.

Bawden's "almost" autobiography, *In My Own Time* (1994), is in part the story of what she refers to as

197

IN MY OWN TIME

PART SEVEN

SPEAKING FOR MYSELF

"Why don't you write a novel like THE CAINE MUTINY?" my
father said, one summer evening in his great old age, leaning
back in his chair with his pipe in his mouth and his beret on
the back of his bald head to keep off the draught from the
window behind him.

He had read very little before he left the sea but since
then he had gone - or, to be more exact, sent my mother - to
the public library two or three times a week. Retiring at
sixty three, and now in his ninetieth year, he had been
blessed with almost a third of his life to catch up on his
reading. He read mainly history, or political memoirs, rarely
novels. But he had read THE CAINE MUTINY and enjoyed it more,
I suspect, than he had ever enjoyed any novel of mine.

A small boy once asked me, bringing a children's book for
my signature at some Book Fair or other, if I had "ever
thought of writing like Shakespeare." My father's equally
innocent question was harder to answer. I said (honestly) that
a writer can't choose the voice that she writes in, and (more
dubiously) that I didn't have the right kind of experience. In
fact, I was flustered. I never really knew my father until he
was old, and had never learned how to talk to him about
something that mattered to me. Now I tried, but made a mess of it,
trying out arguments that sounded specious even
as I ventured them.

Page from the manuscript for Bawden's "almost" autobiography, which was published in 1994 (Collection of Nina Bawden)

"the gamey stew of family life," but it is far more. Chosen by P. D. James as the best book of the year, it is a testament to Bawden's respect for family background and her love of her own family. Filled with vignettes from the past and the present, the book is also an attempt to look at the author's method and assumptions. She speaks of her adult novels as "social comedies" but admits being "reluctantly drawn to the notion that darkness and chaos threaten us all." The central section of the book, which gives the deeply moving history of her schizophrenic son, Niki, provides tragic evidence of her own experience of chaos and suffering. Bawden is a writer who believes in the reality of her characters, needing to know the "streets my characters walk down." She also speaks more than once of seeking "the voice she wishes to write in," a complex notion that suggests a construction of herself as a writer/narrator who is also a truth teller.

Bawden's *A Nice Change* (1997) is set in Nauplion, Greece, a city in which she has a second home. An ill-matched group of package-tour travelers gathers at the luxurious Hotel Parthenon, where the bathrooms are whimsical and the food only sporadically appetizing. The characters include an English member of parliament for the Labour Party, his wife, and his father, as well as his former mistress; an American whose wife has just committed suicide; a young woman doctor; a couple whose riches are of extremely doubtful provenance; and an elderly pair of twins who delight in impersonating each other. As the M.P.'s mistress takes a shine to his father and the M.P. himself manages to save one of the old ladies from drowning, Bawden makes it apparent that this is a group of holidaymakers in flight from themselves; indeed one couple is in flight from the law. The title, *A Nice Change,* a typical Anglo-Saxon cliché, seems something of an understatement in reference to a luxury holiday, but as relationships dissolve and rework themselves the gentle irony of the phrase becomes apparent.

Bawden has written twenty-one novels for adults, most of which are still in print. The novels are regularly reviewed in major newspapers and journals in the United States, England, and the Commonwealth. She has been frequently honored for her work, most recently in 1995, when she was made a companion of the Order of the British Empire. Despite such honors, she seems to have been tagged as a children's writer, and there is a dearth of analysis of her writing for adults.

Writing for *An Encyclopedia of British Women Writers* (1988), Jane Weiss points out that Bawden has "been criticized for skimming too lightly over the issues of morality that she raises," but her clear-eyed satiric studies of men, women, and children have always probed the hypocritical motive and the self-serving response. In her recent novels she has looked at human frailty with a more indulgent eye; even so, her introspective and sophisticated characters "illuminate . . . the attempt to find a believable morality" in daily life.

John Berger

(5 November 1926 –   )

G. M. Hyde
University of East Anglia

and

M. E. de Soissons
University of East Anglia

See also Berger entry in DLB 14: British Novelists Since 1960.

BOOKS: *A Painter of Our Time* (London: Secker & Warburg, 1958; New York: Simon & Schuster, 1959);

Permanent Red: Essays in Seeing (London: Methuen, 1960); republished as *Toward Reality: Essays in Seeing* (New York: Knopf, 1962);

The Foot of Clive (London: Methuen, 1962);

Corker's Freedom (London: Methuen, 1964; New York: Pantheon, 1993);

The Success and Failure of Picasso (Harmondsworth, U.K.: Penguin, 1965; New York: Pantheon, 1980);

A Fortunate Man: The Story of a Country Doctor, photographs by Jean Mohr, text by Berger (London: Allen Lane, 1967; New York: Holt, Rinehart & Winston, 1967);

Art and Revolution: Ernst Neizvestny and the Role of the Artist in the USSR (London: Weidenfeld & Nicolson, 1969; New York: Pantheon, 1969);

The Moment of Cubism and Other Essays (London: Weidenfeld & Nicolson, 1969; New York: Pantheon, 1969);

The Look of Things: Selected Essays and Articles, edited by Nikos Stangos (Harmondsworth, U.K.: Penguin, 1971; New York: Viking, 1972);

Ways of Seeing (Harmondsworth, U.K.: Penguin, 1972; New York: Viking, 1973);

G. (London: Weidenfeld & Nicolson, 1972; New York: Viking, 1972);

A Seventh Man: A Book of Images and Words About the Experience of Migrant Workers in Europe, photographs by Mohr, text by Berger (Harmondsworth, U.K. & Baltimore: Penguin, 1975);

Pig Earth (London: Writers and Readers Publishing Cooperative, 1979; New York: Pantheon, 1979);

John Berger at the time of Corker's Freedom *(photograph by Jean Mohr)*

About Looking (London: Writers and Readers Publishing Cooperative, 1980; New York: Pantheon, 1980);

Another Way of Telling, by Berger and Mohr (London: Writers and Readers Publishing Cooperative, 1982; New York: Pantheon, 1982);

And Our Faces, My Heart, Brief as Photos (London: Writers and Readers Publishing Cooperative, 1984; New York: Pantheon, 1984);

The White Bird, edited by Lloyd Spencer (London: Chatto & Windus, 1985); republished as *The Sense of Sight* (New York: Pantheon, 1986);

A Question of Geography, by Berger and Nella Bielski (London: Faber & Faber, 1987);

Once in Europa (New York: Pantheon, 1987; Cambridge: Penguin/Granta, 1989);

Goya's Last Portrait: The Painter Played Today, by Berger and Bielski (London: Faber & Faber, 1989);

Lilac and Flag: An Old Wives' Tale of a City (New York: Pantheon, 1990; Cambridge: Penguin/Granta, 1991);

Keeping a Rendezvous (New York: Pantheon, 1991; London: Granta, 1992);

Pages of the Wound; Poems, Photographs, Drawings by John Berger (London: Circle, 1994);

To the Wedding (London: Bloomsbury, 1995; New York: Pantheon, 1995);

Mann und Frau, unter einem Pflaumenbaum stehend (Munich: Carl Hanser Verlag, 1995); republished as *Photocopies* (London: Bloomsbury, 1996; New York: Pantheon, 1996);

Isabelle: A Life in Shots, by Berger and Bielski (London: Arcadia, 1998);

King: A Street Story (London: Bloomsbury, 1999; New York: Pantheon, 1999).

Collection: *Into Their Labours* (New York: Pantheon, 1991; London: Penguin/Granta, 1992)—comprises *Pig Earth, Once in Europa,* and *Lilac and Flag.*

MOTION PICTURES: *La Vie a Chandigarh,* screenplay by Berger and Alain Tanner, 1966;

La Salamandre, screenplay by Berger and Tanner, 1971;

Jonas qui aura 25 and en l'an 2000, screenplay by Berger and Tanner, Lausanne, Cinématheque Suisse, 1978;

Play Me Something, screenplay by Berger and Timothy Neat, British Film Institute, 1989.

OTHER: Bertolt Brecht, *Poems on the Theatre,* translated by Berger and Anya Bostock (Middlesex, U.K.: Scorpion, 1961);

Brecht, *Helene Weigel, Actress,* translated by Berger and Bostock (Leipzig: VEB, 1961);

Aime Cesaire, *Return to My Native Land,* translated by Berger and Bostock (London & Baltimore: Penguin, 1969);

Nella Bielski, *Oranges for the Son of Alexander Levy,* translated by Berger and Lisa Appignanesi (London: Writers and Readers Cooperative, 1982);

Bielski, *After Arkadia; The Wickerwork Tram and the Barber's Head,* translated by Berger and Jonathan Steffen (London: Viking, 1991).

John Berger is perhaps the most challenging British writer of his generation. Interdisciplinary, political, and always provocative in the deepest sense, Berger's writings in a wide variety of genres and his way of life have constituted a distinctive artistic statement. Awarded the Booker Prize, Britain's highest mark of inclusion and recognition by the literary establishment,

for his novel *G.* (1972), he donated part of the prize money to the Black Panthers and moved away from Britain. In many ways—his interest in the intersection of fiction and movies, his Marxist orientation, his retention into the eighth decade of his life of a "problematical" approach to literature and the realism central to the novel tradition—Berger has remained true to the most important intellectual trends of the 1960s, when he first began to make his name.

John Berger was born in Stoke Newington, London, on 5 November 1926, the son of S. J. D. Berger and Miriam Branson Berger. His father was born in Liverpool, the son of an émigré from Trieste; his mother was a suffragette who, he says, encouraged him to be a writer, though she never read his work once he did so. Berger attended a preparatory school near Guildford, where he encountered the sadism, torture, and bullying characteristic of a small totalitarian system. At sixteen he ran away. He went to art school and then joined the army in 1944 as a lance corporal.

Twice married and the father of three children, Berger resides in the French Pyrenees. He has not confined himself as a writer to any single genre or type of writing but has produced innovative work in fiction, art criticism, social commentary, and "books of images and words" (the subtitle of the 1975 documentary *A Seventh Man,* produced in collaboration with Jean Mohr, the Swiss photographer). Originally trained at art school (Central and then Chelsea, London) Berger continues to draw, take photographs, make movies, and write plays as well as write novels. The breadth of his works, the result of a deliberate aesthetic that sets out to break down, test, and resynthesize generic and critical boundaries, is central to his project but can create blind spots for critics more used to operating within subject boundaries. As well as breaking generic boundaries, Berger has established for himself a precedent for collaborative work, perhaps in response to the potentially lonely and alienated role of the novelist. He worked with his first wife, Anya Bostock, translating the work of Bertolt Brecht, whose influence can be seen in much of Berger's writing. Two of his children, Jacob and Katya, were the product of this union, and he has also collaborated with Katya, who lives and works in Greece. There is a Greek influence in his late novel *To the Wedding* (1995).

Berger's broad aesthetic and currently unfashionable political commitment means that he has (perhaps deliberately) set himself outside the boundaries of mainstream fiction and its surrounding critical debates. He also seems to avoid his early high-profile media image, which as a working journalist he was well-placed to exploit. Thus, for a writer of his stature there is relatively little biographical detail in the public domain. If

Berger has placed himself outside mainstream debate, however, he is far from exiled from a creative community. Although he lives in the rural Pyrenees, he spends time in Paris and, since his move to Europe, has produced collaborative work with Simon McBernie, the artistic director of the Théatre de Complicité; the film director Timothy Neat; director, cameraman, and publisher John Christie; and the playwright and translator Nella Bielski. In all his work the "unconditional modality of the visual image" is used to question what David Caute has called the "privileged anonymity" of the author. To the extent that the authorial presence and perspective is acknowledged as present in much of the work, including his plentiful essays and journal articles, Berger's work speaks for itself in autobiographical terms.

Berger began his working life teaching painting and drawing and having his work exhibited at several London galleries, including Wildenstein, the Redfern, and the Leicester. He wrote at the same time for the *Tribune* (London) and from 1951 on a regular basis for the *New Statesman,* where he was for ten years a regular art critic, enjoying the support of editor Kingsley Martin. From material published between 1954 and 1959 he assembled his first book of art criticism, the title of which, *Permanent Red* (1960), signifies among other things Berger's Marxist political commitment. In the introduction for a 1979 reissue of the collection, Berger asserts that at the time he wrote it he was "trapped" by the need to express all his feelings and thoughts in "art-critical terms." The sense of enclosure fostered by the cold war was, he says, the reason for the "puritanism" of many of his judgments; he also points out that—Martin excepted—editorial pressure to conform made composition difficult. Robert Hewison's book *In Anger* (1981) shows how Berger's unfashionable championship of realist painting in the early 1950s, especially his exhibition at the Whitechapel Gallery in 1952 of realist work under the title "Looking Forward," aroused much animosity from fellow art critics such as Sir Herbert Read and Patrick Heron, who also worked for the *New Statesman.* The recurring theme of *Permanent Red,* "the disastrous relation between art and property," underlies much of Berger's work. Critics seized on what they called Berger's habit of judging from fixed premises without indicating what they are. Equally annoying to many was his eschewal of the given historical categories of art criticism in favor of an existential engagement with the historical moment of the artist and the work of art.

Berger's effort to humanize bloodless categories leads him to fictionalize the moment of creation and the process of decoding. Even before these essays were collected he had written his first novel, *A Painter of Our Time*

(1958), which explores the relationship between and the function of the painter in a consumer society. The protagonist, Janos Lavin, a Hungarian émigré, unites these themes. His work is perhaps modeled on that of Fernand Leger, who learned how to "discover the spirit, the ethics, the attitude of mind" needed to make use of modern technical achievements. (Berger wrote at length on Leger and technology in a 1963 issue of *Marxism Today*.) The choice of the artist-exile as protagonist focuses the issue of artistic commitment, and the narrative technique—the narrator in the abandoned studio searches in Lavin's diary for clues to his disappearance—juxtaposes document with fiction in such a way as to dissolve their boundaries. The decoding of the journal (which constitutes the plot of the novel) is effectively related to the composition and "reading" of the paintings that form the life of the artist. Elements from this novel—the investigation of abstraction, a structure that plays with a conventional "plot" and the relationship between individual subjectivity and social praxis—are developed further in later novels, particularly those collected as the trilogy *Into Their Labours* (1991), which focuses on the move to abstraction, and *G.,* which reworks the conventions of plot.

As Berger relates in an essay in *The Look of Things: Selected Essays and Articles* (1971), he was close to the Hungarian sculptor Peter Peri, who was living in poverty in Camden. He had, says Berger, the face of a ghetto dweller who carried "a microcosm in a sack," the turmoil of central European culture that he hardly expected the English to understand. "Something of the meaning of being such an exile I tried to put into my novel," says Berger, adding that he discussed the novel with Peri, who was "enthusiastic about the idea of my writing it." Some traits of Lavin are therefore drawn from Peri, others from the Hungarian art historian Frederick Antal, "who, more than any other man, taught me how to write about art. . . . What Lavin and Antal share is the depth of their experience of exile." Berger cautions, however, that Lavin is not a portrait of Peri.

A Painter of Our Time was hostilely reviewed in *Encounter* and elsewhere, and parts of it are awkward and ill contrived, but Berger's intense existential concern with the complex perspectives upon the world that art creates illuminates Lavin's journal. The condition of exile, though not romanticized—rather it is represented as having a high price—is seen to be a necessary condition for artistic freedom in certain kinds of society. Lavin is free to be unimpressed by high-society art patrons, and free to ignore both middle-class values and their alternative, the lifestyle of the coterie. His passionate defense of art against the plausible ethics of ownership is memorable.

Dust jacket for John Berger's 1972 novel, which won the Booker Prize (Collection of William Cagle)

The fictional Lavin echoes Berger's ideas and methods in both political and artistic matters. Reflecting upon art and politics, for instance, Lavin finds an example of the dialectical process in the technique of cross-hatching, where the intersecting lines form a new diamond shape. Similarly, Berger's compositional technique is to counterpose Lavin's journal with the narrator's commentary to create a "cross-hatched," dialectical narrative. Thus, *A Painter of Our Time* incorporates a critique and reworking of fictionality inherent in all of Berger's work. History is thus a kind of unconscious that the work of art, like Sigmund Freud's concept of dream-works, both reveals and conceals. Hence the vivid elliptical shifts between object and concept, fact and metaphor, that are to remain typical of Berger and indeed become more pronounced in his later novels, particularly the last novel of the trilogy, *Lilac and Flag* (1990).

Berger's investigation of the task of the artist and the processes of artistic creation in the modern world are taken further in his work on Pablo Picasso, the modern "artist as hero" in *The Success and Failure of Picasso* (1965). Berger sets out to strip away the ideological

accretions that have made it difficult to "see" Picasso: he demythologizes the "man of genius" (the commodity value that painters have acquired in an age that grants them no effective place in society). There is, Berger believes, a "dualism at the very heart of the bourgeois attitude to art. On the one hand, the glory and mystery of genius; on the other hand, the work of art as a saleable commodity." Berger interprets this belief in terms of the class structure of Spain, Spanish anarchism, and the facts of Picasso's childhood while managing to avoid any crudely Marxist or Freudian generalizations. Thus what Berger calls the "discontinuity" of Picasso's life and work, often related to his perennial youthfulness, is seen as an ambiguous phenomenon inextricably linked to a failure to develop.

Only after establishing these imaginative structures in Picasso's work does Berger turn his attention to the subject matter of his painting (the sympathy with the outcast in his early work, for example) and to the short-lived "promise of the modern world" that cubism heralded. Berger attaches particular significance to the failure or radical inability of cubists—Picasso among them—to respond to the age of "essential politics" inaugurated by World War I, and contrasts the increasing subjectivity of Picasso's art with the public dimension of Leger's. Berger finds that in certain key works Picasso becomes solipsistic by virtue of the fact that "there is nothing *to resist him:* neither the subject, nor his awareness of reality as understood by others." Thus Picasso ended his career as a "national monument," doyen of the West and exploited by propaganda in the East because of his communism.

Berger's second novel, *The Foot of Clive* (1962), studies the life of a hospital in relation to the lives of the patients who temporarily inhabit it. Berger believes that patients are particularly in touch with their bodily functions, and as such they are representative of complex forms of mediation between subjectivity and structure. This microcosmic society, engaged in writing its own history, is intruded upon at the end of part 1 of the novel by a new patient, Jack House the Murderer. Part 2, "The Screens," and part 3, "The Execution," unfold against the background of his ominous presence. House embodies the fear of the unknown and the presence of death "screened off" from the "normal" world. House's presence crystallizes the latent violence in the men: they both need him—he stands for Law and Judgment—and anathematize him. Part 4, "The Survivors," dissolves the precarious synthesis of Clive Ward back into professional objectivity, with the doctors treating the patients as case histories. As the little community opens up onto the outside world, readers are led to reflect upon the kinds of "freedoms" encountered in Clive Ward's uncensored intimacies and the ways in which they relate to the possibility of freedom in the "real" world.

In his next novel, *Corker's Freedom* (1964), Berger creates a central hero, the manager of a small employment agency. Though the method of this novel could be called more traditional and the writing is assured and exact, the basic components of the fiction—hero, plot, and setting—are all made problematic. Berger describes the novel as "partly a film scenario and partly a historical document," a characterization consistent with his wish that "my books transcend the categories into which they are generally forced." In *Corker's Freedom* Berger confronts the problem of representing an individual with limited faculties of self-knowledge and still more restricted powers of self-expression but whose need for the "freedom" of a richer social milieu and more positive field of personal and social action is urgent. The small employment exchange that Corker runs becomes the focus of Berger's critique of a culture that values individuals only for their earning potential. The narrator offers access to Corker's thoughts that he is unable to express himself. Corker dreams of freedom, symbolized by his romantic longing for faraway places, especially Vienna. His utopia is also partially symbol-

ized by a mysterious woman, a theme that is to be taken much further in later novels. In a somewhat sensational climax, two petty crooks burglarize Corker's office while he presents a slide show about Vienna in a local church. Corker ironically realizes his dreams for freedom when he becomes the spokesman for a shabby Pan-European political organization.

The beginnings of "mixed media" effects in *Corker's Freedom* reflect Berger's continuing interest in movies and television. In 1967 and 1975 he produced two major volumes of photographic documentary, *A Fortunate Man* and *A Seventh Man,* respectively, both in collaboration with the Swiss photographer Jean Mohr. *A Fortunate Man* is a documentary record of the work of a doctor in a poor rural community in the north of England. The book creates a landscape "no longer only geographic but also biographical and personal." Initially the doctor sees himself as a man with special skills and responsibilities, while later he enters into relationships with patients, with an ironic sense of his limitations. The community as a whole, Berger points out in a footnote, suffers from the "Corker" problem: "They are deprived of the means of translating what they know into thoughts which they can think." Illness discloses needs and even faculties that lie hidden behind the "common sense" of the group, a common sense that Berger challengingly describes as "the home-made ideology of those who have been kept ignorant."

A Seventh Man depicts migrant workers in Germany, where, as in Britain, one out of seven manual workers is an immigrant. The title of the book, from a poem by Attila Jozsef, indicates that it is also about the absent other, the individual who exceeds the total of his functions or roles in the world at the same time as being constituted by them. Between the two documentaries lie two events: the political and cultural struggles of 1968 and the publication that same year of Hannah Arendt's selection of essays by Walter Benjamin, *Illuminations.* Berger draws on Benjamin's analysis of a photograph in *A Seventh Man.* Characteristically, photography is not a disparate component of the book but a part of its form and rhetorical method. The photograph carried by an immigrant "defines an absence," the family in which the worker no longer fills a space. The photograph makes present the family that is absent but wished for, a contradiction that hangs over all the photographs in the text. The migrants, who stand for all who sell their labor and mortgage their present to an unsure future, sever organic ties with family and future and so become "immortal" in that they are "continually interchangeable. They are not born, they are not brought up: they do not age: they do not get tired: they do not die." Thus Berger defamiliarizes the migrant's predicament and illuminates the contradiction (inherent in the method of the photograph) between individual and society. Berger claims that "the migrant is not on the margin of modern experience; he is absolutely central to it." Based in part upon *A Seventh Man,* Berger was awarded the George Orwell Memorial Prize in 1977.

Berger's influential work *Ways of Seeing* (1972), which nearly thirty years after its publication is still on the syllabus of most art-history courses, pays detailed tribute to Benjamin, especially to his essay "The Work of Art in the Age of Mechanical Reproduction." The same essay may serve to illuminate *G.,* the winner amid much controversy of the Booker Prize, the James Tait Black Memorial Prize in 1973, and the *Guardian* fiction prize. Whereas the author formerly emulated painters, in this novel he emulates a cameraman. Perhaps his hero is the camera itself, penetrating, analyzing, breaking down, and rendering visible hidden gestures much as the psychiatrist discloses hidden desires.

G. himself is more a set of hypotheses or angles of vision than a character; he is the point of intersection of subjectivity and history. As the illegitimate offspring of high-bourgeois society, he embodies its contradictions, flouts its taboos, and initiates its decline in the anarchy of the war. His exploitation of women—he evokes Don Giovanni as well as Giuseppe Garibaldi—is simply the disclosure of the truth about the prevailing ethic of his society. He lays claim to various identities, for instance, Giovanni and Garibaldi, but the narrative makes him less than a hero by accounting for him in terms of an historical process that renders him obsolete (as new technology is rendering obsolete the old bourgeois ethic). The fragmented narrative, composed in terms of cubist "fields of force" rather than as a linear continuum, multiplies contradictions between subjective personal and historical systems of interpretation: at points in the narrative the author intervenes to tell the reader that he has no privileged access to knowledge or to any interpretative schema and even at one point counters a "voice" that accuses him of excessive theorizing. The insurgent crowds of Milan; the exploited Africans of Beatrice's past; the crowds that follow the aviator Chavez, with whom G. is temporarily identified; and the people of Trieste on the eve of war are as central to the action of the novel as G. or the women imprisoned by men (here Berger quotes his own *Ways of Seeing*).

G. is a diffuse and calculatedly unresolved work, a mix of modernism and realism. The realist fragments are held together by Don Giovanni's journey through Europe in search of sexual conquest. Aspects of the "protagonist," G., who can hardly be described as a character, are depicted in part naturalistically, shown from various viewpoints. Yet, the collage of these aspects in G. is as disorientating as a cubist portrait. G. is Don Giovanni chasing women across Europe,

Garibaldi the revolutionary, and Geo, a pilot attempting to cross the Alps. Berger uses a cubist perspective—three different viewpoints of the same object—to depict the force of history. All these characters' individual histories, their individual drives and the correspondence between them make up the force that is history, in a way a conventional historian could not show.

If the search for sex is one constant, the inexorable approach of death is another, reflected in the fact that the moment of cubism ended where the novel ends. Don Giovanni's death is preordained, and Geo ends up mentally destroyed by his attempt at a solo flight in the stone "womb" of the Gondo—another element of G.?—while Garibaldi's revolutionary hopes lead nowhere. All of these individual forms of death coincide with the outbreak of World War I.

G., then, is a radically experimental novel that at the same time retains two important aspects of the conventional realist novel. Berger maintains a semblance of character by the realist fragments that make up the novel. The force of sex, Don Giovanni's unceasing drive for sexual conquest, propels the reader through the novel as if it were the reader's "drive" to complete the text. That this completion is a preordained death is part of Berger's rhetorical plan. Multiple perspectives, derived from cubism, imply rhetorically the breakdown of the Cartesian ego. Berger thus allies himself to a European tradition of postmodernism: death, desire, and the breakdown of the ego are all incorporated as structural elements of the plot.

The critic Geoff Dyer has said that Berger's abandonment of Britain, leaving behind the constricting environment of British ethical debate, was both a literal and an intellectual move. Berger's work after this point reflects the European world both in content and style. According to Berger, his work is now read more in Germany, Spain, and Turkey than in the United Kingdom.

Into Their Labours could only be set in a European environment. The first two novels, *Pig Earth* (1979) and *Once in Europa* (1987), are made up of a series of short stories about the lives of the people that Berger has lived with in the Jura since he left England. *Pig Earth* ends with a trilogy within the trilogy, "The Three Lives of Lucie Cabrol." The early stories are written in a sparse, naturalist style, while "The Three Lives of Lucie Cabrol" begins to incorporate a utopian vision. *Once in Europa,* through its various stories, begins to chart the gradual move into the towns by the peasants. *Lilac and Flag* (1990) is closer to a novel in form; it tells the story of a young couple from "Rat Hill," a city slum. The trilogy is a kind of elegy for the rural peasantry that existed in Europe for centuries, largely uncharted and unrecorded despite making up the majority of the population. The large continental land-

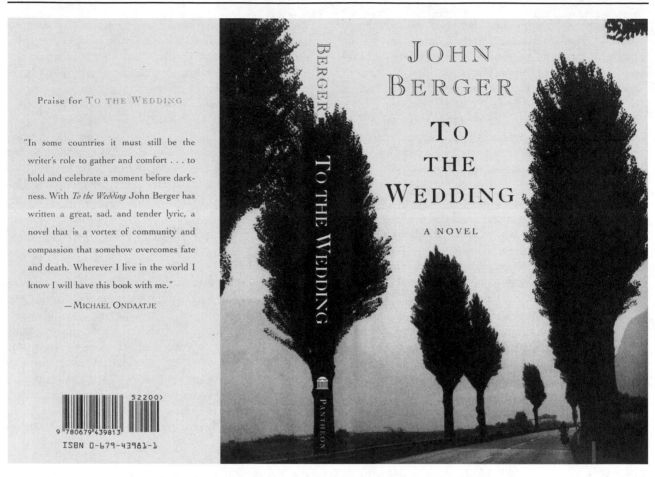

Dust jacket for the first U.S. edition of Berger's 1995 novel, which follows a motorcyclist's journey across Europe

mass has allowed the peasant way of life to exist in Europe long after the industrial revolution destroyed it in England—Berger, in choosing to live and work in the French Pyrennes, has recorded the final days of that ancient culture. His purpose in doing so is clearly laid out in the preface to the first volume, *Pig Earth*.

Pig Earth is strongly attached in time and place to Berger's adopted home in rural France. The community evoked in the novel has a strong oral tradition and culture: its coordinates of time and space are as immediate as a row of melons and as extensive as the maquis and the war, detailed in the section "The Three Lives of Lucie Cabrol." The narrator is only one more storyteller, helping to maintain the identity of the community. Berger unobtrusively appropriates the idiom of one or another of the great storytellers of his adopted culture: Emile Zola, Guy de Maupassant, and Alphonse Daudet are all referenced. *Pig Earth* remains contemporary in tone, however. The epic "The Three Lives of Lucie Cabrol," for instance, demonstrates exactly what Berger means when he speaks of peasants as survivors

and why survival matters also to those who are not peasants. The power of survival is the exact inverse of the immortality of the migrant in *A Seventh Man*. If this formulation implies a kind of conservatism, "it is a conservatism not of power but of meaning," Berger argues. Thus the peasant experience is seen to be peculiarly relevant to the modern world that envisages its destruction: "The peasant suspicion of 'progress' . . . is not altogether misplaced or groundless." With the annihilation of the "survivors," Berger suggests, society may lose not only a complex way of relating to nature and to animals (a major theme of the novel that is also documented elsewhere by Berger): the destruction of the world's peasant population could be "a final act of historical elimination."

In the process of covering the move from a rural way of life to an urban, capitalist one, *Into Their Labours* incorporates a change in style from naturalism to a postmodern style that verges on abstraction. As well as referring to a precedent in painting, this change in style implies that the naturalist mode, with its assumption of authorial omniscience, is no longer sufficient for the developing modern world. Berger's late style is complex and has evolved over the whole of his writing career. There can be seen in his work a continuing involvement with and corresponding evolution of form, a continuing dialectic that covers some consistent themes.

Novels, though, are only a part of Berger's work. While rhetorically questioning the necessity and desirability of atomized genres, Berger respects and develops the potential of each form. An example of this formal open-mindedness is *Pages of the Wound: Poems, Photographs, Drawings by John Berger* (1994), in which Berger presents poems that he describes as generically "born of a sense of helplessness, hence their force," an assertion that would seem to acknowledge the Romantic idea of poetry as an expression of emotion. The book also includes photographs and drawings, the photographs depicting pictures framing part of a woman's body against a backdrop of mountains and trees. In view of Berger's conception, inspired by Benjamin, of photographs as a simultaneous absence and presence, the photographs in this book seem to express an unobtainable desire or potentiality that has no other form or outlet. This depiction of women and nature thus has a utopian quality.

Technical innovation—something Berger has unceasingly, almost fetishistically used throughout his career—is a major feature of high Modernism, in which it was used to express new ideas and changing ideology. More recently, however, technical innovation has become a structural function of the market, related only to the need to produce novelty as a selling point. Perhaps one of Berger's greatest contributions to postmodernism is an ongoing demonstration that aesthetic innovation does not have to carry a commercial function, that it can embrace less fashionable politics at the expense of becoming a less fashionable commodity. Berger's work is always underpinned by his Marxist commitment, in dialogue with previous aestheticians while attempting to find a language for the present and hence the future. Rhetorical innovation and political import are inseparable in Berger's work.

Berger found an inspiration for this aesthetic in cubism, the subject of his 1969 critical work *The Moment of Cubism.* Cubism for Berger was a brief moment of art that had revolutionary potential. "Cubist art points out the partiality of perception—several perspectives must be taken at once and the 'truth' is the interrelation of the various discoveries of those perceptions." This revolutionary potential was cut off by World War I, the historical setting of *G.* Berger's continuing experimentation with form from *G.* onward can be interpreted as a continuation of the cubist movement or "moment."

Cubism influences many features of Berger's work. Perhaps one of the most difficult aspects is his use of multiple perspectives that "must be taken at once." The same form occurring in different manifestations is a characteristic feature of Berger's work as it has unfolded. It is an echoing motif, something more typical of a poetic or musical body of work. This polyphonic quality is a fairly common element of many modernist novels, but Berger's use of it as a rhetorical motif, across his work as a whole, is systematic and wide-ranging—the device has thus become foregrounded.

How multiple perspective functions across the whole of Berger's work can also be seen in his regular yet ambivalent interest in the hero, in particular the figure or personal trope of a male pilot or cyclist. As with *G.,* this figure is polyvalent, suggesting multiple allusions while avoiding absolute interpretation. This polyvalence is both poetic and painterly. The figure of the pilot or cyclist is a recurrent one from *G.* onward. (Berger himself is a keen motorcyclist, though he hates to fly.) A motorcyclist's journey provides the structural backbone for *To the Wedding,* and the figure appears also in *Pages of the Wound* and *Photocopies* (1996), a semi-autobiographical collection of short pieces describing Berger's friends and acquaintances. *The Guardian* ran a short piece by Berger in August 1998 praising the racer Michael Schumacher. The motorcyclist/pilot figure can be seen as Berger's continuing involvement with the Romantic hero. The valorization of a male hero, used by the Romantic movement as a response to the dehumanization of the developing commercial world, is in keeping with Berger's political commitment. The figure of a fighter pilot is one of considerable resonance for the European generation that lived through the world wars. Berger has developed a motif that is tied into an historical occasion.

Berger's characters—for want of a better term—are frequently individuals, but at the same time they represent historical forces. To this extent Berger's late style may be seen as allegorical. The last novel in *Into Their Labours, Lilac and Flag,* follows the lives of an ill-fated couple from Rat Hill, a fictional slum that could be almost anywhere in the developing world. The novel clarifies and develops Berger's method of depicting characters as simultaneously individual and universal. The two main protagonists have two names: Sucus and Zsusa, which refer to their individual identities, and Lilac and Flag, which refer to universal male and female qualities. Lilac, the flower, is frequently associated in Berger's work with the female qualities, just as the figure of the motorcyclist is inevitably male. Flag, as well as connoting a phallic flagpole, is also a flower. That both names represent flowers indicates the ephemeral fragility of the central characters, who are ultimately destroyed. Berger, however, claims not to like allegory. Perhaps it is more useful to look at his personification of abstract ideas from the context of painting, in which figurative painters must always use either people or things or landscapes to depict abstract qualities or ideas. In *Lilac and Flag* the couple are depicted making love in the cockpit of a giant crane on a building site where Sucus is working, and he subsequently gets sacked. The correspondence between the phallic properties of the master crane and the act of love are implicated in a scene that is simultaneously banal, touching, and ludicrous. This scene seems to be a literalization of the concept of reification: the properties of the phallus and love between the two characters have become intertwined with the properties of the crane on the building site. Sexuality, technology, and the economic structures that encompass them both have become reified structures in mutual relation. The overt merging of individual characters and abstract forces becomes an integral, seemingly immutable part of this novel, a tragic vision of late capitalism.

This overt schematization in Berger's later work has the effect of exposing structures that were present in a less developed way in his previous writing. A feature that has come out more starkly in its constancy is the treatment of gender. Although *G.* is dedicated to Anya Bostock "and her sisters in the Women's Liberation Movement," it is not clear that Berger has kept up with the women's movement since the publication of that novel. In *G.* Berger offers a critique of women's "specular prison"—created by the fact that femaleness is constructed in the male eye. While apparently wishing this situation to change, Berger at the same time depicts women continually and obsessively in the "specular range." Not surprisingly, perhaps, he adopts similarly contentious stances in later work, as when in the middle of *Into Their Labours* Berger self-consciously elides his depictions of femaleness and natural or rural-village life into a utopia. In *Corker's Freedom* and the later novels, women are consistently represented as utopian in that they are always in the position of being desired. The difficulty with this kind of schematization is that it often leaves out the individual from the representation, leaving the female reader with no point of identification and even appearing to be sexist. Berger has referred to his depiction of women as working with archetypes, but postmodernism begs the question of for whom the archetypes are intended.

While Berger's presentation of archetypes may provoke the reader to angry realization of the tragic plight of the worker or woman, in some cases the novels become reaffirmations of imprisoning clichés; Berger sometimes avoids this problem through a dialogue between several of his novels. When reading a work such as *Photocopies,* one is struck by the apparent love Berger holds for his subjects, the ingenuity of his depiction, and the beauty of his prose. As one reads several of the novels, certain less temperate concerns emerge, as counterpoints among them become apparent. For example, a parallel plot formation is discernible between *G.* and *To the Wedding,* both of which are made up of fragments held together by a central drive analagous to the cubist "field of force."

To the Wedding signals Berger's continental orientation through a prose style that incorporates a similar rhythm and syntax to spoken French. One of the effects of this stylistic experimentation—radically alienating to an English reader—is to evoke a voice or voices in the text, something Berger does in different ways in many of his novels. His texts are a Barthesian "weaving of voices," and his later use of a "voice" evoked by rhythm and syntax alone is perhaps evidence of a developing interest in the spoken word and, by extension, radio. *To the Wedding* was performed as a radio play by the Théatre de Complicité to honor National AIDS Day—during the writing of the novel Berger's daughter-in-law had been diagnosed with the HIV virus.

The central drive in *G.* is sexual, while in *To the Wedding* it is the literal drive of Don Fererro, the motorcyclist, across Europe to a wedding. Don Fererro is another manifestation of the ambivalent hero figure that appears throughout the later work. Both fields of force are tragic: as Don Giovanni moves toward his preordained death, so Don Ferrero moves toward a paradoxical death, as Berger indicates at the beginning of the novel that the wedding that is the focus of the whole story never actually happened. The bride-to-be dies of AIDS at the age of twenty-three. Both plots are coterminous with social holocaust, the outbreak of World War I, and the mass destruction of AIDS.

The device of a predetermined ending in death is simultaneously metaphorical, paradoxical, and political. These qualities are present in many of Berger's devices, but his use of death is perhaps the predominant motif in his work. Particularly in the context of the novel form's significance to the industrial world, Berger's deathly paradox takes on a frightening significance. A happy ending—or at least an ending that brings the events and characters of the novel to resolution or completion—is a standard element of the realist novel genre. Berger has developed a variation for the end of the century. He seems sympathetic to the idea put forth by György Lukács that the resolution of fictional lives within a novel represents a totality unobtainable in capitalist reality, but Berger's variation is to problematize Lukács by souring that totality at its end. By ending these two novels with preordained deaths, Berger undermines the usual pleasure of the text and hence its reactionary

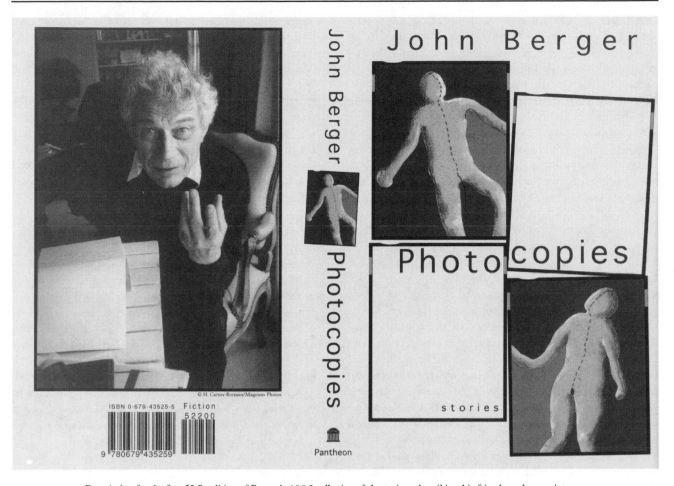

Dust jacket for the first U.S. edition of Berger's 1995 collection of short pieces describing his friends and acquaintances

potential, yet without defying all reactionary expectation. Berger's paradoxical conceit has the effect, consistent with the revolutionary project of his writing throughout his long career, of questioning the ontological status or truth value of the text.

In his novel *King* (1999) Berger takes readers into undocumented worlds of modern urban experience. "I am mad to try to lead you to where I live" are the first words of the central character, a dog. The words express the compulsiveness and difficulty of the task Berger has set for himself. In his most accomplished novel to date, Berger continues his attempt to represent the experience of the late twentieth century in novel form. In this case he is representing lives in an inner-city dump next to a motorway, a place where "there are no words for what make up the wasteland, because everything on it is smashed and has been thrown away." Living among these fragments is a precarious community: an old couple, Vica and Vico; Marcello; Anna, who lives in a block that may have housed an electrical transformer; Joachim and his cat, Catastro-

phe; Malak and Liberto; and Saul, Danny, and Luc. Jack plays landlord to the whole community, policing who comes in and collecting rent in the form of services.

The novel continues the restless aesthetic experimentation characteristic of all Berger's work. At the same time it maintains many of Berger's trademarks. Although the edition published by Bloomsbury does not have the author's name on the cover, its carefully worked prose is unmistakably Berger's. As in most of his work, Berger has reworked the meaning of character. In taking an animal as the narrator of the story, Berger is able to avoid the constraints and clichés of established novelistic conventions. The dog is a composite creation that includes a third-person narrator, an authorial presence that is less overt than in past work. King moves easily and unobtrusively between all the characters, human and otherwise. He also involves the reader in the surrounding landscape and maintains a link, however tenuous, with what wildlife is left in the dump and its surroundings. The dog (whether in body or mind is unclear) visits a nearby beach, where among the eel grass a whelk changes shells. This unexpected and unobtrusive visit demonstrates one of the skills that Berger has developed in his long career as a writer, the ability to depict a richly sensuous immediacy, a linguistic experience that touches the senses while surprising the intellect. In Berger's mature work, words rarely follow established paths.

The novel spans twenty-four hours in the lives of the community. Through flashbacks Berger chronicles the previous lives of Vica and Vico, and he provides everyday details of their lives as near-destitutes: of Vica's trips with "the chariot" (an old trolley) to a motorway lavatory to collect water for washing and cooking, of the brazier made from an old oil can to roast and sell chestnuts on the streets. During the twenty-four hours Jack hears that city officials are planning to send machinery and men to clear the site, which has been sold for development as a sports arena. In its depiction of the threat of destruction to the shantytown, *King* is as bleakly critical of advanced capitalism as any Berger has written, though in the course of the novel this bleakness is counterpointed by tenderness and moments of pleasure: the growing of radishes, the pleasure Joachim takes in his cat, the stars that Vica has painted on the ceiling above the couple's bed, and a hyacinth planted in an old margarine tin.

As with most of Berger's work, *King* can be read on several levels. The everyday lives of the people depicted are as involving as any soap opera. Concern for the outcome of the central drama, Jack's discussion with city hall, provides the dramatic impetus and tension that are generally characteristic of Berger's novels. On one level the novel is a simple and accessible tale. Characteristically, though, the book is also a novel of ideas. Vico, King's master, tells King that among his ancestors was the seventeenth-century historian and philospher Giambattista Vico. Vico—just as Berger, he was particular in the span of his interests—believed that the cyclical developments of history can only be understood through the study of changes in language, myth, and culture. Vico, the philosophical tramp, tells King of the four successive ages: the Age of Gods, the Age of Heroes, the Age of Men, and finally the Age of Dogs. King relates that the language of dogs, graffiti, is a language of the mad and the insane.

The reviews of *King,* while drawing comparisons with great writers of the past such as Charles Dickens, Arthur Rimbaud, and François Villon—show that Berger still has the capacity to incite strong opinions, both hostile and complimentary. The reviewer in the *Times Metro* (20 February 1999) points out that the use of a dog as a central character is not a new device, and suggested that readers turn to Jack London's *Call of the Wild* (1903) instead. By contrast, the reviewer in the *Sunday Herald* (Glasgow) of 21 February 1999 claims that *King* achieves a "poetic lucidity that is genuinely breathtaking" and is as concentratedly powerful as anything Berger has yet written. *King* is Berger's best novel to date, a novel that bears the fruit of a lifetime's experimentation with language and genre.

Little of lasting significance has been written about Berger, although his work has attracted reviews of more than usual passion and coherence. The sophisticated nature of the debate surrounding his work is no accident: more than any other significant contemporary novelist, Berger sees his work as contributing to a continuing dialectic rather than aspiring to classic status. As a novelist of ideas who is continually engaged with problems of literary realism, he perhaps stands outside of the mainstream of contemporary English fiction. The lasting value of his work consists precisely in the intellectual restlessness that makes it necessary for him to cross frontiers between established cultural and social institutions in his pursuit of a synthetic critique of contemporary civilization.

Interview:

Jeremy Isaacs, interview with Berger, BBC Productions, 1995.

References:

David Caute, "What we might be and what we are: The Art of John Berger," in his *Collisions* (London: Quartet, 1974), pp. 135–146;

Geoff Dyer, *Ways of Telling: The Work of John Berger* (London: Pluto, 1987);

Petr Fuller, *Seeing Berger: A Revaluation of Ways of Seeing* (London: Writers and Readers Publishing Cooperative, 1980);

Robert Hewison, *In Anger* (London: Weidenfeld & Nicolson, 1981);

Arnold Kettle, "Trying to re-shape the novel," *New Republic* (7 November 1972): 30–31;

Fred Pfiel, "Between Salvage and Silvershades: John Berger and What's Left," *Triquarterly,* no. 88 (1993): 230–245.

Caroline Blackwood
(16 July 1931 – 14 February 1996)

Priscilla Martin
St. Edmund Hall, Oxford

See also the Blackwood entry in *DLB 14: British Novelists Since 1960.*

BOOKS: *For All That I Found There* (London: Duckworth, 1973; New York: Braziller, 1974);
The Stepdaughter (London: Duckworth, 1976; New York: Scribners, 1977);
Great Granny Webster (London: Duckworth, 1977; New York: Scribners, 1977);
Darling, You Shouldn't Have Gone to So Much Trouble, by Blackwood and Anna Haycraft (London: Cape, 1980);
The Fate of Mary Rose (London: Cape, 1981; New York: Summit, 1981);
Goodnight Sweet Ladies (London: Heinemann, 1983);
Corrigan (London: Heinemann, 1984; New York: Viking/Penguin, 1985);
On the Perimeter (London: Heinemann, 1984);
In the Pink, Caroline Blackwood on Hunting (London: Bloomsbury, 1987);
The Last of the Duchess (London: Macmillan, 1995).

Caroline Blackwood's writing career, which occupied little more than a dozen years, produced noteworthy contributions in several genres. Her books include two collections of stories and journalistic pieces, four novels, a biographical study, and a cookbook. Her novels won almost unanimous praise from the critics, along with some wry expressions of discomfiture. Her first book, *For All That I Found There* (1973), provoked a chorus of shudders at her pessimism and misanthropy. The review in *TLS: The Times Literary Supplement* was headed "Hopeless Cases" and asserted: "reading them consecutively one can only repeat, how near the precipice this time?" Francis King in the *Sunday Telegraph* characterized the "constant theme" of the stories as "destructiveness." Gabriele Annan in the *Listener* described it as "the unbearable," remarking that "she does not seem to like human beings at all." Reviewing Blackwood's latest novel in the light of her whole career, Peter Kemp in the *Listener* began: "Wounds appall and fascinate Caroline

Caroline Blackwood at the time of The Last of the Duchess
(photograph © by Sara Barrett)

Blackwood: her imagination can hardly tear itself away from them." Carolyn Gaiser found in the same novel "a sunniness that manages to be believable without ever becoming sentimental." Her material is anguish, dementia, and despair–injuries of all kinds, insanity, rape, murder, internecine marriages, a disastrous face-lift, and suicidal isolation. Her distinctive power is to direct an unflinching gaze at the intolerable and convey it in elegant, witty, and dispassionate prose.

Caroline Blackwood was born on 16 July 1931, the daughter of an Irish peer, Basil Sheridan Hamilton-Temple-Blackwood, fourth Marquess of Dufferin and Ava, and his wife, Maureen Guinness, Marchioness of Dufferin and Ava. On her father's side she was descended from the dramatist Richard Brinsley Sheridan. She grew up in the beautiful, crumbling, leaky ancestral mansion, Clandeboye, in County Down, the basis for the white elephant of a stately home in *Great Granny Webster* (1977). She recalled Clandeboye as a magical place to be a child. Yet, as an adult she remembered the tedium of Northern Ireland, described her childhood as too painful to talk about, and dismissed the estate in *Great Granny Webster* as "so emotionally and financially draining that, as was obvious to any outsider, it should have long ago been sold."

Blackwood's secondary education was at an English boarding school, and she did not live in Northern Ireland after she was seventeen. She seemed to share some of the detachment of the Anglo-Irish nobility she describes in *Great Granny Webster*. The narrator's grandfather has been educated in England, has sent his children to English schools, reads only English newspapers, and looks forward perpetually to the visits from England of his more loyal and stoic friends. Trapped in Ireland, he "lived in Dunmartin Hall as if it was an English island and he was a man who had been shipwrecked." Blackwood also writes of the province and its doomed, dotty inhabitants in *For All That I Found There*. This collection is organized under three headings, "Fiction," "Fact," and "Ulster." The pieces in the Ulster section are autobiographical. They include an account of the young Caroline's wartime experience of being the only girl at a Protestant boys' school, where she therefore invited, along with the new boys and the neighboring Catholic children, the attention of the school bully. In "Memories of Ulster" she recalls how the Northern Ireland of her youth seemed the archetypal place where nothing would ever happen; she wonders if the troubles in Northern Ireland are in part inhabitants' rebellion against their "internment" in the province. Internment, in all its guises, is a potent theme in her later work.

In her early twenties Blackwood married painter Lucian Freud; his portrait of her, reproduced on the dust jacket of *The Stepdaughter* (1976), shows a young woman of remarkable childlike beauty with a steady gaze and a vulnerable mouth. For a period during her marriage to Freud, Cyril Connolly considered the "good-looking and aristocratic young woman"—whose father had been his schoolmate at Eton—his "muse," as Clive Fisher reports in his biography of Connolly. This marriage ended in divorce. In her late twenties she married American composer Israel Citkovitz, with whom she lived in New York and had three daughters; this marriage also did not last. In 1970 the poet Robert Lowell, then married to his second wife, Elizabeth Hardwick, arrived in England to take up a visiting academic post. He and Blackwood had met four years

before in New York. In *The Dolphin* (1973) Lowell wrote of their love affair, his breakdown and hospital confinement, and the end of his marriage to Hardwick. In one poem of this volume, Caroline, with her "Alice-in-Wonderland straight gold hair, / fair-featured, curve and bone," appears as a mermaid, only half human, symbolic of both love and art. The section titled "Marriage" celebrates their love and the birth of their son, Robert Sheridan, in 1971. In October 1972, after his divorce from Hardwick, Lowell and Blackwood were married. For the rest of his life Lowell continued to teach one semester a year at Harvard so that their time was divided between the United States, Lowell's English country house, Milgate, in Kent, and their London home in Redcliffe Square, Earls Court.

Blackwood's marriage to Lowell coincided with an apparent development in creativity. Blackwood had previously published only journalism, some of which was collected in her first book, *For All That I Found There*. As well as the pieces on Ulster, there are fact and fiction sections, categories that are not sharply demarcated in Blackwood's imagination. The fiction shines with a documentary clarity, and the facts are surreal in their extravagance. The stories are cool vignettes of human vanity, lovelessness, and cruelty; most of them deal, directly or obliquely, with the failures of marriage. One was selected by several reviewers as emblematic of the author: an account of a woman recovering from a face-lift operation that has left her unable to weep or to close her eyes. The factual section includes sardonic, rearguard appraisals of the beatniks, the women's movement, and a progressive school in Harlem. One piece seems characteristic and is frequently recalled in reviews of her later work: an agonizing account of a hospital burns unit, in which one of Blackwood's daughters was a patient.

The Stepdaughter, Blackwood's first novel, was undertaken at her publisher's suggestion. Like all her novels, it can be seen as a modern variation on an established form. It is a miniature epistolary novel that explores the conscience of a threatened and isolated woman. Susan Salter in *Contemporary Authors* calls it "the kind of psychological drama that characterizes the best of her style."

Blackwood's character K has lost her moral and social moorings. The novel is nudged toward modernism by its reference to Franz Kafka's hero and by its brevity—it is one hundred pages long. "People don't really read long books," Blackwood said, and her novel indicates that perhaps their attention span for other human beings is similarly limited. K has been abandoned by her husband in a luxurious penthouse apartment in New York with her small child, her obese and withdrawn stepdaughter, and her maltreated au pair girl. She scarcely speaks to this suffering and neglected trio, but instead writes letters into the void to an imaginary confidant. In these missives K distills her resentment, jealousy, and—most of all—self-hatred. She dislikes herself as much as she loathes her hideous and silent stepdaughter, the symbol of her blighted marriage and her husband's escape.

K is interned: in her apartment, where she also imprisons the other inmates; in the straitened circumstances of her life; and in her own foul and apparently immutable personality. She is not completely the prisoner of her own nature, however. When she finally talks with her stepdaughter, Renata proves to have her own knowledge and perspective to contribute. In the last pages of her book K experiences a change of heart, but it is too late. Ignorant that her stepmother is now prepared to love her, Renata runs away into another freezing and dangerous world outside. The novel ends: "Will only write again if I have good news." Blackwood observed that she could not begin a story until she knew exactly how it would end; her characters certainly seem like hostages of inevitability.

The Stepdaughter was hailed by the reviewer for the *Guardian* as a "small epic of modern neurosis" and was cited by several newspapers in the "Critics' Choice" columns at the end of the year. James Price called it "a notable contribution to the women's movement" as well as "a philosophical and religious work." It was a finalist for the S. E. Arts Literature Prize and was awarded the 1976 David Higham Prize for the best novel of the year.

Great Granny Webster, Blackwood's next novel, is a condensed family chronicle encapsulating the history of four generations in less than one hundred pages. It ends with the funeral of the dour great-grandmother, whose energies have been devoted since 1894 to the merest and most joyless survival. The novel moves through a series of episodes rather than a plot: the great-granddaughter's miserable stay with the grim old lady whose life is restricted to her straight-backed chair and a daily ride in a closed car; ravishing and hedonistic Aunt Lavinia's account of her suicide attempt; the grandparents in their rotting Irish mansion; the grandmother's insanity "in the prison of her marriage"; and the macabrely comic funeral. The form suggests that delighted annals of the family would be redundant. These vignettes tell everything about the characters, frozen in their inheritance. Great Granny sits for decades, rigid in her excruciating chair; she will remain fixed thus in the narrator's memory. Aunt Lavinia will successfully commit suicide when the amusements pall. The same meal is served for lunch and dinner by the helpless cooks in the uncontrollable stately home. The roof will leak forever. Everyone is imprisoned. Out of this bleakly deter-

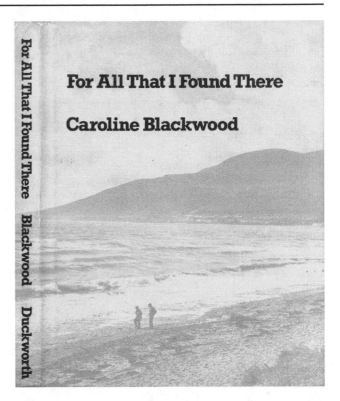

Dust jacket for Blackwood's first book, a short-story collection published in 1973

ministic vision, Blackwood creates an elegant and unforgettable comedy.

Great Granny Webster received favorable response from critics. A typical comment is that of the *Sunday Telegraph* reviewer: "Her world is small and her treatment witty but her vision is drawn from outer darkness." Karl Miller suggested that *Great Granny Webster* had been a successful novel in England both because "the appetite for the eccentricities and sufferings of the privileged never sleeps" and because "without being, in any extensive way, artless or careless, it reads like a long and colorful letter, and has the force of an eager unburdening." The novel was shortlisted for the 1977 Booker Prize.

By 1977 Blackwood's marriage to Lowell had developed problems. He returned to New York and in September died of a heart attack in a taxicab. This loss was followed by other bereavements: the death of Blackwood's second husband, Israel Citkovitz, and the accidental death of her eldest daughter, who had become a drug addict. Perhaps these tragic events contributed to the darkest and most violent of her fictions. Blackwood's third novel, *The Fate of Mary Rose* (1981), teases the reader by its resemblance to a conventional thriller. It is narrated by Rowan Anderson, a historian, whose unloved wife, Cressida, and daughter, Mary Rose, live in Beckham, a charming and historic village,

CORRIGAN

Caroline Blackwood

Provisional publication date: September 1984
Provisional publication price: £8.95

HEINEMANN : LONDON

Paper wrapper for a proof copy of Blackwood's novel about a confidence man who gives a grieving widow a new zest for life

which he occasionally visits. A child from the neighboring housing project is raped and murdered on a night of which Rowan—who can only get through weekends with his family by drinking continuously—remembers nothing. This mystery form encloses questions as disturbing as the identity of the murderer. Cressida, the obsessively pure wife, attempts to create in Beckham a perfect environment for Mary Rose, whose name recalls the sugary, retarded innocence of the enchanted child wife in J. M. Barrie's play of the same name. The crime and the reactions to it reveal that the serpent also lives in this commuter's Eden, however. The detached and rational historian proves to have little understanding of causality, the logic by which his unloved child is unlovable. Puzzled by her drabness, the father does not see that his own lack of interest produces it. He is working on a study of a woman engineer but makes no effort to empathize with the women in his own life. The rape inflames the antagonism between the sexes: the deranged Cressida is the most extreme example of the women's punitive fear and hatred of men. Mary Rose is

destroyed by her mother's paranoia and her father's indifference, as much a victim as the murdered girl. Finally Rowan, like the narrator of *The Stepdaughter,* experiences a change of heart that comes too late to save his child.

The novel was warmly received by the critics, who were equally impressed by its poise and its power to disturb. Shelley Cox wrote in *Library Journal:* "a minutely crafted, intensely unsettling study of three emotionally isolated people, bound in a parody of family life . . . Blackwood expertly plays on the tensions between surface normality and inner emptiness, skillfully exposing the underside of 'normal' family relations." Patricia Craig in *TLS: The Times Literary Supplement* observed: "Caroline Blackwood joins that small group of distinguished woman novelists . . . whose task is to comment obliquely on the dangers and infirmities of contemporary life."

In addition to her novels, Blackwood (with "Anna Haycraft," the novelist Alice Thomas Ellis) completed a cookbook, *Darling, You Shouldn't Have Gone to So Much Trouble* (1980). In rebellion against the traditional, elaborate cooking fashionable in the 1960s, the editors offer shortcut, sophisticated recipes confided to them by various friends and celebrities; the book is aimed at the busy career woman who wants to talk and drink as well as cook. After Blackwood's three fictional exposés of family life, one reviewer expressed misgivings at the thought of her in the kitchen; another wrote a vehemently purist denunciation of corner-cutting and instant potatoes. The book sold well, however, and went through several reprintings.

The Last of the Duchess was written in 1980 but not published until 1995, after the death of Maitre Blum, lawyer to the duchess of Windsor. In 1980 the *Sunday Times* (London) asked Blackwood to write an article about the duchess and to accompany Lord Snowdon to Paris to photograph her. It soon became clear that Maitre Blum would not permit access to the ailing duchess and that almost nobody had seen her for some years. Blackwood even wondered if the duchess were dead. Intrigued, she decided to interview the possessive, eighty-four-year-old lawyer. Maitre Blum's loyalty, vanity, and creativity were clear at their first meeting. Her duchess was a teetotaler who hated nightclubs. The couple liked to stay home in the evenings listening to classical music and reading good books and, though not rich, donated large sums to charity. She threatened to kill Blackwood if she wrote an article unfavorable to the duchess. Blackwood relates further improbable conversations with Maitre Blum and interviews various friends and acquaintances of the Windsors, whose memories of them differ considerably and whose own lives are often pitiful. The book is as much a series of

Dust jacket for Blackwood's nonfiction work about the former Wallis Warfield Simpson, Duchess of Windsor

appalled vignettes of old age as an "unorthodox biography."

Reviewers such as Andrew Barrow were seduced by its "zest, spikiness, outrageous black humour" but cautious about the "extremely subjective account which makes no pretence to biographical correctness or formality. It is written throughout with a kind of wide-eyed schoolgirlish innocence—and mounting sense of horror. Various inaccuracies and solecisms only serve to in-crease the strangeness of it all." Some questioned Blackwood's central thesis that Maitre Blum was in love with the duchess. Zoe Heller concluded: "The Freudian irony at the heart of this book is that Blackwood commits exactly those crimes of which she accuses her subject—recklessly projecting the lurid stuff of her own fantasies and showing herself time and again indifferent to the evidence of a more mundane reality."

Goodnight Sweet Ladies (1983) is a collection of stories about women, exploring again Blackwood's favorite themes of the trapped and the dying. The characters in "Matron," "Olga," "Addy," "Mrs Taft," and "Anglelica" are immured in the terminal ward, the graveyard, and awful social events that feel equally desperate. Families and lovers give no comfort: a son is bitterly jealous of his mother's ravaged charm, even as she nears death; a meeting between a woman and the illegitimate child she has tried to forget is disastrous; a man pretends loyalty to the memory of a fictitious dead wife to protect him from serious relationships with other women; an actress whose career was really ended by stage fright chooses to blame her failure on the birth of her daughter; and a young officer killed in World War I, only a name in the cemetery, seems preferable to any living man. One reviewer made the apt analogy: "The humour is as black as the grave."

The same themes of bereavement and disability recur in *Corrigan* (1984), Blackwood's longest and most ambitious novel, but they are treated with surprising warmth and optimism. Corrigan the Irish "cripple" rolls in a wheelchair into the life of widowed Mrs. Blunt, more genuinely disabled by grief for her husband, the Colonel. He puts on a virtuoso performance and galvanizes her into making large contributions for a replacement wheelchair and to St Crispin's "home for the handicapped" (which turns out to be a greasy pancake shop). He literally breaks up Mrs. Blunt's home: she covers the steps to her exquisite old house with a shocking ramp for his wheelchair and sacrifices her drawing room and hall with its magnificent paneling to create a ground-floor apartment for him. His effect is more creative than destructive, however: Mrs. Blunt designs the ramp herself, at last learns to drive, discovers unexpected entrepreneurial skills to place at the disposal of St Crispin's, and enjoys drinking her husband's favorite wines with Corrigan. The spurious cripple cures the symbolic cripple. Mrs. Blunt's daughter and son-in-law are outraged, disapproving, and anxious about her will. Mrs. Murphy, the obstreperous Irish cleaning lady, sees through Corrigan, as did Mrs. Blunt, the reader learns after her death. Blackwood was too scarred by her own losses to think the bereaved should be fastidious about the sources of consolation and cure.

Arguably Blackwood's best novel, *Corrigan* was well received by the critics. Some praised the comic energy of the narrative and its antihero. Penelope Lively, writing in the *Listener,* described it as "manic, at times demonic." Some found a moral purpose in the demonism. Carolyn Gaiser said that the author's "sly wit and her affection for her characters brings a glow to these pages," and Nicholas Spicer connected the qualities valorized in *Corrigan*–"ingenuousness, the immediate, means over ends"–with the virtues demonstrated in her next book, *On the Perimeter* (1984).

On the Perimeter is an account of a visit to Greenham Common, the site of an occupation by the Women's Peace Movement in protest against the nearby nuclear-missile base. Blackwood powerfully conveys the discomfort and boredom of life in the camp, the fortitude of the women who endured it, and the obscene hostility they provoked in soldiers guarding the base and residents of the neighborhood. Reviewers commended the book's vividness while noting, with varying degrees of disapproval, the lack of argument on this apocalyptic dilemma.

In the Pink, Caroline Blackwood on Hunting (1987) confronts a highly controversial subject with an apparently innocent neutrality. It consists of sketches and impressions of people (hunters, car-hunters, antihunters), of the beauty of the meet on a sunny frosty morning, of clothes, children, accidents, and legends. Anecdotes abound: of the seventy-eight-year-old Lord Longford, who had not ridden for forty years, rashly saying in Ireland that he would love to hunt and being forced into it by generous hosts and thrown by a mettlesome horse; of Prince Charles scandalously appearing in a hat secured with pink elastic; and of a crippled old enthusiast continuing to hunt vicariously by telephone. The book does not offer a history, overview, or debate. Lady Caroline rode with the North Down Harriers in her Irish girlhood and "had never thought of hunting as very cruel" because "the hare never seemed to get caught." Most reviewers enjoyed *In the Pink* and praised its impartiality. Yet, although Blackwood vividly conveys the attractions of the hunt and observes cruelty in the antihunting lobby both to humans and animals, her opposition to the sport is clear. Her last chapter, on myths and legends, concludes: "The primitive fables of the fox-hunt in which the Devil appears as the beautiful huntsman, and the evil tempter . . . appear to spring from a buried guilt that lies rock-heavy on the human conscience. This conscience finds it insufferable and devilish that the human being can derive quite so much pleasure from causing pain to a defenceless animal."

In 1996 Caroline Blackwood decided to move to New York, where she began "Tamara," a novel about a transsexual, a person trapped in the wrong body. The work was not finished, as Blackwood succumbed to cancer. Her friends and family were moved by the grace and patience with which she accepted terminal illness. She was overjoyed by the news that her daughter Evgenia was expecting a baby, her first grandchild. She died on 14 February 1996.

References:

David S. Gewanter, "Child of Collaboration: Robert Lowell's Dolphin," *Modern Philology,* 93 (November 1995): 178–203;

Michael Kimmelman, "Titled Bohemian: Caroline Blackwood," *New York Times Magazine,* 2 April 1995, pp. 32–36.

Malcolm Bradbury

(7 September 1932 –)

Merritt Moseley
University of North Carolina at Asheville

See also the Bradbury entry in *DLB 14: British Novelists Since 1960.*

BOOKS: *Eating People Is Wrong* (London: Secker & Warburg, 1959; New York: Knopf, 1960);

Phogey!; or, How to Have Class in a Classless Society (London: Parrish, 1960); republished with *All Dressed Up and Nowhere to Go: The Poor Man's Guide to the Affluent Society* as *All Dressed Up and Nowhere to Go* (London: Joseph, 1982);

All Dressed Up and Nowhere to Go: The Poor Man's Guide to the Affluent Society (London: Parrish, 1962); republished with *Phogey!* as *All Dressed Up and Nowhere to Go* (London: Joseph, 1982);

Evelyn Waugh (Edinburgh: Oliver & Boyd, 1964);

Stepping Westward (London: Secker & Warburg, 1965; Boston: Houghton Mifflin, 1966);

Two Poets, by Bradbury and Allan Rodway (Nottingham: Byron Press, 1966);

What Is a Novel? (London: Edward Arnold, 1969);

The Social Context of Modern English Literature (Oxford: Blackwell, 1971; New York: Schocken, 1971);

Possibilities: Essays on the State of the Novel (London & New York: Oxford University Press, 1973);

The History Man (London: Secker & Warburg, 1975; Boston: Houghton Mifflin, 1976);

Who Do You Think You Are? Stories and Parodies (London: Secker & Warburg, 1976);

The Outland Dart: American Writers and European Modernism (London: Oxford University Press, 1978);

Saul Bellow (London & New York: Methuen, 1982);

The After Dinner Game: Three Plays for Television, by Bradbury and Christopher Bigsby (London: Arrow, 1982);

The Expatriate Tradition in American Literature (Durham, U.K.: British Association for American Studies, 1982);

Rates of Exchange (London: Secker & Warburg, 1983; New York: Knopf, 1983);

Malcolm Bradbury at the time of Rates of Exchange *(photograph © 1983 by Jerry Bauer)*

The Modern American Novel (Oxford & New York: Oxford University Press, 1983; revised, 1991);

Why Come to Slaka? (London: Secker & Warburg, 1986; New York: Penguin, 1991);

Cuts: A Very Short Novel (London: Hutchinson, 1987; New York & San Francisco: Harper & Row, 1987);

No, Not Bloomsbury (London: Deutsch, 1987; New York: Columbia University Press, 1988);

My Strange Quest for Mensonge: Structuralism's Hidden Hero (London: Deutsch, 1987; New York: Penguin, 1988);

The Modern World: Ten Great Writers (London: Secker & Warburg, 1988; New York: Viking, 1989);

Unsent Letters: Irreverent Notes from a Literary Life (London: Deutsch, 1988; New York: Viking, 1988);

From Puritanism to Postmodernism: A History of American Literature, by Bradbury and Richard Ruland (London: Routledge, 1991; New York: Viking, 1991);

Doctor Criminale (London: Secker & Warburg, 1992; New York: Viking, 1992);

The Modern British Novel (London: Secker & Warburg, 1993; London & New York: Penguin, 1993);

Dangerous Pilgrimages: Transatlantic Mythologies and the Novel (London: Secker & Warburg, 1995; New York: Viking, 1996);

Inside Trading: A Comedy in Three Acts (London & Portsmouth, N.H.: Methuen Drama, 1997)

PLAY PRODUCTIONS: *Between These Four Walls,* by Bradbury, David Lodge, and James Duckett, Birmingham, Birmingham Repertory Theatre, November 1963;

Slap in the Middle, by Bradbury, Lodge, and Duckett, Birmingham, Birmingham Repertory Company, October 1965;

Inside Trading, Norwich, Norwich Playhouse, 28 November 1996.

TELEVISION: *The After Dinner Game,* by Bradbury and Christopher Bigsby, BBC1, 16 January 1975;

"Stones," *The Mind Beyond,* by Bradbury and Bigsby, BBC, 1976;

Love on a Gunboat, BBC1, 4 January 1977;

The Enigma, adapted from a story by John Fowles, BBC, 9 February 1980;

Standing in for Henry, BBC1, December 1980;

Blott on the Landscape, adapted from the novel by Tom Sharpe, BBC2, January–February 1985;

Porterhouse Blue, adapted from the novel by Sharpe, Channel 4, 1987;

Imaginary Friends, adapted from the novel by Alison Lurie, ITV, June 1987;

Anything More Would Be Greedy (series), ITV, July–August 1989;

The Gravy Train, Channel 4, July–August 1990;

The Green Man, adapted from the novel by Kingsley Amis, BBC1, June 1990;

The Gravy Train Goes East, Channel 4, October 1991;

Cold Comfort Farm, adapted from the novel by Stella Gibbons, BBC1, 1 January 1995;

An Autumn Shroud, adapted from the novel by Reginald Hill, BBC1, 30 March 1996;

Ruling Passion and Killing Kindness, adapted from the novels by Hill, BBC1, June 1997.

RADIO: *Paris France,* BBC, Third Programme, February 1960;

This Sporting Life, by Bradbury and Elizabeth Bradbury, adapted from the novel by David Storey, BBC, 1974;

Scenes from Provincial Life, by Bradbury and Elizabeth Bradbury, adapted from the novel by William Cooper, BBC, Radio 4, 1975;

Scenes from Married Life, by Bradbury and Elizabeth Bradbury, adapted from the novel by Cooper, BBC, Radio 4, 1976;

Patterson, by Bradbury and Christopher Bigsby, BBC, Radio 4, 1981;

Congress, BBC, Radio 3, 1981;

See a Friend This Weekend, BBC, Radio 3, 1985.

OTHER: *Forster: A Collection of Critical Essays,* edited by Bradbury (Englewood Cliffs, N.J.: Prentice-Hall, 1966);

E. M. Forster: "A Passage to India," a Casebook, edited by Bradbury (London: Macmillan, 1970);

The Penguin Companion to Literature, vol 3: United States and Latin America, edited by Bradbury and Eric Mottram (Harmondsworth, U.K.: Penguin, 1971; New York: McGraw-Hill, 1971);

The American Novel and the Nineteen Twenties, edited by Bradbury and David Palmer (London: Edward Arnold, 1971);

Victorian Poetry, edited by Bradbury and Palmer (London: Edward Arnold, 1972);

Modernism: 1890–1930, edited by Bradbury and J. W. McFarlane (Harmondsworth, U.K.: Penguin, 1976; Atlantic Highlands, N.J.: Humanities Press, 1978);

The Novel Today: Contemporary Writers on Modern Fiction, edited by Bradbury (Manchester, U.K.: Manchester University Press, 1977; Totowa, N.J.: Rowman & Littlefield, 1977);

The Contemporary English Novel, edited by Bradbury and Palmer (London: Edward Arnold, 1979; New York: Holmes & Meier, 1980);

Introduction to American Studies, edited by Bradbury and Howard Temperley (London & New York: Longman, 1981);

Jay N. Halio, ed., *Dictionary of Literary Biography 14: British Novelists Since 1960,* foreword by Bradbury (Detroit: Gale Research, 1983);

Contemporary American Fiction, edited by Bradbury (London & Baltimore: Edward Arnold, 1987);

The Penguin Book of Modern British Short Stories, edited by Bradbury (Harmondsworth, U.K.: Penguin, 1987; New York: Viking, 1987);

New Writing, edited by Bradbury and Judy Cooke (London: Minerva, 1992);

New Writing 2, edited by Bradbury and Andrew Motion (London: Minerva, 1993);

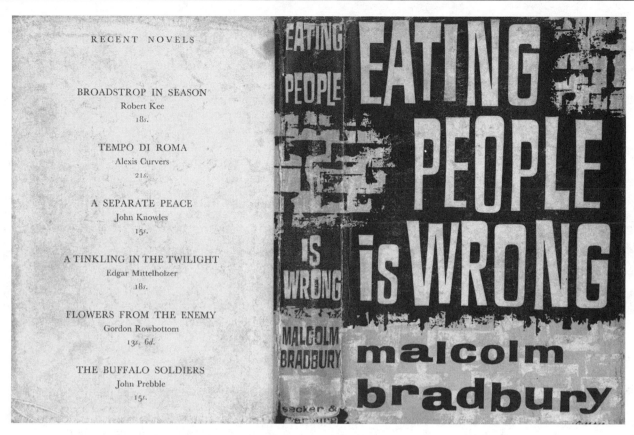

RECENT NOVELS

BROADSTROP IN SEASON
Robert Kee
18s.

TEMPO DI ROMA
Alexis Curvers
21s.

A SEPARATE PEACE
John Knowles
15s.

A TINKLING IN THE TWILIGHT
Edgar Mittelholzer
18s.

FLOWERS FROM THE ENEMY
Gordon Rowbottom
13s. 6d.

THE BUFFALO SOLDIERS
John Prebble
15s.

Dust jacket for Bradbury's first book, a comic novel about an indecisive professor (Collection of William Cagle)

Present Laughter: An Anthology of Modern Comic Fiction,
edited by Bradbury (London: Weidenfeld &
Nicolson, 1994);
Class Work: The Best of Contemporary Short Fiction, edited by
Bradbury (London: Hodder & Stoughton, 1995);
The Atlas of Literature, edited by Bradbury (London &
New York: De Agostini, 1996).

Malcolm Bradbury has been one of the central
figures in British literature since 1960. As a critic, editor,
commentator, entrepreneur, anthologist, and judge for
fiction awards he has tirelessly promoted the vitality
and importance of contemporary fiction, often in the
face of disparagement or declarations that the novel is
dead. As a prolific fiction writer himself, he has written
some of the most incisive and entertaining novels of his
time; beginning as an author of "campus fictions," he
has broadened the scope of his work—in parallel with
his own burgeoning career as critic, pundit, and adap-
tor—so that it may be said to chart the course of the past
forty years in the life of the British literary intellectual.
Further, he helped to found the writing program at the
University of East Anglia, where he taught from 1970
until 1985. The program—as indicated by such gradu-

ates as Ian McEwan, Kazuo Ishiguro, and Rose Tremain—has proven to be influential. Taken as a whole, his
fiction, along with his plays, works of humor and social
commentary, literary histories, and original television
dramas, demonstrate that Bradbury is a busy, versatile,
and important man of letters.

Malcolm Stanley Bradbury was born in Sheffield,
England, on 7 September 1932, the son of Arthur and
Doris (Marshall) Bradbury. His father worked for the
railway in London from about 1934 to 1941, while the
Bradburys lived in the nearby suburbs. Moving back to
Sheffield, they lived through the bombings of World
War II, described by Bradbury as "terror by night and
disturbance by day." Bradbury received a B.A. with
first-class honors from University College, Leicester, in
1953. In 1955 he received an M.A. from the University
of London; he also has a Ph.D. from the University of
Manchester, received in 1964, and has pursued further
graduate study at Indiana University and Yale. He has
received honorary degrees from the Universities of
Leicester, Birmingham, Hull, and Nottingham. In 1959
he married Elizabeth Salt. They have two sons.

A lifelong teacher in higher education, Bradbury
began his career as a staff tutor in literature and drama

in the Department of Adult Education at the University of Hull from 1959 to 1961, where he was employed when his first novel, *Eating People Is Wrong* (1959), appeared. In 1961 he became a lecturer in English language and literature at the University of Birmingham. During his four years there he became friends with David Lodge, another author of campus novels and a sometime collaborator. Lodge attributes his own ability to write humor to his work with Bradbury on comic revues: "My association with Malcolm Bradbury, and the example of his own work in comedy, was therefore a crucial factor in this development in my writing. . . . A few years later, Malcolm left Birmingham for the University of East Anglia. . . . We both regretted the separation, but it was probably a necessary one for the healthy development of our respective literary careers. We are often enough linked, not to say confused, in the public mind, as it is." Both Bradbury and Lodge make playful use of this confusion in their own books, as when an Eastern European in Bradbury's *Rates of Exchange* (1983) asks about "a campus writer Brodge . . . Who wrote *Changing Westward?*"

In 1965 Bradbury moved to the University of East Anglia, one of Britain's postwar (sometimes called "white tile") universities, located in Norwich. He was successively lecturer, senior lecturer, reader in English, and then professor of American studies at the university, becoming a professorial fellow in 1994 and retiring in 1995. In 1970 he founded in collaboration with Angus Wilson, another novelist then teaching at the university, the writing program, an unusual project in Britain, where suspicion of teaching creative writing has always been strong. Ian McEwan, the first graduate of the program, commented twenty-five years later: "I know very few novelists who have not been to the University of East Anglia to read, and it is largely through Malcolm Bradbury that Norwich has gained its international reputation as a place where writers and would-be writers alike are treated well."

During his years at East Anglia, Bradbury has been a frequent visitor to other campuses, having been a visiting professor at Oxford, the University of California at Davis, the University of Zurich, Washington University in St. Louis, and two universities in Australia, in addition to many shorter residencies. Bemused students at the University of East Anglia are supposed to have created the riddle: "Q: What's the difference between God and Malcolm Bradbury? A: God is everywhere; Malcolm Bradbury is everywhere but UEA." Bradbury revised this joke in his *Doctor Criminale* (1992), about a bafflingly universal Eastern European man of letters: "'What is the difference between God and Bazlo Criminale?' 'God is everywhere, Criminale is everywhere but here.'"

In the 1980s Bradbury began adapting fiction for television and film (he had already written several original television plays); he has written scripts made from two of Tom Sharpe's novels, Alison Lurie's *Imaginary Friends* (1967), Kingsley Amis's *The Green Man* (1969), Stella Gibbons's *Cold Comfort Farm* (1932), and three television series, including *The Gravy Train Goes East* (1991), which won a Monte Carlo Award. He chaired the judging panel for the Booker Prize for fiction in 1981 and the Whitbread Prize in 1997. In 1991 he was made a Companion of the Order of the British Empire.

Though he has written no full-length autobiography, Bradbury has often commented on the circumstances behind his novels. His fullest account of the origins of his first novel is in *No, Not Bloomsbury* (1987):

> I began my first novel, as a brylcreemed youth, in the early Fifties, and for a good reason: my experience at the time had been that of some portable identikit anti-hero from everybody's Fifties novel. I grew up down in the lower middle class and in the provinces, a kind of compound of Jim Dixon, Joe Lampton, Arthur Seaton and Billy Liar. I went in 1944 to grammar school, a product of the Butler Education Act, a Richard Hoggart scholarship boy. From there I went as first generation student to a redbrick university, one of the reddest, an institution which started life as the local lunatic asylum and sat across from the local cemetery; Philip Larkin was a librarian, Kingsley Amis was said to be writing some novel about it. Naturally, since I seemed to be living the Fifties novel, I started writing it. Fifties novels were all set either in provincial redbrick universities or around a rugby club in Bradford, and I chose the first, knowing little about rugby. I wrote it about liberal anxieties, and in the prevailing spirit of moral seriousness.

Though morally serious, *Eating People Is Wrong* is a comedy. Moreover, being about "liberal anxieties," it announces a theme that motivates much of Bradbury's writing, both fiction and nonfiction: a consideration of the plight of liberalism and the liberal in the modern world. The main character, forty-year-old Stuart Treece, has been described as a projection of the concerns of the twenty-year-old author. He is head of English at a provincial university—in the English terminology, "red brick," meaning one of the municipal universities set up in the nineteenth and twentieth centuries, such as Sheffield, Birmingham, Nottingham, Liverpool, and Leicester, Bradbury's alma mater, which shares with this fictional university its location in the former city lunatic asylum. Treece is a self-conscious liberal: "It is well I am a liberal, and can love all men, thought Treece; for if I were not, I doubt if I could." His liberalism implies tolerance, decency, being nice to people, and seeing all sides of the question. As the novel demonstrates, it also makes him passive, inde-

*Dust jacket for Bradbury's second novel, about a British novelist's experiences as writer in residence at an American university
(Collection of William Cagle)*

cisive, and weak. His weakness is demonstrated in his relations with students, particularly two "difficult" ones: an older man named Louis Bates, a terrible misfit who clamors for special treatment and ends up in a mental hospital, and an African student, Mr. Eborabelosa, guilty of various offenses against decorum such as keeping animals in his rooms. In neither case can Treece decide on a firm course of action, and his failure to do so proves disastrous.

Likewise, Treece's liberalism has a detrimental effect on his personal relationships; feeling that relationships are the most important part of life somehow makes him bad at them. He has an affair with Emma Fielding, a postgraduate student and a fellow liberal who is troubled by both Bates and Eborabelosa. When Emma eventually denounces him for his shortcomings, Treece liberally sees her point: "I'm simply parasitic on other people and compelled to be so by a force I can't even explain, a lack of responsibility to other people and an inability to form proper relationships. And it's so cruel, because responsibility and relationships are the things I believe in so deeply; they are all there is. I've always believed, you know, in my own goodness, and

thought I could never do anything wrong in the things of love. Yet is seems to me that I have."

The plot of *Eating People Is Wrong* is patchy. Bates and Eborabelosa come to different sorts of grief: Bates falls into the Avon while trying to seduce Emma in a boat, and Eborabelosa suffers a racist assault. A visiting "angry young man" makes Treece feel old, feeble, and priggishly principled. Eventually he has to go into the hospital, and the novel ends with him there, gloomily, fearing he may never escape. The hospital ending was inspired partly by Bradbury's own hospitalization with a serious heart condition, for which he underwent an operation in 1958.

Since 1958 Bradbury has published many more works of literary criticism than novels, of which he seemed to produce no more than one per decade. He has commented on this fact: "it is true that I do tend to think of books as objects for particular cultural periods, partly because I think all writers do anyway, but also because I write very slowly and therefore it takes me almost a decade to write one." Thus his second novel, *Stepping Westward,* did not appear until 1965.

In the meantime he published a study of Evelyn Waugh in 1964 and wrote many humorous pieces, which were published in periodicals such as *Punch* and then collected in two books, *Phogey!; or, How to Have Class in a Classless Society* (1960) and *All Dressed Up and Nowhere to Go: The Poor Man's Guide to the Affluent Society* (1962). These two were republished in 1982 as *All Dressed Up and Nowhere to Go*. This writing is funny, thoughtful, humane, and discriminating. It demonstrates quite clearly the way in which Bradbury, though he makes fun of sociologists here and elsewhere, is a sort of nonstatistical sociologist of postwar Britain. In his introduction he explains that coming back from America had provoked a heightened awareness of cultural contrasts: "I began an American novel, and also, in a frenzy of invention, started writing a number of humorous articles for magazines on both sides of the Atlantic." One chapter, "A Portpholio of Phogeys," illustrates his satiric take on traditional English society (which he steadily contrasts with a consumer society, presumably one more like America): the Phogey Author "read *Lucky Jim* and remarked that if this were what things were coming to he was glad he hadn't lived to see it. The point of this comment was that writers are traditionally upper middle; everyone knows that, and their job as 'civilised beings,' is to give delight, not go on about what they *think*." It is an odd fact that, though all his novels are comedies of some sort, Bradbury is actually much funnier in his nonfiction—such as these books or *Unsent Letters* (1988)—and his parodies included in *Who Do You Think You Are?* (1976) than in any of the novels; *All Dressed Up and Nowhere to Go* manages to be simultaneously funnier and more incisive about the United States than *Stepping Westward*, which relies on the same experience.

Bradbury has called *Stepping Westward* "Henry James in reverse, British puritan innocence seeking American experience." This formulation is explicitly applied to the novel's English main character, James Walker, a Nottingham novelist who goes to America as writer in residence at Benedict Arnold University.

There are some odd features in Bradbury's picture of America. The grasp of American idiom and dialect is shaky: a New York longshoreman says of Walker (who has porridge in his hair): "Take a look a' dis kook . . . Whadya tink? That kind guy dey ouh ta sen hem ride back to Yerrup wit a hart kick up du fanny." Other Americans use English idioms like "fish slice" and "bumf."

In *Stepping Westward* Bradbury proposed to explore "the different transatlantic meanings of liberalism"—an obvious continuation of the study of provincial liberalism surviving in the modern world in *Eating People Is Wrong*—though in fact James Walker's liberalism finds itself in conflict with forces that are hardly liberal. He refuses to sign an oath promising not to overthrow the government, for instance, and, though hardly an inflammatory type, creates a cause célèbre by refusing. "All his values were private values, he believed; if

he had political faiths, he had them because they ensured privacy and independence and personal survival, and he had never known what it was to think of himself as an agent in a cause. He was just James Walker, naked as they come; all else was pretence and role-playing." He is used by an Anglophile American named Froelich in campus political schemes; eventually, after souring on Benedict Arnold and an affair with a young female student, he returns six months early to England.

As well as representing liberalism—here as elsewhere in Bradbury's work, the liberal seems to be "right" but ineffectual—Walker is a discriminating academic in futile combat against dull students and almost equally dull American academics. For example, Harris Bourbon, head of the English department and a former Rhodes scholar, explains Walker's composition course to him: "if they're going to get any benefit out of a U at all, and by that I mean intellectual benefit, they've got to be taught to communicate. So here in the English Dep. we run these courses for entering freshmen, tellin' the kids how to talk and write and pass messages on and avoid parkin' where it says 'No Parkin.'" The only other humane, intelligent, and disinterested person at Benedict Arnold is a European émigré who ends up being fired.

Stepping Westward can be seen fruitfully in relation to such Joseph McCarthy–era campus novels as Mary McCarthy's *The Groves of Academe* (1952) and May Sarton's *Faithful Are the Wounds* (1955); Heide Ziegler and Christopher Bigsby, in their *The Radical Imagination and the Liberal Tradition* (1982), compare the novel to Evelyn Waugh's *The Loved One* (1948), another novel with a "mordant view of America" in which an Englishman is baffled and defeated by the crassness of American culture. Perhaps a useful way of reading Bradbury's novel is to discount his own view that it is a realistic text and see it as a symbolic drama pitting two ways of thought and life against each other, in which liberalism—here represented by Walker—struggles fruitlessly against illiberalism and ignorance.

In the ten years between the publication of *Stepping Westward* and the appearance of Bradbury's "seventies" novel, *The History Man* (1975), Bradbury wrote a collaborative book of poems with Allan Rodway (*Two Poets*, 1966) and three important books of literary criticism and scholarship. *What Is a Novel?* (1969) is a personal statement, seventy-two pages long, that includes some explanation for the versatility of the English novelist. *Possibilities: Essays on the State of the Novel* (1973) is a more substantial study in which Bradbury deals with the dichotomy between two major strains in the contemporary novel—the experimental novel and the novel of journalism—and tries to reconcile them. This work is reminiscent of the project of his friend David Lodge, whose *The Novelist at the Crossroads* (1971) posited a

A

TWO

Three days later, on the Monday morning, Howard Kirk wakes up in an
unhappy temper. Surfacing out of unconsciousness and into being, he finds
the space in the bed beside him empty; Barbara is already up. He groans,
and smoothes his hair down, and looks out of the window: a heavy rain is
pouring down, washing dreariness over the damaged houxses. He gets out of
bed and pads along the landing to the bathroom, to sculpt round the elegance
of his Zapata moustache. He plugs his razor into the two little holes
beneath the bleak round globe of the light. His face comes up in the mirror;
in the cool urban sheen of morning he inspects the Condition of Man. It is
unpromising; in the streaky glass, finger-marked by children, k the beaky
face, all manifest discontent, wearing its moustache like a glower, stares
back at him. He touches and presses the flesh into position and rides the
razor over it. A sense of irritated unfulfillment runs through him and he
recalls that last night he and Barbara had not made love. A depression always
on the edge of his mind settles deeper. 'Beside the bathroom window, the rain
washes over the uneven guttering and thumps down onto the gaunt glass of
the Victorian conservatory beneath; no flowers grow there, and it is d deposit
for children's toys. The razor buzzes and downstairs the children yamp in

Page from the typescript for Bradbury's 1975 novel, The History Man *(Collection of Malcolm Bradbury)*

choice between "the nonfiction novel" and "fabulation." John Spurling, reviewing *Possibilities,* commented that Bradbury "tends to equate humanity with liberal realism. Nevertheless, although he often appears to be no more than another advocate for naturalism (which he calls 'realism'), he does make a genuine attempt to occupy the middle ground." Here, as elsewhere, it is stimulating to read Bradbury on the novel primarily because he is so convinced of its possibilities; while many of his contemporaries brood in a "prevailing cultural gloom" on the irrelevance or futility of literary fiction, Bradbury is always willing to celebrate its potential: "as for the scene as a whole, I find it decidedly exciting. . . ." *The Social Context of Modern English Literature* (1971) neatly combines two of the author's main interests, permitting him to show that all literature, even modernism, responds to describable social forces. Partly taking a sociological approach, he discusses urbanization, the publishing world, and other important influences on the production of literature.

During these same years Bradbury wrote plays, often in collaboration. He worked with David Lodge and James Duckett on the first of two satirical revues performed by the Birmingham Repertory company, *Between These Four Walls* (1963) and *Slap in the Middle* (1965). With Christopher Bigsby, a colleague at the University of East Anglia, he wrote *The After Dinner Game,* which was televised in 1975, as well as a radio play, *Patterson* (1981). He collaborated with Elizabeth Bradbury, his wife, on *This Sporting Life* (1974), *Scenes from Provincial Life* (1975), and *Scenes from Married Life* (1976).

The History Man may be Bradbury's best novel to date. It was the first of his novels to be adapted for television, and it won the Heinemann/Royal Society of Literature Award. It even stimulated interest in his earlier novels and helped to establish him as an important novelist as well as critic. While most of his novels, as he professes, could be considered "books about their decades, their themes, ideas, emotions, hypocrisies, intellectual fashions, and preoccupations," *The History Man* is most fully representative of its particular historic context. It is another university novel, this time set at the University of Watermouth, one of the new universities of the 1960s. Though arguably still a comedy, it is clearly different in tone from its two predecessors; Bradbury marks it as the point when "my books became harsher in tone, more elaborate technically." It would be equally plausible to read *The History Man* as tragedy. As Bradbury says, "There is one character whom you can identify with, but she betrays you."

One indication of the difference between *The History Man* and its predecessors is Bradburys adoption of the present tense for its narration, a technique he has used in several works since. In *The History Man* the present tense is appropriate because characters such as the Kirks are without history, without a past; they live in and for the present. A further difference is that most of the characters in *The History Man* are not ineffectual duffers, poseurs, or too ignorant for the work they have undertaken.

The novel begins and ends with plans for a party to be held by Howard Kirk, a sociology professor, and his wife. Howard is depicted as evil, an antihumanist; he is "a thorn in the flesh of the council, a terror to the selfish bourgeoisie, a pressing agent in the Claimants' Union, a focus of responsibility and concern." Howard is a great one for stirring things up: he foments a political uproar on campus by starting a rumor that Professor Mangel, a scholar whose work on genetic inheritance has resulted in his being branded a racist, has been invited to campus and then launching a campaign against the visit on political grounds. When, to demonstrate that the university can tolerate all views, Mangel actually is invited to speak—on the apolitical subject of the familial behavior of rats—a riot ensues, and one of Howard's colleagues and supposed friends is assaulted. Howard persecutes a conservative student who offends his sensibilities, eventually contriving to have him driven from the university, especially after the student files a complaint against Professor Kirk alleging (truthfully) that he is sleeping with a student and giving her good marks.

Howard is fashionably radical, but whether he is committed to any position is unclear; he is certainly a relativist when it suits him. His most deeply felt commitment apparently is to his own sexual freedom. He and his wife supposedly have an understanding, but his regular and casual infidelity seems to be what drives Barbara to a suicide attempt at their end-of-term party.

Bradbury's one sympathetic character in the novel is Annie Callendar, a new lecturer in the English department who seems to see through Howard from the beginning. She penetrates Howard's cant and defends the student he persecutes, who is her advisee. She is the kind of liberal—a "nineteenth-century liberal," as she calls herself—about whom Bradbury often writes. At the Kirks' first party Howard accuses her of having no social conscience, to which she reponds, "I have a conscience. I use it a lot. I think it's a sort of moral conscience. I'm very old-fashioned." "We must modernize you," says Howard.

The novel's tragic quality results from the fact that he does modernize her by seducing and corrupting her. In a final conversation he tells her: "it's the plot of history. It was simply inevitable." Thus, the one character on whom the reader relies to provide a counterweight to the amoral posthumanism of Howard fails in

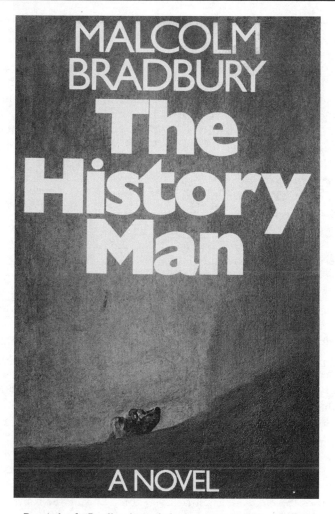

Dust jacket for Bradbury's novel about an amoral sociology professor
(Collection of William Cagle)

the task. Another reason for the chilly quality of the novel is the effaced narration; Bradbury has chosen to eschew almost all inside views and authoritative judgments, has chosen "not to enter the psychology or consciousness of the characters, but to present them from outside by their speech, their signs, their actions, having them reveal themselves by their words and their historical behaviour. . . . The narrative tense is largely the present tense, emphasising the instantaneous and the phenomenal, and reducing causality and explanation."

The History Man is Bradbury's most comprehensive demonstration of the position that the best people lack all conviction while the worst are full of passionate intensity. Howard is not only an adherent of causes that will not stand scrutiny and a totalitarian posing as a liberator; he is the ultimate opportunist. That the University of Watermouth—and, by extension, the system of higher education in the early 1970s—is a setting in which he can not only survive but also flourish constitutes a serious indictment.

In 1976 Bradbury published *Who Do You Think You Are?,* a collection of stories and parodies. "The Adult Education Class" is a modified segment omitted from *Eating People Is Wrong.* "Composition" and "A Very Hospitable Person," which again depict an Englishman teaching composition in America, revisit the theme of *Stepping Westward;* in both cases the English visitor is entangled in a threatening sexual encounter with Americans. "Nobody Here in England" and "A Breakdown" also have academic settings, while "Who Do You Think You Are?" is about a trendy social psychologist. None of these short fictions is particularly original or moving, and several of the later ones illustrate Bradbury's new employment of present-tense narration for a tersely ironic tone. What are more impressive in this volume are the parodies of Angus Wilson, C. P. Snow, Iris Murdoch, John Braine, Muriel Spark, Lawrence Durrell, Alan Sillitoe, J. D. Salinger, and John Osborne. These brief pieces—usually four to eight pages in length—were published originally in such diverse forums as the

Guardian, Punch, and *Transatlantic Review.* Lines such as "'Aye, things have changed,' I said, in the flat northern accent I use when I'm with very expensive people," which appears in the parody of John Braine, remind the reader of Bradbury's comic talents. The parody of C. P. Snow's Oxford novels turns on his repetition of the odd phrase that a draught "struck cold" and contains a delightful encounter between Snow's Lewis Eliot and Kingsley Amis's Jim Dixon, ending with Eliot doing an ape imitation in emulation of Amis's style.

In *Eating People Is Wrong* Emma Fielding thinks about the liberal humanist Treece: "Poor man, he has tried to show us all that foreigners aren't funny; but they are." Bradbury seems to agree with Emma. In *Rates of Exchange,* as well as in his later *Why Come to Slaka?* (1986) and *Doctor Criminale,* a surprising amount of the humor is based on the simple fact that when foreigners speak English they do so differently from native Anglophones. Likewise, their way of pronouncing an Englishman's name—and even their own names—is made to seem funny. The following speech from *Rates of Exchange* is representative: "Comrade Petwurt, you will see many great achievements in your tour.... We hope you like them much and tell them in your country. You will see many beauties of our heritage, but let us make toast to the very best, we know you agree it. Welcome, and please drink to our finest treasure: the beautiful ladies, for the first time."

Rates of Exchange testifies to Bradbury's increasing mobility; as a well-established critic and novelist he regularly traveled to other countries to speak on behalf of the British Council and to attend scholarly conferences. His counterpart, Lodge—who was also a figure of increasingly high visibility and consequently frequently invited abroad—about the same time published his own novel about academic travel, *Small World: An Academic Romance* (1984). Each novel includes some allusion to the other author—*Rates of Exchange* with the Slakan question about a "campus writer Brodge" and *Small World* in a scene at the Modern Language Association conference that depicts a Lodge figure "talking to a tallish dark-haired man smoking a pipe. 'If I can have Eastern Europe,' the tallish man was saying in an English accent, 'you can have the rest of the world.' 'All right,' said the shortish man, 'but I daresay people will still get us mixed up.'"

Rates of Exchange returns to the Bradbury model of an ineffectual central character who is the victim of events. Angus Petworth, a professor of linguistics, has been sent to the Eastern European country of Slaka, still under Communist control, to lecture on the topic "The English Language as a Medium of International Communication." His hosts seem to expect a different Petworth, this one a sociologist at the University of Watermouth. Angus Petworth is a well-meaning non-entity, as the narrator specifies: "Indeed, as brilliant, batik-clad, magical realist novelist Katya Princip will remark, somewhat later in this narrative, he is just not a character in the world historical sense." The novel comprises Petworth's comic misadventures in attempting to do what he thinks he has been sent to Slaka to do; on a deeper level it demonstrates the imperfection of English as a medium of international communication and explores a theoretical substrate of discourse about varieties of symbolic interchange such as currency and language.

Bradbury has summarized the novel as being "about a character who is really not a character caught in the labyrinth of an imaginary language which changes about him as he tries to learn its nonexistent messages." Petworth finds his capacity for language slipping away from him as he tries to communicate with the Slakans or learn their tongue. His own name is mispronounced as Petworthi, Pitwit, Petwurt, and Pervert. His native informant tells him about the Slakan language: "All you must know is the nouns end in 'i,' or sometimes two or three, but with many exceptions. We have one spoken language and one book language. Really there are only three cases, but sometimes seven. Mostly it is inflected, but also sometimes not. It is different from country to town, also from region to region, because of our confused history. Vocabulary is a little bit Latin, a little bit German, a little bit Finn. So really it is quite simple. I think you will speak it very well, soon." During the course of Petworth's stay a political controversy erupts over whether nouns should end in *ü* or *uu,* and consequently the noun endings change twice without explanation.

Rates of Exchange can thus be said to be about sliding signification, which is one of the key ideas of post-structuralist thought. The relation between word and thing is, if not random, at least unpredictable; any counter will do for an exchange if both parties will agree to it, but this agreement is difficult to achieve. Significantly, Petworth tries vainly throughout his stay to acquire some local currency but cannot find out the rate of exchange. Similarly, his local lover, Lubijova, refers to their relationship as an exchange. Even Petworth's larger project—his visit to Slaka—is a sort of academic exchange but, like most of the others in this novel, is an unequal, confused, and even contradictory one. The narrator ruminates, as he describes Petworth waiting to deplane at Slaka airport, "Yes, Petworths are always needed, for isn't everything a language? The grammar of airports is a language. . . . The code of coming and going is a language, though it is the nature of language to function differently in different cultures. So in some societies the opening of a plane door is a signal suggesting to passengers that they may get off. In others, like this one, the same signal may mean something else; for example, that armed men may get on."

Robert S. Burton, writing in *Critique* (Winter 1987), comments on Petworth's usefulness in the novel: "On one level, he represents Bradbury's acknowledgment of post-structuralist theory, functioning as a verbal construction consciously manipulated by the author, clearly not a real-life character but a playful tool of fiction. On another level, Petworth is a realistic character who seems to share many of Bradbury's own liberal views, doubts, and uncertainties." Though the author is quite clearly familiar with poststructuralism and deconstruction, it is hard to tell how seriously he views them, as his treatment of them is almost always placed within some sort of ironic or comic frame; this is true not only of *Rates of Exchange* but also of *My Strange Quest for Mensonge: Structuralism's Hidden Hero* (1987) and "Inspeak: Your Streetwise Guide to Linguistics and Structuralism," reprinted in *Unsent Letters: Irreverent Notes from a Literary Life* (1988).

The first chapter of *Rates of Exchange* is titled "Visiting Slaka: A Few Brief Hints," and it pretends to introduce Slaka, "that fine flower of middle European cities, capital of commerce and art, wide streets and gipsy music. . . ." Evidently Bradbury had so much fun inventing Slaka and the pieces of its language that appear in the novel that he returned to the setting in *Why Come to Slaka?*, which is described on the title page as "A Guidebook and a Phrasebook Translated Into English by Dr. F. Plitplov," a character from *Rates of Exchange*. The work also features an introduction by "Dr. A. Petworth." While this jeu d'esprit is less ambitious than his full-length novels, *Why Come to Slaka?* is an inventive, funny book. Some of the humor is based on backwardness described in comically imperfect English, for instance: "No main autoroutes pass through our country, because we like to keep it nice, but British travellers will be accustomed to this. But Slaka lies not remotely from the route Berlin-Calcutta and Moscova-Sevilla. Slakan roads are often asphalt and many are free of boulders. Foreign drivers are permitted an entry at 3 frontiers, Pilaf, Splat and Vitosk. Insurances and permits of travel may be purchased (75 vloskan) from the boarder. There are more than 15 stations of petrol (bin'zinii) in the country, and tourists may buy with western currency at special high prices."

The work's humor derives from a variety of sources: satire on communism (the state tourist board, Cosmoplot, has the "proud slogo, 'We have ways of making you tour!'"), predictable linguistic drolleries ("dances by pheasants in their long skirts"), and the clever use of the phrase book to create little narratives. The section on dining out, for example, has the follow-

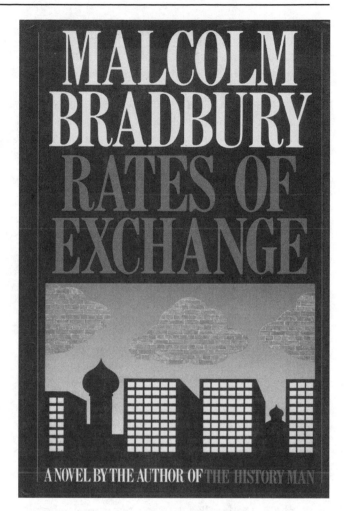

Dust jacket for Bradbury's novel about a linguistics professor's adventures in miscommunication in a fictional Eastern European country
(Collection of William Cagle)

ing translated English phrases: "Do you like to eat a brain? The veal of a sheep? The milk chords of a goat? Our boiled tortoise is world famous. I will try anything once." The section on travel provides another vignette: "Can I get a taxi here? I have waited an hour. Is this an official taxi? Take me to the city centre. You drive very fast. Please drive more slowly. More slowly still. He was only a peasant. His friends will assist him." There are also references to *Rates of Exchange*. In the section titled "Going to the Bank" the traveler is taught how to say "Kindly tell me the rate of exchange. There are many rates of exchange," and in a description of the Slakan language, Katya Princip, who was a character in the earlier novel, writes: "Strange to say, an excellent explication of our language is to be found (of all places!!) in a novellum written by a British liberal-burgerish writer M. Bradburyim, called *Rates of Exchange* (in the Slakan translation it is called *Cursi'Cursii,* but this is really quite hard to get)."

In 1983, the year in which *Rates of Exchange* appeared, Bradbury also published *The Modern American Novel*. His production of fiction accelerated during the 1980s, well beyond his previous one novel per decade. After *Why Come to Slaka?* he published another novella, *Cuts: A Very Short Novel* (1987), which develops from puns and metaphors based around the title. The novel begins: "It was the summer of 1986, and everywhere there were cuts.... They were incising heavy industry, they were slicing steel, they were—by no longer cutting much coal—cutting coal. They were axing the arts, slimming the sciences, cutting inflation and the external services of the BBC." Later the news reveals that "The Tory lead had been cut in the polls. This was likely to lead to cuts in taxes and rates. There might be deep cuts in nuclear arms. Henry pressed a button; Botham was cutting a ball to the boundary." The cuts also affect higher education, where "they were cutting almost everything." The main character, Henry Babbacombe, is a lecturer in English and drama in the Department of Extra-Mural Studies in a small provincial university and a novelist of no reputation. Babbacombe is recruited by Eldorado Television to write a serial, which is good news for his university since it can now cut him guilt-lessly, its budget having been cut by 20 percent. Henry writes the script with difficulty. Actors are recruited, but the lead dies during the filming of a deathbed scene—clearly modeled on the climax of Evelyn Waugh's *Brideshead Revisited* (1945)—and the whole series is cut.

Cuts is witty without being particularly deep. Babbacombe is another Bradbury academic nonentity who is buffeted by events. There are two primary sources of interest in the novel. The first is the serious treatment of what Bradbury calls Mrs. Thatcher's "sado-monetar-ism," defined as the relentless reduction of government services such as higher education, the consequent inflic-tion of pain on those least able to endure it, and the government's heartless use of language to disguise its own motives. The other is the focus on television and the role of an academic in writing a television serial. By this time Bradbury was no naïf like Henry Babba-combe. He had adapted *Rates of Exchange* and Sharpe's *Blott on the Landscape* (1975) into television series and has since the mid 1980s done a great deal more work in the medium. His explanation in *Unsent Letters* is partly ironic, though he has clearly thought much about the relationship between novel and play, creator and adap-tor: "I could also point out that I like undertaking the experience as a kind of commentary, one writer making some sort of creative marriage with another, and that this can be very exciting. But there is another reason why someone who is by nature and custom a novelist, as I am, enjoys writing for television in this way. It does get you out of the house."

Also in 1987 Bradbury expanded an article origi-nally published in the *Observer* on April Fools' Day, 1984, into another short book, *My Strange Quest for Men-songe: Structuralism's Hidden Hero*. The work is another spoof, written with the assistance of Lodge: there is a "Foreword/Afterword" by Michel Tardieu, professor of structrualist narratology, University of Paris, translated by Lodge. Tardieu is actually one of Lodge's characters from *Small World*. This little book pretends to be a study, with what biographical information is available, of one of the central figures of Deconstructionism, Henri Mensonge. Part of the joke is that he is cen-tral because so little is known of him; if, as the post-structuralists claim, the author is dead and every presence is a hidden absence, then Henri Men-songe, by being so resolutely absent, is in some way the most present of all thinkers. Author of only one book, *La Fornication comme acte culturel,* Mensonge is so reclusive that the book is able to include only a photograph of the back of his head. He somehow, the narrator claims, "may be considered our truest, our most necessary philosopher, the ultimate case of Decon-structionist integrity—the man who has out-Barthesed Barthes, out-Foucaulted Foucault, out-Derridaed Derrida, out-Deleuzed-and-Guattaried Deleuze and Guatarri." Tar-dieu identifies Mensonge as the thinker "who had first grasped the fundamental principle of deconstruction, namely, that language ceaselessly undermines its own claim to mean anything, and thus at a single stroke threw the whole structuralist enterprise *en abime*." There is more comedy, partly delivered in the form of a quasi-serious account of poststructuralist thought; partly in academic in-jokes like "the entire Gallic intel-lectual scene, as Yale University is sometimes called"; and much more in the bibliography, which includes real titles by such figures as Roland Barthes and Jacques Derrida alongside Mensonge's own work (*La Fornication* and a disputed piece in the journal *Tel Quel*), invented texts about Mensonge, and nonexistent articles by Bradbury and his friends Anthony Thwaite and Heide Ziegler, as well as by fictional characters Henry Beamish, Anne Callendar, and Howard Kirk of the University of Watermouth. It is a funny performance, written out of "an attitude of sympathetic skepticism towards the ideas it describes."

Two collections of Bradbury's nonfiction writing appeared in the late 1980s. The more serious is *No, Not Bloomsbury,* which takes its title from *Lucky Jim,* an assemblage of the author's critical (and sometimes self-critical) work. Essays that are revealing about Brad-bury include "Writer and Critic," "Campus Fictions," "Bookering and Being Bookered," and "Adapting and Being Adaptable: The Novelist and Television." There are longer, ambitious overview essays that thoughtfully

Dust jacket for the U.S. edition of Bradbury's 1992 novel, about a television journalist's search for an enigmatic intellectual giant

and convincingly comment on fiction and on the related arts and the social conditions in which fiction operates. "'A Dog Engulfed in Sand': Character and Abstraction in Contemporary Writing and Painting" is illuminating on that topic and also makes some important points about *The History Man*. Two other essays convey Bradbury's mastery of literary history: "'Closing Time in the Gardens' Or, What Happened to Writing in the 1940s" and "The Novel No Longer Novel: Writing Fiction after World War Two." Some of the pieces here are updated from *Possibilities;* collectively, they represent the harvest of a busy period of lecturing, reviewing, and writing. Bradbury is always interesting on the novel and novelists, and his comments on John Fowles, Amis, and Wilson particularly are extremely valuable.

Unsent Letters: Irreverent Notes from a Literary Life also draws on previously published periodical pieces but fits them into a different sort of frame, suggested in the title; each essay is couched as a letter to a specific correspondent, usually represented as having written to Bradbury with a question. The first chapter, "The Wis-

senschaft File," begins with a letter from a German student asking about the campus novel; the response is an elegant essay on the subject, complete with some bibliographical suggestions and a discussion of the difficulty of telling Bradbury and Lodge apart. Chapters such as "Remembering the Fifties," "The Adapter's Tale," and "Time Called While You Were Out" are autobiographical; "The Conference: A Lay-Person's Guide" is sociological in its approach; and "Inspeak: Your Streetwise Guide to Linguistics and Structuralism" focuses on linguistics. The letters, though clearly an artificial device, serve to unify the volume. David Wright, reviewing *Unsent Letters,* called it "an on-target critique of contemporary universities, writing, writers' lives, wives—and, come to think of it, of life as lived—a mix of light-handed, lethal drollery and grassroots commonsense."

In the years since *Unsent Letters* Bradbury has accelerated his productivity as a critic, editor, and scholar. He has edited or co-edited four collections: *New Writing* (with Judy Cooke, 1992), *New Writing 2* (with Andrew Motion, 1993), *Present Laughter: An Anthology of Modern Comic Fiction* (1994), and *Class Work* (1995), a collection of stories written by students in the writing program at the University of East Anglia on the occasion of its twenty-fifth anniversary and Bradbury's retirement. The last collection is an impressive demonstration of the number of good writers who have participated in the program. He also edited *The Atlas of Literature* (1996), a treatment of the landscapes important in the background of literature.

Bradbury also published two important scholarly works in the early 1990s: *From Puritanism to Postmodernism: A History of American Literature* (1991), with Richard Ruland, and *Dangerous Pilgrimages: Transatlantic Mythologies and the Novel* (1995). The first of these is a serious literary history of America, one of Bradbury's major interests throughout his career. Though its four-hundred-page length dictates occasional overgeneralization, it is an impressive study. In an introduction the authors refer to it as "a story in two senses—our own tale of a nation's literature, and the fable a country told itself as it tried to understand its own becoming in writing." As one would expect, the literary "fable" is related to social developments. It is particularly interesting to read Bradbury and Ruland on themes that have been at the heart of Bradbury's criticism and fiction, such as liberalism, modernism, and postmodernism, which is described as "an art of stylized and mannered quotation from a splayed and glutted tradition."

Dangerous Pilgrimages is a magisterial study of the transatlantic negotiations of European (mostly English-language) and American literature. It has been, the author notes, a long time in the making, and a good many of its elements have seen previous publication in Bradbury's previous books. Holly Boren, reviewing the book, declared that it "provides a detailed and anecdotal compendium of literary reasons for moving, or at least for travelling, without much venturing to analyse what all this literary to-ing and fro-ing between the Old World and the New might add up to, in aesthetic and social terms."

Perhaps returning to his "novel of the decade" pattern, Bradbury published *Doctor Criminale* in 1992, nine years after his previous full-length novel, *Rates of Exchange*. In some ways *Doctor Criminale* combines the themes of that novel with *My Strange Quest for Mensonge*: set substantially in Eastern Europe and populated by comic foreigners, it is about a quest for one of the central figures of contemporary thought, Bazlo Criminale. Characteristic of Bradbury's new preoccupations, the protagonist is no academic but a well-educated television journalist. The stimulus for the plot of the novel is the development of a television series, "Great Thinkers of the Age of Glasnost," for Eldorado Television, a project reminiscent of Bradbury's *The Modern World: Ten*

Great Writers (1988), a book written to accompany a series with the same title.

Francis Jay is a young journalist who studied literary theory at "the University of Sussex, the Sixties-by-the-Sea," where he reveled in an atmosphere dominated by deconstructionism: "Junior interrogators, literary commissars, we deconstructed everything: author, text, reader, language, discourse, life itself. No task was too small, no piece of writing below suspicion. We demythologized, we demystified. We dehegemonized, we decanonized. We dephallicized, we depatriarchalized; we decoded, we de-canted, we de-famed, we de-manned." Because of this background, perhaps, but more because he drunkenly disgraced himself on television at the ceremony to award the Booker Prize, Jay is chosen to pursue Bazlo Criminale. Criminale (who seems to be the addressee of one of Bradbury's *Unsent Letters,* in which he figures as a conference organizer) is a fantastic figure: a biographer, poet, novelist, economist, photographer, psychopathologist, thinker, arranger of conferences—"by the beginning of the Eighties Criminale had already become to modern thought pretty much what Napoleon was to brandy." He is also the friend of the great, both intellectuals and politicians; a rich man from a poor country (though nobody knows which country, exactly); and an enigma. "He knew everybody, everybody knew him; he was Doctor Criminale. But ask where he came from, who paid him, how he lived so well, which institution he was attached to, and things grew more obscure. He was just that vague and placeless creature, the European intellectual."

Jay's pursuit of Criminale involves unpredictable border crossings, impersonation, attendance at a series of conferences, and many confusing and contradictory accounts by those who know or claim to know Criminale and those who read—and in some cases claim to write—his books. As usual Bradbury mingles fictional and real personalities: Henry Mensonge is on the agenda of one conference but fails to appear, and Jay encounters someone much like David Lodge in Argentina. Eventually Jay discovers enough to know that Criminale, who has lived through the postwar years mostly behind the Iron Curtain, is a compromised man: "Great hero he might be; moral disappointment he definitely was." Finally, in a face-to-face conversation with the great man, Jay is told, "we *all* betray each other. Sometimes from malice, or fear. Sometimes from indifference, sometimes love. Sometimes for an idea, sometimes from political need. Sometimes because we cannot think of a good ethical reason why not to. Are you different?" In part this novel, then, is about the *trahaison des clercs,* in part about the necessary compromises of modern life. Many of the social ills the novel identifies are blamed on "history."

Doctor Criminale is an ambitious book dealing with serious themes. It is occasionally marred by problems of tone—facetiousness, mostly—that are related to the questionable conception of the narrator. Francis Jay is a young man whose education, he tells the reader, was relentlessly postmodern, but from time to time he sounds strikingly like the more recognizable Bradbury man, or even Bradbury himself: "Here I was, a good latter-day liberal humanist, if that isn't too grandiose a term to describe the chaotic mixture of tolerance, permissiveness, pragmatism, moral uncertainty, global anxiety and (as you know) deconstructive skepticism I had come to steer my small life by. I lived (as I knew perfectly well, because all the experts kept telling me) in the age of historyless history, the time after the great meta-narratives." It is an odd kind of deconstructive skepticism that may be seen as a component of liberal humanism, usually figured as its antithesis. Bradbury also gives Jay sentiments that seem more appropriate to a sixty-year-old established writer-critic than a callow journalist on a Sunday paper with a B.A. in literary theory, such as a long disquisition on literary conferences that seems more Bradbury's style than Jay's.

To counterbalance such shortcomings is a funny scene that effectively starts the plot, set at the ceremony for the Booker Prize. Bradbury, who has seen this particular event from both sides, having been one of the shortlisted authors (for *Rates of Exchange*) and later chairing the Booker judges, has Jay relate the Booker to events in the world: "this particular Booker Prize happened to fall right in the lull or dark hollow between the Entrepreneurial Eighties and the Nervous, Nebulous, Nailbiting Nineties. . . . more than forty years of history were daily coming unravelled." Jay denounces the shortlist, calling the books "Granny Novels."

The satisfactions of *Doctor Criminale* are provided by a panoramic set of experiences, a knowing view of the wide literary world, and a serious probe of matters such as the nature of truth and the moral right of the present to judge the past, particularly the past under Communist rule.

In 1996 Bradbury wrote a play, *Inside Trading*, for the Norwich Playhouse. It is a witty exploration of the new world of banking, which could not have taken its current form without the fall of Barings Bank, though it is hardly a retelling of that story. Instead it shows plausibly how a young man, Wickerman, can rise to the top of a bank by discovering, and using ruthlessly, the fact that banking is based on fiction. He invents a fictional project for a moribund company and raises billions of pounds for it. The point is similar to that made by *Rates of Exchange*: banking is, as Wickerman asserts, the exchange of symbols or signs; it is "fiction. A big dream." Such an assessment demonstrates how Bradbury's growing interest in economics—evidenced in *Rates of Exchange, Cuts,* and his play *Standing in for Henry* (broadcast in 1980)—is related to his lifelong interest in fiction.

Interviews:

Richard Todd, "An Interview with Malcolm Bradbury," *DQR: Dutch Quarterly Review of Anglo-American Letters,* 11 (1981): 183–196;

Heide Ziegler and Christopher Bigsby, eds., *The Radical Imagination and the Liberal Tradition: Interviews with English and American Novelists* (London: Junction, 1982), pp. 60–78;

John Haffenden, *Novelists in Interview* (London & New York: Methuen, 1985), pp. 25–56;

"The Man in the Back Row Has a Question V," *Paris Review,* 146 (Spring 1988): 156–179.

References:

James Acheson, "The Small Worlds of Malcolm Bradbury and David Lodge," in *The British and Irish Novel Since 1960,* edited by Acheson (New York: St. Martin's Press, 1991), pp. 78–92;

Bernard Bergonzi, *The Situation of the Novel,* revised edition (London: Macmillan, 1979);

Robert S. Burton, "A Plurality of Voices: Malcolm Bradbury's Rates of Exchange," *Critique: Studies in Contemporary Fiction,* 28 (Winter 1987): 101–106;

Ronald Hayman, *The Novel Today 1967–1975* (Harlow, U.K.: Longman, 1976);

Robert A. Morace, *The Dialogic Novels of Malcolm Bradbury and David Lodge* (Carbondale: Southern Illinois University Press, 1989);

Peter Widdowson, "The Anti-History Men: Malcolm Bradbury and David Lodge," *Critical Quarterly,* 26 (Winter 1984): 5–32.

Papers:

A large collection of Malcolm Bradbury's papers, including correspondence, drafts of his books, and miscellaneous materials related to his teaching, lecturing, and other activities is in the Lilly Library, Indiana University.

Mary Rose Callaghan

(23 January 1944 –)

Jay L. Halio
University of Delaware

BOOKS: *Mothers* (Dublin: Arlen House, 1984; London: Boyars, 1984);

Confessions of a Prodigal Daughter (London & New York: Boyars, 1985);

Kitty O'Shea: A Life of Katharine Parnell (London: Pandora, 1989; San Francisco: Pandora, 1994);

The Awkward Girl (Dublin: Attic Press, 1990);

Has Anyone Seen Heather? (Dublin: Attic Press, 1990);

I Met a Man Who Wasn't There (New York: Boyars, 1996); republished as *Emigrant Dreams* (Dublin: Poolbeg, 1996);

The Last Summer (Dublin: Poolbeg, 1997).

OTHER: "Underwear," in *Wall Reader and Other Stories* (Dublin: Arlen House, 1979), pp. 94–101;

"Julia O'Faolain," in *DLB 14: British Novelists Since 1960,* edited by Jay L. Halio (Detroit: Gale / Columbia, S.C.: Bruccoli Clark, 1983), pp. 580–584;

"The Siege of Fort Bathtub," in *Modern Irish Stories,* edited by Caroline Walsh (Dublin: Irish Times, 1985), pp. 70–75;

"I Hate Christmas," in *A Woman's Christmas,* edited by Terry Prone (Dublin: Martello Press, 1994), pp. 146–155;

"Windfalls," in *If Only,* edited by Kate Cruise O'Brien and Mary Maher (Dublin: Poolbeg, 1997), pp. 47–60.

SELECTED PERIODICAL PUBLICATIONS–
UNCOLLECTED: "Ronnie," *Journal of Irish Literature,* 5 (1976): 89–121;

"Breakfast with Turgenev," *Journal of Irish Literature,* 6 (1977): 14–20;

"My First Bra," *Irish Times,* 27 August 1979, p. 12;

"Two Daffodils," *U Magazine* (August 1981);

"A House for Fools," *Journal of Irish Literature,* 12 (1983): 3–66;

"A Novel Way of Cooking," *Woman's Way,* 28 October 1983, pp. 6, 8, 38–40;

"Sisters–The Pain and Joy of a Lifelong Bond," *Irish Times,* 13 September 1985, p. 13;

Mary Rose Callaghan at the time of I Met a Man Who Wasn't There

"A Far, Far Better Thing," *Image Magazine* (May 1986): 96–102;

"Hold It! These Things Don't Happen in Real Life," *Irish Independent,* 10 February 1987, p. 9;

"How I Saved Thirteen Thousand Pounds," *Journal of Irish Literature,* 17 (1988): 14–31;

"Crybaby," *Shenandoah,* 46 (Fall 1996): 74–79.

The Irish novelist Mary Rose Callaghan focuses primarily on the relationships women have with their mothers, with their siblings, and with each other, as well as those with men–fathers, brothers, lovers, and husbands. Unlike more explicitly feminist writers, who often analyze such bonds from a polemical ideological perspective, Callaghan has asserted that she is first of all a humanist, then a feminist. The humanist aspect of her work is what critics have found most appealing. She has no axes to grind, although as one of her surrogates, Sally Ann Fitzpatrick, says at the beginning of *The Awkward Girl* (1990), "Ireland would make a feminist out of a stone."

Mary Rose Callaghan was born in North Dublin on 23 January 1944 to Michael Anthony and Sheila Sullivan Callaghan. She grew up mainly on a farm near Finglas in the Irish Republic. In the 1950s Finglas was essentially rural, and Callaghan recalls people fetching water from a communal pump. "It was a dark, spooky countryside with huge, old gnarled trees," she adds, and in one of those trees she built a house out of orange boxes. The family's parish was Ballymun, a country village; from the nearest crossroads only two buses ran daily to the city. As her father was always telling ghost stories, she grew up believing in spirits. Her mother often gave her books as gifts, which together with her father's stories kindled her imagination. Among her favorites were Lucy Maud Montgomery's *Anne of Green Gables* (1908) and *Anne of Avonlea* (1909). Although her childhood was a happy time, she was aware of the terrible poverty around her, which influenced her later writing. She remembers barefoot children in Gardiner Street and Mountjoy Square as the family drove to the city.

Callaghan, the second of six children, entered Mount Anville boarding school when she was nine years old. Her recollections of the Catholic school and the nuns who ran it are fictionalized in the stories she began writing in the 1970s, which later provided the basis for her novel *The Awkward Girl*. The nuns were mostly kind, and one of them, who became the model for Sister Rita in the novel, read aloud to the girls from Frances Hodgson Burnett's *The Secret Garden* (1911), and Edith Nesbit's *The Railway Children* (1906). On her own, Callaghan read Charles Dickens's *Oliver Twist* (1838) and was fascinated by the Artful Dodger's pickpocketing.

When Callaghan was thirteen years old, her father became ill, and the family moved to Dun Laoghaire, the scene of various episodes in her fiction. Her mother coped with adversity with great courage. Callaghan spent the school holidays with her brothers and sisters, enjoying brass bands on the pier, swimming, a library, and the Globe Theater.

After completing school Callaghan worked at different jobs while at the same time studying physics and chemistry in hopes of becoming a doctor. Although she started the premedicine curriculum at University College, Dublin, she soon realized she had neither suffi-

cient background nor ability for a medical career and switched to an arts degree program, which also allowed her time also to work. She was a terrible student, she recalls, but after "walking around" for three years she received her B.A. in 1968. She became a teacher, first in Dublin and then in England, ending up at the Rye St. Anthony School in Oxford, where she taught for three years. Callaghan felt from the outset that she wanted to be a writer but lacked the confidence to start anything, except for what she calls some "terrible poetry." In 1973 she took a position as an assistant editor of *Arts in Ireland* magazine. Callaghan not only edited for the magazine but also wrote articles for newspapers, including the *Catholic Standard*, the editor of which, John Feeney, was a great source of encouragement for her.

While on assignment to review a play by Sean O'Casey, Callaghan remade the acquaintance of Robert Hogan, a professor of English in an American university who had taught Callaghan briefly at University College. The two commenced a relationship and were married in December 1979. In 1975 Callaghan moved to the United States with Hogan and lived there with him for nearly twenty years, returning to Ireland in the summers. In America she began to pursue writing in earnest. During these years Callaghan met the British novelist Angus Wilson, who was a distinguished visiting professor several different times at the university where her husband taught. Wilson provided important encouragement for her early fiction efforts. After 1984, when her first novel was published, Callaghan has occasionally taught writing to various groups within and outside of the university. When Hogan retired in 1994, he and Callaghan relocated permanently to Ireland.

Callaghan's first novel, *Mothers* (1984), is the story of three unwed mothers: twenty-two-year-old Ronnie Bourke, an imaginative, and impressionable journalist who has just discovered that she is pregnant; Harriet Roberts, an embittered, early-middle-aged woman whose son by Ronnie's father has recently been killed in a motorcycle accident; and Agnes Legge—author of a play that years before had been highly praised by William Butler Yeats—whose son was taken away from her at the time of his birth and whose family forbade her wealthy lover from ever seeing her again. With skill and sensitivity Callaghan not only develops her three principal characters with distinctive but complementary sensibilities; she also interweaves their narratives so that each one serves as a comment on the others. Callaghan's major technique in the novel is to combine interior monologue from the perspectives of the three mothers with remembered dialogue.

The critical response to *Mothers* was generally positive. Gillian Somerville-Large observed in the *Irish Times* that the writing is "touched with vigour and

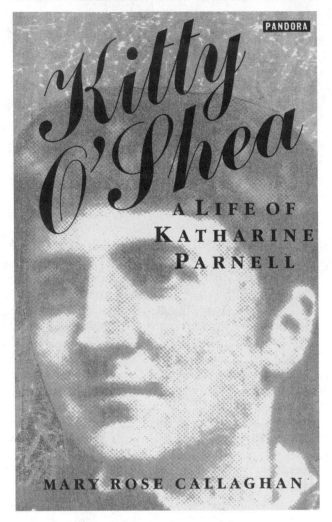

Cover of Callaghan's 1989 biography of the mistress of the Irish nationalist leader Charles Stuart Parnell

humour and two of the three mums come over strongly. In particular, the old spinster Agnes, living in eccentricity in Sorrento Terrace bickering with her equally ancient maid about betting on horses, is a powerful piece of character writing. It's a long time since I enjoyed a novel published in Ireland so much." Mike Duff in the *Irish Echo* wrote that the abortion controversy in Ireland probably stimulated interest in *Mothers* in America and led to the novel's publication there, although the controversy might have hurt sales in Ireland. Hilary Bailey in the *Guardian* wrote of the novel's "fine sense of life going on, in spite of all its imperfections" and "the author's respectful accuracy about people and their ways" that give the book its substance. In the *Irish Press* Sean Breslin wrote: "Mary Rose Callaghan has written a novel which is enjoyable, stimulating and at times trenchantly comic. . . . It is to her credit that she does not make heavy weather from her trio of

unwed mothers but allows their stories to make their own commentary upon the social mores within which each pregnancy is situated." He continued about Callaghan's gift for comedy, which he considers the author's main strength: "It is an American gift, the comedy of language allied to the comedy of the absurd. She has a delightful feeling for the pretentious and the phony. . . ."

Callaghan's gift for comedy is also much in evidence in her second novel, *Confessions of a Prodigal Daughter* (1985). Although the chief character in the novel, Anne O'Brien, is rather a sad, emotionally unstable young woman, she encounters a colorful and comic parade of characters reminiscent of Dickens, a point that Mary-Anne Wessel-Felter also makes in "Commedia: The Fiction of Mary Rose Callaghan" (1994), one of the first articles about Callaghan's fiction. Perhaps the most colorful character is Anne's mother, a flamboyant Irish American who supports Anne and her younger sister, Doone, on a meager income and through various schemes involving the girls' wealthy but grumpy Aunt Allie. As Aoife Feeney wrote in her *Dublin Evening Herald* review of the novel, "Anne's real world is a nightmare, her aunt and mother pulling her apart between them." When Anne suffers a breakdown, her mother reluctantly sends her to a mental hospital. The people she meets there provide some of the comic highlights of the novel: the stuttering psychiatrist Dr. Nirval, who treats her; the alcoholic but caring Mrs. Greene; the "Volga," two elderly and eccentric twin sisters; and old Grundig, who refuses to speak but becomes Anne's champion at a crucial moment. *Confessions of a Prodigal Daughter* anticipates several of Callaghan's later novels, such as the Kelly family trilogy and *I Met a Man Who Wasn't There* (1996), whose protagonist is also named Anne O'Brien but is older and a successful novelist, not a frustrated translator of Dante, as is the Anne in this novel.

Confessions of a Prodigal Daughter did not receive the widespread notice and acclaim that *Mothers* did, probably because its subjects were less controversial. Nevertheless, Diane Menustik in *Washington Post Book Review* called it "a highly accomplished novel and very entertaining read," and Feeney hailed it as "a great achievement." She noticed especially Callaghan's ability to capture "the thought and speech patterns of a romantic teenager whose brain is spilling over with literary allusions." The use of such allusions is even more apparent in Callaghan's subsequent work, but it is particularly apt here, as Anne is absorbed in reading literary works and has a remarkable gift for remembering and quoting lines pertinent to her immediate situation. Anne Haverty noted in *TLS: The Times Literary Supplement* that Callaghan "writes with some grace, though she suffers from a determination to be charming. Her heroine,

Anne O'Brien, undergoes the pangs of adolescence (gaucheness, confusion, first love) and enjoys its escapes from life into literature." Haverty detected the influence of Edna O'Brien in the poor but genteel milieu, the faithful family retainer, the empathy with the mother, and the inconstant richer friend, Nicola; but Callaghan lacks the "anguish" of the older writer: "her characters are picturesque without pathos," she claimed. The reviewer in the *Sunday Press* remarked on Callaghan's "verve and style," and Carol Ames in *The New York Times Book Review* also called the book a "skillful second novel." Robert Nye, writing in the *Guardian,* recognized the grace and amusing qualities in *Confessions of a Prodigal Daughter* and invoked J. D. Salinger's *Catcher in the Rye* (1951) for comparison but warned that Callaghan would do much better when she gets away from "the singularly unpromising material in which her imagination at present wallows."

Perhaps agreeing with Nye's review, Callaghan put fiction aside temporarily and accepted a commission to write a biography of Kitty O'Shea, which was published in 1989. O'Shea was Irish nationalist leader Charles Stuart Parnell's mistress, who precipitated the political downfall of one of Ireland's fighters for independence and was a colorful and interesting personality in her own right. Callaghan made good use of her earlier training in history in preparing to write the biography.

When Callaghan returned to fiction, she reshaped thirteen of her short stories, some of which had been previously published, into her next novel, *The Awkward Girl.* The novel's chapters have as their connecting thread Sally Ann Fitzpatrick, who is introduced as a pupil in a Catholic school probably much like the school Callaghan attended when she was a girl. Sally Ann is not the main character in this opening chapter, "Rita" (first published separately in 1979 as "Underwear"), and she makes only brief appearances in some of the other stories, such as "Jim." Through Sally Ann many different kinds of characters, places, and situations are introduced into the novel. As the novel progresses, however, Sally Ann becomes increasingly the main focus, particularly after her adventures with various young men from her student days. Although her liaison with and subsequent marriage to Richard Sheridan, an Irish American professor of English, seems to provide a measure of happiness, such comfort is short-lived. Some of the novel's episodes are comic, such as the one recounting Gracie O'Malley's visiting professorship at Richard's university, and others are moving, such as the chapter called "Doc," which focuses on Sally Ann's relationship to her widowed father. The final chapter, "Births, Marriages and Deaths," poignantly treats the reactions of characters

from preceding chapters to Sally Ann's death during childbirth. The conclusion of the novel contains perhaps Callaghan's finest writing, her gift for comedy notwithstanding.

Madeleine Keane, in the *Sunday Independent,* found that the individual tales that make up *The Awkward Girl* contain "mesmerising glimpses" into ordinary lives. She noted the variety of techniques Callaghan uses, including that of the epistolary novel as well as first- and third-person narrative, and concluded: "For all its light-hearted, scattery humour, *The Awkward Girl* is a profoundly moving book. Although Sally Ann lives life with a chaotic verve, she never actually achieves fulfilling happiness." In the *Irish Times* Victoria White also noted the novel's variety of narrative techniques but was somewhat put off by the overall structure. Nevertheless, she found that "Sally Ann certainly hooks the reader" and gave special notice to two of the other characters: Sister Rita, the liberated nun; and Mona, the deserted mother giving birth to a second, unwanted child. She also noted the understated feminist aspects of the novel: "Callaghan has shown subtlety in giving us a novel about a woman who, like most women, is a feminist who never was, and even for this alone, *The Awkward Girl* is to be recommended."

Also in 1990, Callaghan's first novel written expressly for young adults, *Has Anyone Seen Heather?,* appeared, winning a special merit award from the Readers' Association of Ireland. The first of a projected trilogy involving the Kelly family, the novel is narrated by Clare, the elder of two sisters. She and her sister, Katie, have been living with their grandfather; their mother, Heather, is separated from Daniel, her American actor husband, and living in London. Heather sends for her daughters on their summer vacation, but when they arrive she fails to meet them. The novel recounts the girls' adventures as they search for Heather and take a variety of low-paying jobs to keep from having to return to Dublin. At one point they hire a private detective, A. Beresford Clarke, to help them, and the novel turns into a thriller as Clarke discovers that a box of chocolates sent to the girls while they worked at a hotel was in fact poisoned.

Suzanne Crosbie, writing in the *Cork Examiner,* rightly notes that many teenage girls would identify with the worries and dreams of adolescence as described in Callaghan's novel. The girls' "hair-raising adventures are told with great verve and while the ending is somewhat 'tidy,' it is good to see contemporary social issues being dealt with." Most prominent among such issues are the problems caused by broken homes and irresponsible, sometimes even abusive, parenting, poignantly expressed throughout the novel by Clare's longing for a normal home life. The novel also focuses

Mary Rose Callaghan

I Met A Man Who Wasn't There

a novel

Dust jacket for the U.S. edition of Callaghan's novel about a writer's investigation of the life of her grandfather

on exploitation of various kinds, following the girls as they work nearly to exhaustion for low pay and a shabby room at a Bayswater hotel after they arrive in London. Patricia Callaghan, the reviewer for the *Cavan Leader,* remarked on the "sinister web of adult deceit, lust, anger and violence" into which Clare and Katie are drawn in London, but she notes that the novel is much more than a mere thriller: "it is a novel about the difficulties and changing atmosphere of modern-day Ireland." Although the sisters return to Dublin and their grandfather to continue their education, the novel does not sentimentalize their homecoming; rather, Patricia Callaghan noted, "It embodies progress and liberation."

Callaghan's next novel, *I Met a Man Who Wasn't There,* begins and ends on an Aer Lingus airplane, perhaps symbolic of Callaghan's intention to leave things up in the air, an indication of the influence of Angus Wilson's early novels. In this novel Anne O'Brien is a successful writer of popular fiction on her way to teach at a small college in the Philadelphia area. En route she

is startled by the sight of a man who looks and acts much like her long-dead grandfather, Marcus Quilligan O'Neil, once American ambassador to the Dominican Republic. O'Neil's ghost haunts her during her stay in America, soliciting her to write his biography and set the record straight about some nefarious doings he was once involved in. Her interest in her grandfather leads Anne to some fascinating research, though at the end she decides she will not write his biography after all and considers the possibility of an historical romance about him instead.

Anne's research is only one strand of the novel's complex plotting, however. She leaves Ireland in part to separate from her husband, Fergal, a former priest whom Anne suspects of having an extramarital affair. Another part of the novel concerns Anne's own affair with a colleague, Chuck Matthews, who is accused of raping one of the students in Anne's writing class. He has been exonerated, and the student is hospitalized in a mental institution; but when Anne discovers that he is really guilty, he nearly kills her.

While Yvette Weller Olson in the *Library Journal* did not recommend the novel, she did notice how "seamlessly" its various strands were woven. For Olson it nevertheless had "too many subplots," which diluted the drama. By contrast, the review in *Publishers Weekly* hailed the novel as a "comic romp," noting how Callaghan skillfully "intertwines the fascinating world of Tammany Hall politics and pre-Prohibition corruption with the life of present-day Ivy League academia, which proves more treacherous than it seems." She "fuses intriguing historical detail onto a psychological thriller that features more than one superbly wrought character. Eccentric and thoroughly enjoyable, this novel offers intelligent, witty entertainment." Sophie Gorman in the *Irish Independent* saw the novel as "the adventures of a 40-something woman, floundering in the search for meaning and purpose as she approaches the second half of her life." The reviewer in the *Cork Examiner* observed that "Callaghan's dialogue is fast and frequently funny" and concluded that "the novel is light but satisfying." While the novel succeeds as entertaining fiction, it also offers perceptive comments about the writing process and how it is affected by the difficulties of married life and other relationships.

In the second novel of the Kelly family trilogy, *The Last Summer* (1997), the family is reunited and living in a rented house in Bray, County Wicklow. Clare's hope for an enduring, normal family life is bound for disappointment, as Daniel's fortunes are subject to the vagaries of an actor's life. Circumstances seem to improve when Dan's army buddy, Luke, spends the summer with them, and he and Dan produce in a small Dublin theater a play Luke has written. Clare hopes that she will be cast in a lead, but Katie is given the role she covets. While Katie seems to take naturally to acting and to boys, Clare is relegated to dogsbody for her father's acting troupe. Meanwhile, much to Clare's irritation, Heather is pregnant again. Like Anne O'Brien in *Confessions of a Prodigal Daughter,* Clare seems destined to postpone her own ambitions and dreams to look after the needs and wishes of others. Although no longer in school, she is still growing up, learning to control the jealousy she feels for her sister and forever placating her father and grandfather, who never seem to get along with each other, even though Dan is dependent on his elderly father-in-law. In a further similarity to *Confessions of a Prodigal Daughter,* this novel has a host of colorful characters, including many of the actors in Dan's troupe and Aunt Brigid, who lives with Granddad and who, despite her age and infirmities, determines to help Dan put on his production.

While intended, as was *Has Anyone Seen Heather?,* for young adults, *The Last Summer* was recommended by reviewers to readers of all ages. "The honest voice of Clare," Teresa Nerney wrote in *Radio-Television Guide,* "makes this a fresh, funny and at times touching read about family living." In the *Irish Independent* Sophie Gorman commented: "Relationships are keenly dissected aided by well-paced and accurate dialogue." Gorman also noted how Callaghan "paints an illustrative and intermittently humourous portrait of a young girl's struggle to define herself." Louise East commented in the *Irish Times* how well Callaghan had captured "the natural speech and slang of all ages and types." In the projected third installment of the trilogy Clare is a schoolteacher; presumably the novel draws on Callaghan's own experiences at Rye St. Anthony.

Mary Rose Callaghan's gift for character portrayal and her insights into women's attitudes and problems, particularly as they emerge from the contemporary Irish milieu, have secured her reputation as a perceptive and sensitive novelist. In addition, she is an extremely literate and historically informed writer who uses allusion both seriously and comically, as Wessel-Felter has remarked. Her novels feature well-crafted plots but are greater than the sum of their suspenseful elements. Callaghan usually has much more to say, whether about getting along as a family or about women trying to deal with a male-dominated society.

Interviews:

Grace Wynne-Jones, "Like a Child That Has Left," *Irish Press,* 15 September 1982, p. 9;

Mary Geaghan, "Dublin Novelist Has Newark Tie," *Wilmington News-Journal,* 11 November 1982, p. 8;

Jennifer Fitzgerald, "Ireland Starts Thinking the Unthinkable," *Guardian,* 24 November 1982;

"The Price of Success," (Dublin) *Evening Herald,* 8 August 1983, p. 16;

Anne Haverty, "Heroine Opts for Motherhood," *Irish Times,* 12 August 1983, p. 8;

Jacinta O'Brien, "A Born Writer," *Woman's Way,* 28 October 1983, pp. 6, 8;

Mike Duff, "Novel Gets Caught in Abortion Controversy," *Irish Echo,* 19 May 1984.

References:

Ann Owens Weekes, "Mary Rose Callaghan," in *Unveiling Treasures: The Attic Guide to the published works of Irish Women Literary Writers,* edited by Weekes (Dublin: Attic Press, 1993), pp. 66–68;

Mary-Anne Wessel-Felter, "Commedia: The Fiction of Mary Rose Callaghan," *Eire-Ireland,* 29 (1994): 139–145;

Wessel-Felter, "Mary Rose Callaghan," in *Dictionary of Irish Literature,* edited by Robert Hogan (Westport, Conn.: Greenwood Press, 1996), pp. 214–215.

Angela Carter
(7 May 1940 – 16 February 1992)

Lorna Sage
University of East Anglia

See also the Carter entry in *DLB 14: British Novelists Since 1960.*

BOOKS: *Shadow Dance* (London: Heinemann, 1966); republished as *Honeybuzzard* (New York: Simon & Schuster, 1966);

The Magic Toyshop (London: Heinemann, 1967; New York: Simon & Schuster, 1967);

Several Perceptions (London: Heinemann, 1968; New York: Simon & Schuster, 1968);

Heroes and Villains (London: Heinemann, 1969; New York: Simon & Schuster, 1969);

Love (London: Hart-Davis, 1971; revised, London: Chatto & Windus, 1987; New York: Viking Penguin, 1988);

The Infernal Desire Machines of Doctor Hoffman (London: Hart-Davis, 1972); republished as *The War of Dreams* (New York: Harcourt Brace Jovanovich, 1974);

Fireworks: Nine Profane Pieces (London: Quartet, 1974; New York: Harper & Row, 1981; revised, London: Chatto & Windus, 1987);

The Passion of New Eve (London: Gollancz, 1977; New York: Harcourt Brace Jovanovich, 1977);

The Sadeian Woman: An Exercise in Cultural History (London: Virago, 1979); republished as *The Sadeian Woman and the Ideology of Pornography* (New York: Pantheon, 1979);

The Bloody Chamber and Other Stories (London: Gollancz, 1979; New York: Harper & Row, 1979);

Nothing Sacred: Selected Writings (London: Virago, 1982; revised edition, 1992);

Nights at the Circus (London: Chatto & Windus, 1984; New York: Viking, 1985);

Black Venus (London: Chatto & Windus, 1985); republished as *Saints and Strangers* (New York: Viking, 1986);

Come Unto These Yellow Sands: Four Radio Plays (Newcastle upon Tyne: Bloodaxe, 1985);

Wise Children (London: Chatto & Windus, 1991; New York: Farrar, Straus & Giroux, 1992);

Expletives Deleted: Selected Writings (London: Chatto & Windus, 1992);

American Ghosts & Old-World Wonders (London: Chatto & Windus, 1993).

Angela Carter at the time of Burning Your Boats *(photograph by Miriam Berkley)*

Collections: *Burning Your Boats: Collected Short Stories,* edited by Jenny Uglow, introduction by Salman Rushdie (London: Chatto & Windus, 1995; New York: Holt, 1996);

The Curious Room: Plays, Film Scripts and an Opera, edited by Mark Bell, introduction by Susannah Clapp (London: Chatto & Windus, 1996);

Shaking a Leg: Collected Journalism and Writings, edited by Jenny Uglow, introduction by Joan Smith (London: Chatto & Windus, 1997).

OTHER: Charles Perrault, *The Fairy Tales of Charles Perrault,* translated, with an introduction, by Carter (London: Gollancz, 1977; New York: Bard, 1979);

Sleeping Beauty and Other Favourite Fairy Tales, edited by Carter (London: Gollancz, 1982; New York: Schocken, 1989);

Walter de la Mare, *Memoirs of a Midget,* preface by Carter (Oxford & New York: Oxford University Press, 1982);

"Notes from the Front Line," in *On Gender and Writing,* edited by Michelene Wandor (London: Pandora, 1983);

Wayward Girls and Wicked Women: An Anthology of Stories, edited by Carter (London: Virago, 1986);

"Truly It Felt Like Year One," in *Very Heaven: Looking Back at the 1960s,* edited by Sara Maitland (London: Virago, 1981);

Images of Frida Kahlo, introduction by Carter (London: Redstone, 1989);

The Virago Book of Fairy Tales, edited by Carter (London: Virago, 1990); republished as *The Old Wives' Fairy Tale Book* (New York: Pantheon, 1990);

The Second Virago Book of Fairy Tales, edited by Carter (London: Virago, 1992); republished as *Sometimes Strange Things Still Happen* (Boston: Faber & Faber, 1993).

During the inventive last ten years of her life—when she produced two of the most festive and disturbing novels of the last years of the century, *Nights at the Circus* (1984) and *Wise Children* (1991)—Angela Carter also reinvented herself. She took on the time-honored role of tale-spinner and storyteller, becoming her era's Mother Goose. In *Come Unto These Yellow Sands* (1985), in an essay about the appeal of writing for radio, she described with relish "the atavistic lure, the atavistic power, of voices in the dark . . . the writer who gives the words to those voices retains some of the authority of the most antique tellers of tales." The shocked obituary tributes that followed her death at age fifty-one all registered her paradoxical authority, which seemed to originate in subliterary or preliterary life. Fellow novelist Margaret Atwood cast Carter in a fairy-tale part:

> The amazing thing about her, for me, was that someone who looked so much like the Fairy Godmother—the long, prematurely-white hair, the beautiful complexion, the benign, slightly blinky eyes, the heart-shaped mouth—should actually be so much like the Fairy Godmother. She seemed always on the verge of bestowing something—some talisman, some magic token you'd need to get through the dark forest, some verbal formula useful for the opening of charmed doors.

Such were the terms in which her canonization, which had been under way for a while, crystallized upon her death. She was a wolf in Granny's clothing to the end, even though she became of central importance to British writing in the later 1980s and 1990s.

She began her career on the margins, as a member of 1960s counterculture—"the savage sideshow," as she wryly called it. "We live in Gothic times," she wrote in an afterword (later dropped) to her 1974 collection of tales, *Fireworks*. At the time she was writing, Gothic tales, along with romance, pornography, science fiction, and fairy tale, were firmly set aside from the literary novel as genre fiction. Carter's assertion implied that since the times themselves were splintered and fraught with violent mythology, such subgenres were now the appropriate and central ones. In her 1972 novel, *The Infernal Desire Machines of Doctor Hoffman*—the product, like some of the *Fireworks* stories, of two years she spent in Japan—imaginary animals step out of paintings and reflections escape from mirrors to invade the realm of the real. Such fantastic plot elements made her early work difficult to characterize. While writers as diverse as Anthony Burgess and John Hawkes expressed great admiration for her writing, other reviewers were unimpressed, greeting it with incomprehension or revulsion. For many readers, the presence of the fantastic was unacceptable when it demanded direct and sustained attention on its own dubious ground. The reception of Carter's writing changed along with the writing itself between the 1960s, when despite being seen as strange she won two major British literary prizes, and the 1970s, when she returned from Japan more radically self-conscious and aggressive in her re-creation of her heritage from the outside. It took several years for her to reacquire an audience. She ended the decade with two books in 1979: *The Bloody Chamber,* a collection of rewritten fairy tales, and *The Sadeian Woman,* a polemical and radically ironic excursion into cultural history (published by the newly founded feminist press Virago, for which Carter was an adviser from its inception). These books marked another turning point in her fortunes.

Angela Carter was born in South London on 7 May 1940 but her journalist father, Hugh Stalker, came from Scotland, and her mother, Olive, from a mining district in South Yorkshire. Her Yorkshire grandmother evacuated herself and her grandchildren (infant Angela and her elder brother, Hugh, who was twelve) to the gritty village of Wath-upon-Dearne, whisking them safely back into the past for the duration of the war. This granny—who may well have been a model for the role Carter herself played on the page and in public readings of her work in the 1980s—was a working-class suffragist and radical, and "a woman of such physical and spiritual heaviness she seemed to have been born with greater degree of gravity than most people. She came from a community where women rule the roost. . . . And she overshadowed her own daughters, whom she did not understand—my mother, who liked things to be nice; my dotty aunt." A good deal of the self-conscious quality of Carter's debut derives from the sense of a lost, deliberately distanced reality—working class, northern, solid—out of which she formed a literary pastiche. She shed the weight of "authenticity" that belonged to her grandmother's time and place; as she related in a 1977 interview, she and her brother "often say to each other, How is it possible that such camp little flowers as ourselves emanated from Balham via Wath-upon-Dearne and the places my father comes from, north Aberdeenshire, stark, bleak and apparently lugubriously Calvinistic, witch-burning country? But obviously, something in this peculiar rootless, upward, downward, sideways socially mobile family" informed her literary vision. Revisiting the past and a different social order—slipping out of a precarious middle-class existence and into a house of fear, desire, and dirt—is the subject of her second novel, *The Magic Toyshop* (1967). Years later, in the preface to a 1982 edition of Walter de la Mare's bizarre tale *Memoirs of a Midget,* Carter wrote that "all fiction is symbolic autobiography." Readers can discern such transformations of her family tree in the surreal symbolism of the novels.

Her postwar childhood took place in the period of free orange juice and cod-liver oil, the National Health Service, and grammar-school education: she passed the "eleven-plus" qualifying examination and attended a local, direct-grant grammar school; after leaving school she became briefly a junior reporter on a London local newspaper, the *Croydon Advertiser.* One news story she worked on, about a self-starving adolescent, struck home: she had been starving herself, as well. Her tall, big-boned body and her intransigent spirit were at odds with the way girls were supposed to be, inside or outside. Looking back to her teenage years, she always made the same joke: "I now recall this period with intense embarrassment, because my parents' concern to protect me from predatory boys was only equaled by the enthusiasm with which the boys I did indeed occasionally meet protected themselves against me." She married in 1960—to Paul Carter, whose name she kept—as a more or less desperate remedy for loneliness; she described her husband as "somebody who would go to Godard movies with me and on CND marches and even have sexual intercourse, though he insisted we should be engaged first." This period of rebellion took the form of a quest for authenticity: the Beats in the United States, the existentialists in France, the Angry Young Men in Britain. At the same time, however, there was a growing sense that realism and authenticity were somehow subtly fake, threadbare, and conformist. Carter's response to this mood was to play games with Gothic, fairy-tale, and fantasy motifs, taking advantage of the decay of realism. Her tone was camp; her texts were full of invisible quotation marks. In her first five novels, all of which

were written in the 1960s—*Love,* published in 1971, was written in 1969—the point of view was vagrant, as readily "male" as "female."

Before Carter published anything, she returned to school, attending the University of Bristol from 1962 to 1965 as a married, older student. She read English and specialized in medieval literature, with an autodidact's resistance to the conventional syllabus, which was still influenced by the maps of the great tradition drawn by F. R. Leavis. Alongside medieval romance and folktales she read widely in psychology, anthropology, and narratology. She also read science fiction and horror comics and watched a lot of movies. Her first novel, *Shadow Dance* (1966)—later renamed *Honeybuzzard,* after its sexy and malign master of ceremonies, in American and paperback versions—was completed during her second summer vacation at Bristol. She settled in Bristol for a time after graduating, and its provincial 1960s version of Bohemia provides the setting not only for *Shadow Dance* but also for *Several Perceptions* (1968) and *Love.*

Carter's first novel is crammed with ideas, themes, and images that its author explored for years to come. It is a Gothic thriller, and its main setting is a junk shop selling newly fashionable Victorian rubbish. A patina of meretricious charm spreads over the characters and their present world, and echoes of fairy tales such as "Beauty and the Beast" and "Bluebeard" and of other fictions lend an eerily familiar and even decorative air to the violent, grubby, chaotic feelings and events of the book. *Shadow Dance* is a shocking novel, particularly in the way that its treatment of sexual politics ruthlessly reflects and anatomizes 1960s mores. Just as in the gender-segregated domain of Jane Austen's novels there are no extended scenes that show men alone together, so in this sexually liberated book there are no scenes between women alone: the female characters are scattered at large in a man's world. The plot involves an ambiguous threesome: impressionable Morris, from whose point of view the story is told; Honeybuzzard, Morris's beautiful, blond hippie partner in the antique business; and Ghislaine, who had used her baby-doll charm to seduce a series of men until Morris, after a disastrous one-night stand with her, asked Honey to "teach her a lesson," and he sliced up her beautiful face. She has returned from the dead, and the pain of her condition is matched only by its stylization: "her face was all sideways and might suddenly . . . leak gallons of blood."

Ghislaine comes to stand for the past, a vengeful emissary from the realm of shadows that Morris and Honey regularly raid. Much of the novel's action consists of scavenging expeditions through derelict houses, where the decay of ordinary possessions into camp "antiques" forms a fitting metaphor for the decay of the characters' experience into theater. The setting is a whole world of leftovers, quotes, copies, and déjà vu: "life imitating rotten art again, as Honey always said it did." Morris admires Honey for his pitiless playfulness. He becomes a toy maker, making jumping-jack caricatures of the other characters (anticipating sinister uncle Philip Flower in *The Magic Toyshop*), high on the freedom of role-playing: "I like—you know—to slip in and out of me. . . . I would like to have a cupboard bulging with all different bodies and faces. . . . There was a man, last night, we were in a club and there was this man, singing blues, and he had a red rose stuck in his shirt. It was red as the cap of liberty. . . . I would like to wear him, tomorrow morning." The reference to the "cap of liberty" worn in the French Revolution signals that Honey is no ordinary monster. Like the Marquis de Sade, he is a radical pornographer who strips away the mystification of sex and sentiment to reveal the workings of power underneath.

In the plot the past devours the three main characters. Carter mirrors this circumstance stylistically, writing about the secondhand trade in a literary idiom that was itself self-consciously secondhand. The ending, when, in a deserted house, Morris discovers Ghislaine's body carefully covered with oilcloth, a bowl of disinfectant under the bed, is an ironic act of homage to Fyodor Dostoyevsky's *The Idiot* (1868). Carter shared her characters' obsession with the realm of shades, of past realities ruined and recycled. Looking back almost twenty years later, she wrote, "I am the pure product of an advanced, industrialised, post-imperialist country in decline."

Shadow Dance is an elaborately, even obsessively structured book, but it also has some interesting loose ends; it is full of unfinished business. Honey's London girlfriend, Emily, for instance, who ends the book pregnant and practical, is a survivor. Morris thinks her hard, but he is surprised by a sudden glimpse of her capacity for insight. Emily is marginal to this story, but she comes into her own in Carter's later writing—in the cool heroines of *The Magic Toyshop* and *Heroes and Villains* (1969) and the bride who outwits Bluebeard in the title story of *The Bloody Chamber*. Some of Carter's male characters have a similar gift: Desiderio, for instance, the narrator of *The Infernal Desire Machines of Dr. Hoffman*, saves himself from being eaten by a tribe of river Indians because he has read anthropologist Claude Lévi-Strauss and can work out what they have in store for him. One of the hallmarks of Carter's narrative style throughout her career is the way she allows certain characters to read their worlds and thus, like authors, escape the script. In *Nights at the Circus* her winged heroine, Fevvers, interviewed by skeptical journalist Walser on the cusp of the fin de siècle, suddenly reveals a cul-

tural historian's grasp of the "decadent" mystification of prostitution, attributing it to the influence of Charles Baudelaire: "'I put it down to the influence of Baudelaire, sir.' 'What's this?' cried Walser. . . . 'The French poet, sir; a poor fellow who loved whores not for the pleasure of it but, as he perceived it, the horror of it, as if we was, not working women doing it for money but *damned souls.*'"

Carter's second novel, *The Magic Toyshop,* a much simpler book than *Shadow Dance,* is the most popular of her early works. It has a classic rite-of-passage plot in which Melanie and her younger brother, Jonathan, are suddenly, bleakly orphaned and find themselves fostered by the unknown Uncle Philip, who makes all-too-lifelike toys. His South London shop, with its vertical, decaying house beetling above, becomes their world, and their nice, clean, vague childishness is sharpened, bit by bit, into vivid definition. Carter has refashioned a conventional tale about growing up into a Freudian fairy tale about supplanting mother—Melanie knows she somehow caused her parents' death in a plane crash when she tried on her mother's wedding dress—and symbolically sleeping with father, played by gross, domineering Uncle Philip, who now stands between Melanie and her future.

This new household, seen with stunned literalness through Melanie's eyes, is a place of timeless enchantment, where Philip like an ogre holds in thrall his starveling Irish wife, Margaret, who was struck dumb on her wedding day, and her two threadbare, wild brothers, Finn and Francie. In the basement he has a private theater, "Flower's Puppet Microcosm," where flesh and wood share a sinister equality: here he wants Melanie to play Leda and be raped by his huge puppet swan. She fights her way out of his world of artifice, joining forces with his desperate Irish captives, who are conducting their own occult rebellion through music, images, incest, and arson. The burning down of houses, a recurrent motif in Carter's books, is first depicted here. Melanie survives to start the world with smelly and sensuous Finn, a parody of the conventional fairy tale's happy ending. Both of them suffer from sudden vertigo and uncertainty once the old man has been dethroned and they are faced with the question of how to enter real time.

The Magic Toyshop won the John Lewellyn Rhys Memorial Prize of 1967. Her third novel, *Several Perceptions,* won the Somerset Maugham Award. It is set in Bristol among a pageantlike array of "fringe" figures and has the same period flavor as *Shadow Dance:* Joseph, the antihero of the hero, attempts suicide in the first chapter in the style of Samuel Beckett's Murphy—exploding the gas—and thereafter is hopelessly disoriented, unstuck in time in a desultory, shiftless sideshow

Dust jacket for Carter's 1971 novel about a macabre triangle

of a world made up of hippies, vagrants, tramps, and a prostitute whose family members were "fairground people." The novel is constructed rather like a strip cartoon or a "flicker-book," in which the motion of the pages turning sets the different characters into illusory motion: a geriatric music- hall artiste playing an imaginary fiddle, a bisexual self- appointed master of the revels, an analyst who tells Joseph, "You're wedged in the gap between art and life." The plot is a benevolent variation on the puppet-master theme, with good magic in the foreground. According to the first edition, the novel was written quickly, between March and December 1967. It is in a sense a Christmas story, a fable of innocence regained: "It was the time of the winter solstice, one of the numinous hinges of the year. . . ."

Around this time Carter seemed to have found her cultural niche as a reporter from the front line of the counterculture. From 1966 on she wrote occasionally for *New Society* and *Guardian,* honing her insights into the iconography of clothes, gestures, and idioms. She did not settle into this role, however. *Heroes and Villains* in 1969 deals with the same kinds of material but pushes the implications of imaginative dandyism to newly radical conclusions. Employing the familiar sci-

ence-fiction convention of a postnuclear dark age, the novel is a speculative allegory, more aggressive and more schematic than anything she had written before. There is continuity with the earlier novels, both thematically and technically (the opening, for instance, parodies the opening of Jane Austen's 1816 novel, *Emma*), but Carter is embarked on a skeptical exploration of the whole mystique of Otherness. The narrative is related from the point of view of Marianne, who runs away from the white tower where she grew up with her Professor-father. Professors live in orderly communities mostly made up of craftsmen and farmers, guarded by soldiers. Outside are forests and the ruins of cities, inhabited by shapeless mutants and tribes of wandering Barbarians, who raid Professor villages from time to time and who have haunted Marianne's imagination ever since she watched one of them kill her brother.

The action of the book concerns Marianne's violent initiation into Barbarian life and her chillingly efficient acquisition of the strategies necessary for survival outside the pale of reason. Barbarian existence, with its bizarre costumes of "furs and brilliant rags," its superstitions, and its collage of half-forgotten, half-invented rituals, is partly code for the glamour of the 1960s guerrilla underground and various counterculture movements. It is also an ironic portrayal of the traditional realm of fantasy and romance as (after all) part of history. When Marianne becomes the ravished "bride" of beautiful, savage Jewel, she discovers with furious disappointment, pain, and even pity that he too suffers from self-consciousness and lack of conviction; he is just "a phallic and diabolic version of the female beauties of former periods." In the book's closing scene on the seashore a pregnant and widowed Marianne contemplates her future role in the tribe: "I'll be the tiger lady and rule them with a rod of iron." In the wilderness the shape of society is laid bare but not left behind. *Heroes and Villains* is at once euphoric and without illusions. Carter, looking back to the 1960s, wrote "truly, it felt like Year One. . . . All that was holy was in the process of being profaned. . . . I can date to that time . . . and to that sense of heightened awareness of the society around me in the summer of 1968, my own questioning of the nature of my reality as a woman. How that social fiction of my femininity was created, by means outside my control, and palmed off on me as the real thing." She had become a deliberate analyst and interrogator of mythologies. In a 1977 interview in the *New Review* she said: "I do think we're at the end of a line, and to a certain extent I'm making a conscious critique of the culture I was born to. In a period like this of transition and conflicting ideologies, when there isn't a prevalent ideology, really all artists can do is to go round mopping up."

The lowlife, picaresque structure of *Heroes and Villains* and the rigorous, allegorical quality of its fantasy disappointed some of Carter's readers. The *New Statesman* reviewer regretted her addiction to the "Gothick," letting spelling imply his distaste for the whole genre, and found the objects of her parody "obscure." Her publishing history suggests that she was becoming too demanding on a mainstream audience's sensibilities: she had been regularly published by Heinemann in England and Simon and Schuster in the United States, but she now became a nomad, with several publishers and no secure home. *Heroes and Villains* was a book that symbolized breaks and new departures—it was one of the first titles published in the 1970s by the new, consciously experimental Picador imprint and in 1981 by the revived King Penguin paperback list. Its wandering, speculative formula became the narrative mode of her fiction for the next decade. In the meantime, however, she rounded out the 1960s with *Love,* an ironic salute to the passing of the decade.

Love is a rewrite of *Shadow Dance,* again set in Bristol's Bohemia and again with a lethal triangle. The craft and indifference of the novel's writing transforms experience into theater. The character of Honeybuzzard has

been split into two half brothers, Lee and Buzz; and undead Ghislaine has a counterpart in Annabel, Lee and Buzz's go-between, who like her predecessor dies horribly, overdosed on role-playing. The novel revises the story of Sleeping Beauty, as well, in that the girl realizes what the script really means by waking up to die instead of living happily ever after. Once upon a time Lee would have delivered sexual redemption, but here he does not—the fact that the narrative point of view is his, that he is supposedly in charge, underlines his failure as a folk hero. When Carter revised *Love* in 1987, teasing out futures for the surviving characters, she asserted that of course Annabel could not be given a future, that the book was "Annabel's coffin."

Carter's own rite of passage was her journey to Japan, which she first visited in 1969 with money from the Somerset Maugham Award and then went there to live for two years. She had left her husband behind—they divorced in 1972—and lived first with a Japanese lover, and later alone. She wrote about her experience at the time, in pieces for *New Society* (some of which were reprinted in *Nothing Sacred,* 1982) and later in some of the stories in *Fireworks,* such as "A Souvenir of Japan":

they seemed to have made the entire city into a cold hall of mirrors which continually proliferated whole galleries of constantly changing appearances, all marvellous, but none tangible. If they did not lock up the real looking-glasses it would be hard to tell what was real and what was not. Even the buildings one had taken for substantial had a trick of disappearing overnight. One morning, we woke to find the house next door reduced to nothing but a heap of sticks and a pile of newspapers neatly tied with string, left out for the garbage collector.

Another *Fireworks* story, "Flesh and the Mirror," describes Tokyo as the city where one can lose and find oneself, the capital of a country of the skin, where "the inside no longer commands the outside" (as Roland Barthes put it in his 1970 book on Japan, *Empire of Signs*). "Flesh and the Mirror" centers on an erotic encounter with a stranger reflected in a mirror on a hotel-room ceiling and is about the vertigo of losing a kind of psychic virginity, one's sense of home. In Japan she completed the project of estrangement begun in England: "In Japan I learnt what it was to be a woman and became radicalised." The remark is in the same spirit as her descriptions of the ethos of the late 1960s in her essay "Truly It Felt Like Year One" (1988): ". . . it started to feel like living on a demolition site—one felt one was living on the edge of the unimaginable."

In a 1977 interview that appeared in *New Review,* Carter described *The Infernal Desire Machines of Doctor Hoffman,* which was published after her return to England in

1972, as "an inventory of imaginary cities." The narrator, Desiderio, looks back at a time when he saved the world from the machinations of the title's mad scientist, a dealer in dreams—a new incarnation of the old patriarchal puppet master. Desiderio tracks him through a whole series of distinct subcultures, from a circus to a tribe of river Indians to a Sadeian brothel peopled with automata and androids to a society of centaurs related to the Houyhynhmns in Jonathan Swift's *Gulliver's Travels* (1726). Throughout his travels Desiderio encounters one lover in many disguises—Albertina, the doctor's shape-shifting daughter—who turns out ultimately to be her father's loyal agent and whom Desiderio finally destroys, only to want her forever. The novel has a primitive, picaresque structure, but its satire is every bit as savage, topical, and cerebral as Swift's: it plays with ideas and assumptions from structuralist thinkers such as Lévi-Strauss and Michel Foucault and is set in Latin America in tribute to the magical realism associated with the fiction of Jorge Luis Borges and Gabriel García Márquez. It ends, in its hero's phrase, with "insatiable regret" that society sustains the possible only by outlawing the impossible.

The Infernal Desire Machines of Doctor Hoffman was ignored or treated with incomprehension and contempt by most mainstream critics, as was Carter's other novel of the 1970s, *The Passion of New Eve* (1977), also a last-days allegory. *The Passion of New Eve* is set in the United States, a near-future New World where society is breaking down into sects and militias who live according to bizarre schemes of their own invention. The novel is a frontal attack on the question of gender, a feminist book though at odds with the "madwoman in the attic" version of a woman's place in the house of fiction. Her own account of the history of her feminism in "Truly It Felt Like Year One" starts with a quotation from one of her favorite poets, the visionary William Blake, from *Proverbs of Hell* (1790–1793): "'If the fool persists in his folly, he becomes wise.' I suppose that was how I came to feminism, in the end, because still and all there remained something out of joint and it turned out that was it, rather an important thing, that all the time I thought things were going so well I was a second class citizen." In *The Passion of New Eve* woman is born out of a man's body again, as in the Genesis story—a moving image of the painful process by which the 1970s women's movement had to carve out its own identity from the unisex mold of 1960s radical politics.

The plot concerns bringing the dead travesty of a woman to life: symbols are acknowledged as such, chief among them Tristessa, a Hollywood goddess in the mold of Greta Garbo, long vanished into seclusion and thus impeccably glamorous, a timelessly erotic shimmer on the silver screen: "Suffering was her vocation, she suffered exquisitely. . . ." Again the form is primitive and picaresque. Evelyn, the English hero and one of Tristessa's fans, rejects his black love, Leilah, in New York and in full flight from his guilt and her bloody abortion sets out westward. He first encounters a technological matriarchy in the desert, where he is surgically transformed into a centerfold Eve; then a commune like that of Charles Manson's "family"; and then the glass mausoleum of Tristessa, who is not a woman but the greatest transvestite of them all. To this grand unreality Carter mates her "new Eve" in a kind of alchemical marriage and again concludes the novel with her heroine pregnant by the shore, conscious of having crossed to the other side of passive suffering.

In 1977 Carter also published an elegant translation of *The Fairy Tales of Charles Perrault*. She had been rereading fairy tales and the works of the Marquis de Sade in tandem and bleakly contemplating the historical interweaving of femininity and pain. In her 1978 radio play, "Come Unto These Yellow Sands"—which is about the Victorian painter of fairy scenes, Richard Dadd, who murdered his father and spent the rest of his life in mental asylums—the "realm of faery" is described as "a kitsch repository for fancies too savage, too dark, too voluptuous, fancies that were forbidden the light of Common Victorian day." During this time she was also developing the thesis of *The Sadeian Woman*, which had been commissioned by the newly created Virago Press: "To be the object of desire is to be defined in the passive case. To exist in the passive case is to die in the passive case—that is, to be killed." The heroine of Sade's *Justine* (1791) "becomes the prototype of two centuries of women who find that the world was not, as they had been promised, made for them. . . . These self-consciously blameless ones suffer and suffer until it becomes second nature." Traditionally, fairy tales too had served this masochistic end.

In *The Bloody Chamber,* however, Beauty and the Beast, Bluebeard, Sleeping Beauty, and Red Riding Hood are pried loose from their timeless roles and persuaded to relive them with different conclusions. The heroines of Carter's earlier fiction, who try on dead women's wedding dresses and step into their mother's shoes, are evoked by the title character of "The Lady of the House of Love," a vampiric sleeping beauty who wears "a hoop-skirted dress of white satin draped here and there with lace": she is "a girl with the fragility of the skeleton of a moth, so thin, so frail that her dress seemed . . . to hang suspended, as if untenanted in the dark air, a fabulous lending, a self-articulated garment in which she lived like a ghost in a machine." The fairy tales exemplify a continuous interweaving of texts, demonstrating how supposedly timeless myths of women's passivity are made and disseminated. Not sur-

Dust jacket for Carter's 1984 novel, about a journalist and a trapeze artist at the turn of the nineteenth century

prisingly, the most popular of Carter's retold tales are those—"The Tiger's Bride," "The Company of Wolves," and "Wolf Alice"—that are about abandoning human separateness and getting permanently lost in the forest.

In the 1980s, in her forties, Carter came into her own. She refined her persona as a yarn-spinner and settled in South London with her partner, Mark Pearce. At the same time she traveled around the world to read and teach writing. She came to appreciate public readings as a means of dramatizing the teasing power of the narrator and providing an added dimension to the written work. In her last two novels, *Nights at the Circus* and *Wise Children,* the protagonists are professional performers.

Nights at the Circus was the only novel Carter published in the 1980s, but the book compensated for this paucity by its size and vaudevillian energy. Its heroine, Fevvers, is a heavyweight trapeze act, a ribald Mae West with wings, and the plot chronicles a gargantuan series of adventures set at the turn of the last century. Fevver's minder, Lizzie, a stand-in for the author, offers a description of the book's carnival progress: "A motley

crew indeed—a gaggle of strangers drawn from many diverse countries. Why, you might have said we constituted a microcosm of humanity, that we were an emblematic company. . . . The hazards of the journey reduced us to a little band of pilgrims abandoned in the wilderness upon whom the wilderness acted like a moral magnifying glass. . . ." The narrative cuts between third-person description, speeches, inset tales, and authorial commentary. The central plot, however, involves the contest and romance between Fevvers and journalist Jack Walser, who comes along to interview and expose her and finds himself caught up in a different story that unravels his skeptical worldview. When he joins the circus undercover as a clown, he begins a journey that culminates in his becoming a shaman's apprentice in Siberia. Fevvers runs out of peroxide and breaks a wing but manages to stay her own woman and keep her mystery throughout. Her given name is Sophia, which means wisdom. She is portrayed as a new kind of being, a music-hall version of the New Woman, a conscious symbol who uses other symbols to make up her own story. In so doing, Fevvers exposes the myths for what they are, thus embodying the artistic principle Carter set forth in a 1983 essay in *On Gender and Writing:* "I become mildly irritated when people . . . ask me about the 'mythic' quality of work I've written lately. . . . I'm in the demythologising business. I'm interested in myths . . . just because they are extraordinary lies designed to make people unfree."

While writing *Nights at the Circus* Carter became pregnant, and her son, Alexander, was born in November 1983. From that time until her death she followed a familiar pattern of keeping her domestic base in South London but traveling frequently, almost always with Pearce and Alexander. Hers was increasingly the life of a woman of letters. She served as judge for contests and literary awards, edited collections, compiled anthologies, and wrote introductions and essays, all with zest—she was for the first time making enough money from writing to live on. In her public persona she took on the mocking character of Mother Goose and spoke with apocryphal authority. Her preface to *The Virago Book of Fairy Tales* (1990), which she edited, celebrates the role of the re-writer:

> . . . the term "fairy tale" is a figure of speech and we use it loosely, to describe the great mass of infinitely various narrative that was, once upon a time and still is, sometimes passed on and disseminated through the world by word of mouth, stories without known originators that can be remade again and again by every person who tells them. . . . Fairy tales, stories from the oral tradition, are all of them the most vital connection we have with the imaginations of the ordinary men and women whose labour created our world.

Her own stories from the late 1970s and early 1980s, collected in *Black Venus* (1985), are not folksy or wholesome, however. She inserts new episodes into ready-made myths, for example, into Charles Baudelaire's and Edgar Allan Poe's life stories; she also revisits the Lizzie Borden murders and rewrites Daniel Defoe. The stories are virtuoso performances that mark out the extraordinary range of her later work. "The Kitchen Child" is the story of a blithe bastard who was conceived while his enormous mother was busy whipping up a lobster soufflé and looking the other way. The reader is led to expect a revelation—that the child is really the heir to great name or fortune—but he is simply the doyen of chefs, who resolutely refuses to be interested in the question of who his father may be. If "The Kitchen Child" is a tribute to anonymous creativity, "Overture and Incidental Music for *A Midsummer Night's Dream*," first published in the science-fiction magazine *Interzone* in 1982, is an irreverent salute to England's national literary hero. The story is set behind the scenes of William Shakespeare's play, where there

are no human characters at all, only fairies and mutants in the dank English woods. In a late interview Carter talked about Shakespeare and about this play in particular, spelling out something of its enchantment for her:

> Shakespeare, like Picasso, is one of the great hinge-figures that sum up the past—one of the great Janus-figures that sum up the past as well as opening all the doors towards the future. . . . I like *A Midsummer Night's Dream* almost beyond reason, because it's beautiful and funny and camp—and glamorous and cynical. . . . English popular culture is very odd. . . . There's no other country in the world where you have pantomime with men dressed as women and women dressed as men. . . . it's part of the great tradition of British art, is all that 'smut' and transvestism and so on.

English theater culture is also the territory of her last novel, *Wise Children,* in which the theme is parenthood, literary and literal. It traces the history of the Hazard theatrical dynasty from its nineteenth-century heyday, when its members colonized their world—or at least the parts colored pink on the map, the colonies—and took Shakespeare to the sticks, to the twentieth-century travesty of its imperial triumph, when the stage has been upstaged in film and television. The Hazards are mirrored and mocked by the illegitimate, female branch of the family, represented by elderly twins Dora and Nora Chance, who had their own vaudeville careers and live in indecorous retirement on the wrong side of the Thames. Dora is the book's narrator, a performer who becomes a storyteller in what could be considered an inversion of Carter's own career. *Wise Children* is a generous and inclusive book, and Carter's death from cancer, coming soon after its publication, hastened its acceptance as one of the canonical texts of the postmodern feminist sensibility.

As the critical responses to Carter's work multiply and the debate over its meaning and significance grows, it has become clear that her writing is more ambivalent, its implications darker, than a label such as "postmodern" suggests. The point about carnival, as Carter said, is that it has to stop: readers are compelled to face mortality with only the fragile armor of their imaginings.

Interviews:

Lorna Sage, "The Savage Sideshow," *New Review,* 4 (July 1977): 51–57;

William Bedford, *New Yorkshire Writing,* 3 (Winter 1978): 1–3;

John Haffenden, "Angela Carter," in his *Novelists in Interview* (London: Methuen, 1985), pp. 76–96;

Kerryn Goldsworthy, "Angela Carter," *Meanjin,* 44, no. 1 (1985): 4–13;

Sage, "Angela Carter Interviewed," in *New Writing,* edited by Malcolm Bradbury and Judy Cooke (London: Minerva, 1992), pp. 185–193.

References:

Cristina Bacchilega, *Postmodern Fairy Tales, Gender, and Narrative Strategies* (Philadelphia: University of Pennsylvania Press, 1997);

Joseph Bristow and Trev Broughton, eds., *The Infernal Desires of Angela Carter: Fiction, Femininity, Feminism* (Essex: Addison Wesley Longman, 1997);

Christina Britzolakis, "Angela Carter's Fetishism," *Textual Practice,* 9, no. 3 (1995): 459–476;

Aidan Day, *The Rational Glass* (Manchester & New York: Manchester University Press, 1998);

Anne Fernihough, "'Is she fact or fiction?': Angela Carter and the Enigma of Woman," *Textual Practice,* 11, no. 10 (1997): 89–107;

Sarah Gamble, *Angela Carter: Writing from the Front Line* (Edinburgh: Edinburgh University Press, 1997);

Michael Hardin, "The Other Other: Self-Definition Outside Patriarchal Institutions in Angela Carter's *Wise Children,*" *Review of Contemporary Fiction,* 14 (Fall 1994): 77–83;

Elaine Jordan, "Down the Road, or History Rehearsed," in *Postmodernism and the Re-reading of Modernity,* edited by Francis Barber and others (Manchester: Manchester University Press, 1992), pp. 159–179;

Jordan, "Enthralment: Angela Carter's Speculative Fictions," in *Plotting Change: Contemporary Women's Fiction,* edited by Linda Anderson (London: Edward Arnold, 1980), pp. 18–40;

Marvels and Tales: The Journal of Fairy Tale Studies, 12, no. 1 (1998), special issue on Carter;

Gerardine Meaney, *(Un)like Subjects: Women, Theory and Fiction* (London: Routledge, 1993);

Paulina Palmer, "From 'Coded Mannequin' to Bird Woman: Angela Carter's Magic Flight," in *Women Reading Women's Writing,* edited by Sue Roe (Brighton, U.K.: Harvester, 1987), pp. 177–205;

Linden Peach, *Angela Carter* (Basingstoke, U.K.: Macmillan, 1998);

David Punter, "Angela Carter: Supersessions of the Masculine," *Critique: Studies in Modern Fiction,* 25 (Summer 1984): 209–222;

Lorna Sage, *Angela Carter* (Plymouth, U.K.: Northcote House/British Council, 1994);

Sage, ed., *Flesh and the Mirror: Essays on the Art of Angela Carter* (London: Virago, 1994);

Lindsey Tucker, ed., *Critical Essays on Angela Carter* (New York: Hall, 1998);

Rory P. B. Turner, "Subjects and Symbols: Transformations of Identity in *Nights at the Circus,*" *Folklore Forum,* 20, nos. 1–2 (1987): 39–60.

Candida Crewe

(6 June 1964 –   )

Merritt Moseley
University of North Carolina at Asheville

BOOKS: *Focus* (London: Collins, 1985);

Romantic Hero (London: Collins, 1986);

Accommodating Molly (London: Heinemann, 1989);

Mad about Bees (London: Heinemann, 1991);

Falling Away (London: Century, 1996);

The Last to Know (London: Century, 1998).

Candida Crewe is one of the most impressive of the generation of British novelists now in their thirties. Her first novel, written while she was still in her teens, deploys the romantic machinery of gilded youth, glittering beauty, glamorous European travel, and thoroughly requited love. Each of her five successive novels has improved on its predecessor. She told an interviewer, "The foibles, weaknesses, and cruelties of human nature inform my novels and my journalism." Indeed, she addresses these characteristics lucidly in her fiction, at times with a satirical and humorous approach and on other occasions with a serious realism that demonstrates the importance of carefully observed or imagined details. She is interested in "how very small circumstances in life can have extreme consequences." Likewise, she uses finely noticed details to build fiction that carries great conviction without sensational events. She writes mostly about female protagonists, and the cruelty that affects their lives is often but not always perpetrated by men.

Candida Annabel Crewe is the daughter of writers: Quentin Crewe and his wife, Angela Howard-Johnson. Her father was a prolific journalist and food critic and the author of travel books and works of biography and autobiography, and her mother is a novelist whose works–novels, plays, short stories, children's books– have all appeared under her maiden name, Angela Huth. Each of Crewe's parents has been married three times. She lived with her mother after her parents' marriage ended, and her encouragement helped Crewe to become a writer. She began writing for her mother, including plays created as birthday presents, which she says were often about "the infidelities of adults."

Candida Crewe at the time of The Last to Know *(photograph © by Donovan Wylie, 1998)*

Crewe was educated at St. Mary's School in Calne, Wiltshire, from 1975 to 1978 and then at Headington School, Oxford, from 1978 to 1982. Based on the results of her A Level examinations, she was not initially accepted into the universities to which she applied; she tried for Oxford with the encouragement of her stepfather, an Oxford don, but was again passed over. At this point she decided not to try for Cambridge and moved to London. She worked in a bookshop and in publishing and began writing books, the first of which, *Focus,* appeared in 1985. Candida Crewe is married to Donovan Wylie, a Magnum photographer. Her first child, a son named Erskine, was born on 11 July 1998.

Except for 1986–1987, when she was a weekly columnist for the *Evening Standard* (London), Crewe has been a freelance journalist and novelist since the success of *Focus*. She has written for periodicals such as *The Times, The Telegraph, The Guardian,* and *The Spectator.* Her journalism includes interviews, book reviews, and general pieces. A report on the Adults-Only Peanut Butter Lovers Convention in Florida, published in the *Sunday Telegraph,* earned her the Catherine Pakenham Award for journalism in 1990. Her novel *Falling Away* (1996) was shortlisted for the John Llewellyn Rhys Memorial Award in 1997.

Focus is a young woman's book in many ways. Its protagonist, Zara Cecil, is wealthy, well connected, and loved by several desirable men; she is a beauty who almost inadvertently becomes a successful model and actress. Crewe wrote the novel at age eighteen "purely as an exercise in self-discipline, to see if I could get however many thousand words down on paper and get them published, and make enough money to write a 'proper' novel." By Crewe's own estimation her first "proper" novel is *Accommodating Molly* (1989). She has subsequently referred to *Focus* as "dreadful."

The plot of *Focus* is that of a traditional women's romance, in which the protagonist is loved by two men, one likeable but unexciting, the other unreliable but sexually appealing. There are similarities between Zara's situation and that of Marianne Dashwood in Jane Austen's *Sense and Sensibility* (1811): like Marianne, Zara has a level-headed sister, but in Crewe's novel the sexy rake comes to terms, and Zara is not expected to settle for the dull but worthy man. Another sort of interest is provided by Zara's job in fashion modeling, her friendships with rich socialites, and her enviable time spent in Venice and New York. There is a jolly excitement reminiscent of best-selling British novelist Jilly Cooper, whose book Zara reads on the plane to New York, in such lines as "Zara leapt into the pink, bubbly water, singing cheerily as she rubbed a bar of raspberry-red glycerine soap all over her. The soap made her hungry because it reminded her of a tempting, glistening boiled sweet." The novel also sounds an occasional note of realism, as when Zara, asked by the man she loves if she intends to be unfaithful to her husband, replies: "Of course I don't intend to be, you fool. But I assume the inevitable. That he will be to me. That goes without saying. And I don't completely rule out the possibility that I might be so myself. I don't mean however that I will or want to. There is a difference."

This occasionally cynical note was developed much more strongly in Crewe's next novel, *Romantic*

Hero (1986), another story of love entanglements featuring a romantic triangle with an unreliable but attractive man at the apex. The main character is India, a successful journalist. As she rides to work on her motorcycle one day, she spots a beautiful man crossing a Soho street. She decides to include him, if she can locate him, in an article she is writing about romantic heroes. She encounters him again starring in a production of *Romeo and Juliet,* which she is attending with another, more solid man, Tom. She commences an affair with Piers, though he treats her badly, lying about his whereabouts; eventually she learns that he has been having an affair with Bethnay, an older American woman whom she has befriended at the gym. Her earlier advice to Bethnay concerning how to handle philandering men becomes ironic when she realizes that they share a lover: "Throw him completely, refer to the other woman in a passing comment, but not with any hint of jealousy. Then carry on as if everything's fine. He should feel so guilty he can't go on with the pretense. If not, either lump it or better, leave him." Her own sangfroid is disrupted by the discovery that Piers has deceived her: she is visiting Tom and his family at their Scottish castle when she discovers that Piers, having told her he would be in Los Angeles over Christmas, is actually in London; wildly upset, she hitchhikes to London to confront him.

India realizes that Tom is the right man for her, that Piers, though physically beautiful, is worthless. Along with this maturing view of relationships, she matures in her professional life. She is a facile journalist, witty and cruel. Tom encourages her to set a loftier goal for her writing. When she tries to defend her article on romantic heroes as "a serious study of the hero with reference to literature, cinema," he insists that it is actually an "elaborate excuse to meet six eligible young men, interview them, have them flatter you and want . . . you. How many of them did you sleep with?" Tom arranges for her to write book reviews for his own more serious-minded magazine, and eventually India is made acting editor of another journal.

Romantic Hero is not without its own qualities of wish fulfillment, though it is written with an irony that contrasts nicely with the rather wide-eyed *Focus*. Though the romantic skeins are untangled to India's satisfaction, there is a lucid awareness of the shakiness of love relations that may be linked to her childhood interest in "the infidelities of adults." India, speaking to Tom, declares, "Women are often masochists. We are, on the whole, only ever attracted to shits. It may be more tragic becoming involved with them, but it's certainly more interesting."

Crewe's third novel, *Accommodating Molly* (1989), is another study of relations between men and women, focusing on the sadness of unhappy marriages and what Crewe perceives as the enormous disparity among contemporary Londoners between women's desire—usually unspoken but nonetheless strong—to marry and men's desire not to. The main character, Molly Almond, is a single woman in her mid twenties, not beautiful, tending to be overweight. The novel begins immediately after her boyfriend Dominic has left her. After this short prologue the novel goes back in time to depict Molly's relationship with her boss, Nick Winter, a bookseller. Nick is charming but feckless and heartless toward women, as evidenced by the three affairs in which he is involved. He worries about death, as he tells Molly: "I was just thinking that a soul is rather like a love letter, the body its envelope. Because the contents are so important, that envelope should be treated with due respect. I happen to take a lot of care of my envelope—fruit, vegetables, fish, exercise. When it's been ripped open and the letter's blown away to burn in Hell or reside in Heaven's golden file, I'm keen that it shouldn't just end up in the bin. It's not an unreasonable wish."

One of Nick's lovers, Helen Hardy, a spinster who lectures in English at University College and is writing a biography of A. E. Housman, has (like Molly) unhappily married parents and an unsatisfactory love life and thinks that "Housman was like a surrogate lover. He was certainly more attentive, reliable, romantic and faithful than Nick Winter. Of course, it was unfortunate that he was both homosexual and dead. 'But, there again, there're drawbacks in all relationships,' Helen said to herself."

A sensitive dread of commitment motivates most of the men in *Accommodating Molly*. Nick, sensing neediness from his lover Georgia, breaks off their affair; she has been excruciatingly careful never to mention marriage or to suggest in any way that she might desire it, but he has broken her heart. Meanwhile, Molly has begun an affair with Dominic De'Ath, who is shy and polite, unlike the rogues she usually becomes involved with. He is also desperately unwilling to make any commitment, however, to regard himself as living with Molly even after he begins dwelling in her flat, insistent on not discussing her family with her, as he interprets this as being "inveigled." Molly knows the symptoms: "There's all these women desperate to get married, all these men desperate to avoid it. Nick's just one who's, well, exploiting the situation, having his cake and eating it. Much though I love him, he's a bit of a bastard." After Dominic leaves her and she meets a friend who is getting married, Molly reflects,

Lucy, I'm very happy for you. I am. Really. But I'm not going to admit that I, too, want to be a wife. You don't admit things like that. Not ever. The rule is you don't let on. Not ever. Women in the latter part of the twentieth century have feminist ideals. They don't think about marriage, unless it slaps them in the face. They certainly don't tell people that in fact marriage is the thing they aspire to more than anything in life.

A husband. Children. Security.

It's not asking much. But one must never ask for it, all the same.

That last line is, perhaps, the theme of *Accommodating Molly*. In fact, Molly does receive a proposal—from the "bastard," Nick Winter—but refuses him, and, in the end, she retreats to Oxford to be with her father, who has been abandoned by his own selfish and unfaithful wife, Cake. Despite the frustration of all love projects in this novel, it is far from dreary. There is beautiful writing in the analysis, in some descriptions, and in such lines as this one, about a guest at a publisher's cocktail party: "He attempted to smile, but his cheeks appeared to be puffed up and bulky like badly distributed cellulite on a fat woman's bottom."

The characters in *Accommodating Molly* are all in some way isolated, through the failures of love, their eccentricities, or selfishness. Like that novel, *Mad about Bees* (1991) is an ensemble study of a group of loosely related Londoners and their mostly fragile relationships. Crewe takes as one of her main characters a man who is beyond mere eccentricity, who suffers from a condition that seems to combine neurosis with some form of Tourette's syndrome. Samuel Sorrell, a science teacher in a comprehensive school in London, has an unreasonable fear of electricity, dreading that at night gas will escape from the electric outlets in his home and kill his family; he also feels compelled to tap his head twenty-four times before drinking coffee, or his children will be run over by a bus. In this novel Crewe adds a political dimension of an anti-Thatcherite kind, with serious reflections on the difficulty of teaching in deprived schools—staff shortages, one textbook per class—and the problems of the National Health System.

Samuel, basically a good man, is infatuated with an English teacher at his school. He performs in *A Midsummer Night's Dream* because she is directing, and one night after rehearsal they go to bed together; the experience seems to have no effect on his marriage and may even help to cure his neuroses.

Samuel's sister-in-law, Nell, has a more difficult love life; her affair with a scientist specializing in bees, the grandson of an aged poet to whom she reads, seems imperiled by another woman who claims to be "mad about bees." Earlier in the novel Nell relates to the old poet, Cillian, her pessimistic view of relationships, which accords with Candida Crewe's childhood interest in the infidelities of adults:

I've seen you, Mum and Dad, and God knows how many others all make a mess of things. To believe in love and marriage after you lot I'd need to be either irredeemably unobservant or unforgiveably naive. Things don't last. That's all there is to it. Part of the human condition. Every association crumbles. Why draw out and exacerbate the inevitable alienations and partings with tedious religious and legal complications? Pointless.

Mad about Bees contains some sharp observation, as readers will expect from Crewe. A horrible man "took a duty-free cigarette with a white filter from a long box, and lit it with a lighter as blatantly gold as the sequins on a showgirl's bra. He didn't offer one to Nell." At a showing of paintings by Nell's friend Hilary, an art bore orates pompously about the work; Nell "winked at Hilary and watched him as the man droned on, reflecting that he had the uncomfortable, slightly desperate air of someone at an opera who feels the onset of a coughing fit."

In Crewe's first four books marriage-minded women are more prevalent than those with feminist ideals. Crewe's fifth novel, *Falling Away,* redresses the balance. The novel alternately relates the present and past circumstances of Dorothy Sheffield, a midwife living in a rundown seaside town in Somerset. As an adult she contentedly practices midwifery, taking a sympathetic interest in her patients; one of her sisters, whose husband batters her; and a dying old woman. The story of her youth, by contrast, is sensational. After a one-night stand under the pier with an older man she became pregnant; her parents made her surrender the baby and then sent her to Glasgow, where she spent nine years effectively imprisoned in Piccadilly Laundry, a home for wayward women. Crewe based Dorothy's incarceration on actual social and historical circumstances, underlining the fact that institutions such as Piccadilly Laundry existed throughout England, Scotland, and Ireland until recently. Dorothy's privations and mistreatment there are reminiscent of Lowood school in Charlotte Brontë's *Jane Eyre* (1837), which is also run by religious fanatics. She escapes once but is caught and returned; later, she leads another, highly publicized breakout.

In the present, Dorothy falls in love with Harold Mills, the nephew of the old woman she visits in a home, and she offers him a harrowing account of her time at Picadilly Laundry:

I was blinded, in a sense, for nearly a decade of my youth. Though I never lost my sight, I was sent to live in an institution which was a working laundry. I and my fellow "moral defectives" had to labour every day, cleaning sheets, cleaning our bodies, cleansing our souls. . . . Such a place . . . existed for the containment

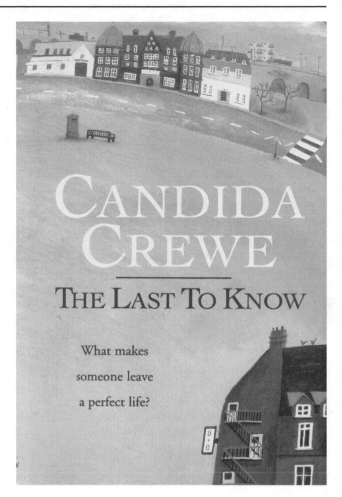

Dust jacket for Crewe's 1998 novel, about a husband who goes out to buy ice cream and vanishes for several months

of women—deaf women; dumb women; blind women; tumorous women; physically deformed women; ugly women; obese women; neurotic women; stultiloquent women; idiosyncratic women; abandoned women; alcoholic women; penniless women; thieving women; violent women; psychotic women; schizophrenic women; insane women; feeble-minded women; morally defective women; spinster women.

Dorothy explains that "falling away" was the term for unmarried pregnancy at Piccadilly: "It's a lovely phrase I always thought, biblical sounding almost. Falling Away. Pity so often it gave rise to such unchristian consequences, such lack of joy at a new life, such wanting of imagination or understanding, such punishment, such heartlessness."

Despite her miserable history, Dorothy believes that people were not meant to live unloved. Even while in the laundry and dreaming of escape she longed for ordinary domesticity: "The overriding fantasy was for family life, simple domesticity. I used to envisage myself dressing the kids for school in their little uniforms, packing their lunchboxes, and cooking my husband's breakfast, all at the same time." The conclusion of the novel allows for at least the possibility of domestic happiness: despite plentiful examples of married misery—especially that of Dorothy's sister—Dorothy and Harold intend to move in together.

Crewe's most recent novel, *The Last to Know* (1998), is likewise based on an actual social phenomenon: the significant number of adults who have simply disappeared without offering any explanation to their spouses. Crewe has said that she is "fascinated by people's capacity for cruelty towards those they purport to love," and *The Last to Know* is a study in exactly this capacity. Kim Black, who one day leaves his wife, Sylvie, and stays away for months, telling himself the entire time that he will soon go back or at least telephone, is hardly a classic sadist or even an unimaginative man. His leaving is essentially unmotivated, and thus his cruelty is almost inadvert. He has no reason to want his wife to suffer or awareness that he felt stifled in his marriage.

The psychological working out of this situation—an abandonment in which the most sensational details have been eschewed—gives the novel its power. Kim and Sylvie have been married, seemingly happily, for twenty-three years. Both are in "caring professions": Sylvie is a court welfare officer and Kim is a hard-working general practitioner. One night in November Kim comes home for dinner, but before it is ready he steps back out to buy some ice cream for dessert. Unable to find ice cream at the local grocery, he begins acting unaccountably, sitting idly in the cold, going to an Indian restaurant, then walking to the center of town and taking a bus to London.

From this almost routine act the novel proceeds to follow Kim around the country. Alternating chapters recount Sylvie's attempts to find him and her emotional reactions. Kim goes to Scotland, where he lives in rooming houses and finds menial jobs. Under the name Tim White he works as a porter in a hospital but loses that job because he saves the life of a patient being treated by an incompetent doctor. Meanwhile Sylvie consults with the police, her friends, and her two grown children. After an uneventful few months, during which he toys with the idea that he is having an adventure but eventually realizes that he is not, Kim returns. He is accepted, but with resentment and suspicion, by his wife.

Kim's portion of the novel is more interesting than Sylvie's, since she is essentially passive. Having found work in Inverness, Kim contemplates calling Sylvie: "Kim consciously acknowledged to himself at last that, for all the abominable cruelty it implied, the inclination was not there yet. Until he found it—which he wished and hoped he would very shortly—and could tell Sylvie where he was and why, his name and circumstances were certainly nobody else's business." Later he reflects that he has been thinking of his flight as "an innocent anomaly, while he enjoyed a temporary little blip of freedom and anonymity. Only now did he acknowledge to himself that this was patent bollocks. He was running away. Must have been. Really wasn't aiming to be traced." Even in this passage he seems to lack volition; eventually he sums up his motives as "whimsical opportunity, egotistical curiosity and diversion by the unedifying notion that chance might just turn up a little amuse-gueule to tickle his fancy." As he thinks these thoughts, he is cleaning garbage from the bottom of a skip at a restaurant. Shortly thereafter he returns home.

The risk Crewe takes in this novel is of writing a story of mysterious abandonment while keeping her characters average and inventing no unusual events. Kim's behavior is obviously not normal, but it comes to seem so because he is himself so normal. Thus, while *The Last to Know* lacks the humor of some of Crewe's earlier fiction, it is a deeper book, a profound exploration of the mysteries of human behavior. In this way it extends the author's mastery of the small details that become resonant through art.

In Kim's absence, Sylvie ponders the past, and her reflections could be said to offer insight into Crewe's fictional technique:

> The so-called ordinary past is for private reflection only. If it ever does inspire the attention of another, it is usually that of the individual in love with its subject, but even then it is not guaranteed an airing. If you were never abused, or an inquisitive type never fell in love with you, you could go through a whole life and no one might ever ask even simple things, like where exactly you were born, what was the wallpaper pattern on your childhood bedroom wall, did you prefer pear-drops or sherbet lemons? But it is surely these seeming trifles, every bit as much as the broad strokes, which reveal so much about the true nature of a particular character.

Candida Crewe is that inquisitive type, that individual in love with her subject, who proves the power of seeming trifles.

Sebastian Faulks

(20 April 1953 –)

Merritt Moseley
University of North Carolina at Asheville

BOOKS: *A Trick of the Light* (London: Bodley Head, 1984);
The Girl at the Lion d'Or (London: Hutchinson, 1989);
A Fool's Alphabet (London: Hutchinson, 1992; New York: Little, Brown, 1992);
Birdsong (London: Hutchinson, 1993; New York: Random House, 1993);
The Fatal Englishman (London: Hutchinson, 1996);
Charlotte Gray (London: Hutchinson, 1998; New York: Random House, 1999).

SELECTED PERIODICAL PUBLICATION–
UNCOLLECTED: "Forever a Mistress," *New Yorker,* 74 (27 April–4 May, 1998): 146–150.

Sebastian Faulks has published relatively few novels but has established a solid reputation. With the enormous critical and popular success of his 1993 novel, *Birdsong,* he vaulted to the front rank of writers born since 1950. Following a career as a literary journalist and three well-received literary novels, he made his mark with a book called by Wilder Penfield in the *Toronto Sun* (29 June 1996) "a wildly acclaimed epic novel" and by Louise Baring in *Vogue* (July 1995) "the most erotic book" she had ever read. In a country where, as Anthony Beevor suggested in the *Electronic Telegraph* (22 August 1998), "the idea of a popular literary novel still sounds like a contradiction in terms," he has become the most highly visible author—and beneficiary—of this anomalous category. Faulks's 1998 novel, *Charlotte Gray,* completes a loose trilogy that includes *Birdsong* and begins with his second novel, *The Girl at the Lion d'Or* (1989).

In terms of genre, Faulks's fiction is difficult to define. Despite his popularity (one of his novels has sold more than one-half million copies), he can be seen as unfashionable in his interests and methods. As Jason Cowley noted in the *Sunday Times* (29 August 1998), "There is a paradox in Faulks's fiction: he is an ambitiously literary writer yet his work can lend itself to interpretations of a kind of inflated sentimentalism."

Sebastian Faulks (photograph by Cornel Lucas) at the time of the U.S. edition of Birdsong

Fellow novelists such as Louise Baring have suggested that *Birdsong* "doesn't qualify for the front rank because it fails to break new ground." With the partial exception of *A Fool's Alphabet* (1992), which fractures chronology and presents its broad story in twenty-six short sections arranged not sequentially but alphabetically, his work is not in any way avant-garde. He has identified his influences as Gustave Flaubert, Marcel Proust, and Emile Zola and has called himself a romantic writer. Faulks's work is hardly romantic in the contemporary sense; what he may mean is that he is unabashedly interested in and good at conveying emotion, including powerful love, terror, dread, and desire, without a distancing scrim of irony or postmodern technique.

If Faulks has subjects or themes that run through all his books, they are France and twentieth-century history, particularly periods of extremity such as wartime. He has spent a considerable part of his life in France, including living in Toulouse in the middle 1990s, and, as he told Jason Cowley, "Ever since I visited France as a student I have felt an intense yearning for the country. In the early Seventies, it seemed a place where the past was imediately accessible. . . . I also feel that its history is emblematic of the 20th century: France is so close to Britain that their experience could so easily have been ours."

A charge regularly leveled against English writers (Scots are entirely different in this regard) is that they are unwilling or unable to write about contemporary life in Britain, choosing instead to write historical fiction. Faulks's *A Trick of the Light* (1984) is set in the present day, and *Birdsong* and *A Fool's Alphabet* have sections that are contemporary, but he generally writes about the first half of the twentieth century. Faulks has chosen a historic period of which he has made himself a master and has found those elements in it that seem universal—human beings under pressure, human relationships at their most intense—and presented them in luminous prose.

Sebastian Faulks was born in Newbury, England, the son of His Honour Peter Ronald Faulks (a judge) and Pamela Lawless Faulks. His father fought in World War II, his grandfather in World War I—two events of interest in his novels—and Faulks mildly regrets that he has had no similar opportunity for heroism. His family background was happy. Compared to the three subjects of his joint biography, *The Fatal Englishman* (1996), all of whom had emotionally remote fathers, he believes his father was "sort of operatic in his affections towards me." He enjoyed a comfortable middle-class upbringing: after Wellington College, a public school, he attended Emmanuel College, Cambridge, receiving his B.A. in 1974. Aspiring to become a novelist, he became first a teacher and, beginning with freelance writing while still a teacher, a journalist. In 1978 he became a reporter for the *Daily Telegraph,* a position he retained until 1982. At the same time he was running the New Fiction Society, a book club. From 1983 to 1986 he was a feature writer for the *Sunday Telegraph.*

In 1986 he rather riskily joined a newly launched national newspaper, *The Independent,* for which he served as literary editor from 1986 to 1989; he was then deputy editor (1989–1990) and associate editor (1990–1991) of its sister publication, *The Independent on Sunday.* The Sunday newspaper had circulation and financial difficulties from the beginning; in 1991 Faulks, who had been unhappy there anyway, was dismissed, with a large severance payment that supported him for a time and thus enabled him to write *Birdsong.* About his dismissal and the ensuing freedom, he told Jason Cowley, "For the first three months after I left I couldn't stop laughing. Every morning I'd wake up and start

cackling wildly, hysterically; I was so relieved to be out of the place." His greatest personal legacy from the years with *The Independent* is his marriage to Veronica Youlten, once his assistant literary editor. They have three children. Since 1992 Faulks has written a regular column in *The Guardian,* but he is essentially a full-time novelist. Since the success of *Birdsong* he has had even less need for journalistic employment.

Published in 1984, Faulks's first novel, *A Trick of the Light,* is extremely accomplished. It tells the story of evil practiced on an innocent and explores the question of whether political ends may justify otherwise unacceptable means. The protagonist is George Grillet, who has come from France to England to recover from a disappointment in love. He stays with his married sister Francoise, her husband, Alan, and their children, Bernadette and Peter. On his arrival in London, George enters a pub and encounters the character who provides most of the moving force in the novel, Wyn Douglas, whom he sees haranguing a group of West Indian youths; soon white hooligans enter the pub and a riot ensues. George takes a room in a flat belonging to Susan, who is friendly with Wyn; Susan is annoying, unreliable, and persistent, pushing herself on the reluctant George while at the same time accusing him of wanting her. Eventually Susan and Wyn deceive George into stealing an audiotape; when a friend from the school where George teaches discovers that the tape is meant to aid the Irish Republican Army in a terror campaign, he erases it. As a result the friend kills himself, and George is kidnapped, tortured, humiliated, and terrified by the IRA. They let him go, but only after threatening to kill his niece.

When George confronts Susan and Wyn, they remain smug and unrepentant:

> "Listen," he said, "I don't want any sympathy. I know very well what you think of me. I don't want you to say you're sorry about what happened to Philip Harrison. I don't even expect you to care if my niece gets kidnapped and killed. But just for one moment admit it was serious. Say for one second that you wouldn't have liked it to happen to you. Just say something in *your own words.*"
>
> He found he was shouting and gripping Susan's wrist.
>
> She flushed as she tried to pull herself free. She was shouting too. "Don't you come the big macho man with me. I'm not interested. Comprende? I don't want you playing out your male chauvinist fantasies with this lady. OK?"

A Trick of the Light is a genuinely chilling study in evil as practiced by those who justify it with political slogans.

Wyn Douglas actually seems a true believer; Susan is worse because she employs only the rhetoric, without convictions.

Formally the novel places George's story in several ways. The main narrative is punctuated occasionally by two- or three-page passages of bitter political analysis and commentary, espousing the sort of leftist radicalism that Wyn exemplifies. They are anonymous but address events in the novel—one says, for instance, "I was far from certain that this George Grillet was the right person"—and the analysis is antiromantic. The passage that discusses George's sex life concludes that "Love is a madness, a loss of perspective; it afflicts only the madman. It's not the basis of any sane man's life. That remains the same; pain and the bond of need. To put it another way, money." The last such interpolation is a shocking confirmation that this is no detached observer but an agent in the action who promises further violence.

Throughout the novel George reads spy thrillers about a CIA agent named Macey. The adventures of Macey, with their moral clarity and purposeful action, provide a crisp alternative to the muddle and futility of George's life (identification with Macey even helps to draw George into the burglary). Near the novel's conclusion, when almost everything has gone wrong for George and he is returning to France, side-by-side passages contrast George with Macey:

> What was left for him now was the problem that had brought him here. How was he supposed to reorder his life to give it back the sense of purpose and joy it had lost? Or, to be precise, how could he stop his waking and his dreaming thoughts from lodging on the single and rather wearisome topic of a plump and stubborn school-teacher with shining eyes?

> "Mission accomplished," said Macey, and permitted himself a thin smile of satisfaction as he handed back the file to Goldman and tossed the snub-nosed Mauser into the older man's bulging in-tray. I don't know where to begin, thought George Grillet, putting the book back into his suitcase and closing it.

Faulks's interest in France is in evidence in this novel, though primarily as a place George comes from and returns to and in the thoughts of his brother-in-law, Alan: when Francoise says, "That's the difference between you and George. He may be a bit dreamy but at least he's got some ideals," Alan responds, "Of course, . . . it's probably different for George standing around with his face dipped in a glassful of wine all day with those simpering Frenchmen with their handbags and immaculate trousers."

Faulks, obviously, does not share his character's thoughtless, stereotypical view of France. In 1989, five years after *A Trick of the Light,* Faulks published *The Girl at the Lion d'Or,* a novel set entirely in that country in the late 1930s. It is an unsensational novel, with most of the dramatic and political elements relegated to the background. Anne, a young woman, arrives in the provincial town of Janvilliers, gets a job at the Hotel Lion d'Or, and commences an affair with a married landowner, Hartmann. The portentous political context of the time is represented by fears of Adolf Hitler's rise to power and extended discussions of the Popular Front government of Léon Blum; at a further remove, events from World War I cast shadows in the novel, as well.

Anne drifts into love with Hartmann, who gives her a gramophone and installs her in her own flat so she can have privacy. When he takes her away for a weekend trip, they become lovers. During the trip Anne tells Hartmann that her father had been an infantryman in World War I, driven beyond endurance when an officer ordered his unit to a pointless attack. He led a mutiny and shot the officer and was subsequently killed by a firing squad of his own comrades. When the circumstances of his death became known some time later, Anne and her mother were tormented by their neighbors, the father's name was chiseled off the local war memorial, and someone poisoned their dog. Eventually Anne's mother killed herself, and Anne went to Paris and lived with an older man, Louvet. Their relationship is shadowy; Louvet acted as a mentor for Anne, telling her that courage is the only thing that counts. On another occasion he attempted to persuade her that "When the good Lord made this world from the infinite number of possibilities open to him and selected—from another limitless pool—the kind of misery that his creatures should be subject to, he selected only one model. The moment of bereavement. Death, desertion, betrayal—all the same thing. The child sent from its parents, the widow, the lover abandoned— they all feel the same emotion which, in its most extreme form, finds expression in a cry." Louvet's vision foreshadows that Anne will experience the pain of bereavement from Hartmann, as she has from her mother and father; he does eventually order her away from his house. She leaves and goes to Paris, wanders around friendlessly, and, at the novel's end, climbs into the garden of Léon Blum's house.

Hartmann is a thoughtful and kind man, not a rake. His wife's discovery of his affair with Anne helps precipitate his ending it, but it is suggested that her family history is an obstacle for him, too:

> There was only his feeling for Anne with which he could comfort himself. There was no atom in him

which did not wish for her happiness and release. But all this fine feeling was of no use when confronted by the simple paradox of her dilemma: she could not be properly loved until she had disclosed the full story of her life; but by choosing him, at that moment in his own life, as the recipient of her trust, she had set in motion a slow but inevitable rejection. Its pattern would duplicate in her the effects of that first abandonment which had so far shaped her existence, and thus ensure that evil would be triumphant, repeating itself as naturally as if by breeding.

Hartmann is himelf a veteran of World War I. In *Birdsong* he appears again as an officer who discusses with his English counterparts the loss of morale in the French armies, indicating that he has personal experience of the kind of mutiny for which Anne's father was executed. He appears also in *Charlotte Gray,* in which his Jewishness becomes an important issue. The war plays a significant role in this novel as well, and not just for Anne and Hartmann: Mme Bouin, the unsympathetic manageress of the hotel, prays every night for her eighteen-year-old son, who was killed and left for ten days in a wall of French dead at the battle of Verdun.

Faulks has spoken often of his love for the "France profonde"—the provincial France, in which history seems yet at hand—and in this novel he creates a convincing tableau of small-town life in Janvilliers in the 1930s. Emily Read's review in *The Spectator* (5 August 1989) commends Faulks for "writing a very good French novel in English."

A Fool's Alphabet (1992) returns to many of the themes that resonate in the first two novels. The main character, Pietro Russell, experiences bereavement so serious that he suffers a breakdown; his father has also been bereaved by the early death of his wife, Pietro's mother. Both world wars figure in the novel. Pietro's father was wounded at the Battle of Anzio in World War II, and his grandfather fought at the Battle of Mons during World War I. The novel begins, in fact, with the father's wounding and convalescence in the home of an Italian family, which leads to his marriage to Francesca, the daughter of the house. Only gradually does Pietro become the novel's focus.

A "fool's alphabet" is a joke based on puns, Cockney mispronunciations, and misunderstanding; for instance, *A* for horses, *F* for vescence, and *N* for a penny. Pietro is not a fool, though he is bewildered and uneasy during much of the novel. After his mother's early death he lives with an uncommunicative father and attends a bad school in London. He becomes a great traveler, first as a sort of rootless hippie and then as a professional photographer, and his wanderings give the novel its geographical reach. Each of the novel's twenty-six chapters is named for a place. *A* is

for Anzio; *Z* is for Zanica, Italy; other prominent locations are Ghent, Uzes, and Mons, the site of another World War I battle in 1914. Although the sections do not appear in chronological order, they are dated, and the reader has no difficulty following the story as it builds through indirection a powerful account of Pietro Russell's life.

In place of chronology Faulks offers a variety of links. For instance, Pietro meets a young woman named Hannah, whom he later marries, in Ghent; in conversation with a friend, Hannah remembers Pietro's comment on "Belgian schoolgirls on a bridge" and how his grandfather would have liked that. Later in the novel (but chronologically earlier) the grandfather comments on how the Battle of Mons had been suspended while a group of Belgian schoolgirls crossed a bridge in the battlefield. Likewise, Pietro's observation of Castellamare Drive in San Francisco is a muted link to his father's recognition of Castellamare in Italy as he is evacuated from the Battle of Anzio.

In response to Jason Cowley's suggestion that he writes premodern fiction, Faulks cites *A Fool's Alphabet* as the novel with which he "tried to do something different with form." More striking than its formal inventiveness, however, is the beauty of Faulks's writing, which makes the normal seem extraordinary. Pietro Russell is really an ordinary man, but, by virtue of Faulks's art, his life comes to seem luminous. The texture of the novel is extremely rich, giving a feeling of the influence of the past on the present and the poignance of lives unlived; in one sweeping passage Pietro's thoughts drift from Yarmouth in Norfolk to southern California, New York City, Rome, and Hong Kong: "He did not cry or feel moved at the thought of the terrifying sea and the unmade journeys it contained. He put from his mind the thought of the Italian shore and his mother, young Italian girl denied the world." Such passages led the reviewer for *Publishers Weekly* to judge *A Fool's Alphabet* "a wonderfully insightful book that reverberates with epiphanies large and small, a celebration of life in all its beauty and tragic brevity."

Even more than its predecessors, Faulks's next novel, *Birdsong,* demonstrates the author's sensitive and powerful awareness of love and his ability to represent it, as well as his concern for men and women in extreme situations. Although Faulks had written about war in *The Girl at the Lion D'Or* and *A Fool's Alphabet,* it was not central to the action; but *Birdsong,* subtitled "a novel of love and war," is focused on World War I. At the beginning of the novel a young Englishman, Stephen Wraysford, is staying in Amiens in northern France to learn about a textile business. He is struck by Isabelle Azaire, the beautiful but unhappy wife of his host, a middle-aged, somewhat brutal businessman;

soon the two are involved in a passionate affair. They run away together, but eventually she leaves him.

The next section of the novel is set during World War I. Another narrative strand, set in the 1970s and featuring Stephen's granddaughter, is intercut with the wartime scenes and comments on the wartime action. Stephen is an officer with the British Expeditionary Forces on the Western Front, caught up in the endless, deadly, and futile trench warfare. He is wounded twice, sees everyone he cares for killed or wounded, and occasionally goes back to England to discover general incomprehension and a feeling of lostness. Stephen is embittered because of his experience with Isabelle, the reader is led to understand, and seems to have few human relationships. While he is stationed near Amiens he reestablishes contact with Isabelle and her sister, though he does not revive his love affair with Isabelle, who eventually goes to Germany with a soldier, one of the occupiers of Amiens. Stephen marries her sister, Jeanne.

The overpowering impact of the war scenes is a result of Faulks's determination "to try and understand WWI, to try to relive it in some way, to explain it to myself and to other people." In fact, *Birdsong* is an old-fashioned novel in several respects, not only because of its realism and essentially chronological arrangement but also because of its didactic intent. Faulks believes it is important for contemporary readers to know more about what happened between 1914 and 1918. As he remarked in his 15 September 1993 column for *The Guardian:* "the men who had fought at the Somme and Passchendaele, who had seen extermination on a scale never before or since witnessed in war, became the victims, to some extent, of their own reticence. Because they could not, or did not care to, describe the scope of what they had seen they became remembered half-ironically: there was no museum of their holocaust, only songs and silence and quaint brown photographs." The vividness with which Faulks conveys the terrors of the war owes much to his sheer knowledgeability about this period of history, which comes across in the novel as simple authority and reliability. He has said that the war was inadequately remembered but amply documented, and his use of documentary material provides solidity without becoming intrusive.

Faulks assigns central importance to 1 July 1916, the first day of the disastrous Battle of the Somme, on which more than thirty thousand British soldiers lost their lives. The Somme has always been a sort of byword for mass slaughter—in *A Fool's Alphabet* one of the participants at the Battle of Anzio makes the point that the fighting is worse than expected: "This is not Gallipoli . . . this is the bloody Somme." Faulks vividly

Dust jacket for the U.S. edition of Faulks's novel about World War I

portrays the experiences of Stephen and his men at the Somme, but even more moving than the horrible fighting is his account of the night before, in which he includes excerpts from the men's letters home, in many cases the last the soldiers will ever write; they contain lines such as "We are going to attack tomorrow, everything is absolutely thumbs up merry and bright and trusting to the best of luck." Other letters are more somber, however: Stephen writes to Isabelle, "Some crime against nature is about to be committed. I feel it in my veins."

A more unexpected choice was to write extensively about the digging and fighting underground. Though Stephen is an infantry officer, he becomes close to a unit of engineers—many of them veterans of the construction of the London Underground—whose job is to dig long tunnels under the German lines, either for listening posts or to explode mines. Their work is extremely tense—the Germans are also mining, and there is occasional fighting underground. Eventually,

Stephen is trapped underground with another soldier, Jack Firebrace.

Stephen is in some ways a burnt-out case, but he recognizes a spiritual dimension to his experiences, physical though they mostly are. When he is first wounded, "under the indifferent sky his spirit left the body with its ripped flesh, its infections, its weak and damaged nature. While the rain fell on his arms and legs, the part of him that still lived was unreachable. It was not his mind, but some other essence that was longing now for peace on a quiet, shadowed road where no guns sounded." He is revived, and after the Somme he takes leave to go back to England. At home in Norfolk, he feels "himself overtaken by a climactic surge of feeling . . . not an assault but a passionate affinity. It was for the rough field running down to the trees and for the path going back into the village, where he could see the tower of the church: these and the forgiving distance of the sky were not separate, but part of one creation, and he too, still by any sane judgement a young man, by the repeated tiny pulsing of his blood, was one with them."

Presumably it is passages such as this that critics have in mind when they mention sentimentality in connection with this book, but Faulks undermines such assumptions when Stephen returns to the war and, just before another pointless but deadly encounter, looks back to this moment: "Where now was the loving unity of the world?"

Ultimately one's judgment of *Birdsong* must rest on one's view of the war and what Faulks has done with it. If he is correct, that it is an event of vast importance and moral seriousness that deserves to be known, understood, and mourned, then *Birdsong* is justified. The sections of the novel set in the 1970s, in which Stephen's granddaughter undertakes an investigation of the war and feels guilty because she knows so little about it, perhaps are intended to represent the perspective of Faulks or the average reader, but they are weaker than the wartime scenes themselves. It would be difficult, however, for the more contemporary scenes to match the emotional impact of the war passages, such as the roll call in Stephen's unit after the catastrophe on the Somme, which describes his comrades as "only granite slabs in place of living flesh, on whose inhuman surface the moss and lichen would cast their crawling green indifference."

Something of this sense of loss underlies Faulks's next book, a nonfiction joint biography called *The Fatal Englishman*. This is an entirely competent but never fully gripping account of three men perhaps burdened by early promise but in any event doomed to an early death. The first is Christopher Wood, an artist who became a fixture in the French avant-garde scene and was taken up by Pablo Picasso and Jean Cocteau. He

developed an opium habit and killed himself at age twenty-nine. Richard Hillary was a fighter pilot during the early days of World War II. Shot down in 1940, he was horribly burned, losing his eyelids as well as most of the use of his hands. He recovered partially after plastic surgery and became a spokesman for the war effort, writing a well-received book, *The Last Enemy* (1942). He convinced the Royal Air Force that he should be permitted to fly again, though Faulks suggests that there was ample evidence that he was not fit. He crashed and died in 1942. The final "fatal Englishman" is Jeremy Wolfenden, who was supposedly the most brilliant man of his generation, though evidence of this brilliance is scarce and rests mostly on the assertion of his contemporaries. He was a journalist, an openly promiscuous homosexual at a time when there were severe legal penalties against sodomy, and an alcoholic. Perhaps compromised by the Soviets, he became murkily involved in spying and died in Washington at the age of thirty-one in such a way that suspicions of murder lingered afterwards. Faulks links the stories through the theme of early promise lost or betrayed.

In 1998 Faulks returned to his great theme, which he has explained by saying, "If you are writing about human beings and their reactions and their relations with others you can hardly put them in more dramatic circumstances" than war. *Charlotte Gray* is set during World War II. It has several connections with both *The Girl at the Lion d'Or* and *Birdsong,* though these may justify calling the three books a trilogy only in a loose sense. Charlotte is the daughter of Captain Gray, Stephen Wraysford's superior officer; Hartmann, Anne's lover and an acquaintance of Stephen Wraysford, is again a character; Levy, the German Jewish doctor whom Stephen encounters on Armistice Day, reappears; and someone even sings the little song with the refrain "and the little boat sailed away," with which Azaire's obnoxious friend Bérard bores Stephen and Isabelle in the opening pages of *Birdsong*. After the success of *Birdsong,* however, it was perhaps inevitable that *Charlotte Gray* was received as a disappointment.

Faulks's choice to set the novel in World War II France results in scenes that are not as innately gripping and involving as the trench warfare scenes, particularly those set during the Battle of the Somme in *Birdsong*. Not only was the later war fought in a different way, but France surrendered in 1940 and thus was at peace, despite a small amount of resistance activity. Further, Faulks's decision to put a woman at the center of the novel reduces the possibility for battle scenes, though Charlotte Gray is an intrepid and resourceful woman who is committed to France and the rescue of her lover, a pilot downed somewhere in France. The novel is not dull, however; although it is slow at the beginning, as some reviewers objected, it builds in excitement as it moves to consider the French contribution to the Holocaust.

Faulks's aim, less insistent than his demand that readers do justice to the men who fought in 1916, seems to be a partial correction of the idealization of the French Resistance, which he has called "a necessary fiction"–necessary, perhaps, immediately after the war as a means to salvage French self-respect, but worth examining more closely at a fifty-year remove. In *Charlotte Gray* most of the French population is happy with the peace, though it was purchased at the price of French capitulation; there is more resentment of the English for sinking French ships or bombing French houses than of the Germans; and the French version of the Gestapo is much more effective than the *resistants,* who are few and unimpressive. Worst of all is the French readiness to round up and turn over Jews, both immigrants and French citizens, to the Germans, with such enthusiasm at times that even the Germans are inconvenienced.

Faulks always attempts in his fiction to place private and public experience in useful relation to each other. In this novel Charlotte has a private grief that is related to her father's experience in the trenches and the fact that he is one of those veterans who, as Faulks notes, "could not, or did not care to, describe the scope of what they had seen." His one faltering attempt to share his emotional burden from service in World War I is transmuted in her memory into some sort of assault, and until the end of the novel she regards her baffled father as some sort of monster.

In addition to provincial French life, this novel has an important strand set in wartime London, where young women party desperately with flyers and the intelligence services conspire to undo the Nazis and Charles de Gaulle at the same time. Ian Ousby, who in *TLS: The Times Literary Supplement* (11 September 1998) judged the novel "a considerable disappointment," asserts that Faulks's 1990s perspective on the events of the 1940s does not change the fact that he has included much predictable material bordering on cliché: "Faulks obviously knows that, however it was reworked and rewoven, a narrative made of such familiar cloth would not be enough." David Robson in the *Electronic Telegraph* (5 September 1998) saw it much more positively: "if the novel defies exact categorisation–is it a wartime romance, a thriller or a psychological mystery story?– that does not come across as a weakness. It merely testifies to the artistry of a novelist who is growing in authority with every book."

Whatever the tractability of his material, there is no question that Faulks writes wonderfully and is interested in important matters, both historically and psychologically. One remembers his own reflections on the fact that, unlike his father and grandfather, he had been given no great historical crisis that would permit him to be heroic. Charlotte Gray is given such an opportunity, however, and her remarks to a French friend who suggests that the problems of lovers are like "the antics of fretful children" may serve as a statement of Faulk's literary approach: "If at the one moment in your life when the chance of something transcendental is offered to you, if you have this chance to move beyond the surface of things, to understand–and you say, No, maybe not, it's just a bore to my friends. What then? how do you explain the rest of your life to yourself? How do you pass the time until you die?" Faulks has demonstrated in his five novels an extraordinary capacity for facing both the surface of things and those transcendental qualities that the best fiction captures.

Interviews:

Erin Graham and Chris Hoover, "Faulks Trot," *R & R* [online magazine], 16, no. 3 (1997);

Antony Beevor, "A Return to Arms," *Electronic Telegraph* [online magazine], no. 1, 184 (22 August 1998);

Jason Cowley, "Blue-eyed Boy," *Times* [online magazine], 29 August 1998.

John Fowles

(31 March 1926 –)

Ellen Pifer
University of Delaware

and

Merritt Moseley
University of North Carolina at Asheville

See also the Fowles entries in *DLB 14: British Novelists Since 1960* and *DLB 139: British Short-Fiction Writers, 1945–1980.*

BOOKS: *The Collector* (Boston: Little, Brown, 1963; London: Cape, 1963);

The Aristos: A Self-Portrait in Ideas (Boston: Little, Brown, 1964; London: Cape, 1965; revised, London: Cape, 1968; Boston: Little, Brown, 1970);

The Magus (Boston: Little, Brown, 1965; London: Cape, 1966; revised, Boston: Little, Brown, 1977; London: Cape, 1977);

The French Lieutenant's Woman (Boston: Little, Brown, 1969; London: Cape, 1969);

Poems (New York: Ecco, 1973; Toronto: Macmillan, 1973);

The Ebony Tower (Boston: Little, Brown, 1974; London: Cape, 1974);

Shipwreck, text by Fowles, photographs by the Gibsons of Scilly (London: Cape, 1974; Boston: Little, Brown, 1975);

Daniel Martin (Boston: Little, Brown, 1977; London: Cape, 1977);

Islands, text by Fowles, photographs by Fay Godwin (Boston: Little, Brown, 1978; London: Cape, 1978);

The Tree, text by Fowles, photographs by Frank Horvat (Boston: Little, Brown, 1979; London: Aurum, 1979);

The Enigma of Stonehenge, text by Fowles, photographs by Barry Brukoff (New York: Summit, 1980; London: Cape, 1980);

Mantissa (London: Cape, 1982; Boston: Little, Brown, 1982);

John Fowles (photograph from The Bookseller, *14 August 1982)*

A Short History of Lyme Regis (Wimborne, U.K.: Dovecote, 1982; Boston: Little, Brown, 1982);

A Maggot (London: Cape, 1985; Boston: Little, Brown, 1985);

Lyme Regis Camera (Wimborne, U.K.: Dovecote, 1990; Boston: Little, Brown, 1990);

The Nature of Nature: An Essay (Covelo, Cal.: Yolla Bolly, 1995);

Wormholes: Essays and Occasional Writings, edited by Jan Relf (New York: Holt, 1998; London: Cape, 1998).

MOTION PICTURE: *The Magus,* screenplay by Fowles, Twentieth-Century Fox, 1968.

TELEVISION: *The Enigma of Stonehenge,* screenplay and narration by Fowles, BBC, 1981.

OTHER: Sabine Baring-Gould, *Mehalah: A Story of the Salt Marshes,* introduction, glossary, and appendix by Fowles (London: Chatto & Windus, 1969);

Henri Alain-Fournier, *The Wanderer,* afterword by Fowles (New York: New American Library, 1971);

Charles Perrault, *Cinderella,* translated by Fowles (London: Cape, 1974; Boston: Little, Brown, 1976);

Claire de Durfort, *Ourika,* translated, with an introduction and an epilogue, by Fowles (Austin, Tex.: W. Thomas Taylor, 1977);

Marie de France, *The Lais of Marie de France,* foreword by Fowles (New York: Dutton, 1978);

Harold Pinter, *The French Lieutenant's Woman: A Screenplay,* foreword by Fowles (Boston: Little, Brown, 1981);

G. B. Edwards, *The Book of Ebenezer Le Page,* introduction by Fowles (New York: Knopf, 1981; London: Hamilton, 1981);

Thomas Hardy's England, edited by Fowles (Boston: Little, Brown, 1984);

Fay Godwin, *Land,* includes essay by Fowles (Boston: Little, Brown, 1985; London: Heinemann, 1985);

Henri Alain-Fournier, *The Lost Domain (Le Grand Meaulnes),* afterword by Fowles (Oxford & New York: Oxford University Press, 1986);

"Golding and 'Golding,'" in *William Golding: The Man and His Books: A Tribute on His 75th Birthday,* edited by John Carey (London: Faber & Faber, 1986).

SELECTED PERIODICAL PUBLICATIONS—UNCOLLECTED: "Is the Novel Dead?" *Books,* 1 (Autumn 1970): 2–5;

"Book to Movie: The French Lieutenant's Woman," *Vogue* (November 1981): 266, 269, 271.

"I've always wanted to write," declared John Fowles in a 1964 essay, "(in this order) poems, philosophy, and only then novels" (published in *Wormholes: Essays and Occasional Writings,* 1998). Though he has established a reputation as a philosopher—both a philosophical novelist and, in *The Aristos: A Self-Portrait in Ideas*

(1964), an accomplished existentialist thinker—and has published books of essays, naturalist writing, and one book of poetry, it is as a novelist that Fowles is firmly established in the first rank of postwar English authors. His six novels, published over two decades, have brought him a combination of popular success and critical and intellectual acclaim that is almost unprecedented in his time. His success in the marketplace derives from his great skill as a storyteller. His fiction is rich in narrative suspense, romantic conflict, and erotic drama. Remarkably, he manages to sustain such effects while, as an experimental writer testing conventional assumptions about reality, he examines and parodies the traditional devices of storytelling. He is one of the few writers over the past thirty years to have commanded the attention of both the mass audience and the literary scholar.

John Fowles was born to Robert and Gladys Richard Fowles on 31 March 1926 in Leigh-on-Sea, Essex, an area that Fowles describes as "dominated by conformism—the pursuit of respectability." A fierce individualist, he attributes his dislike of groups, of "mankind *en masse,*" to the oppressive social pressures of his childhood. Fowles learned, however, to cope with these pressures by developing, in his words, "a facility with masks." This ability to take on various roles helped him to win popularity as a student leader at Bedford School, a suburban London preparatory school he attended between the ages of fourteen and eighteen.

During the years when Fowles was at Bedford School excelling in scholarship and sports, World War II was at its height. At one point his family was forced to evacuate their home in order to escape German air raids, and Fowles left Bedford for a term to join them in Devonshire. There, in the unspoiled southwestern countryside of England, he first encountered the "mystery and beauty" of nature—the beginning of a powerful attraction that is evident in his fiction, philosophy, and lifelong avocation as an amateur naturalist. After preparatory school Fowles served two years of compulsory military service as a lieutenant in the Royal Marines, attending the University of Edinburgh for six months as part of this training. The war ended just at the time his military training concluded, so he never saw combat duty. Instead, he entered New College, Oxford, to read French and German languages and literatures. His study of French, especially, has had a lasting influence on his intellectual and literary development.

When Fowles was at Oxford, the French existentialist writers Albert Camus and Jean-Paul Sartre were being read and discussed widely. Fowles and his friends eagerly took up their ideas and imitated their philosophical stance, although he now points out that there was more fashion than substance to his understanding of existentialism at that time. All the same, much of Fowles's fiction reflects the existentialists' preoccupation with individual freedom and choice. The postwar existentialists were not the only French writers to have an abiding effect on Fowles's literary imagination. Of his other reading at Oxford, he says: "I was to discover later that one field of Old French literature refused to subside into the oblivion I wished on the whole period once I had taken Finals. This field—'forest' would be more appropriate—was that of the Celtic romance." Fowles believes that the origin of modern fiction can be traced to Celtic lore and its influence on medieval French tales of chivalry and courtly love. Many years after his graduation from Oxford, he paid tribute to his Celtic and French precursors. In his story collection *The Ebony Tower* (1974) he includes a translation of Marie de France's twelfth-century French romance, *Eliduc.* In reading *Eliduc,* Fowles says, the contemporary writer "is watching his own birth."

After graduation from Oxford, Fowles left England for Europe, teaching English first at the University of Poitiers in France and then at Anargyrios College, a boarding school for boys on the Greek island of Spetsai. On this island he rediscovered the enchantments of nature in a dazzling Mediterranean guise. The purity of the Greek landscape—the starkness of sea, sky, and stone—inspired his first sustained attempts at writing. Fowles did not think seriously about becoming a writer until he was in his early twenties. Then a strong desire to translate a French poem by Pierre de Ronsard inspired him to attempt it. Fowles attributes his early hesitation about writing to "that stark, puritanical view of all art that haunts England, that there is something shameful about expressing yourself." Although Fowles had done some writing while teaching school in France, his efforts intensified considerably in Greece. The two years he spent there, 1951–1952, proved a formative influence on both his artistic and his personal life.

On Spetsai, Fowles met Elizabeth Whitton, the woman he married three years later in England, after her divorce from her first husband. It was on Spetsai too that he wrote several poems that later made up one section of his published volume of poetry. The Greek landscape had a direct influence on Fowles's first attempts to write fiction as well. In *The Magus* (1965), a novel he began writing shortly after leaving Greece in 1952, the fictive island of Phraxos is directly modeled on Spetsai. Years later, Fowles described the powerful hold that the island landscape of Greece had on his literary imagination: "Its pine forest silences were uncanny, unlike those I have experienced anywhere else; like an eternal blank page waiting for a note or a word. They gave the curious sense of timelessness and of incipient myth. . . . I am hard put to convey the

importance of this experience for me as a writer. It imbued and marked me far more profoundly than any of my more social and physical memories of the place. I already knew I was a permanent exile from many aspects of English society, but a novelist has to enter deeper exile still."

This image of the writer as exile persists both in Fowles's fiction and in his personal life. Since 1966 he has lived in the small coastal town of Lyme Regis, in Dorset, in southwestern England. Hours away from the nearest city, Fowles frankly regards living in Lyme Regis as a kind of exile. He says: "novelists have to live in some sort of exile. I also believe that—more than other kinds of writers—they have to keep in touch with their native culture . . . linguistically, psychologically and in many other ways."

At the end of 1952 Fowles left Greece and returned to England, where he taught for the next decade at various schools in and around London. He was also working on the first draft of *The Magus,* while experiencing an acute sense of loss at having left Greece. Although he has settled permanently in England, he continues to feel spiritually rooted in three countries: France, England, and Greece. Fowles wrote in 1964, "I don't want to be an English writer; I want to be a European one, what I call a mega-European (Europe plus America plus Russia plus wherever else the culture is essentially European)."

On 2 April 1954 Fowles married Whitton and became stepfather to his wife's three-year-old daughter, Anna. For the next ten years the family lived in Hampstead, London, while Fowles pursued a teaching career. He spent a year teaching English at an adult education institution, Ashridge College. At Ashridge, Fowles says, he "took strongly to the trade union and socialist side; and I haven't seen reason to change my mind since." With the success of *The Collector* (1963), his first published novel, he retired from teaching, having last served as the head of the English Department at St. Godric's College in Hampstead. Several years later he and his wife moved to Lyme Regis, where they settled, at first, in an isolated old farmhouse on Ware Commons, a mile west of the town. Eventually finding the solitude too unbroken, the family moved to Lyme Regis in 1968. Fowles has served as honorary curator of the little museum there and has spent time researching the town's history. He has said that his study of local history has supplanted that of natural history, but Fowles regards the two activities as "faces of the one coin." As local historian he has published *A Short History of Lyme Regis* (1982) and *Lyme Regis Camera* (1990), *The Tree* (1979), an essay in Fay Godwin's *Land* (1985), and *The Nature of Nature* (1995).

Anargyrios College of Spetses, Spetsai, Greece, where Fowles taught English from 1951 to 1953. Fowles's portrayal of the Lord Byron School in The Magus *was inspired by his experiences there.*

In 1988 John Fowles suffered a serious stroke, the effect of which has been to end his novels, although he has written about Greece, about his own work, and about that of others since the stroke. In a 1989 interview he said, "I can still enjoy reading. I feel I can still judge books. What escapes me is composing fiction. . . . The other bar to writing is less mysterious. It is something like abulia, loss of will, indecision; but not quite. . . . I have lost all conventional faith or belief in books, in 'literature,' most of that superstructure of self-regard most writers have to erect between themselves and the outside world. . . . I certainly don't feel barren, bereft of ideas, just of the ability to put them into practice." Shortly after his stroke his wife, Elizabeth, died of bone marrow cancer.

The Collector was not Fowles's first effort at writing fiction. By 1963, when this novel appeared in print, he had been writing for more than ten years and had produced seven or eight other manuscripts—most particularly *The Magus,* which was not published until 1965. *The Collector* was the first book Fowles sent to the publishers because in his view it was the first manuscript he

had completed satisfactorily. The others were "too large," and he found he lacked the technical mastery to bring them off. Set in London and its environs, *The Collector* is based on a central dramatic incident: the kidnapping of a young woman by a total stranger. Frederick Clegg, a nondescript clerk who works in a government office, kidnaps a twenty-year-old art student, Miranda Grey, as she is walking home from a movie. Although Miranda's family lives across the street from the town hall annex where Clegg works, their world is remote from his. Miranda enjoys all the privileges of an upper-middle-class background and education. She is talented, beautiful, and surrounded by friends and admirers. Clegg is the son of lower-class parents whose marriage ended in disaster even before Clegg was orphaned at the age of two. Clegg is an introvert who suffers an acute sense of social and sexual inferiority. He spends most of his leisure time collecting butterflies, and he is attracted to Miranda as an amateur lepidopterist is drawn to a rare and beautiful specimen. Secretly he begins to follow her activities, suffering pangs of resentment as he observes her casually going out with other young men. He also indulges in romantic day-dreams, picturing a cozy life with Miranda in a "beautiful modern home." His fantasies remain only that until, one day, he wins a huge sum of money—the equivalent in the early 1960s of £200,000—on the football pools, which he has routinely played for years. Finding himself suddenly graced with "time and money," Clegg begins making plans to realize what before had been only a daydream. He buys a country cottage, furnishes the cellar room, stocks it with books and clothes he thinks Miranda will like, and finally brings her, chloroformed and gagged, to live in captivity.

The first half of the novel consists of Clegg's account of his relationship with Miranda. It is soon apparent that what he calls his "love" for the girl is really his desire to own her, to possess her not sexually but as one would acquire a beautiful object. *The Collector* introduces a theme to which Fowles returns in his later works: how the obsession with "having" has overtaken modern industrial society. Clegg's actions dramatize the confusion inherent in contemporary values—society's failure to distinguish the urge for control from the liberating power of love. Clegg's confusion intensifies when, after he captures Miranda, the real and proximate human being proves very different from the remote and unchanging image he has worshiped at a distance. Miranda's verbal assaults, abrupt shifts of mood, and probing wit unsettle and bewilder her captor. At times driven to retreat altogether from her volatile presence, Clegg consoles himself with photographs he has secretly taken of the drugged and sleeping girl. As he says, "I used to look at them sometimes. I could take my time with them. They didn't talk back at me."

Following Clegg's narration, the second half of the novel launches a second account of the same events, this time from Miranda's perspective. In her diary Miranda secretly records her responses to what has happened, along with an account of the thoughts and memories that occupy her in her cell. Now the reader gains a vivid sense of the stifling tedium and oppression of her daily life in captivity—the misery of confinement that ends only with her death. From Miranda's viewpoint Clegg's attempts to make his prisoner comfortable appear even more absurd. Gifts of perfume and chocolate can hardly compensate for her loss of freedom—for fresh air, sunlight, and the ability to move about unhampered. Yet, to this experience of freedom, precious and inalienable, Clegg remains persistently blind. As Miranda begins to observe and analyze her captor, she recognizes that he is the true prisoner. Trapped in an airless and dead existence, Clegg is mortally afraid of feeling, of human contact, of what is alive in himself and in others. Miranda records the discovered paradox in her diary: "He's the one in prison; in

his own hateful narrow present world." As Miranda vainly struggles to win her freedom, she begins to perceive Clegg's power over her as embodying "the hateful tyranny of weak people." Those who are themselves imprisoned by fear, ignorance, and resentment will naturally seek to repress and confine others, just as those who have a deadened perception of reality will tend to regard other people as objects.

Hoping to convince Clegg to release her, Miranda strives to make him understand that she is a living human being, not a specimen he can keep in his private collection. Although totally in his power—Clegg prepares her food, buys her what she needs, determines whether she may be allowed a five-minute walk in the night air—Miranda nevertheless asserts her natural as well as her social superiority in their relationship. Miranda needles Clegg with questions he cannot answer, scorns his lack of taste in art and books, and even tries to educate him morally and intellectually. To her, Clegg represents the vulgar and unenlightened world of mass taste and education. He is one of the Many, while she is struggling to develop the civilized and liberated values of the Few.

The social dimensions of this conflict between Miranda and Clegg, the Few and the Many, were immediately recognized by critics and reviewers of the novel, some of whom charged Fowles with elitism and even crypto-fascism. Responding to what he considered a misunderstanding, Fowles attempted to explain his intent. "My purpose in *The Collector*," he wrote in 1968, "was to attempt to analyse, through a parable, some of the results" of the historical confrontation "between the Few and the Many, between 'Them' and 'Us.'"

> Clegg, the kidnapper, committed the evil; but I tried to show that his evil was largely, perhaps wholly, the result of a bad education, a mean environment, being orphaned; all factors over which he had no control. In short, I tried to establish the virtual innocence of the Many. Miranda, the girl he imprisoned, had very little more control than Clegg over what she was: she had well-to-do parents, good educational opportunity, inherited aptitude and intelligence. That does not mean she was perfect. Far from it—she was arrogant in her ideas, a prig, a liberal-humanist snob, like so many university students. Yet if she had not died she might have become . . . the kind of being humanity so desperately needs.

Fowles believes that society—the inequities of environment and social class—is largely responsible for the evils men commit against the system. In his next published book, *The Aristos,* he states that "one cause of all crime is maleducation."

The author's expressed belief in the essential innocence of a man such as Clegg may come as a surprise to readers of *The Collector*. It is questionable whether the novel really achieves this intended effect. The reader is naturally horrified as Clegg passively observes Miranda's slow death from pneumonia, which she contracts from the damp and unhealthy air of the cell. Clegg cannot bring himself to take her to a doctor, preferring to watch her die rather than to grant her freedom. At the end of the novel, soon after he buries Miranda's body under a tree, Clegg begins to follow the movements of a young woman in a nearby village who strikingly resembles Miranda. The future is grimly predictable. Considering Fowles's comments about the Few and the Many, is the reader to assume that Clegg would have been a good and productive citizen if he had been given a few of the benefits and privileges enjoyed by Miranda? The intended social parable may be lost on many readers because the immediate effects of Clegg's actions tend to overwhelm any thoughtful consideration of their alleged social cause. Fowles may have intended that the reader perceive Clegg's deadened sensibility as an extreme product of the deceptively ordinary conditions of existence. Miranda observes that Clegg is "so ordinary that he's extraordinary." She recognizes that he is "a victim of a miserable . . . suburban world and a miserable social class"; and she identifies Clegg with "the blindness, deadness," "apathy," and "sheer jealous malice of the great bulk of England." When Miranda violently smashes the china ducks sitting on Clegg's mantelpiece, the reader knows she is expressing her hatred for the stifling banality of conventional taste and wisdom. Yet, perhaps because this novel is rendered with such realistic detail, because the ordinary world is evoked in all its familiarity, Clegg appears too abnormal, too mentally disturbed, to function as a convincing emblem of the "deadweight" of ordinary English life.

The Collector surprised Fowles with its commercial success. Even before the book was published, he had earned several thousand pounds from the sale of paperback, translation, and movie rights. The novel was eventually translated into twelve languages, and a commercially successful motion picture–directed by William Wyler and starring Terence Stamp and Samantha Eggar–was released by Columbia Pictures in 1965. For someone who, until the age of thirty-five, could not at times afford a pack of cigarettes, such financial success must have proved a heady experience. Since then, Fowles has sold many more books and paperback, translation, and movie rights. Yet, what he says he enjoys most about being so well off is not the power to buy, but the freedom to live independently and do with his time what he chooses. Money appears, in fact, to

have freed Fowles from wanting things: "I'm rich in a minor financial way," he says, "rich enough never to buy new clothes, never to want to go abroad, rich enough not to like spending money any more. I'm also rich in having many interests. I always have a backlog of books to read, there's the garden, nature, walking."

Taking advantage of the freedom brought by success, Fowles made his next publication a book that was almost certain not to be a best-seller. A year after *The Collector* appeared, Fowles produced a work of informal philosophy, presented as a series of notes resembling Blaise Pascal's *Pensées* (1844) or Friedrich Nietzsche's more aphoristic writings. As the subtitle to the original edition indicates, *The Aristos: A Self-Portrait in Ideas* is the personal expression of the author's views on a wide range of subjects. "The notion I had," Fowles explains, "was that if you put down all the ideas you hold, it would amount to a kind of painter's frank self-portrait." He admits that *The Aristos* was in part a reaction to the commercial success of *The Collector*: "I didn't want to get docketed as a good story teller or as a thriller writer. *The Collector* . . . was widely reviewed in England as a thriller, it didn't even make the serious novel columns. Which is why I'm certainly tender towards the American critical scene. They at least realized it was simply borrowing something from the thriller form, but that, of course, the deeper intentions were quite different."

The Aristos met with considerable prepublication opposition: "I was told that it would do my 'image' no good; and I am sure that my belief that a favourable 'image' is conceivably not of any great human–or literary–significance would have counted for very little if I had not had a best-selling novel behind me. I used that 'success' to issue this 'failure.'" By making use of his commercial success to bring forth his "failure," he demonstrates his commitment to the moral and philosophical convictions set forth in *The Aristos*.

Presenting Fowles's views on such diverse subjects as human nature, evolution, art, society, religion, and politics, *The Aristos* provides a fruitful introduction to the major themes of his fiction. His main concern in this book is "to preserve the freedom of the individual against all those pressures-to-conform that threaten our century." Like the existentialist philosophers to whom he pays tribute in *The Aristos,* Fowles is urgently concerned with the question of human freedom and the value of independent existence and action. The Greek word *aristos* means, as he explains, "best or most excellent of its kind," and Fowles uses the term to refer to the individual most ideally suited to will and enact excellence under the conditions of existence as he or she perceives them. Fowles takes the word and concept of *aristos* from Heraclitus, a pre-Socratic Greek philosopher whose thought is extant only in a few surviving fragments. From Heraclitus, Fowles also draws his perception of the two opposing forces or principles at work in the universe: "the Law, or organizing principle, and the Chaos, or disintegrating one." The opposition of these two forces is what constitutes the war of existence, the tension between polar forces in which all forms of matter, including human beings, exist. Conflict and hazard, the operation of blind chance, are the inescapable grounds of existence.

Like Sartre, Camus, and other existentialist precursors, Fowles seeks a philosophical basis for human choice, value, and action in a universe that is not, so far as can be known, guided by a supernatural agent or power. Fowles's existential man inhabits a precarious universe that is constantly evolving but has no ultimate purpose. Not only are the welfare and survival of human beings contingencies, but the very world is an accident, a contingent world that happened to "survive where it might not have." Such a world and its survival has purpose only to human beings, because they have the conscious desire to see it survive, along with their race. Human freedom is relative because all people are limited—as Miranda is in *The Collector*—by circumstances and forces beyond their control. Yet, by asserting the freedom to will, choose, and act within such limits, humans can constrain the blind power of chance, or, conversely, seize the opportunities created by chance. By struggling to establish some measure of justice and equality in society, moreover, human beings may inhibit the harsher effects of social and biological inequities.

In 1968 Fowles had a revised edition of *The Aristos* published, stating in his preface that he hoped to clarify both the style and the organization of his ideas. In so doing, he cut much of the original material, restructured and occasionally retitled whole sections, and introduced new material that provides helpful transitions and more ample context for the development of particular ideas. Despite these noteworthy improvements, *The Aristos* is still not a wholly convincing work. Fowles admits that his manner of presentation is dogmatic rather than persuasive. He aims not to plead a case but, by "baldly" stating what he thinks, to provoke the reader into articulating his own ideas. Yet, such statements seem insufficient when the reader is faced with metaphysical questions concerning the origins of the universe and the nature of human consciousness. The loosely linked notes and paragraphs comprising *The Aristos* frequently seem an inadequate mode of discourse for such complex subjects. Moreover, the dogmatic nature of some of Fowles's assertions tends to contradict his avowed belief in the essential mystery of being. The why of existence and of the universe, he says, will never be solved by science or art. But his attitude toward "old religions and philosophies" is often condescending. In the words of critic Walter Allen, *The Aristos* "falls short of what it promises . . . but at least it can be taken as an indication of [Fowles's] ambition." Ambition, Allen adds, "is probably the first thing that strikes one about Fowles's second novel, *The Magus*."

In 1964, the year *The Aristos* was first published, Fowles resumed work on *The Magus*, which he had begun writing twelve years before. Over a span of a quarter century, he worked and reworked this book, so that it became inextricably bound up with his life. As soon as the first edition appeared in print, Fowles knew he was dissatisfied, later remarking that the novel remained the "notebook of an exploration, often erring and misconceived." In interviews over the following several years, he candidly stated that he did not regard the work a success. Finally, in 1977, twenty-five years after it was begun, *The Magus* reappeared in a thorough revision, with stylistic or structural changes occurring on nearly every page.

The novel's protagonist, Englishman Nicholas Urfe, is, like Miranda Grey in *The Collector*, a bright, well-educated person in his twenties. Having graduated from Oxford, Nicholas—for lack of a better idea of what to do with himself—accepts a job teaching English at a private boarding school for boys on a Greek island. As Fowles says in his introduction to the revised edition, he modeled the fictional island of Phraxos after Spetsai. But the school on Spetsai, Anargyrios College, where Fowles taught during 1951–1952, is apparently not the model for the Lord Byron School, where Fowles sends his character Nicholas to teach. Although quickly bored with his job at this school, Nicholas remains enchanted with the gleaming Mediterranean landscape. The azure sea and sky give him the sense of inhabiting a pristine universe, an Eden untouched by human suffering or fear. Walking along the edge of a deserted beach, Nicholas feels like "the very first man that had ever stood on it, that had ever had eyes, that had ever existed, the very first man." But Nicholas is soon stripped of this illusion—the first in a series of illusions from which he will be separated. He meets Maurice Conchis, the wealthy owner of a villa overlooking this Eden. What Conchis says to him about Greece proves a more accurate description of the world Nicholas has entered: "Greece is like a mirror. It makes you suffer. Then you learn."

A cultivated European of Greek and English extraction, Conchis is a man of many and exceptional talents. Both scientist and artist, he has mastered disciplines as various as medicine, music, psychology, and the dramatic arts. What strikes Nicholas upon first meeting him is Conchis's extraordinary vitality: "He had a bizarre family resemblance to Picasso: saurian as

Dust jacket for Fowles's first novel, in which a city clerk kidnaps and imprisons a young woman

well as simian; decades of living in the sun, the quintessential Mediterranean man, who had discarded everything that lay between him and his vitality." Among the things Conchis has discarded are those conventional patterns of thought and behavior that mark an individual as belonging to a particular nation or class. Conchis, like Picasso—or Prospero in William Shakespeare's *The Tempest* (1611), to whom Nicholas later compares him—presides over a world of his own making, a world summoned into being by his creative energies and dominated by his will.

Like Prospero, Conchis is a master of illusion. The "Magus," or magician, of the novel's title, he dominates an island that, like Prospero's, is a stage for dramatic spectacles and masques that bring revelation to their audience. Conchis's audience does not merely observe but participates in the dramatic action, which takes the form of a psychodrama. Nicholas soon becomes involved as actor-audience to the drama, and his spontaneous reactions contribute to the way it develops. What occurs between Nicholas and the Magus is,

in Fowles's words, a kind of "godgame"; Conchis "exhibits a series of masks representing human notions of God, from the supernatural to the jargon-ridden scientific." By staging "a series of human illusions about something that does not exist in fact, absolute knowledge and absolute power," Conchis provokes Nicholas into confronting the essential mystery and hazard of existence. Conchis's motives for devoting his personal fortune and energies to such an elaborate enterprise are never fully explained in the novel. It is suggested, however, that the godgame is the result of a lifetime's study of human nature and the pursuit of a valid philosophy. The participant in the godgame discovers, through a series of concrete actions rather than a system of abstract logic, his capacity for free choice and action.

As Fowles suggests through frequent allusions to *The Tempest,* Homer's *Odyssey,* and medieval romance, the quest on which Nicholas embarks has romantic and mythic parallels. The island of Phraxos resembles that unknown other world to which the hero of ancient myth journeys in search of adventure and, ultimately, his true self. Fowles's final purposes are, however, those of the novelist, not the romancer. Nicholas is in no way an idealized hero, and the larger context for his adventure is the specific social-historical conditions of modern industrial society. Nicholas belongs to Fowles's own generation, coming of age immediately after World War II. Accepting few traditional beliefs or inherited values, Nicholas, like so many of his peers, feels incapable of sustaining a commitment to any person or ideal that might shape the course of his life.

In one sense, Nicholas is both Miranda Grey and Frederick Clegg. He shares with Miranda an interest in art and literature, and, like her, he desires to rise above the unexamined life of the Many, to define himself apart from the stultifying conventions of respectable middle-class life. Yet, Nicholas remains detached from life, an outsider looking in. In *The Collector* Miranda deplores Clegg's inhuman detachment from feeling. The "only thing that really matters," she writes, "is feeling and living what you believe–so long as it's something more than belief in your own comfort." Unlike Miranda, Nicholas has neither found what he believes nor actively begun to seek it. Nicholas treats his emotional relationships with studied casualness. In London, before leaving for his teaching post in Greece, Nicholas meets, and briefly lives with, a young Australian, Alison Kelly, whose affection for him is warm and spontaneous. While he is sexually and emotionally drawn to Alison, however, he refuses to admit fully his feelings for her, much less allow them to flourish. To others and at times to himself he pretends that Alison is a mere convenience. When an old friend from his Oxford days runs into them, privately commenting to Nicholas that Alison is attractive, Nicholas feigns cool indifference. She is, he condescendingly remarks, "cheaper than central heating."

Behind Nicholas's cold and cruel remark lies a host of implications that Fowles directly addresses in *The Aristos*. He describes the values of contemporary industrial society as based almost exclusively on the marketplace. Members of a marketplace or agora society tend "to turn all experiences and relationships into objects." Yet, while he exhibits the confused values of his society, Nicholas seeks to change this condition. The promise of discovering a new mode of existence draws him deeply into Conchis's drama. He experiences "an awareness of a new kind of potentiality," sensing that the "mess" of his life–"the selfishness and false turnings–could "become a source of construction rather than a source of chaos." To Nicholas, the entry into Conchis's labyrinth feels "like a step forward–and upward." Yet, as he seeks the answers to riddles posed by the dramatic scenarios orchestrated by Conchis and enacted by his company of actors, Nicholas discovers

behind each question not an answer but another question, and, mirrorlike, this series of questions seems to double back on the seeker. Nicholas will not be granted, by the god of this game, any ultimate answers to his questions. The twists and turns of the godgame, the false leads and dead ends into which Nicholas is led, are a dramatization of the essential mystery of existence. Existential uncertainty is, for Fowles, the ground of being; in that uncertainty man affirms not the answers to his questions but his freedom to seek them.

The labyrinthine complexity of *The Magus*–the mazes of the godgame, the multiple identities of its dramatis personae, the ambiguous nature of each version of reality devised by Conchis–disturbed many critics and reviewers when the novel first appeared. Yet, the complexity of its form, so unlike the tightly compressed action of *The Collector,* is complemented by a greater complexity of characterization. In the earlier novel the conflict between psychological polarities–between the Few and the Many, freedom and repression, love and possession, individuality and conformity–was played out, rather too neatly and with somewhat melodramatic effect, between Miranda on the one side and Clegg on the other. In *The Magus* that conflict does not take place between polarized characters but within Nicholas himself. Thus, despite the latter novel's somewhat cluttered form and frequently mystifying effects, *The Magus* is a more convincing dramatization of Fowles's vision of human existence. For if, as Fowles believes, existence is conflict, then surely the primary battleground for this ongoing struggle between opposing forces is not merely external reality but the human heart and mind.

In part 3 of *The Magus* Nicholas leaves Phraxos and returns to England. As critic Barry Olshen has noted, Nicholas's journey from England to Greece and back is patterned after "the traditional quest story, involving a voyage to a distant land, the achievement of a mission or the acquisition of special knowledge, and the return home." Having acquired a degree of self-knowledge, Nicholas returns to London to confront Alison and resolve their relationship. Nicholas is not the only one who has been changed by his journey; Alison, too, is not the same. Nicholas learns that she has secretly taken part in the godgame, and in London he discovers that the game is not over. Maurice Conchis is replaced by an equally extraordinary being, Lily de Seitas, who knows where Alison Kelly is and what terms Nicholas may have to fulfill in order to see her. As Nicholas discovers, she and the other actors have all been through the harrowing spiritual journey on which he himself is embarked. This experience is what has given each seeker in the godgame such impressive vitality and courage. De Seitas and Conchis are those rare individuals (and Nicholas may one day join them) who embrace their freedom, reject the values of the market-place, and recognize the Aristos–the ideal individual–as their true model.

At the end of the novel Nicholas and Alison finally encounter each other, but their relationship remains unresolved. They are, as Nicholas realizes, at a "point of fulcrum," an experience of potential freedom that is the goal of the godgame. Here Fowles chooses to leave them, saying only that what happens to Nicholas and Alison after this "is another mystery." The apparent finality of endings is also an illusion. Like Conchis, Fowles believes that mankind "needs the existence of mysteries. Not their solution," for mystery "pours energy into whoever seeks the answer to it." As a novelist Fowles seeks to provide his readers with that energy, too, bringing them to their fulcrum point. At the end the reader recognizes that Fowles's novel is a godgame; the game's two elements, "the one didactic, the other aesthetic," form a paradigm of the novel's strategy.

For the sake of the game, Conchis tells Nicholas, one must "pretend to believe." As a participant in the game between reader and author, the reader likewise obliges, pretending to believe in the staged illusions of the novelist until, in the last pages of the book, the author breaks the spell of his magic-making and announces that the reader, like his "anti-hero," is also "at a crossroads, in a dilemma." "We too are waiting in our solitary rooms where the telephone never rings, waiting for this girl, this truth . . . this reality." The novel, like the godgame, is a metaphor for existence. What Fowles teaches in *The Magus* is not a particular set of truths or solutions but the unique responsibility of each individual to seek his or her own answers. In the foreword to the revised edition of the novel, Fowles emphasizes his reader's freedom of choice: "If *The Magus* has any 'real significance,' it is no more than that of the Rorschach test in psychology. Its meaning is whatever reaction it provokes in the reader, and so far as I am concerned there is no given 'right' reaction."

Though not as great a commercial or critical success as *The Collector, The Magus* won, in Ian Watt's phrase, "a special following among the under twenty-fives." Its popularity with this group may be explained by its being, in Fowles's own words, "a novel of adolescence written by a retarded adolescent." Though he finds this quality to be his novel's weakness, Fowles defends the novelist's right to "regress" in this manner: "The rest of the world can censor or bury their private past. We cannot, and so have to remain partly green till the day we die . . . callow-green in the hope of becoming fertile-green."

Although Fowles was dissatisfied with *The Magus* almost as soon as it was published, the novel aroused sufficient public attention to warrant a film version.

Fowles wrote the screenplay, and he also spent some weeks on location on the island of Majorca. The 1968 film, in Fowles's words, was "a disaster." Directed by Guy Green, it starred Anthony Quinn as Conchis and Michael Caine as Nicholas Urfe, with Candice Bergen and Anna Karina starring in the female leads.

Despite or perhaps because of the failures associated with the first version of *The Magus,* Fowles decided, more than a decade later, to revise this "endlessly tortured and recast cripple." In 1977 he had the new version published, explaining his intentions in the foreword. In rewriting the novel one final time, Fowles did not attempt to answer "the many justified criticisms of excess, overcomplexity, artificiality and the rest that the book received from the more sternly adult reviewers on its first appearance." Fowles did want to rescue this novel from a clumsiness of style and structure: "I do not believe that the intention matters more than the craft, idea more than language; and I do believe that almost all major human evils in our world come from betrayal of the word at a very humble level. In short, I have always felt with *The Magus* like an insufficiently arrested murderer." The novelist thus rewrote phrases and paragraphs on almost every page of the novel and recast whole sequences of action and dialogue. He also corrected "a past failure of nerve" by strengthening the erotic element in two pivotal scenes. The effect is a noteworthy improvement not only in the novel's formal qualities but in thematic clarity as well.

Nicholas's emotional and moral blindness also receives more emphatic treatment in the revised version, as Fowles supplies him more opportunities to act like a cad. Nicholas more openly disavows his relationship with Alison, for instance, clearly betraying past affection as well as present loyalties. Brought to a harsher confrontation with the worst in himself, Nicholas more clearly perceives his own selfishness. Like Pip in *Great Expectations* (1860–1861)–the Dickens novel Fowles most admires and the one that, by his own admission, influenced the writing of *The Magus*– Nicholas sternly judges his past behavior, but the rigor of his self-condemnation is also shown, as in Pip's case, to be a sign of moral growth. The new ending Fowles wrote for the revised edition hints at a greater likelihood for reunion between Nicholas and Alison; yet the final scene is more open-ended. Nicholas demands that Alison choose whether they are to remain together. He then waits for her answer, and in this "frozen present tense" the author leaves his characters, and the reader, suspended.

This withholding of any fixed resolution to the story has troubled many of Fowles's readers, prompting some of them to write him angry letters demanding that he tell the reader what does in fact happen to his char-

Dust jacket for Fowles's 1965 novel, which depicts the playing of a mysterious "godgame" on a Greek island

acters. Yet, Fowles's purpose in sustaining ambiguity is not to shirk his responsibilities as a novelist but to redefine them. In his next novel, *The French Lieutenant's Woman* (1969), he overtly tells the reader that he does not exercise absolute authority over his characters. For him the novelist's traditional role as omniscient god is outmoded and untenable. Victorian novelists adopted this stance because they sought to model themselves after the all-knowing creator of the universe. Fowles, a twentieth-century existentialist, rejects the notion of a universal creator, and in *The French Lieutenant's Woman* he announces his abdication from the throne of literary omniscience. He drives home the point by writing a convincing version of a "Victorian" novel—one that captures with detailed fidelity the manners and milieu of the time—but a Victorian novel that conspicuously lacks the assuring presence of an omniscient author. Thus, eighty pages into the novel, the narrator declares that his character, Sarah Woodruff, remains a mystery even to him. He confesses that his apparent omniscience is only a guise, an aspect of the literary game: "This story I am telling is all imagination," he says. "If I have pretended until now to know my characters' minds and innermost thoughts, it is because I am writing in . . . a convention universally accepted at the time of my

story: that the novelist stands next to God. He may not know all, yet he tries to pretend that he does." A remarkable evocation of the historical and social matrix of the Victorian age, *The French Lieutenant's Woman* is also a parody of the conventions, and underlying assumptions, that operate within the Victorian novel.

While Fowles's narrator draws attention to the contrasts in habits and ideas that exist between Victorian times and our own, he also reminds the reader that the Victorians' apparently stable and unchanging world was, in 1867, about to vanish forever. In that year Karl Marx published the first volume of *Das Kapital;* Charles Darwin's *Origin of Species* had already appeared in 1859– and Fowles's male protagonist is a Darwinian. This modern perspective imbues the historical elements of the novel with poignant irony. An example appears in the narrator's description of Ernestina Freeman, the pretty and pampered young lady engaged to the novelist's protagonist, Charles Smithson. Ernestina's doting parents, the reader is told, worry unnecessarily about their precious daughter's supposedly frail health. To these Victorian parents a genteel young lady is by definition fragile and must be treated like a porcelain doll. The narrator (sounding suspiciously omniscient) then provides the reader with some salient information to counter the assumptions of Ernestina's fond parents: "Had they but been able to see into the future! For Ernestina was to outlive all her generation. She was born in 1846. And she died on the day that Hitler invaded Poland."

Fowles's parodic exposure of Victorian conventions serves as a springboard for testing not only literary devices but also cultural values and assumptions—those of the Victorian age and the present as well. The critical examination of one historical period against the background of another transforms this apparently historical novel into a truly experimental one. In a memorandum Fowles wrote to himself while working on *The French Lieutenant's Woman,* he states: "Remember the etymology of the word. A novel is something new. It must have relevance to the writer's now—so don't ever pretend you live in 1867; or make sure the reader knows it's a pretence." Both the experimental nature of this novel and its display of erudition—crammed as it is with scholarly information on Victorian mores, politics, art, medicine, science—could hardly have prepared Fowles for the extraordinary popular success that greeted its publication.

For many months a best-seller in the United States, the novel also received enthusiastic reviews from distinguished critics such as Ian Watt, who said in *The New York Times Book Review* that Fowles's "immensely interesting, attractive and human" third novel is "both richly English and convincingly existential." Though less enthusiastically received in Britain, as has regularly been the case for Fowles's work, *The French Lieutenant's Woman* was more warmly received there than his previous novels. In 1969 the International Association of Poets, Playwrights, Editors, Essayists, and Novelists gave Fowles its Silver Pen Award for *The French Lieutenant's Woman,* which also won the W. H. Smith and Son Literary Award in 1970. In September 1981, after many difficulties discovering a movie equivalent to the dual perspectives of the novel's narrative approach, a motion picture version of the novel was released with a screenplay by the distinguished British playwright Harold Pinter and starring Meryl Streep as Sarah and Jeremy Irons as Charles.

Fowles was surprised by the critical and commercial success of this novel, whose conception had imposed itself on him while he was halfway through another novel. One predawn autumn morning in 1966, a vision of a woman standing on a deserted quay (one much resembling Lyme Regis harbor, which can be seen from Fowles's garden) came to him while he was still half-asleep. The woman was dressed in black and stood, with her back turned, gazing at the distant horizon. Readers of the novel will immediately recognize the figure as Sarah Woodruff, the French lieutenant's woman. According to Fowles, these "mythopoeic 'stills'" often float into his mind. He ignores them at first, waiting to see if they are of the persistent variety that open "the door into a new world"—the new world, that is, of a new novel. Fowles ignored the image, but it duly persisted, the woman always appearing with her back turned. Her stance, Fowles began to perceive, signaled a rejection of the age she lived in, and Fowles already knew that the figure was Victorian.

Unlike Ernestina Freeman in every way, Sarah Woodruff is, in both senses, the other woman in this novel. Mystifying everyone, including the author, Sarah rejects the values of her age, refusing to live by its conventions. She is an outsider, a nineteenth-century character with a distinctly twentieth-century cast of mind. The daughter of a tenant farmer, she has been sent to boarding school and thus educated beyond her station. Sarah also possesses a strong will, independent mind, and passionate heart—qualities that were hardly viewed as desirable in a young Victorian lady. By nature, temperament, and social circumstance, Sarah breaks the mold of respectable Victorian womanhood.

Between these two women and the opposing values they represent, Charles Smithson, an intelligent though aimless Victorian gentleman in his early thirties, is driven to choose. Already engaged to Ernestina Freeman when he first encounters Sarah, Charles is at once fascinated and a little frightened by this new acquaintance. Rumors that she has been seduced and abandoned by a French lieutenant are adrift in the quiet little town of Lyme Regis, where the novel is set. On this lonely coast Charles first sees Sarah, in chapter 1, staring tragically out to sea. Her isolation from respectable society and her "untamed" nature seem to require that Charles encounter Sarah in the wilds of nature rather than in a well-furnished drawing room. Their relationship thus develops outside the constraining walls of Victorian society.

As this relationship progresses, the mystery of Sarah's nature is not solved but augmented. She eventually tells Charles a different version of the tale concerning the French lieutenant, but she verifies the rumors of her seduction and abandonment. Not until much later, after a great internal struggle on Charles's part to resist her mysterious power over him, does he discover that Sarah's version of the story is also a fiction. She was not seduced by the French lieutenant at all. It is Charles, in fact, who deflowers her, never suspecting that she is still a virgin. Far from being seduced, however, Sarah orchestrates the events that lead to her brief tryst with Charles, who, now in love with Sarah, finds it impossible to go through with his engagement to Ernestina.

Sarah lives outside the bounds of social and moral conventions. While she is drawn to Charles—and even, apparently, loves him—she desires not to make him happy, but to be free. This fierce desire for personal freedom is something that attracts Charles, though he does not understand it. He begins to discover the meaning of personal freedom through this relationship with Sarah. She is the mystery that gives him energy to seek answers; she is the catalyst for the discovery of his potential freedom. This slow and painful process takes place over a period of twenty months, beginning shortly after Sarah vanishes, upsetting all of Charles's romantic expectations. Utterly alone and hopelessly confused, Charles is determined to find Sarah. On a train speeding toward London, Charles, having chosen an empty compartment, is abruptly joined by a bearded stranger who sits down and eventually begins to stare at him with "cannibalistic" intensity. Here the author of this deceptively Victorian novel is making a brief theatrical appearance, in the nineteenth-century guise of a magisterial graybeard in a frock coat. Although his prophet-bearded persona gazes at Charles like an "omnipotent god," Fowles's narrator denies authorial omniscience. "What Charles wants is clear," he admits, but what Sarah, his more inscrutable character, wants "is not so clear; and I am not at all sure where she is at the moment." Appearances—even those of an author in his own novel—can be deceiving.

This playful introduction and ultimate debunking of the author's Victorian persona is a device by which Fowles reminds his readers, once again, that they are not engaged in a Victorian novel. The fact is, the present world of the author and the reader is at a century's remove from the Victorian era, and the enforced awareness of such temporal distance only augments the contemporary reader's sense of disjunction between the world of any era and its fictional representation. The contemporary writer cannot adopt the confident posture of omniscience so favored by his Victorian predecessors because belief in omniscience, like God, is now dead. Fowles's narrator dramatizes his abdication from omniscience by saying that his characters must be granted their freedom. Refusing "to fix the fight" and determine their fate, the author will present, instead, two alternative endings to the story. Now his bearded persona, whose aura of imposing authority has already begun to fade (he later reappears as a dandified impresario), flips a coin to decide which of the two endings shall be given the position of last chapter. The narrator regrets that in the novel's sequential narrative two versions of the ending cannot be presented simultaneously. He laments that the second ending inevitably "will seem, so strong is the tyranny of the last chapter, the final, the 'real' version"—which is exactly what happens in *The French Lieutenant's Woman,* though whether the novelist actually regards it as unfortunate is another question.

The author's expressed determination to grant freedom to his characters is an argument the reader may sympathize with but can hardly accept in a literal sense. Nor did Fowles intend that his provocative statements be taken literally. He has described, in an interview, what he feels to be the freedom of his characters. It is the "bizarre experience" of having his inventions, at some point in the process of writing, suddenly "start up on their own." The novelist, as Fowles sees him, navigates a sometimes treacherous course between the insistent reality of his new world and the formal strictures of artistic creation. In *The French Lieutenant's Woman* he repeatedly draws attention to the paradox of literary creation, of having his characters take life in the imagination even while they are confined to the pages of a written text. This self-consciousness about the processes of art is a hallmark of much twentieth-century fiction. As a writer Fowles is as conscious of the limits on the life of a character as he is of the limits of his own omniscience. The freedom of an author's characters is metaphorical rather than literal, as is the reality embodied in his fiction.

The choices Fowles leaves to both his characters and the reader, in the form of open or alternative endings, reflect his existential preoccupation with human freedom. "How you achieve freedom," he told an interviewer, "obsesses me. All my books are about that. The question is, is there really free will? Can we choose freely? Can we act freely? Can we choose? How do we do it?" One of the ways to do it, Fowles appears to suggest, is through the process of literary creation. For the writer, "the novel is an astounding freedom to choose."

By affirming his characters' freedom, Fowles also reminds his readers of their own. The reader, like the writer, is faced with choices; obviously, however, the choices he or she makes are inextricably bound up with the author's, which have already been made. Art, like life, has its deterministic principle; true freedom, Fowles affirms, "can never be absolute." Any choice the reader makes will be influenced or guided by the artistic choices the author makes—as, for example, when he provides two endings to the same novel. In *The French Lieutenant's Woman,* it is clear, the second ending proves more convincing because the artistry is more complete. This is the "tyranny" not only of the last chapter but of art itself. The author's persona may have flipped a coin in the railway compartment, but the real author, stationed in the wings, is arranging the sequence of endings just as he wants them. True, the novel's first ending is more emotionally satisfying because the lovers are reunited after Sarah has tested Charles, but the reader, no matter how sentimentally inclined, cannot ignore the greater impact of the second ending, even though in it Sarah rejects Charles. In the second ending Charles

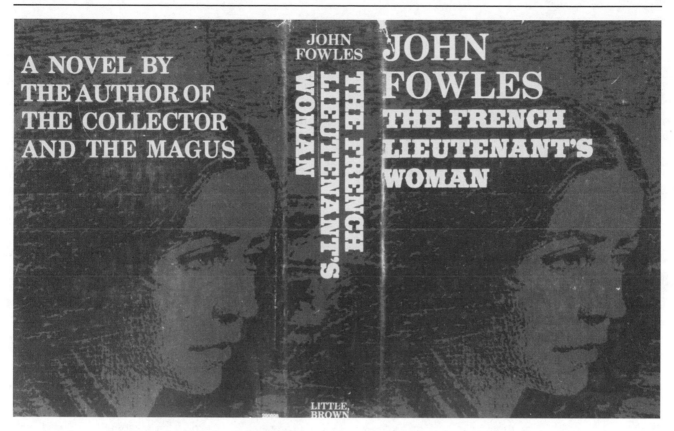

Dust jacket for the first U.S. edition of Fowles's 1969 novel, an examination of Victorian society

does not discover that Sarah has given birth to his child. Only then, bereft of Sarah, past hope and expectations, does Charles discover "an atom of faith in himself, a true uniqueness, on which to build." The second ending, and the final chapter, of Fowles's novel closes with a line from Matthew Arnold's 1852 poem, "To Marguerite": men and women struggle alone, isolated one from the other like islands in the great "unplumb'd, salt, estranging sea."

From the self-conscious artifice of *The French Lieutenant's Woman,* Fowles turned with admitted relief to his next project, a collection of poetry he had begun writing in 1951. This volume, simply titled *Poems,* was published in 1973; it includes poems dating from 1951 through 1972. The personal immediacy of these poems, written in a compressed, even terse style, presents a striking contrast to the richly inventive language and structure of Fowles's major novels. Fowles says he regards poetry as a more honest reflection of the self, because the poet speaks directly from his thoughts and feelings. By contrast, the novel is "first cousin to a lie. This uneasy consciousness of lying," he adds, "is why in the great majority of novels the novelist apes reality so assiduously; it is why giving the game away—making the lie, the fictitiousness of the process, explicit in the

text—has become such a feature of the contemporary novel. Committed to invention . . . the novelist wants either to sound 'true' or to come clean." The novelist's clever and playful persona is a far cry from the quiet self whose voice we hear in *Poems.* "Suburban Childhood" describes a familiar world where "downstairs / the wireless droned immortally / important Sunday hymns." In the poem "In Chalkwell Park" the poet takes a walk with his aging father, quietly hoping that death will not take him soon. Despite the difference in tone and voice, many of the poems echo themes more amply treated in Fowles's novels. The poem "Crusoe," for example, treats the theme of the quest that underlies much of Fowles's fiction. Daniel Defoe's Robinson Crusoe is a symbol of the lonely voyager. People are "Crusoes, all of us. Stranded / On solitary grains of land." The image recalls the line from Arnold's "To Marguerite," with which *The French Lieutenant's Woman* concludes. Cast into the "unplumb'd, salt, estranging sea" of life, each man is an island.

The Ebony Tower, a collection of stories published in 1974, represents a further departure for Fowles from the extended form of the novel, a far more impressive departure than his poetry. It also reflects his continuing fascination with the literature and landscape of France.

Moreover, Fowles includes among the original stories in this collection his translation of a twelfth-century French romance, *Eliduc,* by Marie de France. The love of French literature that Fowles developed during his Oxford years is evident in the many translations and adaptations he has written since. In 1974 his adapted translation of Charles Perrault's seventeenth-century fairy tale, *Cinderella,* appeared. In 1977 he translated two classics of the French theater, Moliere's *Dom Juan* (1665) and Alfred de Musset's *Lorenzaccio,* (1896) for London's National Theatre. His translation of Claire de Durfort's early nineteenth-century novella, *Ourika,* about a young Senegalese girl brought to France as a child and raised among Europeans, was published in 1977. In his foreword to this translation, Fowles admits that "the African figure of Ourika herself," a social outcast, must have subliminally inspired his depiction of Sarah Woodruff in *The French Lieutenant's Woman.*

In "A Personal Note," appended to one of the stories in *The Ebony Tower,* Fowles explains that the working title of this collection was "Variations . . . by which I meant to suggest variations both on certain themes in previous books of mine and in methods of narrative presentation." Each of the stories is also a kind of variation on a mood, setting, or theme found in Marie de France's *Eliduc.* Each of these stories is in some way about art, visual or literary, and at the same time it self-consciously reflects, or exposes, the process of its aesthetic creation. The author plants various self-conscious devices, announcing that "all is fiction" throughout. In the title story, also the longest—just under one hundred pages—one of the characters is reading *The Magus.* David Williams, the protagonist of "The Ebony-Tower," has never heard of the book, however, and assumes it is about astrology and "all that nonsense." The irony, shared by the author and reader, is that David Williams is about to undergo the kind of personal ordeal, or test, that Nicholas Urfe in *The Magus* faces at each stage of the godgame.

An abstract painter who also writes and lectures on contemporary art, David Williams travels to France to interview a renowned British expatriate, the seventy-year-old painter Henry Breasley. Breasley lives with two young female companions in a secluded old manor house in Brittany and possesses a vitality that reminds one of Maurice Conchis or Picasso. Through his encounter with Breasley—and with one of the young women, a promising young painter living at the manor—David finds the orderly solutions of his life suddenly thrown into question. He takes a fresh look at his comfortable but rigid marriage. At Breasley's provocation, he begins to question the enterprise of abstract painting as well. Breasley tells David that abstract painting exists in an "ebony tower," his designation for the

obfuscating tendencies of contemporary art. A modern variant of traditional ivory tower idealism, the ebony tower signifies the contemporary artist's retreat from reality. Obscurity and cool detachment mask his fear of self-exposure and his failure to engage with life's vital mysteries. David gradually recognizes that he is such an artist, camouflaging the "hollow reality" of his paintings under craftsmanship and good taste.

The story culminates in a "point of fulcrum" for David Williams, but, failing to act at the critical moment, he loses the chance of a new existence. Rejecting this chance, David sadly realizes that he has arrested his further development as an artist. "Crippled by common sense," he has failed to embrace mystery, exploit hazard, and discover a way to self-renewal. As he goes to meet his wife at the airport, David awakens from the dream of a freer, more vital mode of existence. He has "a numbed sense of something beginning to slip inexorably away. A shadow of a face, hair streaked with gold, a closing door." With an inward, "drowning cry," David "surrenders to what is left: to abstraction."

Like "The Ebony Tower," Fowles's next story, "Poor Koko," ends with an extended epiphany on the part of the main character. Like David Williams, the protagonist of "Poor Koko" makes a discovery whose meaning extends beyond his personal life. David realizes that abstract painting is one symptom of the malaise in contemporary culture—a retreat from human concerns and reality into the ebony tower. Similarly, the highly literate narrator of "Poor Koko" recognizes in what happens not only his own failure but also the failure of his generation and the breakdown of society. He makes this discovery when he travels to a country cottage in North Dorset, which has been lent to him by friends so that he may finish, without interruption, his critical biography of Thomas Love Peacock (a nineteenth-century novelist admired by Fowles). Just after the narrator arrives at the cottage, a thief breaks in, thinking the cottage empty. The young robber ties up the narrator but does not harm him. In fact, as the thief goes about his business, selecting things of value, he engages the narrator in a long conversation, even offering to make him a cup of coffee before he leaves. Before he goes, the thief suddenly, and without warning, destroys all the books, documents, notes, and drafts the narrator has accumulated—over a period of four years—for his book on Peacock.

This violent attack on his manuscript rather than on his person presents the narrator with an enigma he is still trying to solve nearly a year after the event. His manuscript thrown into the fire, he now perceives that "what was really burned was my generation's 'refusal' to hand down a kind of magic," the power of language. He blames himself, as a member of that generation, for such a catastrophic breakdown of social and cultural values. The younger generation, he perceives, has been deprived of the most vital source of personal energy and power a culture can bestow.

While the narrator of "Poor Koko" solves, at least to his own satisfaction, the enigma of what has happened to him, the mystery of the next story—aptly titled "The Enigma"—is not solved but abandoned. In the process of investigating the sudden and inexplicable disappearance of John Marcus Fielding, a prominent London Member of Parliament, a young police sergeant named Jennings discovers for himself, and the reader, what Fowles had previously suggested in *The Magus:* the quest for answers to a mystery, rather than the answers themselves, pours energy into the seeker. While Michael Jennings searches for clues to a possible "sexual-romantic solution" to the M.P.'s disappearance, he unwittingly embarks on an amorous adventure of his own. *Cherchez la femme,* advises another M.P. whom Jennings questions about Fielding's disappearance, but the woman Jennings finally discovers is not the abstract one for whom he thought he was looking. His investigation leads instead to a remarkable young woman, Isobel Dodgson, who is the former girlfriend of the vanished man's son. Jennings is immediately taken with her, and the mystery of love proves the abiding enigma of this story.

Not only is Isobel Dodgson exceptionally pretty and quick-witted, but she also possesses the electric vitality and independence that characterize a self-motivated individual in Fowles's world. A fledgling writer, Isobel is aware of the parallels between the game of detection in which Jennings is engaged and the conventions of the detective story genre. "Let's pretend," she suggests to him, that "everything to do with the Fieldings, even you and me . . . is in a novel. A detective story. . . . Somewhere there's someone writing us, we're not real. He or she decides who we are, what we do, all about us." By implicitly equating authorial control—being written—with social determinism, Fowles again raises the important question: how does an author who explicitly provokes his reader's awareness of the literary artifice hope to grant to his literary puppets a measure of personal freedom? One way is to insist that those of his characters who reflect human freedom—Maurice Conchis, Lily de Seitas, Sarah Woodruff, Henry Breasley, and perhaps the vanished man Fielding—retain an aura of mystery about them. They are, by virtue of their unpredictable humanity, not wholly solvable or determinable, either by the reader or by the author.

The final story of the collection, "The Cloud," is the most evanescent structurally and thematically. The opening paragraph, with its concrete evocation of a summer's day in rural France, proves nothing short of deceptive. In a matter of hours the azure sky of this "noble day, young summer soaring, vivid with promise," will be transformed by the precipitous appearance of a mysterious cloud, "feral and ominous," the "unmistakable bearer of heavy storm." The style of the opening paragraph is deceptive as well. Its realistic tone and point of view will abruptly give way to a series of shifting narrative perspectives. To begin with, the reader is given a glimpse of the central characters at close range. On a terrace two young women lie outstretched on beach chairs in the sun; three other people, a woman and two men, are ranged about an outdoor table, while three children play below on the lawn. No sooner is this picture sketched than the point of view shifts to a position "across the river," from which the narrator gazes with a painter's detachment at the distant composition of these eight personages in a leafy and "liquid" landscape. The harmony of this composition suggests to the narrator a Gustave Courbet painting; the tranquillity, however, is more apparent than real. "So many things clashed, or were not what one might have expected," he says, adding, "If one had been there, of course." As soon as the narrator reminds the reader that he is indeed not in the scene, he mysteriously finds himself—without any helpful transition—back in the midst of these eight personages. The authorial sleight-of-hand reminds Fowles's readers that they are in a fictive universe, where imagining is the only form of being anywhere.

No matter from which perspective the characters are viewed—and in this story the perspective keeps changing—the sense of their interrelationships and ulterior motives is fleeting and elusive. The indistinct contours of the cloud, after which the story is named, come to suggest the impalpable human emotions lying beneath the visible surface of reality. A vaporous floating island adrift in the azure sky, the cloud also connotes the essential isolation of each of the characters, even as they embark on a group picnic by the river. Most isolated of all is the story's major character, a bitter young woman named Catherine, first glimpsed sunbathing on a beach chair. Since the suicide of her husband, she has lost all sense of continuity in her life. For her everything has become "little islands, without communication, without farther islands to which this that one was on was a stepping-stone, a point with point, a necessary stage. Little islands set in their own limitless sea. . . . And the fear was both of being left behind and of going on." The terror and isolation Catherine feels but cannot express to anyone are revealed in a fairy tale about a lost princess that she tells to her little niece. The princess, having gone on a picnic with her royal family, falls asleep in the forest: "And when she woke up it was dark. All she could see were the stars. She called and called. But no one answered. She was very frightened."

At the end of "The Cloud," Catherine, like the lost princess, has been left alone by the others. As the picnickers, without Catherine, start walking back, the narrative viewpoint once again shifts across the river. The reader watches the characters disappear from the scene, leaving the meadow empty. The landscape is silent, the composition of figures now removed from the setting. All that is left is "the river, the meadow, the cliff and cloud." Catherine, it seems, is lost forever; perhaps she will commit suicide, a possibility that has haunted her throughout the day. Perhaps she is doomed not to death but to that prison of despair from which she cannot call out—or, like the princess, from which she calls out when it is already too late. The events of this story lead to no visible climax. Only the charged atmosphere of unspoken fear, hate, and desire conveys the menace lurking in the otherwise bucolic landscape. The symbolic embodiment of these elusive psychic realities is the cloud. A sign of the bad weather to come, the cloud also serves as a harbinger of impending human disaster.

Writing in *The New York Times Book Review* about *The Ebony Tower,* Theodore Solotaroff qualified his warm praise of these stories by comparing them to Fowles's previous novels, observing that "None of the four long stories . . . has the originality" of *The Magus* and *The French Lieutenant's Woman* "or even the tour de force quality of Fowles's *The Collector* . . . and they do tend to have a kind of relaxed, mopping-up feeling about them." Solotaroff's critical reservations may say less about the intrinsic value of *The Ebony Tower* than they do about the disadvantage any writer faces when he breaks with his past practices and tries a new form or style. Although Fowles returned in his next work, *Daniel Martin* (1977), to the novel form, he was still committed to breaking new literary ground. His description of the novel as "a long journey of a book" is apt, for its writing occupied him for years (during which he also conceived and wrote *The Ebony Tower* and completed his revision of *The Magus*—both published before *Daniel Martin*). Like much of Fowles's other fiction, this novel is patterned on the quest motif, the main character's search for an authentic self. *Daniel Martin* also reflects the author's journey toward greater authenticity as a writer. By Fowles's own admission, this novel is his most personal work. Aware of the obvious parallels between himself and his character, Fowles says: "I was brought up in a Devon village, the one in the book. Quite a lot of my ideas are spoken by [Daniel Martin]. I gave him two or three of my interests." The authenticity as well as the psychological intensity of this novel originate not in its autobiographical elements, however,

but in Fowles's immediate and searching presentation of the main character's inner life.

A few years after the publication of *The French Lieutenant's Woman,* Fowles told an interviewer that he wanted "to write more realistically. *The Collector* was a kind of fable, *The Magus* was a kind of fable, and *The French Lieutenant's Woman* was really an exercise in technique." He added, "of course style is an essential preoccupation for any artist. But not to my mind *the* essential thing. I don't like artists who are high on craft and low on humanity. That's one reason I'm getting tired of fables." In an interview in 1977, shortly after *Daniel Martin* was published, Fowles referred to the novel as his "penance." *Daniel Martin* is not simply nor artlessly constructed; its design is extremely complex. Unlike Fowles's previous novels, however, this one does not proceed with rapid forward momentum, catching the reader up in its ingenious twists and turns. Critics have, in fact, faulted the novel for its long paragraphs of unwieldly introspection and lack of dramatic tension. Fowles's intention, however, is clear. There is nothing superficially compelling about the action or plot of this long, ruminative novel.

The protagonist of *Daniel Martin* is an English playwright turned screenwriter. The idea for a novel about a screenwriter apparently took shape during Fowles's visit to Hollywood in 1969. He had gone there to discuss plans for a motion picture version of *The French Lieutenant's Woman*. With half an hour to kill before his appointment with the head of production at Warner Brothers, Fowles wandered around the studio lot. Since nothing was being filmed, all the sets were empty. He had an intense impression of vacuity, and that sense of emptiness about the moviemaking industry inspired him to begin *Daniel Martin*.

A man in his late forties, Daniel Martin has arrived at a "point of fulcrum" in his personal and professional life. Although materially successful, with an established career in films, he is overcome by a sense of defeat and moral failure. It is, he says, "as if I was totally in exile from what I ought to have been." In an attempt to recover that neglected and abandoned self, Dan begins to contemplate, with considerable trepidation, the possibility of writing a novel about his life. The novel that Fowles's reader holds in his hand appears, at first, to be the one Dan ultimately succeeds in writing. By the end of the novel, however, Dan has not yet begun to work on it. Instead, in the last paragraph of Fowles's novel, Dan suddenly thinks of an apt concluding sentence for his projected work. Then, in the last sentence of *Daniel Martin,* the real author steps in to comment on his character's discovery of a last sentence: "In the knowledge that Dan's novel can never be read, lies eternally in the future, his ill-concealed ghost has made that impossible last his own impossible first." Dan's "ill-concealed ghost" is Fowles himself, who refers the reader to the "impossible first" sentence of his novel. This isolated fragment—"Whole sight; or all the rest is desolation"—makes little sense to the reader when he first encounters it. The full meaning only emerges after he has read Fowles's closing paragraph and returns to the opening of *Daniel Martin* to read the sentence a second time. Fowles's "journey of a book" thus describes a circle, tracing the archetypal pattern of the quest.

At the end of *Daniel Martin,* the protagonist finds himself—like Fowles's other "seekers," Nicholas Urfe and Charles Smithson—poised on the brink of a possible new life, the "chance of a new existence." In contrast to Fowles's other novels, *Daniel Martin* concludes with a definitive happy ending—in the form of the main characters' reconciliation. In another sense Fowles still refuses to offer fixed solutions for his characters or readers. By self-consciously introducing himself, Dan's "ill-concealed ghost," into the novel's concluding sentence, Fowles reminds the reader that his character's projected novel is not the one just read. Dan's book must lie "eternally in the future." Dan's past has been joyfully redeemed, but the future still holds its mysteries.

Most important, however, is the vision of wholeness achieved by Dan at the end of the novel. The discovery of "whole sight" is a culmination of his journey toward self-integration. To be whole, Dan must recover that lost, or potential, self from which he has felt exiled. The stages of this journey toward recovery and integration are embodied in both the events and the narrative structure of the novel. *Daniel Martin* astutely traces a mind's digressive movement back and forth over the critical events of a lifetime. These events loom like islands in the sea of Dan's consciousness, and he journeys back to them in memory while time carries him forward into the future.

This "journey of a book" does not trace the linear movement one associates with a train or car, but the apparently wayward, drifting motion of a sailboat—tacking its way through a populous archipelago and halting at various points of interest. "Forward Backward" is the title of an early chapter in *Daniel Martin,* describing Dan's return to Oxford, England, where an old friend of his is dying of cancer. The friend, Anthony Mallory, is someone from whom Dan has been estranged for many years; in his last hours Anthony wishes to redress old wounds and make amends. The journey to Oxford from London, a literal progression forward in time, is for Dan a journey backward into the past. Here he must confront not only Anthony and his wife, Jane— with whom Dan was in love years ago, when they were

John Fowles, 1980

students at Oxford, and whom he knows he should have married—but also buried regrets, fears, and guilt.

The telephone call that brings Dan to Oxford from Hollywood, where he has been working on a script, is the catalyst for his delayed confrontation with the past and his lost self. When he hears, over the transatlantic telephone wires, the voices of Anthony's wife, Jane Mallory, and her sister, Nell (Dan's former wife), he already knows that the sea and the voyage have claimed him: "The decision is on him, almost before he knows it is there, and he feels—the image is from seeing, not experience—like a surfer, suddenly caught on the crest, and hurled forward."

The forward-backward movement of the novel's narrative also reflects the special Englishness of Dan's elusive nature. These special qualities comprise, according to Fowles, the basic subject of *Daniel Martin.* As Fowles has Dan realize in the novel, the reserve of the English is a manifestation of their "peculiarly structured imagination, so dependent on undisclosed memories, undisclosed real feelings." The Englishman's characteristic withdrawal into the privacy of the inner self is also expressed in Dan's love of the "sacred combe"—the hidden valley or forest retreat that provides sanctuary from the strictures of the everyday world. To this green world, a mythical Sherwood Forest, the English psyche retreats to encounter and be nourished by the essential mysteries of life. In *The Tree,* an essay Fowles wrote to accompany a series of evocative photographs of trees, he describes the green refuge of forest and wood as "the best analogue of prose fiction."

Dan's decision to write a novel is thus an expression of his "longing for a medium that would tally better with this real structure of my racial being and mind . . . something dense, interweaving, treating time as horizontal, like a skyline; not cramped, linear and progressive." Such a medium is embodied in the novel *Daniel Martin.* Dense and interweaving like a forest interior, the novel not only intertwines events from different time periods but also alternates between different narrative points of view. The narrative shifts from third to first person and back as Dan intermittently engages in the "attempt to see oneself as others see one—to escape the first person, to become one's own third." His desire to escape the first person also manifests his fear of subjectivity, of emotion and unreason. He knows that "the objectivity of the camera corresponded to some deep psychological need in him." In some ways Daniel Martin represents a middle-aged version of Nicholas Urfe of *The Magus,* burdened by a sense of personal defeat and failure made heavier by his greater years and experience. The emotional rebirth, or recovery, of self which both characters undergo is, therefore, associated with their renewed apprehension of mystery—the fertile source, the green world, of emotion and unreason.

The novel's frequent shifts in narrative point of view also serve to remind the reader of that authorial presence, Dan's "ill-concealed ghost," standing in the wings, waiting to declare himself at the end of the novel. Fowles's self-conscious references to the act of reading and writing again draw attention to the analogies that exist between life and art. Consciousness makes all human beings readers and writers of reality—writing so that they may be read and interpreted by others. In *Daniel Martin* this literary and existential process is reflected at all levels of the text.

In one sense, the novelist's characters are all versions, or representations, of his inmost self. They are the masks he invents for the purpose of defining what that self is, knows, and experiences. In *Daniel Martin,* then, the author's role is recapitulated by Fowles's central character. As the narrating persona of the novel, Daniel Martin is engaged in the act of "writing himself." But writing himself in the present implies reviewing and interpreting his past. As he sets about doing this, Dan realizes that he has always been writing, pro-

ducing, and acting versions of himself. He sees the Oxford student Dan Martin as a tour-de-force creation—with the author playing the role and serving as the audience, too. "I was writing myself, making myself the chief character in a play, so that I was not only the written personage, the character and its actor, but also the person who sits in the back of the stalls admiring what he has written." Of course, all versions of the self are to some degree masks constructed to act in the world or to protect the individual from its harsh pressures. Some masks are more valuable, or more harmful, than others, however. Some, such as Dan's glib persona at Oxford, may inhibit personal or artistic development by masking a human being's deepest impulses even from himself. Dan thus distinguishes between the "mask of excuse, a sacrificial pawn," behind which the wearer takes refuge from himself, and the mask that serves as "an emblem of some deep truth, or true presentiment."

The drama and destiny of the self is not the only issue confronted in *Daniel Martin,* however. Fowles appears more concerned than ever before with the relationship of the individual to his society, and with the necessary balance between personal freedom and social restraint—what he calls the "printed text of life." Like Gustave Flaubert's *A Sentimental Education* (1869), which Fowles has acknowledged as an influence on his novel, *Daniel Martin* is both the record of a character's personal history and the cultural history of a generation and its failures. Dan's recognition of the narcissism infecting him and his generation appears to convey his author's concern for the ultimate well-being of an entire culture. Significantly, in *Daniel Martin* the sexual-romantic relationships of the protagonist are, unlike those in Fowles's previous novels, linked to family relationships—relationships that bind the individual to society and the generations to each other. When Dan returns to England from America, he breaks off an affair with a younger woman and begins to pick up the pieces of his aborted, mangled friendship with Jane. In the tortuous process of their eventual reconciliation, and the gradual awakening of an affinity that lay in ruin for decades, Dan must examine and rebuild other relationships, too: the one with his daughter, Caro; with Jane's children; even with his former wife, Nell.

This book involves, then, not only Daniel Martin's quest for an integrated self but also his gradual reintegration with others. The bonds existing between Dan's isolated self and others, in both his family and society at large, must be recovered in the quest for wholeness. Dan's renewed sense of loyalty and attachment suggests, within the context of this novel, the necessary commitment required of each individual if a sane and healthy social order is to be achieved. Fowles appears to say that a compromise between the needs of the self and the requirements of society is necessary. Dan comes to recognize, therefore, that compromise is not a denial of personal freedom but its realization in the actual world: "The only true and real field in which one could test personal freedom was present possibility. Of course we could all lead better, nobler . . . lives; but not by positing them only in some future perfect state. One could so clearly only move and act from today, this present and flawed world."

Apocalypse and absurdity seem indelibly written into the texts of life currently produced by the most noted writers of this age. It is, as Dan observes, "like some new version of the Midas touch, with despair taking the place of gold. This despair might sometimes spring from a genuine metaphysical pessimism, or guilt, or empathy with the less fortunate. But far more often it came from a kind of statistical sensitivity . . . since in a period of intense and universal increase in self-awareness, few could be happy with their lot." Perhaps the "cultural fashion" of despair, Fowles suggests, is really a symptom of the age of self, resulting from the extraordinary attention now focused on personal happiness, comfort, and reward. Rejecting the excesses of this age, Daniel Martin refuses to create his novel in "deference to a received idea of the age: that only a tragic, absurdist, black-comic view . . . of human destiny could be counted as truly representative and serious." The thread of optimism that runs through Fowles's novel, affirming the possibilities for moral and social regeneration, suggests that Fowles wants to introduce more than formal innovations into contemporary fiction. In *Daniel Martin* he attempts to free the novel not only from traditional conventions for depicting reality but also from a popular, doom-laden vision of reality itself. The "yes from the heart" of Fowles's novel may well embody the affirmation life can yield when established ways of seeing, as well as writing, give way and the resources of the individual are contemplated anew.

Readers of *Daniel Martin,* as Robert Huffaker points out, "have responded to the book generally less enthusiastically than they greeted his more flamboyant works." The more subdued character of this novel is a direct result of Fowles's decision to guard his integrity as an artist rather than to exploit his talents as a storyteller. Although *Daniel Martin* did not repeat the outstanding popular success of *The French Lieutenant's Woman,* several distinguished critics have regarded it as Fowles's most artistically ambitious work to date. After the publication of *Daniel Martin* in 1977, Fowles published three consecutive works of nonfiction. In each of these books Fowles presents extensive, often wide-ranging commentary to accompany a series of photographic studies on a particular subject. Both *Islands* and *The Tree*

attest to the truth of Fowles's assertion that he "came to writing through nature." In the third study, *The Enigma of Stonehenge* (1980), Fowles turns his attention from natural to man-made wonders. The site of one of the most intriguing artifacts of Stone Age civilization, Stonehenge is the "technological masterpiece" of Neolithic man. Standing on the Salisbury Plain in Wiltshire, England, are large circular formations consisting of huge upright stone slabs and lintels. The function of these massive stones, weighing as much as forty-five tons apiece, has long been the subject of scholarly speculation, and Fowles adds his own voice to the discussion of this ancient enigma. He provides both a detailed account of the archaeological evidence dating the phases of Stonehenge's construction and a survey of the various religious and scientific accounts that have arisen, from medieval times to the present, to explain the original function of this stone ruin.

In the book's final pages, however, Fowles characteristically shifts the focus of his discussion from what is known about Stonehenge to what is still unknown: "There are not yet enough facts about it to bury it in certainty, in a scientific, final solution to all its questions. Its great present virtue is precisely that something so concrete . . . so individualized, should still evoke so much imprecision of feeling and thought." In an "increasingly 'known,' structured, ordained, predictable world," the enigma of Stonehenge—like the mysteries embodied in nature or great works of art—offers the human imagination "a freedom, a last refuge of the self." Here, as in his earliest fiction, Fowles identifies the quest for self and freedom with the presence of mystery and the energy it pours into the seeker. His own quest, it is clear, has centered on the imaginative adventures and the risks of writing fiction.

Mantissa (1982) is the shortest, the least characteristic, and probably the least admired of Fowles's novels. An intellectual fantasy on themes of freedom and necessity, art and sex, it posits an author named Miles Green, who awakes in a hospital room, where he is treated for amnesia by Dr. Delfie, who employs unorthodox means, including sexual congress. Dr. Delfie (Delphi) is also Erato, the novelist's muse, as well as a sort of rock star and male sexual fantasy. She has as her assistant Nurse Cory (or Kore, or Persephone): the underlay of myth and the persistent symbolic quality of all the characters, except perhaps Miles Green, form a powerful part of this novel.

Though John Fowles has always been willing to use the novels of his predecessors in interesting ways in his fiction, *Mantissa* is his most bookish book. It is indebted to Flann O'Brien's *At Swim-Two-Birds* (1939), another metafictional exploration of the relationship between reality and fiction, the creator and the created.

Dust jacket for Fowles's 1982 novel, about the psychiatric treatment of an amnesiac author

Moreover, it includes satire on literary theory and the general practice of academic literary studies.

Fowles comments in the foreword to his *Poems:* "The so-called 'crisis' of the modern novel has to do with its self-consciousness. The fault was always inherent in the form, since it is fundamentally a kind of game, an artifice that allows the writer to play hide-and-seek with the reader . . . giving the game away—making the lie, the fictitiousness of the precess, explicit in the text—has become such a feature of the contemporary novel." Likewise, Miles claims that "Serious modern fiction has only one subject: the difficulty of writing serious modern fiction." Obviously *The French Lieutenant's Woman* is a powerfully self-conscious novel, in which the author not only acknowledges but also celebrates the fictitiousness of his text, using (for instance) the appearance of author John Fowles in the same railroad carriage as his characters and choosing how the novel is to end as original ways of "baring the device." The difference in *Mantissa* is the relative attenuation of the plot, so that the self-consciousness assumes a much larger role in the novel, which consists almost

entirely of a conversation between a writer and his muse, though she does appear in different roles and with different personalities. The exact relationship between Miles and Erato fluctuates, or is contested: whether one of equality (as their sexual relationship would imply) or inspiration (the usual function of a muse to a writer) or domination (as she claims she only speaks words he invents for her). Like *At Swim-Two-Birds,* in which an author's fictional characters drug him so that they can enjoy the freedom of action only available while he is asleep, *Mantissa* delights in confusing realms or rearranging hierarchies.

In addition to its employment of that characteristic modern subject matter, the process of writing itself, *Mantissa* includes a critique of the current literary situation; for instance, Miles declares that the critics "adore downbeat endings. It shows how brave they are, leading upbeat lives themselves." (This comment may be related to the unusually upbeat ending of *Daniel Martin*.) There is a good bit about academia—described as "academic readers, who are the only ones who count nowadays." Erato says that "the French are doing their best to kill the whole stupid thing [that is, fiction] off for good." Through a few jokes about "deconstructivism," Marxism, political correctness and Carl Jung (confused, by the Muse, with Erica Jong) Fowles makes fun of current literary theories and theorists because, as he told an interviewer, "they've been granted altogether too powerful a position on the intellectual side."

Although this may be true, *Mantissa* is hardly likely to right the balance, if only because Fowles treats academic literary practice at such a high level of generalization. There is, furthermore, something slightly heavy about the fun in this novel, which needs (and probably aspires) to be light and astringent. Reviews were (by the standards of Fowles's usual reception) cool. Benjamin DeMott called *Mantissa* "a somewhat sluggishly played *jeu d'esprit* about sex, creativity and theories of literature" and went on to characterize the author's work generally as combining "knowingness, commitment to large topics (humanism, nature) and prolixity." Geoffrey Wolff in *The New Republic* called it silly, meager, nasty, weary, and mechanical and compared Miles to British comedian Benny Hill. Other reviewers, Canadian novelist Robertson Davies for instance, praised it. In general, however, *Mantissa* was seen as a smaller undertaking than readers expect from a John Fowles novel. In fairness, Fowles has taken account of this fact in titling his novel; as he explains, "I did mean the title *Mantissa* (a minor addition) quite literally."

In that same interview he spoke about his next novel, which was then unfinished: "This next novel is going to be readable. I don't think I'm going to play any tricks in it. It's just going to be a straightforward account. I've always liked Daniel Defoe. It will be kind of Defoe-like, I hope." Though set in the eighteenth century, *A Maggot* (1985) is not particularly Defoe-like; and, though it is "readable," it is not really a straightforward account, considering that much of the story is told in a transcript of legal depositions taken by a skeptical attorney trying to get to the bottom of a mysterious, apparently supernatural, disappearance. It begins with a prologue, which declares that the work "may seem like a historical novel; but it is not. It is a maggot"—not much help since, though it may be a maggot in the sense of "whim or quirk" or "the larval stage of a winged creature," it is also, quite clearly, an historical novel. It is the fictional story of the mother of Ann Lee; but Ann Lee was an historical character, the founder of the Shakers, a movement that (unlike most forms of organized religion) Fowles admires.

Like *The French Lieutenant's Woman,* Fowles's conception of *A Maggot* began with a vision: "For some years before its writing a small group of travellers, faceless, without apparent motive, went in my mind towards an event. Evidently in some past, since they rode horses, and in a deserted landscape; but beyond this very primitive image, nothing. I do not know where it came from, or why it kept obstinately rising from my unconscious." As it turns out, those riders–a nobleman in disguise, his handicapped servant who is a sort of doppelgänger, a prostitute portraying his servant, a Welsh brigand posing as an accompanying captain, and an actor pretending to be his uncle–are on their way to the central mystery of the book, which will lead to the disappearance of the nobleman and the suicide of his servant. None of them is what he or she appears to be. The inquiries by attorney Henry Ayscough penetrate some–but not all–of the mysteries.

There are two accounts of what happens in the mysterious cave to which the travelers are bound, both given by the prostitute Fanny or Rebecca. Neither is particularly credible–one of them about sex with the Devil, the other about supernatural travel, in a maggot, to a paradise called June Eternal. The truth is never established. In fact, the novel is a serious investigation of the availability of truth, and thus of the practice of history. Ayscough, a sort of historian, fierce, empiricist, conventional, seeks to find it by cross-examination of the participants (aided by threats). He cannot. The central question raised by the book–what happened to the young nobleman who called himself Mr. Bartholomew–is never solved and in fact becomes increasingly irrelevant to Fowles's interest in Rebecca Lee, the "Quaker maid" of a London whorehouse who shares a vision, of Heaven (or Hell), undergoes religious conversion and, at the end of the novel, gives birth to Ann Lee, the mother of the Shakers.

The text consists of several kinds of material. There is a brief narration of the travelers' activities up until just before the incident in the cave, rendered in third-person present tense; there are long passages of examination of the witnesses by Ayscough; there are interlarded facsimiles from *The Historical Chronicle* of 1736; and there are thoughtful and urbane commentaries, in the form of short essays, by a contemporary narrator looking back on the events of the 1730s, much as the narrator in *The French Lieutenant's Woman* comments in modern terms on Victorian realities. Some of the commentary is simple information–Englishwomen in the eighteenth century wore no underpants; some of it is wry–a form of baseball was played, mostly by girls, and "its traditional prize, for the most skilled, was not the million-dollar contract, but a mere tansy pudding"; and some of it is "philosophical," as when the narrator contrasts Fanny's world with ours:

> Her time has little power for seeing people other than they are in outward; which applies even to how they see themselves, labelled and categorised by circumstance and fate. To us such a world would seem abominably prescribed, with personal destiny fixed to an intolerable degree, totalitarian in its essence; while to its chained human our present lives would seem incredibly fluid, mobile, rich in free will (if not indeed Midas-rich, less to be envied than to be pitied our lack

of absolutes and of social certainty); and above all anarchically, if not insanely, driven by self-esteem and self-interest.

Perhaps Fowles's declaration that *A Maggot* is not an historical novel means just what it says; that instead of positing a narrator of the times, with the perspective of the characters, he uses a modern intelligence and sensibility in part so he can make "anachronistic" explanations of the sort just cited.

In this way *A Maggot* is reminiscent of *The French Lieutenant's Woman,* usually regarded as Fowles's best book. It revisits such themes as freedom and necessity, the possibility of insight into human character, and whether change has brought progress.

A Maggot appeared in 1985; in 1988 Fowles suffered the stroke that apparently ended his career as a novelist. Since then he has written commentary on books influential to him (*The Man Who Died* and more about the natural world and about Lyme Regis. In 1998 a collection of his essays appeared as *Wormholes: Essays and Occasional Writings*—the title refers to "a hypothetical interconnection between widely separated regions of space-time"). This volume brings together several key essays by Fowles, including "Notes on an Unfinished Novel" (1969), "On Being English But Not British" (1964), and "Behind The Magus" (1994), along with introductions to other authors' works and his writings on the natural world, up to *The Nature of Nature* (1995).

Wormholes is a reminder that Fowles is a philosopher and poet as well as a novelist, and yet one would not want to sacrifice the novelist for the "man of letters." It is in the realm of fiction that he has made an indispensable contribution to the story of British fiction since 1960.

As a literary explorer, Fowles has investigated a wide range of styles, techniques, and approaches to writing; the history of this exploration is recorded and embodied in the rich variety of his published work. He has affirmed the resources of language and at the same time delineated the strictures inherent in representing reality within literature and art. By acknowledging these limitations, yet continuing to struggle against them, Fowles has proved himself a dynamic rather than a static artist. Generations of readers will doubtless continue to be enlightened as well as entertained by his fiction.

Interviews:

Roy Newquist, "John Fowles," in his *Counterpoint* (New York: Simon & Schuster, 1964), pp. 217–225;

Richard Boston, "John Fowles, Alone but Not Lonely," *New York Times Book Review,* 9 November 1969, pp. 2, 52, 53;

Daniel Halpern, "A Sort of Exile in Lyme Regis," *London Magazine,* 10 (March 1971): 34–46;

James Campbell, "An Interview with John Fowles," *Contemporary Literature,* 17, no. 4 (1976): 455–469;

Mel Gussow, "Talk With John Fowles," *New York Times Book Review,* 13 November 1977, pp. 3, 84, 85;

Carol M. Barnum, "An Interview with John Fowles," *Twentieth-Century Literature,* 31 (Spring 1985): 187–203;

Robert Foulke, "A Conversation with John Fowles," *Salmagundi,* 68–69 (1985–1986): 367–384;

"The Art of Fiction CIX: John Fowles," *Paris Review,* 31 (1989): 40–63;

Dianne Vipond, "An Unholy Inquisition," *Twentieth-Century Literature,* 42 (Spring 1996): 121–128;

David Streitfeld, "A Writer Blocked," *Washington Post,* 6 May 1996), pp. D1, D4.

Bibliographies:

Barry N. Olshen and Toni Olshen, *John Fowles: A Reference Guide* (Boston: G. K. Hall, 1980);

James R. Aubrey, *John Fowles: A Reference Companion* (New York: Greenwood Press, 1991).

References:

Robert Alter, "Daniel Martin and the Mimetic Task," *Genre,* 14 (Spring 1981): 65–78;

Ronald Binns, "John Fowles: Radical Romancer," *Critical Quarterly,* 15 (Winter 1973): 317–334;

Patrick Brantlinger, Ian Adams, and Sheldon Rothblatt, "*The French Lieutenant's Woman:* A Discussion," *Victorian Studies,* 15 (March 1972): 339–356;

Dwight Eddins, "John Fowles: Existence as Authorship," *Contemporary Literature,* 17 (Spring 1976): 204–222;

Thomas C. Foster, *Understanding John Fowles* (Columbia: University of South Carolina Press, 1994);

Robert Huffaker, *John Fowles* (Boston: G. K. Hall, 1980);

Modern Fiction Studies, special Fowles issue, 31 (Spring 1985);

Barry N. Olshen, *John Fowles* (New York: Unger, 1978);

William J. Palmer, *The Fiction of John Fowles* (Columbia: University of Missouri Press, 1974);

Ellen Pifer, ed., *Critical Essays on John Fowles* (Boston: G. K. Hall, 1986);

Katherine Tarbox, *The Art of John Fowles* (Athens: University of Georgia Press, 1988);

Twentieth-Century Literature, special Fowles issue, 42 (Spring 1996);

Peter Wolfe, *John Fowles, Magus and Moralist* (Lewisburg, Pa.: Bucknell University Press, 1976).

Papers:

John Fowles's papers are at the Harry Ransom Humanities Research Center, University of Texas at Austin.

Stephen Fry

(24 August 1957 –   )

Merritt Moseley
University of North Carolina at Asheville

BOOKS: *A Bit of Fry & Laurie,* by Fry and Hugh Laurie
(London: Mandarin, 1990);

A Bit More Fry & Laurie, by Fry and Laurie (London:
Mandarin, 1991);

The Liar (London: Heinemann, 1991; New York: Soho,
1993);

Three Bits of Fry & Laurie, by Fry and Laurie (London:
Heinemann, 1992);

Paperweight (London: Heinemann, 1992);

The Hippopotamus (London: Hutchinson, 1994; New
York: Random House, 1995);

Fry & Laurie: Bit Number Four, by Fry and Laurie (London: Mandarin, 1995);

Making History (London: Hutchinson, 1996; New York:
Random House, 1997);

Moab Is My Washpot (London: Hutchinson, 1997; New
York: Random House, 1999).

OTHER: Noel Gay, *Me and My Girl,* adapted by Fry
(London: S. French, 1990);

Julian Mitchell, *Wilde,* introduction by Fry (London:
Orion, 1997; Los Angeles: Dove, 1997);

Oscar Wilde, *Nothing–Except My Genius,* introduction by
Fry (London: Penguin, 1997).

Stephen Fry at the time of The Liar

Stephen Fry's youthful success in show business—
including well-remunerated work in television and movies and an adaptation of the musical *Me and My Girl,*
which won an Olivier Award in London and three
Tonys in New York—both preceded and overshadowed
his literary work, suggesting that his fiction is a secondary interest. He maintains, however, as Lynn Barber
reported in the *Observer* (10 May 1998), that "he regards
himself primarily as a writer and that he has 'a more
compulsive need to write than to act.'" His three novels
are witty and imaginative and show a deep concern for
serious ideas.

Stephen John Fry was born in London on 24
August 1957 to Alan John Fry and his wife, Marianne
(née Newman). Alan Fry was an electronics engineer
who formed his own company, operating from his

home in rural Norfolk during Stephen's childhood.
Marianne Fry was Jewish, and Stephen Fry has identified more closely with his Jewish heritage as he has
grown older. He has an older brother and a younger sister. There was, as he has made clear in his autobiography, *Moab Is My Washpot* (1997), nothing at all deprived
about his childhood, though he was a troubled boy,
increasingly prone to lying and eventually expelled
from school. He attended Stout's Hill Preparatory
School, followed by Uppingham, a public school, his
experience in which is echoed in *The Liar* (1991). He
was suspended from Uppingham for a term for stealing

117

Dust jacket for Fry's 1991 novel, an autobiographical account of a young man's homosexual awakening at Cambridge University

money from other boys, then expelled for unapproved absence in London, to which he had been given permission to travel for a meeting of the Sherlock Holmes Society.

Fry then attended another school, The Paston, followed by the Norwich College of Art and Technology. At a low point in his life, caused by unrequited love for a boy at Uppingham and the feeling that his great future was behind him, he attempted suicide, then stole money and a credit card and embarked on two months of travel around Britain financed by stolen funds. Caught and convicted, he spent several months in jail, an experience that seems to have contributed to his feelings of kinship with Oscar Wilde. On his release he matriculated at Norwich City College and excelled in his exams, earning admission to Queens College, Cambridge, from which he received a degree in English in 1981. He also joined the Cambridge Footlights, the theatrical organization that at the time also included others

who have gone on to acting and writing fame, such as Emma Thompson and Fry's future collaborator and costar, Hugh Laurie.

Fry has had a busy career as an actor and comedian since his graduation from Cambridge. He has written for and broadcast on radio, most recently on *Saturday Night Fry* in 1987–1988, and has written scripts for television. He has appeared in theatrical productions of Alan Bennett's *Forty Years On* (1984), Simon Gray's *The Common Pursuit* (1988), Michael Frayn's *Look, Look* (1989), and Gray's *Cell Mates* (1995). His film career includes roles in *The Good Father* (1986), *A Handful of Dust* (1988), *A Fish Called Wanda* (1988), *Peter's Friends* (1992), *I.Q.* (1994), *The Wind in the Willows* (1995), and *Wilde* (1997). Fry has also been a fixture on television. His major credits include supporting roles in three of the *Blackadder* series from 1986 to 1989; *Jeeves and Wooster* from 1990 to 1993, in which he played P. G. Wodehouse's famous butler; *Cold Comfort Farm* (1995), which was also released as a theatrical film; and *A Bit of Fry and Laurie,* which ran from 1989 to 1995, a sketch comedy series Fry wrote and performed with Hugh Laurie, who played also Bertie Wooster to Fry's Jeeves. Four volumes of scripts from the series have been published. His most notorious incident as an actor occurred in 1995: depressed by bad reviews for *Cell Mates,* he disappeared with little notice and turned up several days later in Bruges. Fry has admitted that he was suicidal at this stage of his life. Gray has written an acerbic account of this behavior, to which he attributes the failure of his play, in *Fat Chance* (1995). In 1984 Fry rewrote a 1937 musical comedy by Noel Gay, *Me and My Girl,* which was a critical and popular success in London and New York. He was nominated for a Tony award for his book for the musical.

From 1988 to 1991 Fry was a columnist for *The Listener,* the *Literary Review,* and the *Daily Telegraph.* A selection of his columns was published in the 1992 collection *Paperweight,* which also features many of the radio contributions he made to the series *Loose Ends,* usually in the role of "Professor Donald Trefusis," and a short play called *Latin! or Tobacco and Boys.*

If there is one trait that runs through almost all of Fry's writing, including his columns, his autobiography, and his novels, it is cleverness—to such an extent that he has sometimes been open to the criticism that he is too clever. Max Davidson, reviewing *Making History* (1996) in the *Electronic Telegraph* (24 September 1998), gave vent to such conflicting views when he wrote that Fry "is one of the most naturally talented of the celebrity novelists whose faces clog up bookshop windows, consigning better writers to the remainder pile," and Lynn Barber, in response to Fry's assertion that he thinks of himself as a writer before anything else, asks: "In that case, why doesn't he spend longer on his books and make them better?" A typical column of Fry's television criticism may begin with a quotation from Sir Thomas Browne's *Religio Medici* and go on to discuss "a problem, a twentieth-century mystery, which would appear to be beyond all hope of unravelling, and which would surely have taxed the Masters themselves. The question is this: What is the name of the substance that sloshes about inside the heads of television programme controllers in this country?"

Fry is, of course, aware that he strikes some people as a smart aleck. His strongly autobiographical first novel, *The Liar,* is about just such a character. As the novel opens, Adrian Healey is a pupil at a public school, where he behaves and dresses outrageously and pines with love for a younger boy. At Cambridge he comes under the influence of Prof. Donald Trefusis—a character created by Fry for his radio broadcasts in the early 1980s—a homosexual who encourages Adrian to fake a lost manuscript by Charles Dickens, a pornographic work called "Peter Flowerbuck," and then involves him in espionage. Fry's proclivity to lying from his own years at school here becomes accomplished forgery; the homosexuality that Fry discovered in himself as a student is magnified into Adrian Healey's outrageously camp performance, as in his address to the school's rugby team:

> Adrian checked the orchid at his buttonhole, inspected the spats at his feet, gave the lavender gloves a twitch, smoothed down his waistcoat, tucked the ebony Malacca-cane under his arm, swallowed twice and pushed wide the changeing-room door. "Now, girls," continued Healey, "you're very high-spirited and that's as it should be but I won't have you getting out of hand. I just looked in to applaud a simply marvellous show and to tell you that you are certainly the loveliest chorus in town and that I intend to stand you all dinner at the Embassy one by one over the course of what I know will be a long and successful run."

In one of the pieces appearing in *Paperweights* Fry claims: "When I was at Cambridge it was, naturally enough I felt, my ambition to be approached in some way by an elderly homosexual don and asked to spy for or against my country," and this fantasy is fictionalized and assigned to Adrian Healey in *The Liar.* The novel also involves a machine that compels people to tell the truth, a hint of the science-fiction element that looms large in *Making History.* Evidence to support the argument that Fry writes carelessly may be found in *The Liar:* though finely polished in texture, it has a loose and episodic structure. As the novel progresses, the autobiographical material of the early pages gives way

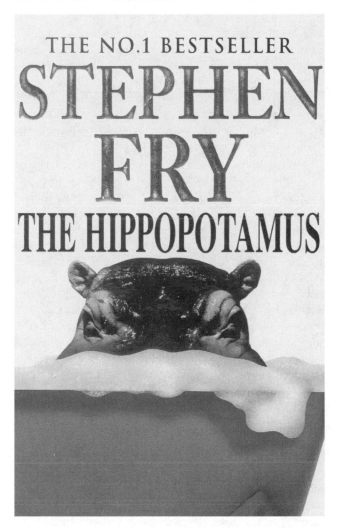

Cover for Fry's 1994 novel, in which a drunken, cantankerous journalist investigates a young faith healer

to alternative inventions that sometimes seem less compelling and more ad hoc.

In the following year Fry published *Paperweight.* Although it was not intended as a unified collection, the journalistic pieces exhibit recurrent themes that shed light on Fry's fiction. One of these is his libertarian attitude toward sex. Though fundamentally homosexual, he declared in a 1985 article in the *Tatler* that he was celibate. Nevertheless, he regularly denounced narrow-mindedness, as in the outcry against the rock singer Freddie Mercury, who died of AIDS: "on reading this and other articles and letters condemning the man's life, I was gripped by an overwhelming urge to behave disgustingly myself: all at once I wanted to be a monster. . . . Would Christ confuse bourgeois smugness with moral strength or judgmental bigotry with neighbourly love?" Fry had gone through a spell of devout Christianity and discussed entering the priesthood but was dissuaded by the bishop of King's Lynn. His regular invocations of a Christian-inspired kindness—for instance, in asking "why the adherents of the gentle and extraordinary Christ who died on the cross two thousand years ago should be so intolerant of those unfortunate enough not to have embraced his doctrines"—position him as a sort of nonpolitical left-winger, though in his support for all sorts of sport and even hunting he seems a more traditional English figure.

Fry's appeals for tolerance may have some connection with his growing willingness to identify himself as a Jew, as did the subplot of his next novel, *The Hippopotamus* (1994). The novel contains much about English anti-Semitism, including the efforts of Jewish refugees from Austria to assimilate, the indifference of the Foreign Office to the plight of European Jewry, and the difficulties of a Jewish pupil in an English school. The major plot, though, concerns Ted Wallace, a cantankerous old drunk who has lost his job as a drama reviewer and investigates what are supposedly miraculous acts of healing at the home of his friend Lord Logan. Ted's circumstances permit Fry to explore several themes of interest to him, including the proper role of spirituality; sex, including gay sex and even bestiality, embodied in a young man with a healing gift who deploys it through sexual contact; and cl   ustinctions and anxieties.

Wallace is fired as a reviewer over, as he puts it, "some frantic piffle about shouting insults from the stalls at a first night." Wallace turns his new freedom to writing a novel, and much humor in the book derives from his difficulties learning to use a word processor, as well as further blasts of opinionated certitude from him, for instance: "If you're a halfway decent human being you've probably been sacked from something in your time. . . ."

The Hippopotamus has too many plot elements, and the narration is divided among narrative devices in a way that contributes little to any overall unity. Moreover, the story of the young man's healing powers ends anticlimactically. As always, however, Fry demonstrates an impressive verbal facility. His impersonation of Ted Wallace is consistently amusing, giving Fry an opportunity to satirize elements of the London world of the arts and letters, as for example when he summarizes the career of Oliver Mills, a member of his old regiment who left the army because of his flagrant homosexuality:

Oliver's first lay billet was with the BBC, a haven for the bent and faithless if there ever was one, where he directed most of those dreary kitchen-sinkers that everyone pretends were the golden produce of the golden age of television, though frankly I'd rather watch John Major dry than sit through any of that self-righteous ullage ever again. Most of the playwrights responsible have died from alcohol poisoning and socialist disillusionment by now, thank God, and Oliver, as you know, specialises these day in rich and loving period adaptations of the classics. . . . Thoroughly amiable and amusing companion (if you like your wit tied in frilly bows) but, when the socialist bit's clamped between his expensively capped pegs, as humourless a lump of dough as ever held a torchlight vigil outside the South African Embassy or stuck an AIDS Awareness ribbon on an unwilling first-nighter.

As Sarah Hudspith noted in the *Independent Students' Newspaper* (23 October 1998), "Reading Stephen Fry is like swallowing a thesaurus: it makes you want to bandy about words like 'mellifluous' and 'discombobulate.' Fry's sharp turn of phrase, witty descriptions and perceptive originality make the book impossible to put down."

Fry's next novel, *Making History*, is a combination of academic satire with the conventional science-fiction positing of an alternate history. The premise hinges on the possibility, through a not-very-well-explained manipulation of time and space, of placing a sterilizing agent in the well from which Adolf Hitler's mother got her drinking water, thus preventing his birth and—or at least so the theory goes—the Holocaust and World War II. Michael Young, the narrator, is a postgraduate student at Cambridge whose specialty is Hitler's early life. He makes friends with Leo Zuckermann, a physicist in his college, who is obsessed with the Holocaust because his father, a physician, was one of the scientists who committed acts of horror against Jews in the camps and he wants to expiate the family curse. Zuckermann and Young together (using experimental materials stolen from the laboratory of Young's former lover) carry out the plan and prevent Hitler's birth.

What results is indeed a change in history, but for the worse. Instead of Hitler, a man named Rudi Gloder (who, according to this account, was in Hitler's unit in World War I) becomes führer. There is a Holocaust that is much worse than the one that really occurred. In fact, the water from the well—poisoned by Young and Zuckermann—plays a role in sterilizing Jews. Ultimately Young has to change history back, permitting Hitler to be born.

Within the broad outlines of the novel's fantasy conceit Fry has packed the book with a variety of themes. There is the idea of changing history itself, along with the somewhat familiar notion that any changes will be for the worse. There is some university comedy. Because all of history has changed somewhat, Young, who in the first half of the book is a postgraduate student at Cambridge, in the second half becomes

Number one bestselling author of *The Hippopotamus*

STEPHEN FRY

MAKING HISTORY

'Stephen Fry at his twinkling best' *Sunday Times*

Cover for the U.S. paperback edition of Fry's 1996 novel, in which a pair of academicians travel through time and prevent Adolf Hitler's birth

"Mikey," an undergraduate at Princeton. Fry posits a particularly conservative society in the United States and at Princeton, including severe intolerance for even the suggestion of homosexuality. The student who becomes Mikey's informant and friend at Princeton is clearly a closeted homosexual terrified of discovery. Mikey simply appears as a student, without any of the knowledge that he should possess, and is challenged to account for such matters as his new and complete ignorance of baseball.

Making History is a comedy on serious themes. Like most comedies it ends happily, though this is probably the wrong term for the restoration of Hitler and the Holocaust to human history. The novel also represents something of an advance for Fry, as it is more tightly and intricately structured than his first two novels. Unlike *The Liar,* which had a convenient biographical structure appropriate to its status as a bildungsroman,

or *The Hippopotamus,* which was built around the personal narrative of a crotchety drunk, *Making History* carefully aligns private and public events. Book 1 (up to the retrospective contraception of Adolf Hitler) is made up of short chapters, the title of each beginning with the word *Making*—for example, "Making Coffee," "Making Friends," and "Making Up"—and includes portions of the "present-day" story of Michael Young and portions of the story of Adolf Hitler in alternation. In book 2 the alternative histories of Young and Rudi Gloder are presented alternatingly in short chapters with titles ending in *History:* "Medical History," "Family History," and "Movie History." The last chapter is "Making History," followed by an epilogue with Michael back at Cambridge.

The reviewer for the *Manchester Evening News* called *Making History* "a joyous display of intellectual wizardry, urbane charm, storytelling at its very best and stunning imagination," while others were more equivocal, such as the reviewer in the *Observer,* who said: "It is good to find a celebrity novelist who can actually write." Like other novelists who have written about the Holocaust, Fry was accused of anti-Semitism and immorality—for instance, by Michiko Kakutani in *The New York Times* (21 April 1998). As he told Cynthia Joyce in an interview that appeared in the online magazine *Salon* (24 September 1998), "my publicist had asked that I put somewhere on the label that I was Jewish, and that a large number of my family had died in the Holocaust. And I said no, I really don't think that it's necessary to wear that as a badge to make the book acceptable."

One year after *Making History* appeared, Fry published his autobiography, *Moab Is My Washpot.* Although some readers were disappointed to discover that he only writes his life up to his admission to Cambridge, he has explained that he did not want to write much of the "what Hugh Laurie is really like" kind of material. At any rate, the book is more than four hundred pages in length despite covering only eighteen years of his life, and it has a definite shape, tracing Fry's descent from a privileged childhood and relatively happy youth into the turmoil of his juvenile years, marked by lying and stealing, alienation from his family, convictions of worthlessness, and ultimately his crime spree and imprisonment. The released Fry tells an academic officer, "If you admit me on to those courses I will get A grades in each subject. I will take S levels in all subjects and get Grade Ones. I will take Cambridge Entrance. . . . I will be given a place to read English at Queens College." He is admitted (though past the deadline for enrollment—in fact, on the day before the beginning of the term), and, more like a character in an old-fashioned novel than an autobiography, all these predictions are made to come true. The book ends with the telegram from Cambridge offering him a scholarship.

Moab Is My Washpot is well written and entertaining, like almost all Fry's work; it has many serious observations, often in the form of long digressions, about education in Britain, homosexuality, and family. Quite a lot of it is familiar, because, as he says, he used his own life liberally in *The Liar:* a familiar exchange,

offered to prove that he was a "cheeky, cocky little runt," shows how he spoke to his schoolmasters:

"Late, Fry?"
"Really, sir? So am I."
"Don't try to be clever, boy."
"Very good, sir. How stupid would you like me to be? Very stupid or only slightly stupid?"

It is too simple to describe Stephen Fry as that schoolboy, still being admonished against cleverness and still unable to resist; but his writing is clever, and the reaction to it is still occasional exasperation. His 1997 publication, the preface to the script of *Wilde*—the film version of the life of Oscar Wilde, in which he played the lead—shows a continuing devotion to cleverness, though Fry writes that he also identifies with Wilde because of his homosexuality and feelings of alienation from the mainstream. Writing in the *Boston Globe* (31 May 1998), Renee Graham paid tribute to "Fry's wit, a great unbridled thing legendary in his native England, at turns erudite, scatological, provocative, and violently funny. An accomplished author, like Wilde he is the quintessential dinner guest turning even casual conversation into a brilliant feast to be savored—rare, filling and delicious." Whichever direction Fry will now turn, whether more acting, further memoirs, television work, or new novels, the result will likely be funny, possibly outrageous, but certainly thought-provoking.

Interviews:

Lynn Barber, "The Fat Controller," *Observer* [online magazine], 10 May 1998;

Renee Graham, "Born to Be Wilde: Stephen Fry Realizes Dream to Play Author," *Boston Globe,* 31 May 1998, p. C11;

Cynthia Joyce, "The Importance of Being Wilde," *Salon* [online magazine], 24 September 1998.

References:

Roger Wilmut, *Didn't You Kill My Mother-in-Law?: The Story of Alternative Comedy in Britain from the Comedy Store to Saturday Live* (London: Methuen, 1989), pp. 164–167, 192, 196, 237, 247.

Maggie Gee

(2 November 1948 –   )

Martha Henn
Birmingham-Southern College

BOOKS: *Dying, in Other Words* (Brighton: Harvester, 1981; Boston: Faber & Faber, 1984);

The Burning Book (London: Faber & Faber, 1983; New York: St. Martin's Press, 1983);

Light Years (London: Faber & Faber, 1985; New York: St. Martin's Press, 1985);

Grace (London: Heinemann, 1988; New York: Weidenfeld & Nicolson, 1989);

Where Are the Snows (London: Heinemann, 1991); republished as *Christopher and Alexandra* (New York: Ticknor & Fields, 1992);

Lost Children (London: Flamingo, 1994);

How May I Speak in My Own Voice?: Language and the Forbidden (London: Birkbeck College, 1996);

The Ice People (London: Richard Coen, 1998).

RADIO: *Over and Out,* script by Gee, 1984; published in *Literary Review,* February 1984.

OTHER: *Anthology of Writing against War: For Life on Earth,* edited by Gee (Norwich: University of East Anglia, 1982);

"Rose on the Broken," in *Granta,* 7 (1983): 107–118;

"Mornington Place," in *London Tales,* edited by Julian Evans (London: Hamish Hamilton, 1983).

SELECTED PERIODICAL PUBLICATIONS–
UNCOLLECTED: "Outside Looking In," *Guardian,* 4 September 1989, p. 15;

"Six Months A-Bookering," *Guardian,* 28 October 1989, p. 25;

"Books for a Lifetime," *New Statesman,* 2 (22 December 1989), p. 46;

"Clinging to the Coat-Tails of Fact," *Times Literary Supplement,* no. 4928 (12 September 1997), p. 10.

Maggie Gee at the time of Light Years *(photograph by Charlie Waite)*

Maggie Gee's importance as a novelist rests on her stylistic innovations and choices of subject matter, which is often political: Gee is, for example, a fierce opponent of nuclear armament. Gee is also known for writing about characters whose lives are often dull and nondescript, whose personalities are somewhat unappetizing, or both. She has studied some of the more arcane and innovative writers of the earlier twentieth century and is herself inventive and artful in the construction of narrative. Her six novels vary in genre and yet frequently share concerns, including most notably the lasting, profound, and unpredictable effects of the actions and events of individual lives on surrounding persons and sequences of events.

Mary Gee was born in Poole, Dorset, on 2 November 1948 to Aileen Mary Church Gee and Victor Valentine Gee. She was educated first at Horsham High School for Girls and then attended Somerville College, Oxford, on an open scholarship, receiving her B.A. in 1969, an M.A. in 1970, and an M. Litt. in 1973, also from Somerville College. She completed a Ph.D. from Wolverhampton Polytechnic in 1980; her career includes four years as a research assistant at Wolverhampton, from 1975 to 1979. Other career accomplishments include a position as an editor with Elsevier International Press in Oxford from 1972 to 1974 and a year in residence at the University of East Anglia, Norwich, as Eastern Arts Writing Fellow, 1982. While at the University of East Anglia she edited a collection of pacifist writings, *Anthology of Writing against War: For Life on Earth* (1982). In 1983 she was named by *Granta* as one of the best British authors under forty years of age. On 6 August 1983 Gee married Nicholas Winton Rankin, and together they have a daughter.

In 1989 Gee was a member of the committee awarding the Booker Prize for fiction, and in the 1990s she has carved out an additional niche for herself as a reviewer. She has published many reviews of art exhibitions, play productions, and fiction, primarily in the *New Statesman, New Scientist, TLS: The Times Literary Supplement,* and *The Guardian.*

Gee has held memberships in the Society of Authors and the Campaign for Nuclear Disarmament. Two novels in particular, *The Burning Book* (1983) and *Grace* (1988), reflect Gee's concern with nuclear issues. Other novels show the influence on Gee of modernist writers Virginia Woolf, Samuel Beckett, and Vladimir Nabokov, who were the subjects of her dissertation. She has also frequently acknowledged the influence of great storytellers such as Charles Dickens and William Makepeace Thackeray, and even repeated readings of her mother's edition of Hans Christian Andersen stories.

Gee remarked of her propensity for complex narrative structures in *Contemporary Novelists* (1986): "I wanted to write stories myself; and I always felt that the difficulty of much 20th-century 'serious' writing must be a problem, not a virtue. If I was difficult, it was despite myself. On the one hand I wanted to write new things, and tell the absolute truth according to my perception of it, which often seems to demand new ways of writing; on the other hand, I've become increasingly aware of the importance of an audience." Gee has, in discussing some of her novels, referred to them as "an attempt to write a new version of a popular genre—thriller, family saga, romance." She has, indeed, become recognized as an experimentalist and at times has been criticized for being obscure and impenetrable because of her difficult plots with their shifting points of view (*Dying, in Other Words,* 1981), embedded subplots (*Grace*), generational crossings (*The Burning Book*), and highly architectural chapter struc-

tures (*Light Years,* 1985). As Gee told *Contemporary Novelists,* her ambition is merely "to appeal to basic emotions, and use basic narrative drives, but to re-work the genre in my own way, and to surprise my readers. All I am conscious of at the time of writing, though, is a desire to show the truth, in ways I never can in speech, and a desire to make structures as beautiful as I can."

When one reads Gee's critical writings it is plausible to accept that she does intend to convey truths as she sees them and uses more complex structures toward that end, rather than for purposes of presenting readers with postmodern pyrotechnics. Consistently throughout her writings as a reviewer and critic she eschews the merely clever and jokey manipulation of genres. Whether she is discussing fiction, visual arts, or drama, Gee values work that makes an honest attempt to reckon with the nature of being human rather than work that shocks or deplores as a matter of policy. For example, in a 1997 *New Statesman* piece titled "The New Metaphysical Art," she quotes approvingly of that movement's manifesto, which "calls for a new art that is 'rooted in the body' but 'moves . . . forward to the spiritual,'" and opposes the "progressive trivialisation of art . . . the uncritical and endless parody and pastiche . . . the ironic and clever habits of postmodernists."

Gee is not a sentimental writer; she grapples with many unpleasant characters and topics, including nuclear destruction, gruesome murder, the tenuousness and frequent dissolution of family life, and selfishness and immaturity. She sometimes, however, allows regret, change, maturation, tenderness, and other redeeming aspects of life and personality to enter into her work.

Positive human qualities are not too much in evidence, however, in Gee's first novel, *Dying, in Other Words.* The novel is centered on Moira Penny, an Oxford postgraduate student of literature with no family ties. Moira is found dead in the opening scenes of the novel and is presented only through odd bits of first-person narrative musings and the recollections of friends, acquaintances, and other characters who are largely peripheral to Moira's life. The novel concludes with what are supposed to be the collected writings of Moira: ephemeral pieces, poetry, and so forth. The novel is self-consciously contrived in its construction, and its seemingly impersonal authorial voice sometimes makes a direct connection between itself and Moira, suggesting that Moira, though dead, is still up in her top-floor flat, authoring the bizarre events recounted in the novel. The novel seems to take seriously the postmodern idea that the author is dead.

Moira's body is discovered early one morning by Bill Dutton, the milkman, while he is making his rounds in the suburban Oxford crescent in which Moira lived. She is found naked, apparently having fallen to her death

W. SUSCHITZKY

"This is the story of Lorna who was born in Wolverhampton, daughter of Mervyn Lamb, who kept the corner shop. When the shop went broke Lorna married Henry Ship, and in a few months she was pregnant.

"This is a contemporary family saga, weaving back through three generations. I chose to write about the family, because it is through our families—love them or suffer them—that most people are connected to the stream of history, and to the future. Henry and Lorna are for the most part too involved in the stuff of their ordinary lives to worry about global issues, so at the end of the book a final war seems to come upon them unprepared, just as their private lives are becoming happier, just as they are working things out. But it is very important to me that the book should not end on that note: we are lucky enough not to be trapped in the book, we still have the power to preserve our own lives. I want this book to shake and grieve my readers, and make them see the reality of the nuclear horrors: but I also want to leave them invigorated with hope and determination."
—*Maggie Gee*

Dust jacket for the U.S. edition of Gee's 1983 novel, which ends with a nuclear holocaust

from the ledge outside her window. As the door to her apartment is locked, the death is assumed to be a suicide; however, no note is discovered and no motive for suicide can be established. Moira's plunge to death is rather like the stone thrown into a still pond: the effects, all sinister, ripple outward, touching those who knew and loved Moira, even those with only a superficial connection to her. The landlady of her flat, lovers, neighbors, and friends all begin experiencing consequences in their own lives, usually of confusion or despair as a result of Moira's death; most of these characters eventually meet their own deaths, through suicide, accident, or murder.

Dying, in Other Words plays with the conventions of the crime thriller. Though the novel comes around again to the question with which it opens (that is, the true nature of Moira's death), it reaches that point almost accidentally, after many circuitous twists and turns. So much drama has passed in between the discovery of Moira's body and the revelation of the true nature of her death that the information seems almost incidental to the tortured sequence of events and deaths recounted in the novel. In place of a plot the novel meanders through the destroyed lives of Moira's acquaintances, drawing connections between them until they seem the product of

some macabre master planner, perhaps the dead Moira herself.

Gee herself, in an opening disclaimer to the novel, cautions that the work is not to be read as a "serious novel." While it does play games with the formulas of crime fiction, it is by no means lighthearted or easy to read. The threads of connection between Moira and the other characters in the book are often difficult to follow, and Gee's use of language is sophisticated and complex. There is the added element of Moira's prose, which is neither explained nor integrated into the rest of the novel. Because of these complexities, some reviewers critiqued *Dying, in Other Words* unfavorably. Gee has called the book her "most technically difficult."

Moira's fall to her death is made into a jumping-off point for the death of others, indicating, as the commentator in *The Feminist Companion to Literature in English* (1990) notes, how the event is "played with, journalistically slanted, recapitulated, made the centre of other stories tending to sinister dying, and seen not to be suicide or murder but accident while trying to survive." In the story's final pages, almost as an aside, the reader learns more about Moira's rigid and stodgy downstairs neighbor, C. Hans, whose noseless face horrifies and repulses Moira; he is the unwitting cause of her death. C. Hans, whose name seems a heavy-handed pun, resents Moira's liveliness and vivacity. One night he lets himself into Moira's apartment to complain about her loud music and suprises her just after a bath. Moira recoils from him in fear, squeezes through the bars onto the icy ledge outside her window, slips and falls to her death. C. Hans locks the door again as he departs. The mystery of Moira's apparent suicide is thus resolved. All of this information comes at the conclusion of the novel, however, by which time "chance" has taken the lives of many other characters.

Besides Moira and C. Hans, occupants of the house in Oxford include the landlady; Clothilde, an ancient Frenchwoman who is Moira's neighbor across the landing; Frank, an unemployed man about whom Clothilde fantasizes; and a trio of violent and ignorant hoodlums whose leader has given himself the moniker of Macbeth. A neighbor and friend, Jean-Claude, is a gay man who is probably closer to Moira than anyone else, but also important is John, a married man from London who is cheating on his wife, Felicity, by sleeping with Moira. A reporter investigating the story and the milkman, Dutton, who is revealed to be a sadistic sex murderer, also figure prominently in the story. These characters, and almost all of the others, are dead through violence or accident by the novel's end. Because these acquaintances of Moira's are "morally and fleshily repellant," as Marion Glastonbury noted in the *New Statesman* (24 July 1981), their deaths "are more monotonous than moving."

Stoddard Martin, writing in the *TLS* (17 July 1981), also commented on the novel's off-putting self-consciousness: "it is inundated with interior monologue and sinks under an endless flow of present participial clauses, many of them inexplicably rhymed. Some of the surrealistic scenery is vivid, but the thickets surrounding are impenetrable. Some of the characters are more appealing than the solipsistic presentation of them lulls one into assuming—they deserve the relief of dialogue." As Martin indicates, the connections between characters, whether tenuous or compelling, are all evinced through interior musings and self-pitying assessments. Characters are full of sorrow and despair over the lost joys or cruel victimizations in their lives, and yet these joys and miseries are made manifest not through any actual human interaction but through bitter and solitary remembrance. This method points to an existential dilemma of human loneliness and whispers of an apocalyptic fate for all.

That apocalyptic whisper in *Dying, in Other Words* becomes a din in Gee's second novel, *The Burning Book,* first published in 1983. The hints of a nuclear apocalypse slowly build during the novel, and at the same time the story points back to the horror of the bombings of Hiroshima and Nagasaki in August 1945. The story on

which *The Burning Book* centers is peppered on occasion with poetic, frozen images from the aftermath of the atomic bombs. In these random vignettes Gee enumerates the absolute devastation to individual lives of a cataclysmic event such as the bombings. By doing so she apparently intends to foreshadow the doom awaiting the small cast of characters who populate the book. Some reviewers judged this technique contrived, but others thought it creates a striking, Janus-like juxtaposition: Patricia Craig, in the *TLS* (5 July 1985), criticizes this novel for its "over-writing and the use of typographical devices to signify disintegration," whereas Linda Taylor, writing in the *TLS* (23 September 1983), promotes these interjections, arguing they have "the quality of a drum beat or a Greek chorus." These sorts of hyperliterary gestures appear less and less often in Gee's subsequent novels.

In *The Burning Book,* which Gee in *Contemporary Novelists* refers to as "a variation on the family saga," the focus is mainly on the marriage of Henry and Lorna Ship, though Gee moves backwards into the family histories of both parties and also spends a great deal of time examining the lives of Henry and Lorna's three children, Guy, George, and Angie. The Ships and their predecessors are intentionally portrayed as remarkably dull, uninspired characters. Gee delves deeply into their sometimes tawdry, sometimes trite lives as they manage to pay no attention to the world events swirling around them. They are utterly unprepared, at the novel's end, for the caustic fate that befalls them. Henry and Lorna manage something of a loving peace and mutuality by the novel's end, but this promise of happiness is annihilated, along with everything else, in nuclear blasts.

Critics generally reacted to the novel as evocative and effective as an antiwar statement but completely lacking in human drama. As Linda Taylor wrote, "It is a relief when the bombs, which we know are coming, have come and gone, when we can awake from the fiction and begin again." Yet, clearly, Gee intends for readers to derive a cautionary theme in her story of plodding characters who ignore the signs of their own doom. Critics agreed that the success of *The Burning Book* lies within its political message rather than its multigenerational storyline. Gee's characters are oblivious and therefore complicit in their own ends; readers may appreciate Gee's evocation of the horror of that end and the need to resist it, but the Ships still inspire little sympathy.

Gee's third novel, *Light Years,* presents Harold Segall and Lottie Lucas, an essentially disagreeable married couple who separate at the novel's opening and spend a year apart learning to regret their own selfishness. In this novel Gee's growing concern for the importance of her audience comes into view, for though Harold and especially Lottie are problematic people, they are rounded and reasonably relatable. While the novel still possesses a complex structure, it is far easier to comprehend than the intricacies of her first novels. The novel is divided into fifty-two chapters, one for each week in a year, and the passage of fictional time is linear, without huge leaps between generations and points of view. *Light Years* utilizes several narrators and spans three generations (from Harold's mother to Harold and Lottie to Lottie's son, Davey), but the shifts in voice are introduced by conventional means such as chapter transitions, and each narrator speaks in the present rather than through visitations to the past or future.

In the first chapter, set shortly before Christmas, an argument erupts between Lottie and Harold that results in Harold storming out. Lottie, who is spoiled and strong-willed, has bought Harold a golden tamarin, a rare monkey, from a disreputable dealer in exotic animals. Harold is horrified by the selfishness of turning an exotic and endangered species into a house pet. To him, the act is emblematic of Lottie's thoughtless whimsy and self-indulgence. He has long been a struggling and somewhat ineffectual scholar until his midlife marriage to Lottie, and yet his already meager productivity has plummeted in the face of the luxurious life Lottie has provided for him. Yet, he clings to a masculine urge to be the provider. He is torn between his fondness for this softer, more lackadaisical life with Lottie and his more ascetic, intellectual pretensions. His own inner conflict bubbles over into the conflict with Lottie.

Lottie's wealth is inherited, and her self-indulgence is deliberate. Her internal musings occasionally allude to a workaholic father who compiled great wealth but led an emotionally sterile existence, and Lottie is determined to live off the money and enjoy a life of pleasure and self-gratification. She has been able to buy her way out of responsibility and overseriousness, employing people, for example, who act in a quasi-parental role to Davey. She is generous with others and exceedingly so with herself, and yet she is fundamentally a selfish and immature woman. Her ability to love is genuine enough, but she resists allowing the love of others to rein her in. Consequently, she is unsympathetic to Harold's reluctance to live off her wealth, unwilling to stay at home for meals or eat at restaurants that Harold could afford on his own. Furthermore, she takes off for a protracted journey to Paris during her separation from Harold in an effort to cheer and distract herself. She essentially abandons Davey, believing that providing for his monetary needs is somehow equivalent to taking care of him. When she meets a man and begins a love affair, the trip gets extended, and she manages to justify to herself this emotional abandonment of her son.

While Harold is a somewhat pathetic creature, more acted upon than acting even despite his walking

out on Lottie, he is not quite as contemptible as she. Lottie is revealed to have genuine impulses and feelings, but more often than not they are self-serving and obviously lacking in any moral grounding or sense of herself in relation to a troubled world. Even when she half confronts and half reaches out to Smeggy, a rather violent and vaguely criminal teenage character with whom her son becomes tangentially involved, her higher motives are tainted by lust and by seeing this human interaction as if it is mere adventure drama.

Despite the fact, though, that we come to view the "emotional battles of Harold and Lottie as ludicrously petty and insignificant," Gee's gift is in making "the self-pitying Harold and the spoiled Lottie as people worthy of our concern." While some of the fifty-two chapters focus on Harold's mother, who dies later in the novel, or on Davey, most are concerned with the actions and petty reactions of Harold and Lottie. Gee uses a device of discussing time and space (hence the novel's title, *Light Years*) and then casting Lottie and Harold somewhat in the role of orbiting planets; one reviewer calls them "lost socks in the laundromat of time."

Both characters go through highs and lows of emotion, rage, surging love, and hate. They are at turns desperate and falsely euphoric, deeply lonely and foolishly headstrong in ill-fated love affairs. Lottie's Paris journey results in an affair with a sexually dynamic man who is eventually revealed to be a comically pornographic sadomasochist, whereupon Lottie abandons him without remorse. Harold's love affair also concludes with a rash journey to Paris; he takes April, a Bournemouth shopgirl who has fallen in love with his middle-aged, professorial bearing. Harold and April are sexually compatible and share some rather hackneyed May-December romance fantasies, but during the course of their weeks in Paris it becomes painfully clear that they have no genuine ties, and the relationship ends in humiliation and regret.

During the year in which the novel takes place, Lottie disappoints Davey, hopelessly alienates her housekeeper, maintains her often-troubled friendship with Cynthia, and has her fling in Paris. Harold flees to Bournemouth during the off-season and holes up in a rented flat with books, has his ridiculous and self-deceiving affair, and endures the death of his mother and a reunion with his father, who has been absent from his life since childhood. The events of the novel are secondary to the tribulations of Lottie and Harold's separation, however; despite their foolishness, their reunion at novel's end is gratifying, and Gee assures the reader that their union will ultimately be a lasting one. Most critics noted Gee's detachment from the antics of Harold and Lottie and her simultaneous ability to make them characters that readers can care about, despite their failings. While in her previous novels critics had judged that the

Dust jacket for the U.S. edition of Gee's novel about a married couple who spend a year apart

Paula is, among other things, a train watcher, charting the movement of trains that carry nuclear waste products through rural and populous parts of England. Paula's lover, Arthur, manages a rundown hotel and is the custodial father of Sally, a young daughter from a previous marriage.

Paula and Grace are watched by Bruno Janes, a loutish figure who has pretensions to greatness as an undercover agent but is in reality a self-deluded, out-of-control, fiery tempered, failed private investigator as well as a split-personality transvestite. His plausibility is somewhat difficult to accept. He lives beside Arthur and has been asked by a shadowy government agency to keep his eye on the couple next door. Believing that if he uncovers damaging evidence against Paula and Grace he will win the agency's respect, he oversteps what is asked of him and deeply invades their lives, breaking into their homes and bugging them, even going so far as to follow them on journeys. In the end he attacks and nearly kills Grace, a circumstance that underlines her connection to Hilda Murrell, about whom Paula is writing a book.

Along with these central characters Gee presents a variety of coworkers and friends. On vacation in a seaside town Grace makes the acquaintance of Faith, an Irish hotel maid struggling with an unwanted pregnancy. During Grace's stay at the hotel a gale blows in, the hotel loses power, and only Grace hears Faith's cries as she goes into a precipitate labor. Grace fetches a doctor and assists in this midnight delivery. The effect of Grace acting as a midwife to Faith's newborn is further evidence that Gee occasionally stretches credibility in the novel through unrestrained appeals to the ridiculous (Bruno) and the sublime (Grace and Faith). One imagines she allows herself such excesses because of her dedication to the cause of the novel, the vilification of nuclear energy. More often than not, however, her choice of symbols, as Paul Oldfield noted in the *New Statesman* (30 September 1988), tends to the "creakily emblematic."

Grace decides to journey to the seaside resort to reflect on her life and also to escape the anonymous phone calls she has been receiving from Bruno. She attempts to get Paula to join her, but Paula is preoccupied with her writing work, her activism, and her life with Arthur and Sally. She endures threats and harassment from government thugs at one point. More worrisome still is her constant ill heath, which she fears is the result of radiation poisoning. Ultimately she learns that she is not ill but pregnant. She goes to Grace's house in Sussex on the day of Grace's return, intending to tell her the news, and she and Arthur arrive just in time to save Grace from Bruno's violent attack. The ending is somewhat contrived: Paula isn't dying but pregnant, and Grace isn't dead but saved.

cleverness of the structure outweighed the warmth of characters and narrative, with *Light Years* Gee begins to reverse this tendency.

Gee's fourth novel, *Grace*, returns somewhat heavy-handedly to her antinuclear themes. *Grace* focuses on the everyday uses and presence of nuclear radiation. The genesis of the novel rests in a factual event, the 1984 murder in Shrewsbury of Hilda Murrell, a seventy-eight-year-old antinuclear activist. Gee centers the novel on two women, an elderly aunt and her adult niece. Grace Stirling is eighty-five years old, an unmarried bookseller with strong leftist ideals and a somewhat colorful past. Her one love affair in life had been with a famous mid-century painter for whom she chucked convention and enjoyed a sexual relationship. It ended after several years over Grace's refusal to have children; she had a feminist bent and felt it would mean sacrificing too much. Throughout her life she regrets the end of the relationship, questions her decision, and ruminates over her life with her lover, who has immortalized her in many of his well-known paintings. Her niece, Paula Timms, is a thirty-something London writer and antinuclear activist.

Like *Dying, in Other Words, Grace* represents Gee's reworking of the crime-fiction genre. The novel alludes to the murder of Hilda Murrell but cannot resolve the mystery surrounding it; the fictional counterpart to that circumstance, the stalking of Paula and Grace by Bruno, is solved. The most significant crime in the context of the novel, however, is the global perpetuation of nuclear radiation through nuclear energy and armament; in *Grace* that crime is identified as not only ongoing but also seemingly protected by an untouchable group of unprincipled government thugs and lackeys who are willing to resort to murder to further the nuclear agenda.

Gee's fifth novel is *Where Are the Snows* (1991), republished in the United States as *Christopher and Alexandra* (1992). The novel is reminiscent of *Light Years* in that Alexandra Court shows the same spoiled and self-indulgent characteristics as Lottie Lucas; even more so than its predecessor, *Where Are the Snows* also depicts in cataclysmic detail the emotional abandonment of children. In *Where Are the Snows* Christopher Court and Alex, his younger second wife, provide financially for their teen-aged children, nineteen-year-old Isaac and seventeen-year-old Susy, and then take off for several decades of globe-trotting. Although they tell the children they are going on holiday, they actually have no intention of returning. As Sybil Steinberg notes in *Publishers Weekly* (13 December 1991), "The story is told in darkly portentous flashbacks from 2005, when the marriage has been rent asunder by infidelity and murder." The Courts' excesses mirror those of late-twentieth-century industrial culture, with its planet-polluting carelessness and self-indulgent monetary policies. While the Courts do sustain their flight of fantasy for quite some time, the same ruin that is slowly choking the planet manages also to crush their endless honeymoon existence.

Just as the love between Chris and Alex eventually comes to ruin, so they leave a trail of destroyed lives in their wake: Alex's family in Ireland, whom she rejects; Chris's spurned first wife, who commits suicide; a neighboring couple, Mary and Matt Brown, with whom Chris and Alex were friends before their departure; Alex's same-time-next-year lover in Spain; and, most importantly, Chris's two children, Isaac and Susy. Isaac finds early success as an artist but succumbs to AIDS, while Susy endures several failed romances and three abortions before attaining a degree of comfort.

Although both Alexandra and Christopher are irresponsible with respect to those around them, it is Alex—as was the case with Lottie in *Light Years*—who is given harsher treatment by Gee. Her selfishness is shown to run deeper than Christopher's, who is willing to give up all else for his love of Alex while she abandons him for other, younger men. Christopher and Alex both face responsibility minimally—they spend time in New York with Chris's son during his illness and death—and Christopher returns eventually to live with his daughter. Alexandra stays away longer, however, coming to maturity and understanding of her poor choices much later and returning to Chris only during her own final illness and death. At the novel's opening she says, "I don't look at other people very much, unless they're beautiful, or interesting," and she holds to that principle throughout the novel. Christopher and Alexandra are able to live their fantasy not because their love is extraordinary or because they are graced by beauty and charm, but by virtue of their wealth and detachment.

As in her other novels, Gee has added an element of commentary about the state of society and the natural world that she does not wholly explain or incorporate into the narrative itself. In *The Burning Book,* for example, she included references to the victims of the atomic explosions at Hiroshima and Nagasaki. In *Light Years* the larger context was conveyed through references to the cosmos. In *Grace* the social concern was creeping nuclear poisoning. *Where Are the Snows,* as its title implies, is concerned with the effects of overpopulation, greed, and global warming on the planet. Christopher had long promised Alexandra a trip to see snow, and yet it is one journey they never get around to making before the dissolution of their life together. When Christopher discovers Alexandra in flagrante delicto with another man in Venice, he shoots his rival. During the subsequent trial Alexandra abandons him. Over the course of the novel global warming is making snow disappear from the earth, until the only place left to see it is in the Himalayas. Christopher and Alexandra wholly miss that opportunity. The slow but steady eradication from the earth of snowfall mirrors the slow corruption of earthly and personal purity.

Aside from the equation of Christopher and Alexandra's fortunes and planetary decline, the novel is actually fairly conventional: as Elizabeth Hawes suggested in *The New York Times Book Review* (15 March 1992), it is "as old-fashioned as it is cutting edge, and its desire to illuminate and explain human behavior is redolent of 1960s idealism." Another critic draws a parallel between Christopher and Alexandra and Tom and Daisy Buchanan of F. Scott Fitzgerald's *The Great Gatsby* (1925), who also "smashed up things and creatures and then retreated back into their money or their vast carelessness." It is a measure of Gee's talent that readers are consistently concerned about the fates of her major characters, despite the fact that they are almost always unlikable.

As with *Where Are the Snows,* a married couple with teenage children are at the center of Gee's sixth novel, *Lost Children* (1994). The novel is centrally concerned with Alma Bennett, whose family life dissolves and then partially reconstitutes itself after her sixteen-year-old daughter, Zoe, runs away. Alma is married to Paul, a school headmaster, and works out of her home as a freelance editor; her world is shattered when Zoe surreptitiously departs one night, leaving behind only a note. Alma has prided herself on her close relationship with Zoe, so close that she has little emotional energy left for elder son, Adam, a law student whose need for love and support seems to have gone largely unmet.

Ultimately Alma is forced to confront the fact that she has deluded herself about her closeness to Zoe and about Zoe's daughterly perfections. Zoe herself remains mostly conceptual in the novel, making only brief appearances at the beginning and end. The novel is primarily focused on Alma and her fractured marriage with Paul, on the relationships she develops at the job she takes with a London realty firm, and on her interaction with Adam, her mother, and her Aunt Eileen. Though not the same sort of spoiled, rich woman as Lottie Lucas and Alexandra Court, Alma Bennett is nonetheless moderately and deliberately selfish, and certainly misdirected, lost, and ultimately rather sour of demeanor.

The implication of the novel's title is that Adam and Zoe are not the novel's only lost children but that all of the characters could be considered as such. Gee presents evidence that most of the novel's characters had miserable childhoods of one sort or another and that their lostness as adults can be traced back to unmet needs or willful mistreatment as children. Alma, through a recurring dream and visits to a therapist, begins to believe that she was probably molested sexually as a child; the perpetrator is unclear and may have been her father, who died under mysterious consequences when Alma was young, her stepfather, or some other shadowy figure.

Lost Children deals consciously with the "inner child" issue that has become germane to the 1990s debates about the nature of selfhood. Alma at first resists the notion of molestation specifically because it has become so faddish to locate the source of all adult dysfunctions in the impenetrable fog of childhood. Such tragedies begin to seem so commonplace that they can explain even the population of homeless people who choose the street in front of Alma's employer to set up an encampment of sorts. As in all her novels, Gee's focus on individuals takes place simultaneously with her investigation of some breakdown of the social order—primarily homelessness, but a spectrum of other issues, too, or "every imaginable liberal bugbear," as Claire Messud characterizes them in the *Guardian* (14

April 1994). As is usual for Gee, the explicit connections between the state of society and the lives of her major characters are left for the reader to make.

Alma grieves deeply over Zoe's disappearance, and her response is to push away those otherwise closest to her. Consequently, she asks Paul for a separation and sends him packing to a rooming house in Ealing. Alma struggles with the incessant lesson of her childhood, to be unselfish, and feels that she has sacrificed too much and been too selfless in tending to Paul and Adam. Adam is upset about Zoe's disappearance, his parents's separation, and Alma's determined indifference to him, but she cannot be reached by either his subtle or not-so-subtle entreaties.

On her journey of personal exploration and reconstruction Alma confronts her mother about her own maternal failings. Alma's mother resists any delving into the past, consenting only under intense pressure from her daughter. At the same time Alma is seriously deluded about her own past as a mother, persisting in the belief that she knows Zoe well and refusing to admit to herself all the ways in which she slights Adam. The insights she does gain are not to be trusted, for they are all over the personal landscape: she decides at one moment that her life with Paul is over and the next that her marriage is salvageable, only to think of it again later as hopelessly adrift. As Messud observes, the novel's "over-earnest, complacent, and self-indulgent characters damn themselves out of their own mouths. They utter painful platitudes and come, internally, to sadly unsubtle insights." Only Adam's attempted suicide, a dramatic act that demands Alma and Paul's attention, brings the family back together in the end.

Gee's six novels have established her reputation, especially in England, as a major contemporary writer. She is known as both a stylistic innovator and a social crusader. Her novels often use complexly constructed plots and devices, draw implicit parallels between individual fates and global issues, and consistently elicit interest and concern from readers despite the difficult persons who populate her fictional landscapes.

Interviews:

Writers on Writing: Creative Writing Course, part 4, "Characters, Setting, Plot." (Northbrook, Ill.: The Roland Collection, 1988);

"Maggie Gee with Sheila McCleod" [videotape] (London and Northbrook, Ill.: Roland Collection/ICA Videos, 1989).

Giles Gordon

(23 May 1940 –   )

Randall Stevenson
University of Edinburgh

See also the Gordon entries in *DLB 14: British Novelists Since 1960* and *DLB 139: British Short-Fiction Writers, 1945–1980.*

BOOKS: *Landscape Any Date* (Edinburgh: Macdonald, 1963);

Two and Two Make One (Preston, U.K.: Akros, 1966);

Two Elegies (London: Turret, 1968);

Pictures from an Exhibition (New York: Dial, 1970; London: Allison & Busby, 1970);

Eight Poems for Gareth (Frensham, U.K.: Sceptre, 1971);

Between Appointments (Frensham, U.K.: Sceptre, 1971);

The Umbrella Man (London: Allison & Busby, 1971);

Twelve Poems for Callum (Preston, U.K.: Akros, 1972);

About a Marriage (New York: Stein & Day, 1972; London: Allison & Busby, 1972);

One Man, Two Women (London: Sheep, 1974);

Girl with Red Hair (London: Hutchinson, 1974);

Walter and the Balloon, by Gordon and Margaret Gordon (London: Heinemann, 1974);

Farewell, Fond Dreams (London: Hutchinson, 1975);

100 Scenes from Married Life (London: Hutchinson, 1976);

The Oban Poems (Knotting: Sceptre, 1977);

Enemies: A Novel about Friendship (Hassocks, U.K.: Harvester, 1978);

The Illusionist (Hassocks, U.K.: Harvester, 1978);

Ambrose's Vision: Sketches towards the Creation of a Cathedral (Hassocks, U.K.: Harvester, 1980);

Aren't We Due a Royalty Statement: A Stern Account of Literary, Theatrical and Publishing Folk (London: Chatto & Windus, 1993).

OTHER: *Factions,* edited by Gordon and Alex Hamilton (London: Joseph, 1974);

Beyond the Words: Eleven Writers in Search of a New Fiction, edited, with an introduction, by Gordon (London: Hutchinson, 1975);

You Always Remember the First Time, edited by Gordon, Michael Bakewell, and B. S. Johnson (London: Quartet, 1975);

Giles Gordon

"Members of the Jury . . . ," edited by Gordon and Dulan Barber (London: Wildwood House, 1976);

Prevailing Spirits: A Book of Scottish Ghost Stories, edited by Gordon (London: Joseph, 1977);

A Book of Contemporary Nightmares, edited by Gordon (London: Joseph, 1977);

"The Thrie Estaitis: Scotch, Scots, Scottish," in *Jock Tamson's Bairns,* edited by Trevor Royle (London: Hamilton, 1977);

Modern Scottish Short Stories, edited by Gordon and Fred Urquhart (London: Hamilton, 1978);

Shakespeare Stories, edited, with an introduction, by Gordon (London: Hamilton, 1982);

English Short Stories: 1900 to the Present, selected, with an introduction, by Gordon (London: Dent, 1988);

The Twentieth-Century Short Story in English, bibliography compiled, with an introduction, by Gordon (London: British Council, 1989);

Christmas Stories, selected by Gordon (London: Bloomsbury, 1995);

The Best of Short Stories 1986–1995, edited by Gordon and David Hughes (London: Minerva, 1995);

Scotland from the Air, photographs by Jason Hawkes, text by Gordon (Weidenfeld & Nicolson, 1996);

William Trevor, *Cocktails at Doney's and Other Stories,* selected by Gordon (London: Bloomsbury, 1996).

Giles Gordon's fiction has been neither widely read nor much discussed critically outside of newspaper reviews; yet, he occupies a significant position among recent British writers as one of those most determined, as he puts it, "to kick fresh life into the novel" in the 1970s. He has been called "the only true inheritor of the late B. S. Johnson's mantle," and in the 1970s he did extend through the 1970s some of the self-conscious, innovative techniques Johnson favored, at the same time showing himself unusually alert to the potential established abroad by the French *nouveau roman.* Such interests contributed to a fiction characterized by its sustained self-reflexivity: his interrogation of the conventions of the novel played a part in consolidating the experimental, postmodern idiom that was being established in British writing at the time.

Giles Alexander Esmé Gordon was born in Edinburgh, Scotland, on 23 May 1940, the son of a distinguished architect, Alexander Esmé Gordon, RSA, and Betsy Balmont McCurry Gordon. He recalls having had few close friends in his early years and turning to the printed word to compensate for a slightly lonely childhood spent in quiet, middle-class areas of Edinburgh–"a very earnest city in which to grow up," in his view. He attended a private, fee-paying school, Edinburgh Academy; he later questioned the Anglified nature of its teaching, recalling that when he first encountered the work of Robert Burns during these school years, he found it incomprehensible because it was written in a Scots language and tradition for which his background and education had not prepared him. Gordon later recorded his Scottishness as a matter of unease, even guilt. This education, the values of which were not altogether those of the nation in which it took place, perhaps added to Gordon's general childhood feelings of isolation, to the sense of estrangement that frequently appears in his later fiction, and to his concern with the separate existence of the self and the problematic nature of relationships.

More immediately, early experience may have contributed to Gordon's readiness to leave Scotland. After he left school in 1957, he studied book design and typography briefly at Edinburgh College of Art and worked as a trainee for the Edinburgh publishers Oliver and Boyd from 1959 until departing for London in 1962 at the age of twenty-two. Though he considered the move to England only temporary, the greater employment opportunities in London's publishing industry kept him there for more than thirty years, living for most of them in a terraced house in Kentish Town. He worked initially at a range of jobs, including as an editor for both Hutchinson and Penguin, before he became editorial director of Victor Gollancz in 1967.

Before leaving Scotland, in 1961 Gordon founded and later helped to edit *New Saltire,* at that time the only literary magazine in Scotland. Under his own imprint he later published pamphlets of poetry, including work by Hugh MacDiarmid and Iain Crichton Smith. Shortly after arriving in London, Gordon began to publish poems of his own. The first volume of these, *Landscape Any Date,* appeared in 1963, and two other collections followed during the 1960s. Throughout 1964 and 1965 he contributed a weekly London column on books and authors to the *Scotsman* newspaper. He also began to publish short stories in various journals.

Gordon's first prose collection, *Pictures from an Exhibition* (1970), introduces many of Gordon's recurrent idioms and concerns. The volume is composed of short accounts of various works of art, often written in a kind of "concrete prose" experimenting with unusual, mimetic typographical layouts. Gordon has suggested that some of the "fresh life" he sought for the novel might be found through relating "it in some degree to aesthetics, to typography and graphic design." Similarly innovative tactics are sustained throughout the pieces, which repeatedly interrogate the nature of the imaginative reality created by fiction and the relationship of words to the world. Fantastically dissociated from everyday reality, stories such as "Balls Balance" and "Thirteen" emphasize their status as linguistic artifacts rather than plausible stories–as does "Construction," which is seemingly concerned with bizarre activities in a strange building but also repeatedly reminds its readers that it is itself a construction, artificial and unreal. Gordon explained that he is "intrigued and fascinated by words, by sentences, paragraphs, pages as sounds, shapes, rhythms as well as senses," and he quotes with approval a critic who asserts regarding fiction that "the only reality it posits is that of its own pages. There is no 'real world,' no specific context to which it refers, and it is subversive precisely because it denies the validity, or stability, of any content. In other words, it is itself. A novel is a novel is a novel." Unsympathetic reviewers have echoed the *Contemporary Authors* reviewer, who called the results of Gordon's complex, perhaps Franco-Scottish approach "vague, convoluted, repetitive, and tedious."

CRITICAL ACCLAIM FOR
GILES GORDON'S
PREVIOUS WORK

"Real talent and promise."
EDWIN MORGAN, *The Listener.*

"Mr Gordon has a gift for sharp social observation
and a flair for domestic comedy-drama."
FRANCIS WYNDHAM, *Sunday Times.*

"He is not afraid to experiment, while still writing
in a manner that holds our attention."
MARTYN GOFF, *Daily Telegraph.*

"What is admirable about Mr Gordon is the
impatience with accepted modes of telling a story
which makes him unusually patient in wringing
the last ounce of meaning from his own stuff."
ROBERT NYE, *The Guardian.*

THE HARVESTER PRESS LTD.
2 STANFORD TERRACE,
HASSOCKS, SUSSEX.

Dust jacket for Gordon's 1978 novel about the relationship of two families

Pictures from an Exhibition shows a range of Gordon's early interests in such now-familiar postmodernist issues. The volume is also typical of the direct, relaxed, colloquial style through which these issues develop in much of his fiction, and–in "Construction" and "The Window" particularly–of his employment of complex, suggestive images through which self-reflexive fictional concerns can be concisely presented.

The eponymous hero of Gordon's first novel, *The Umbrella Man* (1971), remarks, "I had always . . . stared at people through glass, in the bus, in the train, in cinemas." As in "The Window," the image is appropriate to the theme of desired contact with a visible but inaccessible other–in this case, a woman, Delia, whom the lonely umbrella man, Felix, sees from behind glass. Themes of isolation and estrangement are emphasized by the novel's structure, as unusual and experimental as anything in *Pictures from an Exhibition*. Gordon employs three separate but sometimes overlapping points of view: an "objective" third-person voice alongside the first-person narratives of Felix and of Delia, the diverse versions of experience they present dramatizing disparities in their vision and attitudes. Transitions from one perspective to another are not always easy for readers to recognize, and conflicting versions of what may be the same set of events make any clear fictional picture hard to establish, emphasizing the relativity and unreliability of perception itself. In such ways the novel generally sustains what one of its characters calls "an impossible, dream-like quality" rather than "the clear-cut monotony of reality." Another character asks "Do all the people . . . outside this door even exist? Are they figments of my imagination, or are they real?" Readers are forced to negotiate with much the same sort of question. Does Felix actually, for example, drop the corpse of Delia's baby down the funnel of a railway engine as it passes beneath a bridge? Do poppies really sprout, bloom, and wither in a single day? The novel raises, frustrates, and plays with such questions throughout, often presenting improbable or incredible events only to make them seem natural a few pages later, or sometimes vice versa. Not all of its mysteries are ever fully resolved, though it ends with a consummation of the relationship between Felix and Delia that also draws together the novel's hitherto conflicting perspectives into a new, unified, first-person-plural voice.

Gordon has remarked that he writes "two distinct kinds of novel." The experimentation with structure and the nature of narrative that informs *Pictures from an Exhibition* and *The Umbrella Man* defines one of these distinct directions. His second novel, *About a Marriage* (1972), introduces the other, potentially contrary direction—toward fictionalized but realistic autobiography. The novel's first-person narrator, Edward, is a young man with literary aspirations who, like Gordon, has left Scotland to live and work in London. He develops a relationship with Ann, who works as an artist and illustrator, like Gordon's first wife, Margaret Anna Eastoe, whom he married in 1964. Edward and Ann's children even share the same birth dates (August 1968 and May 1970) as Gordon's sons, Callum and Gareth. Flirting only occasionally with self-reflexiveness or fantasy, *About a Marriage* reflects unusually intimately the everyday progress of relationship and marriage, dramatizing details of domestic life the ordinariness, even banality, of which would normally exclude them from the novelist's attention. Though less complex and more conventionally realistic than his earlier fiction, *About a Marriage* is nevertheless not entirely straightforward in structure. Each chapter begins with Edward's account of a series of weekly visits to the park but moves on to recollection of earlier, sometimes troubled, stages of his relationship and marriage with Ann. By the final chapter his reflections have advanced to coincide with the present of Edward's generally happy marriage and trips to the park with his children. As Ann says, his narrative is an attempt to know her "from the beginning again"—a process mysteriously involving encounters in the park with another young mother of the same name—and to rediscover the basis of their present relationship. *About a Marriage* thus shows Gordon once again using an unusual fictional structure to dramatize isolation and the difficulties of relationships but also to emphasize ways they can eventually be satisfactorily overcome.

Girl with Red Hair (1974) returns decisively to Gordon's experimental idiom. He records a possible debt to the detective novels such as *Murder off Miami* (1936), which Dennis Wheatley and J. G. Links published in unbound, dossier form in the 1930s. Of all his fiction, however, *Girl with Red Hair* is the most clearly influenced by the French authors of the *nouveau roman*—Michel Butor and Alain Robbe-Grillet, in particular—for whom Gordon has declared admiration, describing the latter as "To me . . . probably the most influential and intriguing twentieth century fiction writer." Like some of Robbe-Grillet's writing, *Girl with Red Hair* sometimes concentrates on description of inanimate objects almost to the exclusion of character and plot, neither of which is easy to decipher. Like *The Umbrella Man, Girl with Red Hair* presents successive, conflicting

accounts of what may be the same event: a murder may or may not have been committed; the central persona may or may not be connected with it either as investigator, suspect, or witness to events either seen or perhaps just imagined. Like Robbe-Grillet's *Les Gommes* (1953), *Girl with Red Hair* is loosely a detective story, but one that undermines the genre's assumption that the truth about events can be confidently discovered. Gordon further parodies conventional assumptions by providing a semifacetious index of characters and the pages on which they appear. Even the identity of the novel's principal character remains curiously shifty, identified neither as "I" nor "he" but as "you"—a strategy that forces the novel's problems still more firmly upon readers, almost making them protagonists in the fiction. Gordon's tactics may have been derived from Michel Butor's *La Modification* (1957), and another Scottish novelist, Ron Butlin, has since attempted something similar in *The Sound of My Voice* (1987). Second-person narration remains unusual in English-language writing, however, and as Valentine Cunningham pointed out in a *TLS: The Times Literary Supplement* article, Gordon is "one of few serious anglicizers of French modes." *Girl with Red Hair* is his most complete adoption of such modes, thoroughly in accord with his view that "If in terms of its own originality—whatever uniqueness it possesses—the reader of a book has difficulty immediately in interpreting its territory, why shouldn't this be regarded as a challenge?" Like the *nouveau roman, Girl with Red Hair* is as much an act of criticism as of conventional creativity, challenging assumptions about coherence of character and action and interrogating the act of reading itself.

Farewell, Fond Dreams (1975) is another collection of short fictions similar to *Pictures from an Exhibition*. Several more "pictures" are included, though these now range across film, dance, theater, and even newspaper journalism. The collection also extends Gordon's challenge to relations between imagined and actual, fiction and life, into new areas, particularly "faction." With Alex Hamilton, he had published an anthology of material mingling real events and imagination, *Factions,* the previous year. *Farewell, Fond Dreams* contains a long piece, "An attempt to make entertainment out of the war in Vietnam," intersperses accounts of actual events in Vietnam with an imagined correspondence between humorously named politicians in Britain and the United States.

100 Scenes from Married Life (1976) returns to the realistic, autobiographical idiom of *About a Marriage*. Gordon's daughter, Harriet, was born in 1974, and Edward and Ann, now older and more settled, also have a third child: resemblances between Edward and his creator in this work even extend to their sharing the same London telephone number. Like *About a Marriage,*

100 Scenes from Married Life presents the banalities of domestic existence in comprehensive detail, recording with meticulous attentiveness the minutiae of marital relations; parents' Christmas visits; ordinary days of office work; the sudden illness of a child. Its fragmented structure, however, makes it less coherently a novel than *About a Marriage,* and its episodes from domestic life are interspersed with imagined vignettes of more-famous relationships—between Casanova and his wife, for example, and Romeo and Juliet. Witty and bathetic, these brief interludes provide a kind of comic relief as well as an ironic, oblique commentary on the experience of Edward and Ann.

Gordon's next work, *Enemies: A Novel about Friendship* (1978), continues and complicates his interest in marriage, tracing the intimate thoughts and inner reflections arising from relationships within and between two families on holiday in a remote, unspecified European country. Sunny days of leisurely walks and long dinners in the twilight of a splendid garden suggest the families are sequestered safely enough in their own world, until, on the last night of the holiday, the garden is entirely, mysteriously destroyed. This incident may be the first gesture of a rumored revolution, but the occurrence cannot be explained by the characters, and the novel ends without elucidating it. Perhaps it might be rationalized as symbolic of the vanished innocence of the relationships portrayed or of the inevitable enmities at the heart of ostensible friendships, as the title implies. The thoroughly cryptic quality of the novel perhaps also suggests an attempt by Gordon to synthesize hitherto disparate directions in his fiction: toward the self-reflexive puzzles of the *nouveau roman* on the one hand and the detailed, realistic anatomy of relationships on the other. Until its conclusion the novel largely belongs in the latter category, though something of the dreamlike atmosphere of *The Umbrella Man* arises from the mysterious nature of characters' occupations, the vaguely threatening background of revolution, and the unspoken tensions that shape the relationships portrayed. The disappearance of the garden, however, introduces a greater sense of oddity, moving toward the deliberately irreducible mysteries of *Girl with Red Hair*—toward the perplexities of ordering perception in general and not only in deciphering relationships and emotions.

A similar attempt at synthesis of experimentation and more-conventional realism may be said to inform Gordon's 1980 novel, *Ambrose's Vision: Sketches towards the Creation of a Cathedral.* Gordon takes as one of his epigraphs a quotation from John Gower: "I undertoke / . . . to make a boke / Which stant between ernest and game." While *Ambrose's Vision* is an "earnest" or realistic treatment of the world beyond the book, examining creativity and the monuments that result from it, it is also a playful, self-reflexive creation of tenuously connected fantasies—the sketches or visions of a man apparently obsessed with building a cathedral. Though the theme of creativity obviously sanctions a certain self-reflexiveness, different aspects of *Ambrose's Vision* nevertheless seem to cocxist as much as cohere, with Gordon standing between the disparate directions of his fiction rather than achieving a compelling synthesis of them.

Gordon's final collection of short stories, *The Illusionist* (1978), like *Pictures from an Exhibition* and *Farewell, Fond Dreams,* demonstrates the author's interest in diverse subjective perspectives and in relations between illusion and reality, fiction and lived experience. "The Jealous One," about a gunslinging cat, and "Maestro," about a mental breakdown brought on by the complexities of classical music, share Franz Kafka's talent for presenting inexplicable occurrences in straightforward, even colloquial, language that helps to make them seem natural and everyday. Fantasies such as the title story, which depicts a magician who does not just pretend to saw people in half, or "Letter to a Spanish Painter," about a logically impossible correspondence with the surrealist Salvador Dali, owe a clear debt to the elaborate puzzles of Jorge Luis Borges's short fiction. Robbe-Grillet's influence is still apparent in the complex juggling of pattern and perspective in pieces such as "Nineteen Policemen Searching the Solent Shore." The self-reflexive puzzles and fantasies of *The Illusionist,* however, are often more fully and carefully worked out than in Gordon's earlier books. In its investigation of how far the mind can engage with the world beyond itself, *The Illusionist* draws a clear connection to the anxiety the individual faces in relation to other people. Behind many of the stories of *The Illusionist* lies the lonely conviction that the mind is doomed to be separate from the world it envisages and, concomitantly, from the others that inhabit the world. Of a view of London, for example, it is remarked that "there are eight million of us, more or less, in this city and none of us can know even by sight let alone in any more intimate way the rest of us. And each of us feels and is and has his separate, individual being."

Gordon has warned that "the moment you try to relate the mere mortal, a writer . . . to the *oeuvre* . . . you are usually in trouble." Whether or not the sense of separate, individual being so conspicuous in his work should be considered a legacy of a lonely childhood from which the printed word offered some escape, it can be seen to underlie both the experimental and the more conventional aspects of his writing, which are less contrary than they at first appear. The former direction examines ways in which the mind employs fictions and illusions in attempting to reach beyond itself and assimilate experience; the latter—principally the autobio-

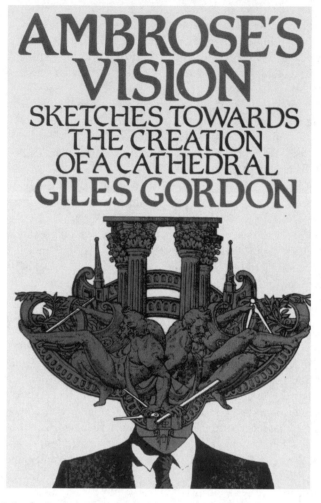

Dust jacket for Gordon's 1980 novel, about a man obsessed with building a cathedral

graphical fiction about marriage—is concerned with ways the isolation of the self can be escaped or transcended through human relationships and love. Gordon remarks of his work that "There is a world out there, beyond the window. There is a world in my head. There is a world I try to pin down on paper. Three separate worlds that should bear some relation to one another." His novels variously use what can be pinned down on paper to examine the window that separates the mind and the world and the chances of reaching beyond it. The autobiographical novels, and to some extent *The Umbrella Man,* analyze the possibility of relationship with people beyond the glass; the experiments and metafictions assess the nature and extent of its translucence.

The limitations of Gordon's work could be considered inevitable corollaries of its strengths. *About a Marriage* and *100 Scenes from Married Life* are unusually intimate, detailed, and occasionally moving investigations of day-to-day relationship issues and ordinary

domesticity, but they run the risk of seeming simply banal, undramatic, or directionless as a result. Likewise, the formal strategy of *The Umbrella Man* successfully highlights disparities of vision between different individuals but does so through repetitious, potentially tedious accounts of the events of the novel. *Girl with Red Hair* and *Enemies* challenge readers to confront the indecipherable in reading or in reality; yet in doing so, each work can also simply frustrate and seem gratuitous in its denial of the novel's conventional capacity to represent and comment broadly on lived experience.

Gordon, in short, is not exempt from the charges of sterility, self-indulgence, or irresponsibility often leveled at metafiction or other modes of postmodernist writing. An element of Gordon's work that tends to offset such charges is his wit, which figures even in his more cerebral, self-reflexive fictions. Gordon himself later complained that "the 'experimental' novelists of the 1970s, except of course myself, utterly lacked a sense of humour. . . . it seems that to be 'experimental' is to be humourless." Reviewers on the whole support this self-assessment. John Mellors in the *Listener* remarked of some of the short stories that "Gordon is one of the few 'experimental' writers to preserve a sense of humour." In his review of *Enemies* for the *Guardian*, Norman Shrapnel suggested that despite its serious themes the novel has a strongly comic effect. Angus Wilson found Gordon "wonderfully entertaining," particularly praising his "courage to use the language with such wit," while Robert Nye called him "one of the liveliest, wittiest and most perplexing young writers."

Since the publication of *Ambrose's Vision,* however, Gordon has not published any more fiction. As he told one interviewer: "Twenty years ago I was mildly confident that I'd write the great novel. I now realise, having published six, that I won't. This comes as a shock to the system. . . . As to poetry, the muse has gone forever, which is probably as well." Instead he has channeled his literary energies into work as an editor, anthologist, journalist, and reviewer. His only book published since *Ambrose's Vision* in 1980 is *Aren't We Due a Royalty Statement: A Stern Account of Literary, Theatrical and Publishing Folk* (1993), an autobiography less concerned with his private life than with the literary celebrities he has encountered in his long professional career. Given Gordon's interest, as indicated in *Ambrose's Vision, Enemies,* and *The Illusionist,* in drawing together the various directions of his work, it seems in one way disappointing that he should have stopped writing fiction at the point he did. On the other hand, it may be that the difficulties of synthesizing disparate interests, also apparent in each of these works, served to discourage further attempts. Gordon has remarked of the 1970s that "'experimental' novelists were all the rage in certain quarters" in the 1960s and 1970s skepticism of social convention encouraged innovations in fictional techniques. British writers grew more interested in "French modes" such as the *nouveau roman* and more sympathetic than some of their predecessors to the broad experimental legacy of modernism. When such inclinations for innovation survived into the anxious 1980s and 1990s, however, it was often in combination with more realistic narrative, as in the work of Martin Amis or Julian Barnes. This hybrid form was what Gordon seems to have attempted, though without complete success, around 1980.

Gordon has suggested that he experienced a kind of exhaustion in his own experimental energies: "the novel . . . is a familiar vehicle. You can only, really, do certain things with it. This is why the 'experimental' novel is more or less bound to fail, although I thought otherwise in my heady youth." In 1972 Gordon became a director of Anthony Sheil Associates (later Sheil Land Associates), literary agents with whom he remained for more than twenty years. His decision to move back to Scotland in 1994 led to his being sued by his employers, a much-publicized case that eventually reached the High Court of Justice. He has since worked in association with the Curtis Brown agency, continuing to act for a large list of authors, ranging from long-standing, distinguished clients to some new Irish and Scottish writers taken on since his move north. His work as an agent also may have contributed to his decision to forego publishing his own fiction: he is "exposed . . . to too many bad or indifferent manuscripts to want to add to them."

Gordon continued to write as a reviewer and a regular columnist for *The Times* from 1993 to 1995. He has also worked extensively as an editor, particularly of volumes of short stories. Several influential collections of experimental writing appeared under his editorship in the 1970s: he was at work on *Beyond the Words* with B. S. Johnson when the latter committed suicide in 1973. From 1986 to 1995 he edited with David Hughes an annual volume of *Best Short Stories* for Heinemann, moving on to assemble other short-story volumes for Bloomsbury Classics since 1995. He has produced collections of Scottish short stories at various points in his career. He has also worked for the Arts Council Literature Panel in the 1960s and served on the committees of the Author's Club and the Society of Authors in Scotland. He was elected to the Royal Society of Literature in 1991.

After the death of his first wife in 1989, Gordon married Margaret Anne McKernan, a publisher, in 1990. They live in Edinburgh with their young daughters, Lucy and Clare. Gordon continues to pursue his interests in theater, opera, and book collecting.

Alan Hollinghurst

(26 May 1954 –   )

David Hopes
University of North Carolina at Asheville

BOOKS: *Confidential Chats with Boys* (Oxford: Sycamore Press, 1982);

The Swimming Pool Library (London: Chatto & Windus, 1988; New York: Vintage, 1989);

The Folding Star (London: Chatto & Windus, 1994; New York: Pantheon, 1994);

The Spell (London: Chatto & Windus, 1998; New York: Viking, 1999).

OTHER: *Poetry Introduction Four,* includes poems by Hollinghurst (London: Faber & Faber, 1978);

LRB Anthology, includes contributions by Hollinghurst (London: Junction, 1983);

Firebird Two, includes contributions by Hollinghurst (London & New York: Penguin, 1983);

Jean Racine, *Bajazet,* translated by Hollinghurst (London: Chatto & Windus, 1991);

New Writing 4, edited by Hollinghurst and A. S. Byatt (London: Vintage, 1995);

The Mammoth Book of Gay Erotica, contributions by Hollinghurst, edited by Lawrence Schimel (London: Baffin Books, 1997).

Though it is too early to judge the significance of Alan Hollinghurst's contribution to English literature or to the more specialized field of gay literature, he has experienced both extravagant praise and impatient dismissal in sufficient measures to keep the debate lively. Both the praise and the dismissal tend to stem from approximately the same features. Critics have applauded the surgical precision of his language, his ability to survey whole landscapes or summarize complex perversities in little more than a phrase. Those who admire Hollinghurst's fiction note the honesty of his portrayal of certain kinds of homosexual relationships as well as of a society that, until the advent of AIDS, saw no particular reason not to refrain from promiscuity. One appreciates furthermore the breathless, enclosed quality of Hollinghurst's fictional environments–reminiscent of the walled garden of medieval allegory–which contain all that is gay and exclude, or admit merely as a sad comparison, all that is not. His enclosed settings are a little larger, though no less fraught with ambiguous gestures and iridescent meanings, than the drawing rooms of Marcel Proust or William Makepeace Thackeray. Hollinghurst's controlled environments are dominated by a homoerotic desire so exclusive that they include scarcely a female character, scarcely characters at all besides prospective sexual partners or former sexual partners, who are remembered with a melancholy ennui evocative of the poetry of Walter Pater.

Hollinghurst's detractors view the same elements from the opposite perspective, claiming that his attention to architectural and anatomical detail leaves no room for a story, that human feeling fades in the glare of the pyrotechnic facility of his language, that the characters are much too deeply immersed in the realm of mystical coincidence, and that once drawn in by beauty, the general reader may feel like an eavesdropper on an intimate conversation.

Alan Hollinghurst was born on 26 May 1954 in Stroud, England. He read English at Magdalen College, Oxford, taking his B.A. in 1975 and his M.Litt. in 1979. He was a lecturer in English at Magdalen in 1977–1978; at Somerville College in 1979–1980; at Corpus Christi College in 1981; and at the University of London beginning in 1982, when he also took up duties as deputy editor at *TLS: The Times Literary Supplement,* where he remained for eight years. He resides in Hampstead.

Hollinghurst was enamored early on with the idea of being an architect like his father, who was forty-four years old when Hollinghurst was born. Later deciding to become a poet, he had a slight volume of poems, *Confidential Chats with Boys,* published in 1982 by Sycamore Press, under the sponsorship of the Florio Society, a literary club of Magdalen College, Oxford. Hollinghurst's earliest writing, though now eclipsed by his novels, earned for him a contract from Faber and Faber in 1985 for a collection of poems. Almost immediately Hollinghurst's "poetry-writing faculty seized

Alan Hollinghurst at the time of The Folding Star *(photograph © 1994 by Jerry Bauer)*

up," but three years later he produced his first published novel, *The Swimming Pool Library* (1988). Hollinghurst's next published work was a verse translation of Jean Racine's *Bajazet,* performed at the Almeida in London and published by Chatto and Windus in 1991.

Hollinghurst began to make his mark on the literary scene as a gay novelist in the late 1980s, perhaps the third decade in which gay literature was a recognized genre. He is appreciated as a craftsman of Proustian observation and as a writer of romances in the manner of Nathaniel Hawthorne and the Brontë sisters. His vision of the excitement of love between unequal partners in an atmosphere of social, medical, and emotional peril, doomed ultimately to disappointment if not tragedy, exactly calculates the fin-de-siécle mood of the late twentieth century.

Hollinghurst is inescapably a genre author, not because of limitation in his talents but because of his invariable subject matter. His works are made up largely of graphically described sexual encounters, and thus they have tended to offend or baffle mainstream audiences. Hollinghurst extends the introspective tradition of gay writers such as Edmund White and John Rechy by producing novels that are full of the minutiae of homosexual longing and balanced on the edge

between romantic celebration and ironic dismissal of a sexual identity. Hollinghurst's novels tend to be about qualities of observation more than incidents. They trace the painstaking, often brilliant, sometimes fey process of revelation and refinement of the identity of the sexually heroic narrator in an erotic or architectural context, or a context in which the architectural and the erotic are scarcely distinguished.

In *The Swimming Pool Library* the young, wealthy, idle, and vainly beautiful protagonist, William Beckwith, saves the life of octogenarian Lord Charles Nantwich by giving him artificial respiration in a public urinal. Though his lordship seems not to remember his benefactor (one of many subtle power strategies in the passive-aggressive, benighted city of the novel), they form a relationship, and eventually Beckwith agrees to write Nantwich's biography. Reading the old man's memoirs, Beckwith gains a feel for the course of gay life from the beginning of the twentieth century and discovers that his own grandfather was instrumental in the failed but vicious crusade against "male vice" in the 1950s, which ended in a peerage for the elder Beckwith and imprisonment for Nantwich. In a twist on Greek tragedy, Beckwith, rather than paying for the ruthlessness of his ancestor, is privileged with a carefree life-

Dust jacket for Hollinghurst's first novel, published in 1988, about the homosexual relationship of an elderly aristocrat and his young biographer (Collection of William Cagle)

style and almost unlimited erotic choice by the sacrifice of his ancestor's victims.

The Swimming Pool Library is a novel about time, presenting one soul who has become a martyred saint of "philanthropic sublimation" and another who has become an icon of hedonism by trying to pursue exactly the same desires at different points in history. To accentuate the theme of a gay heritage or even a gay lineage, the novel glances back to Oscar Wilde and Ronald Firbank and Roman baths—a fragmentary mosaic from one of which is the "swimming pool library" of the title—and laterally to tenor Peter Pears, the companion of composer Benjamin Britten, a gay hero because he was a public and productive, rather than dissolute, figure.

A further shadow hangs over the novel in the form of the omnipresent, if never quite explicit, specter of AIDS, which brings an end to the lifestyle Beckwith inherited from his gay fathers. People die of AIDS or circumstances related to it in Hollinghurst's novels, but the main characters never seem to be impressed by the danger. Edward Manners of *The Folding Star* (1994) irritably buys condoms in case some boy who has caught his fancy requires them,

but he considers them a nuisance. They do not fit with his conception of the world as being based on highly charged aesthetic willfulness.

The reception of *The Swimming Pool Library* in 1988 set the pattern of framing Hollinghurst critically as a sort of gay Henry James, or, as Rhidian Davis suggested in *Attitude* (July 1998), "Jane Austen with cocks." Hollinghurst was called a brilliant commentator on the specialized and self-referential society of gay life. Comparison with James breaks down on the question of reticence, for though Hollinghurst has often been unforth-coming concerning the facts of his personal life, his characters conceal nothing. Fictional elements such as plot tend to be eclipsed by the sheer, effervescent energy of personal revelation in which every passing desire, each incidental impression seems to comprise the core of the narrative. Though one is not always certain of the motivation, mood, and worldview of Hollinghurst's characters, or even of their reactions to the most horrendous personal incidents, their present lives are open books, lavishly illustrated. They respond to sensation without much explanation of anything but its sensory qualities. The prisonlike structure Hollin-

Dust jacket for Hollinghurst's novel about a British tutor's homosexual infatuation with his Flemish student (Collection of William Cagle)

ghurst implies is reality disappears behind a decorative surface.

Based primarily on the merit of *The Swimming Pool Library,* Hollinghurst was named one of the twenty best young novelists in England by *Granta* magazine in 1993. The novel also had the more dubious distinction of being seized as obscene by Canadian customs officials.

Hollinghurst's next novel, *The Folding Star,* was also greeted with accolades. It was shortlisted for the Booker-McConnell Prize in 1994 and won the prestigious James Tait Black Memorial Book Prize for fiction; the American Library Association Gay, Lesbian, and Bisexual Book Award; and the Lambda Award for gay men's fiction. Often compared to Vladimir Nabokov's *Lolita* (1955), *The Folding Star* begins with British tutor Edward Manners's arrival in Belgium after he has fled the cataclysmic decay of his home life for a Flemish town of medieval churches and small, evocative museums. There he becomes infatuated with one of his students, seventeen-year-old Luc Altidore, a tantalizing, unconsciously destructive spirit in the mode of Tadziu from Thomas Mann's *Death in Venice* (1912). Manners lacks the physical perfection of Will Beckwith,

and thus the smarmy confidence that arises from it. He personifies a different segment of the gay life, the lyrical losers who attempt to alleviate a permanent sense of solitude and despair with an occasional affair or anonymous assignation. Manners's love for Altidore does not prevent Hollinghurst's typical feast of promiscuity.

As in *The Swimming Pool Library,* a secret sin is central to the novel, and speaking of it provides some degree of expiation. Paul, the father of another of Manners's students and the curator of a small museum devoted to the work of a nearly forgotten local painter named Edgaard Orst, fell in love with a German soldier during World War II and attempted to save him at the fatal expense of the aged and wheelchair-bound Jewish painter, and of the elderly couple who had been caring for him. Paul tells his story, for which he receives not divine punishment but gentle sympathy from Edward, a touch that demonstrates Hollinghurst's preference for realism over melodrama.

Nevertheless, Manners's pilgrimage from Rough Common to a nameless Flemish town has definite allegorical implications. *Edgaard* is a version of *Edward,* and the painter's story enfolds the teacher's. Luc is analogous to Lucifer, at once the tempter and bringer of

Dust jacket for Hollinghurst's 1998 novel, about four gay middle-class men in 1990s England

light, who in the book is given a pedigree beginning with the Virgin Mary, a trivial Flemish tease descended from the brother of Christ. As Nicholson Baker suggested in the *London Review of Books* (9 June 1994), in the work of a novelist who trades so much on the interplay between past and present, it is appropriate to recall that medieval England sent its raw wool to Flanders to be turned into cloth and tapestry and that the star that presides over the sheepfold, Hesperus, or the evening star, is the folding star of Hollinghurst's title.

The Folding Star is a complicated novel that considers issues of cosmic significance and broad spans of time. A steady parade of characters is introduced and passes through, never to appear again; yet, the reader is induced to care about each of them. The plot hangs absurdly on a string of coincidences and outbursts of inexplicably dramatic behavior at just the right moment. Hollinghurst makes the activity seem not only plausible but also inevitable, even shapely. In the intricacy of its design the novel seems to embody a gay imagination. At times Hollinghurst implies that certain loftier feats of imagination require homosexuality, or at least that one experience a homosexual phase. The hero of *The Folding Star* remarks, "there was always something lacking in those men who had never had a queer phase as boys. . . . it showed in a certain dryness of the imagination, a bland tolerance uncoloured by any suppression of their own, a blindness to the spectrum's violet end."

What those who have remained in their queer phase seem to lack is a conscience. There is neither regret nor remorse in either *The Swimming Pool Library* or in *The Folding Star,* except for unrequited lust. There are sinners, such as the gay-bashing grandfather or the treacherous curator, but they are always counterposed to the hero of the story, whose homosexual desire seems to act as a refining fire that purges all taint of human misdeed.

Hollinghurst's third novel, *The Spell* (1998), takes several risks, first in employing a pared-down style that relies more on plot and incident than his previous novels. The novel is a comic reworking of the grand gestures and subtle symbolic structure of the earlier books, with the vast pageants of time and world affairs replaced by a gossipy group of gay nightclubbers. The lifelong aesthetic commitment that gave meaning to the musing of the heroes of the earlier books is replaced by a cheap party drug, ecstasy, which apparently imparts the same vision with no more effort than swallowing.

In *The Spell* Hollinghurst eschews the exotic locales and refined sensibilities of *The Swimming Pool Library* and *The Folding Star. The Spell* follows the interaction of four gay, middle-class men in London during the 1990s. Robin, an architect, moves to the Dorset countryside with his lover, Justin, a struggling actor who finds life stultifying so far from the dance halls and the erotic possibilities of the city. Danny is Robin's twenty-two-year-old son from a marriage—an almost unheard-of circumstance in Hollinghurst's novels. Perhaps to spite or to balance his father, or perhaps as a recapitulation of his father's unspecified past, Danny is wildly enamored of sex, alcohol, and the glitter of London club life. Alex, a straitlaced civil servant who finds liberation through the use of ecstasy, is a former lover of Justin's and is in now in love with Danny. The ordinariness of the events in the novel is tempered by the sense of excitement these men have about their lives. Hollinghurst successfully conveys to his readers the same tension, the same hope of voluptuous release.

All the characters of *The Spell* are engaging; yet, seemingly against their wills they carry the weight of matters deeper than they seem to comprehend. Their repartee is cleverer than they are, so that the author himself seems a constant spectral presence. Hollinghurst's writing is sufficiently pleasing, however, that the authorial intrusion does not diminish the effectiveness of the book, even though the device becomes increasingly labored as the novel progresses.

The "spell" of the title has several meanings at once. First, it is the pervading erotic anticipation that keeps these men orbiting about each other, trying new sensual combinations and strategies of seduction, always with the hope of finding an abiding fulfillment. The "spell" is the magic that allows them to believe that the same fruitless action in the same spiritually threadbare environment will result in something wonderful. The "spell" also refers to ecstasy, a tab or two of which, dropped at a party, transforms mundane London into a world of splendor and possibility.

In each of Hollinghurst's books, action is initiated by departure into the past, a foreign country, or the phantasmagoria of a drug. Unlike the protagonists of other novels built around journeys, however, Hollinghurst's travelers do not change but affect change in those around them. He portrays his gay wanderer as a catalyst for others, who remains complete in himself against a constantly changing landscape.

In some ways *The Spell* is a throwback to the early days of gay writing, a time of relative innocence and discovery, when homosexual life in literary fiction seemed fresh and exotic. Since then the reading public has learned that gay life is intrinsically no more exotic than straight life. The vitality of Hollinghurst's prose style is such, however, that this recapitulation of the ordinary still seems brimming with possibility.

Nick Hornby

(17 April 1957 –   )

Merritt Moseley
University of North Carolina at Asheville

BOOKS: *Contemporary American Fiction* (London: Vision, 1992; New York: St. Martin's Press, 1992);

Fever Pitch (London: Gollancz, 1992; New York: Penguin, 1994);

High Fidelity (London: Gollancz, 1995; New York: Riverhead, 1995);

Fever Pitch: The Screenplay (London: Indigo, 1997);

About a Boy (London: Gollancz, 1998; New York: Riverhead, 1998).

OTHER: *My Favourite Year: A Collection of New Football Writing,* edited by Hornby (London: Gollancz/ Witherby, 1993);

The Picador Book of Sportswriting, edited by Hornby and Nick Coleman (London: Picador, 1996; New York: Trans-Atlantic, 1996).

SELECTED PERIODICAL PUBLICATION–
UNCOLLECTED:

"Pitch Battle," *When Saturday Comes* (August 1995): 14–15.

Nick Hornby at the time of High Fidelity *(photograph by Charles Hopkinson)*

Nick Hornby appeared on the British literary scene in 1992 with the publication of his imaginative and moving memoir *Fever Pitch,* an account of his years as a fanatic supporter of the Arsenal Football Club. Six years later Andrew Anthony called Hornby "the most successful British author of his generation." (*Guardian,* 25 August 1998) *Fever Pitch* was a nominee for a Whitbread Prize and received remarkable critical praise, including the admiration of many people indifferent or even hostile to British football (soccer). When Hornby followed that success by editing another book about football, he seemed to have placed himself in a niche as the intellectual's football fan; however, though he later co-edited a book of sportswriting, he has also made his name as the author of two well-received and popular novels, *High Fidelity* (1995) and *About a Boy* (1998). What Hornby offers to many readers is honesty about emotion and an awareness of the deficiencies of mod-

ern men, an awareness that is charming rather than defensive or apologetic.

Reviewers have sometimes accused Hornby of being too ingratiating to readers. It is true that his books have sold well and that they make no extravagantly taxing demands on readers' exegetical powers. Approvingly, David Gritten puts it this way: "He is beloved by some people who rarely read books at all, but to whom he appeals on a direct, emotional level. Yet, his status as Our Man on the Terraces"—in other words, in the football stadium, specifically in the sections where the diehard fans stand to watch the game—"is not

Dust jacket for Hornby's 1995 novel, about the obsessively list-making owner of a used-record store

threatened by being lionised by the literary establishment." Andrew Anthony agrees that he has achieved "that most delicate and difficult of acts: a literary writer with mass appeal." In an interview with David Gritten, Hornby commented on his fondness for American writers, as he discussed at length in his first book, *Contemporary American Fiction* (1992), asserting that American writers connect more closely to readers than their English counterparts: "It always struck me that there was a way of writing plainly that didn't alienate people, yet could be reasonably intelligent at the same time." He went on to praise the American novelist Anne Tyler—"She wrote simply with warmth and intelligence. I couldn't find an English writer who did that"—and suggested that English writers "don't seem to believe in emotion or redemption. They think it's vulgar."

Nick Hornby was born on 17 April 1957, the child of middle-class parents who lived in the Home Counties, outside of London. His father, Sir Derek Hornby, is an international businessman. When his parents divorced,

he lived with his mother and younger sister, Gill, who is also a writer. He spent Sunday afternoons with his father, who in his need to find ways to entertain his son took him to a football match, thus beginning the younger Hornby's lifelong obsession with Arsenal. Hornby attended Jesus College, Cambridge, receiving his degree in English. He worked as a petrol station attendant for a year, then took two years of teacher training at Kingston Polytechnic; he then taught English at a comprehensive school in Cambridge. Determined to become a writer, he moved to London and, while trying to make his mark, taught English as a second language, then took a job teaching English to and making social arrangements for Korean employees of the Samsung electronics company. At length he decided to become a full-time writer and wrote reviews and other journalism, as well as his first book, essays on American writers, mostly of the "dirty realist" school.

In 1992 Hornby turned his almost pathological absorption with Arsenal football into the best-selling

Fever Pitch. He was stimulated in part by the late American writer Frederick Exley's *A Fan's Notes* (1968); he explains, "when I saw the book the first time, for some reason I thought, Oh, great, I hope this is an autobiography told through reports of matches and I picked it up and it wasn't, and then I thought, 'Hey, actually that's not a bad idea for a book.'" Thus, each chapter of *Fever Pitch* has a thematic title, such as "Goodbye to All That," but is also keyed to a match—for instance, "Arsenal v Manchester City 4.10.75." *Fever Pitch* is psychologically astute on the pathology of sports followers: Hornby makes it clear that he neither chose to follow Arsenal nor continued doing so because it was pleasurable; even at his first match with his father, he writes, "What impressed me most was just how much most of the men around me hated, really hated, being there. As far as I could tell, nobody seemed to enjoy, in the way that I understood the word, anything that happened during the entire afternoon."

Hornby comments penetratingly, as well, on the effect football has on men's minds and level of maturity. In a passage on the way football helps men to connect with each other, he acknowledges, "I am aware of the downside of this wonderful facility that men have: they become repressed, they fail in their relationships with women, their conversation is trivial and boorish, they cannot relate to their children, and they die lonely and miserable. But, you know, what the hell?" Readers of *Fever Pitch* frequently concluded that Hornby combined a normal man's weaknesses with an abnormal honesty in admitting them and the literary skill to put them into literature. Such a critical response—one interviewer asked him if he felt "a weight of expectation on your shoulders to get to the essence of the male experience"—has also applied to his two novels.

Hornby is appealingly modest. He distinguishes between himself and David Lacey, a professional sportswriter: "The difference between Lacey and me is that I rarely *think*. I remember, I fantasise, I try to visualise every one of Alan Smith's goals, I tick off the number of First Division grounds I have visited. . . . None of this is *thought*, in the proper sense of the word. There is no analysis, or self-awareness, or mental rigour going on at all, because obsessives are denied any kind of perspective on their own passion." Obviously, this assessment is disingenuous, since analysis and perspective on his own passion are the most notable qualities of *Fever Pitch.*

In the aftermath of the success of the book, and particularly when his next book was an anthology of "new football writing," much of it by novelists and intellectuals, Hornby was accused of having "helped turn football into a fashion accessory" and of being part of a "soccerati" that had somehow displaced the sport's tra-

ditional working-class following. In the introduction to *The Picador Book of Sportswriting* (1996) he laments that "those who write about sport still create a whole set of problems for themselves in Britain, many of them relating, predictably, to the subject of class." An educated man from a middle-class background—who admits in *Fever Pitch* that following football has enabled him to impersonate someone different from himself, more rugged and frightening—he nevertheless resents the suggestion that he and his fellow intellectuals "have colonized football stadia and driven out the old working class fan."

In *My Favourite Year: A Collection of New Football Writing* (1993) Hornby includes what may well be a section of *Fever Pitch* that was removed from the book, recounting his period of supporting the small football club Cambridge United. It includes this subtle analysis of addiction:

> In his book *The Easy Way to Give Up Smoking,* Allen Carr likens the smoker to someone who wears tight shoes just for the pleasure of taking them off, and it is a good analogy. Smokers smoke for the pleasure of relieving nicotine withdrawal symptoms—symptoms that only smoking gives them. In other words, we spend a fortune, and take terrible health risks, just to achieve the state that non-smokers maintain effortlessly.

> Football addiction works in much the same way. . . .

Hornby's first novel, *High Fidelity,* is also about a sort of addiction, in this case to rock-and-roll music and the making of lists. The protagonist and narrator, Rob Fleming, is a thirty-five-year-old failure, the owner of Championship Vinyl, a failing shop that sells old records. The novel traces the breakup of his relationship with Laura, his gradual maturation, and their reunion. Reaction to this novel has often focused on the main character either as a pathetic figure or as an uncanny Everyman—or both. Rob is emotionally retarded, unable to maintain an adult relationship with a woman—or, for that matter, a man; he substitutes an encyclopedic interest in old music and a habit of making lists, sharing with the reader, for instance, his "Top Five Bands or Musicians Who Will Have to Be Shot Come the Musical Revolution" and expatiating on his interests in women, interestingly focusing on the unreal:

> Five women who don't live on my street, as far as I know, but would be very welcome if they ever decided to move into the area: the Holly Hunter of *Broadcast News;* the Meg Ryan of *Sleepless in Seattle;* a woman doctor I saw on the telly once, who had lots of long frizzy hair and carved up a Tory MP in a debate about embryos, although I don't know her name and I've never been able to find a pin-up of her; Katharine Hep-

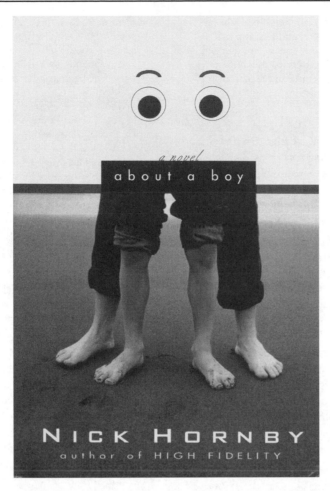

Dust jacket for the U.S. edition of Hornby's 1998 novel, about a single man who pretends to have a son in order to meet women

burn in *The Philadelphia Story;* Valerie Harper in the TV series *Rhoda.* These are women who talk back, women with a mind of their own, women with snap and crackle and pop . . . but they are also women who seem to need the love of a good man. I could rescue them. I could redeem them.

It is fair to say that the plot of *High Fidelity* is slight and conventional. A man loses his lover and grows—erratically, it is true—then regains her. Asked by Cynthia Joyce in an interview for *Salon* to compare himself to Martin Amis, Hornby acknowledged the Amis influence on younger writers who use the demotic in their books but insisted, "I don't think of *High Fidelity* as a real hip book . . . apart from that it has some rock and roll in it. It's sort of redemptive, which isn't very hip." The novel does have a clarity and honesty in its presentation of the main character, who is extremely average. Rob knows this himself and explains: "My genius, if I can call it that, is to combine a whole load of averageness into one compact frame."

The fact that Hornby writes so confidently about the emotionally incomplete has led to some curious reactions. Asked by the *Salon* interviewer if he is like his character, he

explains, "Rob doesn't have an awful lot of perspective on relationships, and I suppose if I didn't, then I wouldn't have been able to write the book." Similarly, he was bemused by reactions to *Fever Pitch* that insisted that football fans were sexist: he knew this already, and had devoted considerable effort and space in his book to saying it himself. Writing in the first person about average men who use obsessions to avoid emotional maturity has apparently invited some readers to identify him with his fictional creations.

One critical approach to Hornby attributes his success to his ability to represent contemporary masculinity, especially its shortcomings. Such a perspective is undoubtedly one of his most notable talents. Rob Fleming observes that it is always "young men who seem to spend a disproportionate amount of their time looking for deleted Smiths singles and 'ORIGINAL NOT RE-RELEASED' Underlined Frank Zappa Albums." On the other hand, as Hornby noted in an interview with Jay Rayner,

One of the things I thought that I was doing was writing about men, but the response to *High Fidelity* in particular from an awful lot of women was that I was writing about them too, and not all of them got the music thing, but in terms of feeling slightly directionless and feeling a lack of self confidence and all kinds of things that are touched on in *High Fidelity,* the gender divide, the response, became a lot more blurred for me after that and I thought I don't really know what I'm doing so I'll just plough on.

About a Boy may be a partial attempt to avoid these two rather confining ways of reading his novels. Though an unmarried man is one of the main characters, he is not the narrator, and there are two other main characters, a woman and her teenage son. The man, Will Freeman, is unattached, thirty-six years old, and–because his father wrote a horribly popular Christmas song in the 1930s and he still receives royalties–comfortably unemployed. Perhaps predictably for a Hornby protagonist, he is self-absorbed, especially in relation to his married, child-raising friends. Will not only does not want any children, he cannot even understand why they seem important to those who have them. *About a Boy* takes this somewhat affectless man and involves him in the lives of two people who have serious problems: Marcus, a young misfit being bullied in school; and his mother, Fiona, a suicidal divorcée unable to cope with her messy life. The plot device that provides the childless Will with a sort of foster son derives from his realization that a single-parents group would be a good place to meet women. To attend a meeting, he has to pretend to have a son, and when challenged to produce him, he brings Marcus along.

Dan DeLuca, reviewing the book in the *Philadelphia Inquirer,* wrote that "*About a Boy* is another guy's book: female characters are drawn with sympathy, but halfheartedly. It's Will and Marcus's world: Girls just live in it." This comment would seem fair: Fiona is certainly a less vivid character than Will and Marcus. Hornby admitted to Jay Rayner some hesitation in writing about women: "I think that I still have a certain degree of caution about it, I think that I've been very hard on the men in my books and I think it would be quite hard for a male writer to be–in this current climate–as hard on a certain kind of woman. I think that Fiona in this book, Marcus's mother, is actually a bit of a disaster area, so I think that's a step forward for me–writing about somebody who has messed up as badly as any man." *About a Boy* differs from *High Fidelity* in having a distributed focus, with Marcus rather than Will sometimes serving as the focal character; it also has considerably more humor, as DeLuca noted when he praised Hornby's "dead-on comic characterizations of no-longer-young males clueless about their own failings." A good example of Hornby's comic gift is the passage that introduces Will and quantifies how cool he is, based on a questionnaire in a magazine:

> This cool: he had slept with a woman he didn't know very well in the last three months (five points). He had spent more than three hundred pounds on a jacket (five points). He had spent more than twenty pounds on a haircut (five points) (How was it possible to spend less than twenty pounds on a haircut in 1993?). He owned more than five hip-hop albums (five points). He had taken Ecstasy (five points), but in a club and not merely at home as a sociological exercise (five bonus points). He intended to vote Labour at the next general election (five points). He earned more than forty thousand pounds a year (five points), and he didn't have to work very hard for it (five points, and he awarded himself an extra five points for not having to work *at all* for it). He had eaten in a restaurant that served polenta and shaved parmesan (five points). He had never used a flavoured condom (five points), and he had both grown a goatee (five points) *and* shaved it off again (five points). The bad news was that he hadn't ever had sex with someone whose photo had appeared on the style page of a newspaper or magazine (minus two), and he did still think, if he was honest (and if Will had anything approaching an ethical belief, it was that lying about yourself in questionnaires was utterly wrong), that owning a fast car was likely to impress women (minus two).

Will Freeman is cool, but he is not cold, and the same thing could be said of Nick Hornby's books. They are, as he acknowledges, "redemptive." They suggest the possibility of human improvement and offer love as a solvent for at least some of life's problems. They are genuinely popular, in some cases with readers who are not customarily bookish, in part because of Hornby's familiarity with contemporary popular culture–rock music, television, and movies as well as football. Popular culture has repaid the interest: *Fever Pitch* has been filmed, with a screenplay by Hornby and a lead performance by Colin Firth, and motion-picture adaptations are planned for *High Fidelity* and *About a Boy,* as well. Hornby began his career writing plays, none of which were ever performed, and may turn to more script writing. In the meantime, his status as the most successful British author of his generation seems secure.

Interviews:

Cynthia Joyce, "Litchat with Nick Hornby," *Salon* [on-line magazine], 14 October 1996;

David Gritten, "Writer's Bloke," *Electronic Telegraph* [on-line magazine], 22 March 1997;

Andrew Anthony, "The Boy Done Good," *Guardian* [on-line magazine], 25 August 1998;

Jay Rayner, "The Observer Interview: Nick Hornby in Edinburgh," *Observer* [on-line magazine], 25 August 1998.

Reference:

Merritt Moseley, "Nick Hornby, English Football, and *Fever Pitch,*" *Aethlon,* 11 (Spring 1994): 87–95.

Dan Jacobson

(7 March 1929 –   )

Anne Fisher Gossage
Pennsylvania State University

See also the Jacobson entry in *DLB 14: British Novelists Since 1960.*

BOOKS: *The Trap* (London: Weidenfeld & Nicolson, 1955; New York: Harcourt, Brace, 1955);

A Dance in the Sun (London: Weidenfeld & Nicolson, 1956; New York: Harcourt, Brace, 1956);

The Price of Diamonds (London: Weidenfeld & Nicolson, 1957; New York: Knopf, 1957);

No Further West: California Visited (London: Weidenfeld & Nicolson, 1957; New York: Macmillan, 1961);

A Long Way from London (London: Weidenfeld & Nicolson, 1958);

The Zulu and the Zeide (Boston: Little, Brown, 1959);

The Evidence of Love (London: Weidenfeld & Nicolson, 1960; Boston: Little, Brown, 1960);

Time of Arrival and Other Essays (London: Weidenfeld & Nicolson, 1962; New York: Macmillan, 1962);

Beggar My Neighbour (London: Weidenfeld & Nicolson, 1964);

The Beginners (London: Weidenfeld & Nicolson, 1966; New York: Macmillan, 1966);

Through the Wilderness, and Other Stories (New York: Macmillan, 1968);

The Rape of Tamar (London: Weidenfeld & Nicolson, 1970; New York: Macmillan, 1970);

A Way of Life and Other Stories (London: Longman, 1971);

The Wonder-Worker (London: Weidenfeld & Nicolson, 1973; Boston: Little, Brown, 1973);

Inklings: Selected Stories (London: Weidenfeld & Nicolson, 1973); republished as *Through the Wilderness* (Harmondsworth, U.K.: Penguin, 1977);

The Confessions of Joseph Baisz (London: Secker & Warburg, 1977; New York: Harper & Row, 1977);

The Story of the Stories: The Chosen People and Its God (London: Secker & Warburg, 1982; New York: Harper & Row, 1982);

Time and Time Again: Autobiographies (London: Deutsch, 1985; Boston: Atlantic Monthly, 1985);

Her Story (London: Deutsch, 1987; Carlsbad, Cal.: Flamingo, 1988);

Dan Jacobson

Adult Pleasures: Essays on Writers and Readers (London: Deutsch, 1988);

Hidden in the Heart (London: Bloomsbury, 1991);

The God-Fearer (London: Bloomsbury, 1992; New York: Scribners, 1992);

The Electronic Elephant: A Southern African Journey (London: Hamilton, 1994);

Heshel's Kingdom (London: Hamilton, 1998; Evanston, Ill.: Northwestern University Press, 1999).

RADIO: *The Caves of Adullan,* script by Jacobson, BBC, 1972.

Writer, critic, and teacher Dan Jacobson's writing seems haunted, both by his South African origins and by his Jewish heritage. A pioneer in South African fiction, he has written strikingly about his homeland and has received acclaim for his literary craftsmanship. His work enjoys considerable popularity with the public, particularly in Great Britain. His fiction includes twelve novels, one a Literary Guild selection, and six volumes of short stories. He has also written autobiographical and travel works, as well as well-respected critical essays and books on literature, religion, and culture. He is professor emeritus at University College, London, where he has taught literature for more than twenty years.

Jacobson has received the Somerset Maugham Award for fiction, the John Llewellyn Rhys Memorial Prize, the *Jewish Chronicle* / H. H. Wingate Award, the J. R. Ackerley Prize for autobiography, and the Mary Elinor Smith Poetry Prize. He has also twice been a creative-writing fellow at American universities and has received a fellowship from the Society of Authors.

Jacobson was born in Kimberley, a small South African town, on 7 March 1929, the youngest son of Jewish immigrants Hyman Michael and Liebe Melamed Jacobson. After graduating from high school at the age of sixteen, he studied English for three years at the University of the Witwatersrand, Johannesburg, and graduated at the head of his class with a bachelor's degree in 1948. After graduation he worked on a kibbutz in Israel for two years before he made his first trip to England and took a job in London teaching English. In 1951 he returned to South Africa, where he held a public-relations job and then worked as a journalist on the *Press Digest* in Johannesburg.

Jacobson had wanted to be a writer since childhood, and he had made several attempts, all unsuccessful. He took admittedly awkward stabs at poetry and short stories at the university, and in London he wrote a novel, which went unpublished. Undaunted, at the age of twenty-three he made two important decisions: that he wanted to write seriously; and that he would ultimately settle in London to do so. First he returned to his hometown, where he worked for two years in his father's business with his two older brothers. Although Kimberley was a hot, dry, rather ugly mining town, it gave him the setting he needed to begin his successful creative work. During this period in South Africa, he wrote a draft of *The Trap* (1955); revised stories, which began to be accepted by magazines; and acquired an agent.

In 1954 he made his permanent move to England after marrying Margaret Pye, a student of mathematics he had met on his previous visit to London. She was originally from Rhodesia, and they were married in Capetown just before leaving for England. The couple has three children.

The Trap was published the year after his marriage. Like six later books and most of his short stories, it is set in South Africa. *The Trap* draws on his boyhood experiences at the two farms his father owned and on his firsthand familiarity with relations between the white ruling class and black serving class of that time. The novel focuses on corruption, violence, and betrayal, particularly those kinds that have been peculiar to the South African social situation.

Van Schoor, owner of a ranch, prides himself on his good relations with his black workers, or Kaffirs, as the whites in the book call them. He believes he is on particularly good terms with Willem, a servant whom he trusts completely. When Willem informs him that Setole, another worker, has been making homosexual advances to him and his son, Van Schoor dismisses Setole at once, despite Setole's ominous warnings that something bad is happening on the farm. Willem then goes secretly to the home of Machlachlan, a dishonest white butcher, to discuss the theft of Van Schoor's sheep. Machlachlan is corruption personified; he not only steals sheep, but when he becomes afraid that he may be suspected of the act, he goes to the police and informs on Willem. Being black, Willem has no power to refute Machlachlan's word. When Van Schoor discovers Willem's disloyalty, he is so upset that he beats the man savagely. It is the first time he has ever beaten a servant, and the book ends with the suggestion that he will continue to use violence, even toward his wife, in the future.

The ranch can be seen as all of South Africa; the situation between Van Schoor and his servant epitomizes the country's racial problem. The worst part about the situation, as described in the novel, is that everyone involved is hurt by what is happening. The social situation is a "trap" that captures all the characters.

The same kind of symbolism is also used in Jacobson's next novel, *A Dance in the Sun* (1956), which, like *The Trap,* is short and has a single-episode plot. Two college students, the narrator and his friend Frank, are hitchhiking to Capetown when they are waylaid at Mirredal, a tiny village along the way similar to Jacobson's hometown of Kimberley. The boys find lodgings in the house of Fletcher, an eccentric, opinionated, middle-aged man, and his wife. During their night's stay, they become involved with the strange goings-on of the place.

First the boys meet Joseph, a black former servant of Fletcher's. As the story unfolds, the boys discover that Louw, Fletcher's brother, has had a child with Joseph's sister. Since interracial sexual relations are forbidden, Fletcher has disposed of the sister and the child and has driven Louw out of town. Joseph wants to know what has happened to his sister, but Fletcher treats him badly—as he treats all blacks—and will not tell him. Louw returns on the same night the boys are staying with the Fletchers and destroys the interior of their house in retaliation for the treatment he has received. While hiding out in the boys' room during his brother-in-law's rampage, Fletcher discovers that they are willing to serve as witnesses on Joseph's behalf, and he breaks down. As the book closes, Joseph has gained power over Fletcher. The house in the novel, like the ranch in *The Trap,* represents apartheid South Africa. The house is divided within itself as well as against the blacks. Louw, ironically, is the most moral character in the novel, because he can accept blacks as people. His frustration with the situation leads him to act against his own race.

The Trap and *A Dance in the Sun,* later combined under one cover, were well received and drew attention to Jacobson as a promising writer. His style in these books, as in the rest of his works, is clear and perceptive, with intriguing characters and settings and a realistic portrayal of human relationships and social tensions. Jacobson has asserted that his direct style was influenced by reading the works of D. H. Lawrence.

The same year that *A Dance in the Sun* was published, Jacobson accepted an invitation to Stanford University as a fellow in creative writing, where he joined Yvor Winters, the poet and critic, and the English poet Thom Gunn on the faculty. After a year he returned to England. The year at Stanford provided Jacobson with time to complete his third novel, *The Price of Diamonds* (1957), which, like his first two novels, is short and is set in South Africa.

The theme of *The Price of Diamonds,* a moralistic, comic novel, is corruption. Gottlieb and Fink, two Jewish businessmen in the diamond-mining town of Lyndhurst, are fast friends. One day Fink, the dominant personality of the two, goes on an errand. While alone in the office Gottlieb mistakenly receives a packet of stolen diamonds, which gives him the idea of making a deal with the illicit diamond buyers of the town to show his partner that he is a real man of action. He does not succeed but instead loses Fink's friendship. The police agent, however, falls in love with Gottlieb's secretary and consequently lets Gottlieb off the hook. Meanwhile, Fink is attacked by hoodlums in the street for taking the side of a black man and is hospitalized. Gottlieb recovers his moral balance, goes to the hospital, and is reunited with his friend. The story ends as Gottlieb, realizing that the price of the diamonds is much too high, throws the bag of diamonds down an abandoned mine pit. This book was not as well received as

Dust jacket for Jacobson's 1970 novel, which retells the biblical story of King David and his children

Jacobson's first two novels. One weakness is that the characters come from stock Jewish humor and are not well developed.

At this point in his career Jacobson made a conscious effort to change the general lack of development in writing. His first few novels could almost be called expanded short stories with their allegorical characters and their focus on a single incident. With his next novel, *The Evidence of Love* (1960), he began to develop greater fullness and complexity. A longer, more powerful tale about an interracial love affair, *The Evidence of Love* portrays relations between the races in South Africa with great psychological depth. The protagonist, Kenneth Makeer, is "Cape colored"—that is, of mixed race. Although Kenneth longs for education, wealth, and other privileges, his position as a colored person in South Africa makes his ambitions seem impossible to achieve. His skin is light enough for him to pass as white, however; therefore, when Miss Bentwisch, a rich, eccentric old lady, takes a fancy to him, she sends him to England to study as a white man, expecting him later to use his position to serve his own "people." Miss

Bentwisch dies while Kenneth is studying, and his resulting sense of freedom causes him to lose sight of this original goal. He courts Isabel, Miss Bentwisch's former protégée, who is also studying in London at the time. Kenneth falls in love with Isabel, and even after she learns he is a Cape colored man, the couple marry.

The ending of the novel does not quite follow from the rest of the story, as one critic noted. The last chapter presents the couple two years later on their way back to South Africa, where they know they will meet resistance to their marriage. They bravely do this as evidence to all of South Africa of their love for one another. Upon returning, they are promptly put in prison for six months.

The Evidence of Love is a transitional work between Jacobson's earlier, simpler books and his final, ambitious novel about South Africa, *The Beginners* (1966). All the themes of his earlier works are present to some degree in this long novel. Starting with the original immigrants to South Africa and ending with a child born in London to the grandson of these immigrants, Jacobson traces the lives of the members of a Jewish family. The book explores the meaning of Jewish identity. Yet, by tracing the individual lives of the members of the family, it shows that the most important ideal to follow in life is one's own human individuality.

The principal figure in the novel is Joel Glickman, a young soldier returning home to South Africa in 1945. Joel worries about the worthlessness of life and struggles to find meaning in it. When he falls in love with a girl involved in the Zionist movement, he becomes involved as well and is sent to Israel to work on a kibbutz. However, his girlfriend, who was to accompany him, marries someone else. Not wanting to make Zionism his life's work, Joel leaves the settlement. He returns to the university and then goes to England, where he marries Pamela, his father's former secretary. Although Joel is never completely satisfied, when he takes his mind off himself he is fairly happy.

The personality of Joel's brother, David, stands in contrast to Joel's. A religious loner, David's inner life is much more stable. Although he does not completely accept the orthodox Jewish religion as his grandmother did, he does have a firm belief in God. Joel's father also presents a contrasting way of life. He is a successful businessman and also a firm supporter of the Zionist movement, although he does not go to Israel until he visits Joel there. Yet, when all his children have grown up, he and his wife settle there. At the end of the novel each of the characters is still, in a sense, beginning. *The Beginners* ends on a happy note, with Joel in England anticipating the birth of his second child.

The Beginners is Jacobson's most autobiographical novel. His work on a kibbutz in Israel gave him the firsthand knowledge to write about Joel's experiences there, although, like Joel, he decided not to give his life to Zionism. Jacobson utilizes other autobiographical details, as well: the senior Glickman owns a butter factory, as did Jacobson's father, and Joel attends the University of the Witwatersrand, Jacobson's alma mater. A Literary Guild selection, *The Beginners* was Jacobson's most widely read novel. It was also well received by critics. *The Beginners* has been called "one of the finest South African novels yet produced."

After *The Beginners* Jacobson moved away from South African subjects. He had written about South Africa in part because he felt the need to expose the social problems of his homeland. After *The Beginners*, however, Jacobson felt that he had done his duty and that he needed fresh material for his work. He therefore went in an entirely new direction to write his most highly praised novel, *The Rape of Tamar* (1970).

Although he took no interest in the Bible as a child, Jacobson developed a strong interest in the Old Testament as he grew older. The idea for *The Rape of Tamar* came when Jacobson was reading 2 Samuel. The plot of the novel is taken from the story of King David's spoiled daughter, raped by her half brother Amnon, whom Absalom, another of David's sons, consequently murders. The novel is narrated by Yonadab, a malignant schemer who calls himself a ghost from the past and moves easily between the time of King David and the year 1970. He encourages Amnon to rape his half sister; then, when Absalom has him beaten for being Amnon's friend, Yonadab becomes Absalom's spy and helps to arrange for Amnon's death. His cynical, entertaining narrative leads the reader to sympathize with his crimes to a certain degree.

The basic theme of *The Rape of Tamar* is the struggle for power in human affairs, illustrated by the conflict between David and his sons and by Yonadab's betrayal of his comrades. The novel offers witty social commentary as well as an entertaining fantasy: the presentation of King David and the high government officials, with their petty self-concerns and weaknesses, satirizes modern-day politics. *The Rape of Tamar* remains one of Jacobson's most popular novels. It was made into a play titled *Yonadab*, which was performed at London's National Theatre in 1985.

The Wonder-Worker (1973) marks another departure for Jacobson. The story, set in London, is about a boy named Timothy who believes he has supernatural powers. He believes, for example, that he can turn himself into objects to escape from the real world. As he grows up, his psychotic delusions become worse, and he finally is driven to theft and murder in order to obey the commands of some power that he imagines controls him.

Jacobson complicates the narrative structure of the novel by having a man under psychiatric treatment relate Timothy's story. As the novel progresses these two planes of reality become intertwined, so that by the end the narrator and Timothy, who have much in common throughout the story, seem to be the same person. Both are lonely characters whose inability to form meaningful relationships with others leads them to lose touch completely with reality. Often interpreted as an exploration of the process of writing fiction itself, *The Wonder-Worker* elaborates on the relationship between reality and literary illusion.

From the time Jacobson had moved to England in 1954 until shortly after *The Wonder-Worker* was published, he had been making a living from his writing, not only novels but also short stories and freelance literary journalism. His books sold well, and one of his short stories, "The Zulu and the Zeide," was adapted into a play. He taught twice more in the United States, once in 1965 as a visiting professor at Syracuse University and once in 1971 as a visiting fellow at Buffalo College of the State University of New York.

Otherwise, he devoted his time fully to writing until 1975, when he took a job teaching English at University College, London. In 1979 he became a reader; in 1988, a professor; and in 1994 he was named professor emeritus. He does not feel that teaching has hindered his writing, although he did stop writing short stories, which some critics feel are his best work; he has had six collections of his stories published.

In 1977 he published his eighth novel, *The Confessions of Joseph Baisz*, which he had worked on for four years. As in *The Rape of Tamar*, the narrator of this novel is malevolent, and betrayal is the central theme. The book is set in the imaginary totalitarian state of Sarmeda, ruled by a dictator, the Heerser; a political party, the Phalanx; and a dreaded police force, the Compresecor. The corruption and violence of this state are mirrored in the actions of Joseph, the main character. Joseph begins his adulthood as a soldier and rises to the position of bodyguard for Serle, a government official whom, on one occasion, he trips down a flight of steps so that he can be alone with Serle's wife, Gita. Later, Joseph also turns on Gita, accusing her of being responsible for his act. Joseph then works for the Compresecor and gets the job of kidnapping two children. After their father commits suicide in grief over the kidnapping, Joseph marries the children's mother.

Joseph has a talent for treachery, and paradoxically he comes to love the people he betrays, feeling a strange, protective power over them. After this job with the Compresecor, Joseph works in a prison, where he has great success, until one day at an assembly he discovers his sister, Beata, calling out to him from the

Dust jacket for the American edition of Jacobson's 1992 novel in which Judaism, and not Christianity, becomes the dominant religion of Europe

ranks of the women prisoners. Rather than be disgraced in the presence of the Heerser, Joseph denies knowledge of her. This treachery is the act that finally undoes him. Previously he had been indifferent to the people he had betrayed. Beata, however, had been a sustaining and loving force in his life, so that when he betrays her, he begins to hate her. Consequently, he comes to hate all his victims, including himself. The story ends with his suicide. Some critics believe the novel, for which Jacobson received the *Jewish Chronicle / H. H. Wingate Award*, to be the author's best.

For the next ten years Jacobson shifted his focus from novels to nonfiction. *The Story of the Stories: The Chosen People and Its God* (1982) is a literary and historical study of the Bible. It shows how the Hebrews' belief that they were God's chosen people explained reality for them in a creative way that controlled the development of Jewish history and by extension influenced the development of Christianity and helped to shape Western culture. *The Story of the Stories* elicited strong responses. The Jewish religious community responded negatively, presumably because Jacobson discusses God as "an imaginative creation." However, literary critics have praised the work because it succeeds both as textual analysis and as a narrative itself, which was Jacobson's goal for the book. This idea that a narrative can control both people and history is also present in Jacobson's novels.

Jacobson's next work, *Time and Time Again* (1985), won the J. R. Ackerly Prize for autobiography. Its thirteen chapters, each describing a key event in his life, read like a novel because of Jacobson's close attention to plot and detail. Many of the concerns apparent in his novels, such as racism and religion, are reflected in the work. *Time and Time Again* also illustrates Jacobson's growing interest in the themes of time and recovering the past through stories.

Her Story (1987), Jacobson's first novel in a decade, continues with these themes and with his interest in the Bible. In the 1989 interview with Michael Freeman, Jacobson says that he conceived of the idea for the novel while he was writing *The Rape of Tamar* and that he thinks of the two novels as a pair, the first being a biblical story about men and the second, about women. In *Her Story* a female narrator from the future introduces a tale written by a twentieth-century woman, Celia Dinan, discovered in manuscript form among Celia's papers, known as "The Dinan Collection." Celia's narrative is about an unnamed woman from an even older era whose son was one of the thieves crucified with Jesus. This story has become an important literary work in the twenty-third century.

At the beginning of Celia's story the woman and her husband travel to Jerusalem for a festival and, like the biblical Mary and Joseph, lose their young son and are forced to return to look for him after the festival is over. Unlike Mary and Joseph, however, they do not find their son. During the passing years the mother ignores her family and her own needs as she continually fantasizes about the possible return of her lost son. Finally, she believes she has found him. Like the historical Jesus, he is a wandering religious speaker. He is imprisoned for stealing clothes and sentenced to death. His mother and Mary make eye contact at the crucifixion, sharing each other's pain.

The strength of *Her Story* lies partly in its psychological portrayal of the bereaved mother. Her belief that her son will return is poignant and realistic. The novel also examines from a female perspective the power of history and of storytelling. Curiously, in a future period when Islam has become the primary religion, it is a woman's story, discovered "quite by chance," that comes to be seen as canonical. Although *Her Story* has not achieved the popularity of *The Rape of Tamar,* its critical reception has been positive.

A discovered text is also central to *Hidden in the Heart* (1991). The novel opens with a physical act of narration—a writer staring at a computer screen, musing on her own power to erase the text she has written. The story she has written is about Adrian Bested, a South African who moves to England and attempts to shed his Afrikaans accent and become a poet. Adrian's one great love is Diana, the wife of his mentor, the established poet Rodney Foxborough. When Diana is mysteriously killed, Adrian publicly blames Foxborough.

Near the end of the novel, however, the narrator discovers a journal entry of Adrian's, written in Afrikaans. In it Adrian confesses in detail to causing Diana's death. He explains that the two had become trapped on some rocks in a high tide and Adrian had pushed her away from him, causing her to fall and drown. After she was dead, he continued to be tormented by her memory until his own death. The narrator, who remains nameless, is obsessed with Adrian in the same hopeless way.

A sense of displacement is central to the novel. Both the narrator and Adrian long for an imagined time in the past when they could have had their lovers all to themselves. Adrian is also displaced geographically. He never becomes a poet and never feels that he belongs in England. He seems to want to forge an identity for himself out of someone else's life—Diana's—and is never able to do so. Neither can the narrator, who tries to capture Adrian by writing about him: the narrative she writes is about other lives, not her own. She remains a ghostly figure, on the margins of her own story. Critics noted minor structural problems with using a narrator who is only marginally part of her own story but praised Jacobson's originality and craftsmanship in *Hidden in the Heart.*

Both *Hidden in the Heart* and Jacobson's next novel, *The God-Fearer* (1992), have been compared to the work of Henry James in their ambiguity and focus on guilt. *The God-Fearer,* an alternate-history novel, explores the mind and memories of Kobus, an octogenarian retired bookbinder living in the early years of the Roman Empire. In this novel, Judaism, practiced by the "God-Fearers," is the dominant religion of Europe, not Christianity. It is the "Christers" who are instead persecuted by the majority. In the 9 July 1992 *London Review of Books* Jacobson says that he got the name "God-Fearers" from a Baptist sect in the United States that had decided that it no longer believed in Jesus and changed its name accordingly. The novel posits the arbitrariness and easy reversibility of religious history: if Jewish and Christian roles in history were reversed, Jacobson suggests, Jews would show the same lack of mercy toward

Christians as Christians have historically shown toward Jews.

Kobus is haunted by a mysterious pair of children who make him recall a key event of his youth, when he betrayed a Christer girl who had been accused of witchcraft by refusing to testify in her behalf. Kobus and the girl had been friends, and Kobus had been afraid to speak in her favor for fear he would be ostracized. His lasting guilt manifests itself in the last few disoriented months before his death in the form of visions of the children, who he believes represent the girl's unborn grandchildren.

Jacobson's depiction of dementia in old age is brilliantly realistic. The regret that Kobus feels for his early mistake comes across clearly and painfully. Yet, there is an inner peace about Kobus, as he is finally able to come to terms with his past. Kobus is an atheist; yet, he is deeply concerned with the immorality of his tragic choice and its consequences. He had been the only one of his people to befriend a Christer. His shame is that he could not stand firm in that friendship.

The idea of betrayal concerns Jacobson greatly. There is evidence of this preoccupation in many of his works, including *The Rape of Tamar, The Trap, The Confessions of Joseph Baisz, Hidden in the Heart,* and especially *The God-Fearer,* which was nominated for the Whitbread Prize.

The Electronic Elephant (1994), a travel narrative, returned Jacobson to his native South Africa to describe the land and people and how they have changed since the early days of colonization. A travelogue as well as a history, it was well received and has reinforced Jacobson's status as both a British and a South African author. Jacobson's latest work, *Heshel's Kingdom* (1998), is also nonfiction, both a biography and an autobiography. It chronicles the life of his grandfather, Heshel Melamed, who was a rabbi in Lithuania, and Jacobson's search for the details of Melamed's life.

Themes such as betrayal, racial strife, religion, the formation of history, and power—including the power of narrative itself—are the major subjects of Jacobson's works. From the social morality and naturalism of his early South African novels to the depth of characterization in *The Beginners* and the focus on history and storytelling in his most recent novels, his writing is gripping and realistic, sensitive and warm. Jacobson has a steady following that includes a solid critical reputation.

In the 1989 interview with Michael Freeman, Jacobson said that authors often write about what they have been "tormented" by. Jacobson writes about themes familiar to an expatriate of a violent country. As he told Richard Lansdown in a 1994 interview, he agrees with Friedrich Nietzsche that conflict is "a condition of all invention and innovation, both for the individual and the culture." Jacobson's novels, about human conflict, succeed because those conflicts are both topical and universal.

Interviews:

Meir Mindlin, "A Talk with Dan Jacobson," *Jewish Affairs,* 14 (August 1959): 22–24;

Ian Hamilton, "Dan Jacobson," *New Review* (October 1977): 25–29;

Ronald Hayman, "Dan Jacobson in Interview," *Books and Bookmen* (February 1980): 45–46;

Michael Freeman, "Dan Jacobson," *Poetry National Review,* 16, no. 1 (1989): 23–28;

Richard Lansdown, "Weapons of Vicissitude: An Interview with Dan Jacobson," *Critical Review,* 34 (1994): 113–132.

Bibliography:

Myra Yudelman, *Dan Jacobson: A Bibliography* (Johannesburg: University of the Witwatersrand, 1967).

References:

Midge Decter, "Novelist of South Africa," in her *The Liberated Woman and Other Essays* (New York: Coward-McCann, 1971), pp. 201–208;

Paul Gready, "Dan Jacobson as Expatriate Writer: South Africa as Private Resource and Half-Code and the Literature of Multiple Exposure," *Research in African Literatures,* 25 (Winter 1994): 17–32;

Sheila Roberts, *Dan Jacobson* (Boston: Twayne, 1984);

Michael Wade, "Apollo, Dionysius, and Other Performers in Dan Jacobson's South African Circus," in *World Literature in English,* 13 (April 1974): 39–82;

Renee Winegarten, "The Novels of Dan Jacobson," *Midstream* (May 1966): 25–29.

Papers:

The Harry Ransom Humanities Research Center at the University of Texas holds a large collection of Dan Jacobson's drafts, professional correspondence, and personal documents as well as materials about Jacobson.

Howard Jacobson

(25 August 1942 –   )

Glyn Turton
University College Chester, England

BOOKS: *Shakespeare's Magnanimity: Four Tragic Heroes, Their Friends and Families,* by Jacobson and Wilbur Sanders (London: Chatto & Windus, 1978; New York: Oxford University Press, 1978);

Coming from Behind (London: Chatto & Windus, 1983; New York: St. Martin's Press, 1984);

Peeping Tom (London: Chatto & Windus, 1984; New York: Ticknor & Fields, 1985);

Redback (London: Bantam, 1986; New York: Viking, 1987);

In the Land of Oz (London: Hamilton, 1987);

The Very Model of a Man (London: Viking, 1992; Woodstock, N.Y.: Overlook, 1994);

Roots Schmoots, Journeys among Jews (London: Viking, 1993; Woodstock, N.Y.: Overlook, 1994);

Seriously Funny (London: Viking, 1997);

No More Mister Nice Guy (London: Cape, 1998).

OTHER: "Travelling Elsewhere," in *Best Short Stories 1989,* edited by Giles Gordon and David Hughes (London: Heinemann, 1989).

Howard Jacobson at the time of Redback *(1986)*

Howard Jacobson's 1996 television series on the nature of the comic and accompanying written study, published in 1997, are titled *Seriously Funny*. That title, at once oxymoron and skittish postmodern catchphrase, reflects Jacobson's fascination with incongruity. Though the incongruous is a feature of most comic writing, Jacobson's predilection for it as the basis of his novels is marked. Reading his work can be a frustrating experience. He can be uproariously funny and delightfully liberating as a breaker of modern taboos and intelligent in his use of the absurd to expose society's sexual and cultural condition. Nevertheless, Jacobson's tendency to set up narrative patterns that require more careful management than he seems prepared to give them sometimes detracts from the pleasure of the nicely realized comic episodes and the mordant comments on life's absurdities. The key to this apparent reluctance to discipline his narratives may well lie in Jacobson's essential themes–the subverting of received structures, flight from constraint, and craving for instant gratification. Readers may differ as to whether Jacobson can be claimed as a "seriously funny" writer in the sense in which he uses the phrase, that is, to describe one whose comic creations deflate any notion humans might harbor of their own tragic grandeur. At his best, however, he is a highly effective wit and jester, both fictively dramatizing and discursively advocating, the therapeutic value of the wisdom of the fools.

If the essence of comic writing is making the familiar seem strange by the processes of skewing and distancing, Jacobson's background equipped him perfectly for the task. A northerner among southerners, a

Jew among Gentiles, an Englishman among Australians, a cultural iconoclast reared in F. R. Leavis's tradition of high moral seriousness, Jacobson's provenance and experience have given him enough bizarrely contrasting influences to last a lifetime of satirical exploration. Born of Jewish parents in Manchester, England, on 25 August 1942, Jacobson was educated at a local grammar school and then, from 1961 to 1964, at Downing College, Cambridge, where he studied English under Leavis, a celebrated critic and teacher. Much of Jacobson's comic capital has been made out of his argument with academia—not surprisingly, since the earlier part of his career was as a university teacher in Sydney, New South Wales, from 1965 to 1968; Selwyn College, Cambridge, from 1969 to 1972; and Wolverhampton Polytechnic in the English West Midlands from 1974 to 1980. Jacobson has many academic publications to his credit dating from this phase of his career, but he left academia to work as a freelance writer and broadcaster throughout the 1980s and 1990s. Fiction and travel writing have been his principal fields, although he also has enjoyed success as a maker and presenter of television programs. Jacobson married Rosalin Sadler in 1978 and has one child from a previous marriage.

Jacobson's first novel, *Coming from Behind* (1983), derives its comic edge and telling accuracy from the author's experience of the drearier reaches of modern British higher education. It is a satire upon the polytechnics: cut-price, municipal institutions created in the late 1960s in order to expand degree-level education. The novel is closely autobiographical, with its Jewish hero, Sefton Goldberg, having studied at Cambridge and taught in an Australian university before becoming stranded as a polytechnic lecturer in the English West Midlands, an unlovely area of urban sprawl rejoicing in the name of the Black Country. Though often compared to Kingsley Amis's *Lucky Jim* (1953), that benchmark for all subsequent campus novels, *Coming from Behind* is less even in its narrative pace and less measured in its irony, closer to farce than to comedy of manners. It should be noted, however, that by the 1980s the face of British higher education had changed significantly, with the new polytechnics, in their more outlandish aspects, inviting just the kind of rough lampooning that they receive at Jacobson's hands.

Jacobson's interest in the comic potential of the way of all flesh is proclaimed in the double entendre of the novel's title. In most of his books progress is almost invariably priapic. In *Coming from Behind* the relative ease of getting a girl and the difficulty of getting a job make up much of the comic substance of the novel. Sefton Goldberg takes his sexual chances where he finds them but has less luck in his overtures to other universities,

whither he is desperate to flee in order to escape the ultimate humiliation of having to teach literature in the stands of a local soccer club leased by the polytechnic. His hopes of salvation are eventually pinned on a fellowship at the Cambridge college of Holy Christ Hall, his translation to which is the culminating point of the novel. Though in the book's closing section Jacobson subjects Cambridge's academic snobbery and rituals to the comic treatment he has earlier meted out to Wrottesley Polytechnic and its crass gestures of modernity and populism, the sense of absurdity is less keenly felt and the satire clumsier. There is no doubt that the real target of Jacobson's wit is the "poly," where the brave new world of expanded educational opportunity turns out to be the misbegotten offspring of the mediocre and the bureaucratic.

Coming from Behind establishes a pattern that all Jacobson's subsequent novels approximate. Underpinned by a concentration upon the misadventures, misalliances, neuroses, and antipathies of a central character (always Jewish and always male), they are otherwise essentially vehicles for totem-busting, cultural jokes, and rumbustious comic episodes. The corollary of this pattern is that the pleasures of a Jacobson novel rarely lie in the plot, which sometimes disappears underground only to reemerge when the reader has almost forgotten about it, or in robust characterization. They lie instead in Jacobson's knack of being able to take a comic situation and draw it out so that the reader can savor it and in his irreverent handling of social and cultural myths.

In both these respects, *Coming from Behind* is probably the richest of all Jacobson's novels. Its memorable opening scene—which has the novel's hero crouched on his office floor performing a graduation day rite of passage with a recent former student but distractedly unable to remember whether he has dropped the latch on his door—is the stock-in-trade of farce. Yet, the comic idea that in the midst of death (in the Elizabethan, sexual sense of the word), one can be irritatingly in life is nicely exploited with the third-person narrator viewing Sefton's predicament from every angle, while Sefton is unable to engineer the only angle that matters: the one that will afford him a view of the latch to his office.

Comic iconoclasm is the book's other great strength. In this novel Jacobson develops the perspective that he exploits again in subsequent ones: that of the Jewish observer of gentile culture, in both its high and popular forms. One of the features of *Coming from Behind* that makes it arguably Jacobson's best novel is the maintenance throughout of a clear identity for the central character. This identity is achieved partly by the author's sustaining a sharp contradistinction between Sefton Goldberg and those British cultural norms

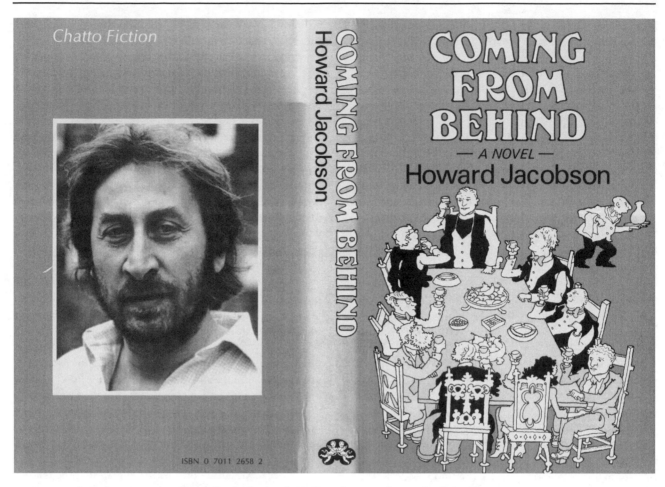

Dust jacket for Jacobson's 1983 novel, set at a dreary polytechnic college

toward which, as a Jew, he is antipathetic and uncomprehending: chiefly, nature and soccer. *Coming from Behind* is undoubtedly at its funniest when the author is discoursing on Sefton's bafflement at the ability of English intellectuals to find the numinous in nature and of the English working classes to find pleasure in watching twenty-two men spend ninety minutes kicking a ball. This debunking of sacred British myths, though digressive, is perpetrated with a quick, fresh, pungent wit and arguably gives us the best moments in all Jacobson's comic writing.

Peeping Tom (1984), Jacobson's second novel, is based on a first-rate comic idea. It concerns a north London Jewish intellectual of middle-class provenance, Barney Fugelman, who was born exactly one hundred years after Thomas Hardy, and who, when under hypnosis, gives voice to Hardy's bitter thoughts and unhealthy preoccupations. The second part of this legacy—the unhealthy preoccupations—has also shaped Barney into a kind of avatar, for his tastes run to voyeurism. Barney attempts to satisfy these tastes in his marriage to the voluptuous Sharon. The stimulus to his acting out his fantasies is his experience, under hypnosis, of infiltrating the mind of Hardy, when, as a boy in Dorchester, the writer had witnessed the public hanging of a woman, Martha Brown, for the murder of her husband. Hardy's sexual frisson at the scene ripples through the ether and manifests itself in Barney as a more benign but rather maladroit kinkiness into which he tries to draw Sharon. Barney's personal predisposition to voyeurism is also linked to his boyhood spying upon his parents' attractive next-door neighbor, Rabika Flatman, with whom, in a later twist to the story, Barney's father elopes and whose husband, Barney's mother confesses to him, is actually his real father.

These tangled relationships are part of the rich mixture of confused and substituted identities that first comes to a boil at the end of part one of the novel. Barney introduces his old school friend, Dr. Roland Fitzpiers, to Sharon and initiates a ménage à trois between them, but he is distressed when Fitzpiers supplants him and begins to take Sharon to wife-swapping parties. Between them, Sharon and Fitzpiers hatch a plan to stage a hypnotic "happening," at which Barney will pour forth the spirit of Thomas Hardy for the benefit of a gathering of Hardy experts and enthusiasts. The plan goes wrong when Barney, angry at his wife for conniving at the staged event, redirects his psychic time-traveling to the other historical character with whom he shares a birthday–the Marquis de Sade. He then erupts into obscene, archaic French and attacks Sharon. Shortly afterwards, Sharon pays him back, and Barney flees the marital home with her raining blows and household objects upon his head. Barney's relationship with Sharon is embroidered by Jacobson with connections to Hardy's life. His introduction of Fitzpiers to her parallels Hardy's introduction of his friend Horace Moule to the cousin with whom he was in love, Tryphena Sparkes. In addition, Sharon's parting shot at Barney is a taunting solicitor's letter, which charges him with paternity of the child she is carrying, sarcastically informs him that it was conceived exactly one hundred years after the alleged birth of a child to Tryphena Sparkes, and alludes to a buzz of speculation in Hardy circles that the writer might have been that child's father.

Though in part 1 alone there is enough material for a whole novel, Jacobson extends it to a second part that functions as a kind of coda. In this section Barney heads for the English West Country to the Alternative Centre for Thomas Hardy Studies, run by the imperious, erotically challenging Camilla Marteline, whom Barney marries and to whom he slavishly subordinates himself. Camilla is one the most memorable of Jacobson's characters. Intellectual, promiscuous, and given to reductive analyses of the male psyche–Hardy's included–she captivates and dominates Barney, until this relationship too comes to grief. In a scene that mocks Barney's earlier undoing, Camilla submits herself to sex with two actors at Stonehenge. She then promptly leaves Barney for Max Loveday, a former academic who runs the seaside candy store in Castle Boterel, bequeathing to Barney the Alternative Centre for Thomas Hardy Studies and a letter titled, "What I think of My Husband." The novel ends with Barney sitting on a Cornish cliff top and dropping the unread letter into the "opal and the sapphire of that wandering western sea." This incident is a culmination of the series of intertextual jokes relating to Hardy and the women in his life that gives *Peeping Tom* its satirical resonance. Here, as elsewhere in his fiction, Jacobson's irreverence inclines him to explore the great themes of literature twice–the first time as tragedy, the second as farce.

Peeping Tom is a richly inventive novel, a sexual comedy of manners, lurking within which is a half-serious fictional commentary on desire and human identity.

Barney's ultimate inadequacies with women widen to take in male inadequacy in general. In a passage of retrospect, after Camilla has left him, Barney imagines her riposte to his anxious supposition that women are beguiled not by mixed-up Jewish ironists but by the easy and authoritative charm of the music-making Celt:

> I've never met a man yet who possesses the softness of tread, the easy stealth, the musical genius, and above all the social confidence to beguile any rational woman of her senses. Men don't come as impressive as that, more's the pity. . . . The idea that they do, the fear that they might lives only in other men's brains. The saucy fiddler is a figure from male mythology. Just like Hardy's flashing Sergeant. You're all hot to know the secret of one another's potency, you men.

Ultimately, though, if the novel has a serious point to make, it is a seriously funny one, exemplified by the disembodied, grubby mind of that great Victorian writer–that the past is full of murky farce, rather than noble tragedy. When Sharon pointedly reminds Barney that Hardy may have been the father of the child his cousin Tryphena may have had, Barney has an insight into the nature of the past: "I immediately grasped something about the past (not just mine, anyone's): it lacked dignity. Parents, family, skeletons in cupboards, hereditary diseases, curses, Atrean atrocities, fatal weaknesses of the line–it was all the stuff of low farce, not tragedy. The last person to have any right to self-respect was Adam; even Eve was compromised by a demeaning antecedence."

If *Peeping Tom* has a weakness, it is that the novel has two substantial parts that are thematically linked but are hinged rather awkwardly on the central character's retrospective narrative. There is much to compensate and bridge over that weakness, however. The digressive jokes, many of them ribald, that are Jacobson's hallmark are funny indeed, begging comparisons between Jacobson and another contemporary Jewish humorist, Woody Allen. Some of the novel's Jewish humor has a specifically British context, as, for example, when Barney opines, "I had never been to Cornwall before. As I've intimated already, Jews don't in the main make for the West Country. Hammersmith is far enough in that direction for most of us." Other passages will resonate with Jewish readers regardless of nationality. When Barney first arrives at Camilla's house, she throws down a sleeping bag for him to use, which occasions a substantial digression on the Jewish aversion to sleeping bags:

> I didn't need to check what the Talmud had to say about that; I possess in full measure the race's instinctive dread of those places where other people's bodies

Dust jacket for the U.S. edition of Jacobson's 1986 novel, which follows the sexual misadventures of a British Jew among Australian political radicals

had been and where alien germs were therefore bound to congregate. And I possessed it in the usual illogical form. I would press my lips to absolutely any part of some girl I'd known for five minutes—in my bachelor days it was my boast that, orally speaking, there wasn't anywhere I hadn't been and wouldn't gladly go again—but I'd invent every kind of fantastic excuse rather than lay my head upon her pillow or slide my unclothed body in between her sheets.

Peeping Tom carries forward the themes developed in *Coming from Behind:* the lure of sexual opportunity and the trap of circumstances, the ambiguous position of the Jew in an Anglo-Saxon culture, and the debunking of cultural idols. It also introduces new themes to satirize, most notably the fashion of the 1960s and 1970s for alternative lifestyles. The "seriously funny" substance of *Peeping Tom,* however, is the delight taken in celebrating what Jacobson's hero Barney Fugelman refers to as "profane innocence": "I had been trying to get other people to see the lewdness of the human body all my life." In Jacobson's novels recognition of the naughti-

ness, compulsiveness, domination, and subordination that attend sexual acts is, paradoxically, release into a kind of prelapsarian dirty-mindedness—a refreshing reversal of D. H. Lawrence's absurd attempt to mystify carnality by solemnizing it.

Jacobson's third novel, *Redback* (1986), is in some ways the least sharp of his three satires on the intellectual life. It is nevertheless pervaded by the mischievous wit that is the main source of pleasure in Jacobson's writing and taps intelligently into that major vein of contemporary debate and anxiety, the power struggle between the sexes. Set chiefly in Australia, the novel deals comically with the manners of the antipodean chattering classes in a period from the liberated 1960s to the dawning of the age of political correctness. Its hero is once more shaped from Jacobson's own life experiences: Leon Forelock, a bright young Jew from the North Country, gains a first-class degree in the Moral Decencies at Cambridge, where he is recruited by the Central Intelligence Agency to act as a kind of cultural counterrevolutionary in Australia. Forelock is naive, priggish, and uptight, in his own words a "swatty women-reared old-fashioned boy." He sets about his mission of propagandizing against the varieties of radical who, in the eyes of the U.S. government, threaten Australia's stability. He seems ideally suited to the job, until he is bitten by the "spider of cynicism," the eponymous redback, whose bite induces the spectacular symptom of priapism. This event, described at the end of the book but alluded to throughout the retrospective narrative, decisively liberates and liberalizes the hero.

The minor characters who people the suburbs and campuses of Sydney are, as is usually the case in a Jacobson novel, lightly drawn foils to the central figure, whose progress in life leads inevitably back to the recesses of his past. One such unresolved circumstance in Leon's life is his relationship with Desley, a feisty Australian woman who years before had registered her dissatisfaction with Leon's sexual prowess by defecating on him in bed. A schoolteacher and leader of a militant feminist collective, she has achieved notoriety by stripping naked in front of a class of children in order to illustrate the joy and power of woman's sexuality. The prospect of sex with Desley has come to represent for Leon not just the chance to expunge from his memory the humiliation of their last encounter but also a symbolic act of congress with the former enemy. Sadly for Leon, his reunion with Desley breaks down over profane semantic quibbling.

Leon has been to Sydney there by his father and his father's mistress, Trilby, queen of the Cheshire suburbs. The elder Forelock's adoration of Trilby has always been complicated by the sheer effort of bringing physical satisfaction to a woman considerably bigger than himself. When his father finally expires, Trilby and Leon, despite the difference in ages, find solace for their grief in each other's arms—much to the disgust of Venie and Maroochie, the Australian synchronized swimmers with whom Leon has been sharing a ménage à trois.

Evident from these summaries of the turn of events in *Redback* is the extent to which the novel revisits the preoccupations of Jacobson's two earlier works: the clash of cultures, the absurdity of intellectual fads, the alienness of nature to the urban Jewish mind, an ambivalent attitude toward dominant younger women, and, the other side of the coin, the lure of indulgent older ones. The cathartic element in Jacobson's work lies in his way of using comedy to work through contemporary social and cultural anxieties. *Redback*, although ostensibly a comedy of modern Australian manners, is really about male psychosexual identity, brought to crisis by the rise of feminism. The fundamental element of masculine identity, the erection, is made risible by being made permanent. The female spider bites Leon just after he has been sexually humiliated by Desley for the second time. The "permanent readiness" that the resultant satyriasis syndrome causes induces in Leon a kind of sexual ennui that brings him all the bittersweet sensations of postcoital melancholy before the event. To the physical absurdity of his condition is thus added a constant reminder of the ultimate emptiness of all desire. It is the age-old male fear of being bitten and consumed by the more powerful female, however, which is at the root of the satire. Leon has had the salutary lesson of watching his father kill himself in the attempt to service Trilby, but Trilby's attraction for him is that she offers him a form of sex not governed by power relations, the demand for satisfaction, or the need for phallic indefatigability: "I am not sure that you can call what we did making love. The phrase is too active. Make love not war, the generation I turned my back on used to say, as if the same ferocious energies could be expended equally on both. Trilby and I had no aggressions to rechannel."

Jacobson's next novel, *The Very Model of a Man* (1992), is marked by the author's strengths and weaknesses writ large and in more or less equal measure. Essentially a revisiting of the story of Cain and Abel enlarged by means of satire into a dramatization of Judaism's argument with itself and God, the novel is central to any claim that might be made for Jacobson as a serious writer. Jacobson himself, in an interview with Rabbi Julia Neuberger in the *Jewish Chronicle*, repudiated the characterization of him as "some American-style Jewish humorist," claiming that his intention was to make serious demands upon his readers' intelligence. *The Very Model of a Man* also, however, taxes their

patience by overelaboration. Jacobson has a gift for wordplay perhaps unrivaled among contemporary British novelists, but in *The Very Model of a Man* it sometimes seems as if the words exceed the meaning striven for.

Jacobson's ambition in constructing a two-stranded account of the life of Cain, counterpointing his version of the events leading to Abel's killing with the experience of his exile in Babel after it, overburdens the novel. The most successful passages in *The Very Model of a Man* are those in which Cain gives selected prominent citizens of Babel his account of Creation's prototypical dysfunctional family. The satire upon Yahweh, Adam, Eve, and their ill-fated offspring is sharp, aphoristic, insightful, and funny. By virtue of his making Cain a self-aware, articulate intellectual, Jacobson's account of the jealous son's complex feelings toward his family is compelling and immediate—the more so for God himself being emotionally embroiled in their turbulent relationship. The novel's early chapters feature its most concentrated writing, with Cain resentful and contemptuous of his mother's twofold yearnings—"her muddy infatuation with my indolent baby brother. And her more stately meeting of minds with the Ethereal." God's fixation upon Eve, and his desire to keep the fixation mutual, leads him to send down a pair of angels to stimulate her flagging interest in the wonders of the firmament. Eve's visitation by the angels Azael and Semyaza affords Jacobson an opportunity for one of his most striking excursions into comic incongruity:

> There was something soiled about them both, as if they had journeyed too far without refreshment, or decided to travel in borrowed plumage. This was an effect partly, as had been noticed on earlier visitations, of a fault in their engineering. Advantageous as it may have been for them, in matters relating to survival, to have arms unencumbered by feathers, in addition to wings, the drawback was an over-elaboration of musculature that impeded ordinary terrestrial movement. Sometimes the wings got in the way of the arms, sometimes the arms interfered with the functioning of the wings. They were not always certain which part of themselves to employ. They walked awkwardly. They toppled easily. The extra load told on the shoulders and the spine, creating problems of posture and any number of dermatological complications.

Jacobson is good at such iconoclasm, which he uses to liberating effect.

In the parallel narrative strand of the novel, Cain is in exile in Babel, and the narrative standpoint is third rather than first person. In the chapters devoted to this strand, the descriptive writing is arch—mock-rabbinical in those places in which Cain's story is linked to other episodes in the Old Testament—and the dialogue is jarringly ventriloquial. Cain's encounters with the dignitaries and intellectuals of Babel, rather than deepening the tragic and mythic significance of Cain's exile, detract from the intensity of the story as he personally relates it. As a result the full imaginative force of Jacobson's project–to ironize the portentousness of the Bible's prototragedy–is much diminished.

It is also unclear exactly what Jacobson is doing with what some feminist critics would claim is the misogyny of the Bible in his retelling of the Cain and Abel myth. In the consciousness of Cain, though, a response to women that ranges from the wary to the contemptuous emerges. He recoils from both his mother, Eve, and the girl Zilpha, daughter of Naaman, the high-ranking civil official of Babel who offers herself to him. Such a response should be read in the context of the book's general Freudian reworking of the biblical story, but whereas Jacobson's earlier portrayals of women suggest the normally confused male feelings of mingled desire and fear, the note struck in *The Very Model of a Man* is sour and troubled.

In argument with Abel, Cain asserts: "Words, too, are among the little we have. . . . So why not play with them?" Cain's way with words is his main weapon as he defines himself in contradistinction to his two fathers, the inarticulate Adam and God. While the biblical Cain has two fathers, however, the fictional Cain has a third in the novelist, who constructs him on the principle that if he cannot have the first word, he might as well try to have the last. This profound attachment to the ludic value of words as the source of liberation, rebellion, and a palliative to the tedium of life is a powerful force of Jacobson's work.

This idea recurs in Jacobson's latest novel, *No More Mister Nice Guy* (1998), the hero of which is, in his own words, "a disputatious man" for whom "criticism is everything." Jacobson's central theme, dealt with from an unapologetically male standpoint, is the cycle of sexual attraction and repulsion, desire and fear. The battlefields may vary in his novels, but the same war between the sexes is always being fought. In this novel there are few subplots to distract from the main subject–the emotional disorientation and sexual nostalgia of a famous television critic who is "looking down both barrels at fifty." Frank Ritz, doyen of the television columns, lives with Mel, an equally successful writer of "feministical erotic" fiction. Mel is resentful of Frank, particularly his past habit of straying sexually, and by the end of the first chapter the two have vented their frustrations and parted. Liberated, Frank takes to the road in his Saab, embarking on a part hopeful, part sentimental search for conquests past and future.

As he revisits the scenes of his youth and the places associated wiht the women he has cared for, Frank plays back to himself in memory of a lifetime of lustful self-indulgence. He reverts to the habit acquired in his Manchester youth of picking up prostitutes, but these transactions fail to bring even simple satisfaction. He commences an affair with D, a feisty comedienne, whom he accompanies on tour, and visits a former lover, Clarice, in Cornwall. Frank then travels to a monastery in northern Scotland, where he finds brief respite among the genial monks. Disappointed by the banal, uncomprehending advice of Father Lawrence, supposedly the wisest monk in the communty, Frank finally realizes that he cannot live without the turmoil and confusion that went with his old life. The novel ends with his return to London and to Mel.

No More Mister Nice Guy received mostly unsympathetic reviews. Catherine Bennett, in the *Guardian* (2 May 1998), associated it with "an emerging literary genre, the misogynistic picaresque, in which ageing, lustful, disappointed men undertake a tour of their sexual conquests, pausing from time to time to deliver sententiae on women." The charge of misogyny is a difficult one to refute, although Frank Ritz's hostility to women is obviously a comic trope, and the novel thoroughly exposes the unpleasant recesses of the male psyche, as well. Moreover, the novel is clearly focused on contemporary issues other than the contradictions of male sexuality, such as the circularity and introversion of the late-twentieth-century preoccupation with television.

Howard Jacobson has in recent years firmly established himself in the British media world as a witty and entertaining critic, commentator, and travel writer. As a novelist, though, he has received less credit. His reputation may also have suffered because he appears to have little respect for political correctness. The robustness of his satire and his exploitation for comic effect of the obscene aspects of human behavior suggest a closer kinship with the seventeenth and eighteenth centuries than the contemporary times. In one of the more intelligent reviews of *No More Mister Nice Guy,* published in the *TLS: The Times Literary Supplement* (24 April 1998) the feminist critic and scholar Germaine Greer convincingly links Jacobson to a scatological tradition that reached its peak in those centuries. Criticism of Jacobson's novels perhaps represents the mainstream critical disposition to favor narrative as an end rather than as a convenient means for exhibiting linguistic playfulness. If so, the judgment on him fails to do justice to the important human concerns that are addressed in his seriously funny novels.

Penelope Lively
(17 March 1933 –)

Ruth P. Feingold
University of Chicago

BOOKS: *Astercote* (London: Heinemann, 1970; New York: Dutton, 1971);

The Whispering Knights (London: Heinemann, 1971; New York: Dutton, 1976);

The Wild Hunt of Hagworthy (London: Heinemann, 1971); republished as *The Wild Hunt of the Ghost Hounds* (New York: Dutton, 1972);

The Driftway (London: Heinemann, 1972; New York: Dutton, 1973);

The Ghost of Thomas Kempe (London: Heinemann, 1973; New York: Dutton, 1973);

The House in Norham Gardens (London: Heinemann, 1974; New York: Dutton, 1974);

Boy without a Name (London: Heinemann, 1975; Berkeley, Cal.: Parnassus, 1975);

Going Back (London: Heinemann, 1975; New York: Dutton, 1975);

A Stitch in Time (London: Heinemann, 1976; New York: Dutton, 1976);

The Stained Glass Window (London: Abelard-Schuman, 1976);

Fanny's Sister (London: Heinemann, 1976; New York: Dutton, 1980);

The Presence of the Past: An Introduction to Landscape History (London: Collins, 1976);

The Road to Lichfield (London: Heinemann, 1977; New York: Grove, 1991);

The Voyage of QV66 (London: Heinemann, 1978; New York: Dutton, 1979);

Nothing Missing but the Samovar, and Other Stories (London: Heinemann, 1978);

Fanny and the Monsters (London: Heinemann, 1979);

Treasures of Time (London: Heinemann, 1979; Garden City, N.Y.: Doubleday, 1980);

Fanny and the Battle of Potter's Piece (London: Heinemann, 1980);

Judgement Day (London: Heinemann, 1980; Garden City, N.Y.: Doubleday, 1981);

The Revenge of Samuel Stokes (London: Heinemann, 1981; New York: Dutton, 1981);

Penelope Lively

Next to Nature, Art (London: Heinemann, 1982);

Perfect Happiness (London: Heinemann, 1983; New York: Dial, 1984);

According to Mark (London: Heinemann, 1984; New York: Beaufort, 1984);

Uninvited Ghosts and Other Stories (London: Heinemann, 1984; New York: Dutton, 1985);

Corruption and Other Stories (London: Heinemann, 1984);

Dragon Trouble (London: Heinemann, 1984; New York: Barron, 1989);

Pack of Cards: Stories 1978–1986 (London: Heinemann, 1986); republished as *Pack of Cards and Other Stories* (New York: Grove, 1989);

Moon Tiger (London: Deutsch, 1987; New York: Grove, 1988);

Debbie and the Little Devil (London: Heinemann, 1987);

A House Inside Out (London: Deutsch, 1987; New York: Dutton, 1987); republished in part as *The Lost Dog and Other Stories* (London: Penguin, 1996);

Passing On (London: Deutsch, 1989; New York: Grove, 1990);

City of the Mind (London: Deutsch, 1991; New York: HarperCollins, 1991);

Judy and the Martian (Hemel Hempstead, U.K.: Simon & Schuster Young Books, 1992);

Cleopatra's Sister (London: Viking Penguin, 1993; New York: HarperCollins, 1993);

Oleander, Jacaranda: A Childhood Perceived (London: Viking, 1994; New York: HarperCollins, 1994);

Good Night, Sleep Tight (London: Walker, 1994; Cambridge, Mass.: Candlewick, 1995);

The Cat, the Crow and the Banyan Tree (London: Walker, 1994; Cambridge, Mass.: Candlewick, 1994);

Staying with Grandpa (London: Viking Penguin, 1995);

The Disastrous Dog (Hemel Hempstead, U.K.: Macdonald Young Books, 1995);

A Martian Comes to Stay (Hemel Hempstead, U.K.: Macdonald Young Books, 1995);

Heat Wave (London: Viking Penguin, 1996; New York: HarperCollins, 1996);

Beyond the Blue Mountains (London: Viking, 1997); republished as *The 5001 Nights* (Seattle: Fjord Press, 1997);

Ghostly Ghosts (London: Heinemann, 1997);

Goldilocks and the Three Bears (Hove, U.K.: Macdonald Young Books, 1997);

One, Two, Three, Jump! (New York: McElderry, 1998);

Spiderweb (New York: HarperFlamingo, 1999).

TELEVISION: *Boy Dominic* series (3 episodes), script by Lively, 1974;

Time Out of Mind, script by Lively, 1976.

OTHER: *One Way of Writing,* audiotape of lecture by Lively (Manchester, U.K.: Manchester Library, Creative Writers Lectures, 1982);

Ivy Compton-Burnett, *Manservant and Maidservant,* foreword by Lively (Oxford: Oxford University Press, 1983);

Compton-Burnett, *A Father and His Fate,* foreword by Lively (Oxford: Oxford University Press, 1984);

Edith Wharton, *The Age of Innocence,* foreword by Lively (London: Virago, 1988);

Willa Cather, *My Àntonia,* introduction by Lively (London: Dent, 1996; Rutland, Vt.: Tuttle, 1996);

Marilyn Bridges, *Egypt: Antiquities from Above,* includes essay by Lively (New York: Little, Brown, 1996).

SELECTED PERIODICAL PUBLICATIONS–UNCOLLECTED: "Children and Memory," *Hornbook,* 49 (August 1973): 400–407;

"Bones in the Sand," *Hornbook,* 57 (December 1981): 641–651.

A prolific novelist and short-story writer, Penelope Lively thus far has published more than forty books for children and adults in a writing career spanning a little less than thirty years. In no way, however, has quality been sacrificed for quantity: she has received half a dozen prestigious literary awards, among them the Booker-McConnell Prize, and was named to the Order of the British Empire in 1989 for her contributions to literature.

Lively began her career as a children's novelist, producing eleven critically acclaimed books for young people before publishing her first adult novel, *The Road to Lichfield* (1977). She has continued to write for both children and adults but has concentrated more and more on adult literature. Such a distinction, however, is in some ways artificial: a definite continuity exists between her children's and her adult fiction and extends also to her two nonfiction books: *The Presence of the Past: An Introduction to Landscape History* (1976), and *Oleander, Jacaranda: A Childhood Perceived* (1994), a memoir of her childhood in Egypt.

Much of Lively's writing in all genres is concerned with themes of time, history, and memory. She likes to explore the interactions of humans with both the natural and the built landscape and to investigate the ways in which place constructs identity and informs relationships. Her protagonists are often amateur or professional archaeologists, paleontologists, architects, or historians who through their frequently accidental discoveries come to a fuller understanding of both their worlds and themselves. A favorite metaphor of Lively's is that of a palimpsest: literally "a manuscript in which a later writing is written over an effaced earlier writing" or a geologic specimen "exhibiting features produced at two or more distinct periods," the word *palimpsest* is used by Lively to denote the layers of experience, memory, and physical data that make up a place or a person. At a broad cultural level, an example of a Livelian palimpsest is the London of *City of the Mind* (1991), a long-inhabited city in which newer construction continually adds onto, yet never fully replaces, what has been built in generations past. At a more intimate level she may write of the palimpsest of personal experience: for example, in *Moon Tiger* (1987) the detritus of papers, small souvenirs, and memories that Claudia shuffles through in the course of her deathbed reverie about her life. The present is never simply the present for Lively but exists always as an accretion of past influences that must be continually reprocessed and accounted for.

Lively's fascination with the complex interplay of past and present, person and place, can be traced in part to her childhood in Egypt, a country, she writes, that "had had two thousand years of foreign occupation, reflected now as then in the emotive wealth of its landscape, in which everything happens at once–Greek temples and Roman forts and the mosques of the Mamluks and eventually the great cosmopolitan jumble of Cairo. With the unimaginable enigmatic reach of the pharonic centuries beyond."

Lively was born in the cosmopolitan jumble of Cairo on 17 March 1933, the daughter of an expatriate English bank manager, Roger Low, and his wife, Vera (née Reckitt). An only child, Lively grew up in the care of an English nanny named Lucy, whom she describes as being "my entire emotional world . . . My parents were satellite figures–occasionally stimulating or provocative, but of a different order." Until the age of twelve, Lively had no formal schooling, instead receiving lessons provided by Lucy–who had little in the way of education. The two of them relied on correspondence material designed for expatriates, and the result was an eclectic mishmash of reading that was "short on expertise, but rich in that crucial element–one-to-one attention."

Lively's childhood idyll came to an abrupt and traumatic end in 1945 when her parents divorced and she was sent to boarding school in England. Although technically English, she had never before been to the country for more than brief visits and experienced herself as "in . . . exile . . . an alien, walking that landscape always with a faint sense of incredulity. Sooner or later, surely, I would wake up and find myself at Bulaq Dakhur . . . and normality would be restored." Instead, normality was forever transformed: Lucy departed; new cultural codes of language and dress had to be learned; and the "slow calvary" of "that particularly barbaric institution, the English boarding school," had to be endured.

Lively's secondary education was profoundly alienating to her. She had always liked reading and was quite ready to learn, but her school "aimed at turning out competent hockey and lacrosse players, and did not encourage other activities." When *The Oxford Book of English Verse* was found in her locker, she was scolded. She would be taught poetry, complained the headmistress, and therefore had no need to read it on her own.

Nonetheless, certain aspects of her new home struck a chord with her, making her once again aware of the continuity of the past in the physical landscape: "I am thirteen. It is 1946. I stand in Cheapside, in the heart of the City of London. . . . All around there is a

Lively as a child in Bulaq Dakhrur, Egypt

sea of rubble–but organized rubble, out of which you can pick the lines of streets and buildings. . . . The bombs have stripped the landscape down to its origins; the medieval street plan, the exposed bastions of the Roman wall. Time is lying there in front of me. . . . something happens to me standing there in the rubble, looking at old walls. I am excited, I am lifted out of the prison of my own head and glimpse something larger." Lively traces her adult preoccupation with the vagaries of historical representation to another adolescent encounter with architecture: touring an old church with her grandmother, she had an epiphany while gazing at a stone effigy, realizing that "this is true; there were actually people like this; this actually happened." The moment was significant enough for her to fictionalize later in her children's novel *The Stained Glass Window* (1976), and it set her on a path of historical inquiry that has woven its way through her entire oeuvre.

Once free of the intellectually repressive confines of secondary education, Lively was finally able to parlay her interest in the past into a course of study. She attended St. Anne's College, Oxford, where she took a B.A. in modern history in 1954. Upon completing her degree she worked for a short period as a research assistant at St. Antony's College, Oxford. There she met Jack Lively, a political theorist. The couple married in 1957 and have two children: Josephine, born in 1958, who became a professional oboist, and Adam, born in 1961, who like his mother is a novelist. Since Jack Lively's retirement from the University of Warwick, he and Penelope have divided their time between a farmhouse in Oxfordshire and a townhouse in northern London.

Making up for the absence of her own parents, upon her marriage Lively threw herself into full-time motherhood—and simultaneously into a demanding program of reading in which she attempted to fill in the gaps left by her irregular education. By the time her younger child entered school, she was ready to try her hand at writing, and she chose children's fiction, as she had read so much of it to her own children.

Lively's first attempt at a novel was, by her own assessment, a fairly awful historical tale. On her second try, however, she produced *Astercote* (1970), which was immediately accepted for publication. In the decades since, hardly a year has gone by in which she has not published a novel or story collection; in addition, she writes scripts, book reviews, essays, and assorted journalism. Like many of her novels—both those written for children and those intended for adults—*Astercote* is not precisely an historical novel but rather a novel about history. Set in the present day, *Astercote* juxtaposes a modern housing estate with the ghostly echoes of the medieval village that predated it. Fact blends with fantasy as the child heroes of the novel must discover and restore an ancient chalice and thus avert the return of the Black Death, which destroyed the original Astercote six hundred years before.

Myth and history join forces once more in *The Whispering Knights* (1971) when a woman trying to route a superhighway through a peaceful village—thus destroying ancient landmarks—is revealed to be a contemporary manifestation of Morgan le Fay. Appropriately enough, she is destroyed when the protagonists lure her into the center of an ancient circle of standing stones that in the distant past served as a protection against evil. *The Wild Hunt of Hagworthy* (1971) also presents a picture of evil spirits from the past raised in the present by the revival of an ancient dance with masks and antlers.

Not all of Lively's historical spirits are malevolent; on the contrary, many are relatively harmless and in fact do much to educate and enlarge the perceptions of the children to whom they appear. The protagonist of *The Driftaway* (1972) is a runaway picked up by an old man, who gradually describes to the boy ghostly visions he once had on the same road down which they are traveling. Soon, the boy is having visions of his own: people from the past telling the story of the road from sometimes conflicting perspectives. Exposed to so many different points of view, the runaway realizes the tricky nature of his own subjectivity and elects to return home to try to understand his family better. *The Driftaway* earned Lively the Children's Spring Book Festival Award in 1973.

Also in 1973 Lively published perhaps her best-known children's novel, *The Ghost of Thomas Kempe,* which won a Carnegie Medal later that year. The eponymous spirit of the novel is a seventeenth-century sorcerer who haunts his former house, currently the home of ten-year-old James. Thomas Kempe is distressed by the incursion of modern science into village life and is making a ruckus trying to put a stop to it. James, in turn, sets out to stop Thomas, as he is being blamed for the poltergeist's activities. Along the way James discovers that Thomas made an earlier appearance in the nineteenth century and that a boy his age had succeeded in exorcising him. Using that earlier boy's diaries and notes, James likewise convinces Thomas Kempe to take long-awaited retirement.

In addition to Lively's books about the overlap of past and present, several of her children's novels—chiefly those intended for slightly younger audiences—are more purely historical fiction. *Boy without a Name* (1975) is set in the seventeenth century and focuses on an orphan who knows nothing of his environment, not even the name of the country he lives in. *Fanny's Sister* (1976), *Fanny and the Monsters* (1979), and *Fanny and the Battle of Potter's Piece* (1980) depict the life of a large, middle-class household in mid Victorian England, centering on the realistic adventures of a nine-year-old tomboy. All three Fanny books were later collected into a single volume, *Fanny and the Monsters: And Other Stories,* published by Puffin in 1982.

Some of Lively's other books for very young readers eschew history entirely. *The Voyage of QV66* (1978) and *A House Inside Out* (1987) are, respectively, a novel and a collection of interlinked short stories told from the perspective of various animals. *Dragon Trouble* (1984), *Uninvited Ghosts and Other Stories* (1984), and *Debbie and the Little Devil* (1987) have contemporary settings and concern children who become aware of supernatural or otherwise mysterious occurrences in their homes.

Lively may have found it possible to move over time into less profound subject matter in her children's books because she discovered an outlet for her more philosophical musings in adult fiction. Three of her novels from the mid 1970s mark this transition in her writing: originally intended for older children, they nonetheless stretch further in the direction of adult readers. While still concerned with the interplay of past and present that characterizes her work from *Astercote* through *The Ghost of Thomas Kempe, The House in Norham Gardens* (1974), *Going Back* (1975), and *A Stitch in Time* (1976) primarily utilize the idiom of realism, not fantasy. History appears to the protagonists of these novels not in the guise of literal ghosts but as a more subtly nuanced sense of the forces of time and place. The books also show a penchant for stylistic experimentation more commonly found in adult fiction and a greater concern with the personal transformation of their protagonists.

The House in Norham Gardens, which has been compared stylistically with the work of Virginia Woolf, concerns fourteen-year-old Clare's discovery of a New Guinea artifact collected by her anthropologist grandfather. Already sensitive to echoes from the past, Clare is prompted by her find to investigate the tribe that produced her grandfather's shield and finds that its members do not understand time as chronological. Because their belief system does not encompass the ideas of past and future, they dwell in an eternal present that coexists with, but bears little relationship to, Clare's world of modern-day Oxford. Lively's narrative structure imitates Clare's discoveries, interspersing scenes of Clare's everyday life with scenes from New Guinea; thus, reader and protagonist come simultaneously to an understanding of the subjective nature of time.

Going Back marks a striking departure from Lively's earlier work, both stylistically and thematically. Although most of the novel describes the experiences of two children on a farm during World War II, the text is framed by opening and. closing scenes of one of these children as a grown woman, and the novel is narrated throughout in the first person, from this woman's adult perspective. The plot of *Going Back* is relatively simple: a brother and sister live in a peace only occasionally shattered by the incursions of their harsh and uncomprehending father; when the brother is sent to an uncongenial boarding school, the two run away briefly to see a sympathetic young man who has befriended them. The simplicity of the plot of the novel, however, belies its far more complicated underlying subject matter: the operation of memory. A Proustian reverie, the story-within-a-story structure of *Going Back* serves as the narrator's attempt not only to recapture her own past but also to understand the elusive way in which her mind has constructed it:

> Remembering is like that. There's what you know happened, and what you think happened. And then there's the business that what you know happened isn't always what you remember. Things are fudged by time: years fuse together. . . .
>
> People's lives tell a story, I thought once: and then, and next, and then. . . . But they don't. Nothing so

Lively in Egypt with her nanny, Lucy, 1943

simple. If it's a story at all, then there are two of them, running side by side. What actually happened, and what we remember. Which is more important, I wonder?

Lively based the environs of *Going Back* on her memories of her grandmother's house in West Somerset, and thus "in describing it I was using that very function of memory that I was trying to suggest in the book—the fragmented, dreamy, preserved quality of selective recollection."

A Stitch in Time, for which Lively won the Whitbread Award in 1976, revisits some of the same territory as *The Ghost of Thomas Kempe* but does so with an increased level of sophistication. Eleven-year-old Maria, a solitary child, is spending a summer holiday with her family in a rented Victorian house in Lyme Regis. During the course of the summer she becomes powerfully drawn to the wide variety of relics that surround her: she learns about the fossils for which the area is famous and also about a girl her age named Harriet, who one hundred years before lived in the house and, like Maria, hunted fossils, producing detailed representations of them in drawings and in a cross-stitch sampler.

The line between fantasy and reality in *A Stitch in Time* is ambiguous. Maria often hears strange noises about the house, but it is left up to the reader to determine to what extent these represent actual spiritual apparitions and to what extent they merely symbolize the echoes of the past picked up by a highly imaginative and sensitive child. Maria is unsure how to characterize her experiences, but with growing maturity—what she describes as "this odd process of changing into someone a little different"—recognizes that there are many different ways beyond a literal haunting for the past to interact with the present: "it came to her, as she turned to go into the house, that places are like clocks. They've got all the time in them there's ever been, everything that's happened. They go on and on, with things that have happened hidden in them, if you can find them, like you find the fossils if you break the rock."

A precursor to many of her later adult novels, *A Stitch in Time* is also significant in that it draws a parallel between the layers of history that go toward making up a place and the similar layers that constitute an individual. Just as Maria learns in growing up to appreciate the complicated interaction of continuity and change in her surroundings, so she discovers that the process of maturation creates a similar effect in her person: "Harriet became Mrs. Harriet Stanton, she thought (a bit stout, with sons), and I'll end up as somebody quite different too, but in a funny way we'll both go on being here forever, aged ten or eleven one summer, because we once were." Thus Maria has stumbled upon the idea that Lively hopes her readers will also find food for thought: that there is an inescapable "interlocking of people with place and time . . . that our lives run for their short span against the greater continuity of history. Even if you are eight or nine or thirteen and as ignorant as sin, you can grasp that astonishing idea and be enlarged by it."

The Road to Lichfield, Lively's first novel marketed for adults, was critically well received, landing her on the shortlist for the Booker Prize that year. The road to Lichfield is, literally, the road that takes Anne Linton from her everyday existence as history teacher, wife, and mother of two to the bedside of her father, who lies dying in a nursing home. The hundred-mile journey, which Anne repeatedly makes over the course of a spring and summer, leads her not only from one place to another but also from ignorance to knowledge of her father and herself. The examination of her father's financial records reveals years of mysterious payments to an unknown woman; investigating, Anne discovers a long-hidden mistress in her father's past. Slightly in shock from this unexpected revelation about his secret existence apart from his role as her father, Anne finds her own conduct unexpectedly mimicking his, as she becomes embroiled in an affair with a former neighbor of his who comes to visit.

Narrated in short, often impressionistic bursts, *The Road to Lichfield* moves from character to character, presenting the reader not only with Anne's point of view but also with those of her father, her lover, her husband, and her brother. Unexpected alliances and sympathies emerge, as well as unexpected divisions. As the summer draws to a close, lives shift and rearrange: Anne's father dies, her love affair whimpers to an unsatisfactory conclusion, and the historic cottage she has been half-heartedly working to save is bulldozed in her absence. Only the road remains, a symbol of the network of human relationships it has both enabled and forever altered: "The night both concealed and revealed. Anne thought: I knew this road, or imagined I did, but now it seems different. . . . places have this way of being unreliable, never quite as constant as you think they are going to be. You think you have them under control, and then find that you have not."

The Road to Lichfield was followed by *Nothing Missing but the Samovar* (1978), a collection of fourteen short stories that won the Southern Arts Literary Prize. A second selection of eleven tales, *Corruption,* came out in 1984; the contents of both books were then republished as a single volume, *Pack of Cards,* in 1986. Lively's short fiction is highly varied in topic and tone: some tales reflect the same interests in time and history that pervade her novels; some are satirical social snapshots; and still others call upon her own adolescent confusion when plunged into English life at age twelve and feature young foreigners attempting to deal with their loneliness and outsider status. In "Bones in the Sand" (1981) Lively claims that her short stories are more explicitly autobiographical than her longer works and has described her dependence on what she calls "the digestion of memory" in writing them: "A number of these have derived from experiences of my own twenty years or more ago; at the time the experiences seemed quite without significance. Years later, I have been able to see them in another light, and use them as the vehicle for a story that illuminates something that was in no way apparent to me at the time." Stylistically, the stories are more concise than the novels, translating the author's epiphanic remembrances into brief but powerful glimpses of moments in their characters' lives. Lively notes that this kind of concision is "the great strength of the short story as a literary form; it gives the writer the opportunity to make a point that could not or should not be expanded into a novel but that may have quite as much impact or significance."

Also by Penelope Lively

THE ROAD TO LICHFIELD

Short-listed for the Booker Prize, 1977

'A beautifully observed story of illicit love and modern marriage, and the subtle influences of the past on the present. Honest, moving, full of quiet quality.'
The Sunday Express

'Time and change is a pattern that recurs constantly in the story of Anne visiting her dying father and loving someone else's husband. Penelope Lively shows her awareness of the relations between individuals: husbands, lovers, children, and parents.'
The Northern Echo

'An ingeniously constructed tale of one of those crucial periods in an individual's life when past and present reach a turning-point. The story slowly but decisively establishes its hold on the reader.'
British Book News

NOTHING MISSING BUT THE SAMOVAR and other stories

Winner of the 1978 Southern Arts Literature Prize

'Thank goodness for Penelope Lively! Her new book shines brilliantly; Her first adult novel established her as a writer of subtlety and compression . . . these stories strongly underline her talent.'
The Daily Telegraph

'Each tale is such an illumination of the human condition that you just have to keep on reading from first to last.'
Good Housekeeping Magazine

'The 14 stories are linked by a pervading sense of menace, a feeling that everything that really matters is on the edge of going wrong – love, children's security, the touch of the supernatural.'
The Birmingham Post

PENELOPE LIVELY
TREASURES OF TIME

PENELOPE LIVELY

TREASURES OF TIME

A NOVEL

Dust jacket for Lively's 1979 novel, in which the making of a television documentary about a deceased archaeologist stirs up resentments among his family

In *Treasures of Time* (1979), Lively's next adult novel, public and private history intersect when a well-meaning but glib television producer undertakes to film a biography of a deceased archaeologist, Hugh Paxton. Drawn into the production are Paxton's widow, Laura; her daughter, Kate; Kate's fiancé; and Laura's sister, Nellie. With the exception of Laura, each of these characters is, like Paxton, professionally involved in the study of the past: Kate is a museum curator; her fiancé, Tom, is a doctoral student researching a seventeenth-century antiquarian; and Nellie is an archaeologist and former colleague of Paxton's. Laura, who is selfish, shallow, and beautiful and, as Tom notes upon first meeting her, has an "extraordinary knack of instantly putting everyone else at a disadvantage," dominates those around her.

As the production gets under way, the significance of Paxton's discoveries pales beside the complicated maneuvers his family and associates undergo in trying to assess and present his life and work for popular consumption. Shifting between the perspectives of each of the major characters, *Treasures of Time* reveals a messy collection of partially obscured truths and disturbing possibilities beneath the neat facade that the documentarian is attempting to construct. Nellie, who worked alongside Paxton for many years, had loved him all the while, even as he married Laura. Laura was insecure and jealous of her husband's friendship with her sister and used her sexual charms to get positive reinforcement from other men. Paxton's work, while valuable, was nonetheless of variable significance.

Meanwhile, the sins and omissions of the past are more than equaled by those of the present. Laura manipulates those around her at every opportunity: most egregiously, she infantilizes and ignores Nellie, who is wheelchairbound and semimute after a stroke. Nellie's mental faculties are as sharp as ever, but clearly, Laura enjoys her sister's dependence and hopes that she will not recover. Tom and Kate, who at the beginning of the novel are contentedly in love, slip further and further apart: he is driven away by Kate's insecurities and irrational jealousy, induced by her mother.

Throughout the novel the complex interplay of the characters' lives is counterpoised with meditations—some from Tom's perspective and some by an anonymous authorial voice—about the nature and role of history and the dangers of romanticizing the past. Laura's evasions and selective memories in private are counterpoised by the public glossiness of the documentary. Despite Tom's misgivings, however, and immediately following a viewing of the completed television program in which he is continually aware of all its inadequacies, the novel closes with his having accepted a job as a researcher for the producer. *Treasures of Time* earned Lively the Arts Council of Great Britain National Book Award.

Judgement Day (1980) shifts Lively's focus firmly from the world of the past to the world of the present. Although set around a village square occupied by an Anglo-Saxon church and loosely revolving around an historical pageant designed to raise money for its renovation, the novel is much more concerned with the everyday lives of the inhabitants of the square. Chief among these are George Radwell, the vicar; Clare Paling, a housewife and new resident; and Sydney Porter, the solitary churchwarden. George is a less-than-ideal priest, lacking both faith and social skills. Clare, with whom he becomes fascinated, is a bright and energetic agnostic who runs rings around him at every encounter. Sydney is a reserved and compulsive man still fighting to keep at bay memories of his wife and daughter, killed in the London Blitz.

Sydney's long-ago brush with the violent mysteries of fate turns out to prefigure the central dramatic elements of the novel and the debate they engender. A freak air accident, shattering an otherwise peaceful day; a senseless act of vandalism, committed by unknown aggressors; and the unexpected death of a child, hit by an errant motorist: in the context of the novel, these events could be either acts of God or pure happenstance. The book concludes with a lengthy exchange between Clare and George, in which each tries to come to terms with the blindness of fate, the balance between faith and hope, and their different, ultimately both inadequate, ways of attempting to make sense of the world.

After the probing questions of *Judgement Day, Next to Nature, Art* (1982) strikes a contrast as Lively's most comic novel. A sharp satire focused on a trendy, for-profit arts-education course, the novel skewers both instructors and students, debunking their mutual illusion that the pursuit of Art somehow raises one above the level of common humanity. The course is taught at a decaying country estate that was once itself a work of art, designed by William Kent to please eighteenth-century aesthetic sensibilities: "twenty-five acres in which the disordered was cunningly turned into a contrivance, in which the physical world was made an artistic product, in which nature became art." Currently, the park is overgrown; the house is falling into disrepair; and the occupants are a motley crew of self-centered pleasure seekers possessed of dubious quantities of talent, judgment, or taste. The limitations of the would-be artists' colony are conveyed by such examples as the piece of statuary that has replaced a vanished Apollo on a plinth at the apex of the woodland ride: sculptor Paula's *Introspective Woman,* "an abstract sculpture of welded bicycle frames and silver-sprayed nylon fruit netting."

Initially impressed by the idea of working with real artists and seduced—in some cases literally—by their instructors' carefully contrived charisma, the eleven disparate members of the course undergo disillusionment at varying rates of speed. The absence of a kitchen staff, the generally seedy nature of the surroundings, and the questionable nature of the productions being touted as art all dovetail with the students' growing recognition of their instructors' feet of clay. The climax of the course is a drunken party, during which fleeting alliances are formed and broken, and utter chaos is barely kept at bay. At the end of a week's "instruction" the disgruntled students return to their daily lives. The opportunistic Tony, owner of Framleigh Hall and organizer of the arts program, has ensured the future of the course by roping in a couple of wealthy investors.

With *Perfect Happiness* (1983) Lively returns from social satire to her more usual finely nuanced explorations into human relationships and emotions. *Perfect Happiness* details the recovery process of forty-nine-year-old Frances Brooklyn after the sudden death of her husband, Steven. The novel centers on the ties between Frances; her daughter, Tabitha; and her sister-in-law and old friend, Zoe—who, as is revealed in a series of flashbacks, is actually Tabitha's birth mother. The narrative takes place over the course of half a year, eight months after Steven's death, and documents Frances's slow reclamation of her life as well as her frequent backsliding into despair. She moves to a new house, develops friends of her own, and, finally, takes a job as an editorial assistant. Throughout this process she is haunted—once to the point of near mental collapse—with flashbacks and memories of her married life. Her ability to take charge of the present, she finally realizes, is dependent on her ability to take charge of her past: "I must not, she thought with sudden clarity, be forever hitched to what has been. Only to such of it as I choose, to such of it that will sustain me."

In *According to Mark* (1984) Lively returns to the theme of collective rather than individual memory and dips into the territory of several of her earlier novels for narrative elements. Like *Treasures of Time, According to Mark* depicts an historical researcher delving into the life of his subject and attempting to reconcile various strands and inconsistencies. Like *Road to Lichfield,* the novel plots the protagonist's discovery of a long-ago affair against the course of his own contemporary one. The researcher in this case is Mark Lamming, a professional biographer; his subject is Gilbert Strong, an early-twentieth-century man of letters "sort of on the edge of . . . Vanessa and Roger and Duncan and Virginia and all that crew." The novel opens as Mark is driving for the first time to Dean Close, Strong's former home, which for financial reasons is currently being run as a combination historic site and Garden Centre.

At Dean Close, Mark makes two unexpected discoveries: a hitherto unheard-of cache of letters and two trunks containing papers in the attic; and Strong's granddaughter, Carrie, who is the proprietress of the Garden Centre. The first find understandably thrills him and draws him back to Dean Close repeatedly for weekend visits. The second is initially uninspiring: Carrie is young, provokingly passive, and shockingly uneducated. Several of the more entertaining passages in the novel consist of meetings between Mark and Carrie, in which she politely and somewhat desperately attempts to make conversation about his work. Far from derogating Carrie, Lively uses such encounters to poke a sly jab at Mark's almost singleminded obsessiveness, implying that a little more perspective might enable him to do his job somewhat better.

Over the course of his increasingly frequent trips to Dean Close, the happily married Mark finds himself inexplicably falling in love with Carrie, and the two are carried into a brief and comic affair. Meanwhile, Mark discovers from the Dean Close papers that Strong had himself had a previously unknown love affair that was neither brief nor comic. As Mark explores the mounting evidence of Strong's secret life, he debates with himself and with colleagues the possibly prurient nature of the biographer's art, as well as the impossibility of coming to a definitive conclusion about a subject's life. As a fellow biographer puts it, "'There are plenty of things . . . we shall never know. One plows on. In pursuit of truth, or whatever.' Mark suppressed a comment about that 'whatever,' which might have been taken amiss. 'It's enough to drive a person to fiction.'" The novel concludes, as does *Treasures of Time,* with Lively's description of a broadcast biography punctuated by her historian protagonist's reflections on its inevitable distortions. *According to Mark* earned Lively her second nomination to the shortlist for the Booker Prize.

With *Moon Tiger* Lively produced what is considered her most accomplished novel and, after her string of honorable mentions, finally won the Booker. A tour de force of kaleidoscopic narrative fragments, *Moon Tiger* represents the deathbed recollections of Claudia

Dust jacket for Lively's 1982 novel, a satire of a would-be artists' colony

Hampton, who is, as she tells her nurse, "writing a history of the world"—or more specifically, "the bit of the twentieth century to which I've been shackled, willy-nilly"—from her perspective as a journalist, historian, lover, and mother. Shifting back and forth from first person to third and periodically interjecting other characters' points of view, Lively weaves Claudia's tale into a vivid and compelling tapestry.

One of the most complex of Lively's protagonists, Claudia is alternately charismatic and infuriating: passionate, self-centered, difficult, and always aware of her own keen intelligence, she has marched through life seeking intellectual sparring partners, casually ignoring the many people—including her only child, Lisa—who do not seem up to the sport. Claudia is also, perhaps, Lively's most articulate spokeswoman on the subject of history: what humans understand it to be, how they make it, how it fits into their lives, and how lives fit into it. Claudia has been passionate about history since she was a child. Her first exposure to the historical method was in her childhood squabbles with her brother, Gordon: "Argument, of course, is the whole point of history. Disagreement; my word against yours. . . . If there were ever such a thing as absolute truth the debate would lose its lustre. I, for one, would no longer be interested."

Claudia is also, as it turns out, passionate about another aspect of her life: the years during World War II when she worked as a war correspondent in Egypt and fell unexpectedly in love with a British tank commander. Although interpretations of history may vary, Claudia notes, she believes that "the past rests upon certain central and indisputable facts. So does life; it has its core, its centre." Her years in Egypt, and her experiences there, form the core of her life, as well as the core of the novel. Living in an alien culture, in the day-to-day fashion that war necessitates, Claudia and Tom Southern meet, fall in love, and find in one another vistas onto worlds outside of themselves. With Claudia, Tom discovers the thought-provoking consequences of "being hitched to one's times in a way one never anticipated"; with Tom, Claudia actually perceives the culture of Egypt for the first time.

Claudia's love affair is brought tragically to a close with Tom's death in the Western Desert campaign. She picks up and moves on; she has other lovers, a child, and a successful career. Yet, Tom is the love of her life, and although she is not destroyed by his death, she is forever shaped by it. A moon tiger, the novel explains, is a mosquito coil that slowly burns away all night, until "its green spiral is mirrored by a grey ash spiral in the saucer." The moon tiger is an apt metaphor for Claudia's life, which spirals about a central core, burning away yet leaving a skeleton behind from which its initial contours may be traced. In *Moon Tiger* Lively manages to explore both the transience of human experience and its enduring effects to depict a vibrant, seemingly unconquerable woman and still make explicit that after her death "the world moves on."

After using *Moon Tiger* to draw for the first time on the landscape and sensations of her Egyptian childhood, Lively returned to England in *Passing On* (1989), a novel set in a small village at the outer rim of the Cotswolds, portraying two middle-aged siblings in the aftermath of their mother's death. Dorothy Glover was not a nice woman, as her children are the first to admit. Nonetheless, Helen and Edward chose to remain living with her in the family house, Greystones, for the better part of their fifty years; only Louise, their much younger sister, managed to break away and move to London. Of the two elder siblings, Edward's stasis is by far the more understandable: he is passive and unbearably awkward, and his only attempt to live away from home proved him to be quite unfit for the task of interacting with others. His life is a seemingly contented round of teaching in a second-rate local girls' school and nature watching in The Britches, a small plot of woodland on the Glovers' property. Helen's position is somewhat more mysterious, and *Passing On* focuses primarily on her thoughts and actions as she sifts literally and metaphorically through the layers of her life with her mother and tries to come to conclusions about both her past and her future.

Over the course of *Passing On,* as Helen sorts through her mother's possessions, cleaning up Greystones in a manner that Edward finds unnerving, both siblings are forced to confront aspects of themselves that they have, with Dorothy's chilling encouragement, denied for many years. Helen finds herself falling in love with their solicitor, the flirtatious Giles Carnaby, but her encounters with him are haunted by her mother's imagined voice, telling her "she was fifty-two years old, no beauty and never had been and would do better to pull herself together and think about something else." Alongside her developing crush, Helen discovers in various locations in the house–tucked into an old coat pocket, for example, or crammed under wastepaper at the bottom of a chest–graphic physical evidence of the way her mother has over the years undermined Helen's forays into love. Edward gazes uncomprehendingly on Helen's infatuation with Giles, yet momentary glimpses past his tight internal defenses allow the reader to see that he too yearns for some kind of human connection beyond that which he has thus far known.

Both Helen's and Edward's sexual awakenings end badly. Helen, discovering that Giles has been toying with her, forces herself to the embarrassing point of admitting her feelings for him and then breaking off their association. Edward, far more traumatically, makes a clumsy pass at a neighbor boy who works in their garden. The boy's father, more concerned with gaining an advantage than with his son's well-being, tries to use the event to blackmail the Glovers into selling him The Britches for development.

At the end of the novel the three Glover siblings sit together, as they had after their mother's funeral, and find that "her presence now was dimmer, she was no longer the insistent unavoidable black hole that she had been on the earlier occasion." Helen and Edward, scarred most by what Dorothy had been in her lifetime and what has come about in the time since her death, are left reflecting on the same theme: "they saw that there is nothing to be done, but that something can be retrieved. Both sniffed the air; each, gingerly, made resolutions."

Following her foray into the solely domestic, personal history of *Passing On,* Lively moves in *City of the Mind* to a broader, more sweeping canvas: the city of London and the many private and public influences that have gone into its construction during approximately two thousand years. As a portrait of a metropolis, *City of the Mind* is in the tradition of such classics of city fiction as Virginia Woolf's *Mrs. Dalloway* (1925) and James Joyce's *Ulysses* (1922). Its finely textured images of streets and squares, sounds and smells, and buildings and their inhabitants convey with vivid intensity both the quotidian life of the city and its recurring moments of crisis.

The plot of *City of the Mind,* like that of Joyce's and Woolf's novels, follows the path of a single character as he traverses the city—in Lively's case, over the course of half a year rather than a single day. Matthew Halland, architect and divorced father, is precisely the kind of man to appreciate and share with readers the many-layered tapestry that is contemporary London: "The whole place is a chronicle, in brick and stone, in silent eloquence, for those who have eyes and ears. For such as Matthew. Through him, the city lives and breathes; it sheds its indifference, its impervious attachment to both then and now, and bears witness." Like most of Lively's protagonists, Matthew is an intelligent, principled, perceptive man, highly attuned to echoes of history in his surroundings and prone to philosophical speculation about his responsibility to the past and to the future:

> This is a pile of bricks. Carefully arranged bricks, I grant you, but bricks nonetheless. You may call it a late Georgian house with a neo-classical portico and Coad stone dressings. Others might just call it a house. . . . You can pull it to pieces in order to build something else with the bricks. You can pull it down in order to use the space it occupies for another building. Or you can give it a new significance because you have stopped thinking about it as simply a pile of bricks. This is what we're doing.

Matthew travels around London visiting potential and actual sites architectural projects for his firm and marveling at the symphony of brick and stone that surrounds him. Like other Lively protagonists, he combines a love of the past with a fierce insistence on the need to see it for what it is, unblinkered by romantic illusions: the eighteenth century produced exquisite Georgian terraces but also its share of filth and disease. In his attacks on mindless antiquarianism, Matthew speaks for his creator, who believes that "the visual past of an object does not exist unless somebody looks at it with understanding." Matthew is not a knee-jerk preservationist, but he struggles daily to find a balance between

Dust jacket for Lively's 1991 novel, which follows a divorced architect in his journeys around London

his desire to respect the past and his need to make his own mark on the city skyline.

Although *City of the Mind* is in some ways the novel of Lively's that is most concerned with public rather than private development, Matthew's architectural walkabouts are complemented by exquisitely rendered scenes of his time with his daughter, Jane, and by his growing love for Sarah Bridges, an art editor he has serendipitously encountered in the course of his rambles. The human element of the novel gains further depth from Lively's insertion of impressionistic scenes from the past in London: Matthew's narrative of the city is periodically punctuated by the experiences of nineteenth-century paleontologist Richard Owen, of a fire warden during the Blitz, of a starving street urchin, and of Martin Frobisher, the Elizabethan navigator after whom Matthew is naming his new Docklands office tower. The novel thus illustrates Lively's belief, expressed in "Bones in the Sand," that "the revelation that there is a collective past is also the revelation that

that collective past is composed of myriad private pasts, that the pursuit of social memory is matched by the need for personal memory." The web of interconnected visions that makes up *City of the Mind* also serves to demonstrate that London, in one sense only a pile of bricks, is given meaning and brought to life by the people who inhabit it, all of whose lives touch one another in sometimes mysterious and invisible ways.

Cleopatra's Sister (1993) shares with *City of the Mind* the narrative element of an utterly serendipitous love affair. In *Cleopatra's Sister,* however, Lively explicitly uses this relationship to underscore her central theme: the fascinating puzzle of historical contingency. The plot of the novel concerns two thirty-something Britons–Howard Beamish, a paleontologist, and Lucy Faulkner, a journalist–and their unexpected involvement with one another and with the imaginary Mediterranean country of Callimbia, which was once, ostensibly, ruled by Cleopatra's sister. The first half of the novel is divided into alternating chapters describing the separate histories of Howard, Lucy, and Callimbia and the string of defining moments that have shaped each of them into what they are. Throughout the novel Lively suggests that free choice and decisive action play only a minor role in the way the world works: "Howard Beamish became a paleontologist because of a rise in the interest rate when he was six years old. His father, a cautious man with a large mortgage, announced that the projected family holiday to the Costa Brava was no longer feasible. A chalet was rented on the north Somerset coast instead and thus, on a dank August afternoon, Howard picked up an ammonite on Blue Anchor Beach."

Just as Howard is brought to his life's work–to which he nonetheless turns out to be perfectly suited–by this early accident of fate, so Howard, Lucy, and Callimbia are brought together at the crucial moment by a series of random occurrences. In the second half of the novel their three narratives converge into a single story: as a result of everything that has previously occurred in their lives, Howard and Lucy both happen to be on an airplane that is bound for Nairobi but instead is forced by mechanical difficulties to land in Callimbia. Callimbia, as it happens, has just had a military coup. Certain enemies of the new regime have fled to Britain seeking asylum; British passengers on the downed flight are held hostage as a bargaining tool, and Howard and Lucy are thrown into an enforced proximity that blossoms rapidly into love.

In "Bones in the Sand" Lively writes that "I am preoccupied, both as a person and as a novelist, with the relationship between private and public life–the way in which we are . . . the children of circumstance, played with by the cruelties and kindnesses of random fate, bound up with an historical process that few people feel they can influence or alter." Throughout *Cleopatra's Sister* she probes this theme, dancing neatly around the fine line between contingency and destiny. Howard and Lucy are soul mates, yet their meeting can be ascribed to nothing more than blind fate. Moreover, they find themselves in precisely the right place at the right time only because they are in the wrong place at the wrong time. In the end Lively advocates embracing the complexities of life rather than throwing one's hands up in helplessness at the capriciousness of fate, as Howard reflects:

> All he could feel, right now, was that explanations and revelations had nothing to do with what had happened and could not be undone, with the whole contingent sequence. He considered this sequence: he dismantled it and looked at its component parts, at moments which could have flown off in some other direction, at the whole precarious narrative. The narrative which had dealt him Lucy and which, by the same token, might yet remove her, in which perhaps there lurked already some fatal twist, some malevolent disposition of events. He stared for an instant at capricious fate, and then turned away, because that is all anyone can do.

With *Oleander, Jacaranda* Lively turns away from fiction into an exploration of the historical contingencies that have made her what she is today. An intriguing narrative set in 1930s and 1940s Cairo, *Oleander, Jacaranda* is both a memoir and a reflection on the nature of childhood and a child's perception of the world. Lively writes, "my childhood is no more–or less–interesting than anyone else's. It has two particularities. One is that I was the product of one society but was learning how to perceive the world in the ambience of quite a different culture. I grew up English, in Egypt. The other is that I was cared for by someone who was not my mother, and that it was a childhood which came to an abrupt and traumatic end." These two particularities structure Lively's account as she details the activities and intense emotional bond she shared with her nurse and attempts to recapture what she calls "the anarchic vision of childhood," all against a background of lush sensory input and cultural confusion.

Oleander, Jacaranda will feel strikingly familiar to regular readers of Lively's fiction–not because of its setting and details, which bear little resemblance to anything other than the Egyptian sections of *Moon Tiger,* but because of the way these details are put together and analyzed. Lively here employs to good effect the kaleidoscopic narrative technique of her best novels, interspersing fragmentary recollections from her childhood with adult reassessments of events, bits of history, and philosophical speculations about the subjective nature of perception. Certain of her novelistic themes emerge,

Lively and her husband, Jack

linked to specific memories, allowing the reader to see the underpinnings of the fiction in the life. The layering of different ages within the self, ruminated on by Maria in *A Stitch in Time* and Claudia in *Moon Tiger,* can be found in Lively's own reported revisiting of childhood scenes, her memories overlaid with the perceptions of subsequent viewings. Her interest in the randomness of fate and how it affects lives, also displayed in *Cleopatra's Sister,* is here grounded in the perplexing childhood pre-occupation with decoding the symbols both of the physical world and of adult behavior: the "curious miscellany" of memories that remain available to her, she writes, "mirrors my own ten-year-old concerns—the dazzling appearance of the world, and the perversity of its ways."

The final short chapter of Lively's memoir deals with her move to England, which she describes as the end of her childhood. She is separated from her childhood home and caregiver and passes from a period of relative happiness and naïveté into one of miserable knowledge. Yet, despite the negative associations of this transition, and despite the fact that *Oleander, Jacaranda* is

a book that celebrates the vision of childhood, the closing mood is not one of despair and loss. For Lively the end of childhood and childhood vision brings with it a valuable new adult awareness of the world beyond herself and of her connection to that world. Like Claudia of *Moon Tiger* before she met Tom, Lively's childhood self did not have the means necessary to process what she saw around her: "A perception of landscape is something learned—it depends on individual knowledge and experience. At the age of ten, a mud hut to me was a mud hut, and could not be seen in the light of prehistory." To Lively adulthood is signaled by the development of the kind of context that will let one think of a mud hut or a pile of bricks as something more. *Oleander, Jacaranda* ends with a further explanation of her adolescent epiphany upon being taken to see the bombed-out city of London, an outing designed to take her mind off her homesickness. A fragment of Roman wall is pointed out to her, and her attention is attracted not only by the interesting association of Roman ruins in London with Roman ruins in Cairo but also by the idea that caring about this, as opposed to her own private misery, is a distinctly adult concern. "It was as though the exposure of that chunk of wall had also shown up concealed possibilities. I sniffed the liberations of maturity and grew up a little more, there amid the wreckage of London and the seething spires of willow herb."

Lively's most recent novel, *Heat Wave* (1996), takes place over the course of a summer in two adjoining nineteenth-century fieldworkers' cottages, known collectively as World's End, that are currently serving to house Pauline; Pauline's daughter, Teresa; Teresa's husband, Maurice; and their baby, Luke. Both Pauline and Maurice are involved in the literary trade: this summer she is editing a promising first novel about romantic love, and he is writing a study of the tourist industry and how it exploits natural and manmade environments. Both topics prove to be curiously apropos as the events of the summer unfold in slow but emotionally intense progression.

Maurice's study of tourism becomes in Lively's hands a metaphor for the way appearances can mislead. What seems quaintly historic may easily be a theatrical stage set or, even if it possesses a genuine antiquity, may still hide unsuspected depths behind its facade. World's End, for example, "is suspended in this landscape like a space capsule, with its machinery quietly humming—its computers, its phones, its faxes. Its microwaves, its freezers, its televisions and videos. World's End in fact is nicely disguised, like one of those turfed-over bunkers kitted out as command posts in the event of nuclear attack." The dual nature of their home—its shifting levels of reality and history—also serves to characterize World's End's inhabitants, who are each an amalgam of experience and memory, presenting different facets in different lights.

These shifting layers of vision are perceived primarily by Pauline, the controlling consciousness of the novel. Her summer is one of peaceful rural retirement and productivity but also almost unbearable anguish, as she sees Teresa reliving traumatic aspects of her mother's past. Pauline's editorship of a novel about love provides commentary on the relationships of the novel: Teresa's surpassing love for Maurice matches the obsessive love Pauline bore for Teresa's father, Harry; and just as Harry betrayed Pauline with a string of mistresses, turning her life for a period of years into a morass of self-destroying jealousy, so Maurice is setting foot on the path of betrayal. As Pauline watches her daughter with her husband and son, she dips repeatedly back into her memories, seeing Teresa both as the child she once was and as the young woman Pauline was at her age. As Teresa becomes more and more unhappy, Pauline becomes more and more enraged.

Equally important to the story of romantic love and infidelity in *Heat Wave* is its story of maternal love.

Lively, always a skilled and compassionate observer of the relationship between parents and children, convincingly portrays the depth of Pauline's painful maternal identification with Teresa and the delicate balance mother and daughter strike as they circle around issues involving the men in their lives. Lively also utilizes a great many of the ideas about childhood perception that she developed in *Oleander, Jacaranda,* portraying the daily life of eighteen-month-old Luke, who lives in a whirl of accelerated time and dazzling physical sensations. At times his infancy seems to place him in a world apart from his adults; sometimes, Pauline speculates, it brings him all too close:

> "Luke is now in a condition of continuous protest. . . . He writhes and roars and weeps. He is a soul in torment, you would think, not someone who is merely bored and tired. And Pauline thinks with wonder of that forgotten turmoil of the emotions. There he is—he shares their days but lives elsewhere, in a place of flaring sensibility, in which anguish supplants ecstasy minute by minute. How can it be endured, survived— this switchback of feeling? Or is it perhaps a violent training for what is to come? A brutal education—a frenetic, accelerated version of what lies ahead."

In 1997 Lively published a third collection of short stories for adults, *Beyond the Blue Mountains* (published in the United States as *The 5001 Nights*), comprised of fourteen tales ranging from the fanciful to the quietly shocking. Many are stories of mild marital discord: "The Five Thousand and One Nights" imagines the subsequent history of Scheherazade and her Sultan, when he begins to tire of her increasingly experimental fiction and takes up storytelling on his own; "Beyond the Blue Mountains" depicts a couple on holiday and the wife's matter-of-fact exposure of her husband's affair; "Marriage Lines" takes place during a single marital counseling session from which husband and wife flee in order to escape their irritating therapist, "bolstered by the familiar private apposition of disagreement and collusion which now seemed a protection rather than a restraint." Building on the fairy-tale theme of the title of the collection, one story, "The Children of Grupp," is an eerie fantasy with an almost medieval feel. Other tales enter with greater or lesser degrees of drama into Lively's speculations about historical contingency and the human inability to control fate. "Season of Goodwill" relates an unsettling encounter between a middle-aged couple out Christmas shopping and the hitchhiker they pick up, a rather dim young man who takes them hostage and robs them. In the aftermath of her ordeal Norma Pocock tells the story of her afternoon to the police, finding that although "she felt almost steady now, . . . as she talked she glimpsed unnerving alternative scenarios which she did not want to contemplate, not now or ever. All that mattered was to get back to her personal struggle to harness the perverse and willful forces all around. She did not want to think about the boy, who was even now continuing his fractured progress from one eventuality to the next." On a lighter note, "The Butterfly and the Tin of Paint" springs out of Lively's fascination with chaos theory and depicts an almost impossibly complex and hilarious string of events that leads from a spilled tin of paint in a bedroom in Fulham to the downfall of a prime minister a fortnight later. With this tale Lively steps in to provide the explanations that, she claims, chaos theory skirts around: "scientists do not always deliver the goods. Real life, on the one hand, and fiction, on the other, leave nothing unexplained."

Over the course of her career Penelope Lively has produced an astonishing quantity of well-crafted, sometimes brilliant work. Critics have called her "one of the best living English children's writers" and, as a novelist for adults, "almost excessively gifted," with "a rare wit and an independence of mind." As a stylist she has displayed an ever-increasing talent for complex, multifaceted, stream-of-consciousness narratives that echo the Modernists. The structural complexity of her texts is matched by their intellectual and moral rigor: seldom possessed of neat resolutions, her adult novels in particular tend to illustrate her view that "I have never come to terms with life, and I wouldn't wish anyone else to do so; if fiction is to help at all in the process of living, it is by illuminating its conflicts and ambiguities."

Nevertheless, despite the challenging nature of many of her novels, they are also quite accessible, pinning their philosophic explorations to realistic situations and likable, fully realized characters. In "Bones in the Sand" Lively describes her work as an attempt to "translate into fictional terms that marvelous process of recollection interspersed with oblivion" of which human consciousness consists. Memory, she explains, is the one common denominator, the key to her writing and to reaching the diverse audiences for whom she writes—"the one thing we all share is the capacity to remember; the novelist tries to convey the significance and the power of that capacity in fictional terms, to make universal stories out of the particular story that we each carry in our own head. At its grandest, this theory is the most compelling in all literature."

Interviews:

Penelope Gilliat, *Penelope Gilliat in Conversation with Penelope Lively* [videotape] (London: Institute of Contemporary Art Video, 1986; Northbrook, Ill.: Roland Collection, 1986);

Christina Hardyment, "Time out of Mind: Penelope Lively (née Low, St. Anne's 1951) Talks to Christina Hardyment," *Oxford Today,* 2, no. 3 (1990): 30–31.

References:

Tony E. Jackson, "The Consequences of Chaos: *Cleopatra's Sister* and Postmodern Historiography," *Modern Fiction Studies,* 42 (Summer 1996): 397–417;

Nicholas Le Mesurier, "A Lesson in History: The Presence of the Past in the Novels of Penelope Lively," *New Welsh Review,* 2 (Spring 1990): 36–38;

Mary Hurley Moran, "The Novels of Penelope Lively: A Case for the Continuity of the Experimental Impulse in Postwar British Fiction," *South Atlantic Review,* 62 (Winter 1997): 101–120;

Moran, *Penelope Lively* (New York: Twayne, 1993);

Moran, "Penelope Lively's *Moon Tiger:* A Feminist 'History of the World,'" *Frontiers: A Journal of Women's Studies,* 11, no. 2–3 (1990): 89–95;

Debrah Raschke, "Penelope Lively's *Moon Tiger:* Re-Envisioning a 'History of the World,'" *ARIEL: A Review of English Literature,* 26 (October 1995): 115–132;

David Rees, "Time Present and Time Past," in his *The Marble in the Water: Essays on Contemporary Writers of Fiction for Children and Young Adults* (Boston: Horn Book, 1980), pp. 185–198;

J. S. Ryan, "'The Tolkien Formation'—with a Lively Example," *Journal of the Tolkien Society,* 25 (September 1988): 20–22;

Louisa Smith, "Layers of Language in Lively's *The Ghost of Thomas Kempe,*" *Children's Literature Association Quarterly,* 10 (Fall 1985): 114–116;

John Rowe Townsend, "Penelope Lively," in his *A Sounding of Storytellers: New and Revised Essays on Contemporary Writers for Children* (New York: Lippincott, 1979), pp. 125–138;

Pierre Yvard, "*Pack of Cards,* a Theme and a Technique," *Journal of the Short Story in English,* 13 (Autumn 1989): 103–111.

Adam Mars-Jones

(26 October 1954 –   )

Kasia Boddy
University College, London

BOOKS: *Lantern Lecture* (London: Faber & Faber, 1981); republished as *Fabrications* (New York: Knopf, 1981);

The Darker Proof: Stories from a Crisis, by Mars-Jones and Edmund White (London: Faber & Faber, 1987; New York: New American Library, 1988);

Venus Envy: On the Womb and the Bomb, Chatto Counterblasts no. 14 (London: Chatto & Windus, 1990);

Monopolies of Loss (London: Faber & Faber, 1992; New York: Knopf, 1992);

The Waters of Thirst (London: Faber & Faber, 1993; New York: Knopf, 1994);

Blind Bitter Happiness (London: Chatto & Windus, 1997).

OTHER: "Structural Anthropology," in *Firebird 1* (Harmondsworth, U.K.: Penguin, 1982); republished in *The Penguin Book of Modern British Short Stories,* edited by Malcolm Bradbury (Harmondsworth, U.K.: Penguin, 1987);

Mae West Is Dead: Recent Lesbian and Gay Fiction, edited, with an introduction, by Mars-Jones (London: Faber & Faber, 1983);

Randall Jarrell, *Pictures from an Institution,* introduction by Mars-Jones (London: Faber & Faber, 1987);

"Remission," in *Best Short Stories, 1988,* edited by Giles Gordon and David Hughes (London: Heinemann, 1988);

"Summer Lightening," in *Best Short Stories, 1989,* edited by Gordon and Hughes (London: Heinemann, 1989);

"The Changes of Those Terrible Years," *The Faber Book of Gay Short Stories,* edited by Edmund Wilson (London: Faber & Faber, 1991), pp. 387–410;

"A Small Spade," in *The Oxford Book of English Love Stories,* edited by John Sutherland (Oxford: Oxford University Press, 1996), pp. 400–442.

SELECTED PERIODICAL PUBLICATIONS–
UNCOLLECTED: "Weaning," *Granta,* 14 (Winter 1984): 232–234;

Adam Mars-Jones at the time of the American edition of The Waters of Thirst *(photograph © 1994 Jerry Bauer)*

"The Book That Launched Clause 28," *Index on Censorship,* 17 (September 1988): 37–40;

"I Was a Teenage Homophobe," *New Statesman,* 19 June 1998, pp. 23–25.

The potential of Adam Mars-Jones, novelist, short-story writer, and essayist was recognized early in his career. Before his first novel was published, he was twice named to the *Granta* magazine list of the best young British novelists (in 1983 and 1993). Mars-Jones's first collection of stories, *Lantern Lecture,* was published in 1981 to great acclaim, and the following year he won the Somerset Maugham Award. He followed this success with a series of stories about HIV and AIDS—some published with fiction by Edmund White in *The Darker Proof* (1987) and others in *Monopolies of Loss* (1992). In 1993 he published a novel, *The Waters of Thirst.*

Adam Mars-Jones was born on 26 October 1954 in London, where he still lives. His father, William Lloyd Mars-Jones, became a High Court judge in 1969 and retired in 1990; his mother, Sheila (née Cobon), who died in 1998, was a lawyer. He was educated at Westminster School, confessing in a 1998 *New Statesman* article that, "in B-movie terms, *I Was a Teenage Homophobe.*" He describes his feelings as "a true phobia: . . . the sort of terror that wants its object obliterated," and attributes them partly to his father's attitudes. "It must have made a difference that my father, a London lawyer with a Welsh village background, considered nothing more disgusting than the twisted desire of one man for another, who could never return it." Gradually exposed to more positive images of gay sexuality in his brother's underground magazines, he was twenty-two years old before he attended his first gay meeting. The comedian Graham Chapman was speaking, and Mars-Jones felt that he could pretend he was simply a Monty Python fan. "It was fifteen years after my coming out to . . . [my father] before he could accept my life without an outward flinch." He went on from Westminster to Cambridge University, where he received a B.A. in 1976. After studying "nothing but classics" from the ages of thirteen to twenty, he turned to American literature in the latter part of his academic career. He then went on to do graduate work on William Faulkner at the University of Virginia. While there, he won the Benjamin C. Moomaw Prize for Oratory in 1980 (for a comic piece on how to educate one's parents about sexuality) and, funded by a Hoyns Fellowship for Creative Writing, continued writing fiction. He lived for a while at the home of Martina Navratilova and Rita Mae Brown; in her 1994 biography of Navratilova, *Martina Unauthorised,* Adrianne Blue describes "the tall, dark, big-boned Englishman" as enjoying joke-telling competitions and playing cocktail piano for the couple.

Published in *Quarto* magazine in 1980, "Lantern Lecture" marked Mars-Jones's first appearance in print. The editor of *Quarto,* poet Craig Raine, showed the piece to Faber and Faber editor Robert McCrum, who signed up Mars-Jones immediately. A collection of three long stories, *Lantern Lecture* was published to a warm reception the following year. All three stories explore and exploit a tension between fact and fiction: "Lantern Lecture" is an achronological biography of a fictional English eccentric, Philip Yorke; "Hoosh-Mi," in which the queen contracts rabies from one of her beloved corgis, is subtitled "a farrago of scurrilous truths" and bears the disclaimer: "The events and characters of this

Dust jacket for the first U.S. edition of Mars-Jones's 1981 collection of stories featuring Queen Elizabeth II and a notorious murderer called the Black Panther

disclaimer are without exception fictitious; any resemblance to persons living or dead is purely coincidental"; "Bathpool Park" is the story of Donald Neilson, alias the Black Panther, who kidnapped and murdered Lesley Whittle in 1975, an event also treated fictionally in V. S. Naipaul's *Guerrillas* (1975).

Galen Strawson, writing in the *TLS: Times Literary Supplement,* (9 October 1981), described the stories as having something "punk in the modern sense of the word" about them. "It's to do with the emotionally deadpanned style of delivery, the technical impassivity of the allusive, cloisonné construction." *Fabrications,* the American edition of the collection, omitted "Lantern Lecture," but it was also well received in the United States: Richard McCann, for instance, writing in the. *Washington Post,* hailed Mars-Jones as "an important discovery." When the book was republished by Faber and Faber in 1990, the *Observer* (1 July 1990) welcomed the reappearance of a collection that was "already something of a classic."

In 1983 Mars-Jones edited *Mae West Is Dead,* an anthology of contemporary lesbian and gay fiction, which he claims "sets itself as much against the expectations of subcultural commerce, as against the studied indifference of the dominant culture." In the introduction he notes the importance of America "in the shaping of gay attitudes in Britain," in particular in promoting a strong gay subculture. This essay, which was republished in *Blind Bitter Happiness* (1997) as "Taking the Yellow View," introduces several enduring concerns: in particular, the relationship between a gay subculture and the mainstream and the differences between the American and British scenes. The book ends with Mars-Jones's story "Slim," written in 1986 after he had read an article about AIDS in Africa that never refers to the disease by name. "The problems attaching to the subject," he wrote in the introduction to *Monopolies of Loss,* "turned out to be overwhelmingly attached to the name. By suppressing that, I was suddenly able to write about the epidemic."

"Slim" was the first of a series of stories on AIDS that marked a radical shift in direction and filled the next ten years of Mars-Jones's writing life. Having read and admired Edmund White's "An Oracle" (1985), he approached the American novelist with the proposal of putting together a collection of short stories about AIDS, none of which would refer to the disease by name. The book set up a series of interesting contrasts by juxtaposing an established American writer who is HIV-positive and a young British writer who is not. Mars-Jones's "The Brake," in which the Englishman, Roger, visits America, explores some cultural differences. "Americans seemed to like jokes to be clearly signalled," Roger muses. "Americans seemed to see camp as an on/off switch, so that something was either campy or it wasn't, whereas he felt that true camp, high English camp, worked like a rheostat, providing endless gradations of frivolity. Perhaps camp was set in fifty years after an empire, in which case America would have to wait a while till the beginning of the next century or so."

The Darker Proof, subtitled *Stories from a Crisis,* came to fruition quickly, even with a "sense of urgency." Mars-Jones and White signed a contract in November and handed in the manuscript in June. During their collaborative process the two became firm friends; White has praised Mars-Jones's "psychological realism and moral exactitude." The reviewer for *Literature and Medicine* argued that the stories "provide a perspective on AIDS impossible to get from the volumes of clinical reportage now available in abundance" and described the "distinguishing feature" of Mars-Jones's writing to be "authenticity of detail."

Both writers went on to write more AIDS stories, although with less urgency. White published his collection *Skinned Alive* in 1995; Mars-Jones published *Monopolies of Loss* in 1992, although he later claimed not greatly to have liked several of the stories, which "I even have been known to wince on re-reading," adding that "The stories after the first batch, starting with 'Remission' . . . seemed somehow less conscientious." In the introduction to *Monopolies of Loss* he argued that the short story was particularly suited to writing about AIDS—"the big issue and the little form had a paradoxical affinity." The short story appealed because "you didn't have to engage with a particular viewpoint in an exhaustive way. AIDS will out-exhaust you somehow. Reading could be a more endurable experience than it is with a novel and also could be less clichéd." His goal was to explore the illness from as many perspectives as possible: how it felt "to be well in a sick world, to be sick in a well world, to be part of a relationship in which sickness was an atmospheric feature, to write about close relationships, personal relationships, and impersonal relationships, the new style of relationship that the epidemic sort of forged."

Although *Gay Times* reviewer Sebastian Beaumont dismissed the stories as "case-studies for trainee volunteer AIDS workers" (November 1992), most critics praised the collection fulsomely. Michael Wood, for example, in his essay "The Contemporary Novel" in *The Columbia History of the British Novel* (1994), noted "its compassion and its range, its sense that AIDS, however fearsome, is not alone among human calamities." John Ryle in the *London Review of Books* (5 November 1992) praised the book's "curbed, celibate style," arguing that its "stylistic austerity has, perhaps, an analogue in sexual restraint." Perhaps more accurately, Geoff Dyer in the *Guardian* (1 October 1992) maintained that although "careful not to over-exert itself, his prose yet takes comfort in its own capacity for eloquence. Even in the last, debilitating reaches of illness, a sentence glows with a faint pride at having made it so effortlessly to the full stop."

During the eleven years between the publication of *Lantern Lecture* and the appearance of *Monopolies of Loss,* Mars-Jones had also been working on a novel. As he recalled, "I was uncomfortably aware that I had written very little to justify having any sort of reputation at all and I was reaching a point when it was better to have a bad book out and then see what I did afterwards." He eventually abandoned a long manuscript that "was started before AIDS and was trying to include AIDS as a fact, which is very difficult—to try to make it hindsight-proof without claiming too much hindsight yourself." He originally conceived of a final installment in his series of HIV stories, one that "would deliberately be about people who seemed not to be affected by HIV at all, people who'd been monogamous since the early eighties." Over the span of two months this idea grew into the novel *The Waters of Thirst*.

The Waters of Thirst was published in 1993 to mixed reviews. According to Mars-Jones, "I was assumed to have carved out my little niche as the AIDS writer, and it was felt to be almost unfair that there was no AIDS in this one." Nevertheless, the *Observer* described it as "a hold-everything-I-must-read-this book," (31 May 1994) while novelist Ali Smith wrote in *The Scotsman* that "Mars-Jones writes like a descendant of Forster; with an innate sense of the rhythms of English" (3 July 1993).

The book is a love story of the "sexual recession." The lovers are an odd couple: Terry, an airline steward, and William, the narrator, who does voice-overs for television advertisements. "Meeting when we did, our monogamy wasn't Aids induced, but I don't see how I can deny it was Aids maintained." William has two obsessions: the porn star Peter Hunter—he brags, "I doubt if anyone in the country has a more complete collection of Hunteriana than I have"—and his diseased kidneys, the care of which is "a full-time job." William narrates the story in a cool, sardonic, and not immediately likeable voice. After all, he admits, "you don't stop being middle class just because you think you're about to be blown to bits." Mars-Jones intended the reader "only gradually to see things from his point of view, or to some extent to be drawn into his emotional world as you began to realise that this apparently very snippy condescending way of referring to other people was not as bad as it seemed." Although praised highly for its detailed realism, the novel is written in a sparse and unsentimental style. Ultimately the effect is powerfully moving. "I expected it to be rather satirical about monogamy but then I found that it was becoming less and less so, and it was acquiring some sort of element of sweetness in there too."

Although anxious about how he was to adapt to the novel form after gaining a reputation as a short-story writer, Mars-Jones found some advantages in extension. "One of the things that pleased me writing was when I dropped a subject or sidelined a topic in the novel and then came back to it, it did seem to return enriched—that somehow by dealing with my hero's obsession with the porn star or the stuff about the specifics of kidney disease, that somehow when you return to a subject, somehow the very opposite topics had nourished each other and somehow defined themselves by opposition." Nevertheless, *The Waters of Thirst* retains the intensity of the short-story form. The narrative is uninterrupted by chapter breaks because, Mars-Jones suggested, that would be "like allowing the reader to

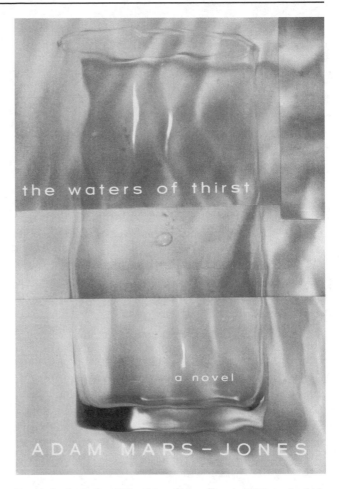

Dust jacket for the first U.S. edition of Mars-Jones's 1993 novel, which chronicles a gay couple's relationship in a time of "sexual recession"

put down their side of the knitting." While the short stories discuss AIDS but never name the disease, in *The Waters of Thirst* kidney disease simultaneously does and does not stand in for HIV, an indirect approach that derives thematic power from its depiction of William's circumstance: "he ends up in exactly the same place as somebody with AIDS even though all his choices seem to have taken him in the other direction."

A central concern of Mars-Jones's work, both fiction and nonfiction, is the family in its varied forms. The essay "Venus Envy" (written for the Chatto Counterblasts series) brilliantly dissects the boastful "new man" father, particularly as exemplified in Martin Amis's *Einstein's Monsters* (1987) and Ian McEwan's *The Child in Time* (1987). On the one hand, "the persona of the father is a liberating construction, allowing for the safe expression of emotion in unprecedented quantities (the key word here is safe)." On the other hand, the new fathers display what anthropologists call "couvade": "patterns of male behaviour that seek to upstage or to appropriate potent moments in the lives of women."

A strong desire neither to upstage nor to appropriate his mother's life informs Mars-Jones's 1996 essay "Blind Bitter Happiness." Commissioned to write the piece for a volume titled *Sons and Mothers,* he originally refused because he did not want to depict what many consider to be a clichéd relationship: "If you are a gay man talking about your mother, it's hard for people, apparently, to read it as anything other than 'he's the only man who will never leave her; she's the only woman he will ever love.'" The essay, thought by many to be one of Mars-Jones's finest achievements, is written in the third person and seems to be about someone who is dead; yet on the last page, Mars-Jones pulls a characteristic trick, revealing that his mother was still alive, and in the last paragraph switching to the first-person voice. The essay is another of the "indeterminate" pieces that Mars-Jones favors, one that hovers between fact and fiction and between easily classifiable lengths.

A highly respected critic as well as a novelist and story writer—he became film critic for *The Independent* in 1986, and in the 1990s he reviewed for the *Sunday Observer*—Mars-Jones has confessed that he finds it hard to suspend his "analytical side," which is "destructive by definition": "Very cheerfully do I put on my goggles and protective mittens when it's somebody else's novel but my own writing obviously has to survive in relatively close proximity to fairly scorching observations about other people's." It is to his readers' great advantage that so much of the fine and elegant writing of this self-deprecatory critic has survived. Compassionate satirists are hard to find; especially with such a graceful touch and such a keen ear and eye for the subtleties of English prose.

In each of his books Mars-Jones has stretched his talents in a new direction. The stories in *Monopolies of Loss* are radically different in theme and style from those in *Lantern Lecture*. In *The Waters of Thirst* he takes on the challenge of the novel with verve and originality. The essays in *Blind Bitter Happiness* are as finely nuanced as his fiction. What unites all Mars-Jones's writings is a sharp intelligence, a distrust of easy emotion (without a rejection of real emotion), and a precise and expert handling of language.

References:

Michael Wood, "The Contemporary Novel," in *The Columbia History of the British Novel,* edited by John Richetti (New York: Columbia University Press, 1994), pp. 969–970, 985–986;

Gregory Woods, *A History of Gay Literature: The Male Tradition* (New Haven, Conn.: Yale University Press, 1998).

William McIlvanney

(25 November 1936 –)

Cairns Craig
University of Edinburgh

See also the McIlvanney entry in *DLB 14: British Novelists Since 1960, First Series.*

BOOKS: *Remedy Is None* (London: Eyre & Spottiswoode, 1966);

A Gift from Nessus (London: Eyre & Spottiswoode, 1968);

The Longships in Harbour: Poems (London: Eyre & Spottiswoode, 1970);

Docherty (London: Allen & Unwin, 1975);

Laidlaw (London: Hodder & Stoughton, 1977; New York: Pantheon, 1977);

The Papers of Tony Veitch (London: Hodder & Stoughton, 1983; New York: Pantheon, 1983);

In through the Head (Edinburgh: Mainstream, 1984);

These Words: Weddings and After. An Essay and Poetry (Edinburgh: Mainstream, 1984);

The Big Man (London: Hodder & Stoughton, 1985; New York: Morrow, 1985);

Walking Wounded (London: Hodder & Stoughton, 1989);

Surviving the Shipwreck (Edinburgh: Mainstream, 1991);

Strange Loyalties (London: Hodder & Stoughton, 1991); New York: Morrow, 1991);

The Kiln (London: Sceptre, 1996).

TELEVISION: *Dreaming,* script by McIlvanney (1991).

OTHER: "Growing Up in the West," in *Memoirs of a Modern Scotland,* edited by Karl Miller (London: Faber & Faber, 1970), pp. 168–178;

Shades of Grey: Glasgow 1956–1987, photographs by Oscar Marzaroli, text by McIlvanney, notes by Joe Fisher and Cordelia Oliver (Edinburgh: Mainstream Publishing in conjunction with Third Eye Centre [Glasgow], 1987).

William McIlvanney (photograph © Jerry Bauer)

In 1975, on the publication of *Docherty,* William McIlvanney was hailed as the most important novelist of his generation in Scotland. *Docherty* was acclaimed not only for its literary qualities—a review in *The Scotsman* suggested that it was the best Scottish novel since MacDougall Hay's *Gillespie* in 1914—but also for focusing on key issues in Scottish culture in the 1970s. This was a period of renascent socialism, as indicated by events such as the Upper Clyde Shipbuilders Occupation in 1971, when workers took over one of the last of Scotland's traditional heavy industries, and the 1974 miners' strike—a socialism that was celebrated by McIlvanney's presentation of the values of a traditional working-class community. It was also a period of a renascent Scottish identity, following the first successes of the Scottish National Party in the late 1960s and the discovery of oil in the North Sea that transformed the

Scottish economy in the 1970s. Despite the emergence of a younger generation of working-class writers in Scotland and his own lengthy detour into detective fiction, McIlvanney remains at the heart of the Scottish working-class literary movement: his 1996 novel *The Kiln* returns to the territory marked out by *Docherty*.

McIlvanney was born on 25 November 1936 in Kilmarnock, Ayrshire, one of four children of William Angus McIlvanney, a miner, and Helen Montgomery McIlvanney. He belonged to the first generation of his class and region that had the opportunity to pursue higher education, and the tensions—both personal and linguistic—of that transition are fundamental to his writing. In the autobiographical essay "A Shield against the Gorgon," collected in *Surviving the Shipwreck* (1991), McIlvanney attributes the source of his creative drive to the moment one winter afternoon when his parents, returning home, woke him. McIlvanney was about eleven years old and had fallen asleep in a chair in the living room:

> What I saw in fact was pretty banal. My father had his hand on the light-switch he had just pressed. My mother was beside him. They were both laughing at what must have been my startled eyes and my wonderment at being where I was. Around them was a room made instantly out of the dark. It was a very ordinary room. But it was wonderful. How strange the biscuit barrel was where my mother kept the rent-money. How unimaginable was the image of Robert Burns with the mouse, painted on glass by my uncle. How incorrigibly itself the battered sideboard became. The room was full of amazing objects. They might as well have come from Pompeii.
>
> And at the centre of them were two marvellously familiar strangers. I saw them not just as my mother and father. I knew suddenly how dark my father was, how physical his presence. His laughter filled the room, coming from a place that was his alone. My mother looked strangely young, coming in fresh-faced from the cold and darkness, her irises swallowing her pupils as she laughed in the shocking brightness. I felt an inordinate love for them. I experienced the transformation of the ordinary into something powerfully mysterious.
>
> . . . if it is impossible to trace any work effectively to all its origins, I'm convinced that that moment in the living-room at St. Maurs Crescent is one of the experiential paradigms from which *Docherty* (and perhaps everything else I've written) grew.

In his essay "Growing Up in the West" (1970) McIlvanney notes that there was a radical division between his working-class childhood, with its Scots speech and traditional value system based around the community, and his preparation for middle-class life by the educational system, which was English in both language and values:

> Much is made of the bright student forging ahead into a new life, while his alienated relatives plod the old ways, bemused and often hurt. . . . Indeed, I've seen so many examples that I've come to believe in a kind of intellectual *nouveau riche,* those who employ their new-found intellectualism to bolster the self-containment of their own lives and to cut their families off. . . . the saddest thing is that the families of such bright ones are frequently masochistically delighted by their "progress." More than once I've heard working-class parents talk with pride about a son or daughter who is "away above us noo."

The McIlvanneys, like many Scottish working-class families, were highly literate; his brother Hugh became a distinguished sports journalist for *The Sunday Times* (London). In an interview published in *Scottish Writers Talking* (1996) McIlvanney recalled that "in that wee house in a housing scheme in Kilmarnock we used to have spontaneous poetry nights when we just—we'd all found poems that we liked and we sat round reading them *at* one another." The supportiveness of his family environment made the challenge of "middle-class" culture all the more stressful, so that he has always felt uneasy about his talent:

> I was aware all the time of a kind of dichotomy in what I was doing, because the people I wanted to write about and therefore as far as possible to write*for,* in the hope that they would read it, were people who you know did not have a lot of immediate love of books. So I've always had the dilemma when I write of justifying what I do as I go along. I've never had the feeling that some people have that—isn't it a wonderful thing to write books—to be a poet—to be a novelist. I've always had the problem is it worthwhile? And on what terms is it worthwhile for me to do?

The dilemma of McIlvanney's relationship to working-class culture continued at Glasgow University, from which he received an M.A. with honors in 1959, and when he became a teacher at Ravenspark Academy in Irvine, Ayrshire, in 1960, for he was directly engaged in training those "bright ones" who would be severed from their family background and their native culture. He married Moira Watson on 23 March 1961; they had two children, Siobhan and Liam.

McIlvanney's biography is paradigmatic of Scottish experience in the post–World War II period: the structure and values of one of the oldest working classes in the world were being steadily destroyed by the decline of the traditional industries of mining, shipbuilding, and engineering and by the failure of government-led initiatives to create modern industries in their place. McIlvanney's family experienced the transition to a new kind of working class and to an alternative version of what constituted Scotland. The use he made of this experience in his fiction, together with his obsessive concern in his essays with what had been lost and what could be revived from that older culture allowed McIlvanney to present himself as the articulator of commonly held but often unspoken values.

Equally, his serious engagement in such iconic elements of Scottish experience as support for the national football team allowed him to straddle the divide between mass and elite culture. Central to both was his profound commitment to socialism. In the preface to *Surviving the Shipwreck* he says:

> I believe that one disaster of our time has not been a physical event. It is something much more widespread, more lasting, more crippling to our subsequent aspirations. It is the perceived shipwreck of social idealism—the loss of belief in our ability significantly to reconstruct society towards a more justly shared community of living. The wreckage of its current failure has washed up most conspicuously in the Soviet Union and Eastern Europe. But debris can be found in many other parts of the world and has been noticed in the recent history of Britain. . . . Many people remark that socialism has failed. I would disagree. I think they are looking at the fragmentation of Marxist-Communism. They have simply insisted that socialism went down with the ship. But I believe it must resurface into survival.

He insists that Scotland is the place in which those socialist values can be maintained, both because of the deep traditions of communitarianism there and because of the power of left-wing politics in resistance to the decade of Thatcherism. In "The Shallowing of Scotland" in *Surviving the Shipwreck* he says:

> Therefore, Scottish socialism, if it is to attempt to realise its potential for power, must separate itself in some way from the rest of the United Kingdom. Those socialists whose internationalism makes a decision like that abhorrent should reflect that there is a world recession in the movement. The only way for it to survive in a serious form is to retrench. Scotland is one of the places where it could effectively do so.

In "A Shield against the Gorgon" McIlvanney says that he began writing in imitation of the models of his education ("ancient Greek or Shakespeare"); he even tried to write a blank-verse play about working-class life. Later it was mainly imitation of American writers ("William Saroyan or Ernest Hemingway") that shaped his style; but the moment when his "love of words had come upon a personal reality it must try to confront" was during his first year at Glasgow University, when his father died of lung cancer.

It is an event that is central to his first novel, *Remedy Is None* (1966): the hero, Charlie Grant—caught, like McIlvanney, between middle-class, English-speaking

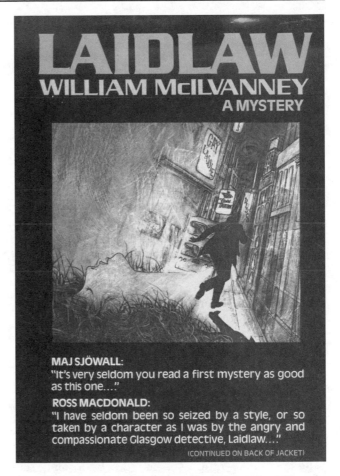

Dust jacket for McIlvanney's 1977 novel, which introduced Glasgow detective Jack Laidlaw

university life and the Scots-speaking, working-class life of his home—is called from Glasgow to the small town in Ayrshire where his father, a miner, is dying. For his father, Charlie's departure to the university had represented the fulfillment of a deeply held ambition to see his children gain all that he had been denied in life; but for Charlie, the university education is a negation of all the bonds that tie him to his family and his community. The pattern of betrayal of working-class values that he feels in himself he sees repeated in his mother, who has left his father for a man who is wealthy, middle-class, and English-speaking. Charlie's bitterness after his father's death leads to an argument during which he kills his mother's new husband, symbolically destroying the middle-class culture that has co-opted him and that puts him on trial for his crime. The power of the novel comes from McIlvanney's rendering of Charlie's situation in a prose style that is ornately English and yet includes and validates the dialect of the working-class community.

Remedy Is None attracted considerable attention and won the Geoffrey Faber Memorial Prize, but the critical consensus is that McIlvanney's anger is only fitfully under control in the novel and that he is trying to say too much. Francis Russell Hart comments that "the figurative psychology of complex and extreme inner states overripens at times, and the authenticity of a simple young rustic's nightmare is occasionally lost in the overanalysis of the university novelist." When the novel was reprinted in 1991, the review in *The Sunday Times* (28 April) said that "although it has flaws, it captures the confused concerns of youth with freshness and sympathy."

McIlvanney's second novel, *A Gift from Nessus* (1968), winner of the Scottish Arts Council Book Award, looks at the issue of class from the other side of the barrier, the side that McIlvanney, by becoming a schoolteacher, had to accept as his own. Its setting is not the working-class districts but the middle-class commuter towns that serve the city of Glasgow. Its central character, Eddie Cameron, is a salesman who is barely keeping up with either his wife's demands for the affluence she expected from their marriage or the demands of his mistress. The plot, which is the most conventional of any of McIlvanney's novels, treats middle-class marital tensions against the landscape of decaying inner-city Glasgow, fragmented by new motorways and blighted by slums. As Eddie climbs the social ladder, he discovers only the nullity of his wife's values, while his mistress is hounded by a family still gripped by the puritanical righteousness of Scottish Calvinism. Eddie is trapped between Scotland's empty anglicized future and its harsh and repressive past, and the book is caught between the English tradition of the novel of manners and the Scottish tradition of engagement with religious and metaphysical issues. Perhaps for this reason, English critics have found it one of the easiest of McIlvanney's novels to accept. Roger Baker in *Books and Bookmen* (September 1968), although noting that "Eddie Cameron's problem might have come directly out of the case-book of a social psychologist," described the novel as "a marvellous piece of work," full of "sharply observed detail (social, personal)" and written "in a language tight with imagery." Scottish critics, on the other hand, have tended to think that there is an ornate preciousness about McIlvanney's style and that here, in particular, it conceals rather than reveals the qualities of his characters. In a long review in *Calgacus* (Spring 1976), Douglas Gifford found the stylistic qualities of *A Gift from Nessus* inadequate: "at no point did McIlvanney use his ability to make his protagonists of almost mythical stature; far from being archetypes . . . the people of *Gift* are all too often stereotypes." Hart, however, commends the work because "milieu and motive are fixed throughout in modern urban Scotland,

and yet the consciousness of being Scottish neither defines the problem nor offers a solution."

McIlvanney worked as a tutor in English literature and creative writing at the University of Grenoble in 1970–1971, as a teacher of English at Irvine Royal Academy in 1971–1972, as a creative writing fellow at the University of Strathclyde in 1972–1973, and as assistant rector for curriculum at Greenwood Academy in Irvine from 1973 to 1975. In "A Shield against the Gorgon" he says that his first two novels, "besides simply being written for themselves–brought me nearer to an understanding of my boyhood experience and heightened the confidence I needed to attempt the finding of a form to express it." That form turned out to be an historical novel about his grandparents' and parents' generations, in which he attempts to come to terms with being a writer from the working classes who could celebrate working-class experience. Of the process of writing *Docherty* he says that although he was aware of precursors–"from Langland's 'field full of folk' to Robert Tressell and the work of Zola and Lawrence and Sillitoe"–he believed that no one had managed to write from within about the "richness and dynamism" of working-class experience. He wanted to avoid negating the culture from which he had come, as D. H. Lawrence had, because "to judge working-class culture, once you have left it, by the standards of the established literary culture you have entered is to judge it by terms which were created to deny it"; "to judge the passion of working-class life by the clinical procedures of middle-class culture is like assembling the data of an autopsy and calling it a life-story." The novel is, therefore, a personal testament to McIlvanney's working-class family, written to assert the heroism of those whose lives are lived in resistance to what he considers the degradation imposed on them by capitalism.

Tam Docherty is a traditional "hard man" of working-class mythology, but his hardness is depicted not as the brutalization of humanity but as a carapace within which a true humanity can survive capitalist exploitation. Tam's three sons exhibit the historical pattern that McIlvanney seems to see as inevitable within the Scottish context. Angus, the eldest, adopts the role of "hard man" but as an individualistic denier of community commitment rather than as the supporter of it that his father was. Mick, the second son, experiences the war as an extension of economic exploitation and, returning wounded and embittered, becomes a communist. Conn, the youngest, inherits Tam's conscientious awareness of others in the community. Like his creator, he is struggling to resolve the tensions of living in "twa minds" and in two cultures. McIlvanney says in "A Shield against the Gorgon" that he avoided making his novel "an escape story with the escapee patronisingly looking back on the lives of those who were still inmates. The vision would be from within, frontal and not tangential. In this connection, Conn's instinctive refusal to seek an alternative life to the one he had is central to the book." Despite McIlvanney's sense of working without precursors, Alan McGillivray sees the novel as McIlvanney's contribution to a long tradition in the Scottish narrative, a "theoretical social or class history of the first quarter of the twentieth century in industrial Ayrshire" similar to the histories of the early nineteenth century written by John Galt in the 1820s that fills in the gaps left by public and official history: "When McIlvanney is creating the history of Graithnock, narrated by old Martin to young Conn, it is the history of Kilmarnock taken from the standard local history by McKay and Findlay, yet in that history there is not a single mention of the coal mines or the miners of Kilmarnock, although when the history was written at the turn of the century these were abundant and important within the life of the town."

The publication of *Docherty* made McIlvanney the most significant of Scotland's younger writers; the work won the Whitbread Literary Award for 1975 and the Scottish Arts Council Award for 1976. Gifford concluded his review in *Calgacus:* "of our modern Scottish novelists he must indisputably be regarded as the most outstanding. . . . McIlvanney is the only novelist in Scotland with the determination, the epic vision, the willingness to wrestle with the endless difficulties of craft and the honesty to push himself to greater achievement."

The success of *Docherty* allowed McIlvanney to give up teaching and become a full-time writer. Instead of continuing the large-scale historical perspective that *Docherty* had opened up, however, over the next sixteen years he produced a series of novels about the Glasgow detective Jack Laidlaw: *Laidlaw* (1977), *The Papers of Tony Veitch* (1983), and *Strange Loyalties* (1991). Even the one nongeneric novel he produced during this period, *The Big Man* (1985), involves criminals and an illegal bare-knuckle fight, events that become the background of *Strange Loyalties*. In the interview in *Scottish Writers Talking* McIlvanney mentioned four motivations for this change in direction. The first was his realization that the audience for his serious novels was an educated elite who could only look at his working-class characters from the outside; by turning to the detective genre he could acquire a readership that belonged to the community about which he wanted to write. The second motivation was his desire to portray Glasgow, with which he had fallen in love during his student days, in a more diverse fashion than he could in a serious novel. The third motivation was his wish to write about contemporary Scotland, from which the long gestation and writ-

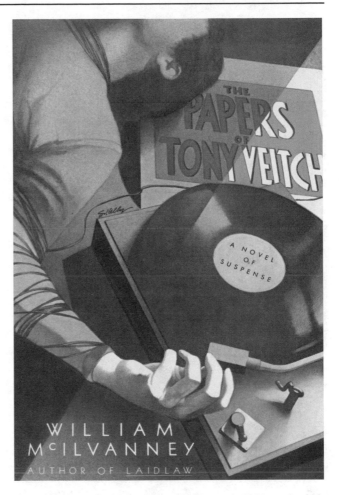

Dust jacket for the first U.S. edition of McIlvanney's 1983 novel, which was awarded the Silver Dagger Award of the Crime Writers' Association of England

ing of *Docherty* had alienated him. Finally, McIlvanney said, he wanted to try to raise the quality of the detective story: "What fascinated me was, here was a form which was popular, and therefore you had the chance that quite a few people might read it. . . . And I thought, here is a form which fights as a fly-weight, when it should at least fight as a middle-weight or maybe even a light-heavyweight. And I thought that was worth trying."

Laidlaw is a detective with a penchant for existentialist philosophy and little sense of commitment to those for whom he works. He says, "A crime you're trying to solve is a temporary mystery. Solved, it's permanent. What can the courts do with this then? Who knows what it is. It's maybe just another love story." He insists, "I'm not just suspicious of the people I'm chasing. I'm suspicious of the people I'm chasing them for." McIlvanney says in "The Courage of Our Doubts" in *Surviving the Shipwreck:* "Laidlaw negates two of the common conventions of the detective story. The first is that

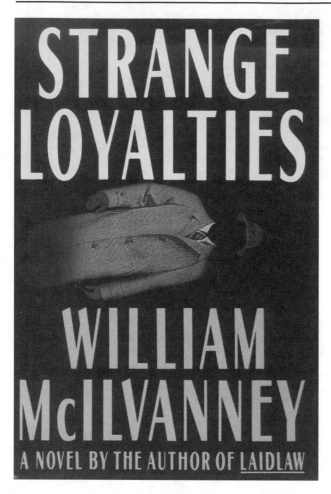

Dust jacket for the first U.S. edition of McIlvanney's 1991 novel featuring Jack Laidlaw

the story fulfills itself in the solution of the crime and the apprehension or dramatic death of the criminal. The second is that the straight world is morally right and the criminal world is morally wrong." Laidlaw's angst-ridden voice and his sympathy with those he chases rather than those for whom he works suggest the depth of McIlvanney's alienation from the world that had replaced the working-class Kilmarnock in which he had grown up and, equally, from the middle-class world he had entered. This alienation was, perhaps, intensified by the failure of his marriage and the isolating circumstances in which he often lived, whether in the bed-sitter in Glasgow that he describes in his text for Oscar Marzaroli's photographic study *Shades of Grey: Glasgow 1956–1987* (1987) or during his periods as writer in residence in Aberdeen in 1980 and in Vancouver in 1987.

The Laidlaw books are not traditional detective novels; they use the genre as a means of exploring the effects of capitalism: McIlvanney regards the criminal

world as an inverse image of the brutality of the capitalist system of the law-abiding. Equally, however, they undercut the traditions of the detective novel by bringing the language of the serious novel to the popular genre. Of criticism that the language *The Papers of Tony Veitch* is too precious, McIlvanney said in *Scottish Writers Talking* that he wanted the language of the novel to be as far from ordinary speech as that of William Shakespeare, Christopher Marlowe, or John Webster was from the ordinary language of their day: "all I'm going to ask, personally, about a book like that, is if it is written with that heightened thing, that the heightening shouldn't be fake, and for me it's not. I suppose what I was trying to do with *Veitch* was to deliberately heighten language, just to let it go, to make everything as packed as I could."

Despite winning the Silver Dagger Award of the British Society of Crime Writers, McIlvanney seems to have become disenchanted with the form and has promised no more Laidlaw novels. The final one, *Strange Loyalties,* virtually deserts the detective-fiction genre to become an exploration of how the idealism of young working-class people in the 1950s is corrupted and destroyed and leaves them embittered inhabitants of the materialistic world of the 1990s. Rather than solving a crime, Laidlaw sets out to understand the death of his brother Scott, a death that is both a reflection of McIlvanney's own experience (one of his brothers died suddenly of a cerebral hemorrhage) and the symbolic death of the Scotland (Scott-land) he had once inhabited. Its conclusion might be considered a reflection of McIlvanney's own relationship with the community about which he had sought to write: "Four experts had an appointment with an ordinary man. They needed him to ratify their findings or anything they achieved would be meaningless. As they drove to meet him, they knocked down a man on the road. He was dying. If they tried to save him, they might miss their appointment. They decided that their appointment . . . was more important than the life of one man. They drove on. . . . They did not know that the man they were to meet was the man they had left to die."

The Big Man, which was filmed in 1991 with Liam Neeson in the leading role of an unemployed Scottish miner who accepts an offer from a mysterious millionaire to become a bare-knuckled boxer, is intended to reveal the extent to which working-class community has been broken down by the destructive effects of late capitalism. The violence of the book and the movie (which was released in the United States as *Crossing the Line*) has raised questions, in many cases from feminists, about McIlvanney's tendency not just to analyze but also to identify with traditional conceptions of male working-class aggression. McIlvanney, however, argued in

Scottish Writers Talking that "violence does seem to me a very, very valid metaphor for a capitalist society."

McIlvanney's exploration of various genres included a television drama, *Dreaming* (1991), which *The Guardian* called "the best one-off play of the year." McIlvanney's success in reaching out to a much broader audience than is usual for a serious novelist turned him into a significant public figure, a regular contributor to Scottish newspapers, and a propagandist for political change. In 1979 he had supported the cause of Scottish Devolution, which had failed to produce a Scottish parliament even though a small majority of the Scottish electorate had voted for it; his poem about the event, "After: March 1979–The Cowardly Lion," which is included in *Surviving the Shipwreck,* became a much-quoted source about the lack of self-confidence that governed Scottish political life. Through the 1980s he became an increasingly significant commentator on Scottish politics, endeavoring to link the traditions of Scottish socialism with the movement toward independence. In "The Shallowing of Scotland" he presents Scotland as a bastion of nonmaterialistic values that can only be mobilized through an effective national politics:

> Scotland was born poor. There are two main ways to react to poverty. One is to fall in love with money, since that is what you do not have. The other is to generate values beyond the economic, since otherwise you acknowledge your own inferiority unless you can acquire wealth. Scotland grew up with the potential to do both.

> The country contained that implicit division within itself, like the internal striations in an apparently solid rock that only needed some natural calamity in order to become a fissure. Scotland's calamity came in 1707. The Act of Union made a separation in the nation that created a unique and confused historical legacy.

> . . . There was on the one side an Anglicised minority, a controlling establishment whose motivation was accepting the materialistic values that made sense of the English connection. There was, on the other side, a more radically Scottish majority whose motivation was the maintenance of a distinctly Scottish identity and for whom the cost of realising that motivation was adopting the deeper, non-materialistic values that were needed to make sense of their determined Scottishness.

In 1991 the Scottish writer Anne Smith declared in *The Sunday Times* (8 December) that "if [Václav] Havel the playwright can lead Czechoslovakia, surely McIlvanney the author could lead Scotland." In the aftermath of the 1992 general election, which produced a fourth consecutive Conservative Party victory, McIlvanney was a leading figure in the founding of "Scot-

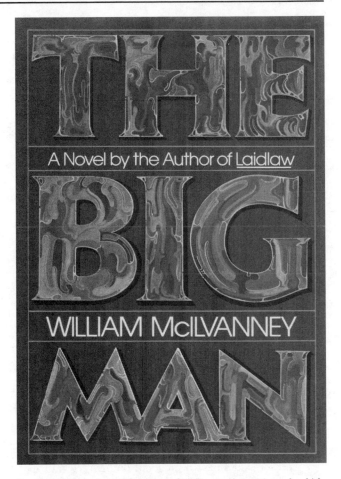

Dust jacket for the first U.S. edition of McIlvanney's 1985 novel, which is set against the backdrop of bare-knuckles fighting

land United," an organization that sought to mobilize people behind the Scottish Constitutional Convention's campaign for a Scottish Assembly. In December 1992 he was the main speaker at a rally of more than twenty-five thousand people in Edinburgh, the site of a meeting of European heads of government, where he suggested that Scotland's sixty-one opposition members of Parliament should boycott Westminster. Scotland finally gained its own parliament in September 1997.

In the meantime, McIlvanney had returned to "serious" fiction with a novel about a writer measuring the distance between the dreams of his adolescence in the 1950s and the realities of the present. The central character of *The Kiln* is Tom Docherty, the grandson of Tam Docherty; one of his friends at school is Jack Laidlaw, the future detective. Tom's life is closely modeled on McIlvanney's: he is the son of working-class parents; he goes to the university; and his father dies of cancer. The linking of autobiography and fiction and the presence of characters from his earlier books shows

McIlvanney establishing his oeuvre as a single tapestry of life in the west of Scotland in the twentieth century.

The Kiln was hailed as McIlvanney's major achievement: Magnus Linklater described it in *The Times* (London) for 21 September 1996 as "a finely judged and beautifully written novel, McIlvanney's most mature and rounded work so far," and Trevor Lewis commented in *The Sunday Times* (29 September 1996) that "McIlvanney controls the elisions of time, place and mood with masterful assurance, a pitch-perfect blend of warm lyricism, limpid observation and excruciatingly funny comedy." *The Kiln* won the Saltire Prize in 1997 and reestablished McIlvanney's reputation as one of Scotland's leading novelists, a reputation that had been severely diminished not just by his resort to detective fiction but also by the arrival in the 1980s of a new breed of Scottish working-class novelists, such as James Kelman, many of whom regarded McIlvanney's use of cultured English instead of dialect as a betrayal of his class. In the interview in *Scottish Writers Talking* McIlvanney argued the necessity for his stylistic choices:

> I spoke Scots until I was five, and I went to primary school, and I was taught English—what I resent is that I was taught English to the *suppression* of Scots. I think it was necessary that I be taught standard English in conjunction, as a harmonious marriage, with my own daily speech—it would have been good! But that having happened, I couldn't sit here and say, 'Well, we'll talk in the mither leid.' . . . And I just think you have to confront what is truly happening and inhibit that, rather than conceptually trying to force things back to a time which has gone.

The new Scottish fiction turned its back on that compromise and was written in dialect, with much less of a sense of the values of traditional working-class community and a much more brutal conception of life in the streets of the modern city than can be found in McIlvanney's works. Robert Crawford said in *The Sunday Times* (17 April 1994) that "other writers are likely to be jealous or to be shown up by what Kelman has done. Compared to his work, for instance, William McIlvanney's earlier west-of-Scotland writing seems embarrassingly purplish." The difference, however, is that whereas Kelman focuses on the ability of his working-class characters to survive exploitation and alienation, McIlvanney wants to use traditional literary forms to establish the heroic nature of the working class. In "A Shield against the Gorgon" he says that his work "is essentially an attempt to democratise traditional culture, to give working-class life the vote in the literature of heroism."

Interviews:

Douglas Gifford, "William McIlvanney Talks to Douglas Gifford," *Books in Scotland,* 30 (Spring 1989): 1–4;

Isobel Murray, ed., "Plato in a Boiler Suit," in *Scottish Writers Talking: George Mackay Brown, Jessie Kesson, Norman MacCaig, William McIlvanney, David Toulmin, Interviewed by Isobel Murray and Bob Tait* (East Linton, U.K.: Tuckwell, 1996), pp. 132–154;

Bernard Sellin, "Rencontre avec William McIlvanney," in his *Modernité de l'Ecosse* (Brest: Centre de Recherche Bretonne et Celtique, Université de Bretagne Occidentale, 1996), pp. 95–106.

References:

Sean Damer, "Sense and Worth," *Scottish Affairs,* 22 (Winter 1998): 112–128;

Simon Dentith, "'This Shitty Urban Machine Humanised': The Urban Crime Novel and the Novels of William McIlvanney," in *Watching the Detectives,* edited by Ian A. Bell and Graham Daldry (Basingstoke: Macmillan, 1990), pp. 18–36;

Beth Dickson, "Class and Being in the Novels of William McIlvanney," in *The Scottish Novel since the Seventies,* edited by Gavin Wallace and Randall Stevenson (Edinburgh: Edinburgh University Press, 1993), pp. 54–70;

Keith Dixon, "Writing on the Borderline: The Works of William McIlvanney," *Studies in Scottish Literature,* 24 (1989): 142–157;

Francis Russell Hart, *The Scottish Novel: From Smollett to Spark* (Cambridge, Mass.: Harvard University Press, 1978), pp. 313–315;

Peter Humm and Paul Stigant, "The Masculine Fiction of William McIlvanney," in *Gender, Genre and Narrative Pleasure,* edited by Derek Longhurst (London: Unwin Hyman, 1989), pp. 84–101;

Jeremy Idle, "McIlvanney, Masculinity and Scottish Literature," *Scottish Affairs,* 2 (Winter 1993): 50–57;

Alan McGillivray, "Natural Loyalties: The Work of William McIlvanney," *Laverock,* 1 (1995): 13–23;

Craig W. McLuckie, *Researching McIlvanney: A Critical and Bibliographic Introduction* (New York: Peter Lang, 1999);

Martin Priestman, *Detective Fiction and Literature: The Figure on the Carpet* (Basingstoke, U.K.: Macmillan, 1990), 179–182, 184;

Robin M. Spittal, "Mac Ilvanney," *Ecosse,* 5–6 (1986): 53–68.

Nicholas Mosley

(25 June 1923 –   )

Peter Lewis
University of Durham

See also the Mosley entry in *DLB 14: British Novelists Since 1960*.

BOOKS: *Spaces of the Dark* (London: Hart-Davis, 1951);

Life Drawing, by Mosley and John Napper (London & New York: Studio Publications, 1954);

The Rainbearers (London: Weidenfeld & Nicolson, 1955);

Corruption (London: Weidenfeld & Nicolson, 1957; Boston: Little, Brown, 1958);

African Switchback (London: Weidenfeld & Nicolson, 1958);

The Life of Raymond Raynes (London: Faith Press, 1961);

Meeting Place (London: Weidenfeld & Nicolson, 1962);

Experience and Religion: A Lay Essay in Theology (London: Hodder & Stoughton, 1965; Philadelphia: United Church Press, 1967);

Accident (London: Hodder & Stoughton, 1965; New York: Coward-McCann, 1966);

Assassins (London: Hodder & Stoughton, 1966; New York: Coward-McCann, 1967);

Impossible Object (London: Hodder & Stoughton, 1968; New York: Coward-McCann, 1969);

Natalie Natalia (London: Hodder & Stoughton, 1971; New York: Coward, McCann & Geoghegan, 1971);

The Assassination of Trotsky (London: Joseph, 1972);

Julian Grenfell: His Life and The Times of His Death 1888–1915 (London: Weidenfeld & Nicolson, 1976; New York: Holt, Rinehart & Winston, 1976);

Catastrophe Practice (London: Secker & Warburg, 1979; Elmwood Park, Ill.: Dalkey Archive Press, 1989);

Imago Bird (London: Secker & Warburg, 1980; Elmwood Park, Ill.: Dalkey Archive Press, 1989);

Serpent (London; Secker & Warburg, 1981; Elmwood Park, Ill.: Dalkey Archive Press, 1990);

Rules of the Game: Sir Oswald and Lady Cynthia Mosley 1896–1933 (London: Secker & Warburg, 1982); republished with *Beyond the Pale* (Elmwood Park, Ill.: Dalkey Archive Press, 1991);

Nicholas Mosley (photograph by Gerhard Cohn)

Beyond the Pale: Sir Oswald Mosley and Family 1933–1980 (London: Secker & Warburg, 1983); republished with *Rules of the Game* (Elmwood Park, Ill.: Dalkey Archive Press, 1991);

Judith (London: Secker & Warburg, 1986; Elmwood Park, Ill.: Dalkey Archive Press, 1991);

Hopeful Monsters (London: Secker & Warburg, 1990; Elmwood Park, Ill.: Dalkey Archive Press, 1991);

Efforts at Truth (London: Secker & Warburg, 1994; Elmwood Park, Ill.: Dalkey Archive Press, 1995);

Children of Darkness and Light (London: Secker & Warburg, 1996; Elmwood Park, Ill.: Dalkey Archive Press, 1997).

MOTION PICTURES: *The Assassination of Trotsky,* screenplay by Mosley and Masolino d'Amico, Cinettel/Dino de Laurentiis Cinematografica/CIAC/Josef Shastel Productions, 1972;
Impossible Object, screenplay by Mosley, Franco-London Films, 1973.

OTHER: Raymond Raynes, *The Faith: Instructions on the Christian Faith,* edited by Mosley (Leighton Buzzard: Faith Press/Community of the Resurrection, 1961).

Nicholas Mosley has long been regarded as one of the most innovative English writers of his generation. He has pursued his chosen course as a novelist with integrity, never being lured away by literary fashions. He has neither sought widespread popularity nor achieved it. It is surprising, however, that he has not attracted a great deal of academic attention in Britain because his complex and thought-provoking fiction lends itself to exegesis and interpretation. One reason for this relative neglect is that Mosley stands apart from the English mainstream. His interest in abstract ideas, his preoccupation with the relationship between words and things, and his experiments with form mark him as more Continental than English in his approach to the art of fiction. It is significant that the first important academic publication about his work was American—an issue of the *Review of Contemporary Fiction* devoted to him in 1982.

What is predictable about Mosley's fiction is its unpredictability. Whereas some of his well-known English contemporaries have developed their own novelistic formulas and stuck to them, Mosley has been determined to avoid repeating himself, especially after his first phase. He usually approaches each novel as a new beginning and has consequently sprung some surprises on his readers over the years. He prefers to take risks rather than play it safe. Although this policy sometimes goes wrong, it can also achieve unexpectedly brilliant results. Never willing to stand still as a writer, Mosley reaches out to invent fictional forms capable of dealing adequately with the complexity of modern life and the perplexing nature of reality.

The second of three children, Nicholas Mosley was born in London on 25 June 1923 into an upper-class family. His parents were Sir Oswald Mosley, a controversial political figure, and Lady Cynthia Mosley, a politician in her own right. A daughter of George Nathaniel, Marquess Curzon of Kedleston, arguably the most successful viceroy of India during the history

of the Raj, Lady Cynthia was among the first women elected to the House of Commons. Also a Labour M.P. for a time, Sir Oswald had a spectacular political career as a young man, becoming a government minister. During the 1930s he changed direction to become leader of the British Union of Fascists. After the early death of his wife, Sir Oswald married one of the well-known Mitford sisters, Diana, in 1936. Because of their prewar contacts with Benito Mussolini and Adolf Hitler, Sir Oswald and Lady Diana were interned for most of World War II as supposed security risks. Becoming the third baron Ravensdale in 1966 on the death of his mother's sister, Nicholas Mosley eventually inherited his father's baronetcy when Sir Oswald died in 1980.

Following the death of his father, Mosley wrote two substantial books about his family history and political involvements, drawing heavily on his father's papers. The first of these personal and partly autobiographical accounts, *Rules of the Game* (1982), begins in the 1890s and ends with the death of his mother in 1933, while the second, *Beyond the Pale* (1983), continues the saga up to the late 1940s with an epilogue to cover the remaining years of his father's life. In part, *Beyond the Pale* is a study of British Fascism, but it also explores the author's frequently turbulent relationship with Sir Oswald. Mosley's autobiography, *Efforts at Truth* (1994), is a decidedly unorthodox contribution to the genre. After a few opening paragraphs he launches into a detailed synopsis of his first novel. In his philosophical quest for the meaning of "truth" as it surfaces in the interplay between his fiction and his life, Mosley devotes a considerable amount of space to his writing.

Mosley was educated at Abinger Hill School and then Eton College from 1937 until 1942, when he joined the army, serving as an infantry officer during World War II. For a daring attack in Italy, described in *Beyond the Pale,* he was awarded the Military Cross. After leaving the army in 1946 he entered Balliol College, Oxford, to study philosophy, but he stayed for only one year. Having decided to devote himself to full-time writing, Mosley produced four novels in the next ten years, *Spaces of the Dark* (1951), "A Garden of Trees," *The Rainbearers* (1955), and *Corruption* (1957). The second of these books has never been published. During this period he also tried writing plays, all of which remain unperformed and unpublished, although one from the late 1950s, "The Good Samaritans," may be seen as the genesis for his 1979 novel, *Catastrophe Practice.* Mosley wrote his first novel in the Caribbean after his marriage to the artist Rosemary Salmond on 14 November 1947. On their return to Britain in 1948 they spent nearly three years on a remote and primitive hill farm in North Wales before moving to Sussex, much nearer London, following the birth of their second child. Mosley's first four novels may be regarded as the first phase in his development as a writer. While the unpublished "A Garden of Trees" is not available for scrutiny, the detailed synopsis and extended quotations Mosley includes in *Efforts at Truth* establish its similarities in theme and tone to the other three.

The stylistic influences of Henry James, William Faulkner, and perhaps Marcel Proust are evident in Mosley's early novels, with their long paragraphs and elaborate sentences, an idiom described as baroque by reviewers. These expansive and self-consciously literary books are deeply analytical about the roots of human behavior. While adhering to the conventions of realism, they also explore beneath the level of society and character to locate a metaphysical or spiritual malaise in modern Western civilization. Mainly set in the postwar world but looking back directly and indirectly to World War II, they reveal the influence of the dominant European philosophical movement of the 1940s and 1950s, existentialism. Alienation, betrayal, moral decadence, despair, nihilism, and intellectual *nausée* are important themes.

The title of Mosley's first and immensely ambitious novel, *Spaces of the Dark,* comes from T. S. Eliot's early "Rhapsody on a Windy Night" (written 1910–1911), a suitably nightmarish and angst-filled poem. Paul Shaun, the central character of Mosley's novel, is a young army officer who returns to England after the war with a terrible, guilty secret. The reason, held back until well into the narrative, is that he deliberately killed his friend and fellow officer John Longmore because John's failure as a commander in battle was endangering the lives of his men. Like the Ancient Mariner and similar Romantic figures haunted by past actions, Paul feels himself to be an outsider separated from ordinary humanity. He can no longer communicate with his family or share their conventional values. Fatalistically he is drawn to the two different young women who had been closest to John: his sister, Margaret, and the bohemian Sarah Thorpe. As Paul's relationships with both women develop, he struggles with increasing desperation to come to terms with his psychological conflicts. Paul's anguish finally ends in death, when he sacrifices his life to rescue the injured Margaret. *Spaces of the Dark* is an attempt by a young writer at the beginning of his career to write a full-scale tragic novel. In *Efforts at Truth* Mosley calls the book "operatic." If he does not succeed, it is because the characters are not sufficiently developed to carry the tragic significance expected of them, but there is no denying the promise or imaginative daring of the novel.

In 1950, while well advanced on "A Garden of Trees," Mosley became interested in Christianity, especially after meeting Father Raymond Raynes, the supe-

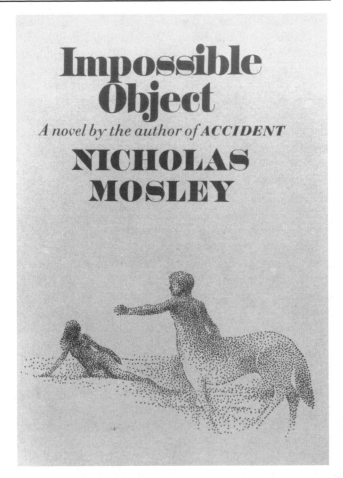

Dust jacket for the first U.S. edition of Mosley's 1968 collection of thematically linked stories illustrating the difficulty of representing reality

rior of the Community of the Resurrection, an Anglican order of monks. The novel was eventually accepted, but Mosley suppressed it in favor of what he and his publishers regarded as his superior third book, *The Rainbearers.* Its publication proved to be fraught with difficulties, as he explains in *Efforts at Truth. The Rainbearers* is less fatalistic than *Spaces in the Dark,* and its denouement lacks the finality of death, but there are similarities between the two books. The central character, Richard, resembles Paul Shaun in being an inhabitant of the postwar wasteland and in being torn by conflicting loyalties to two women: his wife, Elisabeth, and Mary Livingstone, an Anglo-French girl from his past who reenters his life after the war. Through Mary the traumatic experience of World War II colors the novel because she has been in France, helped the Resistance, been tortured by the Germans, and seen her mother shot by the French as a collaborator after the liberation. Richard's lack of direction and his failure to realize his human potential are somehow related to his brief but intense relationship with Mary before his marriage.

When Richard and Mary meet again, they begin their love affair where they left off and enjoy a holiday in Spain. Mary seems to offer Richard fulfillment and happiness, but his inner conflicts, combined with a destructive urge, lead him to leave her just as earlier he had abandoned his wife. Although Richard and Elisabeth are finally reconciled, the novel does not end on a positive note. The emphasis is on loss, failure, and an existential malaise.

Structurally and stylistically, *Corruption* is more complex than Mosley's earlier published novels, which are third-person and chronologically linear narratives with only occasional flashbacks. In *Corruption* Mosley uses a first-person narrator, Robert Croft, and makes extensive use of temporal intercutting between the present and several different pasts to depict Robert's intermittent relationship with his cousin and former lover, Kate Lambourne, since their childhood before World War II. His reminiscences are prompted by their accidental meeting in Venice during his visit to the city with his current girlfriend during the 1950s. Robert finds himself in the same situation as Paul and Richard in Mosley's earlier novels: he is entangled with two women at the same time. More than in the earlier novels, characters serve symbolic as well as realistic purposes; Kate's decadent lifestyle and even Venice itself represent "the corruption and injustice of a dying world." The one-word title could almost be that of a medieval morality play. Yet, in the later stages of the novel the crucial episode of the riot and its accompanying revelations precipitate a lifting of the oppressive bleakness and pessimism to allow a sense of redemption and new possibilities. This radical change is signaled by an abandoning of the intricate and sometimes convoluted prose of much of the novel (and its predecessors) for a simpler, more direct style. Instead of being tragic, as might have been expected, the conclusion is open-ended. With this volte-face Mosley seems to be dramatizing the subversion of his tragic pretensions, as he discovers light at the end of the existential tunnel his fiction had been exploring. The conventional critical view may be that *Corruption* is deeply flawed because the conclusion fractures the artistic coherence of the novel, but this criticism completely misses the point. Mosley deliberately fractures his novel to challenge orthodox ideas about artistic coherence and about art.

Corruption marks the end of Mosley's first creative phase. He did not write another novel for five years, during which time he thought deeply about the direction in which modern fiction had gone, coming to the conclusion that it was largely trapped in pessimistic determinism. After *Corruption* he wrote a travel book, *African Switchback* (1958), an account of his drive from Dakar to Lagos with his friend and fellow novelist

Hugo Charteris in 1957. Beginning in 1958 Mosley served for two years as joint editor for a new religious magazine, *Prism,* launched in 1957 as a monthly platform for advanced theological discussion, specifically Anglican. In 1960 he joined the editorial advisory committee of the magazine, and two years later he was appointed its poetry editor. Mosley was an important contributor to *Prism* before it was absorbed into another publication in 1965, his most significant literary articles being "Christian Novels" (October 1961) and his review of J. D. Salinger's *Franny and Zooey* (July 1962), which he praises as a truly Christian novel. In places this review reads like Mosley's new literary manifesto as a Christian at a time when he was returning to fiction but abandoning determinism for more-open forms: "The importance of this story is that it is about free will, and the way in which one person can touch another, profoundly, when that person needs to be touched. Most clever novels nowadays are about determinism, and the way in which no one has a hope of touching anyone ever."

Mosley's involvement in Christian apologetics led to other books in the 1960s. He gave up the editorship of *Prism* to write a biography of Raymond Raynes (1903–1958), the saintly priest he first met in 1950 and an important influence on his thinking. Research for this book took Mosley to South Africa, where Raynes had spent years working closely with the black community. To coincide with the publication of this biography in 1961, Mosley edited the talks Raynes gave during a mission in Denver, Colorado, not long before his death as *The Faith: Instructions on the Christian Faith* (1961). Another product of Mosley's involvement with *Prism* was his most sustained piece of theological writing, *Experience and Religion: A Lay Essay in Theology* (1965).

Mosley's return to novel writing with *Meeting Place* in 1962 marks the beginning of a new phase in his fiction that lasted for nearly ten years. Determined to break free from his earlier manner and indeed from many widely accepted conceptions of the nature of literature, he simplified his prose, making the sentences and paragraphs shorter and the style more cinematic than analytical. For the first time his writing has a strong visual quality and a hard objectivity in depicting the external world, both of which may owe something to the phenomenology underlying the French *nouveau roman.* The narrative method is also different. It is elliptical and discontinuous, resulting in a much more indeterminate sense of reality than in his previous novels. Whereas Mosley's earlier technique involved explaining everything and leaving out nothing, in *Meeting Place* he is highly selective in what he presents to the reader, who has to piece things together by making connections between the intercut sections. What is particularly sur-

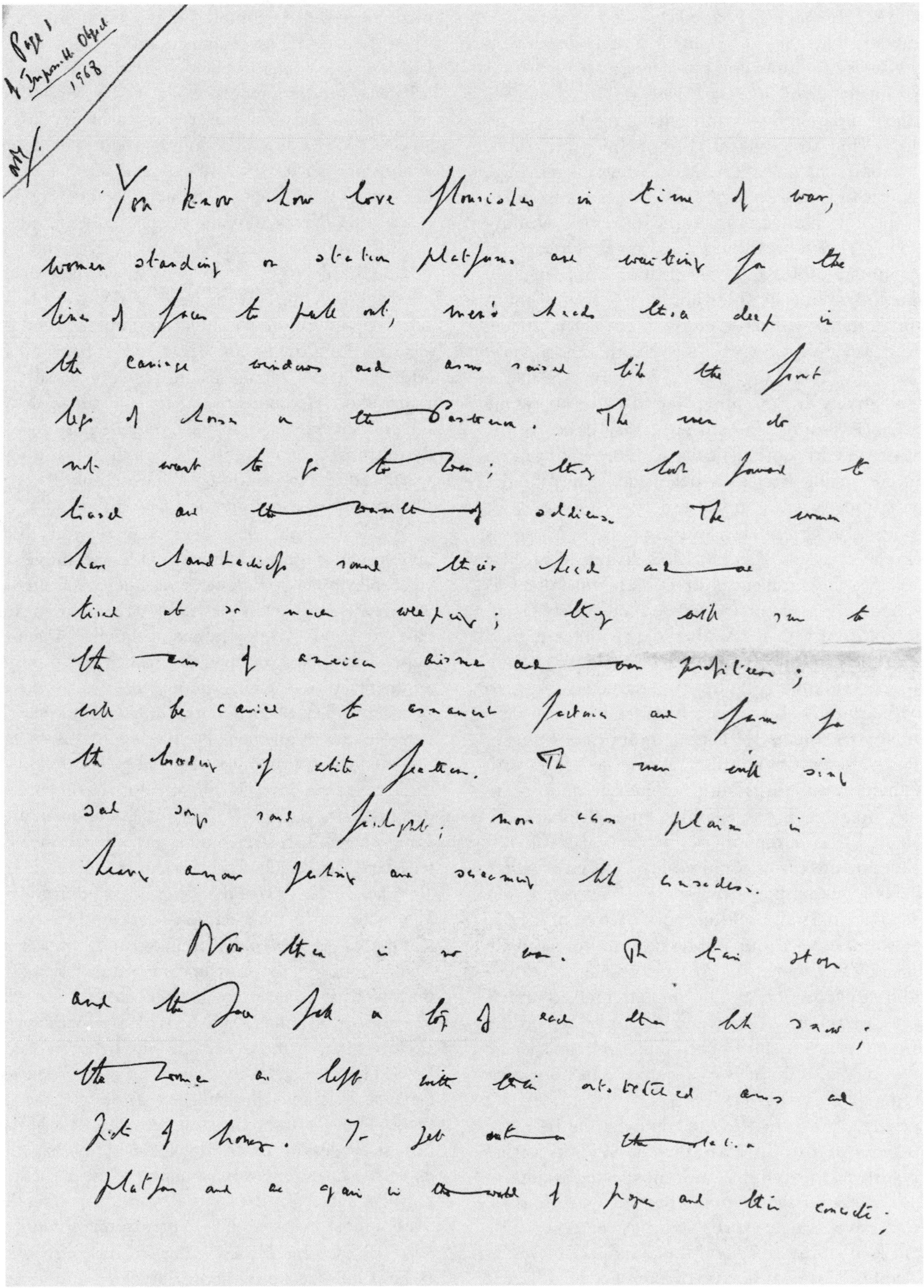

Page from the manuscript for Mosley's Impossible Object *(Collection of Nicholas Mosley)*

prising about *Meeting Place,* and a welcome relief after the somber intensity of Mosley's largely humorless early novels, is the important part comedy plays.

At the center of *Meeting Place* is the idealistic, religious, and fundamentally innocent Harry Gates, who works for a charitable organization, helping social misfits and delinquent teenagers. Meanwhile his marriage to an American is in a state of crisis. Mosley introduces a wide range of characters from the extremely wealthy to the impoverished, including a newspaper tycoon and a former inmate of a Nazi concentration camp, most of whom are linked in a complex network of relationships. This human merry-go-round culminates in Harry being forced to deal with his own problems rather than everybody else's, and following his wife's return to America he acts positively by pursuing her in order to rescue their marriage. Going against the literary trends of the time, the novel ends optimistically with the emphasis on renewal, conveying Mosley's belief in the possibilities of regeneration, growth, and creativity.

While *Meeting Place* is a turning point in Mosley's fiction, his next novel, *Accident* (1965), is one of his best and vindicates the pioneering direction in which he was going. The actual story, narrated retrospectively by an Oxford philosophy don, Stephen Jervis, after a road accident at the beginning of the novel, is simple enough and concerns a small group of characters near to Stephen: his family, his writer friend Charlie and his wife, and two students, William (upper-class English) and Anna (aristocratic Austrian). Anna has affairs with both William and Charlie, and Stephen becomes unintentionally involved in the resulting entanglements, culminating in his suppression of the fact that Anna is responsible for the car crash in which William is killed. What is far from simple is the spare, compressed, and highly selective narration of this story of love, marriage, and the "split between our public face and our private helplessness." The world, as Mosley presents it, is characterized by uncertainty, and human attempts to understand it are extremely tentative. Philosophy, according to Stephen, "does not find specific answers to specific questions, but rather deals with questions to which there are no specific answers."

Mosley's prose in *Accident* could hardly be more different from that of his early novels. With its verbal fragments, staccato rhythms, and unexpected juxtapositions, his writing possesses an intense nervous edginess. Phrases and even single words stand as sentences. The relative lack of connectives and the avoidance of verbal fluency embody the difficulty of connecting different experiences, so that the principle of causality is undermined. Stephen declares, "We are all in fragments, disjointed," and there is considerable tension between his attempt at rational control and the ambiguities, contra-

dictions, and discontinuities of the situation in which he finds himself. This fragmentation helps to explain Mosley's approach to characterization. When William asks why modern novels "can't just be stories of characters and action and society," Charlie replies subversively, "We know too much about characters and actions and society . . . we can now write about people knowing." According to Stephen, "people are not characters but things moving occasionally in jumps and mostly in indiscernible slowness." Elsewhere in the novel Charlie argues, "People don't behave in the way we think they do." At the heart of the novel is the relationship between inner choice and outer event, the subject of a long discussion between Stephen and Charlie after William's fatal accident. Finally Mosley undermines the tragic potential of the narrative, in which a life and several relationships are ended, by focusing on the birth of a baby to Stephen's wife, thus looking forward rather than backward. The emphasis is not on finality but on continuity and new life.

Mosley sold the motion-picture rights to *Accident,* and Joseph Losey eventually made the movie using a screenplay by Harold Pinter, which departs from the novel in a few significant respects. In writing his next novel, *Assassins* (1966), Mosley turned to the thriller genre in the hope of appealing to a wider audience and of negotiating another film deal, which did not materialize. *Assassins* is a political thriller of sorts but is unlike any other. Mosley uses the literary methods he developed in *Accident,* applying them to a broader social and political canvas. The thriller element involves the attempted assassination of a despotic eastern European political leader on an important visit to the British foreign minister. The minister's daughter Mary accidentally discovers the young would-be assassin Peter Ferec, who abducts her, precipitating a situation in which considerable tensions develop between private and public worlds, inner realities, and political facades. Mary seems to have more in common with her kidnapper than with those determined to rescue her, including her unsympathetic father, and Mosley is especially good at exploring the curious relationship between Mary and Peter. Her eventual complicity in his plan produces a particularly ingenious thrillerlike twist before the denouement. The elliptical crosscutting Mosley uses in narrating this story leaves much unexplained, perhaps beyond explanation, and his transformation of the thriller becomes a way of subjecting the political world, including the inner lives of those involved in it, to penetrating scrutiny.

By the time Mosley wrote his next novel, *Impossible Object* (1968), he was no longer involved in organized religion, and his private life had become extremely complex, with his marriage to Rosemary seemingly in terminal decline. In *Efforts at Truth* he writes at length about the novel and the personal involvements behind it. *Impossible*

Object is the most difficult novel of Mosley's second phase, a bewildering assemblage of apparently separate narratives that are nevertheless related. The title refers to trick two-dimensional drawings of supposedly three-dimensional objects that cannot exist in reality. Only from one fixed viewpoint can the three-dimensional version appear as in the drawing. From any other angle it will look quite different. Reflexivity is a feature of Mosley's novels throughout the 1960s, but nowhere more so than in this one, which is preoccupied with the representation of reality and the impossibility of fixing such a relativistic concept as reality: "The object is that life is impossible; one cuts out fabrication and creates reality."

The contents page might suggest that *Impossible Object* is a collection of eight self-contained stories about human relationships, especially love and marriage. Short italicized sections occur before, after, and between the stories, however, and these puzzling interludes, so differently written from the main narratives, act as links by introducing themes and motifs that turn up elsewhere. Most of the stories are narrated in the first person without the "I" being the same throughout; yet, as the reader proceeds from story to story, patterns of repetition begin to emerge, indicating that there are connections between them and that characters do recur. Mosley, however, disguises these lines of continuity rather than drawing attention to them, so that the reader is forced to interpret the text without any confidence that there is such a thing as a correct interpretation. Mosley's technique of multiple viewpoint is far from new, but he pushes it to an extreme of openness and uncertainty in *Impossible Object* in order to demonstrate the folly of trying to impose a rigid pattern on something as fluid as human life.

After making his movie of *Accident,* Losey expressed an interest in a movie version of *Impossible Object.* Mosley worked on a screenplay, but the project failed to develop at that time. It was revived a few years later when the American director John Frankenheimer took it on while trying to break into the flourishing European art-movie market after leaving Hollywood for Paris. Before returning to this screenplay as well as tackling a different one for Losey, Mosley completed a less experimental and more immediately accessible novel than *Impossible Object—Natalie Natalia,* which was widely acclaimed when it was published in 1971 and turned out to be the last novel in his second phase. By this time Mosley had flirted briefly with a career in politics after becoming Baron Ravensdale in 1966. This peerage entitled him to a seat in the House of Lords, and he joined the Liberals, but before long he decided that he was not cut out to be a politician. Nevertheless, the insights he gained into parliamentary life in the Palace of Westminster proved invaluable when he wrote *Natalie Natalia.*

Dust jacket for the first U.S. edition of Mosley's 1980 novel, told from the perspective of an eighteen-year-old who is staying with his uncle, the prime minister

What makes this novel one of Mosley's most exciting is his startlingly unconventional way of treating a story line whose ingredients—love, adultery, shame, and breakdown—are in themselves unexceptional. The narrator, Anthony Greville, is a member of Parliament, and his mistress, Natalia, is the wife of another philandering politician. Because Greville finds her a completely contradictory person, he refers to her by the two names in the title, Natalie indicating her "ravenous" side and Natalia her "angelic" one. To Greville she embodies Johann Wolfgang von Goethe's concept of the daemonic principle as expressed in *Dichtung und Wahrheit* (Poetry and Truth, 1811–1833), from which Mosley drew the long epigraph for *Natalie Natalia.* The novel charts the private and public sides of Greville's life, both of which are in a state of increasing disorder. Greville's secret affair with Natalia and his consequent guilt at deceiving his wife runs parallel to developments in his political career. Although deeply disillusioned with politics, he is sufficiently anxious about a leading black politician interned without trial in Central Africa to become involved in his fate. Eventually, in a state of mental collapse in Africa, Greville rides a bicycle into an empty swimming pool, after which he undergoes a process of psychological and physical recovery. In *Natalie Natalia* Mosley is particularly successful at bringing out the inconsistency of people and the enigmatic nature of human experience. Creating his own particular brand of comedy in the process, he is able to illuminate experience in unexpectedly fresh ways only because he is prepared to take considerable risks with language to convey the truth as he sees it—risks that good poets, unlike many prose writers, regularly take. His originality in using language, stretching its expressive possibilities to encompass the apparently inexpressible, allows him to open the doors of perception.

Right after finishing *Natalie Natalia,* Mosley was nearly killed in a road accident and took almost a year to recover from it. He did not publish another work of fiction for eight years. When Mosley was able to work again, Losey suggested that they collaborate on a movie about the assassination of Leon Trotsky, and this project went ahead quickly. Mosley, however, was not pleased about the way his script was being filmed, so he welcomed the opportunity to write a book about Trotsky, the publication of which would coincide with the release of Losey's movie in 1972 even though he had to write it in just over two months. After *The Assassination of Trotsky,* Mosley returned to his screenplay of *Impossible Object* for Frankenheimer, but again he was disappointed in the finished motion picture, feeling that it lacked the subtlety and irony he had intended. Although never released in either the United States or the United Kingdom, Frankenheimer's movie did enjoy some success on the Continent.

Mosley's next book, another biographical work, came about when his wife's mother, Lady Salmond (née Hon. Monica Margaret Grenfell), died, leaving all her papers to her daughter, including material relating to one of Lady Salmond's brothers, the celebrated soldier-poet Julian Grenfell, who was killed in 1915 during World War I. Mosley had long been interested in Grenfell and welcomed the opportunity to use the papers to write *Julian Grenfell: His Life and The Times of His Death 1888–1915* (1976). As the subtitle suggests, part of Mosley's purpose is to explore Grenfell's aristocratic milieu in an attempt to understand the social and cultural factors, especially the underlying psychological and ideological contradictions, that made World War I possible and even welcome in 1914. By the time the book was published, Mosley's marriage to Rosemary had ended in divorce, and he had married Verity Raymond on 17 July 1974.

During the 1970s, when he went into analysis, Mosley gradually put together his most complex and abstract work of fiction, *Catastrophe Practice,* three "plays not for acting" (each with a preface and the last followed by an essay) followed by a novella. The six principal figures or "actors" reappear in different guises in the various sections of the book, and there is an elaborate arrangement of correspondences and cross-references throughout, producing unity from apparent fragmentation and dislocation. *Catastrophe Practice* marks another important turning point in Mosley's career. He originally intended to follow it with six interlinked yet self-contained novels, each dealing with one of the main characters. Mosley later modified this highly ambitious scheme, reducing the number of "sequels" to four.

Only when he had virtually completed the first book in the series did Mosley come across catastrophe theory, a mathematical attempt to explain discontinuities in the natural world for which orthodox mathematics could not account. Struck by the parallel between this theory and his attempt to investigate discontinuities in human experience using a highly unorthodox literary structure, Mosley was inspired to choose *Catastrophe Practice* as his title. In *Efforts at Truth* Mosley says of this new phase in his writing that "my novels that follow *Catastrophe Practice* are different from the ones that precede it because the protagonists do not feel themselves to be on their own even when they are watching themselves [but] feel themselves as part of some network . . . to do with the recognition, indeed the trust, that if you pay attention to what seems true inside you then something is affected on the outside." Even so, *Catastrophe Practice* is not a complete change of direction for Mosley; rather, it represents a new approach to the issues that preoccupied him in his novels of the 1960s.

The book originated in some experiments by Mosley using dramatic form, reworking ideas from his earlier play *The Good Samaritans.* He began with "Aerodrome," subsequently called *Landfall,* which examines the situation of a group of characters who are apparently trapped on a stage by their scripts, symbolizing their conditioning and inheritance. The issue is whether these "actors" can escape from their allotted roles. Mosley nowhere acknowledges the influence of Luigi Pirandello's *Six Characters in Search of an Author* (1921), but there are obvious resemblances between his "plays not for acting" and Pirandello's dramatic masterpiece. After *Landfall* Mosley wrote the play that precedes it in the published book, *Skylight,* which involves the same "actors" as *Landfall* but in different roles and configurations. Again Mosley employs the metaphor of the stage to investigate ways of experiencing and knowing the world and what is meant by reality. To focus on the relationship between mental activity and the external world, including how the brain constructs reality, Mosley recycles his "actors" in a third play, *Cell.* In *Cypher,* the short novel that follows the plays, Mosley finally identifies his six "actors" as an elderly pair, Eleanor and Max; a young pair, Judith and Bert; and an intermediate pair, Lilia and Jason, all of whom share a way of perceiving the world. At a time of threatening catastrophe and breakup, a crucial issue is the survival of Lilia's baby, who is successfully safeguarded. Indeed the protection of the child, whether unborn or born, is an important preoccupation in this entire series of novels.

Catastrophe Practice is centrally concerned with a major twentieth-century crisis in Western civilization that seems to require a catastrophe (as in the mathematical theory) to produce an evolutionary jump in human consciousness if the drift toward self-destruction is to be avoided. Drawing on several philosophers, including Friedrich Nietzsche, Edmund Husserl, Jean-Paul Sartre, and Karl Popper, as well as both Bertolt Brecht's theory and practice of drama, Mosley attempts to establish a tenable philosophical position for optimism and hope while also struggling to invent forms suitable for articulating such a Weltanschauung. Running through *Catastrophe Practice* is Mosley's belief in the need to liberate consciousness, language, and art from the confines of convention, including such literary models as tragedy and farce. For Mosley much modern literature, with its predilection for disillusionment and despair, possesses a strongly negative bias and inculcates defeatism and pessimism by falsifying reality. *Catastrophe Practice* and the ensuing novels provide an alternative.

Although convinced that *Catastrophe Practice* was his best work, Mosley found it difficult to interest anyone in the book and achieved publication only by contracting to write a book about his father when he died. Reviewers were baffled by the originality of *Catastrophe Practice.* In continuing the series Mosley adopted less-demanding narrative strategies, and his next novel, *Imago Bird* (1980), is comparatively straightforward, presenting few difficulties. Chronologically this work precedes *Cypher* so that Lilia's baby, a crucial element in the narrative, is not yet born. The narrator is Bert, an eighteen-year-old who is staying with his uncle, the prime minister, while waiting to go to Cambridge. Believing the grown-up world to be mad, Bert is trying to make sense of the perplexing, fantastic, and theatrical world of adults and to discover the relation between exterior and interior reality. He is helped by a psychoanalyst, Dr. Anders, who is Eleanor from *Catastrophe Practice.* The process is further complicated by Bert's self-conscious need to understand himself understanding the world and its random discontinuities, recalling Charlie's insistence in *Accident* that the novel today should be "about people knowing." Bert encounters a wide range

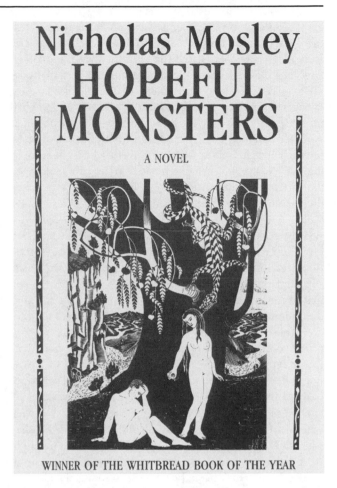

Dust jacket for the first U.S. edition of Mosley's 1990 novel, the final book in his Catastrophe Practice *series*

of people, including pop musicians, Young Trotskyites, leading politicians, and media celebrities. Seen through his innocent yet penetrating eyes, most of these people are unwittingly trapped in linguistics and behaviors of their own devising. They have allocated stock parts to themselves in a melodramatic fiction called life and are intent on acting them out. Instead of accepting things as they appear, Bert probes and analyzes what is considered routine and ordinary in his hesitant, uncertain, and exploratory way, often with startling results. In a more accessible way than *Catastrophe Practice, Imago Bird* is about the imprisoning restrictions imposed by conventions and about the need to escape from the world of illusion they perpetuate if the human potential for creativity and happiness is to be realized.

Serpent (1981), the second "sequel" to *Catastrophe Practice,* is a more complex narrative than *Imago Bird,* including several interwoven strands that are concerned in some way with Israel. The title refers to the story in Genesis about Adam and Eve eating the forbidden fruit of the Tree of Knowledge in the Garden of Eden. Dealing with the biblical Holy Land, *Serpent* is, in its way, about knowing what the Tree of Knowledge involves. The main characters are Lilia and Jason, parents of the child in *Cypher* and *Imago Bird*. The child is now a little older. Jason has been working on a screenplay, and one strand of the novel concerns events on a plane taking Lilia, Jason, and some influential movie people to Israel, where the movie is to be shot. Another strand is Jason's screenplay about the first-century Jewish leader Josephus, who went over to the Romans during the Jewish revolt that culminated in the famous siege at the fortress of Masada in A.D. 73, when many Jews killed themselves rather than surrender. The novel also deals with a contemporary crisis in Israel, a country preoccupied with its survival. At both the individual and the national level, survival in the face of destructive impulses and forces is indeed one of Mosley's principal concerns in *Serpent*. Although historical, Jason's script deals with such perennial issues as the conflict between devotion and reason and the individual's relations with and responsibilities to society. These problems do, in fact, pervade the modern-day action so that past and present echo one another. Jason has to survive the machinations of the movie people, who cannot understand his ironical and reflexive screenplay and so plot against him by trying to arrange Lilia's seduction.

The *Catastrophe Practice* series was progressing well when Sir Oswald Mosley died in 1980. At the time Mosley was working on his next novel, *Judith* (1986), but he put it aside for a few years in order to fulfill his commitment to write a book about his father. So much material about the family came to light from Sir Oswald's voluminous papers that Mosley eventually wrote two books, *Rules of the Game* and *Beyond the Pale*. In *Efforts at Truth* he describes the difficulties he had to overcome, especially from Sir Oswald's widow, in publishing these family histories.

Judith is in the form of three letters from the title character to other main characters in the series. At the narrative level there is a radical discontinuity among these letters, each of which is about a different event in her life. At a metaphorical level, however, these narrative leaps may be seen as a movement toward a new concept of unity. As an actress, Judith is particularly sensitive to the continually changing consciousness with which people play roles, whether on stage or in life. Brecht's influence on the entire *Catastrophe Practice* sequence is particularly evident in Judith's awareness that people often speak as though their words are in quotation marks. *Judith* is a novel about the enigma of human consciousness, including the consciousness of consciousness. Various important themes from earlier narratives recur in *Judith*, especially the birth of Lilia's baby. In the final part of the novel, several years after his birth, Lilia's child is lost for a time during an antinuclear demonstration outside an American airbase in England. The child has entered a military danger zone to look for a mutant, two-headed sheep he calls Hopeful Monster. (For

Mosley the child himself is the hopeful monster.) If the threat of a nuclear holocaust hangs over the world like some Old Testament catastrophe, the child's quest is symbolically a search for a way out to the Promised Land. *Judith* is full of biblical imagery and allusions, including the Garden of Eden, the Tree of Life, and Noah's ark. Judith has a model in the Apocrypha—the Jewish woman who enters the camp of the besieging Assyrians and brings victory from the jaws of defeat by killing their leader, Holofernes. In this respect *Judith* develops elements present in the earlier novels and points forward to the final book in the series, *Hopeful Monsters* (1990).

At one time biologists used the term "hopeful monster" to describe a mutation (such as a two-headed sheep) that seemed monstrous because it was a departure from the norm but could also be considered hopeful in the sense that, given the right conditions, it could survive and prosper to become the norm in the evolutionary scheme of things. In *Efforts at Truth* Mosley says that all the principal characters in his *Catastrophe Practice* series are hopeful monsters, at odds with society and with an unusual way of viewing life: "Their way of seeing things is to do with the faculty of being able with part of themselves to stand back and see the forces and dramas by which other parts of themselves are driven; and by this faculty perhaps to alter the forces and dramas themselves." Mosley's protagonists suggest the possibility of a new mutation in consciousness itself, one that is needed to overcome the destructive and self-destructive patterns of normal human life so evident in the twentieth century, if survival is to be possible in a world that for the first time possesses the capability of annihilating itself.

The Judith and Holofernes story provides an obvious link between *Judith* and *Hopeful Monsters,* in which Mosley ambitiously attempts to pursue the main themes of the series in relation to the political and scientific history, especially the consequences of Albert Einstein's theories. Issues in the philosophies of language and science are interwoven with important historical events. The main characters are Eleanor Anders and Max Ackerman, the elderly pair in previous narratives. *Hopeful Monsters* traces their lives from the 1920s, covering some of the same ground as Mosley's nonfiction books *Rules of the Game* and *Beyond the Pale*. In style too *Hopeful Monsters* is closer to his approachable biographies than to his usually much more difficult fiction. Despite its intellectual content and its considerable length, *Hopeful Monsters* is probably Mosley's most accessible novel.

Until the concluding section, narrated by a "correlator" who proves to be Jason, the narrative alternates between Eleanor and Max, whose paths converge. Jason's coda involves a leap forward in time to just after the end of *Judith*. Eleanor's story begins in Berlin, where her German parents—her mother is Jewish—are active in left-wing politics. Max comes from a family on the fringes of the Bloomsbury Group in Cambridge and London. Eleanor, who is interested in anthropology and psychiatry, and Max, who is concerned with biology, theoretical physics, and cybernetics, employ their knowledge of crucial intellectual problems about matter, reality, subjectivity, and objectivity as a means of interpreting the ideological and existential traumas of Europe, especially between the two world wars. Mosley's narrative includes philosophers such as Husserl, Martin Heidegger, and Ludwig Wittgenstein as well as political figures such as Rosa Luxemburg, Adolf Hitler, and Francisco Franco. Max's involvement in the Manhattan Project to develop nuclear weapons during World War II emphasizes the impossibility of conducting scientific research without considering ethical questions or experiencing political manipulation. *Hopeful Monsters* urges readers not to give up hope in human potentialities even while facing the worst of human catastrophes, including the Spanish Civil War, Joseph Stalin's purges, and the Nazi Holocaust. Mosley's human "monsters" are, above all, hopeful.

For the much-praised *Hopeful Monsters* Mosley won his first literary prize, the prestigious Whitbread Book of the Year Award. He was subsequently invited to be one of the judges for another top British literary award, the Booker Prize for fiction. What he has to say about this experience in his next book, the autobiographical *Efforts at Truth,* is relevant to his own work. After reading more than one hundred new novels, he concluded that the vast majority endorsed a view of life and a conception of fiction that his own novels—especially his *Catastrophe Practice* series but also all his other books since Meeting Place—set out to undermine. When the other judges voted to exclude all six of Mosley's suggestions from the final short list, he resigned, causing waves of consternation in the London literary world. This episode confirmed just how pioneering and forward-looking Mosley's fiction since the 1960s has been in its determination to break out of the confines of so much modernist and postmodernist writing.

On the last page of *Efforts at Truth* Mosley mentions "one more story I might write," and two years later he published *Children of Darkness and Light* (1996). This novel is not part of the *Catastrophe Practice* series, but thematically and stylistically the novel is close to the series. The books share the same preoccupation with uncertainty, evolution, mutation, and knowing about knowing; mythological and especially biblical imagery and allusions abound in all. Incorporated into the narrative of *Children of Darkness and Light* are various catastrophes, including the genocidal lunacy of the Bosnian war after the breakup of Yugoslavia,

the nuclear disaster at Chernobyl, and a lesser incident at a controversial nuclear power and reprocessing plant in Cumbria in northwest England. This plant is not named in the novel, but the episode is based on events at Sellafield, previously called Windscale. In contrast to the destructive and self-destructive catastrophes generated by adults, the children of the title are born into a world of darkness, but they point forward to an alternative world of light. Children are much more in the foreground than in the *Catastrophe Practice* series although in suggesting new patterns that may emerge from the old, exhausted ones they serve the same symbolic function.

The narrator of *Children of Darkness and Light* is Harry, an investigative journalist whose difficult relationships with his wife, Melissa, and son, Billy, become tortuously entangled with his professional work. In the first half of the novel he travels to Cumbria to follow up a story about a group of children who are supposed to have gone into the hills to establish a commune after seeing a vision of the Virgin Mary. Harry has previously written about similar manifestations in Yugoslavia and even interviewed two of the children involved there. Much of what happens to Harry in Cumbria is puzzling and enigmatic, especially as the children's leader, a girl called Gaby, turns out to be a refugee from Yugoslavia. In the later stages of the novel the various narrative strands concerning past and present—involving Melissa, Billy, Gaby, and some other characters in London and Yugoslavia—become interwoven as the novel moves to its climax in war-torn Bosnia, where another group of children escape the adult world of slaughter and carnage under the protection of a woman who claims in the final sentence to be the Blessed Virgin herself. Despite the images of despair and violence in Harry's account of what he sees in the former Yugoslavia, optimistic notes emerge from the children's potential to look forward without being trapped in the past and from the restoration of Harry's relationships with Billy and Melissa, who wants a new baby.

Mosley has discussed the almost miraculous way in which William Shakespeare's last plays, the romances, achieve a hopeful, positive outcome from seeming disaster, thus transcending conventional genres such as tragedy and comedy. In several ways Mosley attempts something similar in his later fiction. Nowhere is the parallel more obvious than in *Children of Darkness and Light,* where Mosley closely echoes the crucial redemptive role given to children by Shakespeare.

Reference:

Review of Contemporary Fiction, special Mosley issue, 2, no. 2 (1982).

V. S. Naipaul

(17 August 1932 –)

Stella Swain
University of the West of England

See also the entries on Naipaul in *DLB 125: Twentieth-Century Caribbean and Black African Writers, Second Series; DLB 204: British Travel Writers, 1940–1997;* and *Yearbook 1985.*

BOOKS: *The Mystic Masseur* (London: Deutsch, 1957; New York: Vanguard, 1959);

The Suffrage of Elvira (London: Deutsch, 1958);

Miguel Street (London: Deutsch, 1959; New York: Vanguard, 1960);

A House for Mr. Biswas (London: Deutsch, 1961; New York: McGraw-Hill, 1962);

The Middle Passage: Impressions of Five Societies–British, French and Dutch–in the West Indies and South America (London: Deutsch, 1962; New York: Macmillan, 1963);

Mr. Stone and the Knights Companion (London: Deutsch, 1963; New York: Macmillan, 1964);

An Area of Darkness: An Experience of India (London: Deutsch, 1964; New York: Macmillan, 1965);

A Flag on the Island (New York: Macmillan, 1967);

The Mimic Men (London: Deutsch, 1967; New York: Macmillan, 1967);

The Loss of El Dorado: A History (London: Deutsch, 1969; New York: Knopf, 1970; revised edition, Harmondsworth, U.K.: Penguin, 1973);

In a Free State (London: Deutsch, 1971; New York: Knopf, 1971);

The Overcrowded Baracoon and Other Articles (London: Deutsch, 1972; New York: Knopf, 1973);

Guerrillas (London: Deutsch, 1975; New York: Knopf, 1975);

India: A Wounded Civilization (London: Deutsch, 1977; New York: Knopf, 1977);

A Bend in the River (London: Deutsch, 1979; New York: Knopf, 1979);

The Return of Eva Peròn, with the Killings in Trinidad (London: Deutsch, 1980; New York: Knopf, 1980);

A Congo Diary (Los Angeles: Sylvester & Orphanos, 1980);

Among the Believers: An Islamic Journey (London: Deutsch, 1981; New York: Knopf, 1981);

V. S. Naipaul at the time of A Way in the World *(photograph © 1994 by Jerry Bauer)*

Finding the Centre: Two Narratives (London: Deutsch, 1984; New York: Knopf, 1984);

The Enigma of Arrival (London: Viking, 1987; New York: Knopf, 1987);

A Turn in the South (London: Viking, 1989; New York: Knopf, 1989);

India: A Million Mutinies Now (London: Heinemann, 1990; New York: Viking, 1991);

A Way in the World (London: Heinemann, 1994);

Beyond Belief: Islamic Excursions Among the Converted Peoples (London: Little, Brown, 1998).

Collection: *Three Novels* (New York: Knopf, 1982)–includes *The Mystic Masseur, The Suffrage of Elvira,* and *Miguel Street.*

OTHER: *Island Voices: Stories from the West Indies,* edited by Andrew Salkey, with contributions by Naipaul New York: Liveright, 1970).

SELECTED PERIODICAL PUBLICATIONS—
UNCOLLECTED: "Honesty Needed in West Indian Writing," *Sunday Guardian* (Trinidad), 28 October 1956, p. 29;

"Reading for Pleasure: The Little More," *Times* (London), 13 July 1961, p. 13;

"The Immigrants: Lo! The Poor West Indian," *Punch*, 242 (17 January 1962): 124–126;

"Trollop in the West Indies," *Listener*, 67 (15 March 1962): 461;

"London: Return to England," *Illustrated Weekly of India*, 84 (14 April 1963): 21;

"London: A Case for Future Historians," *Illustrated Weekly of India*, 84 (28 July 1963): 14–15;

"London Letter: The Race Problem," *Illustrated Weekly of India*, 85 (19 January 1964): 19;

"I Don't Consider Myself a West Indian," *Guyana Graphic* (30 November 1968);

"V. S. Naipaul Tells How Writing Changes a Writer," *Tapia* (Trinidad), 2 December 1973, p. 11;

"My Brother's Tragic Sense," *Spectator*, 24 January 1987, pp. 22–23;

"On Being a Writer," *New York Review of Books*, 23 April 1987, p. 7;

"Argentina: Living with Cruelty," *New York Review of Books*, 30 January 1992, pp. 47–53;

"The End of Peronism?" *New York Review of Books*, 13 February 1992, pp. 47–53;

"To a Young Writer," *New Yorker*, 71 (26 June–3 July 1995): 144–153.

V. S. Naipaul is a gifted contemporary novelist. No important guide to twentieth-century literature is presently without a reference to his work, which has been prolific. In the early stages of his career he was acclaimed as a West Indian and Commonwealth writer. The author's Caribbean upbringing, and the focus on Trinidad in his first novels, led the British literary establishment to position him as a Commonwealth writer, when this term was being newly applied to accommodate writings in English by subjects of Britain's former dominion. However, Naipaul has generally been concerned to resist such categorizations. More recently his work has been termed "postcolonial," but its significance must be acknowledged to exceed that of any particular group interest or experience. His postcolonialism should be understood in the widest sense; this author is not so much the voice of any particular newly independent or decolonized nation, as the chronicler of diverse global experiences of alienation and loss in the wake of European imperialism. His status has long been recognized in the form of important prizes and awards, some received in relation to particular works, others simply acknowledging the overall merit of his

writing. He is a member of the Society of Authors and a fellow of the Royal Society of Literature.

Vidiadhar Surajprasad Naipaul was born in Chaguanas, Trinidad, on 17 August 1932, and is of Indian descent. He was born into the large Brahmin family of Seepersad and Bropatie Capildeo Naipaul. He grew up in Port of Spain with his brother and five sisters. Seepersad Naipaul was a newspaper journalist; his aspirations to be a "serious" writer were disappointed, and Naipaul has remained profoundly moved by his father's sense of failure.

Naipaul's Hindu maternal grandfather migrated at the turn of the century from Utter Pradesh (in Northern India, a region to the South of Nepal) to Trinidad, under the colonial system of indentured labor. This process of migration had been under way since 1845. It was instituted to replace the labor lost on the sugar plantations after the abolition of the slave trade. This mass movement of people from one part of the British empire to another did not cease until well into the twentieth century. As a result of continuous migration, the population of Trinidad is extremely diverse, made up of Caribbeans, Africans, Indians, Chinese, peoples from the Middle East, and Europe. In his work Naipaul observes the multiplicity of races, cultures, and traditions that have come together in this region and the consequent problem of achieving a sense of communal identity. The area, its history, and its inhabitants became the subjects of his fiction and nonfiction writing.

Naipaul's family inherited some wealth on his mother's side. He was educated at Tranquillity Boys School from 1939 to 1942 and the Queen's Royal College, Port of Spain, from 1943 to 1949. He received a schooling derived from the nineteenth-century British educational system that was established in and imported from India. This schooling, as Fawzia Mustafa points out, was in line with Thomas Babington Macaulay's idea, proposed in his well-known "Minute on Indian Education" (1835), that the purpose of colonial education should be to "form a class who may be interpreters between [the British] and the millions whom we govern; a class of persons, Indian in blood and colour, but English in taste, in opinions, in morals and in intellect." This circumstance of his upbringing is of lasting significance to Naipaul throughout his life, in his self-conscious efforts to forge a career as a writer in the European tradition.

In 1948 Naipaul won a scholarship to Oxford University, and in 1950 he left Trinidad for Britain, in excitement and trepidation. However, his destination did not live up to his expectations, and in a 1994 interview with Stephen Schiff he remembered his early years in England as "pretty dreadful," a "long, unbroken period of melancholy" during which he struggled toward find-

Dust jacket for Naipaul's first novel, a satire of Trinidadian politics

ing a secure sense of identity and purpose, as a man and as a writer. His arrival in England, as he later recalled, perplexed him. In *The Enigma of Arrival* (1987) he writes: "In Trinidad, feeling myself far away, I had held myself back for life at the centre of things." However, during his stay in London, he found that he "had come to England at the wrong time": "I had come too late to find the England, the heart of empire which (like a provincial, from a far corner of the empire) I had created in my fantasy." England has, however, remained his principal home since that first arrival. After several moves he settled in Wiltshire in 1970.

The difficulty of his first years in the United Kingdom was exacerbated by the breakdown and death of his father in 1953, which affected him greatly and put a strain on his relationship with his mother. He also had to establish some form of financial security. Following the completion of his time at Oxford, Naipaul began to work for the BBC's World Service, producing occasional pieces for a series called *Caribbean Voices*. He also began to undertake reviewing for magazines and newspapers. Meanwhile, he began to focus his determination to make his living as a writer.

At Oxford University he met a student, Patricia Ann Hale, whom he married in 1955. The couple remained childless. Patricia died after an illness, and Naipaul has since remarried. As Naipaul later said in an interview with Zoe Heller, "I couldn't *bear* the idea of having children. I didn't want a crowd"; this comment is perhaps a reflection upon the conditions of his upbringing. The character that Naipaul projects in his semi-autobiographical writings is of a man who is reclusive and contemplative though profoundly interested in life and in people. He tends to be pessimistic and introspective and values his solitude. He views his personality as having been deeply affected by the anguish of alienation and the effort to establish himself in Britain. Naipaul returned briefly to Trinidad in 1956, felt utterly displaced, and came quickly back to London. This feeling of displacement was to motivate his early works to represent and understand life in the West Indies. He has, since that time, traveled extensively, including journeys to India, Africa, America, and back to the West Indies. These journeys have produced material both for his novels and his travel writing, which explores the bearing travel has had upon his sense of identity. His early writings concentrate upon Trinidad; later he explores the traces left by their political pasts on other countries, including England.

Naipaul's main concern in his work is the human and political debris left in the wake of empire. He offers hard-edged accounts of the chaos, degradation, violence, and political anarchy of twentieth-century life in various postcolonial nations. He disapproves of the aggressive nationalist movements that have arisen. In a letter to author Paul Theroux, published in *The New Yorker* as "To a Young Writer" in 1995, Naipaul wrote, "I do not think that any country that has to surrender judgement on any important issue to its masses can ever make a contribution." He expresses in his work the sense of depletion, betrayal, and dispossession experienced by people whose lives have been profoundly altered and affected by the imperial past. For Naipaul there are no easy answers; idealism of any kind is an unacceptable consolation and a luxury. He examines and articulates the awareness of waste, exhaustion, and lassitude that haunts decolonized nations, and also, to some extent, postimperial Britain. However, the serious philosophical exploration of the human condition in his fiction and nonfiction also seems to exceed such historical contingency.

His writing moves across three generic categories: fiction, autobiography, and travel writing. All of his work is characterized by a strong autobiographical bias. The details of his life that he sees as significant and chooses to make public are amply explored throughout his writing. Notably, they divulge little about his most personal relationships (a reluctance also expressed in interviews). His friend Theroux describes him in *V. S. Naipaul: An Introduction to His Work* (1972) as an "intensely private individual" and suggests that curious readers will be able to deduce from his writing that "Naipaul is not tall, that he is a vegetarian, enjoys cricket, and has no children." He is known to be impatient, fastidious in all matters from cleanliness to good wine, and capable of voicing uncomfortable sentiments. His writings have a great deal to say, however, about his development as a writer and traveler. As he writes retrospectively in *The Enigma of Arrival:* "From the starting point of Trinidad, my knowledge and self-knowledge grew. The street in Port of Spain where I had spent part of my childhood; a reconstruction of my 'Indian' family life in Trinidad; a journey to Caribbean and South American colonies; a later journey to the special ancestral land of India. My curiosity spread in all directions. Every exploration, every book, added to my knowledge, qualified my earlier idea of myself and the world."

A dominant recurrent theme in Naipaul's work is his realization that his becoming a writer was, because of his background, no straightforward task. He realized that he had first to discover or fashion a literary form from the traditions of the European novel, which could accommodate the experience and concerns of the postcolonial, non-European individual, who is without a stable sense of home or history. He had to find a way of making the man and writer into the same person; "it took time—and much writing!—to arrive at that synthesis," he recalls in *The Enigma of Arrival*. This self-consciousness as a writer is closely linked to the personal pain of displacement.

Naipaul's early novels focus on his birthplace in the Caribbean, with the clarity of distance and hindsight provided by being in London. They take a comic look at the inadequate operation of the imported, British political system in the West Indies and, as Michael Thorpe comments, draw upon the "multiracial misunderstandings and rivalries and . . . the ironic contrasts thrown up by the introduction of democratic processes in a largely illiterate and amorphous society." *Miguel Street* (1959) was the first of these "West Indian" novels to be written and the last to be published. It is a collection of farcical character studies that give a colorful account of aspects of Trinidadian life. Their prevailing tone is one of amused and ironic detachment. Naipaul received the Somerset Maugham Award for *Miguel Street* in 1961. It was *The Mystic Masseur,* however, first published in London in 1957, seven years after the author's first arrival in Britain, which gained widespread attention in Britain for Naipaul's writing. It is a sardonic and genial treatment of a colonial politician's career. Pandit Ganesh Ramsummar, the "mystic mas-

seur," is a Trinidadian of Indian descent who seeks to improve his life and status. He becomes first a writer and then a politician, and he sets out to write his autobiography. Finally he rises, fraudulently, as G. Ramsey Muir, Esq., M.B.E., Member of the Legislative Council. The narrative takes the form both of direct narrative and a diary account. Naipaul allows the domestic and public incidents of Ganesh's progress to be communicated with sympathy and humor. In 1958 he received the John Llewellyn Rhys Memorial Prize for this novel.

Naipaul's style in these early writings has been compared to that of Charles Dickens, or rather, the situations he depicts have a Dickensian quality, as Thorpe points out: "As in Dickens's England, the fruits of infant democracy are haggled over by cheap charlatans mouthing hollow ideals; the electorate is already knowing . . . the sustained tone is mock epic." *The Mystic Masseur* was followed by a more focused treatment of West Indian politics in *The Suffrage of Elvira* (1958). Elvira is Trinidad, and the book concerns the running of a Trinidadian election at the beginning of the 1950s, following the introduction of adult suffrage in 1946, when Trinidad was still dominated by Britain. Though there is still an element of the comedy of manners in this novel, the tone is on the whole darker, more ironic, and more impatient with the meanness and stupidity that pervade the struggling community.

Naipaul wrote these books against the background of a growing nationalist movement in the West Indies and an intensifying desire for full autonomy and independence. Following their publication he received a grant from the government of Trinidad for travel in the Caribbean to write a nonfiction work about the region. The West Indian premier Eric Williams, himself a historian, encouraged Naipaul to produce such a study. He returned to Trinidad for a year in 1960.

The following year his next major work of fiction reached publication, *A House for Mr. Biswas* (1961). This book continues the focus upon life in Trinidad between the wars, but the writer's vision takes on a more somber and incisive tone. Mr. Mohun Biswas is an unexceptional man striving to make the best of himself against the odds. The novel is, at one level, about the heroism of the ordinary individual, a traditional concern of the novel genre. The difference here is that Naipaul is transporting this conventionally English literary genre and trope to Trinidad, a place that, as the author was acutely aware, was off the literary map, as drawn by the British literary establishment up to that time. Biswas sets out to be a writer; like Naipaul's father, he wants to be a journalist. He is also a member, like Naipaul and his father, of the displaced colonial community of Brahmins who migrated from Northern India to be laborers in Trinidad. The narrative focuses

Dust jacket for Naipaul's 1959 novel, which offers a farcical account of everyday Trinidadian life

Impressions of Five Societies—British, French and Dutch—in the West Indies and South America (1962). Though he thanks the prime minister of the newly independent state of Trinidad and Tobago in the foreword to this book, his observations about the region turn out to be critical rather than documentary or celebratory. The themes and concerns explored in his earlier fiction are pursued with a cynical, trenchant edge. Nationalism, he says, "was impossible in Trinidad." In the colonial society "every man had to be for himself; every man had to grasp whatever dignity and power was allowed; he owed no loyalty to the island and scarcely any to his group." The book has become notorious for Naipaul's acerbic assessment of his birthplace: "nothing was created in the West Indies." It sparked controversy and antagonism. As Dennis Walder says in his 1993 essay "V. S. Naipaul and the Postcolonial Order," it "shocked and dismayed West Indians at home and abroad for its acid dismissal of Caribbean culture, history and society." Even more upsetting was the "enthusiastic reception it received from English and American critics, who praised its critical detachment and descriptive power."

In 1962 Naipaul traveled to India, principally to research his ancestry and his roots; he remained there for a year. While in Srinagar, he wrote *Mr. Stone and the Knights Companion* (1963), his first novel with English characters. Distance seems once more to have enabled the writer to observe the place he had left. His characters' lives have been damaged by the modern world, by commercialism and city living. It is set in London, which is depicted as a hostile and alienating environment. Mr. Stone is an eccentric, lonely figure, who nurtures fantasies of transcending the limitations placed on him by life. The "Knights Companion" of the title is a circle of friends and former employees of Mr. Stone's company, whom he organizes into an altruistic group. His wish is to re-create a chivalric solidarity; the group is prepared to help individuals abandoned by the modern world. In the end Mr. Stone must come to terms with the futility of such an enterprise and the incompatibility of life as it is with his idealism. Though the novel did not achieve great success, Naipaul received the Hawthornden Prize for it in 1964, which followed his winning the Phoenix Trust award in 1963.

Naipaul's next major publication was *An Area of Darkness* (1964), which draws upon his experiences during his stay in India. He begins by recording details of the voyage from England to India, describing the ports encountered on the way, noting how the character of each changes and how the inhabitants alter. Also, more importantly and unusually (as regards the travel-writing genre), he notices how his own sense of identity and status shifts in relation to those around him. This sensitivity is part of Naipaul's keen awareness of his hybrid-

on the struggle of Biswas to master the art of writing and to own his own house. These struggles come to signify his search for belonging in the world, and for a secure sense of identity. The novel achieves a more profound psychological depth in its characterization. The event at the center of the novel is the destruction of the house by a hurricane. Naipaul's tone in *A House for Mr. Biswas* is distanced, aimed to point out the tragic absurdities of the protagonist's life. In moving away from the observation of island politics, it could be said that the novel achieves a more-pronounced universality, depicting the obstacles encountered by an ordinary individual whose efforts are directed toward obtaining a sense of purpose and achievement in life, yet it also continues the examination begun in the earlier works of the profound complexities of colonial life for the individual.

The book that resulted from Naipaul's 1960 trip to Trinidad was his first travelogue, *The Middle Passage*:

ity and displacement, of being of Indian ancestry but not an Indian. Never having lived in India, he confronts the peculiarity and difficulty that affect his sense of self because of his colonial upbringing. India is part of his family lore, of the narratives told him as a child, but for him it was a mythical, imaginary place, much as England had been.

The book seeks to give an account of Indian history and contemporary life. It includes sketches of the various figures that confront the traveler. They are not all Indian, some are travelers from America and other places. Theroux notes that *An Area of Darkness* is exceptional as a travel book because the voice, presence, and opinions of the narrator are as understated as it possible to be. When Naipaul does report his own speech or actions it can be startling; it is not as an authoritative, appreciative, and eminently respectable guide or observer that he enters the scene, but as an impatient and exacting traveler. Naipaul expresses disappointment with the pervasive dirt, poverty, disorganization, and superstition of India.

The "darkness" of the title is deeply personal; it is not the primitive darkness of Joseph Conrad's Africa, where the colonized nation is made to represent all that the imperial center seeks to distance itself from in order to sustain its superior, "civilized" identity. Instead, for Naipaul, postcolonial India opens up a great void between the India of his mind and past and the actual country he sees around him. The darkness is the sense of loss felt as a result of finding that a place with which the author has an intimate imaginary association, once physically encountered, is further from rather than closer to him. There is an abiding sense that this return to India to discover his roots, to shed light on an area of inner darkness, may simply have made that darkness more profound. Being a stranger and a tourist there further undermines the identity of the displaced narrator; the book concludes with the realization that even though he has "traveled widely over that area which was to me the area of darkness, something of that darkness remains."

In 1966 Naipaul set off from Britain once again, this time to travel in East and central Africa. While there he researched the old Arab slave routes. It was also during this period that he struck up and pursued a friendship and correspondence with Theroux. Some of his subsequent letters to Theroux reproduced in "To a Young Writer" show that Naipaul regarded Theroux's appreciation of his work in his *Introduction* with approval. Naipaul was to draw upon his exploration of Africa in later works.

In 1967 a collection of short stories, *A Flag on the Island,* was published, as well as a novel, *The Mimic Men,* an account of the political career of the main protagonist, Ralph Kripalsingh. To some extent it subverts accepted ideas of third-world postcolonial politics. Singh is writing his memoirs from a hotel room in London. He is seeking to clarify and understand the events that have led him there. His account is not chronological, though it aims to impose order on his own history. It uses the confessional narrative method, presenting a mind in dialogue with itself. Singh's history involves an account of his leaving and return to the place of his birth, a fictional island in the West Indies called Isabella. Like Naipaul, he is critical of his West Indian origins; "to be born on an island like Isabella, an obscure New World transplantation, second-hand and barbarous, was to be born to disorder." He tells of how he returns there to start a new life with the wife he met in London. The account details the process by which Singh attempts to integrate himself into island life and to be a success. He speculates in Coca-Cola and land, becomes a property developer, and gets involved in the political life of the island. Disorder invades his life, however, as his marriage breaks down, violence erupts, and his political career founders. Again he takes flight from the island, wishing he had never returned. The "mimicry" of the title refers to the imposed artificiality of the structure of island life, its emptiness, its mimicking of the ways of the imperial power that once controlled and abruptly abandoned it. The novel examines the contrasts between London, where the account is written, and the island of Isabella. Both are seen to be partially constituted by myth and imagination. The island paradise of memory is juxtaposed to the real island of disorder and wasted effort. Naipaul won the W. H. Smith Award in 1968 for *The Mimic Men.*

The Loss of El Dorado: A History (1969), written in Britain, continues Naipaul's focus upon the West Indies. This factual book gives an historical account of the early European dominance of Trinidad, of the quests for the nonexistent land of El Dorado and of how they came to an end. Naipaul then offers a narrative account of events following the capture of Trinidad from the Spanish by the British in 1797. The British sought to fuel the search for the mythical, inviolate country of El Dorado, characterized by an abundance of mineral wealth. Naipaul traces the effects of this myth on the inhabitants of the region and also catalogues the cruelty of the new British regime and its horrific treatment of Negro slaves. He records the various fates and disappointments of immigrants attracted to Trinidad by the lure of wealth and the legacy both of the myth and of slavery in Trinidadian life. It is a scholarly work, of which Paul Theroux says: "It is not a work of the imagination, and it is not invented, and yet it is an imaginative recovery of a lost history which has much in common with Naipaul's novels. It deals with

Dust jacket for Naipaul's 1961 novel, which follows the daily travails of a Trinidadian of Indian descent

attempts at creation, uprooted individuals, the effects of myth, dependency and exile."

In a Free State (1971) is Naipaul's first treatment of African concerns. It is a sequence of three stories, telling of the experience of a series of individuals who have left the countries of their birth, to which they feel little attachment, to go to other places, where they feel even less at home. They are an Indian in the United States, West Indians in Britain, and an Englishman in Africa. They experience exile and homelessness; they know the pain of constant migration and never arriving. The "freedom" of the title is registered in the narratives in terms of the forms of anxiety that being free—in the troubling sense of being without a home—generates. This kind of freedom is ambiguous, not an ideal state. Freedom is also the perplexed condition of the newly independent and decolonized places from which they come. Dennis Walder calls the book postcolonial because "it takes as its starting point the end of empire and raises the question of what kind of freedom the

departure of the coloniser has left, a question with implications for the First World as well as the Third, the past as well as the present." In 1971 Naipaul received the Booker Prize for *In a Free State*.

This work was followed by the publication of *The Overcrowded Baracoon and Other Articles* (1972), a collection of Naipaul's major articles from newspapers and magazines. He returns to the West Indies in his fiction with *Guerrillas* (1975), which finally gained him considerable attention in America. The setting is an unnamed island, decolonized but still dominated by the United States. The novel is notable for its understated violence; it concerns the corruption of politicians and businessmen and the greed and laziness of those West Indians who involve themselves in trying to acquire power. It is about the fate of revolutionaries and their followers in a postcolonial society. The dominant tone is pessimistic. The hero, Jimmy Ahmed/Leung (Afro-Chinese, Muslim, English-educated), is a political idealist who attempts to set up a commune made up of people from the island's slums. He hopes that they will work the land together, where the plantations used to be; however, other protagonists see the project as a cover for nationalist guerrilla warfare. The novel traces the relationship between Jimmy and Jane, an English liberal who falls for him, but she is subsequently murdered. She had arrived on the island with her South African boyfriend, Roche, who is a hero of the freedom struggle, having escaped torture under the apartheid regime. He is made to confess his moral disillusionment.

Naipaul turns again to India in his next book. *India: A Wounded Civilization* (1977) deals with the emergency declared by Indira Ghandi. It is a nonfiction documentary treatment of contemporary life in India. Naipaul's *India: A Million Mutinies Now* (1990) would be the last of three attempts, beginning with *An Area of Darkness,* to give an account of his encounter with India, expressing and explaining the disappointment and confusion felt by the author during his quest of his roots. Walder concludes that "his failure to settle in India brought with it from the start the realisation that what he finds—instead of a land of achievement based on a whole, living, and long-standing traditional culture—is another fractured, or at least wounded, culture, lost in a 'double fantasy,' a mixture of mimicry of the West and 'oriental resignation.'"

A Bend in the River (1979) is set in postcolonial Africa. Its hero, Salim, is an Indian shopkeeper whose family has lived on the East Coast for generations. He leaves his home to travel into the interior, to take over a store in a derelict colonial town. Salim is the narrator, an incisive observer of the people of this region and the effects of its disintegrative and anarchic political system, which is set against the unchanging life of the river and forest peoples. The novel displays a contempt for the people in Africa (whites and blacks) who remain attached to the colonial past. It also evinces a bitter dejection regarding the future of that country.

Naipaul's next publication, *The Return of Eva Peròn, with the Killings in Trinidad* (1980), includes various studies of Argentina during the guerrilla crisis, Mobutu's Congo, and the Michael X Black Power murders. In 1979 and 1980 Naipaul traveled for several months in the non-Arab Islamic world, including Iran, Pakistan, Malaysia, and Indonesia. The result of these journeys was the travelogue *Among the Believers: An Islamic Journey* (1981). During the 1980s Naipaul's writing was recognized by several prestigious awards: the Bennett Award from the *Hudson Review* in 1980; an honorary doctorate from Columbia State University in 1981; and an Hon.Litt. degree from Cambridge University in 1983. In 1986 he received the T. S. Eliot Award for creative writing from the Ingersoll Foundation, and in 1989 the government of Trinidad and Tobago granted him its highest national award, the Trinity Cross.

Finding the Centre: Two Narratives (1984) is a personal and autobiographical account of Naipaul's experience as a writer. It explores the difficult process by which he came to achieve that status. This theme is also pursued in the analytical and autobiographical *The Enigma of Arrival,* which achieved best-seller status in Britain three years later. This book concerns the author's attempt to settle in Wiltshire. It records his subjective daily experience, as he walks in the surrounding villages and countryside, and becomes involved in relationships with the local people.

Naipaul explores the predicament of being unable to see this English landscape properly. He is aware of his viewpoint as a foreigner whose vision and understanding is informed by the idealistic stories and pictures of England that pervaded his education at the periphery of its dominion. He recalls the extent to which the country once appeared to him in the guise of a promised land. The book shows how people only *see* things that fit into models they already have in their minds. What finds no mental equivalent either goes unnoticed or is troubling in its ambivalence. In a 1993 article, M. Griffiths observes that "the great gain Naipaul claims to make in Wiltshire is gradually to learn to read the landscape accurately through, and despite, the lies of the representations—the crudely colored Constable reproductions or pictures of fat cows on cans of condensed milk—the kind of icons exported to the colonies as part of the imperial project as fixing England as a sign of beauty and an object of desire." The book expresses a "longing for a mythic home which remains elusively beyond his grasp." Naipaul here explores ways in which his narrator, the villagers, and the landed gentry in the area are all bound in "different ways to the sterile, imperial past" and engaged in preserving the traces of that past so as to artificially sustain the identities, relationships, and privileges to which it gave rise.

Following the completion of this book, Naipaul undertook a journey in 1988 through the Deep South of the United States; a journey that gave rise to his third nonfiction study of the New World, *A Turn in the South* (1989). In this exploration of the South and its history, Naipaul is able to draw a comparison between the legacy of slavery in a First World country and its effects on West Indian society. This work, among others, has received an aggressive critical response. Joan Dayan, for example, in her article "Gothic Naipaul" (1993) observes that in his studies of New World societies Naipaul sets up a comparison between the American South and the Caribbean countries that demonstrates his imperialist and colonialist sympathies and his defen-

V. S. NAIPAUL
Mr Stone
and the Knights
Companion

Dust jacket for Naipaul's 1963 novel, in which a lonely eccentric organizes an altruistic group

partly informed by the frustration and difficulty of being a novelist as an outsider to that tradition, but his comments also have a wider significance in that they draw attention to how the novel form, as way of representing a knowable, ordered world, becomes absurd in the context of the postcolonial and postmodern uncertainty that accompanies the dismantling of former political structures and modern epistemologies. Throughout his writing career Naipaul has been concerned with the importance of narrative, which he distinguishes from plot. He sees storytelling as the essential fabric and motivator of life. As he says in an interview with Schiff:

> It's all narrative. . . . Narrative is something large going on around you all the time. Plot is something so trivial—people want it for television plays. Plot assumes that the world has been explored and now this thing, plot, has to be added on. Whereas I am still exploring the world. And there is narrative there, in every exploration. The writers of plots know the world. I don't know the world yet. I began to understand that quite late. I began to understand the full richness of the world that I was in the middle of.

Writers, Naipaul believes, should not write to please or rely on a refined style with authorial flourishes; he should not draw attention to his presence as writer. What the writing says is most important. He enjoys writing that is purposeful and difficult; he writes carefully and slowly; and he expects to be read carefully and slowly, with full attention.

In 1993 Naipaul was the first to receive the David Cohen British Literature Prize in recognition of a "lifetime's achievement by a living author," and in 1994 he was shortlisted for the Nobel Prize. His most recent important publication is *A Way in the World* (1994), a collection of semi-autobiographical stories about various individuals who have visited the West Indies. The book received the 1995 best book prize for fiction in the Canada and Caribbean Division of the Commonwealth Writers Award. The stories take the form of monologues by historical figures, either of some stature, such as Sir Walter Raleigh, or of lesser significance.

Recently the critical response to Naipaul's work has been tremendous, and it continues to grow. His work is of increasing interest to critics and scholars not only because of what he writes, but also because of the historically constituted complexities of the position from which he writes. In the context of the expansion of postcolonial criticism and theory, the question of who he is, as much as how he writes, has drawn attention to his work; the two emphases are, for Naipaul, inseparable. On the whole, the critical response to Naipaul's work has been unusually polarized between disgust and veneration and covers every point between.

sive desire to objectify and denigrate the black races. He is seen to contrast the collapse inward into anarchy and poverty of the Caribbean islands—once slavery was abolished and the imperialists withdrew—unfavorably with the postslavery world of the South, where a strong white influence remained in place. Naipaul, she suggests, "carries on the tradition of mastery while serving the master."

In 1990 two high honors were conferred upon Naipaul: he was knighted by Queen Elizabeth II, and he was awarded the Litt.D. at Oxford University's Encaenia. Naipaul returned to Trinidad in 1992 to lecture for the Beryl MacBurnie Foundation for the Arts. He voiced his pessimism regarding the future of the novel, stating, as Kelvin Jarvis records, "that the novel as an art form has reached its zenith" and that "even when written by sensitive intelligent men" novels turn out to be "versions of what went before, and quite devoid of any atmosphere of discovery." He went on to suggest that travel writing should henceforth be privileged over the novel. In this sentiment he is perhaps

He is a controversial writer whose work is caught up in the emotional vortex of race issues in the contemporary postcolonial world.

Hostile responses to Naipaul's work generally derive from political suspicion; he has been accused of racism, chauvinism, and of displaying a nostalgic collaboration with imperialist ideology. His critics see him as an apologist for white supremacy, disloyal to his roots. Mustafa describes him as writing with a "mannered elegance and fluidity" in the "tradition of English letters," but this style has not always pleased his readers and critics. Non-European readers have taken issue with his tendency to write as if from a privileged, imperial European position about other non-Europeans, whose lives involve the same deracination, displacement, exile, and struggle for identity that he himself has known.

Enthusiasm for his work generally begins from aesthetic and philosophical considerations or from an appreciation of his honesty. Naipaul is lauded as a sophisticated artist whose refined and subtle prose represents the best of contemporary fiction in English. Indeed, his work is understood to have broken the mold of established novelistic techniques and to have achieved an elegant and innovative prose style comparable to that of the most distinguished modernist authors. His nonpartisan presentation of the social and psychological degradation and political corruption left in the wake of the western colonialist and imperialist enterprise is recognized as an astute and thoroughgoing skepticism, an estimable and rational detachment.

These two versions of Naipaul, as heavy-handed racist renegade and poised literary virtuoso, are not easily reconcilable, except insofar as it could be said that the confusion he has caused in his reading public is simply an expression of anxieties and conflicts that already exist. In the sense that his work presses such tensions into articulation and dialogue, it is of great value.

Interviews:

Fitzroy Frazer, "A Talk with Vidia Naipaul," *Sunday Gleaner* (Jamaica), 25 December 1960, pp. 10, 14;

David Bates, "Interview with V. S. Naipaul," *Sunday Times Magazine* (London), 26 May 1963, pp. 12–13;

"Speaking of Writing: V. S. Naipaul," *Times* (London), 2 January 1964, p. 11;

Frank Winstone, "Interview with V. S. Naipaul," *Sunday Mirror* (Trinidad), 26 April 1964;

Derek Walcott, "Interview with V. S. Naipaul," *Sunday Guardian* (Trinidad), 7 March 1965, pp. 5–7;

Stephen Oberbeck, "Angry Young Indian," *Newsweek,* 65 (19 April 1965): 103–104;

Francis Wyndham, "Interview with V. S. Naipaul," *Sunday Times,* 10 November 1968, p. 57;

Ewart Rouse, "Naipaul: An Interview with Ewart Rouse," *Trinidad Guardian,* 28 November 1968, pp. 9, 13;

Ian Hamilton, "Without a Place," *Times Literary Supplement,* 30 July 1971, pp. 897–898;

Alex Hamilton, "Living a Life on Approval," *Guardian,* 4 October 1971, p. 8;

Israel Shenker, "V. S. Naipaul, Man Without a Society," *New York Times Book Review,* 17 October 1971, pp. 4, 22–24;

Jim Douglas Henry, "Unfurnished Entrails–The Novelist V. S. Naipaul in Conversation with Jim Douglas Henry," *Listener,* 86 (25 November 1971): 721;

"An Area of Brilliance," *Observer,* 28 November 1971, p. 8;

Adrian Rowe-Evans, "The Writer as Colonial," *Transition* (Kampala), 40 (December 1971): 56–62;

Eric Roach, "Fame, A Short Lived Cycle, says Vidia," *Trinidad Guardian,* 4 January 1972, pp. 1–2;

Nigel Bingham, "The Novelist V. S. Naipaul Talks to Nigel Bingham about his Childhood in Trinidad," *Listener,* 88 (7 September 1972): 306–307;

Alfred Kazin, "V. S. Naipaul, Novelist as Thinker," *New York Times Book Review,* 1 May 1977, pp. 7, 20, 22;

Bharati Mukherjee and Robert Boyers, "A Conversation with V. S. Naipaul," *Salmagundi,* 54 (Fall 1981): 4–22;

Bernard Levin, "V. S. Naipaul: A Perpetual Voyager," *Listener,* 109 (23 June 1983): 16–17;

Andrew Robinson, "An Elusive Master: V. S. Naipaul Is Still Searching," *World Press Review,* 34 (October 1987): 32–33;

Rahul Singh, "A Miraculous Achievement," *Newsweek,* 48 (3 July 1988);

Andrew Robinson, "An Interview with V. S. Naipaul," *Brick,* 40 (1991): 19–23;

Zoe Heller, "Zoe Heller Meets V.S. Naipaul," *The Independent on Sunday,* 28 March 1993, pp. 2–4;

Dileep Padgaonkar, "An Area of Awakening: V. S. Naipaul in Conversation with Dileep Padgaonkar," *The Sunday Times of India,* 18 July 1993, pp. 10–11;

Mel Gussow, "V. S. Naipaul in Search of Himself: A Conversation," *New York Times Book Review,* 24 April 1994, pp. 29–30;

Stephen Schiff, "Cultural Pursuits, The Ultimate Exile," *New Yorker* (23 May 1994): 60–71;

John F. Baker, "V. S. Naipaul," *Publishers Weekly* (6 June 1994): 44–45;

Aamer Hussein, "Delivering the Truth: An Interview with V. S. Naipaul," *Times Literary Supplement,* 2 September 1994, pp. 3–4;

Alastair Niven, "V. S. Naipaul Talks to Alastair Niven," *Wasafiri,* 21 (1995): 5–6.

Bibliographies:

Kelvin Jarvis, *V. S. Naipaul: A Selective Bibliography with Annotations, 1957–1987* (Metuchen, N.J.: Scarecrow Press, 1989);

Jeffrey Meyers, "V. S. Naipaul: Essays, Stories, Reviews and Interviews, 1948–1992," *Bulletin of Bibliography,* 50 (1993): 317–323;

Kelvin Jarvis, "V. S. Naipaul: A Bibliographical Update," *Ariel,* 26 (1995): 71–85.

References:

Selwyn Cudjoe, *Naipaul: A Materialist Reading* (Amherst: University of Massachusetts Press, 1988);

Wimal and Carmen Dissanayake, *Self and Colonial Desire: Travel Writings by V. S. Naipaul* (New York: Peter Lang, 1993);

M. Griffiths, "Great English Houses/New Homes in England?: Memory and Identity in Kazuo Ishiguro's *The Remains of the Day* and V. S. Naipaul's *The Enigma of Arrival,*" *SPAN,* 36 (1993): 488–503;

Peter Hughes, *V. S. Naipaul,* Routledge Contemporary Writers (London: Routledge, 1988)

Chandra Joshi, *The Voice of Exile: A Study of the Fiction of V. S. Naipaul* (New York: APT Books, 1993);

Feroza Juswalla, *Conversations with V. S. Naipaul* (Oxford: University of Mississippi Press, 1996);

Shasho Kamra, *The Novels of V. S. Naipaul: A Study in Theme and Form* (New Delhi: Prestige, 1990);

Richard Kelly, *V. S. Naipaul* (New York: Continuum, 1989);

Bruce King, *V. S. Naipaul* (Basingstoke, U.K.: Macmillan, 1990);

Judith Levy, *Naipaul: Displacement and Autobiography* (New York: Garland, 1995);

Modern Fiction Studies, special Naipaul issue, 30 (1984);

Fawzia Mustafa, *V. S. Naipaul* (Cambridge: Cambridge University Press, 1995);

Robert Nixon, *London Calling: V. S. Naipaul, Travel Writer and Postcolonial Mandarin* (Oxford: Oxford University Press, 1992);

Kenneth Ramchaud, *The West Indian Novel and Its Background* (London: Heinemann, 1983);

Raghubir Singh, *Bombay: Gateway of India: Conversations with V. S. Naipaul* (New York: Aperture, 1994);

Peggy Smith, *Journey Through Darkness: The Writing of V. S. Naipaul* (St. Lucia: University of Queensland Press, 1987);

Paul Theroux, *Sir Vida's Shadow* (Boston: Houghton Mifflin, 1998);

Theroux, *V. S. Naipaul: An Introduction to His Work* (London: Heinemann, 1972);

John Thieme, *The Web of Tradition: Uses of Allusion in V. S. Naipaul's Fiction* (Hertfordshire, U.K.: Hansib, 1987);

Michael Thorpe, *Writers and Their Work: V. S. Naipaul* (Harlow, U.K.: Longman, 1976);

Dennis Walder, "V. S. Naipaul and the Postcolonial Or-der," in his *Recasting the World* (Baltimore & London: Johns Hopkins University Press, 1993), pp. 82–119;

Timothy Weiss, *On the Margins: The Art of Exile* (Amherst: University of Massachusetts, 1992).

Papers:

In 1994 the MacFarlin Library of the University of Tulsa, Oklahoma, opened the V. S. Naipaul archive, housing most of his existing manuscripts and professional correspondence.

Christopher Priest

(14 July 1943 –)

Andy Sawyer
University of Liverpool

See also the Priest entry in *DLB 14: British Novelists Since 1960*.

BOOKS: *Indoctrinaire* (London: Faber & Faber, 1970; New York: Harper & Row, 1970);

Fugue for a Darkening Island (London: Faber & Faber, 1972); republished as *Darkening Island* (New York: Harper & Row, 1972);

Inverted World (London: Faber & Faber, 1974); republished as *The Inverted World* (New York: Harper & Row, 1974);

Your Book of Film-Making (London: Faber & Faber, 1974);

Real-Time World (London: New English Library, 1974);

The Space Machine: A Scientific Romance (London: Faber & Faber, 1976; New York: Harper & Row, 1976);

A Dream of Wessex (London: Faber & Faber, 1977); republished as *The Perfect Lover* (New York: Scribners, 1977);

An Infinite Summer (London: Faber & Faber, 1979; New York: Scribners, 1979);

The Affirmation (London: Faber & Faber, 1981; New York: Scribners, 1981);

The Glamour (London: Cape, 1984; Garden City, N.Y.: Doubleday, 1985 revised edition, London: Abacus, 1991; revised again, London: Touchstone, 1996);

The Quiet Woman (London: Bloomsbury, 1990);

The Book on the Edge of Forever (Seattle: Fantagraphics, 1994);

The Prestige (London: Touchstone, 1995; New York: St. Martin's Press, 1996);

The Extremes (London: Simon & Schuster, 1998; New York: St. Martin's Press, 1999);

The Dream Archipelago (London: Earthlight, 1999).

TELEVISION: *Return to the Labyrinth,* script by Priest, HTV, 1981;

The Watched, script by Priest, Thames TV, 1981.

Christopher Priest (photograph © Jerry Bauer)

RADIO: *The Space Machine,* script by Priest, BBC Radio 4, 1979;

The Glamour, script by Priest, BBC Radio 4, 12 April 1992.

OTHER: *Anticipations,* edited by Priest (London: Faber & Faber, 1978; New York: Scribners, 1978);

Stars of Albion, edited by Priest and Robert Holdstock (London: Pan, 1979);

Helen Sharman, *Seize the Moment,* ghostwritten by Priest (London: Gollancz, 1994);

Sally Gunnell, *Running Tall,* ghostwritten by Priest (London: Bloomsbury, 1994).

SELECTED PERIODICAL PUBLICATIONS–
UNCOLLECTED: "Science Fiction: Form Versus
　　Content," by Priest and Ian Watson, *Foundation*,
　　10 (June 1976): 55–65;
"The Profession of Science Fiction: Overture and
　　Beginners," *Foundation*, 13 (May 1978): 51–56;
"Outside the Whale," *Vector*, 97 (April 1980): 5–15;
"Leave the Forgotten to the Night," *Vector*, 127 (August/
　　September 1985): 9–10;
"*Christopher Priest* by Nicholas Ruddick," *Foundation*, 50
　　(Autumn 1990): 94–101.

Although Christopher Priest began his career as a science-fiction writer–and is still well known among readers of British science fiction–his dissatisfaction with the generic constraints of the form has propelled him into more-complex areas of the literary fantastic. His third novel, *Inverted World* (1974), won the British Science Fiction Association Award and established his reputation in France, where it achieved best-seller status. By 1983 he had attracted the attention of a wider critical circle and had been named one of the best of young British writers by *Granta* magazine. Later novels also won literary prizes: the German translation of *The Glamour* (1984) won the Kurd Lasswitz award for best novel in 1988, and *The Prestige* (1995) received the James Tait Black Memorial Award. Priest's interest in the reliability of memory and narrative, present throughout most of his fiction but increasingly emphasized after *A Dream of Wessex* (1977), has made his later work as challenging as it is finely wrought. His reputation has grown slowly but steadily with each book, and there are critics who not unreasonably consider him one of Britain's most interesting living novelists.

Christopher Priest was born in Cheadle in Cheshire, a suburb of Manchester, on 14 July 1943. His parents were Walter Mackenzie and Millicent Alice (née Haslock) Priest. In "The Profession of Science Fiction" (1978) he recalls that he "didn't have a miserable or lonely childhood," although his school career was apparently not marked by significant achievement. When he left Manchester Warehousemen Clerk's Orphan School in 1959, he spent nine years in accountancy, during which he discovered science fiction and science-fiction fandom. During this period–and for some time afterward–he published fanzines and contributed to amateur and professional publications. He eventually became a full-time writer in 1968 following his success in selling a series of short stories, beginning with "The Run" in 1965. His first novel, *Indoctrinaire* (1970), was an expansion and revision of two stories, "The Interrogator," which first appeared in *New Writings in SF 15* (1969), and the unpublished "The Maze." Succeeding novels grappled with problems that Priest shared with other writers associated with the New Wave of British science fiction in the late 1960s: how to reconcile ambitious technical questions of structure and viewpoint with the literalized metaphors of science fiction. Not necessarily linked with this concern, but certainly bearing on it, was Priest's position as a reviewer and critic of the genre, which caused him to think deeply about its strengths and weaknesses. He was the reviews editor of *Foundation* for a while, and his critical commentary has appeared in that journal and in other specialist organs of science-fiction criticism. In addition to novels and story collections he has ghostwritten autobiographies of Helen Sharman, the first British astronaut, and athlete Sally Gunnell. He is also the author of two other notable works of nonfiction: *Your Book of Film-Making* (1974), a book for children (Priest's narrative techniques are highly influenced by cinematic devices such as flashback and parallel narrative), and *The Book on the Edge of Forever* (1994), essentially a lengthy polemic concerning Harlan Ellison's long-promised but never-published anthology. Priest lives in Hastings with his wife, Leigh Kennedy (also a writer), and their twin children.

Two biographical details offer insight into Priest's writing–although paradoxically they also warn critics against making too easy connections between life and art. Priest has said of his training as an accountant that "the august profession has never known a more unwilling, bored, lazy or unsuccessful student." He stresses, however, what he learned from his sojourn in accountancy: the concept of "professionalism," of never doing less than one's best, and "a confidentiality about his clients and his intelligence of them." Writing, for Priest, is a painstaking act of creativity, "a process of expression and communication inexpressible and incommunicable." Yet, much of his fiction, as critics such as Paul Kincaid and David Wingrove have pointed out, can be seen to be about the act itself, grappling with the question of the nature of fiction. Priest sometimes seems not unwilling or unable to talk about the act of creation but rather concerned to exercise his perceived duty of confidentiality, of not revealing too much about his professional secrets. Through rereading, or at least reevaluating in light of the events of Priest's work, readers are led to understand the nature of fiction.

Priest relates another significant event in a 1985 article, "Leave the Forgotten to the Night." A childhood accident left him with only minor physical injuries but with no memory, not only of the incident itself but of the previous few days. "When I returned to school I came across innumerable minor mysteries: I had written lessons in exercise books, homework I had handed in came back to me with marks on it, and so on. All was blank to me." In a fascinating reminder of Priest's constant habit of undermining narrative reliability, Paul Kincaid, in his essay "Only connect . . . ," points out that details of this anecdote differ in various tellings. From this seed, says Priest, grew a fascination with memory and how individuals perceive or fail to perceive the stories of their lives. A similar childhood trauma occurs in the life of Peter Sinclair, the protagonist of *The Affirmation* (1981), the novel that marked Priest's departure from science fiction following an acrimonious resignation from the Science Fiction Writers of America. While *Inverted World* can be said to be, in part, about perception, and *A Dream of Wessex* questions the links between "virtual" and "baseline" realities, *The Affirmation* and its successor, *The Glamour,* question the nature of narrative itself. While Priest seems to focus on metafictional trickery—a book that exists in its own fictional world, narrative stances that seem straightforward enough but undermine the viewpoint of the narrator—he also excels as a storyteller. In a novel such as *The Glamour* Priest piles event upon event and reversal upon reversal, in such a straightforward way as to make the novel's ultimate revelations more effective. Later novels exploit readers' expectations of both plain dealing and surprise, as indicated by Priest's choice of stage magic to inform the plot and theme of *The Prestige.*

Priest's novels and short stories are excellently surveyed and analyzed in Nicholas Ruddick's study, *Christopher Priest* (1989), which also contains a full (to that date) bibliography. It is usefully read in conjunction with Priest's largely concurring response in *Foundation 50.* Where Priest disagrees with Ruddick is, interestingly enough, in the depiction (in Priest's words) "of CP as a lonely, dignified figure, wrapped in integrity, heading off to an uncertain future in the world of the literary 'mainstream.'" However, while more-recent novels have incorporated fantastic elements, Priest is no longer published as a science-fiction novelist, and he remains critical of what he sees as the lack of vision and challenge in much recent science fiction, its failure to realize its potential. For the past twenty years he has been not a genre novelist but rather a novelist who uses some of the ideas and limitations of genre to stimulate and challenge the reader. He is one of the few writers of the New Wave who have met the challenge implicit in the movement—that science fiction need not be a literature of undemanding commercialism and trivia. One of Priest's main criticisms of science fiction is its self-imposed limitations: while authors in the genre exploit conventions such as invisibility, alternate worlds, and time travel for their fantasy appeal, they often leave their metaphorical implications underdeveloped, creating "gadget fiction" having little to do with humanity and human relations. Priest's short stories chip uneasily at this generic dissatisfaction, and they are

at their best when most oblique. "Palely Loitering" (1979), for instance, concerns travel through space and time but uses these devices as a means to explore the nature of romantic love. Time is manipulated again in the title story of his 1979 collection, *An Infinite Summer,* as mysterious future beings freeze selected moments—which Priest offers as a metaphor for the eternal quality of art. While his later stories possess the same richly enigmatic qualities of the novels that followed and may be seen as trial runs for some of the themes that are explored in them, Priest's forte is the novel or story cycle, in which his ability to construct both story and self-reflexive literary artifact are developed at length.

Priest at one point more or less disowned his two early novels, *Indoctrinaire* and *Fugue for a Darkening Island* (1972), which have been out of print, apparently at Priest's behest, since 1979. Priest's response to Ruddick's study explicitly rejects both novels. Despite his continued antipathy regarding *Fugue for a Darkening Island,* the novel has reappeared in 1999 as part of a two-volume omnibus reprinting four of Priest's early novels. Although Priest is correct in his assessment of *Indoctrinaire* as flawed and unclear, particularly in its early parts, the novel nevertheless has some fine absurdist scenes. Wentik, a British biochemist, finds himself two hundred years in the future in a world still feeling the effects of the "disturbance gases" that were the subject of his research. He is interrogated and subjected to psychological experiments, and the disorienting effects of his experiences—for instance, a hand grows out of a table and points at him while he is being questioned—interestingly anticipates the way Priest distorts the realities of his characters in later novels. The tangles of the plot are never fully resolved, however.

Fugue for a Darkening Island (published in the United States as *Darkening Island*) is technically and thematically much more ambitious. The title plays with the double meaning of *fugue* as a mental flight from reality and an intricate musical composition. A deliberately disjointed narrative in the manner of the French *nouveau roman,* the novel shows glimpses from the life of Alan Whitman, a former college lecturer in a near-future Britain suffering civil war following a wave of immigration from African refugees after a limited nuclear war has devastated that continent. The novel offers an uncomfortable analysis of middle-class racism. Priest was reportedly hurt by hostile reviews following the novel's 1979 reprinting and "decided it was probably best to let it stay out of sight." Although there are atrocities and dramatic shifts into social collapse in the novel, its most striking quality is the cool restraint of Priest's description. This detached tone in part reflects the increasing isolation of Whitman, whose failing marriage and lack of involvement lead him to spend much

Dust jacket for Priest's 1972 novel, set in a near-future Great Britain plagued by racial strife

of the novel wandering around a small area of a country in chaos. The narrative is divided into fractal-like sections that piece by piece demonstrate the precariousness of Whitman's liberalism, undermined by his lack of commitment.

If *Fugue for a Darkening Island* was Priest's "disaster novel," closer to the fractured narratives of J. G. Ballard than to the plain style of H. G. Wells or John Wyndham—writers to whom Priest has acknowledged debts—*Inverted World* and *A Dream of Wessex* explore other conventions of science fiction and increasingly develop Priest's fascination with perception, reality, and truth. Between these novels came *The Space Machine* (1976), a pastiche "parallel" to Wells's novels *The Time Machine* (1895) and *The War of the Worlds* (1898). The engagingly naive Edward Turnbull is swept off to Mars in the time machine of Wells's novel in the company of Amelia Fitzgibbon, a forthright heroine who takes the lead in attempting to liberate the Martians'

human slaves. Much of the action is shadowed by Turnbull's vision of Amelia's apparent death in a future war—the Martian invasion chronicled in *The War of the Worlds*—although the novel ends romantically and happily. Priest emulates Wells's first-person narrative voice in the novel, with the effect of making the Wellsian narrator himself a character.

Critics had by this point realized that Priest was experimenting with the fundamentals of storytelling: David Wingrove's perceptive 1979 article about the author's early works, for example, characterizes Priest's literary sleight of hand as "legerdemain." A best-seller in France, *Inverted World* is perhaps Priest's most overtly science-fiction novel. Following a prologue inserted at the insistence of Priest's publishers, the novel begins with one of the most quietly startling first sentences in recent science fiction: "I had reached the age of six hundred and fifty miles." On one level, *Inverted World* plays with Einsteinian relativity—specifically, the principle that space and time may be seen as parts of one continuum, which also allows Priest to juggle questions of perception and point of view. Beginning with a first-person narrative from the viewpoint of Helward Mann, an inhabitant of Earth City, who is being dragged across an alien landscape, then shifts to third-person voice but maintains the same individual point of view. The narrative shifts again to Mann's first-person voice, then introduces another protagonist, Elizabeth Khan, a woman from the "real" Earth, as third-person viewpoint character, finally reverting to the original first-person narration of Mann. These alternating points of view enable Priest to examine Mann's increasing insight and alienation while making the reader more aware of the paradox of his situation. The inhabitants of Earth City, who see themselves as living in a finite universe filled with bodies of infinite size, winching their city ever onward to keep it as close as possible to the space-time "optimum," are in the end revealed (thanks to the intervention of Khan) to be dragging themselves across a near-future, somewhat transformed Europe under the influence of an energy generator that distorts their perceptions. Yet, this ending only suggests more questions, as other events in the novel seem to suggest that Mann's physical world is as transformed as his mental one. Even when Khan explains the history of the city to its inhabitants and the generator is shut off, their view of the world remains the same. "It's only your perception," she says to Mann. "I know what I see," he replies. Her answer—"But you don't"—freezes their respective stances into sharp opposition.

Unlike more generic science-fiction novels, *Inverted World* never resolves back into baseline reality. In fact, Mann's perceptions remain as "inverted" as in the beginning. Readers are invited to question precisely what a change in subjective perception means in terms of objective reality, a frequent theme in the science fiction of such writers as Philip K. Dick—but Priest increasingly began to chafe against the generic constraints of the form. *A Dream of Wessex* manipulates the same question but in a subtler way. A group of scientists collectively dream an alternate future in the hope of directing the present toward it, but some of them appear unwilling to return from their fantasy. Into this complex novel Priest weaves a series of interrogations of the constructed nature of reality. Again, Priest uses viewpoint to both soothe and challenge responses to the text. The science-fiction mode of the story manipulates readers to believe in a true present and an imaginary future but also enjoins them from taking this simplistic distinction for granted. The virtual realities of the novel become a series of mirrors as the scientists' project is threatened by the ambitions of one individual, and Priest's fascination with the relationship between mem-

ories and experiences develops as the dreamers, whose lives are as real and concrete in Wessex as out of it, undergo changes in their realities.

With *The Affirmation, The Glamour,* and *The Quiet Woman* (1990) Priest further developed his exploration of the relationship between memories and realities. In *The Affirmation*—the title of which seems intended to echo Priest's 1978 short story "The Negation"—Peter Sinclair's life is a series of escapes after a series of misfortunes. The objectivity of Priest's prose obscures the distinctions between factual events—such as the decoration of a room in a borrowed cottage—and Sinclair's delusions, with only extremely subtle clues enabling readers to tell the difference. On the page, is there a difference between what a character sees and what he imagines he sees? "All prose," Sinclair responds, "is a form of deception." He tries to make sense of his life through ordering its events in autobiography: "It seemed to me important that I should try to impose some kind of order on my memories"; but he increasingly becomes aware that such ordering is not a matter of recording but creating. Dissatisfied with his original attempts, Sinclair "imagines himself into existence" in the imaginary setting of the Dream Archipelago, where he is on his way to receive the immortality treatment he has won in a lottery. He brings with him the autobiographical manuscript he wrote during a crisis of identity a couple of years earlier. During the period of amnesia following the operation, he relies on the manuscript to re-create his identity.

The two worlds of Sinclair's existence reflect and counterpoint each other. Gracia, for instance, with whom he had an affair before his departure from London, is analogized as Seri in the Dream Archipelago. Recovering from his operation, Sinclair experiences "ghost memories" of the "real" Sinclair in a town he has imaginatively created as "London": his aide-mémoire has to be translated from metaphor. In London, Sinclair attempts to rebuild his life with Gracia but is also aware of the presence of Seri.

Tempting as it is to read *The Affirmation* as a novel of madness, such an interpretation misunderstands Priest's intent. If it is a novel of instability, it is one of textual instability. Each conclusion suggested by the text is also undermined by it: the infinite regression it leads to defies resolution. (As Ian Watson remarks, it is its own sequel.) Some of Priest's readers would be aware that the Dream Archipelago of *The Affirmation* is the location for a series of stories, several of which were collected together in *The Infinite Summer*. (The stories were collected as a sequence in a 1981 French collection, and an English edition, which revises the stories and adds new framing material, appeared in 1999.) These stories—many of which, such as "The Watched"

(1978), feature questions of surveillance and identity—are, like the stories in Ballard's *Vermilion Sands* (1971), set against a kind of mental landscape: a neutral zone in a world war fought with weapons reminiscent of the "disturbance gases" of *Indoctrinaire,* where misfits and draft evaders wander uneasily; but their existence gives the imaginary geography of the Archipelago a kind of objective existence outside Sinclair's mind. Priest has created a kind of literary trompe l'oeil effect in which no settled interpretation can be made without immediately including its opposite: the literary analog of an image by M. C. Escher. It is curiously unsettling to read *The Affirmation* in juxtaposition with other Archipelago stories such as "The Miraculous Cairn" (1980), written at approximately the same time, which shares character names and geography with the novel.

This effect is also present in *The Glamour,* which uses the concept of its characters' "invisibility" to develop a powerful metaphor. As was the case in *The Affirmation,* much of the narrative in *The Glamour* is unreliable, made up of false memories and differing viewpoints. What begins as three distinct viewpoints—those of the characters Richard Grey, Sue, and Niall—turn out to be one. Richard, Sue, and especially Niall possess the "glamour" of invisibility (Priest explores the word's double meaning, its contemporary usage as well as its original connotation of a magic spell), the ability to ensure that they are not noticed: a glamour that the author of a fictional text is conventionally understood to have. Richard—significantly, in a novel that has so much to do with viewpoint and manipulated reality, a television cameraman—has to re-create his life after a terrorist bombing has given him amnesia. While this process leads to a startling reversal later in the novel, as Richard's reconstructed memories are revealed to be false, the presence of the profoundly "glamourous" Niall adds even more resonance to the plot. In the end he is either the only "real" character in the novel or the most elusive, fictional viewpoint of all.

Several times revised (the 1996 version published by Touchstone is the author's preferred version), *The Glamour* is a masterpiece of indirection. Both *The Glamour* and *The Affirmation* are metaphysical whodunits in which the question is not who committed a crime but who narrates the text. If the answer reveals endless trompes l'oeil, it is because, as Sinclair affirms, even the most autobiographical writing manipulates the base from which it begins. *The Quiet Woman* enjoys more overt thriller elements. Like Priest's latest novel, *The Extremes* (1998), it is based upon an actual violent incident, in this case the mysterious death of an antinuclear campaigner, but it is also another exercise in misdirection. The main character meditates on one occasion about "deceptive memories," and once more Priest's

descriptive techniques undermine the reader's automatic responses. Several sections of the novel are told from the viewpoint of the son of the murdered Eleanor Hamilton, who perhaps teasingly goes by the name of Sinclair (a character named Seri also appears). The penultimate chapter of the book, however, warns that this viewpoint cannot be trusted. While the lurid sexuality expressed in *The Quiet Woman* threatens to overbalance the story, the sexual descriptions play an important role in stressing what the reader comes to infer must be the truth about Sinclair. The corresponding names and structures suggest that *The Quiet Woman* is in part a darker reworking of the way that *The Affirmation* treats the autobiography.

As several critics have noted, the underlying metaphor of *The Prestige* illuminates Priest's work generally. Indeed, commentators have so often used "prestidigitation," "sleight of hand," and "legerdemain" to characterize Priest's work that it is tempting, although probably misleading, to see the novel as a response to such comments. Although set in the context of a modern man's search for clues to his own family identity, most of the narrative comes from the viewpoint of one or the other of a pair of rival Victorian stage conjurors. Priest explicitly draws the parallel between a conjuror's method of misdirecting his audience by stating the truth while withholding vital information and a writer's ability to be both transparently honest and devious. "As I am an illusionist I can make sure you only see what I wish you to see," says Borden before writing an autobiographical statement that is true in all respects but hides a fundamental assumption that would reveal the secret of his stage act. Borden describes the contract between magician and audience as a "Pact of Acquiescent Sorcery," an obvious reference to Samuel Taylor Coleridge's concept of "willing suspension of disbelief." Another novel about memory and the reliability of texts and narratives (much of the story is told through manuscript and journal entries), *The Prestige* is perhaps Priest's finest work, taking a metaphor that, however apt, is obvious to the point of triteness and reworking it in several contexts, from literary criticism to science fiction. Both Victorian rivals are engaged in perfecting an illusion that apparently enables them to move instantaneously between locations; the present-day narrator of the early part of the novel is convinced that he once had a twin brother. Nikola Tesla, the inventor and pioneer of electrical power, is involved in a complex series of doubling, shadowing, and echoing as Borden's rival, Angier, attempts to surpass Tesla's illusion, "The New Transported Man." Tesla's device is an amusing Victorian variant on one of the best-known science-fiction stereotypes, but again Priest uses this device as metaphor rather than gadget. Priest's portrayal of the profes-

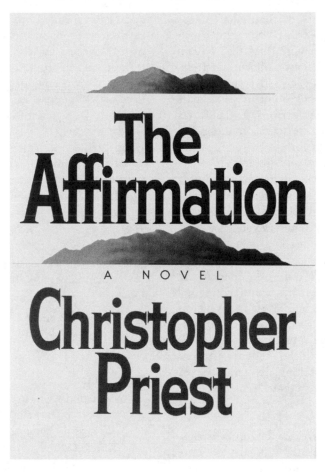

Dust jacket for the first U.S. edition of Priest's 1981 novel, in which a man attempts to reassemble his memories after receiving an immortality treatment

sion of conjuror evokes his early words on the "confidentiality" of the profession of accountancy. A stage magician, like a writer, needs to both involve and distance the audience, creating a dazzling effect through complicated machinery and patter that diverts the audience's attention from what is really going on. The audience knows that stage magic is not "real" magic and that it is being fooled; the audience willingly remains ignorant of how the trick is done, however, and accepts illusion.

Priest's re-creation of the world of Victorian stage-conjuring and its paranoid secrecy is impressive. It is remarkable, also, how little he reveals of the mechanics of the profession, despite his apparent openness. The novel's use of narrative as illusion, however, is its most impressive feature. Playing fair with the reader, admitting openly that the process of writing is itself one of prestidigitation, Priest nevertheless presents a plot that would take a long process of observation and analysis to unravel. Reviewing the novel in *Interzone* (November 1995), John Clute called it "a lesson to us in

the joy of story." However analytical and self-reflective his fiction is, however much it meditates on the act of writing or challenges his audience's sensibilities, Priest remains convinced of the importance of a thoroughly constructed and plotted narrative.

Here, perhaps, he is closest to the magical realists of the European and South American traditions. He has also professed to being a great admirer of John Fowles (who has himself praised Priest's novels), and there is something of Fowles's mastery of narrative strategies and fusion of naturalistic and fantastic modes in Priest's fiction. In the same 1995 interview with Alan Roche in which he referred to Fowles, he spoke of his admiration for Milan Kundera and Vladimir Nabokov.

Priest has several times seemed to verge on greater success; yet, he has never achieved a commercial nor critical breakthrough. Part of the reason might be his slow and careful pace: it was six years before he followed *The Glamour* with *The Quiet Woman*. Nevertheless, the relatively rapid succession of the prizewinning *The Prestige* with a revised, authoritative edition of *The*

Glamour in 1996–following his dramatization of the novel for radio–and *The Extremes* in 1998, together with the revision (including new material) of the "Dream Archipelago" story cycle for a new publisher in 1999, suggests a renewal of Priest's creative energy. *The Extremes,* which takes as a starting point the 1987 mass murder in the small town of Hungerford, England, was developed from an unproduced teleplay; the novel revisits the border between baseline and virtual realities that Priest delineated in *A Dream of Wessex.* An FBI agent attempts to define the parallels between a shooting spree in which her husband was killed and similar events in a small English town. She is trained using a virtual-reality program, "Extreme Experience," in which simulations of life-threatening situations are revisited time and time again until the trainee is able to change the scenario, a metaphor for the human tendency to revisit traumatic events, "rewriting" them until they become less threatening; but Priest also suggests that in doing so one may get lost among the possible realities. Although some of the similarities between *The Extremes* and *A Dream of Wessex* are so close as to suggest that Priest is deliberately reworking the earlier novel, the use of virtual reality to create sensationalistic "Extreme Experience" scenarios is utterly contemporary.

Priest has always seen writing fiction as a challenge and has struggled against the tendency of genre fiction to relax critical strictures and thwart the experimental impulse that he feels is essential in a serious novelist. Certainly, he has not been prolific since the mid 1980s. However, the achievements of *The Affirmation* and *The Glamour,* which brought him to the attention of the wider literary world, are now being matched by novels of equal quality, justifying his slow, painstaking

approach. Furthermore, Priest's reputed relentlessness seems to capture the mood of the times. The excursions of such writers as Martin Amis and Will Self into the territory of science fiction in the years leading up to the turn of the millennium might establish a firmer beachhead for Priest, who has for many years been exploring the same tropes more creatively and thoroughly than almost anyone else. In 1999 for the first time in many years most of Priest's best work will be back in print in revised and omnibus editions. Perhaps these reissues indicate that greater attention will be paid to the work of this sometimes discomforting but always rewarding writer.

Interviews:

Alan Roche, "Outwards from the Centre," *Interzone, 99* (September 1995): 18–20;

David Langford, "Christopher Priest talks to David Langford," *SF Eye,* 15 (Fall 1997): 109–115;

Gary Couzens, "An Interview with Christopher Priest," *Third Alternative,* 17 (September 1998): 42–44.

References:

John Fletcher, "Cultural Pessimist: The Tradition of Christopher Priest's Fiction," *International Fiction Review,* 3 (January 1976): 20–24;

Paul Kincaid, "Only connect...: Psychology and Politics in the Work of Christopher Priest," *Foundation,* 52 (Summer 1991): 42-58;

Nicholas Ruddick, *Christopher Priest,* Starmont Reader's Guide 50 (Mercer Island, Wash.: Starmont House, 1989);

David Wingrove, "Legerdemain: The Fiction of Christopher Priest," *Vector,* 93 (May–June 1979): 3–9.

Barbara Pym

(6 June 1913 – 11 January 1980)

Merritt Moseley
University of North Carolina, Asheville

BOOKS: *Some Tame Gazelle* (London: Cape, 1950; New York: Dutton, 1983);

Excellent Women (London: Cape, 1952; New York: Dutton, 1978);

Jane and Prudence (London: Cape, 1953; New York: Dutton, 1981);

Less Than Angels (London: Cape, 1955; New York: Vanguard, 1957);

A Glass of Blessings (London: Cape, 1958; New York: Dutton, 1980);

No Fond Return of Love (London: Cape, 1961; New York: Dutton, 1982);

Quartet in Autumn (London: Macmillan, 1977; New York: Dutton, 1978);

The Sweet Dove Died (London: Macmillan, 1978; New York: Dutton, 1979);

A Few Green Leaves (London: Macmillan, 1980; New York: Dutton, 1980);

An Unsuitable Attachment (London: Macmillan, 1982; New York: Dutton, 1982);

A Very Private Eye: The Diaries, Letters and Notebooks of Barbara Pym, edited by Hazel Holt and Hilary Pym (London: Macmillan, 1984); republished as *A Very Private Eye: An Autobiography in Diaries and Letters* (New York: Dutton, 1984);

Crampton Hodnet (London: Macmillan, 1985; New York: Dutton, 1985);

An Academic Question (London: Macmillan, 1986; New York: Dutton, 1986);

Civil to Strangers and Other Writings, edited by Holt (London: Macmillan, 1987; New York: Dutton, 1988).

Barbara Pym

Barbara Pym received by far her greatest acclaim, which included frequent comparisons between her work and that of Jane Austen, just prior to and after the end of her life. Her early novels were published with modest success; after her publisher's devastating rejection of her seventh novel in 1963, she lived in obscurity for fourteen years, only to be "rediscovered" in 1977. By this time, however, she had only a short time left to live. Since her death in 1980 posthumous publications have swelled her oeuvre, and she has attracted widespread critical attention.

Pym was born in Oswestry, a town in Shropshire near the Welsh border, on 6 June 1913. Her father, Frederic Crampton Pym, was a solicitor; her mother, Irena Thomas Pym, was one of ten children of an Oswestry ironmonger. Barbara had one sister, Hilary. Her childhood was a happy one, according to Hilary's account. The family was comfortably middle class, lived in a

221

large house, and had servants and a pony. They were devout Anglicans: Mrs. Pym played the organ in the parish church; Mr. Pym sang in the choir; and they regularly entertained curates, an activity that looms surprisingly large in Barbara Pym's fiction.

After a private education at Liverpool College, Huyton, where she chaired the Literary Society but was an average student otherwise, she went on to St. Hilda's College, Oxford, and read English, receiving her B.A. in 1934. Her Oxford years were important to her, providing the background to several of her novels, introducing her to lifelong friends, and involving her in a love affair that, like most of her love affairs, was unhappy. She had an exciting social life at Oxford and an active love life, and—at least according to her journal—spent more time in shopping, cinema going, tea drinking, and thinking about and even shadowing male undergraduates than she did studying. She received a solid grounding in classic English literature, however, especially poetry, touchstones that are everywhere in her novels.

In 1934 Pym visited Germany. Her enthusiasm for the country, and particularly for a German man named Friedbert, blinded her to any worries about the Nazis, and she returned to Germany several times in the following years. After graduation from Oxford she lived on a family allowance, dividing her time between Oswestry and Oxford. She began to write in these years; her first novel took as its subject herself, Hilary, and several of their friends, including her former lover Henry Harvey, as they might be in late middle age. She finished the book, *Some Tame Gazelle,* and submitted it to publishers unsuccessfully; it was eventually published in 1950. In August 1938 Barbara went to Poland, where she was to be an English tutor to a family, but returned because of the worsening political situation, and when war came in September 1939, she returned to Oswestry and her family.

In the early days of the war Pym helped out with domestic chores, wrote fiction (including an unpublished war novel), and served tea at a local military base. From December 1941 to July 1943 she worked in the official Censorship Department (German Division), censoring civilian letters. During this time she lived in Bristol, sharing a house with her sister, who worked for the British Broadcasting Company, and some of her BBC colleagues. Partly because of romantic complications between herself and others in the house, Pym joined the Women's Royal Naval Service, also as a censor; she was stationed at Southampton and, in 1944, in Naples. Her time in the navy was intensely social and enjoyable.

When the war ended, she went to work as an editorial assistant for the International African Institute in London, where she continued until her retirement. She helped to edit the journal *Africa* and came to know anthropology and anthropologists intimately and bemusedly. From 1946 on she again lived with Hilary. Beginning in 1950 she published novels regularly until 1961. Hazel Holt has recalled that they were "praised by the critics, enjoyed a modest financial success, and delighted an ever-growing circle of admirers and enthusiasts."

In 1963 Pym's regular publisher, Jonathan Cape, rejected a novel she submitted, *An Unsuitable Attachment* (1982), with little explanation, leaving Pym baffled and hurt. For most of the next fifteen years she tried various measures to revive her career as a novelist. Worried that her kind of fiction might be too old-fashioned for publishers' tastes, she experimented with harsher plots and with a franker treatment of homosexuality. She fretted about the popularity of Margaret Drabble and William Burroughs's *Naked Lunch* (1959) and what such literary trends portended for her own work. She wrote an academic novel with self-conscious touches of currency. During these years she was sustained by her friends, her continued work at the African Institute, and the sympathetic correspondence of a few literary people, notably the poet Philip Larkin, who had written her a fan letter, and the critic Robert Liddell, an old friend from Oxford. After some incidents of bad health she retired from the institute in 1974; she and her sister had by this time moved to Finstock, a village in Oxfordshire.

In 1977 Pym's fortunes changed dramatically with the appearance of a *TLS: The Times Literary Supplement* feature in which various literary figures nominated the most underrated writer of the century; she was named by two people, Larkin and Lord David Cecil. Almost overnight she was celebrated again. Jane Nardin writes that "only twice during the present century has an English novelist's work, after a period of thorough eclipse, been rediscovered and widely acclaimed for its literary excellence"—the other case being that of Jean Rhys. Her earlier novels were hurried back into print, and the novels she had written in the 1960s were published. *Quartet in Autumn* (1977), her first novel published in sixteen years, was shortlisted for the Booker Prize, and she was invited onto BBC Radio's *Desert Island Discs,* an indication of her celebrity. She wrote one more novel, *A Few Green Leaves* (1980), which reflects Finstock village life, but she was already stricken with cancer—for which she first had surgery in 1971—and died on 11 January 1980. Since her death she has attracted increased critical attention. She never got over her astonishment that, at the end of her life, her books were not only selling again but also attracting academic interest, even in America. She continues to be the subject of new books and articles each year, and her reputation as a major postwar novelist seems secure.

Pym's first novel, *Some Tame Gazelle,* is one of her best. It focuses on a village, a self-important clergyman, and various unmarried women who help out with the church, gossip about the curate, and cook macaroni and cheese—all elements that become familiar to readers of Pym's oeuvre. The main characters are a pair of unmarried sisters, Belinda and Harriet Bede. Belinda maintains an unrequited passion for the married Archdeacon Henry Hoccleve, while Harriet indulges her passions for curates as they pass through the parish. The opening passage is characteristic Barbara Pym:

> The new curate seemed quite a nice young man, but what a pity it was that his combinations showed, tucked carelessly into his socks, when he sat down. Belinda had noticed it when they had met him for the first time at the vicarage last week and had felt quite embarrassed. Perhaps Harriet could say something to him about it. Her blunt jolly manner could carry off these little awkwardnesses much better than Belinda's timidity. Of course he might think it none of their business, as indeed it was, but Belinda rather doubted whether he thought at all, if one were to judge by the quality of his first sermon.

The title of this novel, characteristically, alludes to a couplet from Thomas Haynes Bayly, used as the epigraph: "Some tame gazelle, or some gentle dove: / Something to love, oh, something to love!" As in almost all of Pym's novels, the main women characters seek something or someone to love, and the range of love objects available is unsatisfactory. Men tend to be selfish and unobservant, though the "excellent women" who populate the books forgive them much. The plot is unmomentous; the humor arises from precise social observation, witty phrasing, and the "little awkwardnesses" occurring in social intercourse among gentlemen and gentlewomen in the small world Pym has created. *Some Tame Gazelle* received good reviews, including praise from established writers such as Pamela Hansford Johnson and Antonia White, and Pym moved briefly in literary society, meeting novelists Elizabeth Bowen and Elizabeth Taylor.

In 1952 Pym published *Excellent Women,* the title of which has been appropriated by Charles Burkhart, among other critics, to describe the kind of women about whom she mostly writes. The novel differs from most of her others in having a first-person narrator, a self-deprecating excellent woman named Mildred Lathbury, and in focusing rather more frankly on adulterous relations. It is also—not surprisingly, considering the author's situation at the time—set in London and introduces the theme of anthropology and its practitioners.

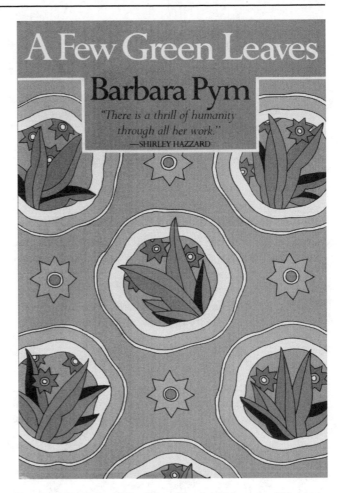

Dust jacket for the first U.S. edition of Pym's 1980 novel, which depicts the effects of the death of a renowned anthropologist

Mildred finds herself caught up in the shaky marriage of Rocky Napier, a former naval officer in Naples, and Helena, his anthropologist wife—neighbors of Mildred's who thoughtlessly exploit her. She meets others in the anthropological world: Everard Bone, whom she at first suspects of an affair with Helena and with whom she becomes involved in a tepid romantic relationship, and the formidable Esther Clovis, who becomes a fixture in later novels, finally dying in *A Few Green Leaves*. Mildred receives an insulting proposal from the brother of a friend, who makes it clear that he cannot love her. She gives of herself to her local church and becomes a confidante to the sister of the vicar, who is himself victimized by a flashy, sophisticated woman. In some ways *Excellent Women* is a study of varieties of women; the title phrase is ironic, since to an extent Mildred's life is dull and even slightly pathetic, but she is redeemed by her character and optimism. Helena Napier's exciting life is counterpointed to Mildred's humble expectations from marriage: ". . . before long I should be certain to find myself at his sink peeling potatoes and washing up; that would be a nice change when both proofreading and indexing began to pall. Was any man worth this burden? Probably not, but one shouldered it bravely and cheerfully and in the end it might turn out to be not so heavy after all."

Published the following year, *Jane and Prudence* (1953) poses a contrast between the two title characters: Jane Cleveland, a former English don, now a clergyman's wife living a rustic life in service to her husband; and Prudence Bold, her former student, now living in London, working in an office, and having affairs. Perhaps neither has fulfilled her promise. Prudence, on a visit to Jane, becomes involved with a narcissistic, rather ridiculous widower named Fabian Driver. She loses him, however, to Jessie Morrow, an unprepossessing spinster with a sharp tongue who is the companion to an elderly woman, Miss Doggett. Though the novel provides support for the view that Pym's novels generally tout the superiority of women over men, at least in terms of capacity for love, unselfishness, and kindness, nevertheless Jessie Morrow, one of her most astute observers, says to Driver: "Yes, you are having the pain now. . . . Women are very powerful—perhaps they are always triumphant in the end." Sometimes their power derives simply from competence, as the domestic scenes between Jane and her husband, Nicholas, reveal.

Less Than Angels (1955), Pym's first novel populated mostly by anthropologists, is one of her finest achievements. The main focal character is Catherine Oliphant, a writer. Catherine is, like Pym herself, an observer, even sometimes a spy. She is in love with an anthropologist, Tom Mallow, who dallies with another woman and eventually dies. In addition to this central love story, the novel is greatly occupied with, in effect, an anthropological study of the anthropologists—their kinship bonds, mating rituals, and procedures for dominance and submission. Two young men, friends of Tom's, compete for a fellowship, while a retired Africanist dons an African mask and performs native rites at his suburban London home. The character Esther Clovis recurs in this novel and, prompted by an offprint inscribed "With all good wishes from Helena Napier and Everard Bone," offers news as to the circumstances of the main characters in *Excellent Women*:

> That had been a most promising partnership which had never come to anything. Two gifted young people, who had worked together, but Helena Napier had a husband and Miss Clovis's efforts in the cause of anthropology had been in vain. After a short estrangement the Napiers had reunited and Helena had retired to the country. Everard had married a rather dull woman who was nevertheless a great help to him in his work; as a clergyman's daughter she naturally got on

very well with the missionaries they were meeting now they were in Africa again.

A Glass of Blessings (1958) is like *Excellent Women*, too, in returning to the use of a first-person narrator, unusually a married woman, though not happily married. Wilmet Forsyth is a thirty-three-year-old woman with a husband who is satisfactory but dull. Her mother-in-law is also part of the family. Events in her life predispose her to an intrigue: the object of her affections is a handsome unmarried man named Piers Longridge, the brother of an old friend. She flirts with Piers, but puzzlingly to no effect. Eventually she realizes that he is homosexual. She meets the man he loves, Keith, of whom she is jealous; there is a third homosexual in the novel, the unattractive Wilf Bason, who serves at the clergy house—like all Pym novels, *A Glass of Blessings* includes elements of Anglicanism. The novel is also representative of Pym's oeuvre in its portrayal of a homosexual man who is the object of a heterosexual woman's love; a portion of *A Glass of Blessings* was published in *The Penguin Book of Gay Short Stories* in 1994.

By the novel's end Wilmet's restlessness has been dampened down, her mother-in-law, Sybil, has a love interest of her own, and Wilmet realizes that her own life is a glass of blessings. The novel ends with a quiet satisfaction. The last sentence gives the quiet flavor: "It seemed a happy and suitable ending to a good day." *Suitable* is, as ever, a key word and concept in Barbara Pym's world.

In 1961 Pym published *No Fond Return of Love*, the last of her novels to appear for a span of sixteen years. The protagonist, Dulcie Mainwaring, is one of her most interesting, a woman much like Pym herself. She works in the world of learning—she is an indexer who works at home—and the novel begins with her attendance at an academic conference in order to recover from her fiancé's revelation that he does not love her. There she becomes interested in Aylwin Forbes, who is to lecture to the conference on "Some Problems of an Editor."

Dulcie launches an investigation of Aylwin, following him and researching him in the library. Pym did this sort of "investigatory work" often from her university years onward, and a description of the process in *No Fond Return of Love* nicely captures the nature of this research:

> For this was really the kind of research Dulcie enjoyed most of all, investigation—some might have said prying—into the lives of other people, the kind of work that involved poring over reference books, and street and telephone directories. It was most satisfactory if the objects of her research were not too well known, either to herself or to the world in general, for it was rather dull just to be able to look up somebody in *Who's Who*,

which gave so many relevant details. *Crockford* was better because it left more to the imagination, not stooping to such personal trivia as marriages or children or recreations.

Dulcie's investigation includes attending a rummage sale at the house of Aylwin's estranged wife's mother, attending a service at the church where his brother is the vicar, going to inspect his house, and finally, along with her lodger, Viola, who is also fascinated by Aylwin, going to stay at his mother's hotel in a West Country resort town. There Dulcie sees Wilmet Forsyth of *A Glass of Blessings,* shopping with Keith, the boyfriend of Piers Longridge—another instance of Pym's practice, about which she sometimes had misgivings, of reusing characters to link her novels. The novel ends ambiguously but with the suggestion of an affair of the heart between Dulcie and Aylwin, hardly an unqualified happy ending, since the author has already made clear Aylwin's egocentrism and shallowness. Dulcie explains to Viola that "perhaps women enjoy that most of all—to feel that they're needed and doing good," a common motif in Pym's novels. Readers may suspect that she will be needed mostly to index Aylwin's books, as Viola has done and as Mildred Lathbury has done for Everard Bone.

In 1963 her regular publisher, Jonathan Cape, rejected *An Unsuitable Attachment.* In a rather bitter letter to Philip Larkin, she wrote, "I suppose it *was* money, really, they didn't think they could sell enough copies. However well they do out of Ian Fleming and Len Deighton and all the Americans they publish, I suppose they can't afford any book that will not cover its cost. (I don't think I *really* feel this!)" Hazel Holt, a longtime colleague of Pym's at the International African Institute who became her literary executor and then biographer, discusses the reasons for this rejection in *A Lot to Ask* (1990), suggesting that Pym's novels had not lost money—her usual sales were between three and four thousand copies, with higher figures for *Jane and Prudence* and *Excellent Women*—but that changes in the economy of publishing and the closure of circulating libraries may help to explain Cape decision.

Pym's next published novel was *Quartet in Autumn,* which she wrote from 1973 to 1976 and which was published in 1977 in the aftermath of her "rediscovery." It was on the Booker Prize shortlist that year. The titular quartet are four lonely people, two men and two women, who work in an office together. The petty issues of a shared office are tellingly portrayed. The four are not particularly fond of each other, and when the two women retire, they go their separate ways. The novel treats loneliness, despair, cancer, and death in a forthright manner; in tone it is significantly different

Pym in Finstock with poet Philip Larkin, her longtime friend

from the novels that went before. Though these people might, like Belinda and Harriet and many of Pym's characters, need and want "something to love," they have had to learn to do without.

Pym followed *Quartet in Autumn* with *The Sweet Dove Died* (1978), a novel written in the 1960s but rejected at that time. The novel is Pym's most bitter. Its main character is Leonora, an unlikable woman who lives by herself in London and derives her satisfactions from the elegance of her life. She turns from her suitor, Humphrey, an antiques dealer, to his nephew, James, whose emotions she toys with; her neighbor Meg has a similar relationship with a young man, Colin, who is repeatedly faithless and insulting to her but always forgiven. Leonora loses James to Ned, an American with an unpleasant, "gnat-like" voice, who is a more ruthless schemer than Leonora and has the youth and vitality that she now lacks.

Pym wrote *A Few Green Leaves* after her return to acclaim, while she was terminally ill with cancer. Published in 1980, the novel returns to some of her previous concerns. Set in a village seemingly composed of absent-minded clergymen, self-centered and self-satisfied bachelors, and a surplus of unmarried older women, the novel is concerned with the changes that accompany the pressures of modern life. The main character, Emma Howick, is an anthropologist who lives with her mother, a college lecturer. Emma travels into London for a memorial service for Esther Clovis, a domineering figure in the field of anthropology who had appeared in several of Pym's novels, and encounters other familiar anthropologists. *A Few Green Leaves* ends unsensationally, even for one of Pym's tales: ". . . Emma was going to stay in the village herself. She could write a novel and even, as she was beginning to realise, embark on a love affair which need not necessarily be an unhappy one."

Pym's death in January 1980 did not bring an end to the publication of additional novels. Under the supervision of Hilary Pym and Hazel Holt, several more books have appeared since 1980. Holt saw *A Few Green Leaves* through the press, though Pym had completed it. The next book to appear was *An Unsuitable Attachment* (1982), the novel rejected by Cape in 1963 and by other publishers thereafter. In a note to the published text, Holt explains that she had discussed the novel with the author and had edited it in accordance with Pym's wishes, at the same time updating a few dated passages.

Although *An Unsuitable Attachment* is hardly the author's best book, it is hard to see why it put a stop to her career. It is unusual in being a bit more loosely focused than some of her others and in having more than one setting; a group of English people from a parish in London take a trip to Rome. Its characters include a clergyman, the Reverend Mark Ainger; his long-suffering wife; an anthropologist, Rupert Stonebird; an unmarried gentlewoman, Ianthe Broome; and secondary characters, mostly comic. Ianthe makes an unsuitable marriage, a misalliance in both age and class, with a colleague at the library where she works. Earlier she is told by Sophia Ainger, "I think you'll grow into one of those splendid spinsters—oh, don't think I mean it nastily or cattily—who are pillars of the Church and whom the Church certainly couldn't do without," again evoking Pym's conception of "excellent women." Ianthe surprises, and to some extent dismays, those who think they understand her, however.

In 1984 *A Very Private Eye: The Diaries, Letters and Notebooks of Barbara Pym* appeared, edited from Pym's papers by Hilary Pym and Holt. The American edition of the collection used the subtitle *An Autobiography in Diaries and Letters,* which probably better describes the mixture of diaries, letters to and from Pym, commentary, and photographs. The journal is of the greatest interest in the picture it provides of her earlier years at Oxford. The collection also provides an account of the rejection of her novel in 1963 that is at times—usually in letters—casual; but her diary indicates the extent of her misery, characterizing 1963 as "a year of violence, death and blows."

The year after *A Very Private Eye* appeared, Holt prepared for publication one of Pym's earliest novels, which is also one of her best and perhaps her funniest, *Crampton Hodnet* (1985). Pym began the novel in 1939, calling it her "north Oxford novel," and completed it in April 1940, sending it to Robert Liddell for his comments. War work intervened to prevent any further efforts at publication, and after the war Pym concluded that it was too dated.

Crampton Hodnet is one of Pym's two academic novels. Set on the fringes of academic life in north Oxford, it features several love affairs, either serious or comic, successful or abortive; the first appearance of Miss Doggett and her companion, Jessie Morrow, who reappear in *Jane and Prudence;* and the comic elopement of impressionable undergraduate Barbara Bird (later to reappear as a novelist in *Jane and Prudence*) with her tutor, Francis Cleveland. Cleveland is one of the self-centered, absent-minded men who frequent Pym's novels; unusually, he is not a clergyman, but his wife is the tolerant, coping kind of woman usually married to such men in her novels. There is a romantic entanglement between Jessie Morrow and a young vicar, Mr. Latimer, and in an effort to conceal their walking out together he contrives a lie about visiting his friend, the vicar of Crampton Hodnet, an imaginary parish. Like many Pym novels, this one ends in much the same place where it began, after a few small upsets and surprises have been smoothed over.

In 1986 Pym's other academic novel appeared, this one frankly called *An Academic Question*. It was judged a less successful book altogether. Left unfinished, with two drafts quite different in execution—one has a first-person narrator, for example, and the other a third-person narrator—it was completed and edited by Holt. Pym had written it in 1971–1972 in an attempt to find something that would interest a publisher; she explained in a letter to Philip Larkin: "I find I have nearly finished the first draft of another novel about a provincial university told by the youngish wife of a lecturer. It was supposed to be a sort of Margaret Drabble effort but of course it hasn't turned out like that at all." In *An Academic Question* she wrote about a milieu she knew only indirectly: she knew about anthropology and scholarship from her work at the International African Institute and about life at provincial universities mostly through correspondence with Larkin, a librarian who was not well informed on the subject himself. Pym introduced some familiar elements into the novel— Esther Clovis and homosexuality, for example—as well as some new ones: Caroline has a small child, a rarity in Pym's novels, and the plot turns on an act of academic dishonesty. The novel lacks sparkle and seems forced, perhaps a reflection of the circumstances of its composition.

A few more of Pym's previously unpublished works appeared in 1987 as part of an omnibus volume called *Civil to Strangers and Other Writings.* Included are *Civil to Strangers,* a complete novel written in the 1930s just after *Some Tame Gazelle;* "Gervase and Flora," part of a novel Pym wrote about her lover Henry Harvey after he left to teach in Finland; part of "Home Front Novel," which, as its title implies, was written on the home front in 1939; and part of "So Very Secret," a spy novel written in 1941. These are all apprentice works, for the most part abandoned by the author. There are also four short stories—a form Pym seldom attempted—and the transcript of a radio talk, "Finding a Voice," delivered after her rediscovery and new fame in 1978. In it she describes her first attempts at fiction, her admiration of Aldous Huxley's *Crome Yellow* (1921), and the unpublished novel she wrote under its influence, "Young Men in Fancy Dress."

Pym's status as one of the major British novelists of the second half of the century is not completely uncontested, though it is widely acknowledged. Much of the critical debate revolves around the nature of her accomplishment: whether she should be regarded as a specialist in somewhat gentle comedies of manners or a sardonic critic of society's arrangements and the roles of men and women in it. Oddly, controversy has focused on whether it is justified to compare her to Jane Austen. Early reviewers occasionally invoked Austen, as did her friends, particularly Liddell and Larkin, in letters. Pym never claimed any such resemblance or equality for herself. As Michael Cotsell observed: "Even the author of her obituary in *The Times* pompously remarked that her qualities 'gained some reputation for her among the discerning. They also drew down on her the injudicious comparison with Jane Austen.'" Mason Cooley, without mentioning Austen, asserts that Pym "is writing a discreetly toned down modern version of the balanced, parallel-loving style of the Augustan Age. But it is also a very modern style in the way so much of the structure underlines questioning, doubt, and continuous revision of perspective." Charles Burkhart, however, explains a fundamental difference between Pym and Austen: "Jane Austen spoke out of an assured and moral culture, while Barbara Pym is afloat in an ebb tide." While no one could argue that Pym is as important a literary personage as Austen, such comparisons have at times led critics to undervalue Pym's achievement. Her work is likely to last,

though, so long as readers like to be amused, to read about love, and to perceive the finer details of character and action filtered through a quick mind and a flexible style.

Letters:

A Very Private Eye: The Diaries, Letters and Notebooks of Barbara Pym, edited by Hazel Holt and Hilary Pym (London: Macmillan, 1984); republished as *A Very Private Eye: An Autobiography in Diaries and Letters* (New York: Dutton, 1984).

Bibliography:

Dale Salwak, *Barbara Pym: A Reference Guide* (Boston: G. K. Hall, 1991).

Biographies:

Hazel Holt, *A Lot to Ask: A Life of Barbara Pym* (London: Macmillan, 1990; New York: Dutton, 1991);

Orphia Jane Allen, *Barbara Pym: Writing a Life* (Metuchen, N.J.: Scarecrow Press, 1994).

References:

Katherine Anne Ackley, *The Novels of Barbara Pym* (New York & London: Garland, 1989);

Diana Benet, *Something to Love: Barbara Pym's Novels* (Columbia: University of Missouri Press, 1986);

Charles Burkhart, *The Pleasure of Miss Pym* (Austin: University of Texas Press, 1987);

Mason Cooley, *The Comic Art of Barbara Pym* (New York: AMS Press, 1990);

Michael Cotsell, *Modern Novelists: Barbara Pym* (New York: St. Martin's Press, 1989);

Robert Liddell, *A Mind at Ease: Barbara Pym and Her Novels* (London: Owen, 1989);

Robert Emmet Long, *Barbara Pym* (New York: Unger, 1986);

Jane Nardin, *Barbara Pym* (Boston: Twayne, 1985);

Janice Rossen, ed., *Independent Women: The Function of Gender in the Novels of Barbara Pym* (New York: St. Martin's Press, 1988; Brighton, U.K.: Harvest Press, 1988);

Dale Salwak, ed., *The Life and Work of Barbara Pym* (Iowa City: University of Iowa Press, 1987);

Annette Weld, *Barbara Pym and the Novel of Manners* (New York: St. Martin's Press, 1992).

Papers:

Barbara Pym's papers and manuscripts are held at the Bodleian Library, Oxford.

Bernice Rubens

(26 July 1928 –)

Annette Rubery
University of Warwick

See also the Rubens entry in *DLB 14: British Novelists Since 1960*.

BOOKS: *Set on Edge* (London: Eyre & Spottiswoode, 1960);

Madame Sousatzka (London: Eyre & Spottiswoode, 1962);

Mate in Three (London: Eyre & Spottiswoode, 1966);

The Elected Member (London: Eyre & Spottiswoode, 1969); republished as *Chosen People* (New York: Atheneum, 1969);

Sunday Best (London: Eyre & Spottiswoode, 1971; New York: Summit, 1980);

Go Tell the Lemming (London: Cape, 1973; New York: Washington Square, 1984);

I Sent a Letter to My Love (London: W. H. Allen, 1975; New York: St. Martin's Press, 1978);

The Ponsonby Post (London: W. H. Allen, 1977; New York: St. Martin's Press, 1978);

A Five Year Sentence (London: W. H. Allen, 1978); republished as *Favours: A Novel* (New York: Summit, 1978);

Spring Sonata: A Fable (London: W. H. Allen, 1979; New York: Warner, 1986);

Birds of Passage (London: Hamilton, 1981; New York: Summit, 1982);

Brothers: A Novel (London: Hamilton, 1983; New York: Delacorte/Seymour Lawrence, 1983);

Mr. Wakefield's Crusade (London: Hamilton, 1985; New York: Delacorte/Seymour Lawrence, 1985);

Our Father (London: Hamilton, 1987; New York: Delacorte, 1987);

Kingdom Come (London: Hamilton, 1990);

A Solitary Grief (London: Sinclair-Stevenson, 1991);

Mother Russia (London: Chapmans, 1992);

Hijack (London: S. French, 1993; New York: S. French, 1993);

Autobiopsy (London: Sinclair-Stevenson, 1993);

Yesterday in the Back Lane (London: Little, Brown, 1995);

The Waiting Game (London: Little, Brown, 1997).

Bernice Rubens

TELEVISION: *Third Party,* script by Rubens, Independent Television, 1972.

OTHER: "The Collector Who Collected Himself," in *Prize Writing,* edited by Martyn Goff (London: Hodder & Stoughton, 1989), pp. 40–49;

"The Comeuppance," *You Magazine (The Mail on Sunday),* 11 October 1988, pp. 71–74.

Bernice Rubens has enjoyed a long and varied career as documentary film writer, director, and novelist. She has received many awards, including the 1968 American Blue Ribbon Award, the Booker Prize in 1970, and the Welsh Arts Council Prize in 1976. Her ninth novel was shortlisted for the Booker Prize in

1978, and she was made a fellow of the University of Wales, Cardiff, in 1982. Born into a Jewish émigré family, Rubens was acclaimed on the basis of her early novels as a witty chronicler of Jewish life. In later novels, however, she diversified, writing in third and first person from the perspectives of men and women, Jews and gentiles. Although her subjects change, her themes are universal: guilt and loneliness are experienced by Jews and gentiles alike. It is a testament to her capacity for compassion that the emotionally crippled (the broken individual, the outsider) take center stage in much of her fiction. Such characters are often conflated with Jewish notions of the Just Man: a messianic figure who is born to take on the world's sufferings.

Bernice Ruth Rubens was born on 26 July 1928 in Cardiff, Wales, to Eli and Dorothy Cohen Rubens. She was the third of their four children. Her father, an Orthodox Jew from Lithuania, had fled Russia intending to go to New York, but his plans were thwarted when a ticket tout at the Hamburg docks, having charged him for the American journey, put him on a boat to Wales. Eli found work as a tallyman and encouraged his children to play musical instruments, starting with the half violin he had brought from Russia. Rubens's siblings all grew up to become professional musicians. Despite her flair for the piano and cello, Rubens dreaded the Sunday visits of her extended family, who listened to the other three children play. She admitted to sitting in the corner with a feeling of inadequacy, though this retreat into herself, and the world of the imagination, soon bore fruit in other ways. One day when a neighbor asked where her mother was, Rubens replied—without knowing why—that she had gone to South Africa. It was the unconscious beginning of her life as a novelist.

Rubens was educated at Cardiff High School for Girls, going on to read English at University College of South Wales and Monmouthshire, where she received a B.A. in 1947. Later she claimed that the study of literature gave her an exaggerated respect for language that had, in turn, hampered her development as a writer. On 29 December 1947 she married novelist and wine merchant Rudi Nassauer, and the following year she took a post as an English teacher at Handsworth Grammar School for Boys in Birmingham. She did not particularly enjoy teaching and, after getting involved in a friend's documentary motion picture about debutantes, decided to embark on a career in movies. In 1950 she resigned from Handsworth Grammar and moved with her husband to Hampstead, North London, where they began cultivating the friendship of writers and intellectuals. After a brief stint on stage in a production of Oscar Wilde's *Salome,* Rubens became involved in making motion pictures for organizations such as the

National Society for Mentally Handicapped Children, the Society for the Blind, and the United Nations. These movies include *One of the Family* (1964), *Call Us by Name* (1968), and *Out of the Mouths* (1970). After her debut as a writer in 1960, some rivalry developed between herself and Nassauer, and their marriage was dissolved in 1970, the year Rubens won the Booker Prize.

Rubens concedes that she married young and in rebellion against her mother. She and Nassauer had two daughters together: Sharon, born in 1952, and Rebecca, born in 1954. When the girls went to nursery Rubens took up novel writing as an exercise that she could "accomplish at the kitchen table without discommoding anyone." The title of her first novel, *Set on Edge* (1960), comes from a verse in the Old Testament book of Ezekiel: "The fathers have eaten sour grapes and the children's teeth are set on edge." The plot charts the terrible consequences of a parent's insensitive act, following the lives of a Jewish family and their destructive matriarch, Mrs. Sperber, whose sole aim is to marry off her eldest daughter. In the Sperber household, money and marriage are interdependent. Gladys Sperber is the impossible piece of goods that her mother must push, while the Sperber siblings—such as the inept businessman Benny, who buys more than he can sell, and Sol, who once rose, Lazarus-like, from an army morgue—point up themes of ill-placed consumerism and the hoped-for redemption at the story's end. The ending is uncompromising: Mrs. Sperber's death leaves Gladys embittered and alone. Ruben's writing manages to be both poignant and satirical, exploring as it does the paradoxical nature of human relationships. For all intents and purposes, *Set on Edge* is based on the story of Ruben's maternal grandmother, though Rubens also drew on her own experiences. The book was a great success. Had it not been, she would not have continued writing, a profession, she insists, that is not to be taken too seriously; it should be treated like any other commercial enterprise.

Reassured by a warm critical response, Rubens continued writing on Jewish subjects. Her second novel, *Madame Sousatzka* (1962), concerns Mrs. Crominski and her young son, Marcus, who is a musical genius. When the renowned Madame Sousatzka offers to teach Marcus the piano, his mother is reluctant to let him spend too much time under Sousatzka's eccentric influence. It is perhaps an oversimplification to call *Madame Sousatzka* a coming-of-age novel, though the early chapters are centered on Marcus's attempts to escape maternal control and the guilt this struggle engenders. One of the most powerful, though underdeveloped, aspects of this novel is the battle between Crominski and Sousatzka for the boy's affections. In her crushing loneliness Sou-

Dust jacket for Rubens's 1991 novel, in which a psychiatrist is unable to cope with his daughter's Down's syndrome

satzka exploits Marcus, taking him away from his mother, just as Felix Manders (the sly impresario) takes the boy from Sousatzka and markets him as the next Wolfgang Amadeus Mozart. Despite the gravity of the theme, there are also moments of high comedy, mostly stemming from the young boy's sense of awkwardness and his ignorance of the other characters' motivations. Again, the novel was a critical success. In 1989 *Madame Sousatzka* was adapted for Cineplex Odeon Films by Ruth Prawer Jhabvala and John Schlesinger, with Shirley MacLaine in the title role.

The role of the Chosen One, or outsider, which Rubens had given to Marcus and also, to a certain extent, to the German émigré Sousatzka, is explored in Rubens's next two novels, *Mate in Three* (1966) and *The Elected Member* (1969). Of all her characters, Ruth Millar from *Mate in Three* most resembles Rubens. The choice of her own middle name seems significant, and not only in biographical terms. Ruth—the biblical paragon of

faithfulness—is an ironic figure in a novel that attempts to explain adultery. The title refers both to the winning position in chess and the presence of a third party intruding in a marriage. It was in fact a highly autobiographical piece, written during a period of marital instability. At the time, Rubens thought that Nassauer had married her in order to spite his mother, who looked down on her because she was a Jew (the book opens with a similar scene, when Jack Millar takes Ruth to visit his parents). Rubens has called *Mate in Three* her worst novel, written as a kind of therapy. The book may in fact have been a direct response to Nassauer's *The Cuckoo* (1962), a painful account of a failing marital relationship. Although many elements of *Mate in Three* are dissatisfying, the idea of human relationships as a game of strategy is effective and recurs in her later work. *The Elected Member,* for which Rubens won the Booker Prize in 1970, is a case in point. Returning to the theme of children hindered by parental expectations, Rubens tells the tale of Norman Zweck, whose early brilliance is exploited by his dominating mother. The events are told in flashback, the book opening with Norman at age forty-one, utterly broken and in the grip of an amphetamine addiction. The book traces Norman's incarceration in an asylum and the subsequent disintegration of the family group. Significantly, Rubens's older brother Harold—the family "child prodigy"—also suffer from mental problems, which Rubens attributed to high parental expectations.

Following the success of *The Elected Member,* Rubens considered giving up writing altogether. Her motion-picture career was thriving: in 1967 she had directed a movie about children in care for Granada Television, and in 1969 she won the American Documentary Film Festival's Blue Ribbon Award for the movie *Stress.* That same year she was commissioned by the United Nations to make a film about agriculture in the Far East. After some deliberation she resolved to continue her literary career but was aware that after *The Elected Member* her writing needed a change of direction. Putting aside the Jewish milieu, she turned instead to an outrageous tale of crime and cross-dressing in the London suburbs, *Sunday Best* (1971), which was well received by both critics and the public. The novel follows the adventures of schoolmaster and occasional transvestite George Verrey-Smith, whose female persona, "Georgiana," stages a gradual personality takeover. After the book was published Rubens's confidence was boosted by the fan mail she received from transvestites testifying to her accuracy and insight.

The first half of the novel is confessional and explores the double identity of its protagonist through childhood memory. As Georgiana begins to assert herself, the narrative viewpoint changes to that of the protagonist's wife, Joy, who recalls the terrible veracity of George's drag act for the Amateur Dramatics Society. The humor is at once bitter and farcical; George's burden is one of self-knowledge, and for this he must make peace with the memory of his abusive father.

An attempt to make peace with her past is something that the heroine of *Go Tell the Lemming* is almost denied. The novel begins with the "lemming" of the title—Angela Morrow—driven to the brink of suicide by her adulterous film-producer husband. Drawing on her own career, Rubens sets the story against the backdrop of a motion picture set; in 1972 she had been involved with Independent Television and, though she said she was not particularly happy writing television drama, it may have inspired her wry observations on screenwriting. In Angela's world, however, art does not imitate life; in fact, her life imitates a kind of bad art in which her lovers utter terrible clichés and her thoughts are those of a "second rate movie." Although Angela comes to accept the events of her past, her newfound freedom is snatched away at the end of the novel when she is brutally murdered. The effect is bleak and shocking and shows Rubens subverting the clichés of her own art by refusing to tie up loose ends. As her divorce progressed, Rubens was also struggling to tie up the loose ends of her twenty-three-year relationship with Nassauer.

I Sent a Letter to My Love (1975) concerns the exchange of letters between the lonely spinster Amy Evans—who has placed a pseudonymous advertisement in the personal column of the local paper—and her disabled brother, Stan, who answers "Miss Blodwyn Pugh." Amy keeps up the charade, surprised at the ardor of her brother's letters, but soon finds herself drawn into this fantasy affair. Like George Verrey-Smith, Amy Evans must confront the dualities of her life, a life that proscribes personal fulfillment in place of duty: "For thou shalt see the land afar off; but thou shalt not go thither," reads the epigraph. Rubens evokes the claustrophobia of a small town where trivial events take on gigantic significance and shows herself adept at catching the idiom of Welsh speech. A dramatic adaptation of *I Sent a Letter to My Love* was performed in 1978 at the Long Wharf Theater, New Haven, Connecticut, with Geraldine Fitzgerald playing Amy; and in 1979 at the Greenwich Theatre, London, with Rosemary Leach in the lead role. Rubens did not adapt the novel for the stage, nor did she write the screenplay for the 1981 French version, *Chère Inconnue,* directed by Moshe Mizrahi and starring Simone Signoret.

Rubens based *The Ponsonby Post* (1977) on a movie-research trip she made to Java in 1969. The plot is more complicated than that of her previous novels, though it is handled with skill. The book attacks the attitudes of Europeans working for the United Nations: a bitterly divided group whose only point of agreement is the wish to separate themselves from the local population. With the exception of the protagonist, Hugh Brownlow, the expatriates are an insensitive clique. Rubens has traveled for most of her working life; her motion pictures for the United Nations and her work in third-world countries as a British Council representative have given her prose a moral edge and a strong sense of humanity. This fine comedy of manners has much in common with the later *Birds of Passage* (1981).

A Five Year Sentence (1978) is Rubens's favorite of her novels and, she says, her most autobiographical. In early middle age her works dealt increasingly with people struggling with the effects of loneliness and guilt. The novel concerns lonely Miss Hawkins, whose retirement gift after forty-six years of service at a confectionery company is a five-year diary. The prospect of absolute solitude prompts Miss Hawkins to consider suicide, but, conditioned from her miserable childhood to obedience, she views the diary as an instruction to go on living. Eventually Miss Hawkins finds companionship and a sexual relationship with Brian Watts, but Brian and the diary soon become the agents of her downfall. Unlike *Mate in Three,* the novel is not literally autobiographical, but the psychology of the heroine reflects that of Rubens. At the time of writing the book she was divorced and living alone, her daughters having grown up and left home. Although this novel was shortlisted for the 1978 Booker Prize, critics were unimpressed with its pathos, which they considered overdone.

In *Spring Sonata: A Fable* (1979) Rubens revisits the theme of parental responsibility. The narrator is the "simple, straightforward" Doctor Brown, who relates the extraordinary tale of Buster, the baby who refused to be born. The fable format allows Rubens to take great liberties: for example, Buster keeps a diary and plays the violin in his mother's womb. Yet, even the womb cannot protect Buster from emotional blackmail—the baby's father, like the impresario of *Madame Sousatzka,* seeks to exploit Buster's prodigious musical talent and in doing so loses everything. The book attracted a cult following in the psychotherapeutic world, despite Rubens's objection to psychiatry as a "criminal" practice. Her device of rendering speech in the form of a play script made the book an ideal subject for radio. In 1994 it was dramatized by Olwen Wymark for BBC Wales.

The opening of *Birds of Passage* describes the friendship of two neighboring couples, the Walshes and the Pickerings, whose mutual privet hedge stretches from one house to the other. When Mr. Walsh, with no respect for synchronicity, dies, leaving Mr. Pickering

Dust jacket for Rubens's 1993 novel, in which a man uses the contents of a dead author's brain to write his definitive biography

still alive and shearing his half of the hedge, Ellen Walsh's resentment grows, for she and Alice Pickering had envisioned spending their joint widowhood on a cruise–an event that Mr. Pickering is delaying. Soon Pickering dies, and, pausing only to poison the offending hedge, the two women set sail for foreign climes. The plot takes a sinister turn with the attempts of the cruise ship's waiter to exploit and torment these vulnerable women. The ending is ambivalent–like the passengers on the ship, the reader is brought back to the place of embarkation. Only the privet hedge has changed: its straggly regrowth seems a symbol of survival in a world poisoned by selfishness. *Birds of Passage* met with a cool reception; critics complained that the characters of Ellen and Alice were not sufficiently differentiated and that Rubens had become repetitive.

This relatively short tale was followed by a novel of epic proportions. In the early 1980s Rubens again considered retirement but persuaded herself to write a final novel, a long historical piece. *Brothers* (1983) traces the persecution of six generations of Jews in tsarist Russia. Rubens was gratified to receive letters from readers who praised her depiction of Odena, a city she had never visited. Her imaginative powers thus affirmed, she resolved to continue writing.

Rubens's next novel, *Mr. Wakefield's Crusade* (1985), is a witty burlesque on the theme of obsession. The dull life of Luke Wakefield, a self-confessed failure, is animated when he sees a man drop dead in line at the post office. Driven by curiosity, Luke steals the dead man's letter, which he takes home to savor in private. The letter is addressed to Marion Firbank and begs forgiveness for a "monstrous act." Rubens uses the letter as a device to keep the reader in suspense; the plot unfurls by way of a sheaf of letters that Luke steals from the dead man's house. Luke's investigation of the Firbank crime conceals a mystery at the heart of its detective: he is a man whose life does not, for some reason, bear analysis; he is completely superficial, not daring to probe his bitterness over his estranged wife, Connie, or his grim obsession with *The Times* obituaries. Luke's crusade turns out not to be for a dead body but for a new lease on life. The novel was successfully adapted for television by Paul Hines in 1992.

The two novels that followed, *Our Father* (1987) and *Kingdom Come* (1990), deal with spiritual issues. The protagonist of *Our Father,* Veronica Smiles, is an explorer. In the opening chapter she is trekking across the Sahara. Halfway across the desert Veronica is accosted by God, and, after returning home to Surbiton, Veronica cannot seem to shake him off. She soon grows irritated by his banal conversation, his fancy dress guises, and his habit of leaving messages on her answering machine. Veronica seems to be hiding something. As she uncovers and sorts her father's papers, each document triggers a flashback, a fragment of Veronica's unhappy childhood that must be faced and understood. Then and only then, she realizes, will God leave her in peace.

Rubens followed *Our Father,* which won the Welsh Arts Council Prize, with an historical take on Jewish themes. *Kingdom Come* is the story of Sabbatai Zvi, founder of a seventeenth-century Middle Eastern messianic cult. The plot follows the growth of the Sabbataian Movement from its infancy in Turkey to Zvi's spectacular martyrdom and apostasy in Jerusalem. He is fanatical, given to trances, and worshiped by a zealous group of disciples. Although the events of the novel are narrated by a skeptic, the reader is left to decide, finally, if Sabbatai Zvi follows God or the devil. *Kingdom Come* was awarded the Wingate Prize for fiction.

A Solitary Grief (1991) is the dark tale of psychiatrist Alistair Crown and his wife, who gives birth to a Down's syndrome child. Rubens sketches the details of Crown's background: the psychiatry practice he shares with his philandering colleague, Gerry; Crown's pathetic obsession with celebrity clients; and his callousness and lack of insight ("He could no more analyse himself than he could mend a pair of shoes"). Traumatized by the birth of his child, Doris, Crown soon takes up with an old girlfriend, scarcely bothering to conceal the affair from his wife. The affair breaks up and Crown—who has developed a phobia about Doris's face—moves out of the family home. The narrative shifts to Crown's peculiar friendship with an exhibitionist he calls "Esau" and a disastrous spree they take to Paris, but when Crown's child goes missing he is drawn back to his wife and home. The subplot might at first seem irrelevant; however, there is a link between Esau, whose hairy appearance constantly prompts him to ask, "Do you not find me beautiful?," and Doris, who Crown fears is ugly. The subjective nature of beauty is clearly an issue here, as is Crown's inability to transcend his own selfishness.

Like *Brothers*, *Mother Russia* (1992) is an epic novel that follows the fortunes of two families: the peasant Volynins and the aristocratic Larinovs. Employing the familiar plot of love across class boundaries, Rubens explores the redeeming nature of family relationships at a time of social upheaval. Ivan Volynin is perhaps the novel's most interesting character. As with most revolutionary spirits, Ivan is torn between political ideals (which must dehumanize individuals for the common good) and personal, familial dramas. His son, Viktor, seeks to revenge himself on Ivan's superior. Ivan's brother, Sasha, is a writer whose artistry leads him into dangerous individualism. Thus Ivan must choose between the conflicting claims of family and nation. Yet, while mothers and the Motherland are strong, the lives of the characters are beset by absent and inadequate fathers. In the face of such disorder, friendship replaces kinship, and psychological ties replace blood ties. Sasha's survival at the end of the novel hints at both the importance of art and the transforming power of love.

Rubens followed *Mother Russia* with *Hijack* (1993), a play set in a London publisher's office. The protagonist, Oscar Anderson, is a philanderer in the mold of Jack Millar of *Mate in Three*. Alone one night in his office, he is hijacked by a desperate writer who demands, at gunpoint, that Oscar read his three-thousand-page manuscript. It is the eve of a long bank holiday weekend—a weekend that Oscar had planned to spend with his lover, having gone to great lengths to sidestep his wife's invitation to Dorset. The writer, Victor, sabotages these plans, however. Victor's novel traces the life of a man named Albert Smith and the various trespasses he makes against his marriage vows. The novel is dramatized within the play—Oscar, his wife, and his mistress doubling as Victor's characters. The self-reflexive nature of this device is confusing although its overall aim is clear. Oscar's confounding inability to commit is enacted, significantly, within another fictional form. As in *Mother Russia*, Rubens

draws attention to the powerful and redeeming qualities of the novelist's art.

Rubens's next book, *Autobiopsy* (1993), is also self-reflexive, taking art and artistry as its main theme. At the center of this work is another writer, one much more desperate than Victor. Martin Peabody has suffered twelve years of writer's block, a humiliation that has not been helped by the success of his friend, the celebrated writer Walter Berry. Yet, when Berry dies, Martin sees a way of recovering the respect of the literary establishment. Claiming to be paying his last respects, he gains access to Berry's death chamber and, using some obscure trepanation technique, extracts his brain. *Autobiopsy* is clearly a robust joke about biography; Martin literally picks his mentor's brains with the intention of writing the definitive Walter Berry memoir. Berry's past is revealed gradually, as Walter laboriously siphons off each thought. However, he is obliged to fill in the gaps of Berry's consciousness and thus the events of his own life come into play. Rubens's theme prompts many questions about the artistic process, not least the overlap of biography and fiction: "My autobiopsy is fiction," Martin explains, "and if at times it occasionally overlaps with fact that is only because the truth of reality is as unreliable as the lie of fiction." Critics spoke of the novel as a masterly exposition of plagiarism, but Rubens objected. *Autobiopsy*, she claimed, was simply a novel about how novels are written. In fact Martin Peabody's writing habits bear comparison with those of his creator. Like Peabody, Rubens is said to interrupt her writing now and again with interludes on the piano—the music of Domenico Scarlatti being a particular favorite.

Yesterday in the Back Lane (1995) concerns seventy-year-old Bronwen Davies, who is a murderer. Much of her story is presented in flashback; at the age of seventeen she stabbed a man who tried to rape her in the lane behind her house. This incident occurs in Cardiff at a precise moment in history when the Russians were repelling a German attack just prior to Britain's entry into World War II. As bombers converge on the city, Bronwen conceals her own terrible, but necessary, act of violence. Years later, realizing she is unable to marry her fiancé, she sentences herself to a life of spinsterhood: a symbolic preservation of her virginity that puzzles and embitters her aging parents. Critics remarked on Rubens's skillful handling of tragedy, played out against the backdrop of ordinary domestic life.

The year 1997 was for Rubens one of bereavement. The death of her brother, the violinist Cyril Rubens, followed by those of her former husband and several friends, prompted a new direction in her fiction. Although she is known for her dark, tragicomic perspective (the so-called Rubens effect), *The Waiting Game*

(1997) was her first direct treatment of aging and mortality. The players of the "game" are the inhabitants of an old people's home who await death. The Hollyhocks Home for the Aged is not quite what it seems, however. The frail Lady Celia Suckling is a blackmailer; Mrs. Hughes is an alcoholic; Mr. Thurlow harbors sadistic tendencies; and Jeremy Cross is a "professional survivor" who keeps tallies of the deaths at Hollyhocks on the back of his wardrobe door. *The Waiting Game* challenges common perceptions of the elderly, much as *A Solitary Grief* explores Down's syndrome and *The Elected Member,* mental illness. There is, in other words, a rejection of stereotypes and a determined facing of the facts. As ever, Rubens demonstrates a mastery of group dynamics. The Hollyhocks Home is an extended family in which roles are conflicting; systems of dominance and victimhood, loneliness and companionship are embodied, as are secrets, betrayals, and hidden identities. In fact, the plot is more intricate and less symmetrical than that of many of Rubens's novels: there are many more characters, and their individual stories merge in complex ways. Critics praised the novel for its lack of condescension and unflinching attention to detail but were hostile toward what they saw as plot acrobatics.

After several failed attempts at retirement, Rubens has, for the moment, ceased contemplating it. Despite a frustrating spell as Booker Prize judge in 1986, she recently joined the judging panel for the 1998 Orange Prize for women's fiction. Although her themes lack diversity, her work is not easily categorized. Her style is somber and unadorned, with emphasis on character rather than physical description. Contradiction interests her; she is drawn by the quirky, the ironic, and the unpredictable. Indeed, her approach is calculated to keep the reader guessing: she claims not to plot books before she begins writing, nor does she revise her work extensively. She has a wry belief in the immortality of the writing process: God would not have the audacity, she says, to take her mid-sentence.

Interviews:

Jan Moir, "The Arts: A Waltz Of Creativity," *Daily Telegraph,* 2 August 1997, p. 5;

Sally Vincent, "Coming Up for More," *Guardian,* 9 August 1997, p. 26.

Reference:

Olga Kenyon, "Bernice Rubens and the Mainstream Jewish Novel," in her *Writing Women; Contemporary Women Novelists* (London: Pluto, 1991), pp. 36–39.

Paul Scott

(25 March 1920 – 1 March 1978)

Margaret Lewis

See also the Scott entry in *DLB 14: British Novelists Since 1960.*

BOOKS: *I Gerontius* (London: Favil, 1941);
Johnny Sahib (London: Eyre & Spottiswoode, 1952);
The Alien Sky (London: Eyre & Spottiswoode, 1953); republished as *Six Days in Marapore* (Garden City, N.Y.: Doubleday, 1953);
A Male Child (London: Eyre & Spottiswoode, 1956; New York: Dutton, 1957);
The Mark of the Warrior (London: Eyre & Spottiswoode, 1958; New York: Morrow, 1958);
The Chinese Love Pavilion (London: Eyre & Spottiswoode, 1960); republished as *The Love Pavilion* (New York: Morrow, 1960);
The Birds of Paradise (London: Eyre & Spottiswoode, 1962; New York: Morrow, 1962);
The Bender: Pictures from an Exhibition of Middle Class Portraits (London: Secker & Warburg, 1963); republished as *The Bender* (New York: Morrow, 1963);
The Corrida at San Feliu (London: Secker & Warburg, 1964; New York: Morrow, 1964);
The Jewel in the Crown (London: Heinemann, 1966; New York: Morrow, 1966);
The Day of the Scorpion (London: Heinemann, 1968; New York: Morrow, 1968);
The Towers of Silence (London: Heinemann, 1971; New York: Morrow, 1972);
A Division of the Spoils (London: Heinemann, 1975; New York: Morrow, 1975);
The Raj Quartet (London: Heinemann, 1976; New York: Morrow, 1976);
Staying On (London: Heinemann, 1977; New York: Morrow, 1977);
After the Funeral (London: Heinemann/Whittington Press, 1979);
My Appointment with the Muse. Essays, 1961–75, edited by Shelley C. Reece (London: Heinemann, 1986); republished as *On Writing and the Novel* (New York: Morrow, 1987).

Paul Scott (photograph © 1980 by Mark Gerson)

TELEVISION: *Lines of Communication,* script by Scott, BBC, 1952;
The Alien Sky, script by Scott, BBC, 1956.

RADIO: *Lines of Communication,* script by Scott, BBC, 1951;
The Alien Sky, script by Scott, BBC, 1954;
Sahibs and Memsahibs, script by Scott, BBC, 1958;
The Mark of the Warrior, script by Scott, BBC, 1960.

OTHER: *Pillars of Salt,* in *Four Jewish Plays,* edited by Harold F. Rubinstein (London: Gollancz, 1948);
"Indian: A Post Forsterian View," in *Essays by Divers Hands* (London: Oxford University Press, 1970).

Paul Scott's worldwide reputation as a novelist has emerged largely since his death in 1978 at the age of fifty-seven. The award of the Booker Prize for fiction in 1977 for his novel *Staying On* finally established him as a serious writer in the eyes of the British literary establishment, which had previously neglected his achievements. Six years later the highly praised television series *The Jewel in the Crown,* based on *The Raj Quartet* (1976), brought his complex and engrossing novels to a much wider public than he might ever have expected. Ironically, most of his career as a novelist had been spent in a state of anxiety about book sales and income; his success came too late to free him from the grueling burden of writing and reviewing that had, according to Hilary Spurling's authorized biography, *Paul Scott: A Life* (1990), increasingly constricted his life and led him to alcoholism and frequent bouts of despair.

Paul Scott was not a child of the empire, that privileged group who returned to England with memories of exotic landscapes and lavish lifestyles far from home. Readers of Scott's novels may feel that the ease and familiarity of his description of the territory and social scene suggest an author who was born in India, but in fact Paul Mark Scott was born in north London on 25 March 1920, the second son of Tom and Frances Scott, both commercial artists. Paul and his brother, Peter, attended the fee-paying Winchmore Hill Collegiate School, but a financial crisis forced his parents to remove him from school before his fifteenth birthday. According to his biographer, Paul blamed his father for betraying his hopes for an artistic future and for deciding that he should become an accountant. Many of his fictional characters share this experience of dislocation and abandoned ambitions, including one of the central characters in *The Raj Quartet,* Hari Kumar. Scott's teenage years were occupied by night classes in accountancy and long days sitting in an office as a clerk. In his few spare moments he wrote poetry.

In 1941, while serving in the British army, Scott married Nancy Edith Avery, a nurse and later a novelist who wrote under the pseudonym Elizabeth Avery. Scott was posted to India in 1943 and worked as an air supply officer, traveling widely throughout India, Burma, and Malaya. In 1946 he returned to England and joined a small publishing firm, Falcon and Grey Walls Press, as company secretary. He left in 1950 to become a literary agent with Pearn, Pollinger, and Higham (later David Higham Associates), and in the ten years following he wrote five novels. The decision to become a full-time writer, to allow himself time to write longer, more expansive fiction, was made more difficult by the fact that he and Nancy by that time had two daughters, Carol and Sally, and a house in Hampstead Garden Suburb to keep.

Scott revisited India in 1964 and there found inspiration for *The Raj Quartet* and *Staying On.* The British Council enabled him to visit India again in 1972 on a lecture tour. In 1976 and 1977 he was a visiting lecturer at the University of Tulsa in Oklahoma, where he spent a happy period teaching creative writing and contemporary British fiction. He was admired by his students and appreciated by the academic staff—the only academic recognition he received during his career as a writer. He was too ill to attend the Booker Prize ceremony in person, and his daughter Carol accepted the award on his behalf.

In all of Scott's novels—most of them set in India or the Far East—there is a concern for what he calls "the common factor . . . this obsession with the relationship between a man and the work he does." His emphasis on work is one of the major differences between the world of *The Raj Quartet* and the world of E. M. Forster's *A Passage to India* (1924), in which, Scott claims, the characters are not adequately defined by the work they do, and, he concludes, "without their aura of occupation they lack what was their chief justification." Scott's imaginative re-creation of the world of the Raj, which he never actually experienced except for his wartime service, begins with an attempt to assess the colonial relationship: the sense that, however tarnished it may appear in retrospect, there was a moral ideal behind service in the empire. Speaking to the Royal Society of Literature in 1968, Scott claimed that the British Raj was "a period and a place in which the liberal philosophy—which now does not excite us—last excited us." Yet, the illusion behind the empire was to become the primary focus of Scott's mature fiction about India.

The idealism that permeates Scott's writing is evident from his earliest published work. In 1941 his long poem *I Gerontius* was included in the Resurgam Series of poetry pamphlets dedicated to "rebuild a new world where men are truly free." *Pillars of Salt*—an early play published in 1948 but not performed—was selected as a prizewinner in a Jewish playwriting competition. Scott finally found his voice not as a poet or dramatist but as a novelist with his first book, *Johnny Sahib* (1952). The book was rejected seventeen times before finally being accepted for publication, when it was awarded the Eyre and Spottiswoode Literary Fellowship Prize. *Johnny Sahib* deals with the tensions between soldiers and their leaders in an air supply unit that drops supplies for the Burma War; the novel draws on Scott's experiences as an officer in such a unit. His play *Lines of Communication* (1952), on a similar subject, was broadcast by BBC radio and television to considerable acclaim.

Scott forged ahead with his next novel, *The Alien Sky* (1953), also set in India and exploring themes familiar to readers of Scott's later, more substantial novels. The concept of work and how it defines the central character, Tom Gower, who has devoted his life to India only to be rejected at independence by those he considered to be his friends, appears repeatedly in Scott's fiction, as does the traveler searching for a lost past.

Although *A Male Child* (1956) is set in England, a cold and miserable place where food and fuel are rationed and returning soldiers are finding difficulty coming to terms with the bleak aftermath of World War II, the two central characters have been on military service in India and the Far East and long to return there. Scott admitted that he longed to return to the warmth and exoticism of the East, and he did so in his next novel, *The Mark of the Warrior* (1958). Scott again depicts the world of men in battle that he first explored in *Johnny Sahib*. *The Mark of the Warrior* is similarly concerned with the nature of the influence that leadership and bravery and with the influence that memories of the past have on the future. Like the rest of his 1950s novels, *The Mark of the Warrior* is thinly characterized and badly in need of development.

Only the last of the 1950s novels, *The Chinese Love Pavilion* (1960), truly hints at Scott's rich resources. Here he first exhibits the leisurely, sensuous prose style that, linked with a more pronounced poetic structure, successfully evoked the fascination that the East has so often held for western visitors. The young officer Tom Brent says that "India was of my bone," and he abandons plans for a settled career as a businessman and flings himself into the country where his family has lived for generations. Scott's own situation at that time was equally unsettled, as he finally decided that in order to satisfy his deepest needs he must choose the frugal life of the writer as opposed to that of the successful literary agent.

The Birds of Paradise (1962) is a worthy antecedent to *The Raj Quartet*. Scott employs a sophisticated blend of narrative techniques to filter the memories of a solitary traveler, William Conway, who is trying to escape from a broken marriage and an uneasy role as a successful businessman in London. Conway is haunted by a brief episode during his childhood in India, when he and his Indian friends had visited an island on a lake in palace gardens, where brilliantly colored, stuffed birds of paradise were suspended in a large, ornate cage. This central image of the mysterious and elusive birds of paradise is used skillfully as a motif throughout the novel, which culminates in a visit to the island by the three friends, now middle-aged. They find that the birds of paradise still reside in their elaborate cage, but they are showing signs of neglect, a poignant comment on the splendor of the Raj and the vanity of the Indian princes as well as on the vague, never-to-be-attained aspirations

Dust jacket for Scott's 1966 novel, the first in The Raj Quartet

of youth, seen from solitary middle age. *The Birds of Paradise* is an elegantly crafted novel, rich enough to allow the emergence of complex, shifting emotions and ideas that had not had a chance to develop in Scott's previous work. At this point, however, Scott began to drink excessively and on occasion behave violently, his charming public persona at odds with the dark, obsessed writer who stayed at home.

Two more novels, both of them unsatisfactory in different ways, followed the artistic success of *The Birds of Paradise*. The autobiographical *The Bender: Pictures from an Exhibition of Middle Class Portraits* (1963) concerns a central character who is left a small legacy so that he does not have to find a job; he manages to exist only on the brink of poverty. It is possible to see in this mildly humorous novel with its satire of fashionable London in the 1960s Scott's preoccupation with the importance of work as a means of defining one's place in life. *The Bender* is also about social class and the British caste system, which is so important in *The Raj Quartet*. Unfortunately, despite Scott's fondness for this novel, its exploration of these issues remains superficial, lacking the necessary psychological depth to engage the reader.

The Corrida at San Feliu (1964) is an unusual, strangely disjointed novel that Scott wrote at a time when an untreated tropical illness was causing him physical and mental distress. Originally subtitled "The Spanish Papers of Edward Thornhill," the narrative is composed of apparently unstructured fragments left behind by the imaginary novelist Edward Thornhill, who with his wife, Myra, was killed in a car crash while returning from a bullfight near their Spanish villa. Scott is clearly preoccupied with the relationship between life and art, between illusion and reality, expressed through Thornhill's literary effects: two short stories, one set in Africa, one in India; two alternative openings to a novel set in India; and a short novel, "The Plaza de Toros." This montage can be baffling when first encountered, but gradually Scott succeeds in building up the memories and experiences that figure in the consciousness of his main character, illuminated by the ever-present image of the bullfight as a comment on life. Patrick Swinden called *The Corrida at San Feliu* "a disturbingly original treatment of some of Scott's familiar themes." It also anticipates Scott's formal experiments in *The Raj Quartet.*

Technically fascinating, the novel was not a commercial success; after the poor sales generated by *The Bender,* Scott found himself under financial and psychological pressure as well as suffering prolonged ill health. His election as a fellow of the Royal Society of Literature in 1963 was one of the few positive features of his life at this time. He signed with a new publisher, Heinemann, in 1962 but continued his long-established association with Roland Gant as his editor. Heinemann made it possible for Scott to revisit India, a trip that his biographer regarded as "a last desperate gamble, one that he had put off as long as he could and risked now only because he could see no alternative for himself as a writer."

Although the four novels of *The Raj Quartet* can be read individually, there are rich rewards to be gained by reading them as our parts of a complete entity. The great achievement that these densely textured novels represent can be seen emerging gradually through Scott's earlier work. His view of the novel as representing "a form of moral dialogue between the writer and the reader . . . much more a series of questions than a set of statements" becomes apparent with *The Raj Quartet,* as does his conviction that "the last days of the Raj are the metaphor I have presently chosen to illustrate my view of life." His success in attempting to fictionalize an historical moment was recognized by the distinguished historian Max Beloff in an article in *Encounter* in May 1976: Beloff acknowledges that "the subject is one

to which the historian's technique, however refined, may not be able to do justice" and that Scott had used the novel form "both to present the circumstances of the case, and through his personages to evoke either directly or through symbolic reference the complex of feelings, physical and moral, that go to make up the experience as a whole."

In one of his comparatively rare public talks about his work, "Method: The Mystery and the Mechanics," given to the Writers' Summer School at Swanwick in 1967 and published in the volume *My Appointment with the Muse. Essays, 1961–75* (1986), Scott describes the image that lies at the heart of the first novel, *The Jewel in the Crown:*

> And there she was, my prime mystery, a girl, in the dark, running, exhausted, hurt in some way, yet strangely of good heart—tough, resilient, her face and figure a sense rather than an observed condition. But she runs.
>
> From what? To where?

He goes on to explain how that image led to the development of the novel: "With knowledge, experience, imagination and creative impulse I bombarded the image of the girl running. I had a beautiful explosion. But that of course was where the real work began—trying to convey that feeling of power and inevitability to others."

The Jewel in the Crown (1966) opens with the uncompromising statement "This is the story of a rape," a crime that still reverberates in the pages of the fourth novel, *A Division of the Spoils* (1975). Daphne Manners is raped by a gang of Indian youths while secretly meeting her Indian lover, Hari Kumar, in the Bibighar Gardens. This crime, and the attack on Edwina Crane, a missionary schoolteacher who has her car overturned and her Indian assistant beaten to death beside her, take place during a time of political turbulence, the "Quit India" riots of August 1942. At that time the ruling British administration was struggling to control civil unrest in India while watching Japanese troops gain ascendancy over the Pacific Ocean in World War II.

Scott's great achievement as a novelist is to weave the lives of individual characters together with historical events and, by doing so, to make history an immediate experience for the reader. Not only do different characters reveal varying views of the same incident, but the incidents are mediated through a variety of literary forms: together with letters, memoirs, formal reports, a journal, a legal deposition, and third-person narration. The reactions of civil and military forces, of Indian judges and English memsahibs, of petty criminals and Indian princesses are all woven together to cre-

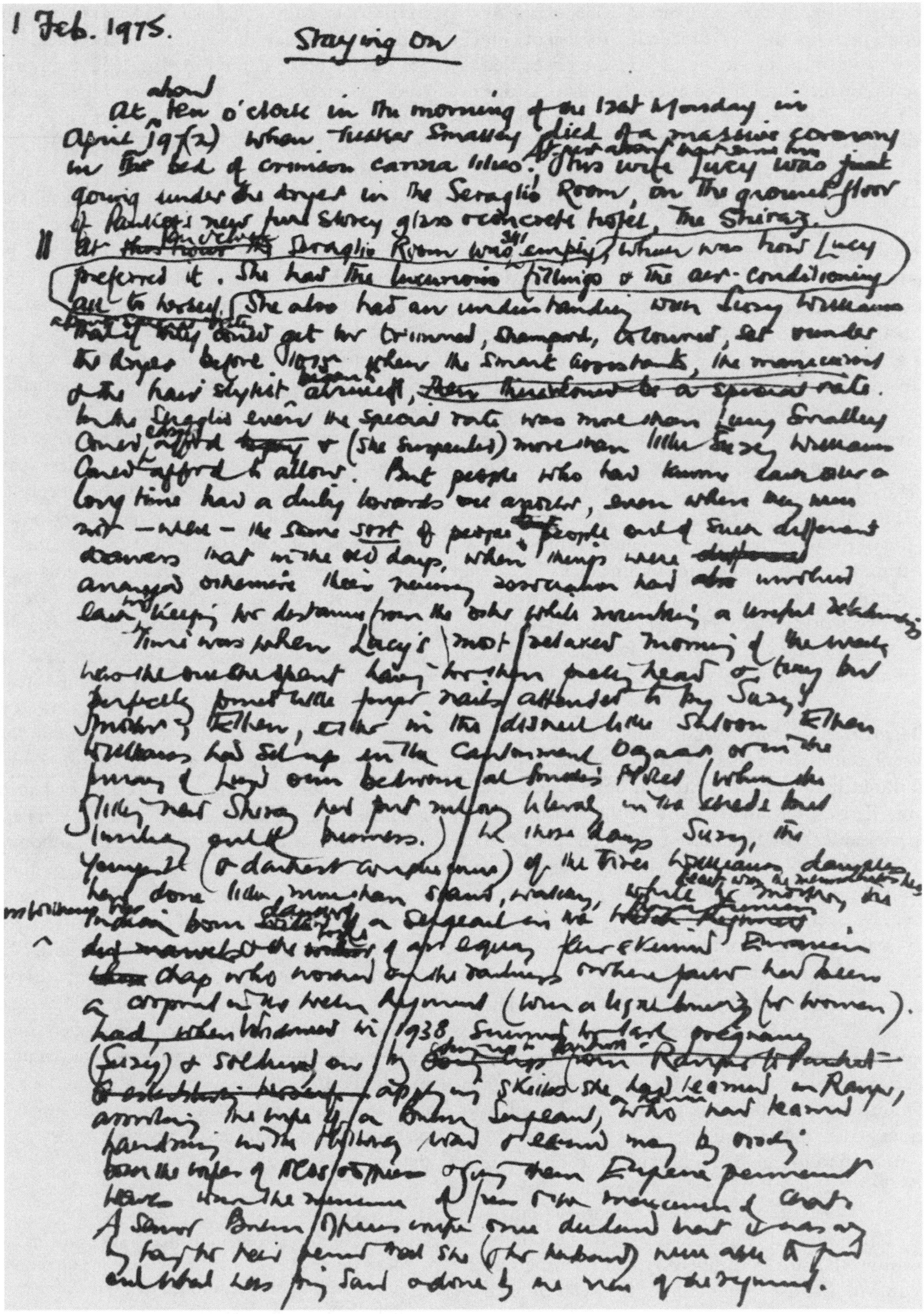
1 Feb. 1975.

Staying On

At about ten o'clock in the morning of the last Monday in April 1972 when Tusker Smalley died of a massive coronary in the bed of crimson canna lilies his wife Lucy was just going under the dryer in the Seraglio Room, on the ground floor of Pankot's new four storey glass & concrete hotel, The Shiraz.

Page from the manuscript for Scott's 1977 novel, a portrayal of the remaining British in postcolonial India

ate a novel rich in texture and moral complexity. As Scott adds layer upon layer of detail to the plot, the reader is drawn into the decisions and the crises that affect the characters, and it becomes clear that making an easy moral judgment of the events or the people involved in them is nearly impossible.

In the vast panorama of *The Raj Quartet,* nearly every character has a precise role to fill, from Sister Ludmila, the European woman who dresses as a nun and rescues the dying from the streets of Mayapore, to the elderly widow Mabel Layton, who works daily in her garden at Rose Cottage in Pankot and quietly sends money to Indian charities. When Hari Kumar returns to India after attending an English public school, he is unable to find work that is in accord with his educational achievements, because the English do not expect Indians to be as cultivated and urbane as he is and the Indians regard him with suspicion as a traitor to his people. Hari does not at first see this social and political gulf dividing him from a future that had at one time seemed full of promise, but his experience of snubs and hostility from the English alienates him from his former life as a member of the privileged public-school world. Straddling two worlds leaves Hari without a social function; his relationship with Daphne Manners is full of misunderstandings, and a catastrophe is almost inevitable.

The arrest and conviction of Hari Kumar for the rape of Daphne Manners polarizes the tensions between the Indians and the British and introduces the ambiguous figure of Ronald Merrick, the corrupt district superintendent of the Indian police, whose outwardly upright character is steadily undermined throughout the four novels. The British establishment may have its secret doubts about Merrick, but his authority is never questioned, even though he is quite clearly an outsider in social terms.

A powerful image haunting all the novels is "The Jewel in Her Crown," a nineteenth-century print of Queen Victoria on her throne accepting tribute from her loyal Indian subjects; India is the jewel in the crown of the empire. In exchange for tribute, the Raj offers that curious paternalistic care known as *man-bap* by the Indians—translated to mean "I am your father and your mother." The print of "The Jewel in Her Crown" appears in many situations, some of them ironic, others poignant. The notion of responsibility on the part of the English administration is codified by this painting and further confirms Scott's recognition of the old-fashioned ideals of the empire.

Scott's portrayal of Ronald Merrick is deepened in *The Day of the Scorpion* (1968), which opens with the arrest of Indian politicians at the time of the "Quit India" riots. More emphasis is placed on the politicians and the soldiers in this novel, and the effect is to circle around the crime in the Bibighar Gardens, portraying it from the viewpoint of Hari Kumar. The events in *The Day of the Scorpion* take place two years after those in *The Jewel in the Crown*. In a dramatic and revealing episode that forms the centerpiece of the novel, Hari at last breaks his silence and tells his story to an emissary from the governor who has come to question him in jail. Daphne Manners has died in childbirth and her aunt, Lady Manners, who is looking after the child, has requested an investigation. Lady Manners arrives at Kandipat Jail heavily veiled in a purdah car to listen unseen to Hari's account. The darkened car, normally used to transport high-caste Hindu ladies still in purdah, adds an aura of seclusion and mystery to her visit. After hearing the startling evidence of Merrick's ill treatment of the prisoners, Lady Manners leaves convinced of Kumar's innocence but also deeply aware of the sense of disaster looming over the relationship betwen the British and the Indians in the final years of colonial rule. "The barrier that separated us was impenetrable," she realizes as, weeping, she gazes at Hari through the thick glass and metal slats of Kandipat Jail.

Political tensions continue to increase as the Congress Party gains in power, and the credibility of British justice is both undermined by the revelations of Merrick's sadistic behavior toward the Indians and strengthened by the reopening of the investigation into Daphne Manner's rape, resulting in the release of Hari Kumar. Balancing the sinister development of Merrick in this novel is the strong presence of Sarah Layton, Colonel Layton's daughter, who lives with her mother, sister, and stepgrandmother in the hill station of Pankot. The wives and family of the officers and bureaucrats who rule the country are skillfully individualized by Scott, who treats them with a mixture of sympathy, sardonic humor, and indignation. Sarah is regarded as "unsound" by the others because of her unorthodox views and is one of the few who can contemplate crossing the boundaries between races and rationally assess the meaning of British involvement in India. Sarah is perceptive enough to see Merrick's ruthless appetite for power:

> She thought: you are, yes, our dark side, the arcane side. You reveal something that is sad about us, as if out here we have built a mansion without doors and windows, with no way in and no way out. All India lies on our doorstep and cannot enter to warm us or be warmed. We live in holes and crevices of the crumbling stone, no longer sheltered by the carapace of our history which is leaving us behind. And one day we shall lie exposed, in our tender skins. You, as well as us.

Siddarta Kak, left, and Tim Piggott-Smith, center, in the 1984 television adaptation of Scott's
The Jewel in the Crown *(Granada Television)*

While Merrick's heroism as an officer cannot be denied—he loses his arm trying to rescue Sarah's brother-in-law from his ambushed jeep in the Burmese jungle—Sarah recoils from his dismissal of the code of conduct, "the whole impossible nonsensical dream" that lies behind the tradition of service in India.

The Towers of Silence (1971) puts even more emphasis on the women behind the British military and civil lines. Most of the novel is set in the hill village of Pankot, and in addition to the Layton family it develops the tragic figure of the retired missionary schoolteacher Barbie Batchelor, who comes as a paying guest to Rose Cottage. Her lower-middle-class background places her outside the circle of the British rulers of India with their private incomes and select schools. Like Lucy Smalley in *Staying On,* who makes the mistake of admitting to knowing shorthand, Barbie is snubbed and persecuted by the memsahibs of Pankot, and these characters allow Scott to explore his concerns with the English class system. Superintendent Merrick plays out his ambivalent role in the background of the novel, but he continues to bring a sense of evil wherever he goes. His presence keeps alive the memory of the "Quit India" riots and the civil disturbance that he ruthlessly quelled.

A Division of the Spoils, the final volume of *The Raj Quartet*, deals extensively with the ultimate retreat of the British and the partition of India in 1947. The clash between Hindus and Muslims becomes a matter of systematic mutual slaughter, and juxtaposed against this pattern of increasing violence is the political discussions of Indian and British politicians, who are incapable of halting the carnage. The violence is particularized in the savage murder of Merrick by the young Indian boys he sexually exploits and in the graphically described butchery of Sarah Layton's friend Ahmed, who is one of a large group of Muslims torn from a train by a Hindu mob and killed before the eyes of the departing British. The horrific presentation of this scene and the bloody aftermath, in which Sarah and her future husband, Guy Perron, try to assist the wounded, is eloquent evidence of Scott's deeply held view that the British were responsible for the deaths of the quarter-million people who were killed after the Indian subcontinent was partitioned into India and Pakistan.

Staying On, a coda to *The Raj Quartet,* is written in a bittersweet, elegiac tone that contrasts sharply to the horrors depicted in *A Division of the Spoils.* Set in 1972, the novel gently satirizes the new India, where Col.

Tusker Smalley and his wife, Lucy, find themselves marooned, an old-fashioned remnant of the Raj in a world of sophisticated, wealthy businessmen and politicians, corrupt property dealers, and fashionable hairdressers. "We should write to Cooks," suggests Lucy, "and ask them to put us on the tourist itinerary. After the Taj Mahal . . . the Smalleys of Pankot."

Tusker and Lucy first appear as background figures in *The Day of the Scorpion,* but in this novel Scott places them centrally, distilling the huge cast of *The Raj Quartet* into these two fragile and rather shabby figures. Tusker's fatal collapse at the opening of the novel leaves the remainder of the narrative to work toward his death in Scott's familiar patterning of memory juxtaposed to the present. The sensitivity of his portrayal of the relationship between Tusker and his wife is heightened rather than destroyed by the humorous handling of their essentially uncommunicative marriage, and the depiction of their Muslim servant, Ibrahim, is a masterpiece of comedy. *Staying On* has the qualities of a miniature painting, especially compared to the vast canvas of *The Raj Quartet:* clarity of definition, minute attention to detail, and total concentration on the subject.

Paul Scott's last fiction, a finely wrought fable titled *After the Funeral* (1979), was published in a private-press edition the year after his death on 1 March 1978. His daughter Sally illustrated the text with imaginative and elegant full-page drawings. Based on Cinderella, it was to have become one of a series of modern fairy tales taken from the Brothers Grimm, whose plots had always fascinated Scott. Despite its brevity, *After the Funeral* could be seen as a reflection of many of the most profound aspects of Scott's thinking, in particular, the recognition that the power of the imagination—Cinderella does not go to the ball in Scott's version, but simply imagines being there—is ultimately life's greatest reward: "It is an old tale, but somewhere in it there is the magic of a persistent wish, as old as earth, but ever-present. The tale is like a looking glass in which you see yourself if you gaze into it long enough."

Even in a magic looking glass, Scott could not have foreseen the enormous popularity that his novels were to achieve when they were adapted for television by Granada in the early 1980s. *Staying On* was the first to be broadcast, with Celia Johnson as Lucy and Trevor Howard as Tusker. Then, Granada adapted *The Raj Quartet* in fourteen episodes with a stellar British cast.

Much critical attention has been focused on Scott since his death. The English academic Patrick Swinden admitted to a "sense of guilt at failing to notice the work of a fine writer" in the preface to his book *Paul Scott: Images of India* (1980), but many others have redressed the balance. K. Bhaskara Rao and Francine S. Weinbaum had the advantage of meeting and interviewing Scott during his visits to the United States in his final years. Critics have broadened their approach in various ways: some have compared him to Forster, Rudyard Kipling, and Joseph Conrad as novelists of the empire; others have contrasted him to Lawrence Durrell, Salman Rushdie, and Ruth Prawer Jhabvala. His creative use of historical sources has been examined by many critics. The publication of his essays and lectures as *My Appointment with the Muse. Essays, 1961–75* threw considerable light on his own thoughts about India and the processes behind his imaginative re-creation of the British Empire in decline.

Biography:
Hilary Spurling, *Paul Scott: A Life* (London: Hutchinson, 1990).

References:
Max Beloff, "The End of the Raj—Paul Scott's Novels as History," *Encounter* (May 1976): 65–70;

Allen Boyer, "Love, Sex, and History in The Raj Quartet," *Modern Language Quarterly,* 46, no. 1 (1985): 64–80;

George W. Brandt, "The Jewel in the Crown (Paul Scott–Ken Taylor): The Literary Serial: Or, the Art of Adaptation," in *British Television Drama in the 1980s,* edited by George W. Brandt, (Cambridge: Cambridge University Press, 1993), pp. 196–213;

Eva T. H. Brann, "Paul Scott's Raj Quintet: Real Politics in Imagined Gardens," in *Poets, Princes and Private Citizens: Literary Alternatives to Postmodern Politics,* edited by Joseph M. Knippenberg and Peter Augustine Lawler (Lanham, Md.: Rowman & Littlefield, 1996), pp. 191–209;

Bruce Degi, "Paul Scott's Indian National Army: *The Mark of the Warrior* and *The Raj Quartet,*" in *CLIO: A Journal of Literature, History and the Philosophy of History,* 18, no. 1 (1988): 41–54;

Yasmine Gooneratne, "The Expatriate Experience: The Novels of Ruth Prawer Jhabvala and Paul Scott," in *The British and Irish Novel Since 1960,* edited by James Acheson (New York: St. Martin's Press, 1991), pp. 48–61;

Gooneratne, "Paul Scott's *Staying On:* Finale in a Minor Key," *Journal of Indian Writing in English,* 9, no. 2 (1981): 1–12;

Donald Hannah, "'Dirty Typescripts and Very Dirty Typescripts': Paul Scott's Working Methods in *The Raj Quartet,*" *Journal of Commonwealth Literature,* 27, no. 1 (1992): 149–170;

Christopher Hitchens, "A Sense of Mission: *The Raj Quartet,*" *Grand Street,* 4, no. 2 (1985): 180–199;

Richard M. Johnson, "'Sayed's Trial' in Paul Scott's *A Division of the Spoils:* The Interplay of History,

Theme and Purpose," *Library Chronicle of the University of Texas,* 37 (1986): 76–91;

F. S. and J. L. Leonard, "The Pivotal Role of the Invert: A Comparison of the Quartets of Lawrence Durrell and Paul Scott," *Deus Loci: The Lawrence Durrell Journal,* 1 (1992): 91–96;

M. M. Mahood, "Paul Scott's Guardians," *Yearbook of English Studies,* 13 (1983): 244–258;

John McBratney, "The Raj is all the Rage: Paul Scott's *The Raj Quartet* and Colonial Nostalgia," *North Dakota Quarterly,* 55, no. 2 (1987): 204–209;

Robin Moore, *Paul Scott's Raj* (London: Heinemann, 1990);

Arthur Pollard, "Twilight of Empire: Paul Scott's *Raj Quartet,*" in *Individual and Community in Commonwealth Literature,* edited by Daniel Massa (Msida: University of Malta Press, 1979), pp. 169–176;

K. Bhaskara Rao, *Paul Scott* (Boston: Twayne, 1980);

Margaret Scanlan, The Disappearance of History: Paul Scott's *Raj Quartet,*" *CLIO: A Journal of Literature, History and the Philosophy of History,* 15, no. 2 (1986): 153–169;

Vasant A. Shahane, "Kipling, Forster and Paul Scott: A Study in Sociological Imagination," in *The Twofold Voice: Essays in Honour of Ramesh Mohan,* Salzburg Studies in English Literature 53, edited by S. N. A.

Rizvi (Salzburg: Institut fur Anglistik und Amerikanistik, 1982), pp. 195–208;

Paul Sharrad, "The Books behind the Film: Paul Scott's Raj Quartet," *East-West Film Journal,* 1, no. 2 (1987): 78–90;

Satya Brat Singh, "Ruby Wiebe, Paul Scott and Salman Rushdie: Historians Distanced from History," *Commonwealth Review,* 1, no. 2 (1990): 146–156;

Hilary Spurling, "Paul Scott: Novelist and Historian," in *Adventures with Britannia: Personalities, Politics and Culture in Britain,* edited by William Roger Louis (Austin: University of Texas Press, 1995);

Patrick Swinden, *Paul Scott: Images of India* (London: Macmillan, 1980);

Janis Tedesco, "*Staying On:* The Final Connection," *Western Humanities Review,* 39, no. 3 (1985): 195–211;

Francine S. Weinbaum, *Paul Scott, a Critical Study* (Austin: University of Texas Press, 1992);

George Woodcock, "The Sometime Sahibs: Two Post-Independence British Novelists of India," *Queen's Quarterly,* 86 (1979): 39–49.

Papers:

Paul Scott's papers are held by the Harry Ransom Humanities Research Center, University of Texas, Austin, and by the Department of Special Collections, McFarlin Library, University of Tulsa, Oklahoma.

Will Self

(26 September 1961 –)

Tim Middleton
University College of Ripon & York, St. John

BOOKS: *The Quantity Theory of Insanity* (London: Bloomsbury, 1991; New York: Atlantic Monthly Press, 1995);

Cock & Bull (London: Bloomsbury, 1992; New York: Atlantic Monthly Press, 1993);

My Idea of Fun: A Cautionary Tale (London: Bloomsbury, 1993; New York: Grove/Atlantic Monthly Press, 1994);

Grey Area and Other Stories (London: Bloomsbury, 1994; New York: Atlantic Monthly Press, 1996);

Junk Mail (London: Bloomsbury, 1995);

The Sweet Smell of Psychosis (London: Bloomsbury, 1996);

Great Apes (London: Bloomsbury, 1997; New York: Grove, 1997);

Tough, Tough Toys for Tough, Tough Boys (London: Bloomsbury, 1998; New York: Grove, 1999).

Will Self became a ubiquitous presence in London media circles in the 1990s. During the British general election campaign of 1997 he was alleged to have taken heroin in the toilet of Prime Minster John Major's plane. He initially denied the allegation but then admitted it, and shortly afterward he lost his job with the London *Observer*. While Self's drug use was hardly a secret, this high-profile incident lent him an additional notoriety. As a result, many of his books are reviewed as if their main subject were drugs and drug addiction, regardless of whether that is actually the case.

This bias on the part of reviewers is unfortunate, since Self is much more than a chronicler of the drug culture: a great satirist of middle England, he offers in his work the kind of debunking of sacred cows that makes him a cult hit with the disaffected children of the terrain he critiques. Self is in that vein of English humor that, in the twentieth century, is still best summed up as Pythonesque. Self's surreal take on the pretensions and mores of England's suburban Home Counties is written with the sensitivity of an insider. His work to date forms a loosely coherent corpus, with characters such as psychoanalyst Dr. Zack Busner and the artist Simon Dykes cropping up in several texts.

William Woodard Self was born on 26 September 1961 in London in the suburb of East Finchley. His mother, Elaine Rosenbloom Self, was an American working in the publishing industry, and his father, Peter Self, was an academic. Their marriage broke up when he was in his teens, and this trauma contributed to his early mental illness. He was diagnosed as a borderline schizophrenic and given drug-based therapy. Self studied philosophy at Oxford University, graduating in 1982. In interviews he comments that he wrote throughout his teens and early twenties but dismisses his early work as "failed pretentious novels."

After leaving Oxford he formed a small publishing company in London, producing trade magazines—an experience, he claims, that taught him the discipline of writing to order. In 1989 Self married Katherine Chancellor, with whom he had two children. Their marriage was dissolved in 1997, the same year in which Self married Deborah Jane Orr. They have one son. Self submitted his first collection of stories as an unsolicited manuscript in 1991: the resulting book, *The Quantity Theory of Insanity*, was lauded by such respected reviewers as Doris Lessing, Martin Amis, and Salman Rushdie, a remarkable achievement for a hitherto unknown author. Self has since worked as a full-time author, mixing fiction writing with work as a journalist and reviewer.

While Self has written two novels to date, his real talent as a writer seems to be in the short story. His longer fiction, reliant upon a similar surreal take on everyday life as his shorter works, lacks the deep inventiveness necessary to sustain an idea across the broader terrain of a novel. Self's trademark prose is wonderfully rich and exuberant, deploying a detailed knowledge of idiomatic English alongside an almost eighteenth-century delight in the richness of nuance available. Indeed, while the debt to modern British writers such as Aldous Huxley, J. G. Ballard, and Martin Amis and to Americans such as William S. Burroughs and Don DeLillo is evident, Self's work at its best is in the long tradition of English satirical writing; time and again in his fiction

Will Self at the time of Cock & Bull *(photograph by Dominic Turner)*

the foibles of contemporary British middle-class culture are held up for ridicule. Although some critics laud Self as a comic writer, it is important to note that his humor works through derision and is thus more aptly labeled satiric.

The Quantity Theory of Insanity is a collection of six short stories offering an introduction to many of Self's characteristic themes and interests. "The North London Book of the Dead" begins with the death of the narrator's mother from cancer but quickly shifts to the fantastic with the revelation that the dead do not go to heaven but, rather, live on in London's suburbia. The story is typical of much of Self's work in its acute observation of the mores and traits of suburban life and in the way that the narrative works for a postmodern undermining of the opposition between the normal and the irrational. It is typical also in that much of its humor depends upon a yoking together of the everyday with

the fantastical. The second story in the collection, "Ward 9," concerns an art therapist working in a psychiatric hospital. Self's work draws heavily upon this kind of hospital milieu, and this story introduces characters who appear elsewhere in his oeuvre—notably Dr. Busner (seen again in the stories "The Quantity Theory of Insanity," "Inclusion," "Grey Area," and the 1997 novel *Great Apes*). The story again trades on the subversion of oppositions—in this case, the doctors are mad and patients, sane—but also exhibits an extensive concern with the role of drugs in regulating mental health in society generally. While Self is often described as a writer of the drug culture, stories such as "Ward 9" should remind readers that his fiction deals with the use of drugs across society and not solely within the world of addicts. "Understanding the Ur-Bororo" concerns Janner, an anthropologist who studies the Ur-Bororo, a tribe of Amazonian forest dwellers whose culture is based upon boredom; once again, this allows Self to satirize the culture of the Home Counties of Britain: Janner brings his Ur-Bororo bride back to Purley with no apparent culture shock.

The title story concerns a team of psychologists who stumble upon a revolutionary theory, namely that "there is only a fixed proportion of sanity available in any given society at any given time." The story satirizes psychology and provides a vehicle for a further teasing out of the opposition between sanity and madness. As with much of Self's writing, there is a strong element of comedy here, largely reliant upon the narration's absolute adherence to the veracity of the created milieu. The story's joke extends to the provision of references that direct the reader to such spurious scholarship as:

Ford, Hurts, Harley, Busner & Sikorski, "Some Aspects of Sanity Quotient Mechanisms in a Witless Shetland Commune," *British Journal of Ephemera,* September, 1974

Ford, H., "Teaching Stockbrokers Ring Dancing," *Practical Mental Health,* January, 1975

The final two stories of the collection, "Mono-Cellular" and "Waiting," also deal with the irrational. The former is a monologue recording the breakdown of a suburban businessman, while the latter deals with the everyday issue of gridlock in London, offering a fantasy solution in the form of Carlos, a dispatch rider who teaches the ability to enter a trance and find gaps in the traffic.

What will strike many readers is that, with the exception of Busner and the other antipsychiatrists of the title story, this collection is memorable more for its rich vein of satiric inventiveness than its creation of credible individuals. Self's debut collection established him as a postmodern writer, remote from the normative conventions of the so-called Hampstead novel, which lovingly re-creates the milieu and attendant crises of the British middle classes.

Self's next work and the first of his texts to be published in America was *Cock & Bull* (1992). The work takes the form of two novellas linked by the theme of sexual identity. "Cock" tells the story of Carol and her alcoholic husband, Dan; Carol grows a penis which, in the story's dramatic ending, she employs in sodomizing her drugged husband in an act of revenge for years of neglect and oppression. The novella contains graphic scenes of sexual violence along with Self's usual dissection of social mores. Yet, "Cock" is an inventive and well-structured tale that unfolds with a good deal of humor. Once again there are many telling observations about English culture, notably concerning drinking (from student parties to seedy unlicenced pubs to meetings of Alcoholics Anonymous) and sex–Carol experiences a brief lesbian phase and Dan suffers from an inability to perform.

In addition the story includes a rich vein of self-consciousness that adds another dimension of complexity. The tale is told by an unnamed first-person narrator who hears it from what at first appears to be an aged professor with whom he shares a train compartment; as the tale unfolds, however, it becomes clear that the don is, in fact, Carol, who has completed her transformation. Self exploits the framing narrative to raise questions about the reader's relationship with the text and, at times, about the relationship between teller and tale: "That's your style, isn't it, being clever and allusive, but what does this really amount to save for trying to get one over on good, ordinary, straightforward people."

While this complaint has been leveled against Self by some reviewers, the whole point of a story such as "Cock" is seemingly to suggest that there is no such thing as an ordinary, straightforward person. Readers are encouraged to question the nature of narration and may wonder if Carol's story is anything more than an elaborate device to hold the narrator's attention as a precursor to the sexual assault that ends the novella.

"Bull" works in much the same way. Its central character, Bull, is a rugby-playing male who wakes one morning to discover that he has grown a vagina behind his knee. As the narrator self-reflexively comments:

There would be no point in implanting a vagina in the back of just any man's knee. You might get some scion of raised consciousness; some almost-Iron John; some acquaintance of Dorothy longing to become a friend. No, much better that this be just a *congruence* understood by us. And much better that it should be Bull, the dubious Bull, the shy Bull, the *conditioned* Bull, who had to bear the weight of this unacceptable transmogrification.

The story's other main character is Bull's doctor, Alan Margoulies, a man whose public persona is that of a caring physician but who in actuality is an egotistical adulterer. On the same morning that Bull discovers his condition, Margoulies walks to work, reflecting upon his adulterous exploits and "lost in the ravenous contemplation" of a vagina "that had yet to be punched from within by a baby's head": the scene is set for his encounter with Bull.

Margoulies is astounded but also attracted to Bull's vagina; he works to keep the truth of the abnormality hidden from his patient, going along with Bull's idea that it is a wound or burn:

. . . the problem was this: Alan was already functioning within the dramatic irony of betrayal. His adulterous liaisons had opened up a gulf between what he knew and what others knew about him. Into this gulf came Bull. . . .

Alan couldn't understand the why, but the more he tried to think about what he should do to help Bull, the more images of Bull that were strictly non scientific started to flood him.

These images are soon turned into action when Alan reveals to Bull the nature of his affliction and then, in consoling him, they come to have sex. From this moment the story becomes more complex, as Self teases out the shifting moods of both central male characters. Things come to a head when Bull, who is attempting to lead a normal life, has his abnormality exposed in a rugby match and in telling of his misfortune reveals to Alan a potential for emotional dependency that causes Alan to resolve to end the relationship. The narrative ends with Bull becoming pregnant and bearing Alan's child. The story's strengths lie in its evocation of the slippery moral terrain that Margoulies moves through and in its charting of Bull's shifting gender identity. In some ways the ending is the weakest part since it insists on taking the events to their rather too-obvious conclusion. This apparent lack of authorial control is only to be expected in a collection that offers itself as a set of cock-and-bull stories: as Self comments in his interview with Martin Amis, included in *Junk Mail* (1995), the collection "is an elaborate joke about the failure of all narrative."

Readers are faced with similar tensions regarding the extent to which they are expected to take the story seriously in Self's most significant work to date, the 1993 novel *My Idea of Fun*. This postmodern bildungsroman tells the story of Ian Wharton, a Home Counties boy who falls under the influence of one of the guests at his mother's caravan park, a Mr. Broadhurst, who is apparently a front for an inhuman entity called–among other things–the Fat Controller, the Magus of the Quotidian, and the Brahmin of the Banal. Half of the novel is told in the first person, which leads to some problems for the reader. Wharton has an eidetic memory–his mind can create images with all the detail of reality; like some yet-to-be-created virtual-reality machine, it allows him to "travel" through space and time to where no Home Counties boy has been before. Broadhurst helps Wharton come to terms with his unusual mental powers, but in return he is made an unwilling party to murder and prevented from engaging in sexual relations because Broadhurst convinces him that expending sexual energy is dangerous.

As Wharton matures, he becomes more disturbed by his relationship with Broadhurst and is eventually referred to Dr. Gyggle, a psychiatrist who helps him realize that he is in fact a casual killer whose murders have been blotted out by the manipulations of Broadhurst and Gyggle himself, who is also an agent of the Fat Controller. It is possible to read the text in such a way that Wharton's experiences with Broadhurst may be regarded as the product of a psychosis or an account of the ways in which the norms and values of everyday life shore up a persona and prevent any manifestation of otherness from being expressed. The novel begins with Wharton wondering how he can explain his secret life to his wife but ends without showing the scene of his confession, leaving the reader uncertain as to the reality of that hidden life.

My Idea of Fun was met with fairly hostile reviews. Julian Evans's response, which appeared in the *Guardian* (14 September 1993), was typical: "Self leaves no adjective unsaid, no metaphor unturned, no synonym unexplored, no tiring digression unpursued. His writing is crippled by this baggage of phrase making. . . . It's paradoxically knowing, even poetical, but quite meaningless. . . . the prose is like styrofoam, modern, slippery and sterile." The apparent sterility of Self's novel, however, makes it profoundly of its era. *My Idea of Fun* knowingly suggests the frequently bewildering heterogeneity of the English character in the late twentieth century. By exploring what the apparently paradigmatic Wharton does for fun, Self seeks to disclose a postmodern culture of difference. Self has commented that he "wanted to explore the nature of the semi-permeable membrane between 'neurosis' and 'psychosis'" as well as wanting Wharton's "lack of sympathetic qualities to point to some wider issue, whether social, psychological or metaphysical."

My Idea of Fun is clearly working for a radical view of late-twentieth-century subjectivity. The novel seeks to confront the reader with an account of the stereotypical 1980s male psyche, hoping to open up issues around masculinity and violence and the relationship between fantasy and reality by its juxtaposition of materialist individualism–exemplified by Wharton's work in marketing–and the obsessive egocentrism of ritual magic as revealed in the Broadhurst plot.

Wharton's eidetic ability makes it possible for him to experience fantasy as reality; for him there is no distinction between what is imagined and what is real. He can inhabit his fantasies and interact with the figures that populate them. From this ability stems his characterization of his own subjectivity as a kind of Möbius strip, a notion that resists the simple 'forked into two chunks' view of the world. For Self, it would seem, the acquisitiveness of 1980s culture is linked to the Fat Controller's insistence on doing what one wants, irrespective of the cost to others. The 1980s promoted an individualism that adhered to this kind of logic, and Wharton's story appears to suggest that in accepting such norms the individual becomes the author of his own despair. As Wharton comments: "Have we lost our collective innocence? Sometimes it seems that way, doesn't it. We feel like we've been thrust into, deflowered by the smirking, brutal world. But on the other hand it also feels as if we were the defilers. . . . How can it be so, this hovering sense of being both victim and perpetrator, both us and them, both me and him."

This sense of being simultaneously a victim and a perpetrator resonates in the novel's presentation of 1980s masculinity: Wharton is the victim of the Fat Controller's machinations but also in his buried life a seemingly willing participant in acts of atrocity. Self explores the relationship between convention and otherness by putting at the novel's center the question of how the diligent student and skillful marketing executive's idea of fun can possibly be ripping the head from a tramp and copulating with the throat of the bleeding torso.

Wharton is consumed by his public persona as marketing man, happy to write off his childhood experiments with Mr. Broadhurst as "an extended delusion" once he has been categorized by Dr. Gyggle as "a borderline personality with pronounced schizoid tendencies." Readers are unlikely to be immediately convinced by this labeling, which is too convenient a gloss on the supposed complexity figured in Wharton's Möbius-like perspective; but as the novel unfolds from this diagnosis, Self uses Wharton to suggest the extent to which men shut off their inner selves and, in so doing, become schizoid.

Self clearly intended for Wharton's story to be received as more than a literary nasty, that it would tell something about the link between Margaret Thatcher's Britain and male violence, much as Bret Easton Ellis's *American Psycho* (1991) did for Ronald Reagan's America. Too often, however, the links are obscured by the fantastic elements of the novel's plot. Because of Wharton's eidetic powers readers are left in a position in which everything might be fantasy, in which Wharton's murders might just be ideas or imagined activities as opposed to actuality. While this ambiguity does not undermine the view of the male as repressed, violent, and unemotional, the turn to fantasy problematizes this perspective by muddying the relationship of the text to the wider cultural context.

My Idea of Fun attempts a subversive use of fantasy: in its account of Wharton's mental makeup it indicates a position from which one can critique the dominant order and its linking of rationality with masculinity. The novel certainly suggests that violence, especially random, unprovoked, and sadistic violence, is a source of deep anxiety in contemporary urban cul-

ture and that masculinity is linked to ideas of fun that can be dangerous and destructive.

Grey Area saw Self return to short fiction as a vehicle for further meditation upon urban Englishness. The title story is concerned with the stasis of modernity: the unnamed female office worker who narrates the story is caught in a life of repetitive actions, and Self expands upon this to imagine a world of Kafkaesque recurrence. As Chris Wright noted in the *Boston Phoenix* (14–21 March 1996), "Self, who has fought his way back from heroin addiction, often touches on the theme of self-control through ritual and habit. But he has also seen the corrosive dreariness of suburbia, and 'Grey Area' seems to point to the insanity engendered by ritualised monotony."

The other stories in the collection, including "Scale" and "Between the Conceits," continue the themes of obsession, ritual, and the craziness of everyday life. Others, such as "Chest" and "Inclusion," continue the vein of satire from his first collection, dealing with pharmaceutical companies, health care, and mental illness. Two stories that stand out are "A short history of the English novel" and "Incubus." The former is a knowing account of literary London in which the central characters find the city populated with frustrated writers, many of whom are waiters. The story seems intended to act as a rejoinder to the widespread critical perception that the English novel in the late twentieth century is in terminal decline. One of the writers encountered laments over the stupidity of publishers: "I have written this book in the grand tradition of the nineteenth-century English novel. I aim to unite dramatically the formation of individual character to the process of social change. Just because I've cast the plot in the form of an allegory and set it in the future, it has to be regarded as a satire." The remark might be read as an account of Self's work: the reliance upon allegory and focus upon the individual as a register of social change are central facets of his writing.

"Incubus" begins in the middle-class world of June Laughton, "a prize-winning gardener," and her philosopher husband, Peter Geddes, who live near Grantham, Lincolnshire, in a house with an odd architectural feature known as the Rood Room: a chapel-like space dominated by a rood screen covered in hundreds of carved phalluses. The chapel was built for a seventeenth-century religious sect called the Grunters, a group for whom "forms of behaviour that orthodox Christians regarded as sinful were in fact to be enjoyed." Geddes awaits the arrival of his new research assistant, Giselle, who comes from a conventional middle-class family and finds her new environment a pleasant change from "the privet-lined precincts of her proper parents." At the center of the story is a dinner

Dust jacket for Self's 1992 collection of two novellas about confusions in sexual identity

party in which Geddes and his old friend Henry Beckwood, a polymer chemist, argue vigorously about free will. This argument about the nature of the self is linked to the lustiness of the rude carvings by a passionate sexual encounter between Giselle and Geddes; the "twist" in this is that Geddes is too drunk to remember what he has done, that he has no real will in this matter. Self critiques the middle-class milieu by suggesting that for all his intellectual sophistication, Geddes is no more in control of himself than a Grunter. The incubus is shown to be the repressed, uncivilized self that Geddes's middle-class veneer seeks to contain. This vision of the libidinous male is a recurrent feature in Self's work.

"Chest" features an alternate incarnation of Simon Dykes, the artist at the center of the novel *Great Apes*. In this story, set in a near future of chronic air pollution, Self offers a parody of Russian short fiction in the vein of Anton Chekhov. The story's semirural setting allows Self to examine a wide swath of middle England, from the adolescents adrift in the local shopping precinct to Hutchinson, a humble shopkeeper, to

the gun-toting landowner Peter Donald. Self creates his alternate future in some detail—everyone has a chest infection or worse, and special occasions revolve around the drinking of cough medicine and the sharing of inhalers. The story ends with Dykes walking alone in the polluting fog on an unfinished Japanese-owned golf course and calling on God to aid him in overcoming the tribulations associated with living under such polluted conditions. Believing that his prayer has been answered, he removes his antismog mask only to be overcome—not by the fog but by the cancer that he has unknowingly been carrying. Dykes's body is found in a bunker on the course by Peter Hanson and his shooting cronies, who comment that "the fellow had the decency not to die on the green," and this bleak ending suggests that the pollution of the country is in some way paralleled by the persistence of rigid class hierarchies and the attitudes that they foster.

The British class system is also evident in "Between the Conceits," which enters into the mind of an obsessive who believes that he is one of "only eight people in London"; the story is a cogent study of mania.

Mental illnesses also featured in "Inclusion," a story that deals with the illegal trial of a new drug designed to control depression and promote "positive engagement" with life. The story is narrated in the second person and places the reader in the position of the recipient of a secret dossier on the drug, which, it is revealed, causes the patients taking it to become so interested in the world that, in a surreal twist, they begin to suck events and people into their psyches. The story again features recurring characters Zack Busner and Simon Dykes. "Scale" is a drug-related tale that also relies on a surreal take on reality: it tells the story of a morphine addict obsessed with motorways and the model village next to his home. By contrast, "The End of the Relationship" is less overtly fantastic–a young woman encounters a sequence of relationships that are at the point of breakup only to return home to the end of her own romance. The weakest story in the collection is "The Indian Mutiny," a feeble tale of schoolboy rebellion.

Self's next publication, *Junk Mail* (1995), is a collection of journalism, reviews, and interviews. The book was praised for its honest insights into drug culture, but the collection's main value from a literary critical point of view rests with the author profiles and interviews that help clarify Self's approach to fiction. Included are two pieces on Martin Amis, a brief account of a lunch with Bret Easton Ellis, and an interview with J. G. Ballard. There is also a selection of book reviews, but these, with the exception of a review of Nicholson Baker's *The Fermata* (1994) that also discusses *My Idea of Fun,* have little to offer in the way of insights into Self's fiction.

"Martin Amis: The Misinformation" is a journalistic profile in which Self discusses Amis as a writer of "psychological interiority" and offers pithy summations of Amis's major works. Many of the general points made about Amis's work can be applied to Self's own work: for example, Self notes "the urge of the critic to elide the writer's moral being with his work," a problem from which Self, after the publication of *My Idea of Fun* and, more particularly, following his high-profile drug-taking, has tended to suffer from. In the interview with Ballard, Self is also dealing with an author whose work has some parallels to his own. The writers share a skeptical view of the world that is easy to label as despair or moral cynicism, and both authors deal with a wholly postmodern milieu in which older models of novelistic practice are hopelessly out of step. As Ballard puts it: "We now live in a huge goulash of competing appetites and dreams and aspirations and activities. The novelist can't take a moral standpoint anymore, he can't sit in judgement on his characters. . . . The writer can only rely upon his own obsessions." *Junk Mail* was praised by Tobias Jones in the *Observer* (29 October 1995) as the work of "a lucid and intelligent man of letters."

A reliance upon his own obsessions is apparent in Self's next fictional work, *The Sweet Smell of Psychosis* (1996), a collaboration with the cartoonist Martin Rowson. The novella is a satirical look at London's media circles in the 1990s and is of interest mainly as a preliminary jaunt through territory to be covered in more detail in *Great Apes.* The members of the Sealink Club are characterized as "transmitters of trivia, broadcasters of banality and disseminators of dreck. They wrote articles about articles, made television programmes about television programmes, and commented on what others had said. They trafficked in the glibbest, slightest, most ephemeral cultural reflexivity, enacting a dialogue between society and its conscience that had all the resonance of a foil individual pie dish smitten with a paperclip." Richard Hermes is a member of this group, a journalist newly arrived in London from the North and the vehicle for many observations about Southern urban culture. Among the inhabitants of media London is Ursula Bentley, a "glibmaiden" with whom Richard is obsessed, and Bell, a hugely successful journalist and media personality. Bell's status allows him to indulge his bisexual lusts and, in particular, to indulge in his favorite vice, breaking up long-established relationships. Hermes, a much-debased messenger for the gods of contemporary culture, works for a self-centered listings magazine. He is very much the innocent abroad; horrified by a cab driver's tale of torture he remarks: "It's awful to think of things like that happening in the world, and we just go on talking about *nothing,* doing *nothing,* just writing on the wallpaper."

Richard progresses to the post of editor, and a platonic relationship with Ursula develops. He is sucked into Bell's clique and develops a serious cocaine habit; he also begins to develop a psychosis in which he imagines that he sees Bell everywhere he goes. The novella ends with Hermes taking Ursula to dinner; returning to her flat they begin to have sex, but in order to prevent himself from climaxing Hermes thinks of Bell only to find that Ursula has metamorphosed into Bell himself. The matter is left uncertain as to whether the incident is some further manifestation of Hermes's psychosis or an actual transformation.

Critics objected that on a certain level *The Sweet Smell of Psychosis* was a rather old-fashioned tale of Northern innocence abroad in the corrupt big city, as Tobias Jones commented in the *Observer* (12 January 1997): "The city cynicism seems to have caused a claustrophobia that has less to do with the metropolis than with a receding imagination; and the up-lift of fine prose can't disguise the lack of an emerging yarn amongst all this urban angst." *The Sweet Smell of Psychosis* merely retreads well-worn ground, in part reprising material from the novella "Bull."

The same sense of repetitiveness mars Self's second novel, *Great Apes,* which tells the story of Simon Dykes, a fashionable artist who awakes one morning in a world in which humans are an inferior species to the apes. The conceit allows Self plenty of scope for his usual satirical look at the foibles of media London, the pitfalls of psychiatry, and the tensions of middle-class life, but the material is stretched over four hundred pages when it would have been far more effective in a novella format.

Nonetheless, there is some effective writing in the novel: Dykes's bewilderment on waking up in an ape world is well done, and the opening pretransformation chapters neatly emphasize the apelike aspects of human life. As Sam Leith noted in the *Observer* (11 May 1997), the first half demonstrates Self's "special genius . . . for taking the sort of whimsical insight that powers five minutes of pub conversation and making deadpan the guiding principle for an entire version of reality." The novel, for all its satiric energy, is traditional in its reliance on character, with Dykes's predicament occupying the center of attention. The novel also features a reappearance by Dr. Busner, the aging antipsychiatrist; much of the novel is taken up with Busner's attempts to rehabilitate Simon into the ape world. In many ways *Great Apes* reworks, less successfully, material and predicaments from *My Idea of Fun:* again the central character's life appears to be split into two separate spheres, and again a psychoanalyst intervenes to help that character piece his world together.

However, unlike *My Idea of Fun,* in which the notion of identity seems to be under investigation, here Self appears to be offering a far simpler tale of London life, given added resonance by its transposition of the familiar into the apparently alien world of "chimpunity." The novel lacks the radical edge of the earlier work, relying on puns and slick one-liners for its effects rather than any sustained reflection upon the fragility of reality. As William Scammell commented in *New Statesman* (13 June 1997): "If Simon was ever more than a name, Sara more than a hole between the legs, Zack more than a peg, the language more than a sputter of smart remarks, the plot more than a rehash of a dozen satirical fables, *Great Apes* might have been as readable as Self's journalism."

Tough, Tough Toys for Tough, Tough Boys (1998) is a collection of short stories, nearly half of which were published in magazines or other short-fiction collections. The collection continues with familiar themes but is loosely linked by a focus on issues of masculinity. The title story details an epic—by British standards—car journey from the North of Scotland to London, bring-

ing together Bill, an alcoholic psychoanalyst who is returning from temporary work in Orkney, and Mark, a morose young Scots hitchhiker who is traveling from Thurso to Glasgow in order to meet up with friends and race Tonka toys down Sauchiehall Street. The story's title is derived from an advertising campaign for the toy vehicles, but any further relevance is left for the reader to deduce. Bill is a loner whose life is "based on exclusion." Mark has separated from his wife and children, and this failed relationship prompts Bill to reflect upon his own abusive relationships with women, whom he imagines as pursuing "Furies." The encounter forces him to recall the neglect of his own child: "He knew all about unanswered phone-calls, crumbled up letters, torn postcards. People said they didn't want children because they didn't want the responsibility. But if you didn't take the responsibility for them—how could you have it for yourself." The story works for the suggestion that masculine toughness is superficial but never labors its point; in many ways it is oddly conventional and character-driven for Self, but this does not mean that it is ineffective.

The collection begins and ends with two tales that share the same milieu: drug-dealing London lowlife. "The Rock of Crack as Big as the Ritz" tells the story of Danny and Tembe, two black British brothers living in East London in a house bought from the money that Danny stole from his employer, Skank, a Jamaican drug dealer. Beneath the house Danny discovers the rock of crack that gives the story its title. This eruption of fantasy into an otherwise dully realist narrative is left undeveloped, offered merely as a device to facilitate the rise of the brother's dealing activities.

The final story in the collection, "The Nonce Prize," returns to the world of Danny and Tembe. By now Danny has become an addict, while his brother has broken his addiction and assumed control of the dealing network. The story deals with the revenge that Skank visits upon Danny, in the form of framing him for the murder and rape of a young boy. Danny is imprisoned and resolves to improve his lot through education: mistakenly signing up for a creative-writing course, he discovers that he has an ability as a critical reader and some flair as a writer and, with the encouragement of his tutor, decides to enter work in a competition for prison writing. Danny's character is developed more fully than in "The Rock of Crack as Big as the Ritz," but Self's authorial voice relies too much on assertive labeling that finds little support in the actions of the characters. The story is further evidence of Self's ability to explore damaged and deranged mental states and offers solid observations on institutionalization and the ways in which it can foster further criminal activity.

Two further stories stand out from this collection as, if not wholly successful, at least worthy of close attention. "A Story for Europe" tells the story of two-year-old Humpy Green, who appears to swap identity with Dr. Zweijärig, deputy director of the Deutsche Bank. The swap takes the form of Humpy speaking business German and Zweijärig suffering a stroke that leaves him babbling incomprehensibly like a two-year-old. Humpy's childish behavior is juxtaposed with assertions in German and scenes from tense business meetings at the bank. Both milieus are carefully drawn, and it is only in their juxtaposition that Self hints at any connection: Humpy plays with cars while Zweijärig imagines driving his Mercedes; Humpy sits in his high chair while Zweijärig sits in his leather office chair. To analyze the humor of the story is to pin down what is left deliberately suggestive.

"Design Faults in the Volvo 760 Turbo: A Manual" also works through juxtaposition and a narrative built with some subtlety. The story is divided into four sections, each with a heading borrowed from a car manual for a vehicle that is a somewhat clichéd register of middle-class status. The tale itself concerns the relationship between Bill Bywater, a psychiatrist, and his mistress, Serena, and their largely futile attempts to consummate their relationship. Bill is obsessed with Serena, with his car, and with the complications of his domestic life. Meanwhile his wife is happily committing adultery with Bill's former colleague—now turned car mechanic—Dave Adler. Once again Self satirizes middle-class masculinity.

The remaining stories in the collection have little to add to an understanding of Self's characteristic themes. "Flytopia" tells of an insect-infested cottage in which man and bug come to a symbiotic arrangement that suits both parties but not the narrator's girlfriend, who becomes a sacrifice to feed the cottage's insect population. "Dave Too" is another story set in the world of psychiatrists and patients, while "Caring Sharing" is set in a near-future New York in which every human has a giant humanoid companion known as an "emoto" that nurtures and cares for its human. Emotos are this sexless society's ideal companions, largely because they "aren't children. They don't grow—they're big already. They don't make demands on you—you make demands on them. They don't have to be dressed, fed, wiped or groomed in any way." This aspect of the emoto is shown to be a superficial veneer in the story's final pages, when the apparent sexless and caring emotos drink, smoke, and have sex with a human passion lacking from their otherwise normal owners.

Self has recently returned to a higher profile position in London's media circus, acting as a pundit on such issues as the death of the English novel and male violence. His literary strengths are in satire, and his fictional territory is resolutely Southern, urban, and middle class. His work is always entertaining, often thought-provoking, and undoubtedly topical. By choosing to work primarily in the rather neglected and, until the 1980s, somewhat genteel field of the English short story, he has been able to carve out a niche. As literary merit is so often viewed in terms of success in the novel, however, it seems fair to say that to date Self has shown promise but has yet to make a contribution to contemporary British fiction commensurate with that promise and his own visibility.

David Storey

(13 July 1933 –   )

Dennis Jackson
University of Delaware

and

Wendy Perkins
Prince George's Community College

See also the Storey entries in *DLB 13: British Dramatists Since World War II* and *DLB 14: British Novelists Since 1960.*

BOOKS: *This Sporting Life* (London: Longmans, 1960; New York: Macmillan, 1960);

Flight into Camden (London: Longmans, 1960; New York: Macmillan, 1961);

Radcliffe (London: Longmans, 1963; New York: Coward-McCann, 1964);

The Restoration of Arnold Middleton (London: Cape, 1967; New York: S. French, 1968);

In Celebration (London: Cape, 1969; New York: Grove, 1975);

The Contractor (London: Cape, 1970; New York: Random House, 1970);

Home (London: Cape, 1970; New York: Random House, 1971);

The Changing Room (London: Cape, 1972; New York: Random House, 1972);

Pasmore (London: Longman, 1972; New York: Dutton, 1972);

Cromwell (London: Cape, 1973);

The Farm (London: Cape, 1973; London & New York: S. French, 1974);

Edward, text by Storey, drawings by Donald Parker (London: Allen Lane, 1973);

A Temporary Life (London: Allen Lane, 1973; New York: Dutton, 1974);

Life Class (London: Cape, 1975);

Saville (London: Cape, 1976; New York: Harper & Row, 1976);

Home, The Changing Room, and Mother's Day (Harmondsworth, U.K.: Penguin, 1978);

Early Days, Sisters, Life Class (Harmondsworth, U.K.: Penguin, 1980);

David Storey, 1974 (photograph by John Haynes)

A Prodigal Child (London: Cape, 1982; New York: Dutton, 1982);

Present Times (London: Cape, 1984);

The March on Russia (London: S. French, 1989);

Storey's Lives: Poems 1951–1991 (London: Cape, 1992);

Phoenix (Woodstock, N.Y.: Dramatic Publishing, 1993);

A Serious Man (London: Cape, 1998).

Collections: *Storey Plays One: The Contractor, Home, Stages, Caring,* includes an introduction by Storey (London: Methuen, 1992);

Storey Plays Two: The Restoration of Arnold Middleton, In Celebration, The March on Russia, includes an introduction by Storey (London: Methuen, 1994).

PLAY PRODUCTIONS: *The Restoration of Arnold Middleton,* Edinburgh, Traverse Theatre Club, 22 November 1966; London, Royal Court Theatre, 4 July 1967;

In Celebration, London, Royal Court Theatre, 22 April 1969; New York: Sutton East Theater, 1977;

The Contractor, London, Royal Court Theatre, 20 October 1969; New York, Chelsea Manhattan Theater, 9 October 1973;

Home, London, Royal Court Theatre, 17 June 1970; New York, Morosco Theater, 17 November 1970;

The Changing Room, London, Royal Court Theatre, 9 November 1971; New York, Morosco Theater, 6 March 1973;

Cromwell, London, Royal Court Theatre, 16 August 1973;

The Farm, London, Royal Court Theatre, 26 September 1973; New York, Circle Repertory Company, 10 October 1976;

Life Class, London, Royal Court Theatre, 9 April 1974; New York, Manhattan Theater Club, 14 December 1975;

Mother's Day, London, Royal Court Theatre, 22 September 1976;

Sisters, Manchester, Royal Exchange Theatre, 12 September 1978;

Early Days, Brighton, 31 March 1980; London, Cottesloe Theatre (National Theatre), 22 April 1980;

Phoenix, Ealing, The Ealing Questors, 7 April 1984;

The March on Russia, London, Lyttleton Theatre (National Theatre), 6 April 1989;

Stages, London, Cottesloe Theatre (National Theatre), 18 November 1992.

MOTION PICTURES: *This Sporting Life,* screenplay by Storey, Continental Films, 1963;

In Celebration, screenplay by Storey, American Film Theatre, 1975.

TELEVISION: *Home,* script by Storey, PBS, 1971;

Grace, script by Storey, based on the short story by James Joyce, BBC, 1974;

Early Days, script by Storey, London Weekend Television, 1981.

OTHER: "On Lindsay Anderson," in *Cinebill: The American Film Theatre—The Second Season* (New York: AFT Distributing, 1975);

"Working with Lindsay," in *At the Royal Court: 25 Years of the English Stage Company,* edited by Richard Findlater (New York: Grove, 1981), pp. 110–115.

SELECTED NONFICTION PUBLICATIONS-UNCOLLECTED: "Robert Colquhoun," *New Statesman* (12 October 1962): 500–501;

"Commonwealth Art Today," *Guardian,* 3 November 1962, p. 5;

"Ned Kelly on Film," *Manchester Guardian,* 7 February 1963, p. 7;

"Cells," *New Statesman* (19 April 1963): 612;

"Nolan's Ark," *New Statesman* (31 May 1963): 840–841;

"What Really Matters," *Twentieth Century,* 172 (Autumn 1963): 96–97;

"Marxism as a Form of Nostalgia," *New Society* (15 July 1965): 23;

"Passionate Polemics," *New Society* (28 January 1967): 137–138.

Few contemporary British authors have had as much success writing in two genres as David Storey in fiction and drama. His first novel, *This Sporting Life* (1960), brought him the Macmillan Fiction Award, and his sixth novel, *Saville* (1976), elicited Britain's most prestigious literary award, the Booker Prize for fiction. He has twice won the *Evening Standard* Drama Award for best play of the year in London and is the only playwright ever to have won the New York Drama Critics' Circle Award three times. He has published nine novels, fifteen plays, and a large volume of poetry, but the vast majority of those works were created in the prolific first two decades of his career, and his rate of publication slowed considerably during the 1980s and 1990s.

His novels, usually written in terse, understated prose, are conventional, realistic works in the tradition of the English social novels. Nearly all of them treat one or both of two themes: the painful and sometimes insoluble conflict between working-class parents and their educated children, and the suffering or psychic disintegration of protagonists—all of them isolated, moody, and self-tortured—who cannot balance their inner spiritual lives with their physical lives and who struggle to achieve a wholeness that would afford them some sort of intellectual or emotional control. All the novels draw somehow on Storey's own experiences, as a professional rugby player, farm worker, schoolteacher, artist, writer, and parent. The novels graphically chronicle the lives of the "north country" people who live amid the smoke- and steam-belching factories, mills, and collieries of gray industrial towns in Yorkshire, where he grew up. The major passage in Storey's life came when he moved away from the people of the West Riding and their value system to join the educated class in London. The effects of his social, geographical, and intellectual uprooting are everywhere delineated in his writing.

David Malcolm Storey was born in the industrial city of Wakefield on 13 July 1933, the third of four sons of Frank Richmond Storey, a Yorkshire coal miner, and Lily Cartwright Storey. The family's second son, Anthony, was himself to become a well-known novelist and screenwriter. The family lived in a housing estate near the Roundwood Colliery, where the father worked. David attended Queen Elizabeth Grammar School on scholarship, where he first developed a fascination with writing and painting. He told interviewer John Haffenden in 1982 that "I decided to become an artist when I was 17 or 18 almost as a political act, as a recoil against everything I was being directed towards." At that point he experienced the first big crisis of his life. As he contended later, in a 1963 BBC broadcast (giving his views on the genesis of his writing career), the world of the West Riding was "an acutely physical one, a world of machines and Labour and commerce, and one in which the artist . . . was not merely an outsider but a hindrance and a nuisance." In fact, in the puritanical working-class community where he lived, physical work was considered "good, and mental work . . . evil." Consequently, acting purely from his sense of guilt over his love for painting and writing, he played rugby union football and became a forward on his school team. His hardworking father had been fiercely determined that his sons would, through the passport of education, escape going "down pit" and would become middle-class professional men. The more David learned, however, and especially the more he pursued his love for art, the more his father came to fear and resent what his talented son was becoming. The young artist became increasingly estranged from his father and laden with guilt that he was not somehow living up to expectations—and the shadow of that guilt is cast long over Storey's novels, reflected everywhere in the relationships of working-class fathers and their educated offspring.

In 1951 Storey enrolled at the Wakefield School of Art, where he attended classes until 1953. He told Haffenden years later that he had been "absolutely desolate" during his two years at the Wakefield school: "They wanted me to become a commercial artist and absolutely refused to . . . write a testimonial for my application" to the Slade School of Fine Art in London. During his second year at the Wakefield School, when he was eighteen years old, the brawny youngster signed a fourteen-year contract with the professional Leeds Rugby League Club, hoping to use the money (his signing bonus of £1,200 was twice what his father earned in a year) to pay his art-college expenses, to help support his family and thereby lessen his continuing depression over the fact that his father was daily bent over in the pits while he sat around painting pictures. Two years after signing with Leeds, he received a scholarship to the Slade, and for the next three years he studied art during the week in London and traveled back to the northern counties for each Saturday's rugby matches. At the Slade School he blossomed as an artist: his works won prizes and were included in London exhibitions. He has told several interviewers that he was expelled from the Slade School for disruptive behavior. Throughout his life he has continued to paint and has frequently designed playbills and dust jackets for his novels.

During this period in the mid 1950s Storey began writing what was to become his first published novel, *This Sporting Life,* which was substantially completed by the time he left the Slade School. His creation of this tale about a brawny but sensitive rugby-league hero was (as he acknowledged in his later BBC talk) an "act of despair," an attempt to make sense of his own schizophrenic condition during those unhappy "nightmare" years when in both the worlds of art and athletics he found himself an outsider. His Leeds teammates, all young miners and mill workers, were somewhat wary of the introverted, long-haired youth who spent his week painting pictures in London; fellow Slade students, thinking him a moody provincial, similarly kept him at a distance.

The weekly, two-hundred-mile train trip across England eventually took on for Storey a metaphorical reality: "those four hours of blackness were a journey across my brain," he later recalled. In his increasing despair he came to think of Leeds and London as being representative of the two poles of his own temperament: its northern, physical, extroverted, masculine aspects and its southern, spiritual, self-absorbed, feminine aspects. In an effort to reconcile these warring elements of his own psyche, he began writing *This Sporting Life,* first scribbling rough notes during his London-to-Yorkshire train rides. In creating his rugged protagonist, Arthur Machin, Storey was trying to isolate and come to terms with the physical side of his own temperament, which had confused and frightened him throughout his youth. Machin, by his own description, is a "super ape," a big, powerful battering ram of a man who thrives on tearing other rugby leaguers "into postage stamps." He is estranged from his parents, is at odds with the working class as well as with the industrialists who own his Primstone team, and has no stable relationships, even with his own teammates. He is vain, strives constantly to dominate others, and frequently discards acquaintances who have become "withered limbs" of his ambition. Yet, he is by no means simply a truculent, destructive brute. As his perceptive first-person narration of the story reflects, he has a decided capacity for self-analysis and sensitive thought and often is shown to have deep, generous feelings for others (feelings he tragically cannot articulate). What emerges from this book is a fascinating image of a man struggling courageously but futilely to find wholeness in his life, to balance the two sharply contradictory sides of his nature.

The novel opens with an account of a rugby game during which Machin has six teeth smashed out—David's brother Anthony had actually suffered such an injury as a professional rugby player. Shortly thereafter, while under ether, Machin drifts back in memory several years to the beginning of his rugby career and to the start of his relationship with his landlady, a dowdy, "not-too-young" widow, Valerie Hammond. The first five chapters deftly shuffle the reader back and forth between such flashbacks and several present-tense scenes depicting Machin's trip to the dentist and a rowdy Christmas party at the home of the team's owner. Later chapters detail in a straightforward present-tense narrative his developing affair with Mrs. Hammond, his movement through the sleazy world of professional sports, and his response to the depressing environment of the sooty industrial town where he lives.

Machin had first been drawn to rugby league while working as a lathe operator in a factory, when he had perceived the sport as his only chance to escape the oppressive lot of the ordinary working man. Once he has gained status as a local hero, he can strut through town, the proud gladiator, relishing the fact that "Machin's a name that means something" to area residents. His exterior successes, however, do not satisfy the lonely, reflective man's longing for roots, for some deeper meaning in his life, and his consequent torment becomes Storey's central concern in the novel.

On one occasion, when Machin's boss's wife tries to seduce him, he refuses, because, as one of his teammates mockingly observes, he "believes in falling in love." As a sports celebrity, he has such "samples" available at every turn but remains faithful to the pitiful, washed-out widow with whom he boards on Fairfax Street. This homely, embittered, withdrawn widow, fearful of life and an unappeasable figure of suffering and defeat (she still keeps her husband's boots polished by the hearth) comes to have a compelling grip on Machin, who becomes obsessed with playing Pygmalion to her Galatea, with having "the real Mrs. Hammond . . . come popping out." He also finds a rather perverse challenge in the woman's willful indifference to his being a hero and in her refusal to express gratitude for his kindnesses. He buys her a television and a fur coat and takes her family for Sunday rides in the countryside, but she offers no response. She has her own good reasons for not committing herself to him emotionally: she fears that he wants only to see her give in, to hear her admit her need of him, before abandoning her. His cockiness and brute force overwhelm her.

Despite the perverse, egotistical nature of his initial attraction to the noncommittal widow, however, and despite his continued "ape-like" behavior around her, Machin gradually comes to feel real love and earnest need for her. In a key passage, which opens a revealing window into Machin's deepest feelings, he acknowledges his awareness that he is not "going to be a footballer for ever" and expresses his longing "to have something there for good," a meaningful, permanent connection with Mrs. Hammond. He needs her, he says, "to make me feel whole and wanted." She is willing to give him sexual satisfaction, but he would have her express "some feeling for me" as well. She never realizes, however, that Machin could indeed be the answer to her psychic needs and a real source of warmth and security for her and her children. Because of her temperament and his own inarticulateness, she and Arthur fail, finally, to make the needed affective connection. She eventually throws him out of the Fairfax Street house, and goes into a decline, dying soon after, with a grief-stricken Machin by her hospital bed.

The final chapter makes no mention of the love affair. It offers a straightforward description of a rugby match. Storey thus meaningfully sandwiches the account of Machin's futile love affair between two slices of savage rugby action. The narrative returns full circle, but Machin himself can make no return to the prospects he had held years earlier as a rookie rugby star. He is left, finally, with nothing more than his loneliness, the ever-dwindling joys of physical contact on the ice-hard pitch, and his growing fears that with his coming retirement he will slip back into the obscurity of the life of a factory worker. Storey told Haffenden that his intent at the end of this novel had been "to create a stoic view of life." Stoicism, he said, is "the only alternative to despair."

In style *This Sporting Life* seems extraordinarily mature and polished as a work of a beginning novelist. The prose—taut, unadorned, matter-of-fact—seems particularly well matched to the narrator's personality, and what pathos exists in the novel (particularly in the climactic hospital scenes) is effectively filtered through Machin's customary understated manner. The author's realistic descriptions of working-class life and precise rendering of his Yorkshire characters' dialect particularly impress, as do his graphic portrayals of the industrial landscape of the dreary provincial town, its sky seemingly forever flushed with a hellish, crimson-orange glare from the collieries' coke ovens. Here, as in later writings, Storey displays an acute sense of visual imagery–something no doubt engendered during his apprenticeship as a painter–and a sharp eye for the detail of his setting.

Perhaps most impressive of all passages in *This Sporting Life* are the young author's vibrant descriptions of rugby, of the bone-crushing, brutish, close-quarters battle. Storey shows that he can write superbly when rendering narrative action. Such violence as recurs both on and off the rugby pitch throughout this first novel was to be a feature in virtually all his later novels, especially *Radcliffe* (1963) and *A Temporary Life* (1973). The reader of *This Sporting Life* is also given remarkable first-hand sensual impressions of the game–the sounds of the whistles, trumpets, and "animal roars" that greet every success of the home team; the smells of sweat, sewage mud, carbolic, liniment, and leather that permeate every changing room; and the visions of players limbering up freshly before competition and afterwards slumping wearily into baths, their bodies slimed with mud and blood.

Storey had grown weary of rugby by 1956, and with the encouragement of his new wife, a language teacher named Barbara Rudd Hamilton, he arranged a release from his Leeds team contract. From 1957 until 1960 he worked as a substitute teacher in some seventeen different schools around London's tough East End and found it a wretched experience dealing with devitalized fellow teachers and disruptive students. Dozens of the afflicted young people in his novels and plays are teachers or former teachers, and virtually all of them are made to voice their creator's disillusionment about the profession. The title character in *Saville,* for example, teaches in a Yorkshire secondary school and says his job is "like being in a prison." Many of Storey's characters who are teachers–such as Howarth in *Flight into Camden* (1960), Colin in *Pasmore* (1972), and Yvonne Freestone in *A Temporary Life*–are on or beyond the verge of mental breakdowns. Teaching drove Storey into severe depression, and in 1959, when he began writing his first play, *The Restoration of Arnold Middleton* (1967, originally titled "To Die with the Philistines"), his subject was a schoolmaster who cracks up. Storey was at the time discouraged because *This Sporting Life* had been rejected by more than eight publishers, and he had begun to doubt that he would ever succeed as a novelist. He thus tried his hand at drama, taking off from teaching for a few days during half term to write the play. He said later that he devoted only three days to writing the play, but it would take him eight years to get it produced. He had had no theatrical experience, and, indeed, had made only a half-dozen or so trips to the theater before attempting to write the play.

Middleton is a history teacher in his thirties and is going mad. Like so many of Storey's characters, he is spiritually impoverished. He longs for a better world of better men and complains that the "greatest threat to the present century" is the pygmy-like condition of modern man's soul. He has studied "kingship" and admires adventurers like Robin Hood, but his own life is one of boring schoolwork done amid cringing, mediocre fellow teachers. He suffers also from pressures brought on him by a jealous, demanding wife, by unnatural demands made by his sensual mother-in-law, and by the memory of a working-class mother whose expectations he had not met. His guilt over things not done for his mother in his youth contributes to his madness. In the play's original version, Middleton kills himself, but in a 1964 revision produced in 1967 in London, Storey allows his hero hope of restoration to normality once he has experienced the "insights that irrationality brings."

Shortly after finishing "To Die with the Philistines," Storey got the news that *This Sporting Life* would be published in America by Macmillan and in England by Longmans. It was published early in 1960 to considerable acclaim. The young author was immediately hailed by and associated with the "angry young men," and critic Brian Glanville in *London Magazine* called Storey "a gifted, serious and unusual" novelist who "seems potentially a more important writer than either Braine or Amis." Storey and his wife were £50 in debt, and their first child was soon to be born, but with the receipt of the $7,500 bounty that accompanied the Macmillan Fiction Award, he was able to quit teaching in 1960 and began devoting full time to writing.

In the flush of enthusiasm over the acceptance of *This Sporting Life,* he sat down and wrote another novel, *Flight into Camden,* in eighteen days. It was published in fall 1960. Like *This Sporting Life* it traces the course of a doomed romance between two working-class lovers who seem as ill-matched in their own fashion as Machin and Mrs. Hammond. After dealing in *This Sporting Life* with what he identified as the northern aspect of his temperament, he turned in *Flight into Camden* to explore "its southern counterpart–the intuitive, poetic" London world, which in his BBC talk he associated with "femininity, with a woman's sensibility and responses." In *Flight Into Camden* the heroine and first-person narrator, Margaret Thorpe, makes the same "flight" from Yorkshire to London that the author had made a few years earlier. Her flight into Camden is made with her lover, an art teacher named Gordon Howarth, who has left behind in the provincial town his wife and two children. *Flight into Camden* chronicles the lovers' struggle to find happiness together while undergoing severe pressures from both their families to end their illicit union.

Dust jacket for the first U.S. edition of Storey's 1960 novel, about the turbulent life of a professional rugby player

Before going to London, Margaret had lived a life of dreary routine divided between her work as a Coal Board secretary and her home, where she had been an emotional pawn of her hectoring older brother and her loving but nonetheless oppressive parents. After her initial joy over the freedom of London, however, she becomes disenchanted with Howarth, who has drifted aimlessly and unhappily back into teaching, and their union further erodes under mounting pressures that their families back in the north country bring to bear on them—Howarth's wife begs by correspondence for his return, and Margaret's father and brother visit Camden to seek her return to the family fold.

The parasitic union of these two weak central characters never commands the reader's attention the way Machin's obsessive passion for Mrs. Hammond does. Margaret Thorpe's psychic development, her progress away from her family's conventional puritan moral vision and toward a more liberated emotional state in which she can show feelings for her lover, is developed by Storey in a plausible fashion. The reader faces difficulties, however, in trying to determine why

Margaret ever develops any such feelings for the indecisive, self-pitying, cynical, and unrelentingly morose Howarth in the first place. Margaret recognizes that he is a moral coward, that he "had only a vast emptiness to turn to." Yet, the reader is meant not to question her compelling passion for this hollow, characterless man, nor to doubt her sincerity when she observes: "I missed Howarth more than I could bear. I was incomplete and lifeless without him." Even less convincingly motivated is the climactic letter that ends their affair. In it Howarth avows his deep, unending passion and tells her he is selling her luggage and plans never to see her again. The reader is left to puzzle over the man's ambiguous reasoning for breaking off the romance and to decipher why Margaret bathes herself in tears upon receipt of this letter from her spineless lover. Much more interesting is her response to her family before and after she takes flight into Camden. As he often does in his writing, Storey sensitively demonstrates the complexity of familial relationships and captures well the fine shades of emotions among the Thorpes during their tense, dramatic confrontations. Margaret's mother and father—decent, religious, working-class folk, full of good intentions, homely maxims, and well-meant aspirations for the success of their children—resemble the north-country parents of the central figures in *Pasmore, Saville,* and plays such as *In Celebration* (1969), *The Farm* (1973), and *The March on Russia* (1989). Invariably the fathers of these families have labored for years (usually down pit) to give their children an education, thinking that would mean for them a passage to a better life. In every case, however, the dream has disappointing results for both generations. The children, in moving beyond their working-class origins, seldom find happiness in their new situations, and the older generations are often crushed by the discovery that education has led their children to compromise or wholly abandon the social and moral values of the parents.

From these roots grow the inevitable—and often insoluble—domestic conflicts that are at the heart of much of Storey's writing. Margaret Thorpe's frustrated father condemns his children's "great educated emptiness," and expresses resentment over their ungrateful attitude toward his sacrifice in the mines. Like most parents in Storey's works, he is an emotional vampire who feeds off whatever love and gratitude he can get from his children. The relationship between Margaret and her father—the complex web of love, hatred, gratitude, and guilt spun between them—is the most fascinating aspect of *Flight into Camden,* and their tortured head-on encounters over her "carrying on" with Howarth form the novel's best scenes. Howarth at one point observes that families can be parasitic and destructive, "like vicious animals, radiant with solicitude and affection until you touch them," and then they "rear up like crazy beasts." He directs this observation squarely at the Thorpes, whom he justifiably sees as his enemies, and, while it is an exaggerated view, it does contain kernels of truth. The Thorpes do indeed "rear up" when their family circle is disrupted, and–though they mean no malice toward Margaret–they use all the means available (expressions of love, tears, agonized looks, timely illnesses) to coerce her away from Howarth and back to Yorkshire.

Through the influence of her older brother, Michael, a university lecturer and an "intellectual gangster," Margaret had developed a contempt for "domesticity and the fatefulness of motherhood." As the novel ends she sunbathes on her brother's Yorkshire lawn while her domestic, pregnant sister-in-law beckons her to tea, a visiting clergyman expresses approval of Howarth's return to his wife, and brother Michael drones on in his overbearing way. This final tableau suggests that Margaret's destiny will involve just such a domestic somnolence as that which Michael, in contradiction to his own "theories," has settled into with his "little mother." Such a life for their daughter would certainly please the Thorpes. The question is, would such a life ever please Margaret?

Flight into Camden lacks the force and compelling drama of *This Sporting Life*. The plot unfolds at a frequently dull, pedestrian pace. Storey has no special problems with his use of a woman as his first-person narrator, but his novel suffers because the woman is mousy, gray, and unremittingly intense and dolorous as she narrates her tale. Margaret simply lacks the diversity of mood and sense of humor that would be likely to sustain a reader's interest. Though *Flight into Camden* created less of a stir with reviewers than had *This Sporting Life,* it won two notable literary awards, the John Llewelyn Rhys Memorial Prize for 1961 and the Somerset Maugham Award for 1963.

Storey felt that reviewers had generally missed the point about the physical/spiritual dichotomy in his characters' lives in the first two novels, so when he wrote *Radcliffe* in 1961–1962 he was in a "state of irritation" and determined not to let his audience misread the new story. Toward that end he steps frequently into the narrative to explain things (something he rarely does in other novels), and has his characters talk–endlessly–about the theme of the divided self. He even has one provide what amounts to a gloss for the entire novel: "But just think what if this separate [spirit] were in one man, and the body, the acting part in another? What if these two qualities were typified ideally in two separate men? Then, just imagine . . . the unholy encounter of two such people!" Storey imagines just such an encounter throughout *Radcliffe:* the story's cen-

tral action is the failure, ending in murder, of a tortured, violently passionate homosexual love between two men, one who is made to represent the soul and the other the body of man. As in his earlier novels, Storey sought in *Radcliffe* to dramatize his powers that stormed in his own being by making one of his protagonists, Victor Tolson, a muscular working-class lad, and the other, Leonard Radcliffe, a self-absorbed, artistic intellectual. "Vic was my body, and I was his soul," Radcliffe explains to his father. "It's the division that separates everything in life now." The reader is thus asked to view the relationship between the two men as symbolic of the deep rift that the social and religious traditions of Western society have wrought in man's nature.

Leonard Radcliffe is the effete last of the line in a decayed aristocratic family and lives in a crumbling Yorkshire manor house where his father acts as caretaker. He first meets Tolson when the lower-class lad rescues him from tormenting schoolmates. Even as a child the brawny, slow-witted Tolson is given to outbursts of sadistic violence, which seem his only means of self-expression, and Leonard often becomes his victim. Radcliffe comes to depend on Tolson's vigorous physical presence, however, and when they are separated for several years, it seems as if he is "physically disintegrating." Only after they are reunited after eight years, when they join a tent contractor's crew, does Leonard once again feel alive, and then his physical dependence on Tolson intensifies when they begin a homosexual love affair among the tents at a work site. Leonard mistakenly assumes that their union also implies an emotional commitment, but Tolson soon demonstrates total disregard for his feelings when he has intercourse with a local tart while Leonard lies sobbing in a nearby tent. Tolson thereafter alternately courts and abuses Leonard, wooing him gently on one occasion and on another viciously smashing him with a hammer. Their relationship continues on such a basis until Tolson brutally rapes the weaker man, pushing him over the edge of sanity and prompting him to murder. The death scene itself is a gruesome, slow-motion nightmare, with Leonard raining bloody hammer blows on Tolson's head. Leonard is subsequently incarcerated in a mental home, where he dies of a brain hemorrhage. After these deaths the novel concludes with the birth of a boy to Leonard's sister, Elizabeth, who had herself been raped by Tolson. This child, with its dark, enigmatic "Radcliffe eyes" and the "energetic movement" of Tolson's body, represents a reconciliation of spirit and flesh that had evaded the story's two protagonists during their own lives. It is difficult to say exactly what this strange reconciliation means, however, and to determine what, if any, metaphysical implications are to be gleaned from this complicated, horrible tale of sexual perversity and violence. For one thing, Storey's meaning seems too often to become entangled in the swirling poetic symbolism and melodramatic turbulence of his narrative. A general murkiness pervades the telling of the tale, a perpetually baffling effort by the narrator to stretch his story into allegory. For instance, the battle between the two homosexual protagonists is to be viewed, as Leonard tells the court, as symbolic of the calamitous body/spirit "split in the whole of Western society." The decaying Radcliffe mansion is further suggested as a symbol of aristocratic old England gone to ruin, a symbol of historic culture and intellectualism as it is threatened by mass society, by the physicality of the workers in the housing estate that threatens to consume it. The faint tom-toms of "significance," the hints that this tale is somehow about the decline of the Western world, sound constantly in the edges of Storey's narrative, but the reader never receives sufficient coordinates by which he can locate this weighty theme in terms of the novel's actual events.

In their efforts to describe *Radcliffe,* many reviewers mentioned comparable works by Emily Brontë, Fyodor Dostoyevsky, and D. H. Lawrence; Storey's tale does indeed often seem an amalgam of the best and worst elements of their works. Like *Wuthering Heights* (1847) it chronicles the tumultuous passions of larger-than-life characters and paints as evocative a portrait of modern Yorkshire as Brontë did with the same terrain in her day. Storey's novel has even more in common with the fictional world of Dostoyevsky. Radcliffe easily brings to mind Dostoyevsky's Raskolnikov as he goes feverishly about town fingering the hammer in his raincoat, and his subsequent murder of Tolson is not unlike the ax murder of the old moneylender in *Crime and Punishment* (1866). Dostoyevsky's hero is evoked again when Leonard confesses and asks the authorities to look on his deed "as if it were the simple illustration of an elaborate theory" (his idea of the "split" in Western man's consciousness). The characters in *Radcliffe* are, like those in Dostoyevsky's books, largely an assemblage of perverse, unpredictable grotesques, and Storey's focus on their bizarre acts of sadism and masochism, of rape, murder, and incest, brings to mind the Russian's own concentration on the base passions of his morally diseased characters. Few streaks of sunshine cross the pages of either writer.

It was inevitable that Storey would be compared to Lawrence, if for no other reason than the striking correspondence in their lives: each was the son of a northern England coal miner; each won grammar school scholarships that helped remove them from their working-class backgrounds; each subsequently suffered through unhappy periods as teachers in London secondary schools; and each took up painting before deciding on a career as a writer. There are important resemblances also in the content of their works. Storey's preoccupation with the duality in man's consciousness, with the problem of sexual relationships, with the relations between parents and children, and with the conflict of British social classes are all major thematic concerns for Lawrence as well. Storey's tale of an artistic young man's struggle for release from stifling family ties in his autobiographical novel *Saville* seems remarkably similar to Lawrence's own autobiographical novel *Sons and Lovers* (1913), and Storey's later novel *A Prodigal Child* (1982) even more strikingly resembles *Sons and Lovers.* Far more than in Storey's other novels, Lawrence's prose style seems to have left its mark on *Radcliffe*—especially in Storey's poetic symbolism, his use of phallic symbols, his habit of investing ordinary activities (for instance, the riding of a motorbike) with erotic significance, and the way he creates an emotion-filled landscape that often mirrors his characters' psychic condition.

Storey, with a self-loathing critical eye that he frequently uses in appraising his works years after their initial release, told Haffenden in 1982 that he had "completely screwed up" *Radcliffe,* that "the style is blatant, so self-conscious and wilful; I can't see any grace in it at all." With its florid romanticism, insistent symbolism, and overheated prose, *Radcliffe* certainly seemed a radical departure from the simplicity and vigorous realism of *This Sporting Life* and *Flight into Camden,* and it created a keen controversy among reviewers in 1963. One called it "worthless trash" and another "one of the sweatiest and most ludicrously symbolified novels in years." To the other extreme, Malcolm Bradbury said it was "full of excellencies," and Jeremy Brooks declared that *Radcliffe* "establishes David Storey as the leading novelist of his generation." The consensus among reviewers, however, fell somewhere between these two positions, and John Mellors's observation that *Radcliffe* was a "clumsy, blundering, groping, and yet oddly impressive book" typified the novel's critical reception.

During the time he was working on *Radcliffe,* Storey supported his family partly by writing articles for British periodicals and by working on various television and film projects. He was also asked by film director Lindsay Anderson to convert *This Sporting Life* into a screenplay. The film starred Richard Harris and Rachel Roberts, and at the 1963 Cannes Film Festival it won the International Film Critics' Prize. It has since come to be regarded generally as a classic of modern cinema. Anderson and Storey's extraordinarily fruitful artistic collaboration was to be extended, eventually, to the British stage, and Anderson, before his death in 1994, directed nine of Storey's plays.

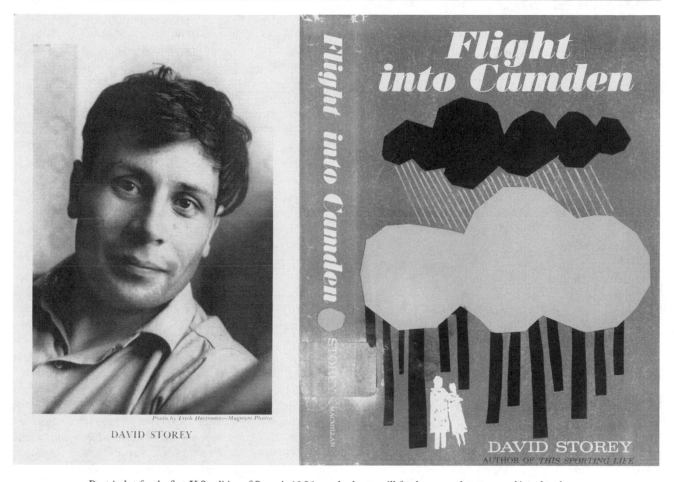

Dust jacket for the first U.S. edition of Storey's 1961 novel, about an ill-fated romance between working-class lovers

After writing the screenplay, Storey was encouraged by Anderson to try his hand again at drama, and he began revising "To Die with the Philistines." It was produced at the Traverse Theatre Club in Edinburgh in November 1966 under its new title, *The Restoration of Arnold Middleton.* Eight months later, the play appeared at the Royal Court in Sloane Square. This nationally subsidized theater, since the mid 1950s a venue for some of the best offerings of British drama, was to produce eight more of Storey's plays in the following decade. After twenty-two performances, the highly praised *Arnold Middleton* was transferred to the Criterion Theatre in the West End, and the *Evening Standard* shortly thereafter named Storey "Most Promising Playwright" for 1967. Buoyed by the success of *Arnold Middleton,* Storey devoted new attention to writing plays, and several just "popped out" (as he later put it) in a remarkably short span of a few months. By 1970 he had written a half-dozen plays, which were all subsequently produced. Within weeks after the July 1967 Royal Court premiere of *Arnold Middleton,* he had written *The*

Contractor (1970), a plotless slice-of-life view of a group of workmen erecting and dismantling a large wedding tent on a lawn. He returned to a novel he had been writing but remained fascinated by the image of a white metalwork table that he had left sitting on an almost bare stage near the end of *The Contractor.* Several weeks after he had finished that play, he began another, *Home* (1970), creating four characters who drift casually onstage to sit and talk at that table—only this time he placed it on the grounds of a mental asylum. His characters are inmates, and *Home* depicts an uneventful afternoon in their bleak lives, when they try futilely to lift their depressions through communication with others around the table. About the same time, in late 1967, Storey spent several mornings laboring on a fourth play, *In Celebration* (1969). It was to become the second of his plays to be produced. It premiered at the Royal Court in April 1969, with Alan Bates playing Andrew Shaw, one of three sons who have returned to the Yorkshire mining town of their birth "in celebration" of their parents' fortieth wedding anniversary. This play, too, won immediate favor with London theatergoers. Six months later, *The Contractor* opened at the Royal Court and was even more warmly received before it was transferred to a West End theater, where it subsequently elicited for Storey the London Theatre Critics Award for 1970. In June of that year *Home* became the third Storey play to open at the Royal Court in a little more than a year. Before the end of the year, the play—starring illustrious British actors John Gielgud and Ralph Richardson—had been transferred to West End and Broadway theaters, and it won both the 1970 *Evening Standard* Drama Award and the 1971 New York Drama Critics' Circle Award (a prize he was to claim again in 1973 with *The Changing Room* and in 1974 with *The Contractor*).

Storey's success as a playwright was not to wane with the production of his fifth play, *The Changing Room,* in November 1971. A documentary-style slice of sporting life—recording a Saturday afternoon in the locker room of a rugby league team in northern England—this play again won recognition as best play of the season in both London and New York. From 1972 to 1974 Storey did a stint as associate artistic director of the Royal Court, and within a nine-month period (August 1973 to April 1974) three more of his plays—*Cromwell, The Farm,* and *Life Class*—had their debut at the theater. None received anything like the critical acclaim that *The Contractor, Home,* and *The Changing Room* had elicited, however.

His plays produced later in the 1970s found even fewer supporters. For instance, when *Mother's Day*—a wild farce about a middle-class English family who engage in a remarkable merry-go-round of rape, adultery, incest, group sex, Oedipal longings, parricide, greed, and extortion—was staged at the Royal Court in 1976, it was widely condemned. Michael Billington, customarily an admirer of Storey's drama, opened his *Guardian* column by declaring, "*Mother's Day* is a stinker." When Storey ran across some London theater critics in the bar at the Royal Court the night after his play's debut, he railed at them and rained blows upon Billington's head. Such violence notwithstanding, critics gave no warmer a greeting to his next play, *Sisters,* another farce about sexual activities on a British housing estate, when it opened in 1978 at the Royal Exchange Theatre in Manchester. *Early Days,* which the small Cottesloe Theatre (National Theatre) produced in 1980, was clearly superior to the farces and received favorable notices, though the elegiac play itself was largely overshadowed by the critical raves given Ralph Richardson in the lead role as Sir Richard Kitchen, who sits in his garden rehearsing the events of his life, his childhood, his marriage, and the days of his political power.

Most of Storey's plays rework themes, characters, or situations dealt with in more complex fashion in his novels. Many of his plays have been direct by-products of the fiction, or vice versa. For example, in 1964 Storey revised *Arnold Middleton* and then turned to material that was published ultimately as *Pasmore.* The title characters of both works are schoolteachers suffering psychic collapses because of marital dilemmas and unresolved problems related to their upbringing and parents. Of all Storey's plays, *In Celebration* seems the most important in relation to his fiction because it deals directly with key themes common to most of his novels. When he got writer's block while working on *Saville* in 1967 Storey put it aside, and, using similar material and transposing characters from the novel, he wrote *In Celebration. Saville* recounts the childhood experiences of the eldest of three sons of a north-country miner who labors desperately to give his children a better life. *In Celebration* takes virtually the same family and describes an incident many years later, when the three brothers (now in their thirties) return to their old Yorkshire home to observe their parents' fortieth wedding anniversary. All three have become externally successful: Andrew as a solicitor; Colin, a labor-relations expert; and Steven, a university teacher. According to Andrew, though, he and his brothers are really "wash-outs," men who have lived lives "measured out in motor-cars." Their move into the middle class has meant for them only spiritual impoverishment and alienation from their work and from themselves. He claims that this psychological and emotional crippling had been set in motion years earlier by their parents' "philistine, parasitic, opportunistic" values and by the "vision of a better life" held perpetually before them by their parents. Steven, the youngest, complains that while their father has found his own work in the mines "significant," the professional work he has educated them for is "nothing . . . at the best a pastime, at the worst a sort of soulless stirring of the pot." *In Celebration* in effect dramatizes the result of what the parents are shown doing to their three sons in *Saville,* and Steven Shaw's observation that he and his brothers had suffered "disfigurement" at the "wholly innocent hands" of their parents states the theme not only of the play but of the novel as well.

The domestic drama of *In Celebration* would be reprised by Storey at least twice more in plays, in *The Farm* and *The March on Russia.* In *The Farm* another family reunion erupts into anger and recriminations between a crusty Yorkshire farmer and his four educated children who have returned home for an anniversary. *The March on Russia* also centers on a family reunion—that of a Yorkshire coal miner, his rigid, unresponsive mate, and their three children, who have come home to celebrate the parents' sixtieth wedding anniversary—and again, as the family gathers, old rivalries and generational conflicts reopen as they reminisce. When *The March on Russia* premiered in 1989 *TLS* reviewer John Wilders observed that it was "so like" *In Celebration* "as to seem a revised version of that original work." It was certainly an *emotional* revision, in what it reflected of the writer's changed attitude toward his parents. Storey's daughter Helen spoke to a *Times* interviewer in 1990 about what a "difficult process" it had been for her father to have written so intimately about his own family members. Another family member had already made it clear how "difficult" it had been for those whom David wrote about. Storey's brother Anthony, in his 1975 novel *Brothers Keepers,* describes how the entire Storey family had attended a performance of *In Celebration* (titled *The Family* in Anthony's narrative) and how the disclosure of "family secrets" on stage had driven their mother to tears and their father to deep anger. By the time *The March on Russia* opened David Storey's relationship with his parents had apparently changed. In comparison to *In Celebration* and *The Farm, The March on Russia* is a much more elegiac play, one suffused with more pathos and more understanding between the professional, educated children and their unreasonable working-class parents. Storey told Haffenden that he was getting along "very well" with his parents, who by that time were living near Scarborough in a retirement bungalow he had purchased for them using money from the film rights for *This Sporting Life*. In the 1960s his father, at age sixty-one, had left the coal mines suffering from pneumoconiosis, with doctors giving him six months to live, but he survived until 1987.

Another of Storey's plays that has close ties to his fiction is *Life Class* (1975), which includes several important parallels to scenes in *A Temporary Life*. The adult characters of the play are lifted straight from the novel and given new names. For example, Wilcox, the deranged art-college principal in the novel, becomes Foley in *Life Class,* and the play's main character, Allott, especially in the sarcastic, ironic tone he often uses, resembles Storey's narrator, Colin Freestone, in the novel. Both are failed artists and failing teachers, and both wind up losing their jobs, Allott because he has allowed the mock rape of his life-class model by one of his students. Much like Arnold Middleton and the title character in *Pasmore,* Allott is a teacher at the end of his tether (especially distraught because his marriage has gone sour), and *Life Class* records the last stages of his crack-up.

When *Pasmore* was published in 1972 reviewers noted its lean, bony prose, its frequent use of dialogue, and the surgical objectivity of its narration. Some of them were led to conclude that the novel showed the result of a new discipline Storey had learned writing

plays during the decade since he had written the relatively tumid, sprawling prose of *Radcliffe*. That was not, however, the case. Much of *Pasmore* had been written in 1964, before Storey had even attempted writing his second play, and he had continued to work hard at fiction all through the years when he was having such phenomenal success in the theater. Writing novels, he told an interviewer in 1971, had been for him "like working in a coal mine," while creating plays had always seemed an easy task, "a holiday."

Pasmore and Storey's fifth novel, *A Temporary Life,* are both actually transpositions from a larger work of fiction written between 1962 and 1967. Storey had piled up enough money writing film scripts that he could devote those five years to writing a "big work" that he projected as a climax to that "campaign for reintegrating myself" that he had begun with *This Sporting Life*. After dramatizing the incompatibility of body and soul in the confrontation of his two lead characters in *Radcliffe,* the author had intended with his fourth novel to bring about a fusion of the warring elements in man's psyche in the figure of one hero, a powerful property developer named Neville Newman. Storey told an interviewer in 1970 that the theme of what he called his "big novel" involved the "division between those who can make society work for them and those who can't," and *Pasmore* is one of those who cannot, a foolish foil for the book's other major characters. In 1967, Storey grew frustrated over his inability to make structural sense of his long work, laid it aside, and began working on plays and on another novel, *Saville,* about an entirely different subject. Subsequently, in order to recoup on his five years of hard work on the "big novel," he sat down and extracted *Pasmore* and *A Temporary Life* from the larger work, extensively reshaping the material as he did so, and the novels were published in 1972 and 1973. In both, the hero of the "big novel," Neville Newman, is glimpsed only briefly as the husband of the mistress of the two books' respective heroes.

As he has so often done throughout his career, Storey in *Pasmore* was reworking situations treated in previous works, looking at them from a wholly different angle. In *Flight into Camden* he had depicted the marital breakdown and psychic disintegration of a college teacher, viewing it from the perspective of the man's mistress. In *Pasmore* such a character is viewed more or less from his own perspective, though in third-person narration. *Pasmore* further shares with *Flight into Camden* an engaging portrayal of the painful conflict between a hardworking coal miner father and an educated child whose values and private torment he cannot comprehend. Despite such circling back over old emotional territory, however, Storey offers in *Pasmore* an interesting, imaginatively conceived story with a subtle ironic tone

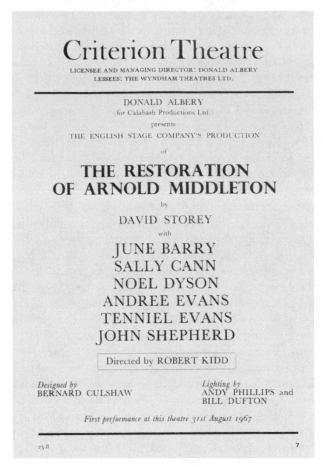

Cover and title page from the playbill for Storey's first play, about the mental breakdown of a schoolmaster

and a sense of humor that makes it superior to the earlier narrative.

Colin Pasmore is almost thirty years old and is going mad. A history teacher at a Bloomsbury college, married with three children, and settled in an Islington house that he has lovingly renovated, he suddenly feels a new "fury," a nameless anxiety that "something was wrong" in his life. His work begins to seem "meaningless and absurd," and, though he loves his wife and children, he cannot bear to be near them. To that point, his life has gone exactly according to the pattern set forth by his working-class Yorkshire parents—he has been a "good and certainly faithful son," a "good and faithful husband," and a "good and faithful teacher." Yet, elements are missing from his life that he cannot identify in terms of his work or family, and he wonders "where had all this faith and goodness got him?" Gradually he drifts from his decent home and respectable marriage into a sparsely furnished flat and a hollow, bloodless affair with an enigmatic mistress named Helen, a wealthy married woman in her late thirties. Her husband soon puts an end to their union, first by offering Pasmore a bribe, then by threats, and finally by having him brutally beaten up.

Colin treasures the sense of jolly control he feels over his gullible, naive wife, Kay, and is disgusted by "her vulnerability. . . her lack of pride . . . the incapacity to stand alone." That statement becomes hugely ironic by the end of *Pasmore,* as their fortunes seesaw and Kay begins to flourish while her husband dwindles into a weak, whining, inert lump of neuroses. She is initially shattered by his desertion but slowly begins taking little steps toward independence, first striking a friendship with a man named Fowler and subsequently insisting rather harshly that Pasmore visit the children only when invited on Sundays. While her prospects rise, his plunge. Having severed all the connections—family, work—that had given his life shape, he sinks into morbid depression and becomes virtually "extinct," spending his long, lonely days at the flat lying in darkness, staring at his ceiling. He becomes increasingly disoriented, and, on the rare days when he does work on his book about evangelical idealists, he scribbles only incomplete sentences. Mostly he sits in slovenly apathy and weeps.

Some reviewers complained that Storey had not properly clarified Pasmore's motivations for withdrawing from his "decent" life into a psychic shell, but they were overlooking the many clues sprinkled through the narrative that suggest that he is another of the Storey characters who suffer, as does Steven Shaw in *In Celebration,* from a "disfigurement" at the "wholly innocent hands" of parents. When Pasmore tells his sister about his problems, she says, "I always felt something would happen. . . . The way my dad sent you out, as his private army." Many other similar passages suggest that Colin's crack-up is a belated reaction to his upbringing. When he travels to his Yorkshire home he is immediately reminded of his painful ties with his parents, when his father rehearses how he had spent his entire life digging coal so his son could escape the pit and when his mother reminds him that "you owe things to people. . . . You can't go shrugging them off." In an effort to induce his son to return to his home, Colin's father resorts to all the same forms of emotional blackmail used by the old coal-mining father in *Flight into Camden,* and, those ploys failing, he finally smashes his son in the face. Colin feels terror when the "ghost" of his "father's reaction" pursues him back to his London flat–giving evidence once again that the root of his problems lies in his old Yorkshire home.

Colin cannot achieve the "feeling of wholeness" he seeks until he has learned to deal with this terror, with the residual guilt over the vague debt he feels he owes to his parents (and to his class) but can never repay. The resolution of his psychic dilemma comes, finally, in a strange purgation by fire. Alone in his flat, Colin feels his own presence "ignited . . . by flames" and imagines himself falling into a "hole in the ground," a gaping pit of blackness that his feverish brain clearly associates with the mines where his father has so labored on his behalf. Once this brainstorm has passed–once he has completely rebelled against the pattern of "faith and goodness" that his parents had set for him, and once he has made his psychic journey into the "pit" to suffer vicariously with his father–he is able to pick up his life again and is soon reconciled both with his parents and with his wife and children.

The ending of *Pasmore* is a qualified happy one. Colin is still aware that "somewhere underneath" the Yorkshire landscape his father is still slaving away, and he himself still dreams of the "pit and the blackness." His despair persists even after he has returned to the Islington nest, and his past still exists "all around him, an intensity, like a presentiment of love, of violence," reflecting again his ambivalence toward his parents and

the origins of his psychosis. He has obviously not, as the book's dust jacket claims, experienced "redemption and renewal," exactly. He has gained some sort of self-knowledge that helps him cope better with the terror caused him by his past, however, and while that may not qualify as a truly happy ending, it is certainly the most upbeat conclusion in Storey's first four novels.

Storey told Victor Sage in 1976 that "it suits me temperamentally to describe things through gritted teeth," and the short, tightly structured *Pasmore* certainly seems to be narrated through clamped jaws, with none of the intrusive attitudinizing that mars *Radcliffe.* Its spare, noncommittal prose leaves readers to make what they will of the story's events. Some reviewers thought the prose too laconic, that it was, as one critic put it, a "deeply evasive and artless novel." On the whole, the critical response to *Pasmore* was lukewarm, at best: even those who defended it generally overlooked what may be its chief merit, the irony and understated humor involved in Pasmore's domestic adventure. The author's three previous novels had been unremittingly humorless. Barry Cole, writing in the *New Statesman,* thought *Pasmore* similarly showed "no sign of wit, humor, or verbal irony. At times it sounds like a case history from a doctor's notebook." There is strong comedy in *Pasmore,* though it is subtly presented and the reader often has to labor to make the comic connections for himself. For example, a certain dark humor inheres in the mafioso-style warnings that Helen's cuckolded husband gives Pasmore to keep hands off his wife–four dark-suited men suddenly appear at the flat to deliver a coffin, a hearse parks outside, and funeral wreaths soon follow. The narrator never overtly directs the reader's attention to the fact, but there is a highly humorous contrast between these methods used by Helen's husband to retrieve his wife and the way Pasmore subsequently reacts when he discovers "another man, in public, in possession of his wife." Instead of confronting this other man directly, as Helen's husband had done, Pasmore warns his wife that Fowler is not the sort of person he would have associating with his children, and–in one of the novel's high comic moments–he condemns the other man for being unstable. Pasmore never recognizes the irony there, nor in the hilariously priggish telegrams he composes (but lacks the nerve to send) to Fowler: "Leave my wife alone homebreaker," he warns. "Adulterer beware"; "Fowler do you believe in the sanctity of marriage." About homebreaking and adultery Pasmore of course knows much, but he sees no connection between his former behavior and his newfound moral stance. Broad comedy exists also in some of the scenes of Colin's darkest moments–as, for example, when he is arrested for loitering outside his own house or when he later has to be pried loose from his own furniture as he clings to it and begs pitiably to be readmitted to the house and the family he had so stoutly rejected the year before. In one telegram to Fowler, he cries that there is "no justice in the world." However, plenty of comic justice is dealt in the fictional world of *Pasmore,* and the reader is meant to enjoy at least some of the agony experienced by the protagonist as the tables are turned on him. *Pasmore* won the Geoffrey Faber Memorial Award for 1973.

As he transposed it from his "big novel," Storey heavily revised the material that went into *A Temporary Life.* The original story had been set in London and had been narrated by the master builder Neville Newman. In its final form, the story is narrated by an art-college teacher named Colin Freestone, and the action takes place in a Yorkshire town where he is living temporarily in order to be near his institutionalized wife. The story focuses on his engagement with wildly idiosyncratic characters in three different and only tenuously connected worlds: the farcical world of the Municipal College of Fine Arts, with its hilariously eccentric majordomo, R.N. Wilcox; the tragic world of Colin's lovely but deranged wife, Yvonne, who resides at Westfield Mental Hospital; and the intensely violent and perverse world of the rich, powerful property dealer Neville Newman. Increasingly it becomes clear that the bizarre inhabitants of all three arenas of the novel's action are mad and that the outside world is even more a madhouse than the asylum where Yvonne stays.

Reviewers of *A Temporary Life* praised Storey's humorous portrait of "Skipper" Wilcox, the more-than-disturbed principal of Colin's art school, who patrols classrooms obsessively seeking out smokers; packs his own lavatory with stolen art objects and bottles filled with his own excreta; lectures against bread, blaming it for the world's "interdenominational strife"; and repeatedly asserts his belief that art is simply a matter of "good digestion." The novel's comic highlight—and one of the most marvelous passages in all of Storey's fiction—comes in the description of Freestone's dinner engagement at Wilcox's cold, dark cottage, when he dines on an unusually frugal meal that includes a toadstool cocktail. Through Wilcox's world of zaniness Colin sails relatively unscathed, but he does not so easily move through the sea of madness and pathos that surrounds Yvonne. Her breakdown is analyzed with clinical skill, and Storey makes her one of the most engaging of all the afflicted personalities in his writings. Again like so many of his characters, Yvonne has been psychically wounded by a well-meaning father, who had slaved in the Yorkshire mills so his "ray of sunshine" could go to college and "get out of here." Once out of the working classes, she had become burdened with guilt over her inability to give back to her own class "some of the things she's had," to repay her father's sacrifice. She has compensated by taking on all the world's suffering, spending her life in a sacrificial round of service to old people and other charities. In this abstract caring about people, however, she has failed to live up to the expectations of her parents and has failed to make contact with the people close to her, to Colin, for instance, who finds more and more that he cannot communicate across the barrier of his wife's madness.

The figure of the mad but compassionate Yvonne overshadows all else in *A Temporary Life,* and her character becomes an especially meaningful counterpoint to the brutal, insensitive Newmans, into whose strange orbit Colin is drawn when he becomes involved with the wife of the wealthy property developer. In contrast to Yvonne and her belief that "it's caring about people you don't have to care about that counts," Elizabeth Newman "couldn't give a damn about anything." The fluorescent-cool affair she has had with Colin is just another brief stop in her quest for pleasure, as her own daughter acknowledges matter-of-factly: "Mummy has her men." Elizabeth seems well-matched with her manipulative, nihilistic husband, who in a broader, more devastating sense is also on the make and careless of anyone who gets in the way. He and his company are, by his reckoning, "harbingers of progress," constructing modern industrial estates before moving on to "revitalize" other towns. In Freestone's eyes Newman is viewed as the arrogant, greedy head of a villainous system that somehow mangles people in its wake. Of Newman and Company Colin observes: "They try and undermine you first by attempting to rouse in you feelings of common decency. . . . Failing that, they clobber you. . . . Failing with that, they compromise you . . . by offering you positions. . . . The one thing you can refuse them is cooperation, until the whole system . . . collapses of its own volition." Just such ploys are indeed tried against Colin, but he holds out against Newman at every juncture. He refuses to abandon Elizabeth even after Newman's henchmen have clobbered him severely, persisting, as much as anything, out of his own perversity of will, his desire to thwart the powerful businessman. The contest of wills between the two men comes to a bloody climax following a party at Newman's house, where Colin goes berserk and attacks one of his host's aides. Colin is eventually beaten unconscious, and when he awakes, Newman—true to Colin's assessment of his methods—offers him a job. Colin refuses cooperation again, and defiantly sneers, "Do I get your wife as well?"

He will not get Elizabeth at any rate, for she is herself a member in good standing of the corrupt Newman world Colin labels a "circus." She masochistically provokes her husband to jealousy and violence, and Colin recognizes that such behavior is part of the Newman family routine, in which not only Elizabeth's adultery but even Newman's retaliation are known quantities. "Wherever we go it gets like this," their daughter acknowledges. Another member of their entourage adds, "It's always the innocent with them . . . who suffer." In the delineation of this Newman world—with its wild weekend parties of the rich and mighty, the exaggerated behavior of their hangers-on, the drinking, promiscuity, and sudden violence—there is a strong whiff of F. Scott Fitzgerald's *The Great Gatsby* (1925), though Storey's narrator certainly has little in common with the moralizing Carraway who narrates Fitzgerald's tale.

The Newmans finally move on to seek other affairs and further violence in other towns. Colin is left (thanks to Newman) without a job at the college and winds up sweeping streets for a living. Even that is a gesture of defiance against Newman, however, who had predicted that he would never "work around here . . . again." Colin is not, finally, a "victor"; rather, he is a survivor. He has answered Wilcox's absurdities in kind (for example, by scribbling graffiti on school walls and by unearthing the secrets of the principal's lavatory); he has come to terms with Yvonne's psychic withdrawal through his own stoicism and understanding of her plight; and he has met Newman's bullying challenge without flinching. One reviewer of *Pasmore* complained that Storey had not made his hero "a man worth feeling for," and the same complaint was voiced in different words about *A Temporary Life,* though the novel generally received warmer reviews than any Storey novel since *This Sporting Life.* Freestone, to be sure, is no ideal man, nor even an especially likable one. Like Elizabeth, he seems not to "give a damn about anything at times," and his perpetual cynicism wears thin after a while. He has redeeming qualities, however: he seems to have genuine feelings for his wife; he is attractive in his cockiness and pugnacity, in his willingness to engage the enemy; and he has something that no other Storey protagonist consistently displays—a sense of humor (sardonic, but nonetheless refreshing).

The same year *A Temporary Life* appeared, Storey published a strange volume titled *Edward* (1973). It is essentially a book of drawings by Donald Parker with a slight text supplied by Storey. Some bibliographers categorize *Edward* as juvenile literature, but that it is certainly not—Parker's drawings frequently include images of naked women and are typically irreverent (in one, a dazed nun inspects a lineup of naked bishops). The wonderfully funny drawings are vastly superior to the text, which focuses on the tale of a bishop who finds a mysterious key and cannot discover what it fits. Storey's

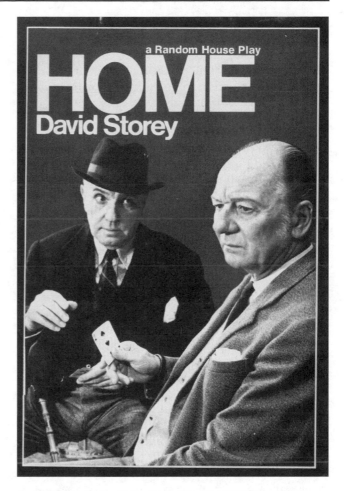

Dust jacket for the first U.S. edition of Storey's 1970 play, depicting an afternoon in the lives of a group of mental patients

enigmatic, scattered text often seems ill-connected to the drawings.

He began his sixth novel, *Saville,* in 1967, after he had for the time abandoned his "big novel," and over the next half-dozen years he worked on it, as he told Victor Sage, "as a kind of relaxation from writing plays." Much longer than his previous novels (it ranges over five hundred pages), *Saville* gives a richly detailed account of the childhood, adolescence, and early manhood of a northern England miner's son, who ultimately struggles to escape the strangling bonds of family affection and duty and the oppressive environment of his small pit village to take flight into London. *Saville* is, as one reviewer noted, "the kind of novel you live in," a curiously old-fashioned, naturalistic tale that traces the fortunes of a family of six in the village of Saxton in south Yorkshire during the 1940s and 1950s. The book gives a firsthand view of the family environment that is so often blamed for having "disfigured" the adults in Storey's earlier works. The evocative descriptions of the activities and people of this tiny village give the feeling of firsthand acquaintance, and *Saville* seems unmistakably autobiographical in tone. Colin Saville resembles Storey in the way he is born in the early 1930s in a north-country industrial town, begins a process of social mobility by winning a scholarship, excels at rugby, loves writing poetry, works as a farmhand during holidays, and finally flees to London and a new freedom of spirit.

Saville is narrated in Storey's typically minimalist style that holds the material at arm's length from the reader. All things are reported dispassionately with little explanation. The third-person narration is generally limited to Colin's consciousness, and the novel's structure basically imitates his memory—the early descriptions of family and village life are mundane and particular, reflecting the narrow perceptions of the growing youngster, and the novel's later portions become more abstract and dialectic, reflecting the impact his education has had on his thinking. Little suspense is created through the first two-thirds of the novel, but Storey commands his reader's attention through his creation of richly idiosyncratic characters and finely etched depictions of village life. He masterfully captures the dialect, syntax, and peculiar rhythms of the language of the West Riding people. As always, his descriptions of physical activities—for example, of Colin's toil with other sweaty farmworkers cutting corn—form some of the novel's best writing. Also good are the accounts of Colin's experiences as a student at King Edward's Grammar School and as a teacher at Rawcliffe village; the closely observed encounters between the bullying masters and their raw young charges are as good as any schoolroom dramas in English fiction. Finally, Storey's painting of the gray old village of Saxton—with its towering colliery headgears, ash heaps, smoke-filled skies, and stinking sewage ponds—recalls the best of Lawrence's sketches of Midlands mining towns.

More than all Storey's other works, *Saville* is a powerful social document, illustrating objectively the poverty, squalor, and hard lives of the working classes in northern England. "Some men grow out of their environment," says Colin's friend Bletchley. "Whereas others just seem to sink into it." They are the only two Saxton men of their generation to rise out of their backgrounds through education. By their community's material standards, Bletchley becomes a success, as a manager with a manufacturing firm, while Colin becomes only a teacher and poet. Their friends all "sink" into the pits to become "factory fodder," however. The vast inequities in the British social class system are dramatized in the contrast between the harsh lives of all the working-class lads and that of Colin's friend Stafford, the son of a mill owner, who glides smoothly through his youth toward an army commission, Oxford, and a life of ease.

Nowhere in all of Storey's writings is the dignity of the undignified man better portrayed than in the character of Colin's father, Harry. Despite the dismal social conditions he lives in, the elder Saville is proud, industrious, and determined to keep his sons out of the pit where a man is "just another piece of muck." He sends Colin forth as an ambassador to live the life he had himself been denied. Together they sit in the kitchen laboring over Colin's homework, and when his son wins the scholarship that will be the key to his deliverance out of the working class, the father bursts with pride. Colin begins questioning his father's work ethic and values, however, and weighs the truth of a cynical friend's assertion that the Saville family's philosophy can be boiled down to a matter of "material progress backed by a modicum of religious superstition." Such self-scrutiny feeds his growing bitterness over how he has been misshaped "not through force" but "through love" by his father. He has never, Colin claims, been allowed to decide for himself what he wants to do, and "in most ways I feel set against what I've been told to become, or felt I ought to become." Once he has become what in his family's eyes is a success—working as a teacher—he draws his father's envious contempt and suffers when he hears his father mock his easy job with long holidays, "no sweating out your guts." Saville derides Colin's "sitting still" and "writing poetry" while others his age are out doing physical things. Thus Colin suffers, as Storey himself had in early manhood, as he strives to reconcile these warring worlds of the intuitive and the physical and as he tries to adjust his inner aspirations and needs to the expectations of his Yorkshire family and community. Colin's attempt at self-definition is helped along by his relationship with a middle-aged woman named Elizabeth, who becomes his surrogate mother and is able to articulate some of the nineteen-year-old boy's psychological problems, which he cannot himself perceive. "You don't really belong to anything," she tells him. "You're not really a teacher. You're not really anything. You don't belong to any class, since you live with one class, respond like another, and feel attachments to none." She accurately claims that he has remained in Saxton because he is still so "bound up" with his parents. "I owe them something," he explains. When he repays that debt in material goods, however, in household furnishings, he complains loudly to his parents, "It's supposed to be enlightenment I've acquired, not learning how to make a better living."

As his depression deepens, his relationship with his family grows stormier. He brutalizes his brother Steven, whose complacent personality is the antithesis of the earnest, industrious Colin. The older brother envies Steven's insouciant nature and reproaches his parents for giving his brother "chances of freedom I've never had," for not "moulding" Stephen to fit their ambitions as they had him. In his mounting frustration over his brother's lack of determination to "succeed" (after failing exams, Steven goes blithely down pit), Colin becomes to him as much an intellectual gangster as ever Michael does to his sister in *Flight into Camden*.

Colin has an even more significant and dramatic relationship with another brother—the one he had never met, Andrew, who had died of pneumonia six months before Colin's birth. His parents had looked on Colin as a "bewitching recompense," as a mystical replacement for the dead child, and Colin belatedly resents the fact that he has been burdened by being the repository of two sons' shares of parental hope and ambition. It is through his own search for this artistic, "unruly," freedom-loving boy that Colin discovers what he himself must be. As a child, Andrew had been "trouble," had repeatedly wandered off from home, spending his short, happy life in constant careless flight. Colin comes to view the child as the symbolic antithesis of his own bound being. Andrew had also been an incipient artist—"He had the nature as well as the gift" to be a painter, his mother reports. The dead boy begins to haunt Colin, and in a strange cemetery scene, an image of the "wild, anarchic boy" comes to Colin's mind and he feels an "invisible bond with that figure in the ground," consequently leaving the graveyard with a new "sense of mission."

It is still a long time thereafter before he acts on this new "mission" and takes flight to London. His growing rage and swelling sense of the possibilities inside himself finally propel him to make the break, however, and the novel ends as he watches the last trail of "blackish smoke" over Saxton as his train moves south. He thus escapes the bondage of his class and village, as well as the obsessive love of his family, and bears his emptiness into the larger world. His future is open, though he seems destined to pursue his dream of writing, dragging his painful past behind him—until, perhaps, in just such a reunion scene as that dramatized in *In Celebration*, he will be able to exorcize the demons of his past. When *Saville* was published in 1976, it received what one critic accurately termed "hysterically enthusiastic reviews" in England. The ultimate accolade paid Storey's sixth novel was the awarding of the £5,000 Booker Prize for fiction, Britain's most important literary award.

During the 1960s and 1970s Storey lived with Barbara and their four children in Hampstead in north London. After *Saville*, he launched work on another similar, but less ambitious, novel, *A Prodigal Child*. Like *Saville*, it is a straightforward, naturalistic tale of a north-country boy's development through adolescence to early manhood and the threshold of an artistic career. "Concrete and specific," the motto of the art room where Storey's young hero, Bryan Morley, sculpts, also provides a clue to the author's greatest strength here—the rich details that cause the provincial Yorkshire world to spring to life, particularly in the opening chapters that chronicle the growth of Stainforth, a new estate where "pioneer" tenants are building homes, carving gardens, and forming new friendships. Beyond those early chapters, though, *A Prodigal Child* suffers from prolonged patches of flat dialogue and from the fact that the story is past midpoint before its chief dramatic conflicts become clear.

The novel concentrates first on the domestic life of Morley's parents, a beer-swilling farm laborer and his sullen wife, but most of the story focuses on the strange alliance Bryan forms in the 1930s with an older woman, Fay Corrigan. She and her rich husband take him into their mansion at Crevet and virtually adopt him, paying his way into a private school where he can study sculpting. Bryan feels wholly cut off from his parents and brother and welcomes this escape from the lowly life of Stainforth estate. He believes himself a "prince" of "special destiny" and yearns to create something that, without him, "could never have existed." His development as an artist is less intriguing, however, than his obsessive fixation on Mrs. Corrigan, a woman several decades his senior. He feels she is destined to play "princess to his prince," and even as a shy schoolboy his attraction to her is sexual (in school he sculpts her nude figure in clay). Their relationship becomes not only that of surrogate mother and son but also, perversely, that of surrogate husband and wife (the Oedipal drama is played out here as prominently as it is in Lawrence's *Sons and Lovers*, which Storey's novel strongly resembles). This relationship—Bryan himself calls it "odd, maybe even mad"—is tolerated, even welcomed, by Fay's weak husband, who hopes it will keep his promiscuous wife at home. It does not, and, during the seven years Bryan is at Crevet and Mrs. Corrigan is waiting for her young charge to grow into manhood and become her mate, she engages in frequent affairs. Belatedly she realizes that her alliance with Bryan is a "disease" and becomes despondent over the inevitability of losing him to her spunky niece Margaret, in whom Bryan sees "a youthful Mrs. Corrigan." At story's end, a fast-maturing Bryan does indeed seem destined to mate with Margaret, who has all along served as muse to his art and his desire to become "someone special," and he is enjoying new success as a sculptor. Like Colin Saville, he plans to pursue his art in London. Unlike Saville and other Storey protagonists

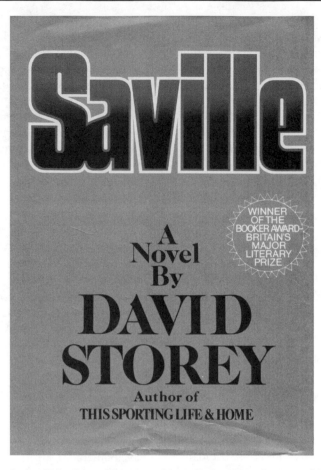

Dust jacket for the first U.S. edition of Storey's autobiographical 1976 novel, winner of the Booker Prize

who have taken similar flights south, however, Bryan is reunited with his past before he leaves to meet his future. Admitting to his father that he has "made mistakes," he expresses his desire to return home and make a "fresh beginning" with his family before going to London. He returns to Stainforth in time for a community-wide party, and, as he watches his neighbors dancing on the estate grounds, he feels it "strange how everything that is full of life has come back here," to the working-class world he had abandoned years before when he had gone to live at Crevet and pursue his art career. As he views his parents and their neighbors, he declares, "this is my kingdom, the kingdom of the heart . . . and we are all a part of it." No other previous Storey protagonist has been able to make such an acceptance of family and class. Bryan seems to have achieved a wholeness of character, an intellectual and emotional control that had evaded the grasp of virtually every tortured character in Storey's earlier works. This ending is not justified in terms of the plot, though, as Storey realized. Shortly after *A Prodigal Child* was published, he told Haffenden: "the conclusion was willed, and to that

extent false. I got so fed up with the characters that basically I jacked it in. The book was supposed to show how the working class has sold its inheritance, and the end was supposed to be ironical. . . . The irony can't be picked up by the reader because of the peremptory nature of the ending; it becomes specious."

Nonetheless, critics generally praised *A Prodigal Child* for its rich scenic background and thoughtful treatment of the aspirations and temperament of the developing artist. Some reviewers complained about Storey's customary "reticence" regarding character motivations, and several agreed with Bryn Caless's assertion in *British Book News* that Storey was again attempting "to rewrite D.H. Lawrence's fiction" but had produced only a "Lawrentian shadow instead of his own substance."

Storey remarked in 1982 that his work is "about groups, the relationship of the individual elements to the group—a football group, a group of people putting up a tent, or the family group. The group dominates the individuals in it, to the extent that they seek to escape from it but in the end are fetched back either to their salvation or to their damnation." In *Present Times* (1984), a novel he began in spring 1982, he continued focusing on the family group but reconfigured its dynamics. Conflict in this narrative arises not between working-class parents and educated offspring but between a middle-class parent and his rebellious teenagers who resent his traditional values and consider him to be redundant. Frank Attercliffe, the central character, suffers a sense of dislocation between himself and his family who are firmly entrenched in "present times." This dislocation spurs him to question his role as a good parent as he struggles to hold his family and life together.

The novel begins with a compelling plotline that focuses on the dysfunctional Attercliffes. Frank, a forty-seven-year-old former footballer, sportswriter, and father of five children lives with his two teenage daughters in an "executive-style" house in Morristown (another reincarnation of Wakefield). Unlike previous Storey protagonists, Frank appears at ease with his past and his progression into the middle class. He is not content, however, with his relationship with his children and neurotic, estranged wife, Sheila, who throughout the novel struggles to reclaim the home she abandoned two years earlier when she pursued a promiscuous romp with a richer man, who in turn dumped her. His eldest child, Elise, supports her mother, ennobling her as a symbol of everywoman in feminist battle against masculine oppression. Frank's counter—that her mother had left him of her own free will and now expects to return home and to continue her adulterous ways while he pays the mortgage—falls on deaf ears. His other teenage child, Catherine, not only sides with her mother, but also insists Frank is a racist and conformist when he has trouble accepting her relationship with a young black criminal.

The clash between ideologies provides the novel's best scenes: Sheila's outrageous ploys to fend off potential buyers for the house she claims is rightfully hers, and Frank's campaign against the inadequacies of his children's state-school system. Despite Frank's protestations, Sheila lays claim to the house, forcing him to move into a one-room apartment. When he tries to sell the house and split the profits, he and his agent are met at the door with flying shoes. Later, Sheila walks the agent and a potential buyer through the house she has just methodically trashed, passing a wall splashed in red paint with the warning "this house is not for sale," all the while apologizing for the general untidiness. In another memorable scene Frank questions the educational practices of his daughter's teachers. When he asks why they do not assign homework, he is told that that tradition is too "discriminatory," and that their goal is to keep the children happy. Attercliffe's set-to with the

authorities over what he perceives as slovenly educational standards is based directly on Storey's own protracted skirmishes from 1974 to 1976 with the board of a Hampstead Comprehensive School that his children attended. Storey won, forcing the school to require more homework and to more carefully evaluate students' classwork. These scenes of Sheila's fits of pique and Attercliffe's quarrel with school officials further demonstrate Storey's underrated comic talents, exhibiting the crisp dialogue that had previously won him high praise.

The novel nonetheless fails ultimately to live up to its initial promise, however. Most reviewers complained that the narrative soon turns into not much more than an endless rant against modern times (with such subjects as union demands, juvenile delinquency, lax school discipline, and the women's movement each receiving pointed attention). At the center of all stands the Job-like Frank, passively enduring the most vitriolic attacks. It is difficult not to grow impatient with his passivity as he is hit with an endless barrage of problems: his editor fires him; his best friend dies; his daughter brings home pot-smoking criminals, is arrested, and later moves in with prostitutes, drug dealers, and thieves; his crazed wife forces him out of his home; his other children join the accusing voices that blame him for the family's breakup. A *TLS* reviewer insisted that Storey "piles up Attercliffe's burdens with sadistic intent and masochistic relish" and argued that Storey's touch is "so heavy" that "any residual sympathy it might arouse keeps leaking away from Attercliffe's case because of the dementedness of its presentation. The argument is obviously, and unfairly, loaded, the general nastiness too clearly fixed, the wife and daughters too contrived and wooden in their horrid hostilities." Because of the stark absence of judgment from the narrator (much of the story is conveyed through passages of sustained dialogue), readers are left to ferret out for themselves what, exactly, motivates the characters and what, if any, political intentions lie buried in the text. The *TLS* reviewer proclaimed Frank's "extraordinary threnody of despair" to be a tract attacking "The Way Things Are Going for Middle-Aged White Men in Our Britain." A London *Times* reviewer was not so certain, and proposed only tenuously that the novel "might suggest" that Storey is "a zealot for the right-wing revival" of the 1980s. Storey admitted to a *Times* reporter in 1984 that "nearly every character is an idiot, trapped into living by some horrendous orthodoxy which they think is some glorious freedom." His narrative detachment in *Present Times* never allows readers to understand why these "idiots" adopt "horrendous orthodoxy," however, nor why they repeatedly target Frank for their abuse. As a result, they appear too histrionic and Frank too passive and whiny, so none ever compel sympathy.

As with *A Prodigal Child,* the ending of *Present Times* does not seem a logical outcome of the narrative. Attercliffe is the most morally attractive of all Storey's protagonists and seems to deserve a happy resolution to his problems. He does achieve success as a playwright with the production of his first effort, "Players" (a reincarnation of Storey's *The Changing Room*); and when Frank's daughter attends the premiere and his wife offers her congratulations, Storey seems to be suggesting the possibility of the family's coming together again. He offers no convincing signs, however, that this family will discard their ideological armor and stop harassing poor, stoic Frank or that the quality of his life will be substantially altered. Malcolm Pittock, in fact, saw the ending as the novel's "central failing," arguing that "when Attercliffe's luck changes, it changes not only dramatically but incredibly." Frank wins support for his educational reform ideas because the Morristown education committee is chaired by a former rugby player who admires Frank's old athletic exploits. Pittock added that when Attercliffe emerges as a successful dramatist, Storey "is not only moving into fairy-tale country but seriously damaging the novel. In terms of his theme it is necessary that Attercliffe should have a representative function. But an ex-provincial sports journalist who hits the jackpot with his first play . . . has no representative resonance at all." Thus, Pittock contended, an air of "improbability" hovers over the novel's ending.

Storey's only major book published between 1984 and 1997 was—to the surprise of his readers—a collection of poetry, *Storey's Lives: Poems 1951–1991* (1992). Occasionally he had cast individual poems into plays, as if they were the work of a given character, but no one expected the 275 pages of *Storey's Lives.* Written over a stretch of forty years, from his eighteenth to fifty-eighth year, the poems chronologically convey the trajectory of a life from youth nearly to old age, and in doing so form a rough sort of spiritual autobiography. He remarked in 1992 that writing the poems had been "extraordinarily therapeutic." *Storey's Lives* drew a largely negative appraisal from reviewers, though most found things to admire. A *Sunday Times* critic thought the poems "undeniably forceful—but more at the level of testimony than achieved work." A *Times Saturday Review* writer praised their "urgent and cohesive" nature but lamented their "inert vocabulary, obscurity, abstraction, embarrassing persistence with rhyme," and "general heaviness." At the least, these poems will have value in the light they shed on themes and motifs in Storey's plays and fiction.

Valerie Grove reported in 1996 that Storey claimed to have "binned about 30 plays," but his activity in the theater has been sparse since the early 1980s. Since 1981 only three of his previously unpublished plays have appeared in print—*Stages* (1992), *Caring,* (1992), and *Phoenix* (1993). (*Caring,* a Beckett-like one-act play, has never been produced.) The highlight for Storey in theater since the early 1980s may well have been the successful revival of *The Changing Room* at the Duke of York's Theatre in 1996, to mark the twenty-fifth anniversary of its opening at the Royal Court. By the early 1980s Storey was complaining that the Royal Court had lost interest in his new works, and that seems indeed so, *Mother's Day*—in 1976—having been his last play mounted on that stage. He grew increasingly disenchanted with British theater, telling Haffenden that in England the critics "seem to like didactic theatre, grim and humourless. They have an . . . intellectualizing approach, and don't approach theatre in terms of life and experience and feeling. There's a huge new philistinism in the approach to art in this country." Between 1981 and 1998 only three Storey dramas reached the stage: *Phoenix,* which played only in England's northern provinces after being premiered in 1984 by an amateur group; *The March on Russia,* which premiered in 1989 at the Lyttleton Theatre in the Royal National Theatre complex; and *Stages,* produced at the Cottesloe in 1992. Of these, only *The March on Russia* drew fairly good reviews.

Storey vented his frustration over the state of British theater and its general disregard for his work after the mid 1970s in *Phoenix.* The play is set in the northern provinces in the Phoenix Theatre, which has lost its government subsidy and is due to be demolished. Its artistic director, Alan Ashcroft, holes up there for the theater's final twenty-four hours. Like Storey's typical heroes, he is a miner's son, a boxer turned artist, a man beset by alcoholism and a myriad of personal problems (he has lost his wife, mistress, and home and faces prison on assault charges). He literally lives at the theater, sleeping on the stage. Ashcroft's diatribes make clear Storey's theme that the fate of England's subsidized theater lies in the hands of "philistines." The play ends with a spectacular onstage explosion set off by Ashcroft that demolishes the Phoenix in a hail of flying debris. This explosive conclusion seems to be an impressively unambiguous statement of what Storey thought about contemporary British theater.

The most recent staging of a new Storey play, that of *Stages* in 1992, is interesting not for the merit of the one-act play but for the direct relation it bears to his novel, *A Serious Man* (1998). The Cottesloe production—with Lindsay Anderson directing and Alan Bates starring—showed promise of being, as Benedict Nightingale wrote in *The New York Times,* "the play that regalvanizes a playwriting career that has been somewhat becalmed of late." Instead, the play drew nearly universal condemnation, with reviewers complaining variously that "it feels more like a poignant, meditative poem than a play," that it was a "closet drama" not accessible to a theater audience, that it was "an outpouring of obsessive melancholia . . . better suited to a psychiatric couch than a theater." Carole Woods of the Glasgow *Herald* thought it "would have made a much better novella." Perhaps Storey agreed that the material in *Stages* would work better in a different genre—at any rate, *A Serious Man* offers precisely the same protagonist, situations, and themes as those in *Stages*.

An *International Herald Tribune* review of *Stages* said it seemed "at times immensely autobiographical." Indeed, the tale of Richard Fenchurch—as dramatized in *Stages* and delineated in *A Serious Man*—does often seem to be Storey's own story: that of a working-class lad (son of a Yorkshire miner) who excels as an athlete; who works as a tent-erector to pay for art school; who suffers lingering guilt over his choice to become an artist in London and effectively to cut himself off from his parents and his northern roots; and who struggles upward to become a painter and an award-winning playwright and novelist. In both works this Storey-like protagonist has subsequently fallen out of fashion as an author and crashed into a midlife depression and writer's block (a psychiatrist in the novel tells him, "You're written out"). Beyond that—as is so often the case with Storey's art—it is dangerous to speculate how far the author's own life story extends into that of Fenchurch's.

In both play and novel Fenchurch is recovering from yet another mental breakdown and performs for all who will hear him an emotional postmortem, dissecting his family origins, his loves, the sacrifices made for his art, and all the various "stages" of his life that have led him into mental collapse. As much as any creative writer in history, Storey has evidenced a career-long fascination with madness and its representation in literature. The madness of the hero in *The Restoration of Arnold Middleton* anticipated the psychic disintegration of dozens of Storey's future characters in plays and novels. Storey's literary world is peopled with comic crazies who talk at cross-purposes, who collect bottles of their own urine, who go down on all fours and bark like dogs, and, much more frequently, with darkly tragic madmen who withdraw into lonely fantasy worlds. Few of these mad figures ever manage to retrieve any fragile sort of mental balance. Storey has denied having been influenced by the theories of British psychiatrist R.D. Laing—who reached a mass audience with such books as *The Divided Self: An Existential Study in Sanity and Madness* (1959)—but critics have often noted similarities between Laing's ideas and Storey's own understanding

and depiction of madness (Laing may be a model for the "celebrated" psychologist Mackendrick in *A Serious Man*). Laing has argued that the modern family often imposes on its members crippling, alienating psychological burdens that lead to madness, and Storey obviously has been obsessed with this theme throughout his career.

Readers are left to discern how much of his own psyche Storey has projected into his isolated, brooding protagonists, although it would seem to be a lot. His daughter, Helen, told the *Times* that as a child she tended to think her father "an extremely depressed person." In 1982 Storey told Haffenden: "I've never actually broken down myself, but I've projected my potential to do so into plays and novels. On a personal level, as an artist, I've always been able vividly to evoke that catastrophe, and I've witnessed it in friends and colleagues." A decade later he admitted to Morrison that at age forty-eight he had experienced "a mid-life crisis": "I'd wake each morning in a state of abject terror, anything could cause it—a fold in a curtain, a sound, a leaf on a tree." His wife, alarmed, sent him to a psychoanalyst, "but he pronounced me an unsuitable case for treatment," Storey said, adding, "I took a sort of pride in sweating it out and digging myself free and going on writing." Storey candidly admitted to Andro Linklater that Fenchurch's breakdowns in *Stages* were taken from his own life. Attempting to explain the origins of his emotional troubles, Storey traced them back to the trauma his mother suffered when his older brother, Neville, died unexpectedly at age six at a time when she was three months pregnant with him. The mother became suicidal, and Storey has told interviewers that he believed this tragedy somehow was imprinted upon his own embryonic nervous system and caused him to become a silent, morose child and a reclusive, melancholic adult. "I was born very depressed," he told Jasper Rees in July 1998. He said then that he experienced a sort of "catharsis" in 1987, in the days between his father's death and cremation. His father's apparition would visit him at night, he explained, and once, as they sat on a sofa, his father told him, "My life has been distressing, but it is at an end. The pain has gone and I'm happy." Storey said he then "had a powerful sense that I therefore need not suffer any more."

Much of this sense of relief is cast into both *Stages* and *A Serious Man*. Storey has given no indication which work he created first. In 1998 he told Rees that *A Serious Man* was written about 1986. He recounted how he has continued slaving over that "big work" that he began in 1962 and abandoned in 1967 (and from which he later extracted material that became *Pasmore* and *A Temporary Life*). He had found himself unable, in the 1960s, to

Dust jacket for Storey's 1984 novel, which focuses on the difficult familial relations between a retired football player, his former wife, and their teenaged daughters

make structural sense of that large work, so he laid it aside. "It just became a challenge to get it into some kind of shape," he told Rees. "About two years ago, I got it out again, having had well over 30 or 40 goes at it, and found a way of cutting through it. I was so relieved that I typed out this novel which I had finished 12 years ago."

At any rate, *Stages* and *A Serious Man* are both structured as extended reminiscences by the artist whose life has gone to pieces. *Stages* is basically an elegiac monologue by Fenchurch, interrupted by four women in his life (his daughter, his former wife, Bea, his psychiatrist, and a neighbor). Gradually he lays bare the secrets of his life, the stages of his plunge into despondency. In the course of his revelations he details a clandestine affair he has carried on passionately for almost thirty years with Bea's mother, Isabella Corrigan. (Bella has the same last name as Mrs. Fay Corrigan, the older woman whose affair with the young Bryan is central to *A Prodigal Child*.) Fenchurch first became mentally unhinged when his beloved Bella, at

age seventy-nine, died (just as Arnold Middleton's madness was caused in part by his relation to his sensual mother-in-law, Edie, though that situation is barely explored in that play). Fenchurch's latest breakdown is brought about by the suicide of his alcoholic mistress, Vivien ("Vivienne" in *A Serious Man*), who drank bleach. In the play and the novel, Fenchurch had met this woman when she auditioned for a film version of one of his novels. Bea, in an apparently vindictive act, had left him to marry a younger man (she was at the time fifty-one, the same age her mother was when she began her affair with the nineteen-year-old Richard).

Both play and novel offer an up-close portrait of the mind's fragility, as Fenchurch analyzes his bleak past—his guilt over how his father had to labor so hard in the pits while the son dabbled at the arts; his guilt over the affair with Bella and his broken marriage to Bea; his failed union with Vivien/Vivienne; his realization of the sacrifices he has made in love and in life to his art; his pique over the "philistinism" of the British audience toward his writings, and the marked dropping off of his reputation as fewer and fewer of his works have been made available by publishers and theaters; and the writer's block that has accompanied his dark depressions.

The big question posed in *Stages* is whether or not Fenchurch should give up his London home and return to Yorkshire to live with his daughter in the house that had once belonged to Bea's parents. His daughter, his former wife, a psychiatrist, and a neighbor encourage him to make the move north, but he remains obstinately immovable, and as the play ends he dances frenziedly, declaiming poetry fragments as he obviously heads for deeper "blacknesses." He rejects seeking help and refuses to go north.

By way of Fenchurch's recollections, *A Serious Man* rehearses with greater detail virtually every theme, motif, character, and plot situation presented in *Stages,* and the novel's opening could be taken as the play's next act—with Fenchurch having finally given in and accompanied his daughter Etty back to her Yorkshire home. Fenchurch is now sixty-five (Storey's own age in 1998), six years older than the Fenchurch of *Stages* (Storey had been fifty-nine when that play was produced). His long-suffering daughter has brought him north in hopes that he will heal, that the place will help "re-animate those areas of [his] mind that previously existed." She had become alarmed that he was living alone in a London "hovel" and that his behavior had grown increasingly erratic. Fenchurch relates, "I've been ill; how ill I can't recall." He can recall how, for years, he has been "in and out" of mental hospitals, how he has seen many psychiatrists in visits that "have not done me, on the whole, a lot of good." His melancholia had intensified with the death of his second wife, Vivienne, who killed herself because (as he tells Etty): "The pain . . . became too much. More . . . than people like you, with humdrum jobs and humdrum minds (with humdrum feelings and humdrum reflections) can possibly imagine." Etty has brought him back to the home where he once courted Bea and, intermittently for three decades, carried on an intense affair with Isabella Corrigan, whom he now acknowledges as his muse and as the love of his life. It is a house full of old memories, just as *A Serious Man* is a novel full of old memories. Fenchurch constantly rehearses these memories—especially recalling his relationship with Bella—as he pads about the house and the former mining community, talking to himself, talking about himself to all within earshot, to Etty and to strangers he encounters at bus stops, in shops, and on the golf course. His notebooks and old love letters spill out into the novel, and he often quotes his own award-winning works as he buttonholes strangers to talk about his art, the failures of the British working class, education, and many other "things that

count." His mind flows constantly in and out of the past—resurrecting old conversations that intrude on present ones, telescoping events and people from his younger days into his present interactions—and his narrative thus demands intense concentration by readers who must track the path of his meandering mind.

Etty reminds him that he has been told "not to dwell in the past," but that is precisely what Fenchurch does throughout the 359 pages of his rolling monologue in *A Serious Man*. This choice of material for the novel seems particularly interesting in light of what British critic Malcolm Pittock had argued in his 1988 essay "Storey at the Crossroads," that Storey in both drama and novel had reached a creative cul-de-sac because of his inability "to emancipate himself from a preoccupation with his own past." Pittock noted that the title of *Present Times* indicated a desire by Storey "to make a decisive break with the past" but argued that the novelist failed in that effort, creating "implausibilities" and problems in his narrative by transferring the Attercliffe family's London experiences to Storey's familiar old territory of Yorkshire/Wakefield. The "obsessional relationship" Storey has to his native area, Pittock contended, may "be a sign of the existence in [the author] himself of an area of personal experience with which he has not finally come to terms." Pittock questioned "whether Storey has a creative future in the novel." For a decade Pittock's observation—that Storey had reached a crossroads beyond which he might never go with his art—seemed prophetic. Storey expressed anxiety over the ebbing of his powers in his poem "Return," when he wrote: "The old fires / that went with creativity / have gone." *A Serious Man* demonstrates well that the old fires still burned effectively in Storey, however, as he answered Pittock and his other critics by successfully creating an entire novel filled with little more than an intense preoccupation with his own past—or at the least with that of his creation, Fenchurch.

Much of the fascination of *A Serious Man* lies in the frequent expressions of Fenchurch's opinions regarding art and its value to society. Fenchurch voices his aversions to art used as a commodity, to art lecturers who tried to get him and other students to design record sleeves and "useful" art. He laments the irrelevance of art in the lives of the working classes he came from. He attacks the "philistines" who dictate the offerings of modern theaters and tells Etty, "The novel is dead: at least in its humanist tradition—and I have died with it." In response she encourages him: "You're not old enough to give up!" Elsewhere Etty criticizes the absence of political awareness or engagement in his writings, telling him that for this reason "those theorists . . . despise your work." Readers have come to his writings, she says, "looking for an appetite for change—even revolution" but found none there. As he defends his work as an art of "revelation" rather than of revolution, one can easily suspect that all this has deep resonance not only in Fenchurch's life and art but in Storey's as well. Throughout *A Serious Man* Storey seems to be addressing–through Fenchurch's rambling discourse– what he views as his problematic relationship with his audience in the years since he had been perhaps the most celebrated playwright and novelist of his time.

A Serious Man poses not only the question of whether or not Fenchurch can be healed, but also whether or not he should be–whether or not his madness is for him a necessary mode of survival in that world of people with "humdrum jobs and humdrum minds (with humdrum feelings and humdrum reflections)" that he so loathes. At any rate, he ends up back in the south, having achieved in his return north a certain measure of reconciliation with his past. ("Don't you see I've come full circle?" he tells Etty, as he announces his intention to return to London.) There is no way of knowing if he will indeed be able to live on his own, as he is determined to do, free of psychiatric drugs and no longer facing inevitable reinternment in a mental hospital, nor if he can marshal his scattered mental resources enough to again create great art with the blank canvasses and sheets of paper he faces once he is back home in the south.

A Serious Man was greeted with more widespread enthusiasm from British reviewers than any Storey novel since *Saville*. Most warmly welcomed his return to the novel after a fourteen-year gap, and many recognized it as his best work since he won the Booker Prize in 1976. *A Serious Man* was hailed as an "unmistakably important book" *(Sunday Times)*, "a major novel and a genuine work of art" *(The Times)*, a "splendid, many-layered novel" "as powerful as anything he has written" *(The Independent)*. With its deliberately disjointed, digressive narration, it is a difficult book to read–following Fenchurch through his tangled thicket of depression and mental collapse is not easy–but nearly every reviewer agreed with Allan Massie's appraisal in *The Scotsman* that "there is so much that is rewarding and satisfying in this novel that the demands made by Storey on his readers are ultimately justified."

Storey has mentioned his work on a philosophical book about the structure of the psyche and has also given strong indications that at long last he is near completion of that "big work" of fiction he began in 1962. No matter what his future holds, he has left a powerful mark on British literature of the second half of the twentieth century. Critics have recently increased their scrutiny of his work, making it the subject of three substantial critical books and of several dozen graduate theses. At the least Storey will likely be remembered, with

Edward Bond, as the leading playwright of what has been called the "second wave" of contemporary British drama. *The Changing Room, Home,* and *The Contractor* will long be respected for the impact they had on theater in the early 1970s, and the play that many of his readers most admire, *In Celebration,* has been translated into more than thirty languages and staged successfully in various countries. *Saville* remains his most highly acclaimed fiction thus far, though many readers still prefer the raw, powerfully evocative depiction of working-class life in his first novel, *This Sporting Life,* which Storey began writing during those lonely London-to-Yorkshire train rides.

Interviews:

Special Correspondent, "Speaking of Writing–II: David Storey," *Times* (London), 28 November 1963, p. 15;

Bernard Bergonzi, "Novelists of the Sixties," Programme 1, BBC, 20 February 1968;

Brendan Hennessy, "David Storey Interviewed by Brendan Hennessy," *Transatlantic Review,* 33–34 (1969): 5–11;

Michael Billington, "Making Life Work on Two Levels," *Times* (London), 4 April 1970, p. 21;

Ronald Hayman, "Conversation with David Storey," *Drama* (Winter 1970): 47–53;

Martha Duffy, "An Ethic of Work and Play," *Sports Illustrated,* 38 (5 March 1973): 66–82;

Mel Gussow, "To David Storey, A Play Is a 'Holiday,'" *New York Times,* 20 April 1973, p. 14;

Peter Ansorge, "The Theatre of Life: David Storey in Interview with Peter Ansorge," *Plays and Players* (September 1973): 32–36;

Victor Sage, "David Storey in Conversation," *New Review* (October 1976): 63–65;

Frances Gibb, "Why David Storey Has Got It In For Academics, the Critics, and 'Literary Whizz-Kids,'" *Times Higher Education Supplement* (London), 2 February 1977, p. D9;

Gussow, "Talk with David Storey, Playwright and Novelist," *New York Times Book Review,* 28 August 1977, p. 11;

Peter Stothard, "Right in a Class of His Own: The Times Profile: David Storey," *Times* (London), 3 May 1984, p. 10;

John Haffenden, "David Storey," in his *Novelists in Interview* (London: Methuen, 1985), pp. 262–280;

Michael Cable, "Top Storeys," *Times* (London), 21 October 1990, pp. 13, 16;

Blake Morrison, "Interview: This Writing Life," *The Independent* (London), 15 March 1992, p. 25;

Andro Linklater, "The Outsiders," *Daily Telegraph Magazine* (London), 7 November 1992, p. 128;

Jeremy Kingston, "Waiting to Hear a Storey," *Times* (London), 16 November 1992, p. 35;

Caroline Boucher, "How We Met," interview with Storey and Lindsay Anderson, *The Independent* (London), 6 December 1992, p. 77;

Peter Lewis, "Profile: This Writing Life," *Sunday Times* (London), 19 June 1994, pp. 6–7;

Valerie Grove, "The Valerie Grove Interview: Why David Storey has decided he never wants to go back to the North again," *Times* (London), 9 February 1996, p. 15;

Jasper Rees, "The Last of the Angry Young Men," *Independent* (London), 14 July 1998, p. 10.

References:

James Gindin, *Postwar British Fiction: New Accents and Attitudes* (Berkeley & Los Angeles: University of California Press, 1962), pp. 96–104;

William Hutchings, *The Plays of David Storey: A Thematic Study* (Carbondale & Edwardsville: Southern Illinois University Press, 1988);

Hutchings, ed., *David Storey: A Casebook* (New York & London: Garland, 1992);

Herbert Liebman, *The Dramatic Art of David Storey: The Journey of a Playwright* (Westport, Conn.: Greenwood Press, 1996);

Frank McGuiness, "The Novels of David Storey," *London Magazine,* 3 (March 1974): 79–83;

John Mellors, "Yorkshire Relish: The Novels of John Braine and David Storey," *London Magazine,* 16 (October–November 1976): 79–84;

Malcolm Pittock, "David Storey and *Saville:* A Revaluation," *Forum for Modern Language Studies,* 32, no. 3 (1996): 208–227;

Pittock, "Revaluing the Sixties: *This Sporting Life* Revisited," *Forum for Modern Language Studies,* 26, no. 2 (1990): 96–108;

Pittock, "Storey as Poet," *Cambridge Quarterly,* 22, no. 4 (1993): 370–382;

Pittock, "Storey at the Crossroads," *Cambridge Quarterly,* 17, no. 3 (1988): 203–221;

Pittock, "Storey's *Radcliffe,*" *Durham University Journal* (June 1991): 235–248;

Jonathan Raban, "Howarth," in his *The Technique of Modern Fiction: Essays in Practical Criticism* (London: Arnold, 1968), pp. 173–179;

John Russell Taylor, *David Storey,* Writers and Their Work 239, edited by Ian Scott-Kilvert (London: Longman, 1974).

D. M. Thomas

(27 January 1935 –)

Jago Morrison
Leeds Metropolitan University

See also the Thomas entry in *DLB 40: Poets of Great Britain and Ireland Since 1960.*

BOOKS: *Personal and Possessive* (Walton-on-Thames, U.K.: Outposts, 1964);

Two Voices (London: Cape Goliard, 1968; New York: Viking, 1968);

Modern Poets 11, by Thomas, D. M. Black, and Peter Redgrove (Harmondsworth, U.K.: Penguin, 1968; Baltimore: Penguin, 1968);

Lover's Horoscope: Kinetic Poem (London: Purple Sage, 1970);

Logan Stone (London: Cape Goliard, 1971; New York: Viking, 1971);

The Shaft (Gillingham, U.K.: Arc, 1973);

Symphony in Moscow (Richmond, U.K.: Keepsake, 1974);

Lilith-Prints (Cardiff, U.K.: Second Aeon, 1974);

Love and Other Deaths (London: Elek, 1975);

The Rock (Knotting, U.K.: Sceptre, 1975);

Orpheus in Hell (Knotting, U.K.: Sceptre, 1977);

The Honeymoon Voyage (London: Secker & Warburg, 1978);

The Devil and the Floral Dance (London: Robson, 1978);

The Flute-Player (London: Gollancz, 1979; New York: Dutton, 1979);

Protest: A Poem after a Medieval Armenian Poem by Frik (Hereford, U.K.: Thomas, 1980);

Birthstone (London: Gollancz, 1980; New York: Viking, 1980);

The White Hotel (London: Gollancz, 1981; New York: Viking, 1981);

Dreaming in Bronze (London: Secker & Warburg, 1981);

Selected Poems (London: Secker & Warburg, 1983; New York: Viking, 1983);

News from the Front, text by Thomas and Sylvia Kantaris (Todmorden, U.K.: Arc, 1983);

Ararat (London: Gollancz, 1983; New York: Viking, 1983);

Swallow (London: Gollancz, 1984; New York: Viking, 1984);

D. M. Thomas at the time of The White Hotel *(photograph by Joyce Ravid)*

Sphinx (London: Gollancz, 1986; New York: Viking, 1987);

Summit (London: Gollancz, 1987; New York: Viking, 1988);

Memories and Hallucinations (London: Gollancz, 1988; New York: Viking, 1988);

The Red River, by Thomas, Frank Turk, and Jan Ruhrmund (Manchester, U.K.: Cornerhouse, 1989);

Lying Together (London: Gollancz, 1990: New York: Viking, 1990);

The Puberty Tree and Selected Poems (Newcastle-upon-Tyne, U.K.: Bloodaxe, 1992)

Flying in to Love (London: Bloomsbury, 1992; New York: Scribners, 1992);

Pictures at an Exhibition (London: Bloomsbury, 1993; New York: Scribners, 1993);

Eating Pavlova (London: Bloomsbury, 1994; New York: Carroll & Graf, 1994);

Lady with a Laptop (New York: Carroll & Graf, 1996);

Alexander Solzhenitsyn: A Century in His Life (London: Little, Brown, 1998; New York: St. Martin's Press, 1998).

OTHER: *The Granite Kingdom: Poems of Cornwall,* edited by Thomas (Truro, U.K.: Barton, 1970);

Poetry in Crosslight, edited by Thomas (London: Longman, 1975; New York: Longman, 1975);

Anna Akhmatova, *Requiem and Poem without a Hero,* translated by Thomas (London: Elek, 1976; Athens: Ohio University Press, 1976);

John Harris, *Poems from the Earth: Selected Poems of John Harris, Cornish Miner 1820–84,* edited, with an introduction, by Thomas (Padstow, U.K.: Lodenek, 1977);

Akhmatova, *Way of All The Earth,* translated by Thomas (London: Secker & Warburg, 1979; Athens: Ohio University Press, 1979);

Yevgeny Yevtushenko, *Invisible Threads,* translated by Thomas (Basingstoke, U.K.: Macmillan, 1981);

Alexander Pushkin, *The Bronze Horseman and Other Poems,* translated, with an introduction, by Thomas (London: Secker & Warburg, 1982; New York: Viking, 1982);

Yevtushenko, *A Dove in Santiago: A Novella in Verse,* translated by Thomas (London: Secker & Warburg, 1982; New York: Viking, 1982);

Akhmatova, *You Will Hear Thunder: Poems,* translated by Thomas (London: Secker & Warburg, 1985; Athens: Ohio University Press, 1985); republished as *Selected Poems* (Harmondsworth, U.K.: Penguin, 1988);

Pushkin, *Boris Godunov,* translated by Thomas (Leamington Spa, U.K.: Sixth Chamber, 1985);

Sandi Felman, *The Japanese Tattoo,* introduction by Thomas (New York: Abbeville, 1986).

Within contemporary British literature D. M. Thomas stands as a novelist, poet, translator, and biographer of distinction as well as a figure of considerable controversy. Early in his career he was honored with the Translator's Award of the British Arts Council for his work on the Soviet poet Anna Akhmatova. He also received the Chomondeley Award for poetry in 1978, and his first novel, *The Flute-Player* (1979), gained him substantial recognition with the Guardian-Gollancz Fantasy Novel Award. *The White Hotel* (1981), which remains Thomas's most important literary achievement, was the recipient of both the Cheltenham Prize and the *Los Angeles Times* Book Award in 1981. Nominated for the Booker Prize, *The White Hotel* established Thomas's literary reputation and shocked the British literary establishment to its roots. The novel was passed over for Britain's most prestigious literary award in favor of Salman Rushdie's *Midnight's Children,* which a decade and a half later won the prestigious "Booker of Bookers." Works by Thomas have been translated into twenty languages.

The emergence of *The White Hotel* brought with it not only a good deal of popular acclaim, including features in *Time* and *Newsweek,* but also a flood of controversy from which Thomas has never been able to separate himself. In his earlier work he had already shown himself to be fundamentally concerned with the interrelationship of death and sex. However, Thomas's presentation of Holocaust testimony directly alongside passages of lurid sexual fantasy in *The White Hotel* almost inevitably became the subject of intense debate when the novel became a best-seller in the United States. While Thomas's work continued throughout the 1980s to pursue provocative and sexual subject matter, it was more than a decade before his distinctive engagement with Freudian analysis and the legacy of the Holocaust were seriously addressed again, in *Pictures at an Exhibition* (1993) and *Eating Pavlova* (1994). Where *The White Hotel* had publicly announced Thomas as a novelist of immense promise and literary daring, however, the judgment of some critics was that *Pictures at an Exhibition* had crossed the line into pornography and exploitation. Such accusations and their denial have been a constant and fascinating feature of Thomas's reception as a major British novelist.

In the twelve years that separated the publication of *The White Hotel* and *Pictures at an Exhibition,* Thomas produced the five novels that together constitute his "Russian Nights" sequence. Focusing on improvisation and storytelling, these novels most strongly reflect the writer's great passion for Russian literature. In 1982 he published a translation of Alexander Pushkin's verse collection *The Bronze Horseman and Other Poems* and in 1985 a new edition of *Boris Godunov.* Pushkin's work is also a constant influence on Thomas's "Russian Nights" novels. Crowning his achievements as a translator of Russian writers, Thomas published a major biography of Alexander Solzhenitsyn in 1998, once again to widespread critical acclaim.

Donald Michael Thomas was born in Redruth, Cornwall, on 27 January 1935, the son of Harold Redvers, a builder, and Amy (née Moyles). He was educated at Redruth Grammar School and subsequently at the University High School in Melbourne, Australia. After a period of national service he attended New College, Oxford, where he was awarded a first-class honors degree in English in 1958 and an M.A. in 1961. He has been married and divorced twice and has two sons, Sean and Ross, and a daughter, Caitlin.

After many years in Hereford and Oxford, Thomas now lives in Truro, Cornwall, with his second wife, Denise. Although the couple are no longer married they continue to live together, just as Thomas did with his first wife, Maureen, after their divorce. Throughout the course of both these relationships, he is candid about the regularity of his extramarital affairs, from a young girl pupil at the school where he worked in Devon in his late twenties, to the family hairdresser. Despite these various intimacies, he professes to being a reticent man whose writing has often kept him occupied in his study to the almost total exclusion of family life. Indeed, his son Sean's own novel of 1996 is tellingly entitled *Absent Fathers*. The scope of Thomas's writing process—he has produced a novel most years throughout the last two decades, as well as poetry collections and translations—is reflected in the complex structure and intensity of many of the texts themselves. In their different ways each of Thomas's writing projects has been intellectually provocative, often appropriating ideas and texts from other writers in new and challenging combinations.

In 1988, after a long period of intellectual exertion, Thomas suffered a nervous breakdown and other health problems from which he was not to recover for months. His son Sean's arrest and trial for rape in the period immediately following left other scars, although the experience of visiting and supporting his son in detention during his period of remand led for the first time to a close and productive relationship between them. Despite such setbacks, Thomas has reemerged in the mid 1990s as a writer of wit, invention, and continued renown.

Growing up in the 1930s and 1940s, Thomas was a plump, awkward child who played truant from school and had difficulty with sports. Relatively speaking, World War II had limited direct effect on Thomas's family. Perhaps the most deeply shocking and life-changing experience of the war for him was seeing news footage of the survivors of Belsen.

At the age of fourteen, sharing a cabin below the waterline with his father and four other men, Thomas immigrated to Australia. Despite a difficult adjustment, Thomas and his father were committed to working for two years in repayment for their free passages. This period was one of rapid maturation for Thomas. On the long voyage he had been exposed for the first time to adult reading material, and his first experience with female peers in school in Perth was an affecting one. In his poetry collections two decades later he still recalls the poignancy of his feelings for the young schoolgirls. Indeed, *Two Voices* (1968) in particular displays an explicitness about desires and encounters with girls that jeopardized Thomas's position as a schoolmaster when it was published in 1968.

From the beginning of his career the ideas that have prompted Thomas to write have often been disturbing and unusual. Thomas's introduction to using the Russian language was an unusual one. During his two years of national service in the latter half of the 1950s, he was chosen for training in the interrogation of Russian prisoners of war. His first interrogation ended abruptly with a linguistic mistake. Demanding to know the subject's rank, he confused a crucial word, substituting *chlyen* for *cheen*—inadvertently he had inquired instead about the state of the subject's genitals. Despite these unlikely beginnings, the study of Russian language and culture and the literary exploration of death and sexual attraction can be identified as the great intellectual passions of Thomas's life. After leaving the army, his first serious attempts at writing were as an undergraduate at New College, Oxford. As a working-class student, however, he was never fully at ease in the Oxford environment, and it was not until his period of teacher training in Plymouth that his own inspiration can be said to have shown itself. For Thomas this inspiration was the disturbing sight of a young girl involved in a car accident. As he writes in *Memories and Hallucinations* (1988): "I felt a prickly sensation at my nape. I knew suddenly, I wanted to be a poet, more than anything else."

Thomas's first novel, *The Flute-Player,* clearly draws on Russian literature and culture and especially on the work of Anna Akhmatova. Three years before the novel appeared he had already published a translation of Akhmatova's *Requiem and Poem Without a Hero* (1976), and in 1979 a translation of *Way of All the Earth* was published within a few months of the novel. Thomas's remarkable confidence in his subject matter was shown by the fact that, by his own account, *The Flute-Player* was completed in as little as two or three hundred hours of work. Despite being unconventional by the standards of the fantasy novel—its setting is both Leningrad and everywhere, both real and imaginary—Thomas's first serious attempt at writing fiction was rewarded with the Gollancz Fantasy Novel Prize.

The main thematic concerns of *The Flute-Player,* literature, sex, and death, are ones to which Thomas has returned in different forms throughout his writing career. Its main character, Elena, is a passive protagonist who suffers and witnesses the sexual and political violence around her. Thomas sets the novel in a totalitarian regime where food rationing, street violence, and summary justice are as common as the sound of jackboots on the stairs at night.

Elena is the receptacle not only for a succession of men's desires but also for their hatred. Early in the novel she is raped by the janitor of her apartment block and, later, arrested and subjected to sexual torture by government security agents. After a change of regime, Elena's image clutching a baby appears on posters throughout the city, as an official exhortation to motherhood. Indeed, the book is full of such reversals. At the same time, the boundaries between narration, memory, and dreams are deliberately blurred and unstable.

If the novel does hold out one overriding conviction apart form the horror of totalitarianism, it is that of the power and value of the written word. Elena is a vehicle not only for physical love and hatred but also for literature. Although she lacks any deep intellectual understanding of poetry herself, she offers up her memory for the preservation of the poetry of her friend Michael and other endangered literary figures. Thus ultimately Elena is presented as both the muse and medium of their writing. Such passive, damaged your women figure prominently in Thomas's later writing, particularly in *The White Hotel.*

Between 1960 and 1979 Thomas worked as a lecturer at Hereford College of Education, rising steadily to a senior lectureship and finally to head of the literature department, writing poetry for publication in his spare time. With the end of the Labour administration of the late 1970s and the dawn of Thatcherism, governmental budget cuts initiated a protracted period of decline before the college finally closed in 1979. Encouraged by the success of *The Flute-Player,* Thomas wrote *Birthstone* (1980), partly as an escape from the realities of working life. *Birthstone* began as a collaboration with the poet Elizabeth Ashworth. As Thomas's professional situation worsened and the closure of the college loomed, however, he became increasingly emotionally attached to the project. The partnership became more and more strained. When Ashworth withdrew, Thomas continued on his own. Nevertheless, this second attempt at fiction was not an easy undertaking. In *Memories and Hallucinations* he remembers that "like an inexperienced, panicky cook, I threw every ingredient I could think of into the pot. The result was an over-flavoured, indigestible dish, even after a second attempt at it."

The novel revolves around a woman, Jo, who meets Californians Lola and Hector while on a coach holiday in Cornwall. High on the Penwith Moors they arrive at the Birthstone, a Bronze Age *men-an-tol* (a Cornish "stone with a hole") credited with great healing powers for anyone who might dare to crawl through its narrow central hole. After doing so the frail and elderly Lola begins to undergo an amazing process of rejuvenation. For Hector, on the other hand, the aging process seems to be radically accelerated. In shaping the characters of Lola and Hector, Thomas draws explicitly on his parents' early life together in California. The central character of Jo, however, is less easy to pin down. Thomas adds a further, complex dimension to the story by revealing Jo to be only one of a lengthening list of multiple personalities. More radically even than Elena's in *The Flute-Player,* Jo's life is constantly encroached on by others, especially the dominating presence of her male alter ego, Joe, who seduces women and gets in trouble with the police, and another female personality, Joanne, whose sexual exploits with the local priest are an increasing source of embarrassment.

As Thomas has admitted, *Birthstone* attempts to juggle with too many thematic elements to achieve adequate focus and coherence. From the beginning an analogy is made between literary creation and psychic instability, and the novel's unstable form may be seen partly as an attempt to explore this notion. As Jo suggests, "creative power seemed a compensation given to all disintegrated personalities." Not until Thomas's next and best novel, *The White Hotel,* however, was this nexus of ideas explored with real effectiveness and insight.

After the publication of *The Flute-Player* and *Birthstone,* and with the closure of the college to which he had devoted a part of his life, Thomas decided to make a virtue of necessity and return to Oxford University. There he worked on a B.Litt. thesis on translating Pushkin under the supervision of John Bailey. At Oxford many of the disparate elements and ideas that were to form *The White Hotel* began to come together. He began to return again to adolescent dreams and fantasies. In his younger years he had been repeatedly troubled and excited by a dream of a girl sitting opposite him in a railway carriage. Later, traveling home during his teacher training, exactly the same scenario had repeated itself in real life. As Thomas left the train, the girl had leaned out of the window and called out to him that she wished he would go with her on holiday to Sweden. For years he regretted his decision not to jump back on the train.

At Oxford, Thomas read Sigmund Freud and C. G. Jung, applying their psychoanalytic insights to new and muddled dreams of journeys and hotels. In his poetry during this time, especially "The House of Dreams" and "The Woman to Sigmund Freud," it is possible to see the development of themes and ideas that finally find full expression in *The White Hotel.* The

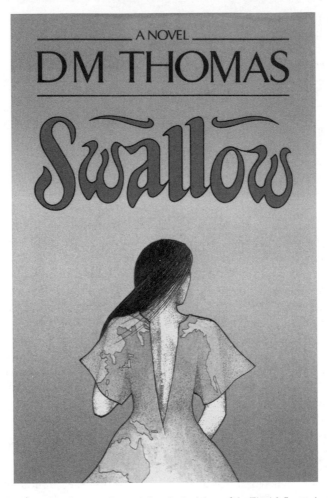

Dust jacket for Thomas's 1984 novel, set against the backdrop of the Finnish Improvisation Olympics

latter poem is in fact a direct creative response to a specific case of Freud's in which a young woman claimed to be having an affair with Freud's son. The poem is framed essentially around four elements: water, fire, earth, and air. The sexual experience of the speaker is thus interwoven with four elements of natural disaster—first the flooding and then the burning of the hotel, then a fatal avalanche, and finally the image of airborne skiers falling to their deaths from a cable car.

With a modest reputation already established, in 1980 Thomas arranged a two-week reading tour in the United States. It was by chance at the beginning of this trip that he discovered Anatoli Kuznetsov's *Babi Yar* (1970). Reading Kuznetsov's treatment of the Babi Yar Massacre of 1941, he was both horrified and moved. In Freud's work he had become fascinated by the interrelationship between Eros and Thanatos, the pleasure principle and the death drive. Together, all these themes began to form a compelling unity. In the Nazi atrocity at Babi Yar, Thomas already perceived the same the-

matic elements: victims fired upon and falling to their deaths, the covering of bodies with earth, and the final flooding of the Babi Yar gorge under Kiev's Soviet administration.

Thomas used "The Woman to Sigmund Freud" with limited revision as part 1 of the novel. Mindful of the effects of plunging readers immediately into this erotic verse fantasy, however, he decided to preface the novel with a series of fictitious letters between Freud, Jung, and other contemporary figures, outlining the circumstances of a young woman patient called "Frau Anna" for the purposes of analysis.

After these letters, Frau Anna's poem, entitled "Don Giovanni," follows as part 1 and is itself followed by an elaboration in prose of the same erotic and violent fantasy in part 2. In each of the two texts the young woman, an opera singer, meets a recently demobilized soldier on a train. As the train empties, the intimacy between them increases; their caresses are interrupted only when the woman's hair is set on fire by the young man's cigarette. They decide to interrupt their respective journeys with a few days together at a white hotel beside a mountain lake. Both accounts of this sojourn are filled with explicit sexual description, punctuated regularly by images of death and of the natural disasters that surround the couple. In Thomas's surrealistic presentation of the white hotel, death and sexual pleasure are presented as disturbing coextensions of each other.

In part 3, "Frau Anna G.," Freud meditates on the development of her case and on the verse and prose fantasies that she has submitted as part of her therapy. Frau Anna's case is outlined and readers are presented with its key documents before being privileged to participate in Freud's analysis. Thus, this section of the novel works to put the reader in the position of psychoanalyst. Indeed, one aspect of *The White Hotel* that was widely admired by critics is the authenticity of its portrayal of Freud and his methods. As Paul Ableman suggested in the *Spectator* (17 January 1981), "the document is so finely-attuned to the style of the founder of psychoanalysis that it seems merely fortuitous that 'Anna G.' never occupied the famous couch in the Berggasse."

Thomas's own admiration for Freud's work is beyond doubt. In his foreword he gives Freudian psychoanalysis the status of science. At the same time he also sees Freud's cases as stories of seduction: "A troubled young woman came in and lay down on a couch; Freud, his cigar flaring, got to work on her, striving to strip her naked. Day after day the struggle went on, behind closed doors. Her powerful resistance made it all the more exciting. At long last, and quite unexpectedly, he broke through, drawing blood from the hymen. She writhed, panted, fought, but he went inexorably on. Afterwards, bruised, weeping, she talked it over with him. He began to lose interest."

Part 3 of *The White Hotel* follows exactly this pattern. Freud slowly draws painful memories and realizations from his subject concerning her mother's death and adultery, the sexual assault she suffered in her teens at the hands of anti-Semitic sailors, and her homosexuality. After the patient Anna (now identified as a Russian Jewish singer, Lisa Erdman) has completed her therapy with Freud, the novel continues as a narrative of her subsequent life and involvement in Russian opera. Inexorably her premonitions of death draw nearer as the narrative approaches the era of Nazism and her execution at Babi Yar. She finds herself being herded with thousands of other Jews from their ghetto in Kiev toward the Babi Yar gorge. In this penultimate section much of Thomas's prose is lifted directly from the testimony of the only survivor of the massacre, Dina Pronicheva, which is included in Kuznetsov's book. As Thomas explained, "my unique character, Lisa, was now becoming a part of history, part of the amorphous mass of victims. So I wanted the events to be authentic. It would have seemed immoral had I, a comfortable Briton, fictionalised the holocaust." Protesting that she is a German housewife caught up by mistake, Lisa is allowed by the soldiers to withdraw to a hill within the compound, a vantage point from which she is able, like Pronicheva, to witness the full horror and extent of the massacre. Then, as a dangerous witness to the atrocity, she is led to the brink of the gorge and machine-gunned. Later, lying paralyzed among the heap of corpses, her death comes finally from a soldier's bayonet in an obscene refiguring of events at the white hotel. Swerving from such a bleak and disturbing ending, the novel concludes with a further section featuring a reunion of the dead, including Lisa and her mother, in an afterlife landscape that seems simultaneously to be both purgatory and Palestine.

Perhaps because of its daring and unusual form and thematic content, initial critical reactions to *The White Hotel* in Britain were less than enthusiastic, with accusations both of plagiarism and pornography. In the United States, however, the overall reaction was different. In *The Nation* (2 May 1981), for example, Thomas Flanagan hailed the novel as "a book of extraordinary beauty, power and audacity—powerful and beautiful in its conception, audacious in its manner of execution." For Flanagan *The White Hotel* was "as stunning a work of fiction as has appeared in a long while."

With the auction of publication rights for *The White Hotel* in the United States the financial rewards of Thomas's fiction began to be significant. All the more surprising, then, was perhaps the choice of his next writing project. The popularity of *The White Hotel* had not yet crested in 1983 when Thomas published the first of a series that eventually extended to five novels, collectively entitled "Russian Nights." The choice of improvisation as the subject matter for this quintet appeared to be a much more conventional and approachable starting point for fiction writing than the multiform and fragmented structure of *The White Hotel.* Nevertheless, none of these novels received anything like the critical recognition accorded to that work. Even so, the writing of the series occupied Thomas's energies for almost the whole of the 1980s.

The first novel, *Ararat* (1983), sets out to elucidate the idea of improvisation. Like a series of Russian dolls, each one waiting for discovery inside the shell of another, *Ararat* consists of a series of narrative layers. Set in the early 1980s, it begins with an arranged meeting between a distinguished poet, Sergei Rozanov, and a blind research student, Olga, who is writing a thesis on his work. After an awkward episode of lovemaking, the poet begins at her suggestion to improvise a story on the theme of improvisations. His story features three writers who meet at a writers' congress. Each tries to outdo the others with their skill in improvised storytelling. A competition begins on the theme of "Ararat." Already two sublayers of narrative have been enveloped within the frame of the novel. The first of Rozanov's improvisatores, Victor Surkov, is a character who frequently reappears throughout the novel sequence. In Surkov's improvisation (introducing yet another narrative layer) he imagines himself as Pushkin, just then beginning to write his tale "Egyptian Nights," in which Cleopatra offers a night of love in return for death. In a curious return to the real, part of *Ararat* is therefore taken up with Thomas's own translation of Pushkin's unfinished story. In the novel "Egyptian Nights" is completed in two different ways, one of which involves the murder of Pushkin himself. In a further complication, Surkov's improvisation is later appropriated as a drunken dream within the improvisation of the next competitor. Increasingly, the reader must struggle against the mounting threat of disorientation.

Thomas's complex fascination with improvisation can be traced on one level to his family roots in Cornwall. According to a family legend, his great-great-grandmother was seduced as a young woman by a charming Italian improvisatore, who later abandoned her with two daughters. Thus by a direct genetic tie Thomas claims connection to the great Italian tradition of improvisation.

In the opening of the second "Russian Nights" novel, *Swallow* (1984), the improvisation theme is extended further. Again the opening is a sexual encounter, this time between an Italian improvisatore, Corinna, and a young Japanese boy whose death immediately follows. This opening sequence is revealed to be a dream of Corinna's, who is preparing to compete in the Finnish Improvisation Olympics. Initially it appears that *Swallow* is going to be a straightforward rerun of *Ararat*. Instead, *Ararat* is itself enfolded within the narrative as Corinna's own competition entry. This repetition of *Ararat* in a female voice can be seen partly as Thomas's response to critical attacks on the earlier novel for its apparently male-chauvinistic and exploitative portrayal of women. As Thomas says in "Thinking about Women" (*TLS: The Times Literary Supplement*, 3–9 June 1988), "had a woman writer, such as Fay Weldon, written the novel, I feel sure she would have been praised for showing what scoundrels men are; but because I am male I was attacked for chauvinism. This gave me the idea for a sequel."

On another level the novel can be seen as a response to the accusations of plagiarism that had greeted Thomas's use of Kuznetsov and Pushkin in previous novels. Similarly, his portrayal of the 1915 massacre of Armenians carried out by Turkish forces prompted his-

torian Christopher Walker angrily to accuse Thomas of lifting his material on this subject. In his foreword he provocatively acknowledges the use of H. Rider Haggard's *King Solomon's Mines* (1885), "scandalously amended." *Swallow*, like *Ararat*, is a novel of improvisation, appropriation, and intertextuality that is partly an explicit exploration of plagiarism itself. Thomas's own position in *Memories and Hallucinations* is that "all that matters is whether a work has an original force, taken as a whole."

In *Sphinx* (1986) Thomas pushes these questions even further, appearing as a character in his own right. At a writer's international conference in London he is amusingly challenged by other writers (characters of his own invention) for equal acknowledgment in the writing of the "Russian Nights" sequence. Thus the boundaries between fiction and the real, writer and character, are again placed directly in question. Despite its air of confidence and wit, *Sphinx* was not an easy text to write. As in *Birthstone*, the proliferation of ideas was constantly in danger of getting out of his control. "I grew oppressed with a thousand pages of rough abandoned sheets, stuffed with unlived events." Over the two years following the publication of *Swallow* in 1984, the text of *Sphinx* slowly developed as a trio of separate sections, one dramatic, one in narrative prose, and one in verse. Again the novel reflects the writer's interest in Russian literature, and again it cleverly encloses its prequels. In the opening, for example, the character of Nadia is pictured flying home to Leningrad, dreaming erotically of Pushkin and clutching a copy of Thomas's *Swallow*.

Critical reaction to both Thomas's second and third "Russian Nights" novels was at best muted. Despite hostile responses from some quarters the level of Thomas's artistic commitment to the larger project was demonstrated over the next three years by the production of two more novels. During this time Thomas also struggled with serious illness: a kidney ailment and a nervous breakdown in 1988. Perhaps surprisingly in the light of these problems, the final novels of "Russian Nights" seem deliberately controversial. In particular, Thomas makes more, and more problematic, figures. In an episode in *Sphinx*, for example, the narrator rapes a young woman while under the fantasy that she is Margaret Thatcher. Similarly, *Summit* satirizes the 1985 Geneva "Fireside" summit. The characters of O'Reilly and Grobichov are transparently caricatures of Ronald Reagan and Mikhail Gorbachev, each involved in a web of intrigue, both sexual and political, with each other's wives and daughters. In the final novel in Thomas's sequence, *Lying Together*, published in 1990, an infatuated Margaret Thatcher saves the character Victor Surkov from a rape charge by a personal intervention on his behalf.

The treatment of rape in *Sphinx* and *Lying Together* certainly reflects Thomas's painful experience related to his son Sean's trial for the same crime in 1988. Hearing in court an intimate dissection of his son's heroin addiction and sadomasochistic encounters was a traumatic and defining experience in Thomas's life. Sean Thomas successfully defended himself against the charges by his former girlfriend, partly by citing the violence that could be intrinsic to some sexual relationships. Thomas's work of this period addresses this same issue. For example, in *Sphinx* he presents rape in such a way that it could almost be seen as a natural extension of male desire. This kind of treatment of potentially offensive material is one of the most controversial features of Thomas's writing.

Thomas's interest in the boundaries between the historical and the fictional again found expression in his first free-standing novel for a decade, *Flying in to Love*. Drawing its title from the name of the Dallas airport, Love Field, *Flying in to Love* is a reexploration of the Kennedy assassination. In 1963 Thomas's own reactions to the killing, as he stood by the television while a hairdresser arranged his wife's hair, had been contradictory: "The news came through, I felt sick, felt—I still do—the world would never be the same: yet I was pleased the BBC didn't cancel the succeeding comedy show because it was one that I liked. I drove the hairdresser home and we fondled in a lay-by."

Written almost two decades later, the novel partly reflects these confusions. It offers not one but several revisionings of Kennedy's fate. In this way the novel explores the question of what it can mean, amid all the hypotheses and popular conspiracy theories, to talk about the "real" events of 22 November. Sometimes in the novel Kennedy has survived the motorcade unscathed. His successive deaths and resurrections have an almost cartoonlike quality, accentuated by the fact that Thomas's portrayal of Kennedy often borders on caricature.

This self-conscious and often provocative experimentation with history received widely varying critical reactions. For many, *Flying in to Love* was considered ingenious. According to Michael Wood in the *London Review of Books* (13 February 1992), "the novel manages to communicate a genuine anger and distress."

The reaction to *Pictures at an Exhibition*, however, was more generally one of distaste. Published in 1993, this novel draws directly from the subject matter of *The White Hotel*. Again the Freudian dualism of Eros and Thanatos provides the work's structuring opposition. In the earlier novel "Anna G's" hysteria is intermixed with premonitions of the Holocaust. *Pictures at an Exhibition* is more specifically concerned with Auschwitz and its legacy. Where *The White Hotel* explores the interconnectedness of sex and death through the fantasies of its protagonist, the later novel is more direct, for example, in its focus on sexual "experimentation" carried out by the SS in the death camps. In the hysteria of contemporary London, the novel suggests, the trauma of Nazi abuses can still be traced. In a way that reflected early reactions to *The White Hotel*, critical reactions to *Pictures at an Exhibition* were sometimes openly hostile. For Bryan Cheyette in the *TLS* (29 January 1993), the novel was unambiguously offensive. In Cheyette's eyes the work was "a cold and calculated piece of writing, extremely self-conscious about its intentions, and designed to make its author a great deal of money."

Thomas's 1994 novel, *Eating Pavlova*, stands out in his oeuvre for the relative restraint with which its subject matter is treated. The novel opens with an aging Freud dying of mouth cancer in his home in Hampstead. As Freud's consciousness drifts from memory to daydream to narration, the theme of clairvoyance established in *The White Hotel* returns. Under the influence of morphine, he envisions scenes from before his own birth, involving figures such as Sir Isaac Newton and Charles Darwin. At other times he is able to foresee the future beyond his own death. As long as his daughter is alive, the novel seems to suggest, Freud will survive intact in her consciousness. This literary device allows Thomas to extend the scope of Freud's mediation impossibly, bringing his gaze to bear on events such as the trial of Adolf Eichmann and even the Vietnam War. This portrayal of a vulnerable younger woman again echoes of Thomas's presentation of the muse in his earliest work. In the same way as Elena in *The Flute-Player*, Anna becomes the receptacle for Freud's consciousness until her own death in 1982.

In different ways both *Pictures at an Exhibition* and *Eating Pavlova* represent a return to the themes of Thomas's most acclaimed work, extending its engagement both with the Holocaust and with the Freudian imagination in fascinating, controversial, and provocative ways. One of the most remarkable features of *The White Hotel* is the way it unifies and encapsulates the different strands of Thomas's intellectual concerns: his literary preoccupation with themes of sex and death, his interest in Freud and psychoanalysis, his passion for Russian culture, and his engagement with the Holocaust and its legacy. This complex of ideas has continued to shape the works of later years.

With the publication of eleven novels in fifteen years, in addition to his considerable achievements in poetry and translation, Thomas's unique place in the literary landscape of Britain and the United States is undeniable. When Thomas was approached by St. Martin's Press in 1987 to write a life of Solzhenitsyn, he was pleased to add biography to his repertoire. As Thomas writes, "What clinched it was that his life stretched from 1918 to the present day, and that he'd gone through every facet of modern Russia. So I saw it more as a chance to write a love story, of my love affair with Russia and its history." Written with the lyricism and grace that is a hallmark of all his best work, the publication in 1998 of *Alexander Solzhenitsyn: A Century in his Life* brought a flood of critical admiration, continuing the cycle of praise and rejection that has been a prominent feature of Thomas's reception as a literary figure. At the extremes of his career Thomas has been hailed as a genius, praised as a scholar, and dismissed as an unreadable degenerate. It remains to be seen in which combination his reputation will finally be fixed.

Interviews:

Elizabeth Alley, "Sex and the Southern Cross," *New Zealand Listener,* no. 2312 (1985): 49–51;

David Brooks, "D. M. Thomas," *Helix* (Spring 1985): 21–22, 33–41;

Anthony Clare, "Sons and Lovers," *Listener,* 124 (6 September 1990): 10–12;

Rosa Casademont, "Art and the Unseen Pattern in the Universe: An Interview with D. M. Thomas," *European English Messenger,* 3, no. 2 (1994): 7–12;

Sabine Durrant, "The Sins of the Father," *Observer,* 8 September 1996, Life section, p. 14.

References:

David Cowart, "Being and Seeming: *The White Hotel,*" *Novel: A Forum on Fiction,* 19, no. 3 (1986): 216–231;

Richard K. Cross, "The Soul Is a Far Country: D. M. Thomas and *The White Hotel,*" *Journal of Modern Literature,* 18, no. 1 (1992): 19–47;

M. D. Fletcher, "Thomas' Satire in *Summit,*" *Studies in Contemporary Satire,* 18 (1991/1992): 9–17;

Krin Gabbard, "*The White Hotel* and the Traditions of Ring Composition," *Comparative Literature Studies,* 27, no. 3 (1990): 230–248;

David Leon Higdon, "Solomon's Fair Shulamite in D. M. Thomas' *The White Hotel,*" *Journal of Modern Literature,* 19, no. 2 (1995): 328–333;

Mary Joe Hughes, "Revelations in *The White Hotel,*" *Critique: Studies in Modern Fiction,* 27 (1985): 37–50;

Robert Lougy, "The Wolf-Man, Freud, and D. M. Thomas: Intertextuality, Interpretation, and Narration in *The White Hotel,*" *Modern Language Studies,* 21, no. 3 (Summer 1991): 91–106;

John MacInnes, "The Case of Anna G.: *The White Hotel* and Acts of Understanding," *Soundings: An Interdisciplinary Journal,* 77 (1994): 253–269;

Mary Robertson, "Hystery, Herstory, History: 'Imagining the Real' in Thomas's *The White Hotel,*" *Contemporary Literature,* 25, no. 4 (Winter 1984): 452–477;

Laura Tanner, "Sweet Pain and Charred Bodies: Figuring Violence in *The White Hotel,*" *Boundary 2: An Interdisciplinary Journal of Literature and Culture,* 18, no. 2 (1991): 130–149;

Rowland Wymer, "Freud, Jung and the Myth of Psychoanalysis in *The White Hotel,*" *Mosaic: A Journal for the Interdisciplinary Study of Literature,* 22, no. 1 (1989): 55–69.

Rosemary Tonks

(1932 –   )

Julie Rak
McMaster University

See also the Tonks entry in *DLB 14: British Novelists Since 1960*.

BOOKS: *On Wooden Wings: The Adventures of Webster* (London: Murray, 1948);

Wild Sea Goose (London: Murray, 1951);

Notes on Cafés and Bedrooms (London: Putnam, 1963);

Opium Fogs (London: Putnam, 1963);

Emir (London: Adam Books, 1963);

Iliad of Broken Sentences (London: Bodley Head, 1967);

The Bloater (London: Bodley Head, 1968);

Businessmen as Lovers (London: Bodley Head, 1969); republished as *Love among the Operators* (Boston: Gambit, 1970);

The Way Out of Berkeley Square (London: Bodley Head, 1970; Boston: Gambit, 1971);

The Halt during the Chase (London: Bodley Head, 1972; New York: Harper & Row, 1973).

SELECTED PERIODICAL PUBLICATIONS–
UNCOLLECTED: "C. P. Cavafy," *Encounter*, 66 (April 1973): 39–42;

"On Being Down, But Not Quite Out, in Paris," *Times* (London), 12 May 1976;

"Baudelaire," *Parnassus: Poetry in Review*, 5, no. 2 (1977): 206–221.

Rosemary Tonks

During her period of most concentrated literary activity, in the late 1960s and the early 1970s, Rosemary Tonks wrote fierce yet humorous novels about the difficulties and small triumphs of British women looking for social, financial, and sexual independence. Unlike other female writers of her generation who joined the women's liberation movement in response to the restrictions they and their female protagonists experienced, Tonks ultimately chose, for her protagonists and for herself, to defy conventional social restrictions on women and then to renounce them totally. Her poems detail the more personal, anguished aspects of this struggle from her own point of view. In these same poems her detailed descriptions of her beloved city, London, established her in the eyes of many as "the poet of the modern metropolis," like the poet she most admired, Charles Baudelaire.

Writing novels in a highly personal style that at times approaches the tone of Evelyn Waugh in its cynical observations of urban living, Tonks has had a mixed critical reception at best, although her critics admit that her grasp of the English language and her sense of London are sharp at times. Her novels are a type of fictional autobiography in which she plays not only the leading role but one or two supporting roles as well. She includes incidents and experiences directly from her past, often with only a thin fictional veil to disguise them. Some critics considered this tendency a fault and labeled the autobiographical dimension of her writing as "feminine" in a negative sense; others decided that her directness was invigorating and showed the distinctiveness of her voice, making for a lively fictional world. Tonks's poems and novels deal with aspects of her life up to 1972, when her last novel was published. Her fiction in particular moves from a dissatisfaction with urban living in satiric novels such as *The Bloater* (1968) and *Businessmen as Lovers* (1969), to a pronounced loathing of middle-class materialism in her later work. Her distaste for materialism meant that Tonks also developed an interest in the movement of symbolism that eventually led her to a conception of spirituality as the only alternative to materialism. This embrace of what she called "the invisible world" ultimately led her to distrust the act of writing itself and to abandon writing as a career.

As her last published novel, *The Halt During the Chase* (1972), indicates, Tonks's anger at materialism marks the beginning of a spiritual journey for Sophie, the main character. Tonks shared this desire to leave behind the world of British professionals and restless intelligentsia, and Sophie's final decision to leave the cloying world of British matrons and their handsome, successful, but dull husbands in order to study mysticism became Tonks's own decision. By the late 1970s she had converted to evangelical Christianity and given up writing. Although this renunciation of a prolific writing career must have been painful, it forms a logical coda to a writing life conducted with an awareness of spiritual possibilities awakened when Tonks saw the ghost of Baudelaire in Paris.

Rosemary D. Boswell Tonks was born in England in 1932. Her father had just died of blackwater fever in Africa (she was called Rosemary "for remembrance" and named Boswell after James Boswell, an ancestor). She spent her early childhood in baby homes and boarding schools. At the age of nine she began to invent things: cameras with drawings of her friends already "developed" inside them; airplanes that dropped two or three parachutes at carefully spaced intervals; and many other gadgets that revealed an already active imagination. While at Wentworth in her early teens, she began writing poetry. Although she was at the top of her class year after year, she was dissatisfied with the curriculum. She resented the absence of worthwhile lessons and considered the tasks assigned to her asinine. Tonks turned to her own amusements, including what she described to Terry Coleman in 1970 as "gang warfare. Heavy fighting in the cellars with taking of prisoners." At sixteen she was expelled. Tonks once said it was for general frivolity, but officially it was for stealing tomatoes. Being expelled surprised her at the time. When Coleman asked her why in a 1968 interview, she replied, "I don't know. It never occurs to you you'll be rejected." That same year she published her first book, an adventure story for children called *On Wooden Wings: The Adventures of Webster* (1948).

Tonks convinced her mother to rent a flat for the two of them in London, where her real education began. She discovered libraries but, as she told Coleman in 1970, discovered that "there was nothing very good in them." She began writing stories for the BBC and received in return "rapturous letters and 10 to 12 guineas each." When she was eighteen, she read the works of James Joyce and Baudelaire, who remained the most important and admired influences on her poetic voice and her choice of subject matter. At nineteen she married Micky, a civil engineer, and a few years later they went to Karachi, Pakistan. She began to write poetry seriously there, but her progress was halted when she contracted typhoid fever and had to return to England. Back in Karachi soon afterward, she contracted poliomyelitis and for months was paralyzed from the neck down. She continued writing poetry, including an epic in free verse that has not been published. Again she returned to England, but finding it full of relatives—and thinking that "in illness you want to be alone"—she went by herself to Paris while her husband remained in Karachi. In a later essay called "On Being Down, But Not Quite Out, in Paris" (1976) she wrote that "the facts of my life, when you looked at them soberly, couldn't have been worse. I had only tropical clothes and little cash. . . . I didn't know a soul. I had managed to get a little room under the roof, with an annex which had a cold water basin in it. At the only table . . . in the middle of the freezing little bedroom" she began to assemble the poems for her first volume of poetry, *Notes on Cafés and Bedrooms* (1963), and wrote part of an unnamed novel there. In Paris she encountered what she later believed to be the ghost of Baudelaire. It was evening and she was coming back across Ponte Marie from the Right Bank when it happened: "I saw a man from the nineteenth century. . . . He wore a stovepipe hat, pale waistcoat, frock coat, narrow trousers, pale gloves, and he looked at me as he passed. I was shaking with fright, and had to prop myself up against a dirty wall." It occurred to her that she may have seen an actor returning from a fancy dress party, but twice afterward, when she returned to the bridge at exactly the same time, she had a similar experience.

After recuperating fully from the polio attack, Tonks returned to London, the source of much of her inspiration. In a poem collected in *Iliad of Broken Sentences* (1967), she wrote of the city's imaginative power:

"From a pestle and mortar—roof, floor, walls, doors, / My London, stuffed with whisky-dark hotels, / Began to pant like a great ode!" She published *Notes on Cafés and Bedrooms,* which received mixed critical reaction. R. K. Burns, writing in the *Library Journal* (1964), found her poems, stark, daring, sensuous, and totally humorless, while Denise Levertov in *The New York Times Book Review* (21 June 1964) saw in them "a brash, bouncy quality." Despite differences of opinion about the mood of the poems, there was a consensus on her literary techniques and content. Usually eschewing regular rhyme or meter, the poems in the volume concentrate on city life and often manage to combine the different flavors of metropolitan boredom, excitement, evil, and malaise, as in these lines from "Escape":

It is among the bins and dormitories of cities
Where the busker wins his bread
By turning music on a spit, and the heavens
Have the dirt of the great sky upon their sides,

That one goes to gourmandize upon Escape!
Where alleys are so narrow that the Fates
Like meatporters can scarcely pass
With their awkward burden in muslin bandages,
And carry off the rabble safely to their graves. . . .

As Norman MacCaig remarked in the *New Statesmen* (12 April 1963), the images and metaphors in Tonks's poems "dance maniacally through the ruin of syntax, sometimes bumping head on . . . in loops and swirls and rosy fogs of language." Tonks herself recognized the profusion of images in her poetry, which she described to Coleman in 1968 as part of her creative process: "I'm really trying to make new music out of natural speech. I can't otherwise cope with large thoughts. No one else is trying to do this so far as I know, though my direct literary forebears, Baudelaire and Rimbaud, were both poets of the modern metropolis. A poet's job is to excite, to send the senses reeling."

In the same year that her first volume of poetry appeared, Tonks also published her first novels for adults, *Opium Fogs* and *Emir.* Tonks always called herself a poet in interviews and seemed to hold her novels in some contempt—calling them "mud" in one interview for *The Guardian* and referring to them in another interview as "porridge"—and intimating that she wrote prose for money. Curiously, although she once called *Emir* "the best prose work I have written," it is not listed along with her other works, including two books for children, in the front matter of her subsequent publications.

While it is not clear which novel she wrote first, *Opium Fogs* appeared just before *Emir.* The story relates directly to Tonks's experiences upon returning to England after recuperating from polio. It is about a bizarre group of Londoners—artists, ne'er-do-wells, "continental Englishmen," and others—who seem to spend most of their energies finding new and better ways to torment each other and themselves. Into this society returns Gabriella, "a moody little beauty of twenty-two" who had left England some eighteen months before and spent ten of them paralyzed in India. For Gerard, her former lover, she was "the only woman with whom I could ever have lived, and for whom there was any reason to live." Gerard is determined to win her back but only briefly succeeds. After a month's pursuit in cold, grimy London, culminating in a few hours of wild, impassioned lovemaking in an old Victorian house, Gabriella abandons Gerard at last. Overcome by self-recrimination, she can still sum up the situation in this way: "I am not even an extension of his personality—but an escape route; a new drug which melts his brains." Recognizing that Gerard's self-destructiveness and the "transforming madness" they share eventually will leave them nothing but "marvellous wreckage," she concludes: "I would rather occupy five hours of his life on which he looks back with regret, than try to build a future on the quicksands of that temperament."

The novel's style is highly metaphorical, which led critics at the time to view it as a prose poem. It also features a literary device that gives it the quality of a radio play: the plot advances through the rendition of sharp, personal encounters conveyed through dialogue (in double quotes) studded with thoughts uttered to oneself (in single quotes). This device also appears in *Emir,* but Tonks dropped it in her later novels in favor of a first-person narrative technique. Above all, *Opium Fogs* captures the backbiting, egocentric mode of life that links Tonks's vision of London society in the 1960s with its counterpart in Baudelaire's Paris.

Like *Opium Fogs,* the action of *Emir* moves through a limited range of scenery, which floats in and out of the consciousness of its main character, in this case a twenty-two-year-old poet named Houda Lawrence. Like Gabriella, Houda is pursued by an admirer who wants to be her lover, a middle-aged aesthete and intellectual named Eugene. Although Houda despises him, especially after he wrecks her room looking for her address when she is on holiday in the country, Eugene is convinced that her attacks against him are merely inverted compliments and therefore persists in his attentions. Nevertheless, Eugene's pursuit has its attractions for Houda. "To get drunk—on someone else's soul, Eugene, you have instructed me in the most fabulous of appetites," Houda says to herself. The conflict between the two is finally resolved only when Houda shows Eugene her poems, which appall him.

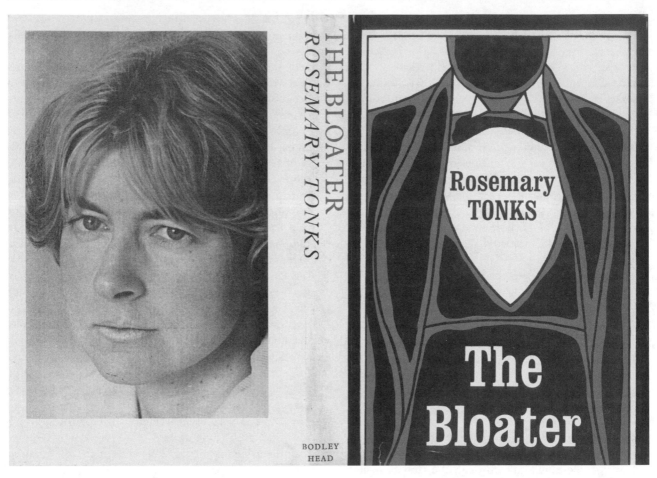

Dust jacket for Tonks's satirical 1968 novel, in which the protagonist fends off the determined romantic advances of an obese opera singer

Tonks uses her protagonist's consciousness to voice what are probably her own views. For example, Houda thinks that "Cézanne's agony made the public learn its lesson all too well, for now they will buy any stupidity with a frame around it." Tonks makes similar observations in interviews. Her portrait of London and its inhabitants is similar to the one in *Opium Fogs,* and her style is identical in both books. Houda, unlike Gabriella, rejects bourgeois existence, however: "Yes, chaos is fearful, but order is much worse because it is boring." Houda and Gabriella reveal what may be different, often contradictory, aspects of Tonks's own view of life at the time. The choice—at the end of a sexual pursuit—between sedentary life with a faithful man and a more rootless existence as a single artist reappears in her later prose in various forms.

Although critics have often faulted Tonks for poor syntax and shallow plot, they usually give her credit for having a biting wit, a light tone, and interesting characters. As Oswald Blakeston wrote in *Punch* (4 September 1968), Tonks "could be classified as a lethal weapon when it comes to witty attacks on cosiness." Tonks, however, told Coleman in 1970 that she wishes people would stop regarding her as light-minded, because in reality she is deadly serious: "but I don't believe in weighing down the reader with a ton of suet so I begin a novel lightly as the only way to convey information."

On the centenary of Baudelaire's death in 1967, when her second book of poems was about to come out, Tonks, in an anecdote that shows the kinship she felt with Baudelaire, went to visit his grave in Montparnasse cemetery. There she lay down on his life-sized effigy and found that she was the same height. She has viewed herself as the albatross of Baudelaire's poem, "encumbered on the ground with the same wings which enabled her to fly." It is an apt reference: her second volume of poetry, *Iliad of Broken Sentences,* never takes off. Critics either ignored it or, as did the critic for the *Listener* (19 October 1967), dismissed Tonks as "shrill." The poems in this volume are often autobiographical, filled with bitter references to herself as "worn out like this, and crippled by brain-fag," to lovers whom she pushes away in disgust, and to contemporary authors of "mud" novels, the hotel-, discotheque-, and café-haunting literati, as in these lines: "All this sitting about in cafés to calm down / Simply wears me out. / And their idea of literature! / The idiotic cut of the stanzas: the novels, full up, gross. . . ." As a critic wrote in *TLS: The Times Literary Supplement* (9 November 1967), "Miss Tonks is creating a style, very calculatedly exotic and dramatic. . . . This is not loose writing." At their best, the poems achieve a toughness and self-mocking wit approaching T. S. Eliot's in individual lines such as: "And this was an ode shaken from a box of rats," but the overall tone remains too bitter and high-pitched without many consistent images to sustain it, and the collection ultimately failed to attract much popular or critical attention.

Tonks continued to write fiction at a rapid rate. She composed her third and best-received novel, *The Bloater* (1968), in only four weeks. Tonks is at her wittiest in this short satire of the London intelligentsia. The protagonist of *The Bloater,* Min, is pursued by a determined would-be lover and the novel's namesake, a gargantuan opera singer whom she repeatedly but not always successfully fends off. Unlike Houda, free-spirited Min is married, but just barely. Her husband is mentioned a few times and appears only at the end, when Min says to him: "I'm terribly sorry, I'm afraid I may have ruined your life." Min's time is split between amusing Claudi, her urbane older neighbor, laughing at the sexual escapades of Jenny, her coworker at the recording studio where she works, and having tête-à-têtes with Billy, her musicologist friend. The plot is resolved when Min and Billy fall in love on a walk in Hampstead. *The Bloater* ends with the couple gleefully planning a holiday involving a train journey to Italy. Although the dialogue has the artificial quality of film noir, *The Bloater* was written in the style of the diary Tonks kept at the time, a style that is, as the critic for *Encounter* (January 1969) recognized, "glancing and impersonal: that is, ideal for confidences." It shows a firm grasp of novelistic techniques without a wholesale sacrifice of the brisk wit and zest that characterize her earlier prose.

Businessmen as Lovers (1969), Tonks's next book, continues the light, satiric style of *The Bloater* and even continues the final aspect of its plot. This time, Caroline and Mimi have set off for Italy on holiday. Caroline is to meet Killi, her humorless financier husband, and Mimi goes with her to be reunited with her lover, Beetle. Later they are joined by Caroline's children and a variety of other eccentric British holiday-makers. In keeping with the novel's light tone, Caroline and Mimi travel by train through the Paris uprising of 1968 and view it as an extension of their own high spirits: at one point Mimi says of the fires made by student groups during the revolution: "Crikey. What fun. Do we join in?" before going back to laughing at her arcane Italian phrase book. Almost plotless, the novel is narrated in the first person by Mimi, who describes the antics of the British on holiday, culminating in a bedroom farce that defeats the attempts of Dr. Oskar Purzelbaum to inflict a combination of psychoanalysis, dentistry, and hot-bath treatments on Mimi's host and her friends. Critical reception of *Businessmen as Lovers* was cool, with most critics preferring the more caustic wit of *The Bloater.*

Tonks's next novel, *The Way Out of Berkeley Square* (1970), has a more serious tone and more highly developed characters, although the critical reception continued to be ambiguous, with the reviewer for the *Observer* (5 October 1970) labeling it "over-ornamented." This time the protagonist is Arabella, a possible throwback to Gabriella, who faces similar choices but draws different conclusions from them. At first, Arabella is held in thrall by three men: her spoiled, tyrannical, and self-indulgent father, who has made her a virtual slave in their Victorian family home; her twenty-year-old rebellious brother, Michael, who is attempting to live an idealist life in Karachi as a poet; and a married, middle-aged, attractive businessman whom Arabella refers to only as Wolf. The opening sentence announces the basic situation, as Arabella proclaims: "I'm thirty, and I'm stuck." Arabella knows that Wolf does not offer a true escape from Berkeley Square, with its upper-middle-class London population of successful stockbrokers and their desperate yet well-bred wives; nor does Michael, who contracts polio and angrily returns to England once Arabella betrays him and tells her father about his illness. Instead, Arabella places herself in the center of their lives as a caregiver on her own terms. She finally allows Wolf to have a love affair with her, which truly begins on her father's easy chair after she has written him a vicious note in order to bring him to heel. Meanwhile, her father is forced to admit to Arabella when he learns from her of Michael's illness that "the whole house revolves around you, you know," while at the end of the novel, Michael's return is clearly to her, not to her father. The hallmarks of Tonks's mature style are evident in this novel—the small power games between Arabella and her father and the sad yet enervating courtship with Wolf are drawn in painful detail and with a sense of emotional realism unrelieved by the bitter jokes Tonks uses in her poetry. As Arabella finally concludes in a frame of mind that emphasizes her weary acceptance of events, the strange painful love she has for the men in her life "doesn't feel like pleasure, so it must be fate."

The Way Out of Berkeley Square

a novel by

Rosemary Tonks

Dust jacket for the U.S. edition of Tonks's 1970 novel, about a woman's turbulent relationships with her father and brother

Tonks's last novel, *The Halt During the Chase,* is the story of Sophie, who is a slightly older version of Arabella. Instead of a domineering father for whom she keeps house, Sophie has a lively, humorous mother whom she does not live with but still must look after. Among the other characters are Rudi Horder, a wealthy antiques dealer, and his two sons: Philip, a successful, clever, and handsome bureaucrat who is Sophie's lover; and Guy, like Michael in *The Way Out of Berkeley Square* a rebellious and tormented young man whose sojourn in Paris on the Ile Saint Louis closely resembles Tonks's at the same age—he too tells of meeting Baudelaire's ghost. Although she is at first much in love with Philip, Sophie realizes one evening when they spend the night in a hotel that Philip's devotion is and always will be shallow and that he has no intention of marrying her. In a moment that probably parallels Tonks's growing desire to embrace spirituality, Sophie observes that the gulf between Philip and herself is total: "He didn't believe in the invisible world; and it was obvious to me that I was getting ill without it." The shock of this revelation

proves to be freeing. Her eventual break from Philip is aided by her recent studies in Eastern mysticism, the counsel of a clairvoyant in Brighton, and a holiday in Normandy provided by her friend, Princess Melika, at a house inhabited by a charming French family. There, despite Philip's pursuit, Sophie awakens to a full consciousness of herself and to full freedom. At last she understands what the lectures on mysticism she attended with Guy were about: "that it was your job to develop yourself, as the primary purpose of life; the chase is inward." She understands, too, that she must now avoid "the company of those who limited you and themselves." She lets Philip go, since his presence would end both her development and his. The novel ends in the living room of Princess Melika, who, despite her increasing poverty, gaily celebrates with Sophie the beginning of her new life.

The Halt During the Chase was widely reviewed, and critical opinion was varied. Some critics enjoyed Tonks's sense of humor and her merciless portrayal of Philip. The reviewer for *TLS* (28 April 1972) praised the book without reservation, saying that it is "buzzing with ideas, and full of details that stick because they are not ornament but belong." Others disliked the novel's slight plotting: the reviewer for *Bookseller* (15 September 1973), for example, compared it unfavorably to the work of Barbara Cartland. Relative to her previous novels, however, *The Halt During the Chase* is the most firmly plotted and carefully structured of all Tonks's fiction, and it reveals a maturing style and purpose. The pursuit that all her novels feature has become spiritualized and has turned inward. As some of her critics noted, however, the novel still has moments of wry humor, and the prose still contains sharply defined images notable for their economy of language, as in this description of telegraph poles in St. Emilion: "They were driven into the body of the countryside; just pegs to earth the surplus electricity in the winter sky." Throughout the novel expressions of genuine feeling, humor, and pointed repartee recur along with Sophie's emerging, clearly delineated quest.

Tonks's tendency to use her novels to express her own ideas extends to her nonfiction as well. In a 1973 article on the poetry of C. P. Cavafy, Tonks praises this writer because she sees him as someone capable of writing historical epic poetry, where creativity becomes a feint, a way of making history more real. Tonks's opinion could equally be applied to her own poetic treatment of her life's events. In the same article she writes that "form in its truest sense is the organization of the poem's inner life: the model made in advance by the thoughts." Here also is Tonks's own view of poetry, since it matches her use of free verse, which still retains a formal, ornamented quality to match the poetry's weighty subject matter. Later, in a 1977 article on Baudelaire, her last piece of published writing, Tonks's interests in mysticism and aesthetics coincide. She discusses Baudelaire as a fabricator of images that are akin to Jungian archetypes. In Tonks's view, the power of Baudelaire's images is ultimately mystical: "For they derive from a knowledge of force, which controls all forms and their behavior in the Universe, and whose mysterious, educating presence in the body of man is dependent for its conscious realization, ultimately, upon the innermost, private workings of his unstable heart. They are the secrets of mysticism." For Tonks the mission of a poet such as Baudelaire is to bring these hidden, mystic images to light and to make the ideal possible in the reader's imagination: "thus Baudelaire renews the world by restoring to it ideal conceptions of what it is already." Clearly Tonks herself had begun to turn from considering in her creative work the figure of Baudelaire's *flanêur,* who travels as a rootless, sardonic witness to urban decay, to the idea of the artist as the transmitter of truths that are buried in culture and language.

The literary results of Tonks's latest journey remain unknown. After the publication of *The Halt During the Chase* Tonks began a long novel, which she spent more than five years writing and which grew to become her longest sustained piece of fiction (ninety thousand words) before she abandoned it. During the late 1970s her growing interest in the spiritual matters that she had delineated in her fiction and nonfiction led her to stop writing, perhaps because she seemed to be able to describe only the reality that she wished to escape. She burned the manuscript of the major novel she had been working on, withdrew her poems from new anthologies, and withdrew, by 1984, from writers' directories as well. Sophie's words in *The Halt During the Chase* probably give Tonks's own feelings about writing and why she could no longer continue: "I was suddenly exceptionally tired of having to justify myself. Tired of being judged by standards which were heartless and narrow, and which I didn't believe in." As a writer who had devoted her career to chronicling the failures of women attempting to break free of confining relationships in the merciless, valueless world of "the modern metropolis," she had finally abandoned that world and embarked on a spiritual journey that has required her silence in the world of literature to be total.

Interviews:

Terry Coleman, "Bloater, Billy, and Min," *Guardian,* 27 June 1968;

Coleman, "Rosemary for Remembrance," *Guardian,* 24 October 1970;

William Foster, "A Poet of the Modern Metropolis," *Scotsman,* 21 November 1970.

Joanna Trollope

(9 December 1943 –)

Helen Clare Taylor
Louisiana State University-Shreveport

BOOKS: *Eliza Stanhope* (London: Hutchinson, 1978; New York: Dutton, 1979);

Parson Harding's Daughter (London: Hutchinson, 1979); republished as *Mistaken Virtues* (New York: Dutton, 1980); republished as by Caroline Harvey (London: Corgi, 1995);

Charlotte, as Harvey (London: Sundial, 1980); republished with *Cara* and *Alexandra* as *Legacy of Love* (London: Octopus, 1983);

Alexandra, as Harvey (London: Sundial, 1980); republished with *Charlotte* and *Cara* as *Legacy of Love* (London: Octopus, 1983);

Leaves from the Valley (London: Hutchinson, 1980; New York: St. Martin's Press, 1980);

The City of Gems (London: Hutchinson, 1981);

Britannia's Daughters: Women of the British Empire (London: Hutchinson, 1983);

Cara, as Harvey (London: Octopus, 1983); republished with *Charlotte* and *Alexandra* as *Legacy of Love* (London: Octopus, 1983);

The Steps of the Sun (London: Hutchinson, 1983; New York: St. Martin's Press, 1984); republished as by Harvey (London: Corgi, 1996);

The Taverners' Place (London: Hutchinson, 1986; New York: St. Martin's Press, 1988);

The Choir (London: Hutchinson, 1988; New York: Random House, 1995);

A Village Affair (London: Bloomsbury, 1989; New York: Harper & Row, 1989);

A Passionate Man (London: Bloomsbury, 1990);

The Rector's Wife (London: Bloomsbury, 1991; New York: Random House, 1994);

The Men and the Girls (London: Bloomsbury, 1992; New York: Random House, 1992);

A Castle in Italy, as Harvey (London: Doubleday, 1993);

A Second Legacy, as Harvey (London: Corgi, 1993);

A Spanish Lover (London: Bloomsbury, 1993; New York: Random House, 1997);

The Best of Friends (London: Bloomsbury, 1995; New York: Viking, 1998);

Next of Kin (London: Bloomsbury, 1996);

Joanna Trollope (photograph by Charles Green)

Faith (London: Bloomsbury, 1996);

The Brass Dolphin, as Harvey (London: Doubleday, 1997; New York: Viking, 1999);

Other People's Children (London: Bloomsbury, 1998).

OTHER: *The Country Habit,* edited by Trollope (London: Bantam, 1993; New York: Bantam, 1993).

Joanna Trollope's first novels were meticulously researched historical romances. It was not until she began writing about contemporary women in provincial settings that she gained a wide readership and critical attention. Two of these later books, *The Choir* (1988) and *The Rector's Wife* (1991), were adapted for television and broadcast in the United States on PBS, which enhanced Trollope's burgeoning reputation in America. Her nonhistorical fiction, written since 1988, explores the restrictions placed on women by family and small-town society in contemporary Britain; she is particularly interested in the ways in which the traditional parameters of church and squirearchy still obtain for women in English provincial life. In this way Trollope is a conscious inheritor of the great tradition of novels about English village society, which includes the work of Jane Austen and George Eliot, as well as Trollope's Victorian forebear, the novelist Anthony Trollope. While her characters wrestle with ordinary domestic and emotional crises, Trollope's greatest skill lies in recording how the community often acts as a web in which every woman is caught. She told Joanne Kaufman in 1995 that like Anthony Trollope, to whom she is a "remote kind of cousin," she is interested in "the psychology of the human dilemma, the map of the human heart."

Joanna Trollope was born in Gloucestershire on 9 December 1943 to Arthur George Cecil Trollope and Rosemary Hodson Trollope. Her father was a royal engineer who was absent during World War II, and she was raised in Surrey at the home of her maternal grandparents in "a very cold house with not quite enough food, but books were everywhere." Even given the effect of wartime rationing on the nation's food supply, this remark, together with the fact that her grandfather was a rural vicar, indicates the same kind of upper-middle-class, short-of-cash gentility that she describes in her novels. Trollope was educated at Reigate County School for Girls and St. Hugh's College, Oxford, where she studied English as a Gamble Scholar and received an M.A. in 1972. From 1965 to 1967 Trollope worked in the information and research department of the British Foreign Office, where she focused on China. She married David Roger William Potter in 1966 and had two daughters, Antonia and Louise (the marriage ended in 1983). From 1967 to 1979 she taught English at both secondary and adult education levels, as well as English as a second language. She has also sold children's clothing and worked for the Save the Children's Fund.

Eliza Stanhope (1978) was Trollope's first published historical romance. "It only took me twenty years to become an overnight success," she told Kaufman about the reception of these earlier books, some of which were published under the pseudonym Caroline Harvey. Although they may have enjoyed brisk sales, these romances did not receive the critical respect granted to her later novels with contemporary settings, beginning with *The Choir*. Trollope is clearly concerned about keeping the two kinds of fiction separate, even having some of the romances, such as *Parson Harding's Daughter* (1979), which was originally published under her own name, republished under her pseudonym in 1995 to maintain the distinction between what she calls her "CHs" from her "JTs." Of her romance-writing alter ego she told David Finkle in 1997: "I see her as given to Anita Brookner cardigans and perhaps with a cat." In 1985 Trollope married Ian Bayley Curteis, a playwright, who adapted *The Choir* for television and who initially suggested to Trollope that she change her focus from historical romance to contemporary fiction. They live in Coln St. Aldwyns, Gloucestershire. *Parson Harding's Daughter* won the Historical Novel of the Year Award, presented by the Romantic Novelists Association in 1979, and in 1980 the same novel won the Elizabeth Goudge Historical Award. In 1996 Trollope achieved the highest acknowledgment that she had become a figure of national importance: she was awarded the Order of the British Empire by Queen Elizabeth II.

Like many of Trollope's historical romances, *Eliza Stanhope* alludes to and reflects the great nineteenth-century novels that Trollope claims as her favorite reading. The story is set during the Napoleonic wars, although the first part of the plot is concerned not with historical events but with love and marriage. The tomboyish, red-haired heroine of the novel, Eliza, is counterbalanced by Ju-lia, her handsome, languid cousin, a pairing reminiscent of William Makepeace Thackeray's Becky Sharpe and Amelia Sedley in *Vanity Fair* (1847–1848) or Austen's Marianne and Elinor Dashwood in *Sense and Sensibility* (1811). In Trollope's historical romances, however, the characters are not fully drawn in keeping with the genre's characteristic emphasis on plot. Eliza wins her handsome husband despite, or perhaps because of, her hoydenish ways, and he is subsequently shipped off to fight with Wellington against Napoleon at Waterloo. Trollope can thus describe the same glittering society in Brussels in 1815 on the eve of the great battle as Thackeray does in *Vanity Fair*. Eliza's refusal to dwindle into the role of a conformist wife, however, gives this version a twist; dressed as a boy, she follows her husband to the battlefield and helps save him after he is wounded. Trollope goes beyond Thackeray by describing the gory details of the battle from two points of view—that of the men in battle and that of those watching from the hillside, Eliza among them. While full of dramatic action, Trollope's novel, unlike Thackeray's, seldom treats anything other than surface issues.

Parson Harding's Daughter also follows a fairly conventional plotline that suggests the influence of nine-

Dust jacket for Trollope's 1995 novel, in which the failure of one couple's marriage tests another married couple's stability

lished romantic fiction depicting English women in foreign situations, including a trilogy, *Charlotte* (1980), *Alexandra* (1980), and *Cara* (1983), later collected as *A Legacy of Love* (1983). The settings of these novels range from Afghanistan in 1841 to London during World War II. Another romance novel, *The Steps of the Sun* (1983), is set mostly in South Africa during the Boer War. Other titles include *The City of Gems* (1981) and *The Taverners' Place* (1986). In the midst of a string of these books, which did not gain critical attention, she published a nonfiction work, *Britannia's Daughters: Women of the British Empire* (1983), which explores the lives of women in the colonies. Much of the research for this book and for her historical romances must have overlapped. Several of the books written prior to 1988 are out of print; they did not create much stir, and most serious criticism is focused on the "contemporary" books, published after 1988.

While Trollope has fleshed out each story with careful research and allusions to contemporary issues, these earlier novels follow predictable patterns centered on courtship and marriage. Like Georgette Heyer, an accomplished practitioner of the historical romance to whom she has been compared by reviewers, Trollope creates independent-minded heroines struggling to make lives for themselves in the face of convention. This element provides the connection with the later books, as the historical backgrounds become less important than the gradual dislocation of female characters from their paternalistic cultures. In *Leaves from the Valley* (1980), for example, the reader follows Sarah Drummond to the Crimean War, where she eschews her sister's frivolity and her brother's rigid attention to duty to work in hellish conditions with soldiers' families at the hospital in Scutari. Inevitably, she meets Florence Nightingale, but Trollope resists associating Sarah overmuch with the extraordinary deeds of this Victorian figure. Trollope's growing interest is in the problem of the thinking woman caught in a culture that does not value what she thinks. Her protagonists are concerned less with heroic acts than with palliating the Victorian ideal of abnegation of self with a fulfilling inner life mirrored in outward action. Sarah's impassioned plea to her brother Edgar for independence anticipates that of Anna Bouverie, the protagonist of *The Rector's Wife:* "I have endured enough, bowed enough and from now on I shall do as *I* think I should. I can bear my uselessness no longer." In response to his objection that she does not know what she is saying, Sarah retaliates by claiming, "I have never been more myself, Ed-gar, never in all my life. I have always been something other people wanted." The confining attributes of family and society as they dictate women's social roles suggest the parameters of her later, more complex fiction, whose ideas are

teenth-century fiction. Caroline Harding is plain and dull; she is bullied by her horrifically bossy older sister and dismissed as boring by the polite society of her village. In many ways the novel suggests the structure and characterization of Charlotte Brontë's *Jane Eyre* (1848), as Caroline comes through her trials—sailing alone to In-dia, being married off to a heartless drunk, painting miniatures to earn a sustenance—to captivate a dashing older man who appreciates her for her wit and tenacity rather than for her beauty. Caroline refuses to be his mistress mostly because to do so would be to lose independence; she finally marries him after her husband dies in a fire (another parallel with Brontë's novel). The settings of novels such as this reveal the breadth of Trollope's skill. Her evocation of the sights, sounds, and smells of Calcutta in 1776 demonstrate considerable powers of description.

In several subsequent romances Trollope also uses exotic locales that she paints convincingly and with great detail. Between 1980 and 1988 she regularly pub-

sufficiently complex as to obviate the need for historical or exotic contexts.

In 1988 Trollope shifted from historical romances to her first novel dealing with contemporary issues, *The Choir*. Trollope told Michael Sims in *Bookpage* (1997) that she did "an enormous amount of research in a cathedral" for the plot of this novel, which was apparently inspired by a real-life dean who gave her the germ of the story at a lunch party. The novel is set within the linked communities of a smallish town and its cathedral close, which are connected not only by location but also by differing responses to spirituality. These responses become distorted by politics and attempts at personal aggrandizement, as the dean of the cathedral knocks heads with a venerable Labour councillor, Frank Ashworth, who also happens to be the grandfather of one of the cathedral choirboys, Henry Ashworth. When the dean chooses to disband the choir so that he can afford to restore the cathedral, Henry becomes involved with the attempt to save the choir, which is led by the dean's rebellious daughter, Ianthe, and by the choirmaster, Leo Beckford, who is having an affair with Henry's mother. For Trollope these enmeshed relationships represent the web of community, where each action eddies out to affect the lives of others. The plot pulls the characters in different directions, forcing them to face themselves and to assess their places in the intricacies of conflicting loyalties. The choir's adversity causes crises in several marriages, in the life of the cathedral school, and in the relationships between several fathers and their children. All are forced to reassess the ties that bind in light of their respective stands on the issue of the choir. As in her later novels, in *The Choir* Trollope studies the effect of conflict and change in relationships, or, as she has put it, the point when ordinary people cease to be passive players in their own lives but have to "take the steering wheel for themselves."

Many of Trollope's later novels are set in villages or small towns, not only because the role of the community in personal issues is a profound one, but also because the response in a quiet village to even a small crisis can be immense and powerful. "Any incident that's slightly out of the norm is more pronounced and has so much more visibility. It's like a skyscraper in the desert," Trollope told Kaufman about her choice of settings. She pursues this theme in *A Village Affair* (1989), a title that, in a gentle pun, suggests the appropriation of private life that results from living in a small rural community. The novel focuses on Alice Jordan, a painter who has moved to an idyllic house in the kind of English village that real estate agents label "sought-after." She thinks that the move will complete her happiness, but her real problem is that she lacks a sense of identity. She expects that external events—marriage,

children, the patterns of village life—will impose this identity on her. Soon she has her wish, as Clodagh Unwin, the daughter of the local squire, impels her into a lesbian relationship. Having been granted a new view of herself, Alice faces the inevitable crisis in her marriage as well as a storm of rumor and resentment in the village after her affair becomes public. These events, especially the alienation that they cause, force Alice to sidestep the village, her marriage, and the affair to live on her own in a dismal house that she plans to decorate herself. This act becomes a strong personal statement, as Alice refuses to adopt any identity but that which she has imposed from within.

The themes of *A Village Affair* run parallel to many ideas in *The Choir*, but a distinguishing focus is the idea of home and its symbolic uses. Houses, a traditional symbol of the self, play important roles in Trollope's fiction; in this novel Alice first inhabits the wrong house, which she had thought would bring happiness, only to move to the right house—outwardly ugly—as a sign of self-knowledge at the end of the novel. In the interview with Finkle, Trollope stated, "There's a Sylvia Townsend Warner letter about life being a series of losses of homes. The first home is the womb, isn't it?" Survival of these losses and the ability to adapt to the changes that they bring become a defining characteristics of Trollope's fiction. As her historical romances contain vivid and realistic descriptions of exotic places, her contemporary novels abound with finely painted details of home interiors, with colors, fabrics, textures, and kitchen smells as rich backdrops to the interior struggles of her characters.

After this novel Trollope wrote *A Passionate Man* (1990), again set in a small village. The protagonist is Archie Logan, a thirty-something country doctor. The novel charts the effect of his actions on the women in his life, especially his wife, Liza, and his long-widowed father's new mistress. Archie has exerted great power over Liza, wooing her at the party celebrating her engagement to someone else; he fears his father's new romantic happiness will diminish his own importance in his father's affections. After his father's sudden death on his honeymoon, Archie blames his new stepmother and feels powerless in his loss. At the same time his tranquil position in the village is threatened with erosion by a new subdivision on the edge of his property. These events combine to force Archie into a crisis. His method of regaining control is to seduce his stepmother, which has disastrous consequences for his marriage, his family, and his medical practice. Once again, Trollope assesses the impact of a personal predicament on an individual's family and community to conclude that in a village, public and private life are virtually inseparable.

Dust jacket for Trollope's 1996 novel, which depicts the effect of a woman's death on her family and their dairy farm

A successful television adaptation of Trollope's next novel, *The Rector's Wife,* brought her greater prominence, especially in the United States. The idea of home and its connection to identity again dominates this book, which begins with the dilemma of a woman who must save her daughter from bullying but cannot afford a private school. Anna Bouverie is caught between the power nexus of the church and the squire; she is a country vicar's wife and has no identity or independence outside that function. Even her home, the village rectory, belongs to the church, and by convention she is not allowed to have a job. The economic and personal restrictions this situation force upon her are exacerbated by her husband's bitter disappointment in being denied a promotion. He turns increasingly to his spiritual duties, leaving Anna invisible and almost nameless in a community that proscribes any real freedom.

Again Trollope confronts the problematical life of women who live outside the big cities; she reminded Mary Loudon in the *Guardian Weekend* (11 March 1995)

"how limited the options for escape are for provincial, rural women." To be a country woman is to be doubly marginalized in a society that still emphasizes the role of the church and the landed gentry. Accused—like Barbara Pym, to whom she is often compared—of glorifying the trivial, Trollope uses her domestic settings to interrogate the status of women such as Anna, who must, as Trollope puts it, "turn protagonist" at the expense of her conventional role to break out of her restrictive existence. Trollope still takes her research as seriously for these contemporary novels as she did for her romances with faraway settings. For *The Rector's Wife* she worked in a supermarket to learn the intricate details of pricing and presenting products that Anna must master in her rebellious job at "Pricewells."

Trollope has earned a great deal of praise for the realistic milieu and ordinary agonies that *The Rector's Wife* explores. Jenny Turner, writing in the *Guardian* (28 March 1995), comments on the dignity of Trollope's heroines but admonishes her for the "cop out" of the ending of this novel; Anna's difficult husband is killed in a car accident, leaving her technically and morally free. Trollope has said that she does not like "easy" endings as she thinks they patronize the reader. She takes her own dictum seriously in her next book, *The Men and the Girls* (1992), which, like Charlotte Brontë's *Villette* (1853), suggests but does not confirm what happens in the end. The novel is set in Oxford, which is depicted as essentially provincial despite its famous university. The theme of age and the trouble caused by age discrepancies in relationships forms the backbone to the plot of the novel. The women in the novel range in age from the elderly Miss Bachelor, whose wise, no-nonsense optimism bolsters everyone, to the teenage Joss, who is searching for a home and an identity. The plot centers, however, on Kate Bain, a woman in her thirties who decides to leave her comfortable home to strike out on her own. Here again, Trollope uses homes as a correlative for a woman's desire for independence. Eschewing the large, airy house owned by her older lover, James, Kate chooses and furnishes a tiny room where she can live with Joss, her daughter, who soon decides to move back "home" with James, forcing Kate to reconsider her own decisions. At the same time James's friend Hugh, whose wife is much younger, flees his perfect cottage and overly understanding wife to move in with James, Joss, and (at least part time) Miss Bachelor. In all this moving around each character seems to mediate the cliché that "home is where the heart is," which is thrown into focus by Kate's work at a refuge for battered women. Ironically, Kate is beaten by her new lover and, representative of her displacement from her life, ends up at the refuge herself. She realizes that perhaps her old home (and the relationship with

James) is not such a terrible prison, especially after she compares her life with those of the women who have fled homes and relationships defined by violence and control. Trollope, who worked in a battered women's refuge to gather information for this novel, closes the tale before the reader learns whether James is willing to take Kate back into his life and home again.

A Spanish Lover (1993) is hung "on the peg of twins," as Trollope put it to Michael Sims, in a comment indicating that Trollope begins with a problem or an issue that she can play out in the lives of several characters, such as age (in *The Men and the Girls*) or grief (in *A Passionate Man*). In this book she explores the push and pull of sibling rivalry complicated by proximity of birth. Frances Shore and Lizzie Middleton have a competitive relationship: the latter is married with a family and a successful retail business; the former is the unmarried owner of a growing travel agency. Lizzie pities her sister's unmarried state, and Frances's desire to escape the stifling attention of her family is represented by her decision to spend Christmas alone in Spain. As Frances falls in love and grows more and more happy and successful, Lizzie's life is complicated by financial worries and by the ensuing stresses on her family. Trollope has said that she is playing with clichés in this novel; northern, slightly uptight Frances is wooed and won by a generous and sensual Spanish lover—all of which worries Lizzie even more. Unlike Trollope's historical romances with their predictable patterns, this novel does not end happily for all of the characters. Frances has made a choice, and Trollope's point is that she must learn to live with the consequences of that choice, good and bad.

As Trollope's style has matured her plots and characters have become more complex. They obviously do not fit into the easy categories that the early books were bound by genre to do, but there has also been a progression from the more mature novels such as *A Village Affair,* which, Trollope commented to Loudon, "retrospectively . . . seem to me slightly overdone." The more subtle nuances and shades of meaning stem from her growing confidence in her art; she usually keeps her plots confined to a specific cultural and social milieu but knows she has something important to say about the effects of change in ordinary lives. "All my novels focus on what making a choice really means because I think sacrifice through choice is something that happens to almost everybody," she asserted. *A Spanish Lover* was a great critical success; in *Booklist* (1 February 1997) a reviewer commented: "This book is a marvel—for its crystal clear prose, skillful construction with flashbacks seamlessly woven in, and wonderful full-bodied and fallible characters. A rich, mature novel dealing with growth, change, loss and survival, this is as entertaining

as it ought to be enduring." Trollope has moved from being a lightweight purveyor of romantic fiction to a significant chronicler of her time.

This solidity of purpose, however, seems to be belied, in terms of publication dates, by a brief reversion to historical romances with two books, *A Castle in Italy* and *A Second Legacy,* both published under the pseudonym of Caroline Harvey in 1993. Trollope has said that these books were written out of financial necessity; they were actually both written in 1990, before *The Rector's Wife* began selling well. Clearly Trollope finds this kind of book easier and quicker to construct because, she told Finkle, they are "not as rich and as deep." Both books return to the formulae of her earlier novels, with *A Second Legacy* continuing the family saga begun in the three volumes of *Legacy of Love.*

The Best of Friends (1995) is another novel whose plot contrasts a pair of women, seen again in the context of marriage and family business. The best friends are actually Gina and Laurence, who has been friends with Gina since before his marriage to Hilary. The emotional crises in this book provide a test on these interconnected couples, beginning with the sudden end of Gina's marriage to Fergus, who, in a memorable statement, tells Gina that like a good surgeon, he will "cut very deeply but quickly and only once." Trollope, like Jane Austen, often uses a scandal or disaster to test her characters' reaction. As Archie Logan responds to the death of his father, or Lizzie Middleton to the pregnancy of her twin sister, so Gina and her daughter, Sophy, must cope with Fergus's abrupt departure. Gina chooses, as one solution to her pain, to sleep with Laurence; Hilary chooses not to overreact to this situation. Meanwhile their children, all teenagers, are providing their own responses to the tangled mess of their parents' lives, as the drama in the lives of the central characters touches and changes everyone in their social circle. Critics have said that the most powerful character in this book is sixteen-year-old Sophy, who is drawn with an empathetic detail that is totally convincing. The book finally comes to center on her, reminding the reader that she has a whole life ahead of her to negotiate the pitfalls confronted by her parents and their friends.

Trollope narrows the focus of her next novel, *Next of Kin* (1996), even further by setting it not in a provincial town or village but on a dairy farm run by an extended family with a variety of hired help. This focus allows her to pinpoint enmeshed family ties and the effects of financial hardship as they influence Robin Meredith and his daughter, Judy, after the death of his American-born wife, Caroline. The effects of this death are explored, as Robin's family, especially his brother, Joe, struggles to assess the meaning and impact of Caroline's loss. For Joe this struggle becomes a damaging and surprising analysis that ends in his suicide. In turn, Robin's parents, Joe's wife, the farm workers, and Zoe, a new friend of Judy's, reposition themselves and meditate on change and its repercussions on the individual's relationship to the family unit. *Next of Kin* indicates that Trollope has become an experienced chronicler of the effects of loss and pain. She is also a countrywoman, and in this novel the vicissitudes of human existence resonate with the rhythms of rural life.

The agricultural setting of this book is thus different from Trollope's earlier "provincial" novels not only in its tighter focus, but also in its treatment of class. Most of the characters in Trollope's oeuvre (including the historical romances) come from the upper middle class, where private schools, good clothes, and a certain satisfaction with life are par for the course. In an interview with Mary Loudon, Trollope objects to criticism that this social status makes her characters appear too comfortable: "What I'm intent on showing . . . is *not* how cosy a prosperous middle-class world is, but how fragile it is." She attempts in all her fiction to study reaction to trouble, whether it be romantic, financial, or emotional in some vaguer sense. The farm location of *Next of Kin,* together with the American classlessness of the dead Caroline and the elfin mysteriousness of Zoe, perhaps indicate an attempt at transcending this kind of criticism. Trollope has been accused of "confusing material prosperity with spiritual well-being" (*Guardian,* March 28, 1995), and in *Next of Kin* she presents a cast of characters who have neither. This fact certainly makes the novels seem "less comfortable," which is what the critics want, but it is also a foreshortening of Trollope's usual vision.

Similarly, *Faith* (1996), which is effectively a short story published as a "Bloomsbury Quid" (a pocket-sized book selling in England for £1) is set in Canada, and in 1997 Trollope published a new "Caroline Harvey" novel, a return to her historical romances—*The Brass Dolphin* is set in Malta and Africa during World War II. Such diversity may be Trollope's way of demonstrating her range to the critics who have dismissed her as penning complacent "Aga-Sagas," in reference to a kind of stove found usually in upper-middle-class English kitchens.

Over the decades Trollope's work has matured into serious art, as her handling of plot and structure reflect issues and ideas of compelling interest. Her fiction is more complex, not only as she gains skill as a writer, but also as her interests have become more philosophical. She meditates on the meaning of real problems, especially those facing women confined by family and culture. When asked by Loudon if her novels will last, that is, whether they will endure as serious literature, Trollope said that she does not "think they will. They don't feel as if they will." Here, however, she is more modest than her sales figures or her rating with critics seem to merit. Trollope is not only an entertaining writer, but also a thoughtful one, reminding her readers that life in the provinces is regulated by concerns and strictures of which urban folk, particularly women, have no real experience.

Interviews:

Mary Loudon, "Another Country," *The Guardian Weekend,* 11 March 1995, pp. 24–26;

Joanne Kaufman, "Literary Legacy," *People Weekly,* 44 (6 November 1995): 37;

Michael Sims, "Interview With Joanna Trollope," *Bookpage* (February 1997);

David Finkle, "Joanna Trollope: Family Plots with Untidy Endings," *Publishers Weekly,* 244 (3 February 1997): 80–82.

Jeanette Winterson

(27 August 1959 –   )

Ann Hancock
University of the West of England, Bristol

BOOKS: *Oranges Are Not the Only Fruit* (London: Pandora, 1985; New York: Atlantic Monthly Press, 1987);

Boating for Beginners (London: Methuen, 1985);

Fit for the Future: The Guide for Women Who Want to Live Well (London: Pandora, 1986);

The Passion (London: Bloomsbury, 1987; New York: Atlantic Monthly Press, 1988);

Sexing the Cherry (London: Bloomsbury, 1989; New York: Atlantic Monthly Press, 1990);

Written on the Body (London: Cape, 1992; New York: Knopf, 1993);

Art and Lies: A Piece for Three Voices and a Bawd (London: Cape, 1994; New York: Knopf, 1995);

Great Moments in Aviation; and Oranges Are Not the Only Fruit: Two Filmscripts (London: Vintage, 1994);

Art Objects: Essays on Ecstasy and Effrontery (London: Cape, 1995; New York: Knopf, 1996);

Gut Symmetries (London: Granta, 1997; New York: Knopf, 1997).

TELEVISION: *Oranges Are Not the Only Fruit,* script by Winterson, BBC2, January 1990;

Great Moments in Aviation, script by Winterson, BBC2, 11 November 1995.

SELECTED PERIODICAL PUBLICATIONS–
UNCOLLECTED: "All Teeth 'n' Smiles," *New Statesman and Society* (22/29 December 1989): 32–33;
"Better than Sex," *Guardian,* 22 July 1997, pp. 1–3.

OTHER: *Passion Fruit: Romantic Fiction with a Twist,* edited by Winterson (London: Pandora, 1986).

Jeanette Winterson is one of the most admired and discussed of her generation of British novelists. Her first novel achieved remarkable success and, although her succeeding ones have often been more controversial–she is capable, whether intentionally or not, of polarizing readers and reviewers in a way unlike any of her contemporaries–she has continued to be a major

Jeanette Winterson at the time of the U.S. publication of The Passion *(photograph © 1988 by Jerry Bauer)*

force in recent British writing. Some consider her to be a feminist icon; she is also the most visible lesbian writer in mainstream British culture.

Born on 27 August 1959, Jeanette Winterson was raised in Lancashire by John Winterson and Constance Brownrigg, who adopted her in infancy. She does not know the identity of her natural mother and father and has never sought them out. The life of a typical Pentecostal evangelist working-class family–her father was a factory worker–is explored in Winterson's first novel, *Oranges Are Not the Only Fruit* (1985). Although the writer has denied any suggestions that her novel is a veiled autobiography, the bare facts of her early life run parallel with events in the novel. As an only child, she was conditioned by her parents' aspirations that she should be a preacher and ultimately a missionary; her world was dominated by biblical teachings and religious devotion. Winterson's accounts of her childhood depict it as an austere existence that she rejected in her teens when she broke away from the church after being publicly denounced for a romance with a local girl. Yet, she has attested many times in her fictions and interviews to the power and influence of that evangelical background, and the unworldliness of her upbringing, with few comforts and little money, has clearly affected her adult lifestyle.

After leaving home at the age of fifteen, Winterson studied at a further education college while employed variously as the driver of an ice-cream van, a makeup assistant at a funeral parlor, and a domestic in a mental hospital. In September 1978 she gained a place at St. Catherine's College, Oxford, to study English, supporting herself throughout her undergraduate years. Her time at Oxford was undistinguished and followed by another series of jobs, briefly in stockbroking, publishing, and the theater.

It was the publication of *Oranges Are Not the Only Fruit* that established Winterson, at the age of twenty-six, in the work that she has since made her full-time career. She claims that her initial motivation for writing was financial: "I needed £1000 and there seemed no other useful and acceptable way to earn it." An editor at Pandora Press, Philippa Brewster, was interested in Winterson's account of her story and encouraged her to write the novel.

Oranges Are Not the Only Fruit charts the childhood and early adulthood of Jeanette, in particular her emerging lesbian sexuality and the conflicts she experiences when, having become a preacher in her church, she is exposed for displaying "unnatural passions." Jeanette's relationship with her eccentric, driven mother, who is "Old Testament through and through" and absolutely set on sending her adopted daughter out into the missionary field, is central to the tale. In form the novel is a conventional linear narrative, interspersed with reflections by the narrator and two stories in fairy-tale style that refer obliquely to themes of the novel.

In terms of both Jeanette's religious and sexual experiences, the novel is a comically rendered story of nonconformity. At school she sews a sampler in black depicting the "terrified damned" with the legend "The summer is ended and we are not saved," while classmates opt for village scenes, pretty colors, and "To Mother with love." Treated with suspicion and hostility by the outside world, she finds a place within the church community until she falls in love with Melanie, one of her converts, and has to leave both home and church. The chapters of the novel are all named after books of the Old Testament and derive their theme loosely from those biblical stories. In the final chapter, "Ruth," Jeanette returns to visit her mother only to find everything much the same. "My mother was treating me like she always had; had she noticed my absence?" Jeanette is clearly still searching for the love she desires but has been drawn back to her mother, who "had tied a thread around my button, to tug when she pleased." She is in limbo, unable to leave her family or find another one.

On the whole, *Oranges Are Not the Only Fruit* was positively received. Roz Kaveney in *TLS: The Times Literary Supplement* thought it an "excellent first novel," though Ursula Hegi in *The New York Times Book Review* criticized Winterson for the way she "glosses over the core," that is, Jeanette's acceptance of her sexuality and rejection of her religious beliefs. Winterson's handling of sexual issues has produced a range of critical responses, though feminist critics have been on the whole gratified by the success of a novel that ridicules pervasive stereotyping of lesbianism. Winterson's comments in the 1991 Vintage edition of the novel make the kind of claims for which the writer has become notorious; she describes it as "an experimental novel," with a "complicated narrative" and "large vocabulary," which, she suggests rather obscurely, may be read in "spirals." G. P. Lainsbury took her to task for such comments, accusing her of patronizing her readers and failing to temper her remarks with the proper humility, observing also that Winterson seemed unable to place her work in a literary context of postwar narrative experimentation. *Oranges Are Not the Only Fruit* paves the way for some of her more challenging works, with its incorporation of fairy tale and fantasy and its tentative hold on realism, but could not be credited with much technical innovation. The book won the Whitbread Prize for a first novel and the television adaptation, scripted by Winterson and shown by the BBC in early 1990, received two BAFTA awards, for best television drama serial and for best actress. *Oranges Are Not the Only Fruit* was quickly followed by another novel, *Boating for Beginners* (1985), and a workout book, *Fit for the Future: The Guide for Women who Want to Live Well* (1986). Also published in 1986 was *Passion Fruit: Romantic Fiction with a Twist,* a collection of stories edited by Winterson and including works by writers such as Angela Carter, Fay Weldon, and Marge Piercy.

Boating for Beginners is classified as a "comic book" on the jackets of Winterson's novels and is rarely given serious assessment; Rebecca O'Rourke has described it as "silly," while Anne Duchêne, in a review of *The Passion* (1987) for the *TLS* (26 June 1987), commented on its "laborious larkiness." Although slight in comparison with Winterson's later works, it is not without interest, however. David Lodge, in an article on Winterson for *The New York Review of Books,* said that *Boating for Beginners* (which has not been published in America) gave him more "simple pleasure" than either *Oranges Are Not the Only Fruit* or *The Passion* and described the work as "an extremely funny travesty of the Book of Genesis, which transfers the story of Noah to our own commercialized and media-ridden times."

The novel is a herald of what was to come in terms of Winterson's abiding literary preoccupations: breaking with realism; a fascination with the power of myth; exploration of the quest theme; the use of fantasy and magic; preaching and storytelling; nonconformity; and an interest in time. A young girl, Gloria, is in search of herself but is hampered by her mother, a benign version of Mrs. Winterson in *Oranges Are Not the Only Fruit*. She is drawn into the family of Noah, a media mogul whose success has been assured by his manufacture of God. In a passage drawn nearly verbatim from Mary Shelley's *Frankenstein* (1818), the reader learns how Noah/Frankenstein created the "Unpronounceable" (Yahweh) from a slab of ice cream, bringing about the invention of Fundamentalist Religion and multiple marketing opportunities. The novel is packed with jokes, parody (the portrayal of romance novelist Bunny Mix draws heavily on Barbara Cartland), and an assortment of biblical and cultural references.

With the publication of her third novel, the highly popular *The Passion*, Winterson established her literary reputation. The novel was well received and won the John Llewellyn Rhys Prize. It was judged by Anne Duchêne in the *TLS* to be the fulfillment of earlier promise, "a book of great imaginative audacity and assurance." A more challenging novel than the previous two, *The Passion* moves into "full-blown magic realism," as David Lodge characterizes it, in a tale set variously in France, Venice, and Russia at the start of the nineteenth century. It opens in a cold and bleak military camp in France, where Henri, one of the two narrators of the novel, is a soldier in the service of Napoleon and currently employed in the kitchens, helping to satisfy the emperor's gluttonous appetite for chicken, the first demonstrable "passion" in the novel. While Henri worships Napoleon and is indefatigable in his task of wringing chickens' necks, he is unfit for army life. In a macho world of power, lust, and greed, exemplified by both Napoleon and the repugnant cook with whom Henri works, he exhibits characteristics culturally defined as feminine: he is physically slight and weak, closely attached to his family, God-fearing, shy, emotional, virginal, and sensitive to the sufferings inflicted by war.

The second narrator, Villanelle, inhabits decadent Venice, the "city of disguises," "an enchanted isle for the mad, the rich, the bored, the perverted." Venice is identified with night, darkness, and casinos; the lure and the risk of gambling, with cards and with love, are highlighted in the recurrent pronouncement: "You play, you win. You play, you lose. You play." Villanelle is the

"She is the most interesting young writer I have read in twenty years."—*Gore Vidal*

JEANETTE WINTERSON

THE PASSION

FICTION

Dust jacket for Winterson's 1988 novel, which follows a mysterious woman through nineteenth-century Venice, France, and Russia

daughter of a boatman and, contrary to a tradition that attributes this quality only to male children, she has inherited webbed feet, as well as the ability to walk on water. She is an enigmatic, bisexual character, who dresses at times as a man both for her protection and for fun. As a man she meets both Henri's enemy, the cook, now a supplier of meat and horses to the army, and a married woman, called only the "Queen of Spades," with whom she falls passionately in love at first sight. Villanelle's love for this woman is the most tangibly rendered passion in the novel. Winterson takes the commonplace notion of someone "stealing the heart" of a lover and enacts it literally: in one of the more fantastic moments of the novel Henri retrieves Villanelle's heart from the woman's house, where it has been kept in a jar, and hands it to her: "I heard her uncork the jar and a sound like gas escaping. Then she began to make terrible swallowing and choking noises and only my fear kept me sitting at the other end of the boat, perhaps hearing her die."

The stories of the two narrators come together in Russia, where Henri finally becomes disillusioned with

Napoleon and Villanelle wishes to desert her post as *vivandière* (prostitute for the officers), a fate inflicted on her by the cook, who, having married her, sells her to the army. They return to Venice, where eventually Henri goes mad, perhaps for love of Villanelle (who sleeps with him but feels only a sisterly affection toward him) but largely as a result of his murder of Villanelle's husband, who had threatened to reveal their whereabouts. At the end of the novel Henri is incarcerated in San Servelo, a prison for the insane, unwilling to leave despite Villanelle's attempts to buy his freedom after the birth of their daughter.

The Passion was much admired for its humor, poignancy, inventiveness, and compelling storytelling. The directive "I'm telling you stories. Trust me" is repeated several times in the novel. Her idiosyncratic style—a mixture of short, aphoristic statements or commands to the reader, intensely evoked physical detail and occasionally overwritten flights of fancy—and fabulous stories impressed many critics and readers.

Feminist interest in Winterson has often concentrated on her representations of sexual identity. In *The Passion* she shows, according to Laura Doan in *The Lesbian Postmodern* (1994), that "the search for clear-cut distinctions where gender is concerned is futile." The representation of Henri and Villanelle suggests that biological sex and culturally acquired gender do not necessarily go hand in hand. In *Sexing the Cherry* (1989), which earned Winterson another literary prize, the E. M. Forster Award, she continues to explore gender issues, partly by using again the device of two narrators, male and female, with changes in voice marked by symbols at the beginning of each section. One narrator, known only as the "Dog Woman," is indicated by a banana; the second narrator, her adopted son, Jordan, is represented by a pineapple. While the majority of the novel is set in seventeenth-century London, Winterson also includes contemporary passages narrated by Nicholas Jordan (introduced by a pineapple split in half) and a 1990s environmentalist who launches a "one-woman campaign" to rid British rivers of mercury poisoning (introduced by a broken-off banana).

Like *The Passion*, *Sexing the Cherry* is in part a fictionalization of history; major events are seen through the eyes of the kinds of isolated nonconformist characters in which Winterson specializes. The Dog Woman, a giant who in a heavyweight contest sends an elephant hurtling from the scales into the sky, tells most of the rewritten history: the English Civil War; the trial and execution of Charles I; the adventures of John Tradescant, the king's gardener; disasters such as the Black Death and the Great Fire of London; and, more mundanely, the arrival in Britain of the first banana and pineapple. She is capable of enthusiastic murder in the

cause of natural justice; yet, she has a curiously good-natured innocence of the ways of the world. Her battles against Puritanism lead her to take to heart the Old Testament adage "an eye for an eye and a tooth for a tooth," assembling, to the horror of her associates, "119 eyeballs, one missing on account of a man who had lost one already, and over 2,000 teeth." The physical realities of seventeenth-century London are illustrated with a Rabelaisian gusto; sounds, smells, and strange sexual habits are graphically described by the Dog Woman.

Jordan, whom the Dog Woman had rescued like Moses from the "stinking Thames" and brought up as her son, provides an altogether different story. His dreamy, philosophical reflections and lovesick quest contrast with the earthy, practical adventures of his mother. Rather like Henri, he is driven by a hopeless love for Fortunata, one of the Twelve Dancing Princesses whose stories of entrapment into marriage and escape through desertion or murder take up a single short section of the novel. Jordan's pursuit of Fortunata and his apprenticeship to John Tradescant take him around the world. During his travels he speculates on the nature of reality and time, and he appears to find Fortunata, although it may be merely a fantasy. Jordan wants to be "brave and admired and have a beautiful wife and a fine house" but sees in his mother, not himself, the "masculine" attributes of strength, self-sufficiency, and an absence of self-doubt.

Sexing the Cherry was reviewed with enthusiasm for the quality of Winterson's writing and the boldness of her experiments with form and content. Gary Krist in the *Hudson Review* (1991) thought the novel had much to recommend it and observed that "it actually has an agenda to advance—something quite rare these days," suggesting that it could be read "as a polemic against narrowness, inflexibility, pedestrianism." Winterson is not afraid to preach to her readers, and many of her novels are driven by an overt moral and political force.

The publication of Winterson's next novel, *Written on the Body* (1992), revealed some resistance to the public persona she had established and to the direction her writing was taking. By this time Winterson had become a wealthy woman fully in charge of her affairs. She had ceased to use a literary agent and had set up Great Moments, a company run from her home that dealt with all of her literary business. Her private life, in particular the coterie of dedicated women who surrounded her, was the subject of speculation, inflamed by Winterson's own comments in interviews. While on the one hand Winterson has always professed to abhor intrusion into her life by journalists, on the other she was dubbed by Nicci Gerrard in a 1 September 1989 interview in *New Statesman and Society* as a "consummate self-publicist, articulate and anecdotal," well-known for fabricating colorful incidents in her life to such an extent that few biographical facts can be established as reliable. She is also free with her provocative, often unfashionable, views on art and life and frequently applauds her own talent; such self-confidence and conviction inevitably stimulate response.

Winterson has represented her life in various ways throughout her career. In one version she lives an ascetic and modest existence as a scholarly loner, devoted to writing, book collecting, gardening, cats, vegetarianism, and her partner of some years, Margaret (Peggy) Reynolds, an academic, broadcaster, and writer. Another version, perpetuated in Jenny Turner's 18 June 1994 interview in the *Guardian,* for example, has had "many, many" lovers, claims to have worked as a lesbian prostitute in her youth (for which she received payment in Le Creuset kitchenware), and denies her family, failing even to go to her mother's deathbed. These versions of Winterson are united in their scorn for modern life and the mundaneness of ordinary lives.

Partly responding to developments in Winterson's writing but also hostile to her self-representation, reviewers and observers seemed to be withdrawing the enthusiasm that had been hers since the publication of *Oranges Are Not the Only Fruit,* and *Written on the Body* did not receive the approbation accorded her earlier novels. Many felt that Winterson had taken too many risks in her writing and had become self-indulgent. It was felt that she had not avoided the potential dangers of her approach to writing, outlined by David Lodge in *The New York Review of Books* (29 September 1998), who suggests that if Winterson were to lose her redeeming humor, which he already saw abating in *The Passion,* and become too confined by the Romantic mode, she could find herself "lacking in the ironical self-consciousness that saves a writer from bathos and pretentiousness." He hoped that Winterson would not set off "in pursuit of high seriousness." Winterson's detractors in the early 1990s complained that she had taken such a course.

The narrator of *Written on the Body* is nameless and of unspecified sex. S/he has had many casual sexual relationships with men and women, which are relayed by anecdotes throughout the novel, and is cynical about commitment and marriage: "the self-exhibition, the self-satisfaction, smarminess, tightness, tight-arsedness." For a while s/he has been uneasily settled with Jacqueline in a comfortable but loveless relationship when s/he falls passionately in love with Louise, who is married to Elgin, a rich and eminent doctor. After a brief period of agonizing, Louise moves in with the narrator, and they are blissfully happy. Problems arise when Elgin informs the narrator that Louise has leukemia. In order to save her life, the narrator abandons Louise to the care of her husband, who can obtain for her the best cancer treat-

ment. Overwhelmed with grief, the narrator moves to a rundown cottage in Yorkshire and devotes much time to an investigation of cancer and the human body. The central sections of the novel, "The Cells, Tissues, Systems and Cavities of the Body," take the form of a "love-poem" to Louise, "embalming" her in the narrator's memory. It is only after several months, when Elgin fails to report on Louise's progress, that regret sets in and the narrator sets out to search for Louise. S/he fails to find her, although s/he discovers that Elgin is now with another woman and returns to Yorkshire. The story ends with a hallucination of Louise arriving at the door.

Written on the Body is in form and subject matter a departure from the magic realism of *The Passion* and *Sexing the Cherry;* indeed, it is a more conventional novel than one might expect from such an adventurous author. It has been described by its more jaundiced reviewers as a version of the North London adultery novel and reminiscent of Erich Segal's *Love Story* (1970), with perhaps insufficient irony to lift it from cliché. While its strengths are evident—poetic intensity, eroticism, emotional power—its perceived weaknesses have attracted much criticism.

Winterson's aims seem to be to reclaim language, in particular the clichés of love, and to eroticize the body through the minute examination of areas absent from romantic discourse—"The lining of your mouth I know through tongue and spit. Its ridges, valleys, the corrugated roof, the fortress of teeth. The glossy smoothness of the inside of your upper lip is interrupted by a rough swirl where you were hurt once"—and to blur gender boundaries by using a sexually indeterminate narrator. On one level this strategy is successful; the sense of an overwhelming, tactile passion is remarkably well conveyed. What has aroused criticism is the grandiose style of the novel and the perceived egotistical self-indulgence of the narrator's passion; the other characters, especially Louise, the love object, tend to lack substance. One might see Winterson merely adhering to literary tradition here, however. Her self-absorbed lover is little different from those given voice by John Donne. To some extent Winterson is regarded by her critics as guilty of transgressing gender boundaries in her appropriation of a masculine discourse of love.

The function of the unsexed narrator is difficult to assess. For some critics it is merely a gimmick; for others the narrator takes on a masculine role and simply reproduces oppressive male/female power relationships in his attitude toward many lovers, as Helen Barr observed in the *English Review* (April 1993): "Winterson's narrator experiences sexual happiness in expressly masculine terms of quest and exploration: 'Let me pene-

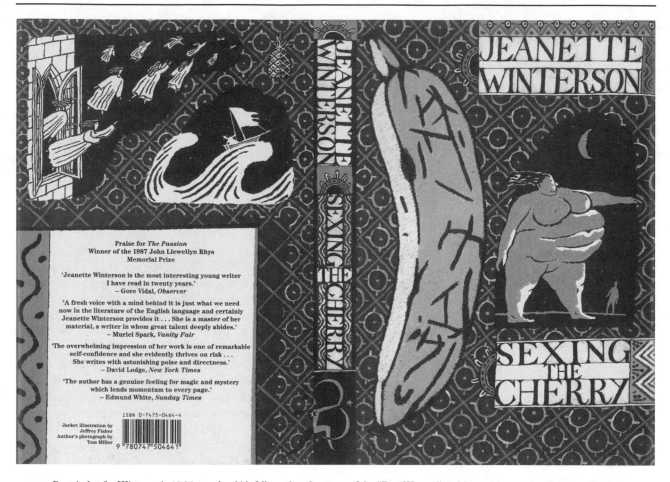

Dust jacket for Winterson's 1989 novel, which follows the adventures of the "Dog Woman" and her son in seventeenth-century London

trate you. I am the archaeologist of tombs."" The view that Winterson reinforces, rather than eradicates, gender distinctions is not shared by Heather Nunn in *Women: a Cultural Review* (1996), who sees the work as an "affirmation of lesbian love, pleasure and desire" that emphasizes fluidity of desire and identity.

Although by the late 1980s Winterson was being vigorously attacked in the press, her status as a novelist remained high. In her 1989 interview, Nicci Gerrard described Winterson as "one of the most exciting and acclaimed authors of her generation"; in January 1993 she was included on the W. H. Smith list of the twenty best young British novelists. While reviewers seemed to have lost sympathy for Winterson's literary projects, her reputation and significance as a feminist icon were assured with literary critics, especially feminists, who found much that was genuinely innovative and impressive in her work. Academic interest in the novels has been considerable and continues.

Winterson's sixth novel, *Art and Lies: A Piece for Three Voices and a Bawd,* was published in the summer of 1994. Profiles and reviews appeared in all the major British newspapers. One in particular, written by Ger-

rard, the deputy books editor of the *Observer,* sparked off a media incident that intensified some people's suspicions that Winterson had become lost in narcissism. This perception had already been fueled in March 1994 by Winterson's assertion that she was the greatest living writer: "No one working in the English language now comes close to my exuberance, my passion, my fidelity to words." Gerrard's article, though not overtly hostile, was critical of what she saw as Winterson's hypocrisy, arrogance, and contempt for a world she had lost touch with. Shortly after the article appeared, Winterson and Peggy Reynolds appeared at Gerrard's door late one evening, demanding an explanation for the criticism. This scene, recorded by Gerrard and commented on by many observers, was not without precedent and emphasized Winterson's stark polarizing of people—rather in the manner of the characterization of Mrs. Winterson in *Oranges Are Not the Only Fruit*—into friends and enemies. Winterson was described at about the same time in the *Sunday Times* as the "books page version of royalty," "a high-profile recluse whose contempt for the media is only matched by her mastery of it." She had become a legend, and stories were rife, ranging from her demands that men in shorts be excluded from her book readings to gossipy accounts of her lovers to stories about the "coven" that existed in her large North London home, with devotees relieving her of the domestic drudgery of everyday life.

Art and Lies is a complete departure from realism, a move that has not been appreciated by all critics and reviewers. It again uses multiple narrators—three in this case—whose life stories are loosely brought together by a shared train journey and some obliquely revealed connections among them. For example, Handel, a doctor, is called at one point to the house of "Picasso" (her real name is Sophia) when her parents demand her admission to a psychiatric hospital. The novel takes the form of a series of dramatic monologues in which Handel, variously a castrato singer, priest, and doctor; Picasso, a painter and abused child; and Sappho, a contemporary lesbian and the reincarnation of the Greek poet, offer their rhapsodic stories. Occasionally a third-person narrator intervenes with descriptive passages in the manner of Virginia Woolf, and readings from a pastiche eighteenth-century pornographic tale of Doll Sneerpiece mark a change from the prevailing somber tone to the bawdiness of *Sexing the Cherry*. It is a self-consciously erudite novel, with a lengthy passage in Latin as early as the third page, much literary allusion and reference, and a recondite vocabulary. Its themes are the continuity of culture, the idea that "all art belongs to the same period," and an attack on modern technology and the dulling of emotions that Winterson attributes to the banality of everyday life. Handel, a cold, remote character, expresses poignantly the absence of feeling in his life, while Sappho, "drunk on words," rails against the dreary world of the "executive zombies, the shop zombies, the Church zombies, the writerly zombies, all mouthing platitudes, the language of the dead" and experiences instead the (verbal) rapture of love.

Reactions to *Art and Lies* were mixed. A few reviewers, generally male, were savage in their criticism of Winterson's pretensions, the absence of originality in her reworking of modernist themes and methods, and her "gender-spite"; the reviewer for the *Sunday Times* (26 June 1994) wrote of a "talent more and more dispiritingly debased by self-worship." Others, often women, were much more receptive to Winterson's writing. Rachel Cusk in the *Times* (London) (20 June 1994) found the novel infuriating in its inaccessibility and apparent contempt for the reader but also exciting and moving; Winterson, she wrote, has "such a depth of feeling for everything she touches."

Winterson's next publication was a collection of essays, *Art Objects: Essays on Ecstacy and Effrontery* (1995); one chapter, titled "The Psychometry of Books" also appeared, slightly edited, in *The Independent* magazine just prior to the publication of *Art Objects* under the title "My Hardback Heaven." The essays express Winterson's views on modern life and the place of art in a different—and for many readers more engaging—way than *Art and Lies*. In her forthright manner Winterson addresses the reader directly with her views on the centrality of art to life, on the need for silence and contemplation, and for an experience of life that is not made up of "microwave moments." She writes with passion about the things that mean most to her: collecting books, especially first editions; Woolf, Gertrude Stein, and the modernist movement; and the enduring power of true art. Her adherence to modernism seems at times perverse and willfully neglectful of all that has happened since, though it is consistent with her professed disregard for late-twentieth-century writing: "I can find little to cheer me between the publication of *Four Quartets* (1944) and Angela Carter's *The Magic Toyshop*." Winterson fails, however, to justify with complete success why anyone in the 1990s should feel the need to replay the call to "make it new" or go over the ground of T. S. Eliot's "Tradition and the Individual Talent," as she does in this book. The traditional views about artistic truth that she expresses coexist uneasily with the contemporary focus she has in her fictions on the fluidity of identity and the unstable nature of reality. The final essay in *Art Objects,* "A Work of My Own," is an explanation of her aims in her novels and perhaps a rejection of those who fail to understand her. She concludes with an implicit rejection of the middle-aged establishment reader, stating that "it is for a new generation that I write." Though some reviewers continued to take Winterson to task for arrogance and careless writing, others found pleasure in these essays and believed that she had something important to say, if the reader could forgive her lapses into whimsy or excessive solemnity.

Gut Symmetries followed in 1997. At the heart of the novel is a love triangle. Stella has been married for many years to Jove, who has an affair with a younger woman, Alice. After Jove rather deviously ensures that his wife finds out about his infidelity, the two women meet and begin an affair themselves. Thus is worked out one kind of "gut symmetry," as the reader learns that there are other connections to be made between the trio; for instance, it becomes apparent that Alice's father had an affair with Stella's German mother, Uta, many years before. As in *Art and Lies,* there is plentiful life-history in the novel, recounted primarily by Stella and Alice, whose voices are often difficult to differentiate. The stories and the love affairs are at once conventional and fantastic. There are gestures toward realism, but Winterson does not depend on plausibility. The reader is asked to believe that Stella has a diamond embedded in her spine, caused by her mother's greed for hard stones during pregnancy, and that Alice's grandmother still works as a cleaner at the age of ninety.

As she has proved before, Winterson's talent for evoking the physicality of passionate feeling is impressive. A scene in which Stella ransacks the marital apartment on discovering Jove's affair with Alice is vigorously conveyed: "Where was she? Under the carpet? Pressed between the glass and window frame? I was breathing her. Her dust, her molecules, the air was fat with her, the droppings and gatherings of a living body." The lyricism of Winterson's descriptive writing can be masterful.

What is less successful in this novel is the incorporation of contemporary scientific theory and the relentless scavenging—through quotation or allusion—of literary forebears. Addressing science has been popular in recent fiction, for example in the work of Ian McEwan, but here the scientific content threatens to overload the narrative, particularly when added to references to tarot, astrology, Kabbalah, and the Bible. Both Alice and Jove are scientists and discourse on Grand Unified Theories (another reference for the *gut* of the title) and other popularized ideas. One of the themes of the novel concerns living in a state of flux, but it does not fully justify the range of scientific reference. Similarly, the inclusion of a character called Captain Ahab, referring to Herman Melville's *Moby-Dick* (1851), and a cabin boy called Friday in reference to Daniel Defoe's *Robinson Crusoe* (1720) seem self-conscious and unnecessary.

Gut Symmetries showed that Winterson remained capable of antagonizing her critics. Those who disliked the novel found it pretentious, too abstract, the writing considerably varied in quality, and the aim too ambitious. However, Marianne Wiggins in the *Times* (26 December 1996) praised its "wisdom" and "joy" and the enormous potential in Winterson's writing. Michèle Roberts in the *Independent on Sunday* (5 January 1997) pointed out that Winterson has broken the implicit rule that girls do not show off, as much of this novel proclaims its own brilliance. James Wood concluded his regretfully negative review in the *Guardian* (2 January 1997) by suggesting that Winterson's writing is robust enough to stand the strain of criticism and that "she will produce something of importance."

Winterson has become a highly controversial figure, but few would deny her talent for writing extraordinary and inspiring prose. As she says at the end of *Gut Symmetries:* "Whatever it is that pulls the pin, that hurls you past the boundaries of your own life into a brief and total beauty, even for a moment, it is enough."

Interviews:

Nicci Gerrard, "The Prophet," *New Statesman and Society* (1 September 1989): 13;

Harry Eyres, "Unpeeling the *Oranges* Psyche," *Times* (London), 10 September 1990, p. 17;

Helen Barr, "Face to Face," *English Review,* 2, no. 1 (1991): 30–32;

Claire Messud, "The Body Politic," *Guardian,* 26 August 1992, p. 29;

Alice Thomson, "Passionate Apostle for the Lexicon of Love," *Times* (London) supplement, 26 August 1992, p. 5;

Justine Picardie, "Making Things Up," *Independent,* 5 September 1992, pp. 44–46;

"Writer with a Tongue of Flame," *Bookseller* (29 April 1994): 32–33;

Jenny Turner, "Preacher Woman," *Guardian,* 18 June 1994, pp. 18–19, 22, 25.

References:

Catherine Belsey, "Postmodern Love: Questioning the Metaphysics of Desire," *New Literary History,* 25, no. 3 (1994): 683–706;

Laurel Bollinger, "Models for Female Loyalty: The Biblical Ruth in Jeanette Winterson's *Oranges Are Not the Only Fruit,*" *Tulsa Studies in Women's Literature,* 13, no. 2 (1994): 363–380;

Christy L. Burns, "Fantastic Language: Jeanette Winterson's Recovery of the Postmodern World," *Contemporary Literature,* 37, no. 2 (1996): 278–306;

Laura Doan, "Jeanette Winterson's Sexing the Postmodern," in *The Lesbian Postmodern,* edited by Doan (New York: Columbia University Press, 1994);

Hilary Hinds, "*Oranges Are Not the Only Fruit:* Reaching Audiences Other Lesbian Texts Cannot Reach," in *New Lesbian Criticism: Literary and Cultural Readings,* edited by Sally Munt (Hemel Hempstead, U.K.: Harvester Wheatsheaf, 1992);

G. P. Lainsbury, "Hubris and the Young Author," *Notes on Contemporary Literature,* 22, no. 4 (1992): 2–3;

Sally Munt, "Is there a Feminist in This Text? Ten Years (1979–1989) of the Lesbian Novel: a Retrospective," *Women's Studies International Forum,* 15, no. 2 (1992): 281–291;

Heather Nunn, "*Written on the Body:* An Anatomy of Horror, Melancholy and Love," *Women: a Cultural Review,* 7, no. 1 (1996): 16–27;

Rebecca O'Rourke, "Fingers in the Fruit Basket: A Feminist Reading of Jeanette Winterson's *Oranges Are Not the Only Fruit,*" in *Feminist Criticism: Theory and Practice,* edited by Susan Sellers (Hemel Hempstead, U.K.: Harvester Wheatsheaf, 1991);

Judith Seaboyer, "Second Death in Venice: Romanticism and the Compulsion to Repent in Jeanette Winterson's *The Passion,*" *Contemporary Literature,* 38, no. 3 (1997): 483–509.

Appendix:
Literary Prizes and British Literary Culture

Richard Todd, in his *Consuming Fictions: The Booker Prize and Fiction in Britain Today* (1996), argues that at "about the beginning of the 1980s, Britain's literary culture in respect of the novel began to undergo a series of rapid and fascinating changes. Prior to this time–in other words during the immediate postwar period until well into the 1970s–Britain's serious literary novelists were likely to achieve notice through either (a) the production of one title that captured the public imagination, or (b) a steady output that contrived to reach a faithful, and usually increasing, readership." The changes that have marked the past two decades in British fiction, Todd explains, are most obvious in the much greater visibility and importance of literary prizes. The British have always had a prize-giving culture. The long tradition of school prizes, prize poems, and even yearly ranking of universities according to whose graduates receive the highest percentage of first-class degrees–another prize–finds a counterpart in the panorama of literary prizes and awards. More than just a love of ranking seems to explain the popularity of literary prizes; there is also a love of ceremony and a desire by people with money to associate themselves with literature. As Simon Brett declared while announcing the 1997 Society of Authors awards, "As Robin Hood found out–apart from Maid Marian, there are few more enjoyable human activities than handing out someone else's money."

The economic developments that came to be known as Thatcherism, after the election of Prime Minister Margaret Thatcher as a radical apostle of market forces in 1979, along with incidental developments in the literary world, dramatically increased the importance of literary prizes. One change that reflects this new significance is the increasing monetary amounts of the awards. While it is an honor to receive a named prize with an accompanying check for ten guineas, it is even more satisfying to receive one that accompanies the honor with £20,000, a figure that several prizes currently exceed. The increased monetary value of the literary prize is likely to be a consequence of the financial interests of the sponsoring institution. A prize underwritten by the estate of a deceased author may not be any more pure in intent than one funded by a large multinational corporation; but the large multinational, in addition to having more money to award, is ultimately interested in publicity. Such self-interest is true, though perhaps to a lesser extent, of such sponsors as the Book Trust–which hopes to increase sales of books rather than meat or beer–W. H. Smith, booksellers, or the Society of Authors, a guild interested in improving the lot of Britain's writers.

Literary prizes have always been controversial. Some authors refuse to be nominated for them. Christopher Hope, who has been a nominated novelist, wrote acidly in the *New Statesman* (21 June 1996) that "a literary prize is . . . a sum of money given by sponsors no-one has heard of to writers few have read, in the hopes of improving the reputations of both. . . . these competitions are an assault on writers in which writers often collaborate." Other observers, while showing no objection to literary prizes as such, fear their proliferation: in the *Independent on Sunday* (20 September 1998) George Walden, a former chairman of the Booker Prize judges, says that the "Booker has tried to maintain its standards, but it becomes a problem if you get into the situation we have in schools, where everyone must win something." Clearly there is some way to go before Walden's fears will be realized; Todd estimates that in the 1980s as many as seven thousand novels eligible for the Booker were published each year, and the number has risen since then. Of course there are also observers, novelists among them, who accept the idea of prize giving but disagree with the judges over their selection of winners, leading to vigorous and usually healthy debate about standards of literary quality, inclusiveness, realism versus experimentalism, and The Fate of the Novel.

Though the Booker Prize attracts the most media attention, it has been awarded only since 1968 and has in fact achieved its blaze of publicity only after about 1980. The Hawthornden Prize for imaginative literature was established in time to make its first award in 1919; the James Tait Black Memorial Prize has been awarded since 1920 (for books published in 1919) and has the distinction of having been given to D. H. Lawrence in its second year.

Many of the prizes, for example, the Hawthornden, the Yorkshire Post, and the W. H. Smith, are not limited to novels. Authors have received those prizes over the years for memoirs, travel, poetry, biography, and history as well as (perhaps somewhat disproportionately) prose fiction. Among the various literary awards the criteria for eligibility vary; though all are for English-language works, for some of them authors from the Commonwealth are entered alongside citizens of the United Kingdom; one award is specifically for Commonwealth and U.K. authors. One award is only for women. Another is only for Irish authors. Several are for young, or first-time, or even young and first-time novelists. Others are restricted to older authors. The amount of prize money awarded varies widely, as can the purposes to which it is supposed to be put: one award encourages the winner to travel abroad; another gives the winner money to pass along to another deserving recipient.

Looking at the awards offered by only one organization, the Society of Authors, one finds the Cholmondley Awards for poets (endowed by the late Dowager Marchioness of Cholmondley in 1966), the Encore Award (sponsored by Miss Lucy Astor) for second novels, the Eric Gregory Awards to encourage promising poets under the age of thirty, the Richard Imison Memorial Award for the best dramatic work broadcast by a writer new to radio (created in 1994 and sponsored by the Peggy Ramsay Foundation—Peggy Ramsay is a recently deceased literary agent), the McKitterick Prize for first novels written by authors over the age of forty, the Royal Society of Medicine Awards for medical writing and illustration in electronic form, and the Sagittarius Prize for a published first novel by an author over the age of sixty. There is a biennial Tom-Gallon Award to fiction writers of limited means on the basis of a short story. The Society of Authors also administers the more important Somerset Maugham Awards and the Betty Trask Prize and Awards.

Deciding on which is the most prestigious of the literary awards is a difficult matter, though there is a near consensus that, for the novelist, the Booker Prize is the most desirable. Whether this is because of its high monetary value (though it is not the most valuable prize), its limitation to novels, the distinguished names of its previous winners (though several outstanding books and authors have been quite shockingly passed over, while some of the winners look, in retrospect, peculiar), or simply intelligent and effective marketing, the Booker is considered most worth winning. To some extent other competitions, particularly the Whitbread, seem to rectify Booker oversights. The Whitbread Book of the Year award, worth £23,000, is an important recognition; but in the case of the Whitbread, unlike in the Booker judging, a novel has to compete against another novel, a biography, a children's book, and a volume of poems. The Orange Prize, awarded only to women, is well publicized and well funded and is seen by many commentators as helping to protect women's writing from the invidious male-dominated standards of other competitions; on the other hand, several distinguished women novelists, most notably Anita Brookner and Doris Lessing, have refused to be considered for the Orange.

Objections to the leading awards as elitist have focused on the Booker. In 1987, for instance, the *Sunday Express* Award was created by then literary editor Graham Lord, who believed that the novels that tended to win the Booker were too often "precious, pretentious, self-regarding, immensely dull and often unreadable." The new prize, worth £20,000 (at that time the most valuable fiction prize in Britain), was judged by practicing novelists and could be given to any book first published in Britain, irrespective of the author's nationality, that was judged to be "not only literate, intelligent and very well written but also compulsively readable." The *Sunday Express* Award was terminated in 1993 on grounds of economy; difficulties in achieving any notice of a newspaper-given award in other newspapers played a role as well. In 1992 W. H. Smith began the Thumping Good Read Award, designed to recognize a "really good page-turner" and specifically focused on "accessible" rather than "literary" titles.

Given the existing profusion of competitions and awards, and their variety of aims and inclusiveness, any listing of British literary prizes is bound to be incomplete. What follows is a discussion of the major British and Irish literary prizes given (though not exclusively) to novels, arranged chronologically from oldest to newest, and lists of the winners since 1960. Years omitted from the following lists are those in which a work of nonfiction, poetry, or short stories won the award. Years in which no prize was given are identified as such.

The Hawthornden Prize

The oldest of the major British literary prizes was founded in 1919 by Alice Warrender. It is awarded annually to an English writer for "the best work of imaginative literature," which is liberally interpreted and thus may include biography, travel, and art history, for instance, as well as fiction and drama. There is no competition; books cannot be submitted. A panel of judges decides the winner. Young authors are particularly encouraged. The current value of the prize is £10,000.

1960 Alan Sillitoe, *The Loneliness of the Long Distance Runner*

1962 Robert Shaw, *The Sun Doctor*

1964 V. S. Naipaul, *Mr. Stone and the Knights Companion*

1965 William Trevor, *The Old Boys*

1966 no award

1967 Michael Frayn, *The Russian Interpreter*

1970 Piers Paul Read, *Monk Dawson*

1971 no award

1972 no award

1973 no award

1975 David Lodge, *Changing Places*

1976 Robert Nye, *Falstaff*

1978 David Cook, *Walter*

1979 P. S. Rushforth, *Kindergarten*

1982 Timothy Mo, *Sour Sweet*

1984 no award

1985 no award

1986 no award

1987 no award

1992 Ferdinand Mount, *Of Love and Asthma*

1993 Andrew Barrow, *The Tap Dancer*

1994 Tim Pears, *In the Place of Fallen Leaves*

1996 Hilary Mantel, *An Experiment in Love*

1997 John Lanchester, *The Debt to Pleasure*

1998 Charles Nicholl, *Somebody Else*

The James Tait Black Memorial Prize

Headquartered in Edinburgh, with a distinguished list of winners from the United Kingdom, the James Tait Black Memorial Prize was founded and endowed by Janet Coats Black in memory of her late husband. Mrs. Black's endowment is now supplemented by the Scottish Arts Council. The winner is chosen by the professor of English literature at the University of Edinburgh; there is an award for the best work of biography as well as for the best work of fiction–in each case, the best work published in the English language in the United Kingdom–during the previous year. The value of each is £3,000.

1960 Morris West, *The Devil's Advocate*

1961 Rex Warner, *Imperial Caesar*

1962 Jennifer Dawson, *The Ha-Ha*

1963 Ronald Hardy, *Act of Destruction*

1964 Gerda Charles, *A Slanting Light*

1965 Frank Tuohy, *The Ice Saints*

1966 Muriel Spark, *The Mandelbaum Gate*

1967 Christine Brooke-Rose, *Such*
Aidan Higgins, *Langrishe, Go Down*

1968 Margaret Drabble, *Jerusalem The Golden*

1969 Maggie Ross, *The Gasteropod*

1970 Elizabeth Bowen, *Eva Trout*

1971 Lily Powell, *The Bird of Paradise*

1972 Nadine Gordimer, *A Guest of Honour*

1973 John Berger, *G.*

1974 Iris Murdoch, *The Black Prince*

1975 Lawrence Durrell, *Monsieur, or the Prince of Darkness*

1976 Brian Moore, *The Great Victorian Collection*

1977 John Banville, *Doctor Copernicus*

1978 John Le Carré *The Honourable Schoolboy*

1979 Maurice Gee, *Plumb*

1980 William Golding, *Darkness Visible*

1981 J. M. Coetzee, *Waiting for the Barbarians*

1982 Salman Rushdie, *Midnight's Children*
Paul Theroux, *The Mosquito Coast*

1983 Bruce Chatwin, *On the Black Hill*

1984 Jonathan Keates, *Allegro Postillions*

1985 J. G. Ballard, *Empire of the Sun*
Angela Carter, *Nights at the Circus*

1986 Robert Edric, *Winter Garden*

1987 Jenny Joseph, *Persephone*

1988 George Mackay Brown, *The Golden Bird: Two Orkney Stories*

1989 Piers Paul Read, *A Season in the West*

1990 James Kelman, *A Disaffection*

1991 William Boyd, *Brazzaville Beach*

1992 Iain Sinclair, *Downriver*

1993 Rose Tremain, *Sacred Country*

1994 Caryl Phillips, *Crossing the River*

1995 Alan Hollinghurst, *The Folding Star*

1996 Christopher Priest, *The Prestige*

1997 Graham Swift, *Last Orders*
Alice Thompson, *Justine*

1998 Andrew Miller, *Ingenious Pain*

The *Mail on Sunday* / John Llewellyn Rhys Prize

Founded in 1942 by Jane Oliver in memory of her late husband, John Llewellyn Rhys, a young writer killed in World War II (who won the Hawthornden Prize in 1942 for a book of poems called *England Is My Village*), this prize is administered by the Book Trust. Sponsorship by the *Mail on Sunday* is a recent development. Any work of literature, fiction or nonfiction, written by a British or Commonwealth writer under the age of thirty-five is eligible if written in English and published in the United Kingdom. Publishers submit entries. Previous winners are not eligible. The winner receives £5,000, and the runners-up receive £500.

1960 David Caute, *At Fever Pitch*

1961 David Storey, *Flight into Camden*

1964 Nell Dunn, *Up the Junction*

1965 Julian Mitchell, *The White Father*

1966 Margaret Drabble, *The Millstone*

1967 Anthony Masters, *The Seahorse*

1968 Angela Carter, *The Magic Toyshop*
1969 Melvyn Bragg, *Without a City Wall*
1971 Shiva Naipaul, *Fireflies*
1973 Peter Smalley, *A Warm Gun*
1974 Hugh Fleetwood, *The Girl Who Passed for Normal*
1975 Tim Jeal, *Cushing's Crusade*
1978 A. N. Wilson, *The Sweets of Pimlico*
1982 William Boyd, *An Ice-Cream War*
1983 Lisa St. Aubin de Teran, *The Slow Train to Milan*
1985 John Milne, *Out of the Blue*
1986 Tim Parks, *Loving Roger*
1987 Jeanette Winterson, *The Passion*
1988 Matthew Yorke, *The March Fence*
1993 Matthew Kneale, *Sweet Thames*
1994 Jonathan Coe, *What a Carve Up!*
1997 Phil Whitaker, *Eclipse of the Sun*

The Somerset Maugham Award

Created and endowed in 1947 by W. Somerset Maugham to enable British authors under the age of thirty-five to enrich their writing by spending time abroad, the Somerset Maugham Award may be best known for its being given to Kingsley Amis in 1955 for *Lucky Jim,* which Maugham had reviewed, pronouncing its author "scum." Amis, who famously disliked foreign travel, used the money to write a book called *I Like It Here.* The award is administered by the Society of Authors; recently there have been several winners each year, each of whom receives £3,500. The awards are not limited to fiction, though dramatic works are excluded from consideration.

1961 V. S. Naipaul, *Miguel Street*
1963 David Storey, *Flight into Camden*
1964 John Le Carré, *The Spy Who Came In from the Cold*
1965 Peter Everett, *Negatives*
1966 Michael Frayn, *The Tin Men*
      Julian Mitchell, *The White Father*
1967 B. S. Johnson, *Trawl*
1968 Paul Bailey, *At the Jerusalem*
1969 Angela Carter, *Several Perceptions*
1970 Jane Gaskell, *A Sweet Sweet Summer*
      Piers Paul Read, *Monk Dawson*
1971 Susan Hill, *I'm the King of the Castle*
      Michael Hastings, *Tussy Is Me*
1972 Gillian Tindall, *Fly Away Home*
1973 Peter Prince, *Play Things*
      Paul Strathern, *A Season in Abyssinia*
      Jonathan Street, *Prudence Dictates*
1974 Martin Amis, *The Rachel Papers*
1975 no award
1976 Dominic Cooper, *The Dead of Winter*
1978 Nigel Williams, *My Life Closed Twice*

1979 Helen Hodgman, *Jack and Jill*
      Sara Maitland, *Daughter of Jerusalem*
1980 Julian Barnes, *Metroland*
1981 A. N. Wilson, *The Healing Art*
1982 William Boyd, *A Good Man in Africa*
1983 Lisa St Aubin de Teran, *Keepers of the House*
1984 Peter Ackroyd, *The Last Testament of Oscar Wilde*
1985 Jane Rogers, *Her Living Image*
1986 Patricia Ferguson, *Family Myths and Legends*
      Tim Parks, *Tongues of Flame*
1987 Stephen Gregory, *The Cormorant*
1988 Matthew Kneale, *Whore Banquets*
1989 Alan Hollinghurst, *The Swimming Pool Library*
      Deirdre Madden, *The Birds of the Innocent Wood*
1990 Sam North, *The Automatic Man*
      Nicholas Shakespeare, *The Vision of Elena Silves*
1991 Peter Benson, *The Other Occupant*
      Lesley Glaister, *Honour Thy Father*
1992 Lawrence Norfolk, *Lempriere's Dictionary*
1994 A. L. Kennedy, *Looking for the Possible Dance*
1996 Alan Warner, *Morvern Callar*
1997 Rhidian Brook, *The Testimony of Taliesin Jones*
      Philip Hensher, *Kitchen Venom*
1998 Rachel Cusk, *The Country Life*

The W. H. Smith Award

Founded in 1959 to "encourage and bring international esteem to authors of the British Commonwealth," the W. H. Smith Award is for an author whose book (not necessarily a novel) "makes, in the opinion of the judges, the most significant contribution to literature." Authors from the United Kingdom, the Commonwealth, or the Irish Republic are eligible. Judging is done by an independent panel of three judges, who call in books from publishers. After they have chosen a shortlist, a guest judge joins them for the selection of the winner. The current value of the award is £10,000.

1959 Patrick White, *Voss*
1960 Laurie Lee, *Cider With Rosie*
1962 J. R. Ackerley, *We Think the World of You*
1963 Gabriel Fielding, *The Birthday King*
1966 R. C. Hutchinson, *A Child Possessed*
1967 Jean Rhys, *Wide Sargasso Sea*
1968 V. S. Naipaul, *The Mimic Men*
1970 John Fowles, *The French Lieutenant's Woman*
1973 Brian Moore, *Catholics*
1974 Anthony Powell, *Temporary Kings*
1981 Isabel Colegate, *The Shooting Party*
1983 A. N. Wilson, *Wise Virgin*
1985 David Hughes, *The Pork Butcher*
1986 Doris Lessing, *The Good Terrorist*

1993 Michèle Roberts, *Daughters of the House*
1994 Vikram Seth, *A Suitable Boy*

The Geoffrey Faber Memorial Prize

Founded in 1963 as a memorial to the founder of the Faber and Faber publishing firm, the Geoffrey Faber Memorial Prize is awarded each year to an author chosen by a panel of three judges who are book reviewers. The prize alternates between a work of prose fiction (which may be a collection of short stories rather than a novel) and a work of poetry, chosen as the work of that type published during the previous two years "of the greatest literary merit." There are no submissions for the prize; instead, the sponsors invite nominations by editors and literary editors of newspapers and magazines that review new fiction and poetry. Eligible authors must be under forty years of age and citizens of the United Kingdom, the Commonwealth, the Republic of Ireland, or South Africa. The value of the prize is £1,000.

1965 Frank Tuohy, *The Ice Saints*
1967 William McIlvanney, *Remedy Is None*
        John Noone, *The Man With the Chocolate Egg*
1969 Piers Paul Read, *The Junkers*
1971 J. G. Farrell, *Troubles*
1973 David Storey, *Pasmore*
1975 Richard Wright, *In the Middle of a Life*
1977 Carolyn Slaughter, *The Story of the Weasel*
1979 Timothy Mo, *The Monkey King*
1981 J. M. Coetzee, *Waiting for the Barbarians*
1983 Graham Swift, *Shuttlecock*
1985 Julian Barnes, *Flaubert's Parrot*
1989 David Profumo, *Sea Music*
1991 Carol Birch, *The Fog Line*
1995 Livi Michael, *Their Angel Reach*

The *Guardian* Fiction Award

Awarded since 1965 by the *Guardian*, one of England's leading "quality," or broadsheet, daily papers, this prize is worth £5,000 to the winner. The selection is made by a panel of critics and writers, chaired by the literary editor of the *Guardian*. The award is the oldest and most established of the awards sponsored by a newspaper; sponsorship by one newspaper however, has a somewhat negative effect on publicity since other newspapers are less willing to publicize the winner than they are for prizes such as the Booker Prize or Somerset Maugham Award.

1965 Clive Barry, *Crumb Borne*
1966 Archie Hind, *The Dear Green Place*

1967 Eva Figes, *Winter Journey*
1968 P. J. Kavanagh, *A Song and a Dance*
1969 Maurice Leitch, *Poor Lazarus*
1970 Margaret Blount, *Where Did You Last See Your Father?*
1971 Thomas Kilroy, *The Big Chapel*
1972 John Berger, *G.*
1973 Peter Redgrover, *In the Country of the Skin*
1974 Beryl Bainbridge, *The Bottle Factory Outing*
1975 Sylvia Clayton, *Friends and Romans*
1976 Robert Nye Hamish, *Falstaff*
1977 Michael Moorcock, *The Condition of Muzak*
1978 Neil Jordan, *Night in Tunisia*
1979 Dambudzo Merechera, *The House of Hunger*
1980 J. L. Carr, *A Month in the Country*
1981 John Banville, *Kepler*
1982 Glyn Hughes, *Where I Used to Play on the Green*
1983 Graham Swift, *Waterland*
1984 J. G. Ballard, *Empire of the Sun*
1985 Peter Ackroyd, *Hawksmoor*
1986 Jim Crace, *Continent*
1987 Peter Benson, *The Levels*
1988 Lucy Ellman, *Sweet Desserts*
1989 Carol Lake, *Rosehill: Portrait from a Midlands City*
1990 Pauline Melville, *Shape-Shifter*
1991 Alan Judd, *The Devil's Own Work*
1992 Alasdair Gray, *Poor Things*
1993 Pat Barker, *The Eye in the Door*
1994 Candia McWilliam, *Debatable Land*
1995 James Buchan, *Heart's Journey in Winter*
1996 Seamus Deane, *Reading in the Dark*
1997 Anne Michaels, *Fugitive Pieces*
1998 Jackie Kay, *Trumpet*

The Booker-McConnell Prize

Called the Booker, this is by common consent the most prestigious award available to British novelists. Sponsored by Booker-McConnell plc, a food-wholesaling company, it has been offered since 1969. In 1993 Salman Rushdie's *Midnight's Children,* the 1981 award winner, was named the "Booker of Bookers," the outstanding Booker winner of the first twenty-five years. It is administered by the Book Council; publishers submit nominated books, though the judges can request others; the panel of judges consists of five persons, usually literary editors, novelists, and nonliterary celebrities, and they announce a shortlist of finalists, usually five books, four or five weeks before the ceremony at which the winner is revealed. Large sums of money are wagered on the Booker Prize, odds for which are established by bookmakers immediately after the shortlist is announced. The award ceremony itself is a gala affair at London's Guildhall, televised live.

Any novel written by a citizen of the United Kingdom, the Republic of Ireland, or the British Commonwealth is eligible to win the Booker for a novel that must have been published in the English language and initially in the United Kingdom. The prize is currently worth £21,000.

1969 P. H. Newby, *Something to Answer For*
1970 Bernice Rubens, *The Elected Member*
1971 V. S. Naipaul, *In a Free State*
1972 John Berger, *G.*
1973 J. G. Farrell, *The Siege of Krishnapur*
1974 Nadine Gordimer, *The Conservationist*
1975 Ruth Prawer Jhabvala, *Heat and Dust*
1976 David Storey, *Saville*
1977 Paul Scott, *Staying On*
1978 Iris Murdoch, *The Sea, The Sea*
1979 Penelope Fitzgerald, *Offshore*
1980 William Golding, *Rites of Passage*
1981 Salman Rushdie, *Midnight's Children*
1982 Thomas Keneally, *Schindler's Ark*
1983 J. M. Coetzee, *Life and Times of Michael K*
1984 Anita Brookner, *Hotel du Lac*
1985 Keri Hulme, *The Bone People*
1986 Kingsley Amis, *The Old Devils*
1987 Penelope Lively, *Moon Tiger*
1988 Peter Carey, *Oscar and Lucinda*
1989 Kazuo Ishiguro, *The Remains of the Day*
1990 A. S. Byatt, *Possession*
1991 Ben Okri, *The Famished Road*
1992 Michael Ondaatje, *The English Patient*
     Barry Unsworth, *Sacred Hunger*
1993 Roddy Doyle, *Paddy Clarke, Ha-Ha-Ha*
1994 James Kelman, *How Late It Was, How Late*
1995 Pat Barker, *The Ghost Road*
1996 Graham Swift, *Last Orders*
1997 Arundhati Roy, *The God of Small Things*
1998 Ian McEwan, *Amsterdam*

The *Yorkshire Post* Book Award

First given in 1964, the *Yorkshire Post* Book Award has changed more than most competitions. In 1972 there were awards for best book, finest fiction work, best first work, and runner-up for best first work. Later books were named novel of the year. There have also been awards for music and art books. This award is unusual in its relatively slight emphasis on fiction. Only once, in 1988, has the book of the year gone to a novel; more often the most honored book is a work of history—often military history—travel, or biography. Since 1991, when there have been awards for book of the year and best first book, the win-

ners in the former category have all been biographies or histories and the winners of the best first book award are as likely to be travel or science writing as novels. The book of the year now receives £1,200 and a scroll; the best first book receives £1,000 and a scroll. Subscribers to the *Yorkshire Post* series of literary luncheons help to support the prize through donations. Publishers are invited to submit nominations for the award, from which selections are made by a panel of judges headed by the *Yorkshire Post* literary editor. Eligibility is normally limited to British authors; the award to Charles Frazier appears to be an anomaly.

1965 Muriel Spark, *The Mandelbaum Gate* (finest fiction)
1966 Rebecca West, *The Birds Fall Down* (first prize)
1967 Laurens van der Post, *The Hunter and the Whale* (finest fiction)
1968 P. H. Newby, *Something to Answer For* (finest fiction)
1969 Iris Murdoch, *Bruno's Dream* (finest fiction)
1970 Edna O'Brien, *A Pagan Place* (finest fiction)
1971 Paul Scott, *The Towers of Silence* (finest fiction)
1972 Margaret Drabble, *The Needle's Eye* (finest fiction)
    Jennifer Johnston, *The Captains and the Kings* (best first work)
1973 Evelyn Anthony, *The Occupying Power* (finest fiction)
1974 Kingsley Amis, *Ending Up* (finest fiction)
    Anne Redmon, *Emily Stone* (best first work)
1975 David Lodge, *Changing Places* (finest fiction)
    Sian James, *One Afternoon* (runner-up, best first work)
1976 Nina Bawden, *Afternoon of a Good Woman* (finest fiction)
    Rhoda Edwards, *Some Touch of Pity* (best first work)
    Sasha Moorsom, *A Lavendar Trip* (finest novel)
1977 Olivia Manning, *The Danger Tree* (finest fiction)
1978 Sîan James, *Yesterday* (finest fiction)
1979 Jennifer Johnston, *The Old Jest* (finest fiction)
1980 Anthony Burgess, *Earthly Powers* (finest fiction)
    Sally Emerson, *Second Sight* (runner-up, best first work)
1981 Paul Theroux, *The Mosquito Coast* (finest fiction)
1982 Elizabeth Jane Howard, *Getting It Right* (novel of the year)
1983 Francis King, *Act of Darkness* (novel of the year)
    Richard Masefield, *Chalkhill Blue* (runner-up, best first work)
1984 Kingsley Amis, *Stanley and the Women* (novel of the year)
    James Buchan, *A Parish of Rich Women* (runner-up, best first work)
1985 Alice Thomas Ellis, *Unexplained Laughter* (novel of the year)
    Patricia Angadi, *The Governess* (runner-up, best first work)
1987 Anne Spillard, *The Cartomancer* (best first work)

1994 Romesh Gunesekera, *Reef* (best first work)
1995 Stephen Blanchard, *Gagarin and I* (best first work)
1996 Martyn Bedford, *Acts of Revision* (best first work)
1997 Charles Frazier, *Cold Mountain* (best first work)

The Whitbread Prize

Founded in 1971, and sponsored by Whitbread Breweries, and administered by the Booksellers Association of Great Britain and Ireland, the Whitbread Prize is considered second only to the Booker in esteem and is considered by some a more important award. There are actually five Whitbread genre prizes each year–best novel, best first novel (beginning in 1981), best biography, best book of poems, and best children's book–from which one is chosen as Whitbread book of the year. Authors who have lived in Great Britain or Ireland for more than three years are eligible. Category winners receive £2,000; the Whitbread book of the year (winners are indicated below by an asterisk) receives £23,000, one of the richest of all literary awards.

1973 Shiva Naipaul, *The Chip Chip Gatherers*
1974 Iris Murdoch, *The Sacred and Profane Love Machine*
1975 William McIlvanney, *Docherty*
1976 William Trevor, *The Children of Dynmouth*
1977 Beryl Bainbridge, *Injury Time*
1978 Paul Theroux, *Picture Palace*
1979 Jennifer Johnston, *The Old Jest*
1980 David Lodge, *How Far Can You Go?* *
1981 Maurice Leitch, *Silver's City*
     William Boyd, *A Good Man in Africa* (best first novel)
1982 John Wain, *Young Shoulders*
     Bruce Chatwin, *On the Black Hill* (best first novel)
1983 William Trevor, *Fools of Fortune*
     John Fuller, *Flying to Nowhere* (best first novel)
1984 Christopher Hope, *Kruger's Alp*
     James Buchan, *A Parish of Rich Women* (best first novel)
1985 Peter Ackroyd, *Hawksmoor*
     Jeanette Winterson, *Oranges Are Not the Only Fruit* (best first novel)
1986 Kazuo Ishiguro, *An Artist of the Floating World**
     Jim Crace, *Continent* (best first novel)
1987 Ian McEwan, *The Child in Time*
     Francis Wyndham, *The Other Garden* (best first novel)
1988 Salman Rushdie, *The Satanic Verses*
     Paul Sayer, *The Comfort of Madness* (best first novel)
1989 Lindsay Clarke, *The Chymical Wedding*
     James Hamilton-Paterson, *Gerontius* (best first novel)
1990 Nicholas Mosley, *Hopeful Monsters*
     Hanif Kureishi, *The Buddha of Suburbia* (best first novel)

1991 Jane Gardam, *The Queen of the Tambourine*
     Gordon Burn, *Alma Cogan* (best first novel)
1992 Alisdair Gray, *Poor Things*
     Jeff Torrington, *Swing Hammer Swing!* (best first novel)
1993 Joan Brady, *Theory of War* *
     Rachel Cusk, *Saving Agnes* (best first novel)
1994 William Trevor, *Felicia's Journey* *
     Fred D'Aguiar, *The Longest Memory* (best first novel)
1995 Salman Rushdie, *The Moor's Last Sigh*
     Kate Atkinson, *Behind the Scenes at the Museum* * (best first novel)
1996 Beryl Bainbridge, *Every Man for Himself*
     John Lanchester, *The Debt to Pleasure* * (best first novel)
1997 Jim Crace, *Quarantine*
     Pauline Melville, *The Ventriloquist's Tale* * (best first novel)
1998 Justin Cartwright, *Leading the Cheers*
     Giles Foden, *The Last King of Scotland* (best first novel)

The Betty Trask Awards

Endowed by a bequest from the late Betty Trask, a somewhat reclusive author of more than thirty romance novels, this award is administered by the Society of Authors. Writers under the age of thirty-five are eligible for a first novel; an unusual feature of the award is that the winner need not have been published. The terms of the bequest specify that the award is to recognize "a romantic novel or other novel of a traditional rather than experimental nature," though the judging panel seems to have interpreted these instructions liberally. Each year there is one Betty Trask Prize, worth £12,000 (indicated by an asterisk), and several more Betty Trask Awards, worth £5,000 or £1,500.

1984 Ronald Frame, *Winter Journey* *
     Clare Nonhebel, *Cold Showers*
     James Buchan, *A Parish of Rich Women*
     Helen Harris, *Playing Fields in Winter*
     Gareth Jones, *The Disinherited*
     Simon Rees, *The Devil's Looking Glass*
1985 Susan Kay, *Legacy* *
     Gary Armitage, *A Season of Peace*
     Elizabeth Ironside, *A Very Private Enterprise*
     Alice Mitchell, "Instead of Eden" (unpublished)
     Caroline Stickland, *The Standing Hills*
     George Schweiz, "The Earth Abides Forever" (unpublished)
1986 Tim Parks, *Tongues of Flame* *
     Patricia Ferguson, *Family Myths and Legends*
     Philippa Blake, *Mzungu's Wife*
     Matthew Kneale, *Whore Banquets*

J. F. McLaughlin, "The Road to Dilmun" (unpublished)

Kate Saunders, *The Prodigal Father*

1987 Helen Flint, *Return Journey* *

Peter Benson, *The Levels* *

James Maw, *Hard Luck*

Catherine Arnold, *Lost Time*

H. S. Bhabra, *Gestures*

Lucy Pinney, *The Pink Stallion*

1988 Alex Martin, *The General Interruptor* *

Candia McWilliam, *A Case of Knives* *

Georgina Andrewes, *Behind the Waterfall*

James Friel, *Left of North*

Glenn Patterson, *Burning Your Own*

Susan Webster, *Small Tales of a Town*

1989 Nigel Watts, *The Life Game* *

William Riviere, *Watercolour Sky*

Paul Houghton, *Harry's Last Wedding*

Alasdair McKee, *Uncle Harry's Last Stand*

1990 Robert McLiam Wilson, *Ripley Bogle* *

Elizabeth Chadwick, *The Wild Hunt*

Rosemary Cohen, "No Strange Land" (unpublished)

Nicholas Shakespeare, *The Vision of Elena Silves*

1991 Amit Chaudhuri, *A Strange and Sublime Address* *

Mark Swallow, *Teaching Little Fang*

Suzannah Dunn, *Quite Contrary*

Lesley Glaister, *Honour Thy Father*

Nino Ricci, *Lives of the Saints*

1992 Liane Jones, *The Dreamstone* *

Peter M. Rosenberg, *Kissing Through a Pane of Glass*

Tibor Fischer, *Under the Frog*

Eugene Mullen, "The Last of His Line" (unpublished)

Edward St. Aubyn, *Never Mind*

1993 Mark Blackaby, *You'll Never Be Here Again* *

Andrew Cowan, *Pig*

Simon Corrigan, *Tommy Was Here*

Joanna Briscoe, *Mothers and Other Lovers*

1994 Colin Bateman, *Divorcing Jack* *

Nadeem Aslam, *Season of the Rainbow*

Guy Burt, *After the Hole*

Frances Liardet, *The Game*

Jonathan Rix, *Some Hope*

1995 Robert Newman, *Dependence Day* *

Mark Behr, *The Smell of Apples*

Martina Evans, *Midnight Feast*

Robit Manchanda, "A Speck of Coaldust" (unpublished)

Juliet Thomas, "Hallelujah Jordan" (unpublished)

Philippa Walshe, "The Latecomer" (unpublished)

Madeline Wickham, *The Tennis Party*

1996 John Lanchester, *The Debt to Pleasure* *

Meera Syal, *Anita and Me*

Rhidian Brook, *The Testimony of Taliesin Jones*

Louis Buss, *The Luxury of Exile*

1997 Alex Garland, *The Beach* *

Josie Barnard, *Poker Face*

Ardashir Vakil, *Beach Boy*

Diran Abedayo, *Some Kind of Black*

Sanjida O'Connell, *Theory of Min*

1998 Kiran Desai, *Hullaballoo in the Guava Orchard* *

Nick Earls, *ZigZag Street*

Phil Whitaker, *Eclipse of the Sun*

Gail Anderson-Dargatz, *The Cure for Death by Lightning*

Tobias Hill, *Underground*

The Commonwealth Writers Prize

Since 1987 the Commonwealth Writers Prize has been awarded by the Commonwealth Foundation to "reward and encourage the upsurge of new Commonwealth fiction, and to ensure that works of merit reach a wider audience outside their own country." Determinedly cosmopolitan, the foundation holds each final judging and award ceremony in a different one of the fifty-three Commonwealth countries. Its shortlisting procedure is designed to ensure this cosmopolitanism. For the purposes of the award the Commonwealth is divided into four regions: Africa, the Caribbean and Canada, Eurasia (which includes the United Kingdom), and Southeast Asia and the South Pacific. In each region a best book and a best first book are chosen: these comprise the overall shortlist. The regional winners each receive a prize of £1,000; the winner of the book of the year receives £10,000; and the winner of the best first book receives £3,000. For its first two years the second prize was awarded to a "runner-up" instead of a best first book.

1987 Olive Senior, *Summer Lightning* (Jamaica)

Witi Ihimaera, *The Matriarch* (New Zealand), runner-up

1988 Festus Iyayi, *Heroes* (Nigeria)

George Turner, *The Sea and Summer* (Australia), runner-up

1989 Janet Frame, *The Carpathians* (New Zealand), best novel

Bonnie Burnard, *Women of Influence* (Canada), best first novel

1990 Mordecai Richler, *Solomon Gursky Was Here* (Canada), best novel

John Cranna, *Visitors* (New Zealand), best first novel

1991 David Malouf, *The Great World* (Australia), best novel

Pauline Melville, *Shape-Shifter* (Guyana), best first novel

1992 Rohinton Mistry, *Such a Long Journey* (Canada), best novel

Robert Antoni, *Divina Trace* (Bahamas), best first
novel

1993 Alex Miller, *The Ancestor Game* (Australia), best
novel

Githa Hariharan, *The Thousand Faces of Night* (India),
best first novel

1994 Vikram Seth, *A Suitable Boy* (India), best novel

Keith Oatley, *The Case of Emily V.* (United Kingdom),
best first novel

1995 Louis de Bernières, *Captain Corelli's Mandolin* (United
Kingdom), best novel

Adib Khan, *Seasonal Adjustments* (Pakistan), best first
novel

1996 Rohinton Mistry, *A Fine Balance* (Canada), best novel

Vidram Chandra, *Red Earth and Pouring Rain* (India),
best first novel

1997 Earl Lovelace, *Salt* (Trinidad), best novel

Ann-Marie MacDonald, *Fall on Your Knees* (Canada),
best first novel

1998 Peter Carey, *Jack Maggs* (Australia), best novel

Tim Wynveen, *Angel Falls* (Canada), best first novel

The *Sunday Express* Fiction Award

Awarded from 1987 to 1993 and conceived of as an
anti–Booker Prize, the *Sunday Express* Fiction Award was
worth £20,000 for the winner and £1,000 for each of
the five shortlisted authors. Judging was by well-known
novelists who chose the winner from a list of novels
suggested by other authors and reviewers—not academics. Nominated books were "novels of real quality that
would also appeal to a wide, intelligent readership."

There was some overlap with the Booker lists,
despite the intentionally different aims and scope. The
first three winners were all on the shortlist for the
Booker Prize.

1987 Brian Moore, *The Colour of Blood*

1988 David Lodge, *Nice Work*

1989 Rose Tremain, *Restoration*

1990 J. M. Coetzee, *Age of Iron*

1991 Michael Frayn, *A Landing on the Sun*

1992 Hilary Mantel, *A Place of Greater Safety*

1993 William Boyd, *The Blue Afternoon*

The *Irish Times* Literature Prizes

The *Irish Times* awards two prizes. Founded in 1988, the
prizes were initially sponsored jointly by the newspaper
and Aer Lingus, the Irish national airline, and thereafter
by the *Irish Times* alone. The awards are described as
"offering Irish writers, novelists as well as those in other
categories, a new opportunity to work towards a prize
which is comparable with that available to writers in

other countries. . . . The institution of an award with an
international dimension in addition to a purely Irish
award, will allow Irish writers to be judged against
international standards." Thus, there is a group of Irish
literature prizes, awarded for poetry and nonfiction as
well as fiction, and an international fiction prize, which
is given to the author of a work of fiction written in
English and published in Ireland, the United Kingdom,
or the United States, and which has usually gone to a
North American. The international fiction prize is
worth IR£7,500, and the Irish literature prizes are
worth IR£5000 each. The judges are a panel of literary
editors and critics who call in books from publishers
and choose the winner from a shortlist.

1989 Frank Ronan, *The Men Who Loved Evelyn Cotton*

1990 John McGahern, *Amongst Women*

1991 Colm Toibin, *The South*

1992 Patrick McCabe, *The Butcher Boy*

1993 no fiction award

1995 Kathleen Ferguson, *A Maid's Tale*

1997 Seamus Deane, *Reading in the Dark*

BRITISH AND IRISH INTERNATIONAL PRIZEWINNERS

1990 A. S. Byatt, *Possession*

1997 Seamus Deane, *Reading in the Dark*

The W. H. Smith Thumping Good Read Award

Awarded since 1992, the Thumping Good Read Award
is for books more accessible than the more "literary"
choices of the Booker or Whitbread. Genre fiction—
murder mysteries, espionage thrillers–is considered;
American authors are eligible, as the award to Dominick Dunne illustrates. It also concentrates on less-estab-
lished, younger authors. Judging is done by a panel of
W. H. Smith customers. The value of the prize is
£5,000.

1992 Robert Goddard, *Into the Blue*

1993 Robert Harris, *Fatherland*

1994 Dominick Dunne, *A Season in Purgatory*

1995 Tom Eidson, *St. Agnes' Stand*

1996 Andrew Klavan, *True Crime*

1997 David Baldacci, *Absolute Power*

1998 Douglas Kennedy, *The Big Picture*

The David Cohen British Literature Prize in the English Language

First awarded in 1993, the Cohen Prize is administered
by the Arts Council. It is unusual in that the general
public is invited to nominate prize winners. Its total
value of £40,000 makes it the most lucrative British lit-

erary prize; of that sum, £30,000 is for the winner to keep and £10,000 is for the winner to use in encouraging younger writers and readers. Muriel Spark gave the £10,000 to the Edinburgh school on which she had based *The Prime of Miss Jean Brodie,* to encourage pupils to develop their creativity. It is awarded every other year. The funds are provided by the David Cohen Family Charitable Trust and the Arts Council. It recognizes lifetime achievement and is not limited to novelists; in 1995 playwright Harold Pinter won the award.

1993 V. S. Naipaul
1997 Muriel Spark

The Orange Prize for Fiction

Announced in 1994 and first awarded in 1996, the Orange Prize is unique in that it is limited to women authors. This restriction was a response to the announced "dissatisfaction of senior women in the book world—publishers, agents, literary editors, booksellers, journalists and writers—with the neglect of women writers shown by the major fiction prizes." Though only women are eligible, they can be of any nationality, so long as the novel is in English and has been published in the United Kingdom. A panel of judges makes the award, which, at £30,000, is one of the most lucrative British literary prizes. Though the prize is named for a mobile telephone company, the award, and a bronze sculpture that also goes to the winner, are said to be anonymously endowed.

1996 Helen Dunmore, *A Spell of Winter*
1997 Anne Michaels, *Fugitive Pieces*
1998 Carol Shields, *Larry's Party*

Checklist of Further Readings

Acheson, James, ed. *The British and Irish Novel Since 1960*. New York: St. Martin's Press, 1991.

Adelman, Irving and Rita Dworkin. *The Contemporary Novel: A Checklist of Critical Literature on the British and American Novel Since 1945*. Metuchen, N.J.: Scarecrow Press, 1972.

Allen, Walter. *The Modern Novel in Britain and the United States*. New York: Dutton, 1964.

Astbury, Raymond, ed. *The Writer in the Market Place*. London: Bingley, 1969.

Bergonzi, Bernard. *The Situation of the Novel*. London: Macmillan, 1970.

Bergonzi, ed. *The Twentieth Century*. Volume 7 of *History of Literature in the English Language*. London: Barrie & Jenkins, 1970.

Blair, John G. *The Confidence Man in Modern Fiction: A Rogue's Gallery with Six Portraits*. London: Vision, 1979; New York: Barnes & Noble, 1979.

Bradbury, Malcolm. *Dangerous Pilgrimages: Transatlantic Mythologies and the Novel*. London: Secker & Warburg, 1995; New York: Viking, 1996.

Bradbury. *The Modern British Novel*. London: Penguin, 1993.

Bradbury. *No, Not Bloomsbury*. New York: Columbia University Press, 1988.

Bradbury, ed. *The Novel Today: Contemporary Writers on Modern Fiction*. Manchester: Manchester University Press/Totowa, N.J.: Rowman & Littlefield, 1977.

Bradbury, ed. *Possibilities: Essays in the State of the Novel*. London & New York: Oxford University Press, 1973.

Bradbury and Judy Cooke, eds. *New Writing*. London: Minerva, 1992.

Bradbury and David Palmer, eds. *The Contemporary English Novel*. London: Arnold, 1979; New York: Holmes & Meier, 1980.

British Council. *The Novel in Britain and Ireland Since 1970: A Select Bibliography*. London: British Council, 1994.

Burgess, Anthony. *Ninety-nine Novels: The Best in English Since 1939. A Personal Choice*. London: Allison & Busby, 1984; New York: Summit, 1984.

Burgess. *The Novel Now: A Guide to Contemporary Fiction*. London: Faber & Faber, 1967; New York: Norton, 1967.

Burns, Alan, and Charles Sugnet, eds. *The Imagination on Trial: British and American Writers Discuss Their Working Methods*. London & New York: Allison & Busby, 1981.

Cassis, A. F. *The Twentieth-Century English Novel: An Annotated Bibliography of General Criticism*. New York: Garland, 1977.

Cope, Jackson I., and Geoffrey Green, eds. *Novel vs. Fiction: The Contemporary Reformation*. Norman, Okla.: Pilgrim, 1981.

Crosland, Margaret. *Beyond the Lighthouse: English Women Novelists in the Twentieth Century*. London: Constable, 1981; New York: Taplinger, 1981.

Federman, Raymond, ed. *Surfiction: Fiction Now . . . and Tomorrow*. Chicago: Swallow Press, 1975.

Firchow, Peter, ed. *The Writer's Place: Interviews on the Literary Situation in Contemporary Britain*. Minneapolis: University of Minnesota Press, 1974.

Fletcher, John. *Novel and Reader*. London & Boston: Boyars, 1980.

Gindin, James. *Post-War British Fiction: New Accents and Attitudes*. Berkeley & Los Angeles: University of California Press, 1962.

Glicksberg, Charles I. *The Sexual Revolution in Modern English Literature*. The Hague: Martinus Nijhoff, 1973.

Gray, Nigel. *The Silent Majority: A Study of the Working Class in Post-War British Fiction*. London: Vision, 1973.

Gunn, James. *Alternate Worlds: The Illustrated History of Science Fiction*. Englewood Cliffs, N.J.: Prentice-Hall, 1975.

Hall, James. *The Lunatic Giant in the Drawing Room: The British and American Novel Since 1930*. Bloomington: Indiana University Press, 1968.

Hazell, Stephen, ed. *The English Novel: Developments in Criticism since Henry James*. London: Macmillan, 1978.

Jameson, Storm. *Parthian Words*. London: Collins & Havrill, 1970.

Kaplan, Sydney Janet. *Feminine Consciousness in the Modern British Novel*. Urbana: University of Illinois Press, 1975.

Klaus, H. Gustav, ed. *The Socialist Novel in Britain: Towards the Recovery of a Tradition*. Brighton, U.K.: Harvester, 1982; New York: St. Martin's Press, 1982.

Lee, Alison. *Realism and Power: Postmodern British Fiction*. London & New York: Routledge, 1990.

Lewald, H. Ernest, ed. *The Cry of Home: Cultural Nationalism and the Modern Writer*. Knoxville: University of Tennessee Press, 1972.

Lodge, David. *After Bakhtin: Essays on Fiction and Criticism*. London & New York: Routledge, 1990.

Lodge. *The Art of Fiction: Illustrated from Classic and Modern Texts*. London: Secker & Warburg, 1992; New York: Viking, 1993.

Lodge. *Language of Fiction: Essays in Criticism and Verbal Analysis of the English Novel*. London: Routledge & Kegan Paul/New York: Columbia University Press, 1966; revised edition, London & Boston: Routledge & Kegan Paul, 1984.

Lodge. *The Modes of Modern Writing: Metaphor, Metonymy, and the Typology of Modern Literature*. London: Arnold, 1977; Ithaca, N.Y.: Cornell University Press, 1977.

Lodge. *The Novelist at the Crossroads and Other Essays on Fiction and Criticism*. London: Routledge & Kegan Paul, 1971; Ithaca, N.Y.: Cornell University Press, 1971.

Lodge. *The Practice of Writing: Essays, Lectures, Reviews and a Diary*. London: Secker & Warburg/New York: Viking, 1996.

Lodge. *Working with Structuralism: Essays and Reviews on Nineteenth- and Twentieth-Century Literature*. London & Boston: Routledge & Kegan Paul, 1986.

Madden, David. *A Primer of the Novel: For Readers and Writers*. Metuchen, N.J. & London: Scarecrow Press, 1980.

Massie, Allan. *The Novel Today: A Critical Guide to the British Novel 1970–1989.* London & New York: Longman, 1990.

McEwan, Neil. *The Survival of the Novel: British Fiction in the Later Twentieth Century.* London: Macmillan, 1981.

Miles, Rosaline. *The Fiction of Sex.* London: Vision Press, 1974; New York: Barnes & Noble, 1976.

Morris, Robert K. *Old Lines, New Forces: Essays on the Contemporary English Novel, 1960–1970.* Rutherford, N.J.: Fairleigh Dickinson University Press, 1976.

O'Connor, William Van. *The New University Wits and the Ends of Modernism.* Carbondale: Southern Illinois University Press, 1963.

Palmer, Helen H., and Anne Jane Dyson. *English Novel Explication: Criticism to 1972.* Hamden, Conn.: Shoe String Press, 1973.

Parker, Peter. *The Reader's Companion to the Twentieth Century Novel.* Oxford: Fourth Estate, Helicon, 1994.

Ross, Stephen D. *Literature and Philosophy: An Analysis of the Philosophical Novel.* New York: Appleton–Century-Crofts, 1969.

Schlueter, Paul, and Jane Schlueter. *The English Novel: Twentieth Century Criticism, volume 2: Twentieth Century Novelists.* Chicago, Athens, Ohio & London: Swallow Press/Ohio University Press, 1982.

Shapiro, C. *Contemporary British Novelists.* Carbondale: Southern Illinois University Press, 1965.

Smith, David J. *Socialist Propaganda in the 20th-Century British Novel.* Totowa, N.J.: Rowman & Littlefield, 1978.

Spilka, Mark, ed. *Towards a Poetics of Fiction.* Bloomington & London: University of Indiana Press, 1977.

Staley, Thomas F., ed. *Twentieth-Century Women Novelists.* London: Macmillan, 1982.

Stevenson, Randall. *The British Novel Since the Thirties: An Introduction.* Athens: University of Georgia Press, 1986.

Sutherland, John. *Fiction and the Fiction Industry.* London: Athlone Press, 1978.

Swinden, Patrick. *The English Novel of History and Society, 1940–80.* New York: St. Martin's Press, 1984.

Swinden. *Unofficial Selves: Character in the Novel from Dickens to the Present Day.* London & New York: Barnes & Noble, 1973.

Taylor, D. J., *A Vain Conceit: British Fiction in the 1980s.* London: Bloomsbury, 1989.

Todd, Richard. *Consuming Fictions: The Booker Prize and Fiction in Britain Today.* London: Bloomsbury, 1996.

West, Paul. *The Modern Novel.* London: Hutchinson, 1963.

Wicker, Brian. *The Story-Shaped World: Fiction and Metaphysics.* London: Athlone Press, 1975.

Wilson, Colin. *The Craft of the Novel.* London: Gollancz, 1975; Salem, N.H.: Salem House, 1986.

Ziegler, Heide, and Christopher Bigsby, eds. *The Radical Imagination and the Liberal Tradition: Interviews with English and American Novelists.* London: Junction, 1982.

Contributors

Elizabeth Allen . . . . *Regent's College, London*

Kasia Boddy . . . . *University College, London*

Cairns Craig . . . . *University of Edinburgh*

Ruth P. Feingold . . . . *University of Chicago*

John Fletcher . . . . *University of East Anglia*

Anne Fisher Gossage . . . . *Pennsylvania State University*

Jay L. Halio . . . . *University of Delaware*

Ann Hancock . . . . *University of the West of England, Bristol*

Martha Henn . . . . *Birmingham-Southern College*

David Hopes . . . . *University of North Carolina at Asheville*

G. M. Hyde . . . . *University of East Anglia*

Dennis Jackson . . . . *University of Delaware*

Margaret Lewis . . . . *Hexham, England*

Peter Lewis . . . . *University of Durham*

Priscilla Martin . . . . *St Edmund Hall, Oxford*

Tim Middleton . . . . *University College of Ripon & York, St. John*

Jago Morrison . . . . *Leeds Metropolitan University*

Merritt Moseley . . . . *University of North Carolina at Asheville*

Wendy Perkins . . . . *Prince George's Community College*

Ellen Pifer . . . . *University of Delaware*

Julie Rak . . . . *McMaster University*

Annette Rubery . . . . *University of Warwick*

Lorna Sage . . . . *University of East Anglia*

Andy Sawyer . . . . *University of Liverpool*

Gerda Seaman . . . . *California State University, Chico*

M. E. de Soissons . . . . *University of East Anglia*

Randall Stevenson . . . . *University of Edinburgh*

Stella Swain . . . . *University of the West of England*

Helen Clare Taylor . . . . *Louisiana State University-Shreveport*

Glyn Turton . . . . *University College Chester, England*

James Whitlark . . . . *Texas Tech University*

Cumulative Index

Dictionary of Literary Biography, Volumes 1-207
Dictionary of Literary Biography Yearbook, 1980-1998
Dictionary of Literary Biography Documentary Series, Volumes 1-19

Cumulative Index

DLB before number: *Dictionary of Literary Biography,* Volumes 1-207
Y before number: *Dictionary of Literary Biography Yearbook,* 1980-1998
DS before number: *Dictionary of Literary Biography Documentary Series,* Volumes 1-19

B

C

F

G

M

Cumulative Index

Q

Cumulative Index

Strittmatter, Erwin 1912- DLB-69

Strniša, Gregor 1930-1987 .... DLB-181

Strode, William 1630-1645........... DLB-126

Strong, L. A. G. 1896-1958........... DLB-191

Strother, David Hunter 1816-1888....... DLB-3

Strouse, Jean 1945- DLB-111

Stuart, Dabney 1937- DLB-105

Stuart, Jesse 1906-1984.....DLB-9, 48, 102; Y-84

Stuart, Ruth McEnery 1849?-1917...... DLB-202

Stuart, Lyle [publishing house] DLB-46

Stubbs, Harry Clement (see Clement, Hal)

Stubenberg, Johann Wilhelm von 1619-1663...................... DLB-164

Studio DLB-112

The Study of Poetry (1880), by Matthew Arnold................ DLB-35

Sturgeon, Theodore 1918-1985 ..... DLB-8; Y-85

Sturges, Preston 1898-1959 .... DLB-26

"Style" (1840; revised, 1859), by Thomas de Quincey [excerpt] DLB-57

"Style" (1888), by Walter Pater DLB-57

Style (1897), by Walter Raleigh [excerpt].................... DLB-57

"Style" (1877), by T. H. Wright [excerpt].................... DLB-57

"Le Style c'est l'homme" (1892), by W. H. Mallock.................. DLB-57

Styron, William 1925- DLB-2, 143; Y-80

Suárez, Mario 1925- DLB-82

Such, Peter 1939- DLB-60

Suckling, Sir John 1609-1641? DLB-58, 126

Suckow, Ruth 1892-1960 .... DLB-9, 102

Sudermann, Hermann 1857-1928....... DLB-118

Sue, Eugène 1804-1857.............. DLB-119

Sue, Marie-Joseph (see Sue, Eugène)

Suggs, Simon (see Hooper, Johnson Jones)

Sukenick, Ronald 1932- DLB-173; Y-81

Suknaski, Andrew 1942- DLB-53

Sullivan, Alan 1868-1947 .... DLB-92

Sullivan, C. Gardner 1886-1965........ DLB-26

Sullivan, Frank 1892-1976 .... DLB-11

Sulte, Benjamin 1841-1923 .... DLB-99

Sulzberger, Arthur Hays 1891-1968..... DLB-127

Sulzberger, Arthur Ochs 1926- DLB-127

Sulzer, Johann Georg 1720-1779........ DLB-97

Sumarokov, Aleksandr Petrovich 1717-1777 .... DLB-150

Summers, Hollis 1916- DLB-6

Sumner, Henry A. [publishing house] DLB-49

Surtees, Robert Smith 1803-1864........ DLB-21

Surveys: Japanese Literature, 1987-1995................... DLB-182

A Survey of Poetry Anthologies, 1879-1960.................... DLB-54

Surveys of the Year's Biographies

A Transit of Poets and Others: American Biography in 1982 .... Y-82

The Year in Literary Biography Y-83–Y-98

Survey of the Year's Book Publishing

The Year in Book Publishing.............. Y-86

Survey of the Year's Book Reviewing

The Year in Book Reviewing and the Literary Situation........................ Y-98

Survey of the Year's Children's Books

The Year in Children's Books Y-92–Y-96, Y-98

The Year in Children's Literature Y-97

Surveys of the Year's Drama

The Year in Drama Y-82–Y-85, Y-87–Y-96

The Year in London Theatre.............. Y-92

Surveys of the Year's Fiction

The Year's Work in Fiction: A Survey....... Y-82

The Year in Fiction: A Biased View........ Y-83

The Year in Fiction.. Y-84–Y-86, Y-89, Y-94–Y-98

The Year in the Novel Y-87, Y-88, Y-90–Y-93

The Year in Short Stories................ Y-87

The Year in the Short Story......Y-88, Y-90–Y-93

Surveys of the Year's Literary Theory

The Year in Literary Theory Y-92–Y-93

Survey of the Year's Literature

The Year in Texas Literature.............. Y-98

Surveys of the Year's Poetry

The Year's Work in American Poetry Y-82

The Year in Poetry........Y-83–Y-92, Y-94–Y-98

Sutherland, Efua Theodora 1924- DLB-117

Sutherland, John 1919-1956........... DLB-68

Sutro, Alfred 1863-1933 .... DLB-10

Swados, Harvey 1920-1972 .... DLB-2

Swain, Charles 1801-1874............. DLB-32

Swallow Press.................... DLB-46

Swan Sonnenschein Limited.......... DLB-106

Swanberg, W. A. 1907- DLB-103

Swenson, May 1919-1989.............. DLB-5

Swerling, Jo 1897- DLB-44

Swift, Graham 1949- DLB-194

Swift, Jonathan 1667-1745...... DLB-39, 95, 101

Swinburne, A. C. 1837-1909........ DLB-35, 57

Swineshead, Richard floruit circa 1350 .... DLB-115

Swinnerton, Frank 1884-1982 .... DLB-34

Swisshelm, Jane Grey 1815-1884 .... DLB-43

Swope, Herbert Bayard 1882-1958....... DLB-25

Swords, T. and J., and Company........ DLB-49

Swords, Thomas 1763-1843 and Swords, James ?-1844........... DLB-73

Sykes, Ella C. ?-1939 ....DLB-174

Sylvester, Josuah 1562 or 1563 - 1618.............. DLB-121

Symonds, Emily Morse (see Paston, George)

Symonds, John Addington 1840-1893 ....DLB-57, 144

Symons, A. J. A. 1900-1941 .... DLB-149

Symons, Arthur 1865-1945 .....DLB-19, 57, 149

Symons, Julian 1912-1994 .....DLB-87, 155; Y-92

Symons, Scott 1933- DLB-53

A Symposium on The Columbia History of the Novel Y-92

Synge, John Millington 1871-1909 .....DLB-10, 19

Synge Summer School: J. M. Synge and the Irish Theater, Rathdrum, County Wiclow, Ireland Y-93

Syrett, Netta 1865-1943 ....DLB-135, 197

Szymborska, Wisława 1923- Y-96

T

Taban lo Liyong 1939?- DLB-125

Tabucchi, Antonio 1943- DLB-196

Taché, Joseph-Charles 1820-1894 .... DLB-99

Tachihara Masaaki 1926-1980........ DLB-182

Tadijanović, Dragutin 1905- DLB-181

Tafolla, Carmen 1951- DLB-82

Taggard, Genevieve 1894-1948 .... DLB-45

Taggart, John 1942- DLB-193

Tagger, Theodor (see Bruckner, Ferdinand)

Taiheiki late fourteenth century........ DLB-203

Tait, J. Selwin, and Sons.............. DLB-49

Tait's Edinburgh Magazine 1832-1861 ..... DLB-110

The Takarazaka Revue Company.......... Y-91

Talander (see Bohse, August)

Talese, Gay 1932- DLB-185

Talev, Dimitr 1898-1966 .... DLB-181

Taliaferro, H. E. 1811-1875 .... DLB-202

Tallent, Elizabeth 1954- DLB-130

TallMountain, Mary 1918-1994........ DLB-193

Talvj 1797-1870................. DLB-59, 133

Tan, Amy 1952- DLB-173

Tanizaki, Jun'ichirō 1886-1965......... DLB-180

Tapahonso, Luci 1953- DLB-175

Taradash, Daniel 1913- DLB-44

Tarbell, Ida M. 1857-1944 .... DLB-47

Tardivel, Jules-Paul 1851-1905.......... DLB-99

Targan, Barry 1932- DLB-130

Tarkington, Booth 1869-1946 .... DLB-9, 102

Tashlin, Frank 1913-1972.............. DLB-44

Tate, Allen 1899-1979......DLB-4, 45, 63; DS-17

Tate, James 1943- DLB-5, 169

Tate, Nahum circa 1652-1715........... DLB-80

Tatian circa 830................... DLB-148

Taufer, Veno 1933- DLB-181

Tauler, Johannes circa 1300-1361 ....DLB-179

Tavčar, Ivan 1851-1923 ....DLB-147

Taylor, Ann 1782-1866 .... DLB-163

Taylor, Bayard 1825-1878 .... DLB-3, 189

Taylor, Bert Leston 1866-1921 .... DLB-25

Taylor, Charles H. 1846-1921 .... DLB-25

Taylor, Edward circa 1642-1729 .... DLB-24

Taylor, Elizabeth 1912-1975........... DLB-139

Taylor, Henry 1942- DLB-5

Taylor, Sir Henry 1800-1886........... DLB-32

U